THE UNITING OF EUROPE

CONTEMPORARY EUROPEAN POLITICS AND SOCIETY

Anthony M. Messina, Series Editor

THE UNITING

OF

EUROPE

POLITICAL, SOCIAL, AND ECONOMIC FORCES
1950–1957

ERNST B. HAAS

Foreword by Desmond Dinan

New Introduction by Ernst B. Haas

UNIVERSITY OF NOTRE DAME PRESS
Notre Dame, Indiana

Published by the University of Notre Dame Press
Notre Dame, Indiana 46556
www.undpress.nd.edu
All Rights Reserved

Manufactured in the United States of America

Library of Congress Cataloging-in-Publication Data

Haas, Ernst B.
    The uniting of Europe : political, social, and economic forces,
1950–1957 / Ernst B. Haas ; foreword by Desmond Dinan ; new introduction
by Ernst B. Haas.
        p.   cm. — (Contemporary European politics and society)
    Originally published: Stanford, Calif.: Stanford University Press, 1958.
    Includes bibliographical references and index.
    ISBN 0-268-04346-9 (cloth : alk. paper)
    ISBN 0-268-04347-7 (pbk.: alk. paper)
    1. European federation.   2. European cooperation.   I. Title.   II. Series.

JN15.H215   2004
341.24'2—dc22   2003070256

∞ *This book is printed on acid-free paper.*

To Hil and Peter

CONTENTS

PART ONE

INTEGRATION: IDEOLOGY AND INSTITUTIONS

PART TWO

PROCESSES OF INTEGRATION AT THE NATIONAL LEVEL

PART THREE

PROCESSES OF INTEGRATION AT THE SUPRANATIONAL LEVEL

FOREWORD

Desmond Dinan

Two events of great importance in the history of European integration happened in 1958. One was the launch of the European Economic Community; the other was the publication of Ernst Haas's *The Uniting of Europe*. It may seem far-fetched to put them on a par with each other. Yet their fates became inextricably linked. As economic integration deepened in the 1960s, interest in integration theory intensified. Just as the launch of the EEC came to be seen as a decisive turning point in the history of European integration, so, too, did the publication of *The Uniting of Europe* become the foundation of a rich and varied literature on integration theory.

The success of the EEC, and with it the impact of *The Uniting of Europe*, were not assured. Most Western Europeans were unaware of or uninterested in the negotiation and ratification of the Rome Treaty. The signing ceremony in March 1957 passed without much notice. The launch of the Community in January 1958 did not strike interested observers as the beginning of a brave new world. If anything, advocates of deeper integration were disappointed with the EEC, which was less supranational than its precursor, the European Coal and Steel Community.

Nor did *The Uniting of Europe* give them grounds for unalloyed optimism. Haas's book was not a pro-integration polemic. On the contrary, although it developed the famous idea of spillover (the notion that integration in one functional area would almost certainly lead to integration in others), *The Uniting of Europe* did not posit the inevitability of European union. Critics later panned Haas and his disciples for painting a false dawn; for forecasting an ever-upward trajectory for ever-closer union. More discerning observers, including Haas himself, appreciated the potential pitfalls of European integration and saw *The Uniting of Europe* as a tentative step forward rather than the definitive last word on integration theory.

Haas grew up in Frankfurt. His family fled Nazi Germany and moved to the United States when he was fourteen. Haas started college in Chicago but was drafted after his freshman year. Following a stint in the U.S. army, he studied at Columbia University, where he received his Ph.D. in political science. Competing with a lot of other ex-soldier scholars, Haas landed a job at Berkeley in 1951 on the strength of a written application (there were no interviews). He stayed there for the rest of his long life.[1]

Within political science, Haas studied international relations because of his background and experience. Having suffered at the hands of the Nazis, Haas wanted to know how the state and the state system could change, and how communities beyond the state might come into being. He was intrigued by the integrative impact of international organizations. For obvious personal and professional reasons, developments in postwar Europe attracted his attention. The Coal and Steel Community was a wonderful laboratory. He spent a year in Luxembourg (1955–1956) observing it in action.

The Uniting of Europe, his ensuing magnum opus, did two things. One was to describe the origins and development of the Coal and Steel Community. Although celebrated for its theoretical contribution, *The Uniting of Europe* is also a much-neglected contemporary chronicle of the making of Europe's first supranational organization. It was one of a number of excellent inquiries at the time into the functioning of the Coal and Steel Community.[2]

The book's other, better-known achievement was to extrapolate from the experience of the Coal and Steel Community the conditions under which sovereignty-sharing and transnational community building could take place. Haas built the idea of spillover not on economic determinism, but on changes in the attitudes and behavior of governments, parties, and, especially, labor and business interest groups. His key conclusion was that "group pressure will spill over into the federal sphere and thereby add to the integrative impulse."[3]

The Uniting of Europe received mixed reviews. C. Grove Haines, a noted authority on European integration, announced at the time that "one is frankly disappointed, after the elaborate and somewhat pedantic formulation of the testing methods subsequently employed in 'dissecting' the processes of integration, to see what little fruit they yield in the way of clarifying those processes or of providing fresh and illuminating gen-

---

1. For an overview of Haas's life and work, see Harry Kreisler, *Science and Progress in International Relations: Conversations with Ernst B. Haas*, http//globetrotter. berkeley.edu/people/Haas.

2. The two other leading inquiries in English into the Coal and Steel Community were William Diebold, *The Schuman Plan: A Study in Economic Cooperation, 1950–1959* (New York: Praeger, 1959), and Hans A. Schmidt, *The Path to European Union: From the Marshall Plan to the Common Market* (Baton Rouge: Louisiana State University Press, 1962).

3. Ernst B. Haas, *The Uniting of Europe: Political, Social, and Economic Forces, 1950–1957* (Stanford: Stanford University Press, 1958), p. xiii.

eralizations on the manner of forming political communities among sovereign states."[4] Nevertheless, *The Uniting of Europe* became the basis for the dominant neofunctionalist theory of European integration, advanced by Haas and others in the 1960s. In retrospect, the book assumed an importance that was not apparent when it first appeared.

In a lukewarm review published in 1959, William Diebold remarked that "if the time comes when [the anti-EEC] Ludwig Erhard and Michel Debré preside over the destinies of the Common Market, we shall really learn something about the extent of political integration."[5] By the mid-1960s Erhard and Charles de Gaulle, Debré's boss, were indeed in control, and the Community's political fortunes looked bleak. More important for the fate of integration and neofunctionalism were the economic recession and ensuing Eurosclerosis of the 1970s. Far from spilling over, European integration appeared to be spilling back. Yet the revival of European integration in the late 1980s brought with it a revival of neofunctionalism, as well as a reaction against it in the form of liberal intergovernmentalism, a theory of major inter-state decisions propounded by Andrew Moravcsik.

Haas was not a doctrinaire neofunctionalist. His ideas about European integration were not frozen in time but, as the introduction to *The Uniting of Europe* on the occasion of its reissue by the University of Notre Dame Press makes clear, evolved considerably over time. Nevertheless, it is for the theoretical contribution of *The Uniting of Europe* that Haas is famous in the annals of European integration studies and political science generally. Little wonder that *Foreign Affairs* selected *The Uniting of Europe* as one of the most significant books of the twentieth century on international relations. In a short review of *The Uniting of Europe* on that occasion, Stanley Hoffmann wrote that the book provided "the solid foundation of what is now a huge theoretical edifice."[6]

As a long-time student of European integration, and a member of the editorial board of the Contemporary European Politics and Society series of Notre Dame Press, I am honored that Tony Messina of the University of Notre Dame asked me to write this foreword. I would like to thank

---

4. C. Grove Haines, review of *The Uniting of Europe: Political, Social, and Economic Forces, 1950–1957*, by Ernst B. Haas, in the *American Historical Review* 64, no. 3 (April 1959), p. 630.

5. William Diebold, review of *The Uniting of Europe: Political, Social, and Economic Forces, 1950–1957*, by Ernst B. Haas, in *World Politics* 11, no. 4 (July 1959), p. 628.

6. Stanley Hoffmann, review of *The Uniting of Europe: Political, Social, and Economic Forces, 1950–1957*, by Ernst B. Haas, in *Foreign Affairs* 76, no. 5 (September–October 1997), p. 226.

Tony Messina and Barbara Hanrahan, director of the Press, for taking the initiative in reissuing *The Uniting of Europe*. Unfortunately, Ernst Haas did not live to see it. Long out of print, *The Uniting of Europe* is now available in paperback with the added value of an introduction that the author finished only weeks before his death. The reappearance of *The Uniting of Europe* is a fitting memorial to Ernst Haas, a pioneer of European integration studies.

INTRODUCTION:
INSTITUTIONALISM OR CONSTRUCTIVISM?

Ernst B. Haas

IS NEOFUNCTIONALISM STILL RELEVANT?

The organization analyzed in these pages ceased to exist on July 1, 1967: the European Coal and Steel Community (ECSC) merged with what was then called the European Communities, now the European Union (EU). My study ends in 1957. In 1958 the inauguration of the European Economic Community shifted the focus of regional integration from Luxembourg to Brussels; from coal and steel to the scrapping of almost all tariffs, the creation of rules of competition for industry, and the subsidization of agriculture; and from talk of well-defined economic sectors to the creation of political unity.

Social scientists were interested less in the substantive activities and achievements of these organizations than in the theories seeking to explain the success of regional integration, of the entirely voluntary submersion of national sovereignties in a larger entity. Never before had sovereign nation-states consented to be peacefully unified on such a scale. This study contributed one such theory: neofunctionalism (NF). It is the fate of NF that justifies continued attention to events which transpired forty-odd years ago and to organizations which no longer exist.

NF became more than an explanation of regional integration in Europe, as scholars applied its propositions to regional integration efforts elsewhere and even to the theoretical study of global politics and global organizations. A reexamination of the original setting for NF is an occasion for contemplating the reasons why the experience of European integration remains unique.

More important, because NF's relationship to general theories of International Relations (IR) remains contested, I make it my purpose in this introduction to restate my theoretical objective in advancing the theory. I shall compare it with some of its challengers and commentators in order to arrive at a new statement, which stresses its relevance to "constructivism," a theory of which NF may be considered a forerunner as well as a part.

NF was developed explicitly to challenge the two theories of IR dominant in the 1950s, classical realism and idealism. Classical realism, in its American version, was personified by Hans Morgenthau, Arnold Wolfers, and Nicolas Spykman; in its British version, by Martin Wight, Hedley Bull, and Herbert Butterfield.[1] I wanted to show that the fetishizing of power, the *Primat der Aussenpolitik*, was far less of a law of politics than claimed by these scholars. But I also wanted to show that the Kantian idealism that saw in more international law the road to world peace was as unnecessary as it was (and is) naïve. I wanted to show that there are other ways to peace than either power or law. In this I was heavily influenced by E. H. Carr and by David Mitrany, as well as by the American theorists of democratic pluralism, David Truman and Robert Dahl. Today's constructivism continues to draw on these sources in challenging contemporary neorealism, neoliberalism, peace theory, and IR notions derived exclusively from rational choice models. NF has become part of this challenge.

NEOFUNCTIONALISM AS DEFINED IN THIS BOOK

States, instead of struggling for power, are expected to defend their preferences and to cooperate when cooperation is deemed necessary for their realization. State preferences are seen as resulting from changing domestic competitions for influence; there is no fixed and knowable national interest. Preferences of political actors are formulated on the basis of the values held; they, in turn, determine an actor's sense of interest. In short, NF carried the assumptions of democratic pluralism over into policy formulations relating to international matters by disaggregating the state into its actor-components.

Regional integration was expected to occur when societal actors, in calculating their interests, decided to rely on the supranational institutions rather than their own governments to realize their demands. These institutions, in turn, would enjoy increasing authority and legitimacy as they became the sources of policies meeting the demands of social actors.

---

1. The NF approach also challenges Marxist theories of IR, as currently represented by world systems theory, though it has more in common with them than with realism and idealism. It rejects them because the concepts of class and of class interest as the core building blocks are jettisoned in favor of groups and group interests, including noneconomic and nonmaterial forces. In short, for NF capitalism is not a mode of production, but a set of interest groups representing business, agriculture, and labor. Agency takes the place of determinism.

Originally, NF assumed that integration would proceed quasi-automatically as demands for additional central services intensified because the central institutions proved unable to satisfy the demands of their new clients. Thus, activities associated with sectors integrated initially would "spill over" into neighboring sectors not yet integrated, but now becoming the focus of demands for more integration.

ECSC experience has spawned a theory of international integration by indirection, by trial and error, by miscalculation on the part of the actors desiring integration, and by manipulation of elite social forces on the part of small groups of pragmatic administrators and politicians in the setting of a vague but permissive public opinion. "Functionalism" and "incrementalism" rather than "federalism" and "comprehensive planning" are key terms for describing the theory.[2]

Its ontology is "soft" rational choice: social actors, in seeking to realize their value-derived interests, will choose whatever means are made available by the prevailing democratic order. If thwarted they will rethink their values, redefine their interests, and choose new means to realize them. The alleged primordial force of nationalism will be trumped by the utilitarian-instrumental human desire to better oneself in life, materially and in terms of status, as well as normative satisfaction. It bears repeating that the ontology is *not* materialistic: values shape interests, and values include many nonmaterial elements.

Many challenges to this view have been articulated over the years. I shall refer only to those that eschew an exclusive interest in the doings of the EU, and concentrate on those tied to theoretical concerns involving all of IR. The link between integration theory and IR in general has always been the same for me: how do sovereign states cease to be sovereign of their own free will? How do nations shed their penchant toward intolerance for the other? The study of integration is a step toward a theory of international change at the macro level.[3]

Thus, the following authors challenge aspects of NF while also remaining interested in macrotheoretical concerns. One school is interested

---

2. NF is superbly summarized by Ben Rosamond, *Theories of European Integration* (New York: St. Martin's Press, 2000), chs. 3 and 4.

3. Hence I shall not consider the many theories about "European governance" and "European policymaking" (mainly British) now being developed, approaches which by and large either challenge or ignore NF, intergovernmentalism, and all other approaches linked to IR theory and to basic social science *à l'américaine*. For a searching discussion see Rosamond, *Theories of European Integration*, ch. 5, and the list of works following this introduction. Nor am I concerned with the debate of whether the study of EU "properly" belongs to IR or to comparative politics.

primarily in multilevel governance as an emerging feature of international and national society, of which the EU is the most striking example.[4] It includes Phillipe Schmitter, Fritz Scharpf, Thomas Christiansen, Liesbet Hooghe, and Gary Marks. Another is concerned with subsuming integration studies under the revived interest in institutions considered as independent variables, sometimes identified (misleadingly) as the "new institutionalism." Prominent practitioners include Wayne Sandholtz, Alec Stone Sweet, and Neil Fligstein, as well as Thomas Christiansen. Still others favor networks and discourse analysis as foci for studying major changes, such as Giandomenico Majone, Christopher Ansell, and Ole Waever. Finally, under the label of "liberalism," Andrew Moravcsik revived the debate between believers in the survival of the sovereign state and supranationalists (such as all the schools mentioned above) by claiming that everything of importance that has happened in Europe since 1950 is due to the doings of actors at the national level, both government and private. All of these approaches, despite their differences, raise issues that NF writers should have addressed but neglected.

Multilevel governance is an obvious fact in a setting in which the nation-state has neither faded away nor retained its full powers. Recognizing this fact as real invites us to think of global politics as tending toward multilevel governance even in the absence of supranational organizations, as is done in aspects of regime theory and notions of "global turbulence." NF neglected to recognize that Europe is nested in a global set of interdependencies.

An appreciation of multilevel governance implies continued respect for one crucial level: national governments, embattled though they may be. It is not true that NF downplayed these actors in the interest of puffing up supranational organizations. But it is true that NF exaggerated the rate at which national governments were expected to lose out to them.

NF neglected the consideration of institutions, except to affirm that enmeshment in supranationalism offers constraints and opportunities not available earlier in international politics. But that affirmation did not touch on the arguments now raised by the new institutionalists. They show that integration results in a decisive increase in the density of institutional ties, both formal and informal. This density acts as a constraint

---

4. The relevant works are all listed following this introduction. Much of this literature is concerned with arguing that the study of European integration is properly a part of comparative politics, and not the kind of IR perpetrated by American scholars. I am not concerned with this silly debate. British (and French) scholars seem never to have forgiven their American colleagues for having invented social science–based integration studies of Europe.

on the freedom of maneuver of other actors, regional and national; inter-group relations are not examined by NF writers even though they seem eminently relevant to any complete study of regional integration. In short, new developments in IR theory force us to reconsider the NF presented in this book.

The most important of these developments—of which the approaches mentioned above can be considered a part—is constructivism, a theory that claims to be a superior alternative to neorealism, neoliberal institutionalism, world systems theory, and peace theory.[5] Our job is to see how NF, as amended by these challengers, can become a part of a respectable constructivism.

Varieties of Constructivism

In terms of substantive differences, there are three clearly distinguishable strands of constructivism, which primarily share a commitment to the social construction of reality as the basis of collective behavior and which reject a structural account. In other words, constructivism is committed to explanations and inquiries that focus on large-scale changes, such as the gradual weakening of the nation-state in Europe. These types are labeled, respectively, organizational, systemic, and normative constructivism.[6] The salient characteristics and differences between neofunctionalism and each type of constructivism are summarized in Table 1.

---

5. Despite Moravcsik's claims to having defined a novel theory of IR, I find that his description conforms exactly to the main ideas of NF. Moreover, while he is absolutely right in insisting on the continuing importance of nation-state–based political forces in Europe, he overstates his case by totally neglecting the departures from state-determined decisions which abound in the day-to-day affairs of the EU and in its legal system, as shown especially by the institutionalist critics of NF. Hence I find that a moderate intergovernmentalism is quite compatible with a scaled-down argument for supranationalism. See Andrew Moravcsik, "Taking Preferences Seriously: A Liberal Theory of International Politics," *International Organization* 51 (1997), pp. 513–53. See the critique of Moravcsik in Martin Saeter, *Comprehensive Neofunctionalism* (Oslo: Norwegian Institute of International Affairs, 1998).

6. This material condenses my treatment in "Does Constructivism Subsume Neofunctionalism?" in Thomas Christiansen, Knud Erik Jorgensen, and Autje Wiener, eds., *The Social Construction of Europe* (London: Sage, 2001). My typology competes with several others; see notes 13–21 of the essay just cited. Authors identified with organizational constructivism are largely students of constitution writing and interpretation and analysts of courts. Systemic constructivists include, prominently, Alexander Wendt and Nicholas Onuf. Normative scholars include Martha Finnemore, Christian Reus-Smit, Michael Barnett, Kathryn Sikkink, and Margaret Keck.

Table 1. Comparison of Neofunctionalism and three Constructivisms

Dimension	Neoconstructivism (Haas version)	Organizational	Systemic	Normative
Dependent Variable	political community	international cooperation; value/policy integration	types of anarchy and conflict	international cooperation; value integration
Agent/Structure Relationship	agency favored	structuration; agency favored	structuration; structure favored	structuration; agency favored
Chief Actors	organizations (all kinds)	organizations (all kinds)	states	states, groups governments
Level of Analysis	second image favored	3rd/2nd image tension; 2nd image favored	third image favored	unresolved tension between 3rd and 2nd images
Derivation of Actor Interests	values and material needs	collectively defined values and needs	socially defined identities	values, norms
Dominant Epistemology	Weberian; pragmatism	Weberian; Durkheimian; pragmatism	scientific realism; Durkheimian;	unclear

NEOFUNCTIONALISM AMENDED

The publication of two volumes on European integration that draw explicitly on a reworked version of neofunctionalist theorizing (NF) prompts the following comments.[7] Unexpected historical events, as is usual in the social sciences, also have a lot to do with these comments.

In my 1975 self-critique of NF, couched in terms of the notion of "turbulent fields," I mentioned several shortcomings of the original NF. These became evident during the wave of globalization that emerged in the 1970s and the social travail in advanced industrial societies associated with the stagflation of those years.[8] These events and the contemporaneous Eurosclerosis suggested that there is no automaticity and no reliable spill-over process in the march of European integration, making the original theory obsolescent, to put it charitably.

Events since 1985 now suggest that this diagnosis was wrong. The phoenix-like evolution of the European Communities into the European Union has triggered a modest renaissance of NF-type analyses, of which the two volumes in question are an example.[9] However, they contain several important amendments to NF that I wish to acknowledge and endorse. They also contain formulations with which I am not totally at ease.

What is the benchmark or "original" version of NF against which this new effort is to be judged? I use as my point of departure the version of NF contained in the second edition of *The Uniting of Europe* (1968) and the early work of Philippe Schmitter (1971).

I shall not use the numerous other NF-like studies of the early 1970s, such as Lindberg and Scheingold's *Europe's Would-Be Polity*.[10]

---

7. Wayne Sandholtz and Alec Stone Sweet, eds., *European Integration and Supranational Governance* (New York: Oxford University Press, 1998), especially ch. 1; Alec Stone Sweet, Wayne Sandholtz, and Neil Fligstein, eds., *The Institutionalization of Europe* (New York: Oxford University Press, 2001).

8. Ernst B. Haas, *The Obsolescence of Regional Integration Theory* (Berkeley: Institute of International Studies, University of California, 1975).

9. For instance, the article on the Economic and Monetary Union by David Cameron, "Creating Supranational Authority in Monetary and Exchange-Rate Policy," in Sandholtz and Stone Sweet, *European Integration and Supranational Governance*, pp. 188–216, as well as several other case studies in this volume.

10. Leon N. Lindberg and Stuart A. Scheingold, eds., *Regional Integration; Theory and Research* (Cambridge, MA: Harvard University Press, 1971), especially the articles by Lindberg, Puchala, Nye, and Schmitter; Leon N. Lindberg and Stuart A. Scheingold, *Europe's Would-Be Polity* (Englewood Cliffs, NJ: Prentice-Hall, 1970), which anticipates some of the concepts and arguments of Sandholtz et al. Other works of that time couched in neofunctionalist terms include J. S. Nye, *Peace in Parts* (Boston: Little Brown, 1971); J. S. Nye, *Pan-Africanism and East African Federation* (Cambridge, MA: Harvard University Press, 1965); Stuart A. Scheingold, *The Rule of Law in European Integration* (New

Sandholtz, Stone Sweet, and Fligstein (SSF) employ a much more open-ended dependent variable than did the original NF. They envisage a continuum anchored in intergovernmental politics at one end, and in supranational politics at the other. They also conceptualize the outcome of concern to them as institutionalized governance for an emerging "European space." The core concepts are "institution" and "institutionalization," roughly, the emergence of a dense network of rules and organizations binding member governments, interest groups, bureaucracies, and politicians in ever-tighter interdependencies. NF postulated a European federal state as the outcome, the professed goal of one set of actors, an outcome relaxed in 1975 by postulating various possible emerging constellations consistent with the idea of turbulence. I now have no difficulty in accepting the SSF formulation.

The original NF conceived of the spill-over process as confined to economic sectors. Dissatisfaction with the performance of already integrated sectors was thought to trigger reforms requiring the integration of additional, cognate, sectors. A perfect example of the spill-over process at work is given by David Cameron's explanation of the origins of the Economic and Monetary Union.[11]

SSF extend the concept to deal with the unintended growth of any kind of EU institution, whether related to economic activity and policy or not. It also covers the growth of administrative and judicial rules and organs. Since the logic underlying their usage is no different from NF's, I also accept this change.

Institutions were not given special attention in the original NF. The studies were done, for the most part, before the pioneering work in the theory of public organization of Philip Selznick, Herbert Simon and James March, and James D. Thompson. SSF reflect the renewed interest in sociological institutionalism. But their version is far superior to the majority of theoretical work in that field because it seeks to understand change, whereas the orthodox canon of sociological institutionalism is concerned with explaining stability and equilibrium in collective behavior. Insofar as this feature was neglected, its prominent inclusion in the list of variables—whether dependent or intervening—is welcome.[12]

Haven: Yale University Press, 1965); Leon N. Lindberg, *The Political Dynamics of European Economic Integration* (Stanford: Stanford University Press, 1963).

11. Cameron, "Creating Supranational Authority in Monetary and Exchange-Rate Policy."

12. In self-justification I note that institutional and organizational dynamics were a prominent feature in my study of the International Labor Organization, which "tested" NF principles in the setting of an organization with universal membership and a mandate for

SSF pay careful attention to the manner in which supranational policies relate to the character and aims of domestic interest groups, especially in explaining the evolution of legal rules and practices. The original NF proceeded somewhat differently in practice, though not in principle. Instead of carefully studying and sorting domestic interests, it took these largely for granted, as "given" by the pluralist theory of democratic politics to which NF was tied. Pluralism predicts that interest groups would act in certain ways; NF writers (with the exception of Lindberg) accepted this as true and proceeded from there. Again, the SSF version is clearly superior to the original effort.

In my judgment, both the original NF and the SSF version make the same mistake with respect to a vital point: the "automaticity" of the integration process once the initial rules of the game are set. NF assumed that once a politically significant segment of collective life is subjected to supranational authority, the logic of spill-over will take care of the future. The process is seen as irreversible, though not necessarily linearly progressive. SSF seem to make similar assumptions about the continuation of institutionalization. The preface to the second edition of *The Uniting of Europe* (1968) already expressed doubts about automaticity, and my 1975 self-critique further elaborated the caveat. In the meantime, Philippe Schmitter had worked out the logics of spill-backs and spill-arounds to show why integration based on spill-over logic is far from automatic.[13] SSF would do well to worry about the limits of the institutionalization process they sketch.

Another difficulty is presented by the notion of "rules." Too much is packaged in it: "An institution is a complex of rules and procedures that governs a given set of human interactions." And, "Rules prescribe appropriate behavior in a particular setting and thus are collective attributes. Procedures are those rules that determine how actors and organizations make all other rules."[14] Rules seem to be prior to the actors who make them and change them. How can a rule be a collective attribute? Of whom or what? This formulation is consistent with aspects of sociological institutionalism that reify rules (or institutions) as something logically prior to actors. The integration "game" is seen as revolving around who makes, who interprets, and who implements the rules. The possibility that integration involves debates about people's identities and futures gets lost

---

global integration of social policy. See my *Beyond the Nation-State* (Stanford: Stanford University Press, 1964).

13. Philippe Schmitter, "A Revised Theory of Regional Integration," in Lindberg and Scheingold, *Regional Integration*, pp. 232–64.

14. Stone Sweet, Sandholtz, and Fligstein, *The Institutionalization of Europe*, p. 6.

in this approach. In SSF, rules are made prior to interests, objectives, and values in the conceptualization of collective action.

Moreover, institutions are empty of content. What seems to matter to SSF is the creation and multiplication of organizations that make, interpret, and enforce rules, not the interests and objectives of actors who "inhabit" them. A consistent adherence to a spill-over logic, however, mandates a concern with interests because, presumably, they will determine which rules will be favored by actors. SSF sidestep the issue by holding that social structure and agency are mutually constitutive, without one being prior to the other; they see "institutionalization as a process that binds together, into a system of tight interdependence, the domain of social structure and the domain of agency."[15] Yet they also concede that analysis may proceed from the rationalist basis of actor interests. If that is so, the logic of structuration does not hold. They can't have it both ways.

Path Dependence or Unintended Consequences as Engines of Integration

The idea of path dependence (PD) had not been invented when NF was formalized. However, the logic of spill-over in its original version contains similarities to what was later labeled path dependence. What is this similarity? Is it consistent with the revised and scaled-down version of spill-over? Was it taken over by SSF? Should it have been taken over? I shall focus on only two features of path dependence: positive feedback and lock-in, as explained by Paul Pierson.[16]

A given policy, after being permitted to run long enough so that its effects can be experienced by an appropriate number of people, is likely to be experienced positively by this constituency. More people will per-

---

15. Ibid., p. 9.
16. Paul Pierson, "Increasing Returns, Path Dependence, and the Study of Politics," *American Political Science Review* (June 2000), p. 251ff. Curiously, Pierson's contribution to *European Integration and Supranational Governance* sounds more like NF. In refuting the intergovernmentalism of Andrew Moravcsik, he stresses that institutional evolution rarely corresponds to the preferences of the founders at the time of founding. Founding states suffer disappointment (he calls them "gaps") with respect to those preferences because any or all of the following may occur: supranational organizations assert their own preferences, politicians are capable only of short-term calculation, major unintended consequences attend policy decisions, and member governments develop new preferences. Pierson, "The Path to European Integration: A Historical-Institutionalist Analysis," in Sandholtz and Stone Sweet, *European Integration and Supranational Governance*, pp. 27–58.

ceive themselves as enjoying benefits and therefore bestow increasing legitimacy on the policies and those who fashioned it. In short, the institutions associated with the policy reap *positive gains*, which have the result of reenforcing the entire system. As a result, the procedures and attitudes associated with these institutions are "locked in": they can no longer be easily changed without offending large numbers of people and thus causing politicians to lose credit. In short, a path-dependent view of European integration sees the process as partly shaped by the initial institutional choices of the founders (no matter what their substantive objectives were) and likely to go on as long as the positive gains continue. Historical institutionalists devoted to this type of thinking like to point out that neither General de Gaulle nor Margaret Thatcher was able to reverse the process of integration, despite claiming that their countries had suffered negative gains.[17]

This view has a lot in common with the spill-over idea as it stood before the rethinking triggered by de Gaulle's vetoes and driven home by the Eurosclerosis of the early 1970s. NF also played with the idea of irreversibility, with a lock-in, even though positive gains were never envisaged in quite the form chosen by Pierson. Moreover, the reasons for NF's version of lock-in are the same as Pierson's. Instead of developing a notion of positive gains, the spill-over was driven by a postulated fear by the actors of suffering losses *unless* further sectors were integrated.

SSF accept this reasoning, along with also endorsing the principal-agent version of rational choice theory. This is curious since the two embody different logics. SSF especially accept as well the idea, shared by NF and PD, that unintended consequences are a powerful pro-integration force because they compel actors to improvise new systems-enhancing rules when they run into unforeseen trouble.

I maintain that these perspectives are not congruent. Principal-agent theory, PD, and rational choice theory are not concerned with specific actor values and interests; NF, using the logic of unintended consequences, is. The idea that different actors entertain different hierarchies of values and interests is factored out by the former, while it is the mainstay of research for the latter. NF is centrally concerned with pinpointing what does and does not spill over, and which consequences are both unin-

---

17. Path dependence literature suffers from a curious terminological confusion. Positive and negative gains are sometimes called feedbacks. In normal systems-theory–inspired discussion (derived ultimately from electrical engineering), positive feedbacks weaken or destroy the system while negative feedbacks reinforce it. Is a negative feedback (gain) really a loss? If so, then spill-over theorizing, because it stresses fears of loss by actors, relies on negative feedbacks.

tended and unwanted. Unlike SSF's emphasis, integration *as such* is never seen by NF as desirable or undesirable for its own sake, except by a relatively small set of actors, national and supranational.

Pierson's version of path dependence is not opposed to rational choice theory, but it is not clearly in that tradition either. Rational choice theory postulates clear equilibrium outcomes, though not a unique optimum. Path dependence merely claims that actors perceive the status quo as preferable to undoing past policies and institutions, whether they have reached equilibrium or not. Path dependence projects the results of earlier choices without also believing that these choices were uniquely efficient (i.e., rational) responses to some challenge. Hence I conclude that the pure version of rational choice theory is not compatible with an acceptance of path dependence.

Neither is it really consistent with featuring the logic of unintended consequences as an explanation of integration. That logic holds that actors at all levels, when confronted with results of past policies they do not like, will devise new policies not initially foreseen. In the European context, it is likely that this will happen as a result of a coalition between supranational actors, certain member governments, and certain interest groups (national and/or supranational). The composition of such coalitions will vary with the issues in question. I stress that this logic can work in a direction that moves toward as well as against integration.

Thus, the logic of unintended consequences is clearly different from both spill-over and path dependency thinking. Making it the centerpiece in an explanation of major changes dispenses with the mechanical aspects of both. It moves the empirical scope of study well beyond the expansion of economic ties and networks, by making *any* concrete policy domain and *any* constitutional issue subject to its logic.

Students of European integration are certainly not the only contemporary social scientists concerned with the exploration of major change. My own concern with the routinization of norms of international behavior is rooted in the same concern. Among the major approaches currently being advocated we find historical institutionalism, sociological in-stitutionalism, rational choice models, and path dependency. These approaches overlap. All of them must be examined to determine their usefulness in the possible revision of NF. All compete with constructivism, which also competes with NF. We now turn to an exploration of these themes. Our first order of business is to clarify the relationship between constructivism and NF. My own efforts at this task are complemented by those of Schmitter and of Sandholtz, Stone Sweet, and Fligstein.

A PRAGMATIC-CONSTRUCTIVIST ONTOLOGY

I want to understand the process(es) whereby norms governing behavior in international politics are routinized, as a way of concretizing my more deep-seated interest in developing a pragmatic-constructivist ontology. Various kinds of sociological institutionalism offer one possible source of help. They, along with all other kinds of institutional analysis, can be examined for the answers they provide to five core questions, which any pragmatic-constructivist inquiry into the interaction of agency and structure also must address. The questions, and a range of possible answers, are as follows:

1. What is the character of the constraint on agency? (a) Choice is limited by being embedded in a self-organizing system; (b) choice is part of a superordinate cycle of events; (c) choice is determined by the actors' initial decisions (path-dependency); (d) incorporation into "networks" determines choice; (e) habit alone conditions choosing.
2. Given constraints, how can change occur? (a) Endogenous change is not possible; (b) endogenous change can occur only as a result of actors' deriving lessons from unintended consequences of earlier choices; (c) exogenous shocks explain change.
3. How do actors choose? (a) Unchanging explicit interests, material and nonmaterial, explain choice; (b) interests explain choice, but they result from strategic interaction among actors; (c) interests are explained by power needs alone; (d) choices derive from frameworks and scripts produced by institutions; (e) choices derive from symbolic needs and their rhetorical articulation.
4. How do actors match ends and means? (a) They engage in cost-benefit analysis; (b) they apply the "logic of appropriateness"; (c) they determine instrumentally "whatever works best"; (d) they rely on rational choice routines.
5. How do actors deal with surprises and shocks? (a) They deny such events; (b) they adapt by selecting new means to attain unchanging ends; (c) they examine and change their ends, and then choose means, i.e., they learn; (d) they fail to respond at all.

Provisionally, the pragmatic-constructivist ontology might answer questions 1–5 as follows. But let us bear in mind that the units thought of as actors are not individuals, but long-lived collective actors professing important common values and concerns, such as states, nations, bureaucracies, or social movements:

1. Constraints may originate as deep-seated habit or be limited by the behavior of a network to which actors belong.
2. Change is due to exogenous shock or to drawing lessons from unintended consequences of earlier actions.
3. Actors choose by seeking to realize changeable interests derived from prior cognitive frameworks which are subject to reexamination.
4. Means are matched with ends by choosing what works best, purely instrumentally.
5. Actors often adapt to shocks and sometimes learn.

We shall see next how much, or how little, this ontology owes to sociological institutionalism.

PRAGMATIC CONSTRUCTIVISM: SPECIFIED ASSUMPTIONS ABOUT COLLECTIVE BEHAVIOR

It is time to delineate pragmatic constructivism (PC) more sharply.[18] PC assumes that agency is constrained by the actors' enmeshment in networks, formed by institutions and by habit, not by structural forces. These constraints, however, do not predict the results of agency or action itself because PC also assumes that actors adjust their later behavior in light of the perceived failure of earlier behavior to realize the actors' perceived interests. Put differently, later choices are the result of unwanted and unforeseen consequences.

While actors are assumed to change on the basis of their perceived interests, they remain constrained not only by institutions and habit but also by strategic interactions and calculations regarding other actors and by their own symbolic needs. Actors match ends and means by following an instrumental logic of "whatever works best." This is not to say that the logic of appropriateness is never used, but PC assumes that such a recourse can never be taken for granted.

Most importantly, actors are assumed to change their interests by adapting to surprises. Occasionally, they even learn to abandon a habitual way of attributing causality and to search for a new one, often more complex than the former way.

---

18. See Peter Haas and Ernst B. Haas, "Pragmatic Constructivism," *Millennium: Journal of International Studies* (December 2002), for a full statement.

SOFT RATIONAL CHOICE AND COLLECTIVE ACTION

These PC assumptions about collective behavior beg the question: is PC part of the "rational choice" ontology? Only in a trivial way, as the following defined terms suggest.

1. Values: a collectively-held repertoire with beliefs concerning rectitude and proper collective behavior. A value or a set of values can be considered "irrational" if, in the judgment of observers, it is not realizable in terms of the generally accepted view of the world that prevails in the society/polity in question.
2. Objectives: values expressed as ideas that are to shape the relevant society/polity. Objectives are "irrational" if, in the judgment of observers, the means chosen to implement objectives are inappropriate and/or impractical.
3. Interests: objectives expressed as formal demands by an organized group against the relevant society/polity. Interests are "irrational" if, in the judgment of observers, the actors fail to adjust means to ends in case of unintended consequences deflecting the attainment of the original ends. Interests are also "irrational" if they are too inflexibly defined to allow for adjustment.
4. Choice of policy: collective choices defining a set of measures (usually legal). Since interests in a polity are seldom wholly consensual, policy choices normally reflect compromises among actors. Choices are "irrational" as described in the case of interests.

What features distinguish "soft" rational choice from the "hard" variety?

1. There are no equilibrium outcomes in the soft variant; the concept of equilibrium is irrelevant.
2. There are no fixed interests because there are no predefined values, beliefs or preferences.
3. There is no overarching concept of rationality as there is in markets, games, or institutions as structures.
4. All choices are made on the basis of "satisficing."
5. Crisp predictions are not possible but ranges of outcomes are specifiable.

THE NEW INSTITUTIONALISM

I begin with the type of pragmatic constructivism known as the "new institutionalism" (NI). In order to explore this possibility, the nature of NI must first be established. I use the magisterial treatment of Walter Powell and Paul DiMaggio as the canonical characterization of NI.[19]

NI is conceived, above all, as an ontological stance that totally breaks with the "behaviorist" tradition of considering the rationally calculating individual as the prime unit of analysis for explaining collective action. NI rejects rational choice explanations, along with attempting to get rid of functionalist assumptions as agents of causality. It argues that actors should not be conceived as seeking to realize identifiable objectives by means they choose deliberately. Nor do organizations engage in calculated goal-seeking. I shall have more to say on these topics when I examine the relevance of rational choice theory to pragmatic constructivism.

Powell and DiMaggio identify several approaches to the study of institutions that they reject as not being properly part of NI because these approaches retain too many traces of utilitarian thinking, even though they break with "behavioralism." Thus, institutional economics retains a functionalist ontology. Rational-choice political scientists who focus on explaining the workings of institutions of government still cling to the notion of goal-seeking organizations (and individuals) attempting to realize equilibrium outcomes. Neoliberal regime theory in IR suffers from the same shortcomings.

Still, these theories agree with NI in that they are "united by little but a common skepticism toward atomistic accounts of social processes and a common conviction that institutional arrangements and social processes matter."[20] My approach to the study of norms also accept such a commitment. I agree that institutions—whatever they may be—"matter" and

---

19. Walter W. Powell and Paul J. DiMaggio, eds., *The New Institutionalism in Organizational Analysis* (Chicago: University of Chicago Press, 1991). I rely on the editors' introduction, pp. 1–40. I follow the convention suggested by the editors that NI is to be understood exclusively as that part of a larger sociological institutionalism that deals with organizations. Since states and non-state actors are invariably "organizations," i.e., congeries of individual actors "organized" for collective action, I find no incongruity in adopting this convention.

For a different conceptualization of institutionalism that offers an insightful constrast of the sociological with the economic kind, see Michael Rowlinson, *Organizations and Institutions* (Houndsmill: Macmillan, 1997). The literature reviews and paradigmatic summaries offered are very valuable.

For an outstanding comparison of PC, as used by myself, and sociological constructivism, as used by Alex Wendt, see Anne Clunan, "Constructing Concepts of Identity," in Rudra Sil and Eileen M. Doherty, eds., *Beyond Boundaries* (Albany: State University of New York Press, 2000), pp. 87–116.

20. Powell and DiMaggio, *New Institutionalism*, p. 3.

that large-scale change should be thought of as a "social process" animated by various forms of collective action. Remaining questions include: *what* counts as an "institution" and *how* do these entities shape collective action?

In their eagerness to avoid behavioral explanations of social processes, NI scholars run the risk of reifying whatever they end up considering as entities, forces, or influences that shape, constrain, or inspire human agency. They often conflate institutions with culture. Sometimes either or both are also considered to be a "system," within which agency must be explored. Moreover, social structure, a ubiquitous term, shows up as apparently isomorphic or even synonymous with institutions, culture, and systems. In short, NI obfuscates what causes what, or what is prior to what.[21] Whether a given characterization refers to actors or observers often remains obscure. Reliance on "structuration" as an ontological solvent confuses causality even more and offers no help in arriving at consensual definitions of core terms.[22]

NI, in featuring institutions as independent variables, stresses the notions of "institutional environments" and "organizational fields." These refer to the networks of discrete organizations in the same economic or social "sector" and the overall social settings (culture, structure) that allegedly constrain organizational action, as opposed to more localized influences. NI is concerned with persistence due to the embeddedness of social action in deep-seated forces.

---

21. As expressed by Powell and DiMaggio, NI has "an interest in institutions as independent variables, a turn toward cognitive and cultural explanations, and an interest in properties of supraindividual units of analysis that cannot be reduced to aggregations or direct consequences of individuals' attributes or motives. In the sociological tradition, institutionalization is both a 'phenomenological process by which certain social relationships and actions come to to be taken for granted' and a state of affairs in which shared cognitions define 'what has meaning and what actions are possible.' Whereas economists and public choice theorists often treat *institutions* and *conventions* as synonyms, sociologists and organization theorists restrict the former term to those conventions that, far from being perceived as mere conveniences, 'take on rulelike status in social thought and action.'" Ibid., pp. 8–9, emphasis in original. The first quote in this passage is from Lynne Zucker, "Organizations as Institutions," in S. B. Bacharach, ed., *Research in the Sociology of Organizations* (Greenwich, CT: JAI Press, 1983), p. 2; the second is from Mary Douglas, *How Institutions Think* (Syracuse, NY: Syracuse University Press, 1986), pp. 46–48.

22. See, for example, Powell and DiMaggio, *New Institutionalism*, p. 9, and the chapter by Lynne Zucker in the same volume. See Margaret S. Archer, *Realist Social Theory: The Morphogenetic Approach* (Cambridge: Cambridge University Press, 1995), for a withering attack on structurationism as resolving none of the major sociological conundra, on grounds derived from her version of scientific-realist thinking.

HISTORICAL INSTITUTIONALISM:
SLOGAN IN SEARCH OF A CLEAR ARGUMENT?

We are primarily concerned with two core questions with respect to historical institutionalism (HI). One concerns the issue of whether explanation that stresses path dependency is part and parcel of HI, or whether that approach can also be followed without making "path" assumptions. The other challenges us to sort out various approaches to historical-institutionalist explanations that stress structure, favor agency, or seek to combine the two. I address this concern first.

The empirical universe inhabited by historical institutionalists is shrouded in the fog of confusion noted by students of classical battles. Practitioners claim to be analyzing any political phenomenon whose form is shaped by a historical context. It is difficult to think of a phenomenon that does not fit this bill, provided only that human agency is somehow constrained by "institutions." All historical institutionalists sharply limit freedom of the will.

Considerable conceptual uncertainties make one suspect that historical institutionalism is merely another name for historical sociology as practiced by such scholars as Charles Tilly, Michael Mann, Reinhard Bendix, and Perry Anderson. True, these writers are concerned with large-scale events unfolding over centuries, while contemporary historical institutionalists deal with single policies that emerge over mere decades. Nevertheless, the two do not seem to differ markedly in basic concerns or assumptions.

I begin with a comparison of two searching efforts to define HI, one by Kathleen Thelen and Sven Steinmo, and the other by Ellen Immergut.[23] The difference in the two conceptualizations that interests me is the matter of agency. Thelen and Steinmo tend to favor structure over agency, whereas Immergut reverses the emphasis. Both treatments lead to the conclusion that HI is not a theory, but rather a way of emphasizing a certain type of causality.

For all three authors, the chief purpose of HI is to correct the causal assumptions associated with behaviorism and with Marxism, by showing

---

23. Kathleen Thelen and Sven Steinmo, "Historical Institutionalism in Comparative Politics," in Sven Steinmo, Kathleen Thelen, and F. Longstreth, eds., *Structuring Politics* (Cambridge: Cambridge University Press, 1992), pp. 1–32; Ellen M. Immergut, "The Theoretical Core of the New Institutionalism," *Politics and Society* (March 1998), pp. 5–34. Unlike other writers on the "new institutionalism," Immergut considers rational choice and organization theory as parts of this approach, along with HI. I am concerned here only with her treatment of HI.

how behavior is shaped by causally prior forces called institutions. These prominently include all arrangements that define decision-making processes, constitutions as well as ideas and interests. Interests are socially constructed by actors as a result of the historical context shaping actors' perceptions. Choice is structured by the legal rules in which decisions must be made, as well as by timing and sequencing pressures. Political power is relational: it depends on the network or coalition of which the actor is a part, and where in the overall institutional structure the actor is placed.

That said, emphasis among our definers diverges. Thelen and Steinmo explain change by stressing structure and context. Broad changes in socioeconomic context determine which institutions gain prominence. Such changes also determine adaptations in old institutions as new actors enter the game. Major exogenous changes trigger the articulation of new institutional objectives on the part of established institutions. The actual choices flesh-and-blood political actors make result from these larger dynamics. Their perceptions, not the analyst's, provide judgments of what is good or bad about choices.

Immergut, by contrast, insists that HI has a normative component in that it offers judgments of what is to be considered progressive or regressive. She insists that the true preferences of actors cannot be known and that individual preferences cannot be aggregated into collective ones; hence, normative results from choice cannot be specified ex ante. HI stresses historical contingency at the expense of the structural dynamics that appeal to other practitioners of HI. And a considerable amount of free will remains in the actor's repertoire:

> Institutions do not determine behavior, they simply provide a context for action that helps us to understand why actors make the choices that they do. Facing the same sets of institutional hurdles, self-reflective actors can make creative decisions about how to proceed. Thus, institutions—even when defined in the broadest sense— neither mold human perceptions to such an extent that individuals are incapable of recognizing competing definitions of identity and interest nor do they force human action along a single track.[24]

HI does not have a standardized list of independent variables, or even of core concepts that can be regularly adduced as explanations of change. Nor does it have a clear dependent variable. It simply postulates a black

---

24. Immergut, "Theoretical Core," p. 26.

box—institutions—as a variable intervening between any number of possible dependent variables and a large number of possible explanatory ones.[25]

STRUCTURE DOMINATES EXPLANATION OF CHANGE

HI features relatively few authors who put their emphasis on structural features in dealing with change. Those who opt for a structural emphasis also mention path-dependent arguments as a kind of afterthought. Our examples of this approach are articles by Stephen Krasner and John Ikenberry.[26]

Krasner and Ikenberry are not overly concerned with systematizing either history or institutions. Both are eager to show that adaptive choices on the part of actors seeking to cope with changing environments are hemmed in by the results of prior choices, which have acquired the force of brakes on free will. Institutions, as a result, are reified. Such terms as "system," "structure," "institution," and "institutional structure" are used as synonyms. Krasner says that "an institutional perspective regards enduring institutional structures as the building blocks of social and political life. The preferences, capabilities and basic self-identities of individuals are conditioned by these institutional structures. . . . The range of options available to policymakers at any given point in time is a function of institutional capabilities that were put in place at some earlier period."[27] Ikenberry concludes that "the general point that emerges from this perspective is that the appropriateness of system-, society- and state-centered theory is grounded in the larger set of historical dynamics that undergird institutional structures and policymaking."[28]

---

25. For a scathing indictment of HI along these lines, see Michael J. Gorges, "New Institutionalist Explanations of Institutional Change: A Note of Caution," *Politics* 21, no. 2 (2001), pp. 137–45. Gorges includes all forms of "new" institutionalism in his condemnation; HI is singled out on pp. 138–39. He also notes that most of the explanatory factors adduced by HI are accepted in many other theories and deployed more effectively. He shows how the social program of the Maastricht Treaty of European Union can be explained as an episode in institutionalization without recourse to HI. See his "The New Institutionalism and the Study of the European Union," *West European Politics* (October 2001), pp. 152–68.

26. Stephen Krasner, "Sovereignty," *Comparative Political Studies* (April 1988), pp. 66–94; G. John Ikenberry, "Conclusion," *International Organization* (Winter 1988), 219–43.

27. Krasner, "Sovereignty," p. 67.

28. Ikenberry, "Conclusion," p. 233.

There is nothing very specific about the historicity of the activities thus described: some choice in the past resulted in the evolution of a pattern of behavior (any law, norm, or practice) which persists. Krasner uses this pattern to explain the persistence of suboptimal institutions, such as the system of sovereign states; Ikenberry employs it to explain the difficulties of changing foreign policies. Endogenously-caused change is minimized, as are actor cognitions in their devising of adaptive behaviors. Almost every one of these authors' arguments could have been made without any reference to HI whatever.

AGENCY AS THE ENGINE OF HISTORY

Authors writing in the HI tradition who favor agency in their explanation of change tend to stress constraints on choice due to enmeshment in networks or commitment to earlier decisions. Actors benefit from their analysis of unintended consequences of earlier decisions. They choose on the basis of their interests, perceived directly or as a result of interactions with other players. Means are matched to ends on the basis of cost-benefit thinking in the process of adaptation. In short, a human dimension is restored to institutions, as is an assumption about rational behavior.

Thus, Jack Goldstone downgrades structural determinants by showing how identical structural conditions nevertheless did not produce identical or even similar outcomes because ideological motives intervened.[29] Other writers stress the enmeshing power of rhetoric, or repetitive normative discourse, in channeling actor decisions. Here, rhetoric as practice acquires the characteristics of institutions.[30] This argument is made with particular force by students of international law, who thus account for its efficacy despite the absence of an authoritative enforcer.[31] It is worth

---

29. Jack A. Goldstone, "Comparative-Historical Analysis and Knowledge Accumulation in the Study of Revolutions," in James Mahoney and Dietrich Rueschemeyer, eds., *Comparative Historical Analysis in the Social Sciences* (New York: Cambridge University Press, 2003), ch. 2. The article specifically challenges the accounts of Barrington Moore and Theda Skocpol as overly structural.

30. See, for instance, Frank Schimmelfennig, "The Community Trap," *International Organization* (Winter 2001). The author argues that the verbal commitment to the consolidation of democracy in eastern Europe on the part of European Union members compelled them to negotiate the eastward expansion in the face of many material objections.

31. Thomas M. Franck, *The Power of Legitimacy among Nations* (New York: Oxford University Press, 1990); Harold Hongju Koh, "Why Do Nations Obey International Law?" *Yale Law Journal* (June 1997), pp. 2599–2659. Koh identifies himself as a constructivist, though he does not make clear which type of constructivism he favors. He also sees strong affinities between his view and the British school of realism. However, his downplaying of the role of international society makes me question his claim.

stressing that authors who hold this view also maintain that a state *interest* in a given rule of law or treaty provision is insufficient for explaining the *habit of compliance* that states allegedly develop. Mere membership in international society, similarly, may be a necessary condition for compliance, but is not a sufficient one. Repetitive discourse by domestic audiences is also required.

This line of thinking has been most fully conceptualized by Jeffrey Checkel. He is concerned with studying the diffusion of norms originating in the international system (as represented, for instance, by multilateral organizations). He finds the microfoundations of local acceptance in the perceptions of national actors, both mass and elite. Hence he sees diffusion as an instance of social practice, that is, as an institution. Its success is mediated by the kinds of national institutions and norms (also called cultures and domestic structures) that the new superordinate norms encounter. Checkel states:

> More formally, both domestic structures and domestic norms are variables that intervene between systemic norms and national level outcomes. Domestic structure is used "to investigate and explain the decision process by which various initial conditions [systemic norms in my case] are translated into outcomes"; . . . for me, it also predicts, across countries with different state-society relations, the likely domestic agents empowering norms. Domestic norms determine the degree of cultural match, and thus predict, in a probabilistic sense, whether norm-takers in a particular country will be open to prescriptions embodied in systemic understandings.[32]

These legal arguments should be juxtaposed to ones that explain the efficacy of international law essentially in terms of the perceived interests of states, a distinctly nonconstructivist argument. See Abram and Antonia Handler Chayes, *The New Sovereignty* (Cambridge, MA: Harvard University Press, 1995); Louis Henkin, *How Nations Behave* (New York: Columbia University Press, 1979).

32. Jeffrey T. Checkel, "Norms, Institutions and National Identity in Contemporary Europe," *International Studies Quarterly* 43 (1999), p. 91. The embedded quote is from Alexander George. Checkel considers his constructivism as compatible with, but more inclusive theoretically than, that of others who, respectively, locate their microfoundations in symbolic interaction theory, role theory, attribution theory, and cognitive evolution. See pp. 90–91. His empirical work shows no evidence of any such transtheoretical integration. See, for instance, his "The Europeanization of Citizenship?" in Maria Green Cowles, James Caporaso, and Thomas Risse, eds., *Transforming Europe* (Ithaca, NY: Cornell University Press, 2001), pp. 180–97.

INDETERMINATE HISTORICAL INSTITUTIONALISM

The bodies of HI literature surveyed so far more or less clearly distinguish between a predominant dependence on structure and a predominant dependence on agency in explaining norm formation and normative change. In addition, we encounter HI arguments that insist on having it both ways, thus depriving us of a clear conceptualization.

One such provocative work offers a version of HI that causes it to lose its identity.[33] The authors think that all versions of HI and all other versions of institutionalism can learn from each other. They pay a high price, however, for this uplifting thought in the loss of clarity for all varieties. They posit a "calculus"-based HI, which sounds almost exactly like rational choice analysis, and a "culture"-based type, which resembles sociological institutionalism. HI differs from both, they argue, in not being preoccupied with issues of power and its persistence. Where path dependence fits in is unclear, along with the role of unintended consequences, in triggering institutional change. In fact, apart from the sequential character of all change, it is not evident that historicity has any marked role in this conceptualization.

Another group of authors, all concerned with explaining change and persistence in the institutions of social policy in advanced countries, and all claiming the mantle of HI, seem to mean nothing more elaborate than that timing and sequencing matter in explaining the origin of social welfare institutions (laws and bureaucracies), and that political institutions provide the "veto points" that prevent change. No claims are made that *particular* sequences imply *particular* outcomes, or that *specific* coalitions predict *specific* institutional arrangements, such as we see in the work of Barrington Moore and Gregory Luebbert.[34]

Analysts who privilege international organizations as masters of norm-creation and perpetuation confuse the issue of assigning causal significance. Some argue that international bureaucracies are powerful agents of norm-creation—or are they structures? But they lose power when the norms become less relevant in the face of changing environmental conditions (a euphemism for self-interested states that spurn the

---

33. Peter A. Hall and Rosemary C. R. Taylor, "Political Science and the Three Institutionalisms," *Political Studies* 44 (1996), pp. 396–57.

34. Essays by Bo Rothstein, Margaret Weir, Immergut, and Hall, in Steinmo, Thelen, and Longstreth, *Structuring Politics*, pp. 33–56, 57–89, 90–113, and 188–216, respectively.

norms).[35] Again, it is unclear whether these states are agents or speak in the name of some institutional structure, such as sovereignty. Constructivism does not benefit from this kind of confusion.

WHAT IS MISSING?

Some practitioners of HI are their own harshest critics. It has not escaped them that the causal conundra I have sought to illustrate obscure the power of the approach. Hence the suggestion has been made that HI is still "just history," unless its accounts of events are disciplined with the inclusion of two cognate approaches that stress *path dependency* and *critical junctures*.[36] Path dependency will be considered separately. It accounts for the continuity in institutions, for "locked-in" practices and organizations. Critical juncture analysis seeks to account for the origin of the institutions later locked in by path-dependent processes. It studies "big events" that change the trajectory of entire societies, and it does so by seeking to systematize the actors and their objectives and to match them with recurring outcomes.

But how far will that take us? Consider the following story, as told by Mark Blyth.[37] The corporatist institutions enabling the chief interest groups of the Swedish political economy to participate in shaping social and economic policy were created in the 1930s in a "critical juncture"– like context, and the policies enacted in them were shaped essentially by the Social Democratic Party and its affiliated trade union federation until the late 1970s. When the nonsocialist parties won control of Parliament in 1976, the institutions and policies erected by their antagonists were not challenged because the ideas on which they were based were "locked in": the new majority had no alternative ideas, seemingly a clear case of path dependence that kept the election from being a critical juncture. However, another event proved to be critical: when the Social Democrats were

---

35. For example, Michael N. Barnett and Martha Finnemore, "The Politics, Power and Pathologies of International Organizations," *International Organization* (Autumn 1999), pp. 699–732.

36. One such critic is Kathleen Thelen. See her admirable "Historical Institutionalism in Comparative Politics," *Annual Review of Political Science* (1999), pp. 369–404. For more self-criticism and a discussion of path dependence and critical junctures as additions to HI, see Jacob S. Hacker, "The Historical Logic of National Health Insurance," *Studies in American Political Development* (Spring 1998), pp. 57–130. The classical "critical juncture" comparative study is Ruth Berins Collier and David Collier, *Shaping the Political Arena* (Princeton: Princeton University Press, 1991).

37. Mark Blyth, "The Transformation of the Swedish Model," *World Politics* (October 2001), pp. 1–26.

once again victorious, in the next election, they "overreached" by attempting to alter the corporatist institutions so as to weaken industry and strengthen labor. This attempted power grab inspired representatives of industry to refuse their continued participation in the corporatist councils and to favor free-market policies, once the conservative-liberal coalition won the following election.

Blyth concludes from this story that whatever path dependence had produced during the forty-odd years of Social Democratic dominance was not stable enough to withstand a crisis. Actually, he had to invent a type of "cognitive path dependence" in order to make the story credible. He also concludes that institutions *by themselves* explain nothing. It is necessary to specify which ideas animate their role occupants before any institutional explanation becomes persuasive. Whether the 1980s will turn out to be a critical juncture in the history of the Swedish welfare state will not be known until we discover whether it will give way to the power of global free markets. Critical junctures, without the benefit of a long hindsight, may not turn out to be a powerful analytic tool.

THE POVERTY OF HISTORICAL INSTITUTIONALISM

No constructivist would deny that history matters, that timing is important, and that different patterned sequences of events can have important differential consequences. But unless we can systematize these insights we are really saying very little. Moreover, the empirical narratives of HI are almost exclusively about democratic-industrial countries, not the majority in a world of changing nation-states. The narratives, even if mindful of critical junctures and path dependence, do not do justice to change. If critical juncture analysis deals with the origin of institutions and path dependence with their reproduction, nobody deals directly with change, that is, with the arrival of new critical junctures.

Pragmatic constructivism does deal with change. It is concerned with the impact of new ideas on new norms of conduct. And it features as a mechanism of change the logic of unintended consequences, which most studies of path dependence ignore. Actors must cope with situations not experienced earlier. They must make efforts to reduce uncertainty about the future by using new cognitions or new knowledge—if they wish to flourish. In short, they must conceptualize how and why the consequences of customary patterns of behavior turned out badly, given the interests of actors. Little in HI seems to explain how they accomplish this task. No doubt, HI studies have made numerous descriptive contributions, primarily in the areas of modern social welfare and economic policy in advanced democracies. They have neglected studies of other issue areas and of changes in poor and nondemocratic countries. Worse, their treatment of causal mechanisms remains unsystematic and hence noncumulative. Few HI studies tell us in a disciplined way *why* actors adopt new ways or persist in old ones; they tell us only *how* they do it. One major conceptual failing, as noted by Immergut, is the lack of precision in the use and specification of preferences, interests, and choices. Pragmatic constructivism, too, can greatly benefit from these possible improvements in HI.

THE NEW INSTITUTIONALISM AND THE OLD

An older institutionalism (OI) allows for change and endows organizations (and their inmates) with a great deal of autonomy. NI is thought to differ from OI thus:

1. Conflicts of interests—along with "interests" in general—are not important, as opposed to OI, where they are crucial.
2. Inertia in spurring organizational action derives from lack of legitimacy, not from the desires of vested interests.
3. The relationship between an organization and its environment is constitutive, not based on calculated co-optation.
4. Institutionalization occurs in the surrounding environment or field, not within the organization.
5. NI questions the theory of action associated with utilitarianism because it involves lack of reflection by actors; OI stresses inadequacies in the way utilitarians deal with the aggregation of individual interests into a collective interest and with their neglect of unanticipated consequences.
6. NI focuses on classifications, routines, scripts and schemas used by actors constrained by institutions, whereas OI puts the emphasis on the norms, values and attitudes associated with institutions.
7. NI relies on attribution theory in its reliance on cognitive social psychology, OI on socialization theory.
8. Actors, in NI thought, act on the basis of habit and practice; in OI they act on the basis of commitment.

How do these characteristics apply to the development of a pragmatic constructivist ontology in IR? We are concerned with the way norms—ideas and values embedded in the minds of actors, not floating freely in "cultures" or sticking out of "social structures"—become routinized into practices. Put differently, we must be concerned with how identifiable collective actors with names like "British foreign ministry" or "Indian manufacturers association" or "Amnesty International" come to change their behavior toward one another as a result of adopting new beliefs about what constitutes legitimate conduct.

NI practitioners are of several minds about how or whether norms serve as constraints and sanctions. While my research allows for the differential impact of norms on action—some are more powerful than others—the fact that norms exist and are of some causal importance remains my unshakable assumption. Hence, NI perspectives that stress "deep" cognitive constraints as central to the study of institutional impacts are incompatible with pragmatic constructivism.[38]

Ontological suppositions that, in essence, deny any rational component in decision making are also incompatible with pragmatic constructivism. NI formulations are ill at ease with even the very "soft" rationality imputed to organizational behavior by James March, Herbert Simon, and Johan Olsen. Not much is left to even the impaired rational faculties of decision-makers in bureaucratic units if everything is explained by scripts and habits.

SOCIOLOGICAL INSTITUTIONALISM AND INTERNATIONAL RELATIONS

Pragmatic constructivism is based on the conviction that ideas matter in decision making in the way they shape and reshape actors' perceptions of their own interests. Pragmatic constructivists believe that the acceptance and the routinization of norms are related to actors' perceived interests, rather than emanating from a separate, free-floating moral entity. It follows that even though aspects of OI are compatible with pragmatic constructivism, NI definitely is not. I demonstrate this with a summary of the Stanford school's application of sociological institutionalism to IR.[39]

The Stanford authors claim that

> Many features of the contemporary nation-state derive from worldwide models constructed and propagated through global cultural and

---

38. I call attention to the work of Philip Tetlock on what he calls "cognitive complexity." That version of perception and cognition allows for the kinds of sensitivities on which pragmatic constructivism relies in its theory of change.

39. This section is based entirely on John W. Meyer, John Boli, George M. Thomas, and Francisco Ramirez, "World Society and the Nation-State," *American Journal of Sociology* 103, no. 1 (July 1997), pp. 144–86. They argue that their theory of IR does for culture what world systems theory attempts in economics and economic history. Structurally and in terms of the substantive argument, the two are identical.

associational processes. These models and the purposes they reflect (e.g. equality, socioeconomic progress, human development) are highly rationalized, articulated, and often surprisingly consensual. Worldwide models define and legitimate agendas for local action, shaping the structures and policies of nation-states and other national and local actors in virtually all of the domains of rationalized social life—business, politics, education, medicine, science, and even the family and religion.[40]

The core terms of the argument are "world model," "world system," "world culture," "world society," "dominant model," and "rationalization." All but the last exist "out there," antedating the nation-state and most of its institutions, indeed constituting them. The dominant model (i.e., the modern West in its entire cultural manifestation in western Europe and north America) shapes the rest of the world because non-western elites have been brainwashed into believing that this model alone guarantees progress.

The underlying mechanism of domination is the notion of a self-governing and self-perpetuating global system, animated not by the interests and malign intentions of the developed world's elites, but by the innate structural properties of the system itself. All development is due to exogenous forces. Actors do not choose policies or norms; policies and norms impose themselves from the oustide in the form of institutions.

Far from being able to learn, actors merely benefit from gaps and contradictions in the dominating external institutions. Non-western actors may subvert bureaucracies by decoupling local traditions from imposed rules, or by resisting the imposed rationalization with still viable local practices.[41]

Much of the work in this area is merely pretentious relabeling of familiar structural-Durkheimian argumentation. The core terms, often defined circularly, are used as snynonyms for one another, not as distinct elements in a complex directional argument in which causality can be identified. Mechanisms for linking units or forces at micro and macro

---

40. Ibid., p. 144.

41. The Stanford authors are unclear about the moral status of their argument. Emphasis on weaknesses in the world culture's ability to mold local cultures suggests that the authors really consider the world model to be the Sauron of an evolving Middle Earth. Yet they wax rhapdosic in praising that model for enhancing individual human rights and gender equality.

levels are missing. The authors insist on a single dominant model, not several competing ones. Most disturbing of all, it is often unclear whether the argument refers only to processes perceived by the observer or whether actors are expected to be aware of what goes on, even if active agency is completely eliminated in this scheme.

The concept of culture tends to be used as a hegemonic device for the minimization of agency. The actual substantive content of norms then becomes less relevant than their sanctioning quality for explaining behavior. If the culture is consensual, this quality alone will continue to integrate the society. In the terminology of one theorist, culture-derived norms function as social capital or as scripts. Hall and Taylor, for instance, favor habit for the persistence of institutional constraint, see little endogenous change, and credit institutions for shaping cognitive frameworks, which in turn make actors rely on the logic of appropriateness in making decisions.[42] The full application of this way of thinking to the study of international institutions would imply the impossibility of any normative change—since the cultural-normative frameworks are far from consensual—unless the developed world's dominance is used as the *deus ex machina*.

MOVING TOWARD PRAGMATIC CONSTRUCTIVISM

The possible relevance of sociological institutionalism to the creation of a pragmatic-constructivist ontology is dependent on finding formulations that moderate the constraints of structure so as to allow a good deal of leeway for agency. None of the works we surveyed come close to meeting this condition. At the same time it must be shown how and why structures constrain actors. We now survey works that may move in the desired direction.

This ambiguity is cleared up by Y. N. Soysal, *Limits of Citizenship* (Chicago: University of Chicago Press, 1994). Putting to work the Stanford conceptualization, she argues that the older dominant model of the nation-state forced the denial of cultural and other rights for immigrants in western Europe and kept them from being considered anything other than "the other." But she also argues that a new dominant model is being created by means of discourse among elites, resulting in the legitimation of multicultural nation-states, and thus reinforcing the Stanford school's argument that the new discourse is progressively moral.

42. Hall and Taylor, "Political Science and the Three New Institutionalisms." See also Victor Nee, "Sources of the New Institutionalism," in Marcy C. Brinton and Victor Nee, eds., *The New Institutionalism in Sociology* (New York: Sage, 1998), pp. 1–16.

One constraint on pure choice is the stricture of rationality. Rational choice is not a concept dear to sociological institutionalists; most abhor and shun it. But there are exceptions, notably Arthur Stinchcombe and James Coleman. In addition, James March and Johan Olsen allow for a great deal of agency while distancing themselves from rational choice explanations.

Coleman allows for the shaping of actor interests by institutions as well as by cognitive frameworks. Though he privileges decision making that follows a rational calculus, he allows for important exceptions. Stinchcombe seeks to explain organizational behavior in terms of how actors manage to cope with uncertainty, and with how they process and use information. "The best way to describe the individual as an information-processing structure is by the *routines* he or she can use, and then by the *principles* he or she uses to decide which routine to invoke."[43] Deliberate organizational design is the way to create organizations that improve information processing, and hence social welfare. This approach places the development of norms squarely in the realm of human calculation, while seeking to specify the wide limits on choice left to the actor by social structure.

March and Olsen lack respect for these residual traces of rational choice theorizing. The constraint on choice derives from path dependency: the actors are locked in by the consequences and benefits of earlier choices. Later change is due to endogenous forces in the drawing of appropriate lessons derived from the unintended consequences of earlier decisions.

Actors choose on the basis of their perceived material and non-material interests using the logic of appropriateness. They change their behavior by adaptation, choosing new means to attain fixed ends. Except for the reliance on path dependency and the featuring of the logic of appropriateness, this formulation comes close to a pragmatic-constructivist position.[44]

---

43. James Coleman, "A Rational Choice Perspective on Economic Sociology," in Neil J. Smelser and Richard Swedberg, eds., *Handbook of Economic Sociology* (Princeton: Princeton University Press, 1994). The quote is from Arthur Stinchcombe, *Information and Organizations* (Berkeley: University of California Press, 1990), p. 32, emphasis in original.

44. James G. Marsh and Johan Olsen, *Rediscovering Institutions* (New York: Free Press, 1989); Olsen amends this treatment in "Europeanization of Nation-State Dynamics," in S. Gustavsson and L. Lewin, eds., *The Future of the Nation State* (New York: Routledge, 1996). He argues that macro-level changes, such as the ones taking place in Europe now, can only be explained by actors' responding to exogenous shocks which cause them to doubt the legitimacy of existing institutions. This happens if established

Toward Reintroducing Change

A more satisfactory formulation of the issue is suggested by Beate Kohler-Koch's study of the origin of norms in the European Union.[45] By tracing the actual development of some norms she shows that the metaphor of the network captures the decentralized and relatively open-ended process of norm-creation. The loose constraints implied by being part of a network do constrain the freedom of maneuver of all actors because of the dynamic of multiple strategic interactions. But subsequent endogenous change occurs because of the actors' adaptation to unintended consequences. The matching of means and ends takes place on a purely instrumental basis. These constraints on choice leave a great deal to agency. Only the remaining power of states to call a halt to the entire process, or to leave the Union, acts as a macro-level structural brake on choice.

An even more promising sociological-institutionalist approach deliberately focuses on the dynamic elements of institutionalization, not on the reproduction and stability of institutions.[46] This approach is different from both the old and the new institutionalism. Change is conceived as the alterations in whatever system is being studied, and its transformation into another system, only to yield to still another later in the process. There is no final system.

The core concept is the "field." A field consists of the systematic relations among domains of interest: legal, political, and economic. The actors inhabiting these domains, in their interactions, act out their interests and in doing so assert and transform their mutual ties. The core collective actors in each domain are courts and the legal profession, bureaucracies and legislatures, and firms. Regional and global organizations and regimes are here reconceptualized as fields. Their evolution transforms global systems.

I call attention to the special features associated with fields because they will determine the utility of this conceptualization for pragmatic

---

norms are seen as failing to perform as expected and thus clashing with alternative norms. In short, a modicum of rational choice reappears as part of agency.

45. Beate Kohler-Koch, "The Strength of Weakness," in Gustavsson and Lewin, *Future of the Nation State*, pp. 169–210.

46. Neil Fligstein and Alec Stone Sweet, "Constructing Polities and Markets; An Institutionalist Account of European Integration," *American Journal of Sociology,* forthcoming; Neil Fligstein, *The Architecture of Markets* (Princeton: Princeton University Press, 2001); Sandholtz and Stone Sweet, *European Integration and Supranational Governance*; Stone Sweet, Fligstein, and Sandholtz, *The Institutionalization of Europe*; Alec Stone Sweet, *Governing with Judges* (Oxford: Oxford University Press, 2000).

constructivism. The interests driving actors are derived from transaction cost economics. Interests do not change, but the interactions and ties among actors do, as the circumstances under which perceived interests are acted on undergo change. It follows that actor calculations based on the logic of appropriateness are alien to this way of thinking. So are considerations that endow institutions with affect, making them valued for their own sake. Attachment to institutions remains instrumental so long as interests derived from market rationality remain ascendant.

Much of this approach ought to be seductive for pragmatic constructivism. Yet enough of the static, system-reproducing biases remain embedded in it to make us hesitate. The underlying logic is essentially functionalist: fields represent the stylized needs of interdependent actors. In the chamber music of inter-domain change, there is a haunting theme of a built-in need to change, a *leitmotiv* of actors' doing what the composer wants them to do. As a result the power of agency is once more put in doubt; the "needs of the system" achieve control, much as in Parsonian functionalism.

Institutions are really treated as abstract structures, even though they are supposed to be instruments for the realization of actor interests. The substantive stuff of the collective action in them is of little importance. In the case of European integration, what matters is the increasing quantity of acts performed within them, never mind their kind and quality.[47] Hence, such matters as the causal role of ideas, unintended consequences, inter-issue linkages, and actors' capacity for practicing cognitive complexity cannot be addressed, and actor learning remains unexplored.

HARD VS. SOFT RATIONAL CHOICE

Scholars who believe in the "emergent properties" contained in and by all kinds of systems have a quasi-mystical faith in the logic of "becoming." Potentially, this belief provides a structural pillar for "hard rational choice" as part of institutionalism. As demonstrated by Ilya Prigogine in chemistry, and as applied to almost everything by the Santa Fe Institute, computer simulation of the behavior of units in a complex system can disclose the ways in which the units can multiply, mutate, combine to do new tasks, go extinct, and adapt to do yet newer tasks. The pattern that emerges after tens of thousands of runs, as the principle of natural selec-

---

47. This conclusion applies more to the empirical work of Fligstein than to that of Sandholtz and Stone Sweet.

tion tells us, is superior to all of its predecessors in its ability to solve problems, and it dispenses with intentionality and motivation as explanation.

From this insight it is but a short step to argue that the emergent pattern is also wiser and more moral than its program-generated ancestors. Robert Axelrod's *The Complexity of Cooperation* makes exactly that argument about cooperation among human actors as played out in computer simulations.[48] If he is right, many of the puzzles about the origin and evolution of norms of international conduct may disappear. We will no longer argue among ourselves about the respective roles of path dependency and institutions, variations of rational choice by agents, and the different perceptions collective actors entertain about their interests. More generally, computer simulations will clean up one ontological battlefield.

One of the puzzling aspects of Axelrod's approach is the value one should attribute to his use of such key terms as "genetics," "mechanism," and "learning." Are these terms to be taken literally? Do they have specific meanings in the languages of artificial intelligence or complex self-organizing systems? If so, do these meanings carry over into the discussion of human collective behavior, or even individual behavior? Or are these terms to be taken as analogies to stimulate thought experiments—to make us imagine human interactions not readily observed or explained? More generally, is it acceptable to argue by analogy when the terms used in the argument come from fields far from human collective action? It is clearly acceptable if we merely wish to stimulate original thinking, but is this enough for an explanatory argument?

Axelrod's treatment fails to give us an institutionalist support for soft rational choice, for the following reasons:

1. Norms are never specified in terms of their content.
2. "Metanorm," a crucial item in explaining origins of norms and their robustness, is not a norm at all in the usual sense, but a condition of politics or an attribute of the international system. "Precondition" would have been a happier term.
3. "Mechanism" is really best translated as "accompanying condition," which makes it sound less deterministic.

---

48. Robert Axelrod, *The Complexity of Cooperation: Agent-Based Models of Competition and Collaboration* (Princeton: Princeton University Press, 1997). My comment concerns ch. 3, "Promoting Norms," ch. 6, "Building New Political Actors," and ch. 7, "Disseminating Culture."

4. With respect to other "mechanisms," it is unclear whether these are more than just "conditions," that is, whether they are lessons actors learn on the basis of trial and error.

Fritz Scharpf, in *Games Real Actors Play*, offers another approach that promises to link agency with structure in a "rational" form.[49] Real actors do not really play the games Scharpf analyzes. His objective is to improve the understanding of policy processes by treating them analogously to games. He does so by stressing "actor-centered institutionalism." Actions are fatally influenced by institutional opportunities and constraints, but nevertheless determined on the basis of a variety of choices open to actors in interdependent relationships, some cooperative and others antagonistic. Scharpf's theory is a case of the "new institutionalism."

This sounds as if it could combine institutionalism with constructivism: but this is not so. Ideas do not matter. Actors do not change preferences during the game, but rather they recalculate advantages. Agreement on the value of benefits and costs of losses is assumed. The public interest is also assumed to be an objective that governments may seek, as opposed to mere private interests. Rival assessments of benefits, shaped by prior ideas or ideologies, are still excluded. Learning, in the sense of reassessing values, does not operate.

Scharpf offers definitions that sound as if they could bridge rational choice with constructivist arguments.[50] He calls this a framework rather than a theory.[51] On the other hand, he avoids the circular explanations found in norm-type constructivism, where culture, institutions, and norms are defined with reference to one another.

Margaret Levi offers a serious discussion of how to adapt rational choice approaches to the analysis of major institutional developments by avoiding some of the overly economistic approaches.[52] Her "analytic narratives" come close to pragmatic constructivism. But the justifications and extensions are much more questionable and require critique. A major objection is that the empirical referents for elaborating and testing are all trivial with respect to the macro issues supposedly being probed. The same is true of Levi's discussion of conscription.

---

49. Fritz Scharpf, *Games Real Actors Play* (Boulder, CO: Westview Press, 1997).
50. See especially ibid., pp. 21–23, 34, 37–39, 40–41.
51. Ibid., pp. 29–30, 37.
52. Margaret Levi, "A Model, A Method, and a Map: Rational Choice in Comparative and Historical Analysis," in M. J. Lichbach, ed., *Culture and Structure* (Cambridge: Cambridge University Press, 1997), pp. 19–37.

All versions of institutionalism make the incontrovertible point that agency is indeed constrained or channeled by institutions, however defined. This point was deemphasized in the original NF, which treated institutions—if at all—in largely utilitarian terms consistent with PC. Various contemporary efforts seek to improve NF. Thus, Rosamond, citing Stone Sweet and Sandholtz, says:

> We view intergovernmental bargaining and decision-making as embedded in processes that are provoked and sustained by the expansion of transnational society, the pro-integrative activities of supranational organizations, and the growing density of supranational rules. And . . . these processes gradually, but inevitably, reduce the capacity of the member states to control outcomes.[53]

The conclusion seems overstated because it is offered in disregard of the substantive tasks of the institutions concerned. But if we focus on the Court of Justice and the Councils of Ministers of the ECSC, this emphasis is entirely compatible with their amended NF, as summarized above. Schmitter, unlike SSF, stresses the functions of institutions rather than their territorial basis, subsuming NF under what he calls polycentric governance without defined-uniform territory. The dynamic of collective action remains rational in the sense that agency is instrumentally interest-driven.

> "Irrational" postures or strategies—whether for dogmatic/ideological or personal/emotive reasons—are never absent from social action, even at the international level, but they are from this theory. They fit very uncomfortably within it. "Instant brotherhood" as a motive and "all or nothing" as a strategy make its operation exceedingly difficult. Unless some policy area can initially be separated out as jointly manipulable and unless some possibility of subsequent compromise involving tradeoffs or side payments exists, international integration, as conceived herein, is not likely to occur. The model assumes that integration is basically (but not exclusively) a rational process whereby actors calculate anticipated returns from various alternative strategies of participation in joint decision-making structures. More recently, this has been called the "soft rationality" assumption by Ernst B. Haas.[54]

---

53. Rosamond, *Theories of European Integration*, p. 127.
54. Philippe C. Schmitter, "Neo-Neo-Functionalism: Déjà Vu, All Over Again?" unpublished paper, July 2002, p. 16.

From this "soft rational" version of agency and mild institutional constraint, Schmitter defends some important hypotheses of neo-neofunction-
alism:

1. Spill-over effects resulting in more powerful regional entities are
    possible but not very likely.
2. The integration process is highly dependent on a large number of idio-
    syncratic and random exogenous conditions. "The model is, therefore,
    a very poor predictor of the initiation of integration movements and
    of the consequences of their first decisional cycles. It does not purport
    to synthesize such sufficient causes. If, however, it has any analytical
    validity, the residual proportion of variance attributable to these idio-
    syncratic and random events should decline. In other words, predicta-
    bility should increase with successive 'upward-grading' cycles as the
    movement approaches a political community. . . . One might call this:
    'hypothesis of increasing mutual determination.'"[55]

Schmitter thinks in terms of clearly demarcated phases of the integration
process which can take the form of regular cycles if the basic model correctly fits conditions on the ground. Phases and cycles are the least
conceptualized aspects of Schmitter's NF. Had he seriously considered
the implications of path dependency, despite shortcomings vis-à-vis PC
discussed above, the analytic plausibility of the cycles could thus be increased and illustrated.

All efforts to improve NF used to take claims of network theory
more seriously—their major debt to sociological institutionalism—and
also discourse analysis so as to do justice to what the inmates of institutions say to each other. After all, PC aims at showing how normative
orders change.[56]

MEDIATING BETWEEN HARD AND SOFT RATIONAL CHOICE

Schmitter's current work in amending NF to rid it of some of its earlier
missteps also implies a reconciliation with aspects of institutionalism.

---

55. Ibid., p. 21.
56. On this, see especially Clunan, "Constructing Concepts of Identity." Christian
Reus-Smit, however, overstates that argument by embedding the state and its institutions
entirely in culture and civilization, thus blending the work of Hedley Bull and of Adda
Bozeman's *Politics and Culture in International History* (Princeton: Princeton University
Press, 1960). See Clunan's *The Moral Purpose of the State* (Princeton: Princeton University Press, 1999).

This is achieved by means of Schmitter's idea of integration cycles. He distinguishes between (1) initiation, (2) priming, and (3) transformative cycles in the life of efforts at regional integration. The cycles differ in the way in which variables are distributed, as follows:

1. changes in the equitable distribution of costs and benefits among members derived from regionally induced transactions;
2. rate of regional group formation: "pattern of formation and active participation of new non-governmental or quasi-governmental organizations representing some or all members across national borders and designed explicitly to promote the interest of classes, sectors, professions and causes at the regional levels";[57]
3. differences in the extent of puralism (freedom) allowed private-actor groups;
4. differences in complementarity, particularly in view of the mobilization of group expectations regarding costs/benefits of regional integration;
5. differences in dependence on extra-regional actors and events.

The initiation cycles cover the period of the origin of events and the initial expectations and fears, and therefore trigger group formation. During the priming cycles, these trends either weaken or intensify. The transformative cycles describe events as the integration process leads to massive new regional institutionalization—or fails to do so. The value of this conceptualization resides in the measures for observing change. Thus, Schmitter advances these specifications concerning the priming cycles:

1. The less change in the relative size and power of national actors (vis-à-vis each other), the more likely that perception of benefits will be equitable.
2. The greater and more varied the changes in rates of transaction, the more likely that the rate of regional group formation and of the development of a distinctive regional identity will increase.
3. The greater the increase in internal pluralism within and across member states, the more likely are transnational groups to form and regional identities to emerge.
4. The more that complementary elites come to acquire similar expectations and attitudes toward the integration process, the easier it will be to form transnational associations and to accept regional identi-

---

57. Schmitter, "Neo-Neo-Functionalism," p. 25.

ties. Similarly, the joint sensitivity of elites to variation in international status is likely to become stronger.

5. The greater the previous scope and level of regional institutions and
    the more "upward grading" their decisional style, the more likely are
    regional bureaucrats to engage in reform-mongering.

6. The effect of changes in extra-regional dependence seems particu-
    larly paradoxical or parabolic. Both the marked rise or decline in
    global economic dependence may heighten sensitivity to interna-
    tional status. In the former case, new regional institutions may come
    to be regarded as the only bulwark of defense against further deteri-
    oration; in the latter, they may be at least partially credited with the
    relative success. Specific attempts by extra-regional authorities to in-
    fluence the integration process likewise may have a dual effect.

7. Actors who perceive their returns from integration as equitable—in
    line with anticipated returns and in proportion to those of others—
    will not reevaluate their integrative strategies (unless forced to do so
    by less satisfied actors) and eventually will opt for encapsulation.
    Only actors dissatisfied with the equity of returns will promote or re-
    consider alternative strategies. Within a certain negative range the
    most likely response is a positive one—push the process into new
    areas or provide central decision-makers with more resources or au-
    thority to redistribute returns. Beyond that negative range, the re-
    sponse will probably be negative in either scope or level or both.

8. Regional change processes "interdetermine" national actor strategies
    or, better, they set certain parameters within which alternative strate-
    gies are selected. Contrary to integovernmentalism, which postulates
    that these strategies for pursuing the (allegedly) unitary national in-
    terest will only be determined by "domestic actors," this theory
    stresses the extent to which such strategies may come to be influ-
    enced by transnational (regional or global) actors.

9. During the initiation cycle(s), the probability that a given national
    actor will push a spillover policy is relatively low, if only because
    initial insecurity and mistrust of partners is likely to make all negoti-
    ations more cautious.

The probability described above changes, however, during the priming cycles. As regional processes begin to have a greater effect, national
actors may become more receptive to changing authority and compe-
tences of regional institutions. "Spill-around"—the proliferation of
functionally specialized, independent, but strictly intergovernmental or-

ganizations—is a particularly attractive and easy strategy due to the ready availability of a large number of unexploited and relatively noncontroversial policy areas. "Build-up"—the concession by member states of greater authority to a regional organization without expanding its mandate—is more difficult because of the "untried" capacity of such a newly formed organization. It may prove more attractive where a competent but encapsulated one already exists and where its members are strongly but unequally affected by regional changes in a single sector. Disintegrative ("spill-back") strategies are, of course, less costly early in the process due to lower sunken costs, less entrenched patterns of benefit, and weaker symbolic engagement. It is the most likely strategy for an actor weakly affected by regional group formation, the development of regional identity, and the international status effect, but highly sensitive to perceptions of inequity on comparative rate of return. Characteristically, this takes the form of a single country defecting and, thereby, bringing the entire process of regional integration to a halt.

But the most likely strategy to prevail, once the priming cycles have kicked in, is "spill-over." Herein lies the core dynamic of neo- (and neo-neo-) functionalism—namely, that the regional processes mentioned above will dispose national actors to resolve their inevitable dissatisfactions by increasing both the level and the scope of common institutions.

Only regional integration experiments that make it through the priming cycles are likely to transform themselves into something qualitatively different. They will have exhausted the potentialities inherent in functionally integrating their economies and will dedicate more and more of their efforts to functionally integrating their polities. In the jargon of Mitrany's functionalism, they will "transcend" their initial commitment. In the jargon of Euro-speak, they will, at long last, define their *finalité politique*.

Needless to say, any theory about how (not to mention, when) this happens has to be purely speculative. No existing nation-state integrated itself in this fashion. They all used other means: war, revolution, dynastic marriage, anti-colonial struggle, and so forth. The European Union is, at the present moment, the only plausible candidate for entering this transformative cycle by cultivating complex interdependence, negotiating a sequence of voluntary (and unanimous) agreements, and foregoing even the threat of using force to produce a successful outcome. Clearly, the dynamic of institutionalization of decision processes is a crucial component of neo-NF, as is the idea of rational choice based on actor commitment to utilitarian thinking.

Revised NF and Future Research

The EU faces a number of curious challenges that could provide the occasion for research based on the model inspired by soft rational choice and by PC. What are these challenges?

Eastward expansion poses the following problems: is institutional pluralism compatible with group institutions and expectations that exist in the West? Is democratic decision making to be taken for granted in dealing with actor dissatisfaction? Is the growing complementarity of elite values with the West's likely? Not every politician west of the Oder is a Václav Havel.

The future for new policies poses similar questions. How are groups and politicians coming from different ideological families going to respond to environmental/energy measures, to a reduction in agricultural subsidies, and to immigration controls? Europe is attempting to write a new constitution for itself.

If the European Union has already entered or is about to enter into a transformative cycle, what processes might operate to bring this about? The higher order hypothesis of neo-neo-functionalism is that this will not come from below, i.e., from a convergence of changes in national institutions and interests, but from above, i.e., from innovations in exchanges and power relations at the regional level.

The first major innovation would be an increase in the "reform-mongering" role of regional bureaucrats within the EU institutions. With their capacity and resources augmented by previous redefinitions of scope and level, they are more likely to step up their efforts at directly influencing regional processes, even bypassing intervening changes at the national level. By negotiating directly with regional NGOs (and subnational governments), by inventing and promoting new symbols of regional identity, and by bargaining as representatives for the region as a whole with outsiders, they could begin to affect virtually all these processes rather than, as during the priming cycles, being confined to a few of them.

Regional institutions are also most likely during this cycle to begin in earnest their attempts at externalization. Their extended scope and level, together with the previously recorded and consolidated strength of regional change processes, provide the internal resources for such an effort; the impact of regional discrimination on nonparticipants is likely to provide external stimulus. These outsiders are going to begin to insist on treating the region as a new international bargaining unit and may even insist that it shoulder additional responsibilities in such areas as defense and security.

Finally, a new process of regional changes could well emerge. Let us call it the Domestic Status Effect. The redefined scope/level of regional institutions will tend to affect relative status and influence in the domestic politics of its member states.

None of this is predictable by the old NF. All of it can be conceptualized and studied systematically with an NF that has benefited from some parts of institutionalist thinking. Regional integration theory has a new lease on life; it is no longer obsolescent.

FURTHER READING

Alford, R. A., and R. Friedland. *Powers of Theory: Capitalism, the State, and Democracy.* Cambridge: Cambridge University Press, 1985.

Archer, M. *Culture and Agency: The Place of Culture in Social Theory.* Cambridge: Cambridge University Press, 1988.

Archibugi, D., and D. Held, eds. *Cosmopolitan Democracy: An Agenda for a New World Order.* Cambridge: Polity Press, 1995.

Armstrong, K., and S. Blumer. *The Governance of the Single European Market.* Manchester: Manchester University Press, 1998.

Brugmans, H. *Fundamentals Of European Federalism.* London: British Section of the European Union of Federalists, 1948.

Burgess, M. *Federalism and European Union: Political Ideas, Influences and Strategies in the European Community, 1972–1987.* London: Routledge, 1989.

Buzan, B., C. Jones, and R. Little. *The Logic of Anarchy: Neorealism to Structural Realism.* New York: Columbia University Press, 1993.

Cerny, P. G. *The Changing Architecture of Politics: Structure, Agency and the Future of the State.* London: Sage, 1990.

Christiansen, T., and K. E. Jorgensen. "The Amsterdam Process: A Structurationist Perspective on EU Treaty Reform." *European Integration On-Line Papers* 3 (1), http://eiop.or.at/eiop/texts/1999-001a.htm.

Christiansen, T., K. E. Jorgenson, and A. Wiener, eds. *The Social Construction of Europe.* London: Sage, 2001.

Chryssochoou, D. N., M. J. Tsinisizelis, and K. Ifantis. *Theory and Reform in the European Union.* Manchester: Manchester University Press, 1999.

Cowles, M. G., J. Caporaso, and T. Risse, eds. *Transforming Europe.* Ithaca, NY: Cornell University Press, 2001.

Dehousse, R. *The European Court of Justice.* Basingstoke: Macmillan, 1999.

Deutsch, K. W., S. A. Burell, R. A. Kann, M. Lee, M. Lichterman, R. E. Lindgren, F. L. Loewenheim, and R. W. Van Wangeren. *Political Community and the North Atlantic Area: International Organization in the Light of Historical Experience.* Princeton: Princeton University Press, 1957.

Deutsch, K. W., L. J. Edinger, R. C. Macridis, and R. L. Merritt. *France, Germany, and the Western Alliance: A Study of Elite Attitudes on European Integration and World Politics*. New York: Charles Scribner's Sons, 1967.

Duchene, F. *Jean Monet: The First Statesman of Interdependence*. New York: Norton, 1994.

Fawcett, L., and A. Hurrell, eds. *Regionalism and World Politics*. Oxford: Oxford University Press, 1995.

Gorges, M. J. *Europcorporatism?* Lanham, MD: University Press of America, 1996.

Grant, W. *The Common Agricultural Policy*. Basingstoke: Macmillan, 1997.

Griffiths, M. *Realism, Idealism and International Politics—A Representation*. London: Routledge, 1992.

Groom, A. J. R., and P. Taylor, eds. *Frameworks for International Cooperation*. London: Printer, 1994.

Held, D., A. McGrew, D. Goldblatt, and J. Perraton. *Global Transformations: Politics, Economics and Culture*. Cambridge: Polity Press, 1999.

Hesse, J. J., and V. Wright, eds. *Federalizing Europe? The Costs, Benefits, and Preconditions of Federal Political Systems*. Oxford: Oxford University Press, 1996.

Hix, S. *The Political System of the European Union*. Basingstoke: Macmillan, 1999.

Hollis, M., and S. Smith. *Explaining and Understanding International Relations*. Oxford: Clarendon Press, 1991.

Hooghe, L., and Gary Marks, *Multi-Level Governance and European Integration*. Lanham, MD: Rowan and Littlefield, 2001.

Jorgensen, K. E., ed. *Reflective Approaches to European Governance*. Basingstoke: Macmillan, 1997.

Kegley, C. W. *Controversies in International Relations Theory: Realism and the Neoliberal Challenge*. New York: St. Martin's Press, 1995.

Keohane, K. O., and S. Hoffman, eds. *The New European Community: Decision-making and Institutional Change*. Boulder, CO: Westview, 1991.

King, P. *Federalism and Federation*. London: Croom Helm, 1982.

Lindberg, L. N. *The Political Dynamics of European Economic Integration*. Stanford: Stanford University Press, 1963.

Lindberg, L. N., and S. A. Scheingold. *Europe's Would-Be Polity: Patterns of Change in the European Community*. Englewood Cliffs, NJ: Prentice Hall, 1970.

Lindberg, L. N., and S. A. Scheingold, eds. *Regional Integration; Theory and Research*. Cambridge, MA: Harvard University Press, 1971.

Mansfield, E. D., and H. V. Milner, eds. *The Political Economy of Regionalism*. New York: Columbia University Press, 1997.

Marks, G., F. W. Scharpf, P. C. Schmitter, and W. Streek. *Governance in the European Union*. London: Sage, 1996.

Middlemas, K. *Orchestrating Europe: The Informal Politics of the European Union, 1973–1995.* London: Fontana Press, 1995.

Milward, A. S. *The European Rescue of the Nation State.* London: Routledge, 1992.

Milward, A. S., F. M. B. Lynch, F. Romero, R. Ranieri, and V. Sorensen. *The Frontiers of National Sovereignty: History and Theory 1945–1992.* London: Routledge, 1993.

Mittrany, D. *A Working Peace System.* Chicago: Quadrangle Books, 1966.

Moravcsik, A. *The Choice for Europe: Social Purpose and State Power from Messina to Maastricht.* London: UCL Press, 1998.

Nelsen, B. F., and A. C. G. Stubbs, eds. *The European Union.* Boulder, CO: Lynne Reinner, 1998.

Ojanen, H. *The Plurality of Truth.* Aldershot: Ashgate, 1998.

Pentland, C. *International Theory and European Integration.* London: Faber and Faber, 1973.

Peterson, J., and E. Bomberg. *Decision-Making in the European Union.* Basingstoke: Macmillan, 1999.

Pinder, J. *European Community: The Building of a Union.* Oxford: Oxford University Press, 1991.

Robson, P. *The Economics of International Integration.* London: Routledge, 1998.

Rosamond, B. *Theories of European Integration.* New York: St. Martin's Press, 2000.

Rosenau, J. N. *Turbulence in World Politics: A Theory of Change and Continuity.* Princeton: Princeton University Press, 1990.

Ross, G. *Jacques Delors and European Integration.* New York: Oxford University Press, 1995.

Ruggie, J. G. *Constructing the World Polity: Essays on International Institutionalization.* London: Routledge, 1998.

Sandholtz, W. *High-Tech Europe.* Berkeley: University of California Press, 1992.

Sandholtz, W., and A. Stone Sweet. *European Integration and Supranational Governance.* New York: Oxford University Press, 1998.

Schmitter, P. C. "Imagining the Future of the Euro-Polity with the Help of New Concepts." In G. Marks, F. W. Scharpf, P. C. Schmitter, and W. Streek, *Governance in the European Union.* London: Sage, 1996.

Sidjanski, D. *The Federal Future of Europe.* Ann Arbor: University of Michigan Press, 2000.

Smith, S., K. Booth, and M. Zalewski. *International Theory: Positivism and Beyond.* Cambridge: Cambridge University Press, 1996.

Stone Sweet, A., W. Sandholtz, and N. Fligstein, eds. *The Institutionalization Of Europe.* New York: Oxford University Press, 2001.

Taylor, P. *International Organization in the Modern World: The Regional and the Global Process.* London: Printer, 1993.

Tranholm-Mikkelsen, J. "Neofunctionalism: Obstinate or Obsolete?" *Millennium: Journal of International Studies* 20, no. 1 (1991).

Tsoukalis, L. *The New European Economy Revisited.* Oxford: Oxford University Press, 1997.

Wallace, H., and W. Wallace, eds. *Policy-Making in the European Union.* Oxford: Oxford University Press, 2000.

Wheare, K. C. *Federal Government.* 4th ed. London: Oxford University Press/ Royal Institute of International Affairs, 1963.

AUTHOR'S PREFACE, 1968

I

THE central institution analyzed in these pages ceased to exist on July 1, 1967. The European Coal and Steel Community (ECSC) lost its identity as a separate institution when, on that date, its executive organ—the High Authority—was merged with the Commissions of the European Economic Community (EEC) and the European Atomic Energy Community (Euratom) to form the common executive of the European Community. The merger of the three executives presages an eventual fusion of the separate treaties constituting these central agencies of European economic and political integration.

This study ends in 1957. In 1958 the inauguration of the EEC shifted the focus of integrative and disintegrative activity from Luxembourg to Brussels, from coal and steel to tariff cutting, rules of competition, and agriculture, from talk of well-defined economic sectors to talk of political unity. ECSC continued to exist, but only as a shadow of the vital institution described in this book. It had become a technical agency concerned with improving the quality of steel and increasing the demand for steel products, with negotiating (unsuccessfully) a common European policy for oil, gas, nuclear energy, and coal, with adapting a dying coal-mining industry to the demands of a different market for energy. It was no longer concerned with the more politically infused activities of regulating prices, eliminating subsidies, and standardizing transport rates. The High Authority's supreme attempt to assert supranational powers by imposing coal production quotas in 1959 was rebuffed by three of the six governments. Why then republish this book?

There are two justifications for republication: to retain a factual and descriptive account of the adaptive ability demonstrated by men, political and economic groups, and entire nations with respect to new international institutions and powers; and to throw into bold relief the theory of regional integration that follows the "principle of the hiding hand," to use Albert O. Hirschman's suggestive phrase.[1]

The factual record shows the behavior of interest groups in a democratic-pluralistic setting when confronted with decisions and powers from new sources, superimposed on long familiar national governments. It offers parallel material on the adaptive activities of political parties. Technical administrators and bureaucrats, who play a particularly important role in industrial societies, are observed and their creative manipulations of politicians and interest groups highlighted. But if these groups and individuals are so important and their activities so crucial, why have they not resulted in a united Western Europe? What makes these actions worthy of being recorded? Are we not endowing the free will of the actors with a little too much weight?

Discovering, recording, and presenting a body of factual material that is no longer part of an ongoing reality is worthwhile only if it is relevant to the explication of a process that is still very much with us. The ECSC experience has spawned a theory of international integration by indirection, by trial and error, by miscalculation on the part of the actors desiring integration, by manipulation of elite social forces on the part of small groups of pragmatic administrators and politicians in the setting of a vague but permissive public opinion. "Functionalism" and "incrementalism" rather than "federalism" and "comprehensive planning" are the key terms used in describing this theory. Have events in Western Europe since 1958 validated or weakened that theory? What limitations of the theory have been discovered? How must the theory be amended in order to remove these limitations? These are the big questions that must still be answered before the justification for republication of this work is wholly persuasive. My preface is devoted to answering these questions rather than to summarizing the original theory and placing it into context, a task accomplished by the prefatory remarks to the first edition.

II

The central maxim of this theory is the Nietzschean saying that "that which does not destroy me, makes me stronger." But for

---

[1] *The Public Interest*, No. 6 (Winter, 1967), pp. 10–23.

the empiricist the validity of this aphorism must first of all rest on the demonstration of the continued temporal validity of the processes culled and induced from the factual survey. If I may be forgiven the normal pride of authorship, studies of the European Communities completed in the last few years seem to attest to the essential soundness of the processes and patterns described in *The Uniting of Europe.* Britain's continued efforts to penetrate the Six testify to the reality of the spill-over as experienced by the trade and defense partners of the Community countries. The Commission of the EEC evolved a decision-making process not vitally different from that of the High Authority of the ECSC. The political behavior of the Council of Ministers of the European Economic Community and Euratom surprised nobody familiar with the pattern of negotiation and discussion in the ECSC's Council of Ministers. The unique "supranational" style evolved in Luxembourg of basing European economic decisions on permanent interaction between Commission and Ministers was carried over to Brussels. Interest groups that cautiously organized at the level of the Six in order to assure the voicing of their demands at the supranational level did not evolve beyond the confederal mode in Luxembourg; neither had they in Brussels ten years later. Political parties, in their national parliaments and in the European Parliament in Strasbourg, first learned to make themselves heard supranationally and assert their powers of "control" over the executives under ECSC auspices; their pattern of organization and their effectiveness have not changed dramatically under the aegis of the EEC. As for public opinion, it favored "European unity" in general and unsophisticated terms in the earlier as well as in the most recent periods of history, but it still remains impressionistic, weakly structured, and lacking in patterns of demands and expectations—except among young people.[2]

---

[2] The following works provide the most complete studies of the political significance and methods of the EEC: Leon N. Lindberg, *The Political Dynamics of European Economic Integration* (Stanford, 1963); Stuart A. Scheingold, *The Rule of Law in European Integration* (New Haven, Conn., 1965); U. W. Kitzinger, *The Politics and Economics of European Integration* (New York, 1963); R. Colin Beever, *European Unity and the Trade Union Movement* (Leyden, 1960); P.-H.J.M. Houben, *Les Conseils de ministres des communautés européennes* (Leyden, 1964); Gerda Zellentin, *Der Wirtschafts- und Sozialausschuss der EWG und Euratom* (Leyden, 1962) and *Budgetpolitik und Integration* (Cologne, 1965); Henri Manzanarès, *Le Parlement européen* (Nancy, 1964). Much light on the way the Commission saw its duty and role is shed by Walter Hallstein, *United Europe* (Cambridge, Mass., 1962). See also the excellent articles by John Lambert, Dusan Sidjanski, Gerda Zellentin, Etienne Hirsch, and J.-R. Rabier in *Government and Opposition*, II, 3 (April-July, 1967). Also Ronald Inglehart, "An End to European Integration," *American Political Science Review*, LXI, 1 (March, 1967), 91–105, and Guy Van Oudenhove, *The Political Parties in the European Parliament* (Leyden, 1965).

These findings are reassuring to the author because they confirm the persistence of the patterns discerned earlier; but they should also shake his faith in the functional theory. After all, ten years after the completion of the study the various spill-over and adaptive processes still had not resulted in a politically united Europe. The theory predicted institutional and group behavior with considerable accuracy, but that behavior failed to result in the integrative political consequences anticipated. What went wrong? I can now perceive, with the benefit of hindsight, comparative integration studies, and the lessons taught us all by General de Gaulle, that the functional theory erred in not giving sufficient weight to four considerations:

(1) The functional theory neglected the important distinction between *background* variables, such as are treated most often in studies of regional transactions, and heterogeneity, conditions, and expectations prevailing *at the time* a union is set up, as well as new aspirations and expectations that develop *after* the initial experience. The emergence of a new style of leadership at the national level, such as a single charismatic figure who is able to rule because of a crisis in a portion of the union, is an example of such a development, and underscores the need for distinguishing between the causative role of these three temporally differentiated sets of conditions.

(2) The original theory, implicitly if not explicitly, assumed the existence of the condition we have come to label "the end of ideology." Therefore, the conditioning impact of nationalism was defined out of existence but not empirically examined. I do not regret having done this, because an important point was made in the process: the mutability of the concept of "nation" and of the intensity of national feeling was underlined. But the point was made too strongly, because a new kind of national consciousness has since become discernible, particularly in France.

(3) Functional theory also neglected to treat the world setting or the external environment in which the integration took place, except in the most cursory fashion. Again, I have no regrets in having overemphasized a point that had previously been shrugged off with assertions that regional unions result from the balance of power and other mythical animals. But in stressing the purely internal determinants of integrative behavior, I created the impression that external stimuli do not exist. The impact of the

East-West détente on the speed and focus of European integration has taught us otherwise, as has the direction of Gaullist foreign policy. Our argument that an external *military threat* was not sufficient to account for integration overlooked the fact that the international system contains stimuli other and more subtle than common external enemies, such as new international opportunities.

(4) Finally, the functional theory here developed failed to spell out the massive transformations of European society and political style that occurred contemporaneously with, but *autonomously* of, the integration process. Highly industrialized society and the behavior patterns associated with it are the internal environment in which the forces here described took shape. Massive changes in economic and social organization owed very little to the integration process, but the forces of integration depended largely on these changes.[3]

We must attempt to explore some of these oversights.

III

Let us start with a discussion of the phenomenon of nationalism. To the self-conscious nation the preservation of its independence is the minimal and most cherished aim. Politics is the means to keep independence; politics must take precedence over everything, certainly over the economics of a common market. How true is this to the reality of modern Europe?

Following Stanley Hoffmann, we may think of nationalism as the explicit doctrine or "ideology" of certain elites, suggesting positive values with respect to one's own nation and less positive ones for outsiders, and certainly implying specific policies for the state to follow. Hoffman contrasts this notion of nationalism with "national consciousness," the feelings of the inhabitants of the state that they "belong" to the community of people living under one government, or wishing to do so. Finally, Hoffmann suggests the existence of a "national situation," a condition in time and space describing the power, freedom of maneuver, and rank of one's own nation

---

[3] These afterthoughts and refinements in the theory are worked out in my "International Integration: The European and the Universal Process," *International Organization* (Summer, 1961); "Technocracy, Pluralism and the New Europe" in S. Graubard (ed.), *A New Europe?* (Boston, 1964); "Economics and Differential Patterns of Political Integration," *International Organization* (Autumn, 1964); "The Uniting of Europe and the Uniting of Latin America," *Journal of Common Market Studies* (June, 1967).

vis-à-vis others. The national ideology produces foreign policy on the basis of the firmness of national consciousness and limited by the nature of the national situation.[4]

Supranational integration becomes explicable, therefore, whenever a certain relationship between these three aspects of nationalism happens to exist. Thus, in 1950 Europeans saw their national situations in very gloomy terms. Moreover, *each* nation experienced this pessimism. Germans strongly felt the stigma of guilt inherited from the Nazi period and searched for a way to reattain international respectability. Italians shared this sentiment. Both attributed their plight to an earlier national ideology and therefore did not value their own national identities very highly. Frenchmen saw themselves as a defeated power, barely able to control inflation and begin economic reconstruction, living in the protective shadow of the "Anglo-Saxons." The Benelux countries experienced their dependence and weakness more than ever, having seen their neutrality ignored and their foreign trade manipulated by forces beyond their control. Britain and the Scandinavian countries, by contrast, saw their national situations in more optimistic terms.

National consciousness reflected this reasonably objective picture of the situation. The trauma of the war and the reconstruction period seemed to make a mockery of the proud national feelings of the prewar period in the Europe of the Six. National consciousness was practically lacking in Germany and Italy; it was far from people's minds in France, Belgium, and the Netherlands when the tasks of the moment seemed to be hard work, investment, the search for new export markets, nationalization of industry, expanded social security coverage, and a perceived threat of communism that struck all of Europe in approximately equal terms.

The national ideologies of the ruling elites in 1950 were therefore far from ebullient, self-confident, assertive, or hostile. On the contrary, national consciousness and the objective national situation combined to make desirable a search for policy alternatives that would guarantee security and welfare, peace and plenty *without* repeating the nationalist mistakes of an earlier generation of statesmen. The result was the drive for a united Europe—maximally by way of federal institutions, minimally through a tight network of intergovernmental organizations, and, after 1952, most consistently

[4] Stanley Hoffmann, "Obstinate or Obsolete? The Fate of the Nation-State and the Case of Western Europe," *Daedalus* (Summer, 1966), pp. 867–69.

by way of supranational "communities" devoted to specific functional tasks with great indirect political importance.

What does the Europe of the Six look like in 1967? The national situation of each country is vastly different. As the recent history of NATO shows, only Germany is still concerned with a Communist threat. Living standards have soared; industrialization has been pushed to the point where it rivals that of the United States; consumption patterns are those typical of the most highly developed countries; various kinds of economic planning are routinely accepted; from a recipient of aid, Europe has become an international donor. France is a small nuclear power; Italy has a labor shortage; Holland is wealthy and self-confident enough to have a peace corps, as do the Scandinavian countries. West Germany is once more one of the leading industrial nations, with a far-flung network of international trade. And so is France.

Does this picture of new vigor imply a rebirth of the older national consciousness? Apparently it does not. Self-satisfaction and a desire to enjoy the fruits of industrialism seem to have taken the place of the older passions. In the Benelux countries there seems to be general agreement that the safeguarding of these boons requires a continental vision and policy, not exclusive loyalty to the nation, especially when the supranational scheme does not call for a conflict of loyalties between the nation and the European Community. Italians still do not seem to be able to rally to the old slogans. While we hear sometimes of a revival of German nationalism, there is little evidence that a set of popular values closely resembling the Nazi visions is developing. Only in France is there a revival of "great power thinking" that reflects the new national situation; but by no means all groups and parties share this feeling, and few of the elite groups of France are willing to follow their leader into scuttling the Common Market for the sake of a pure national French identity.

National ideology reflects these conditions. For Italy and the Benelux countries the change in the national situation has implied no major change in national consciousness and ideology: their aim is the continuation of the integrative process, albeit by unspectacular and hardly federal means. For West Germany it has implied a certain rebirth of self-confidence that makes itself felt in an effort to secure German aims by alternatively negotiating with and courting France, Britain, and the United States. From a guilt-struck satellite, Germany has become a cautiously independent actor on the international stage, still accepting European unity as an economic and military aim to resolve her conflicts in policy, even if the supranational method has become less important.

France is the deviant case. Here a marked change in the national situation has brought a partial change in national consciousness that was translated by General de Gaulle into a very major change in national ideology and policy. Still, many elite groups in the economy and in public life, while welcoming some measure of increased national self-confidence, remain committed to integration and the downgrading of the General's nineteenth-century concept of sovereignty. Nevertheless, it is the change in national situation and consciousness in France that enables de Gaulle, a true nineteenth-century nationalist, to follow the pro-sovereignty policy now, whereas he failed in the same attempt in 1950.

The postwar national situation in each West European country later involved in the European Community was such as to make people look for solutions to their problems in a framework larger than the discredited nation-state. The nation-state seemed unable to guarantee economic welfare, military security, or the enjoyment of democracy and human rights. Each nation possessed many groups that questioned the utility of national autarky, even if each group did so for its own reasons. However, the disenchantment was shared across the frontiers so that the lack of faith in the nation was expressed in the formation of a series of regional voluntary associations of diverse ideological persuasions, each eager to safeguard the new lease gained on the democratic way of life as a result of the defeat of fascism. Some wanted merely freer trade and investment; others wanted a full-fledged federation; all shared a sense of frustration. But far from wanting to create a new society, to innovate, to make a new kind of man, each sought only to safeguard an *existing way of life* given a new birth through victory in World War II. Regional unification, in a sense, was a conservative impulse: it sought to innovate in order to preserve something already existing.

Federalism was the initial watchword. European unity was hailed with glowing phrases by Winston Churchill, Léon Blum, Alcide de Gasperi, Salvador de Madariaga. A "European Movement" was formed that sought to achieve federation by stressing the cultural unity of Western civilization and that drew heavily on the misery of Europe, overshadowed by the new giants of East and West. The pan-European ideal first enunciated by Count Coudenhove-Kalergi in 1923, extolling Europe to seek survival in a world increasingly dominated by the United States and the Soviet Union, was hailed once more. The result was failure: no federal institutions were created, no uniform enthusiasm for federation could be mobilized in equal measure on the continent, in Britain, and in Scandinavia. The record of failure stretched from the creation of the far-from-federal Council of Europe through the defeat of the European Defense Community treaty to the burial of the European Political Community project in 1954.

Something else happened instead. Not cultural unity but economic advantage proved to be an acceptable shared goal among the Six. The failure of the federalist European Movement saw the rise of the "functionalist" school of technocrats led by Jean Monnet, the architect of France's postwar economic planning structure. Each of the Six, for individual national reasons and *not* because of a clear common purpose, found it possible and desirable to embark on the road of economic integration using supranational institutions. Converging practical goals provided the leaven out of which the bread of European unity was baked. It was not the fear of the Soviet Union nor the envy of the United States that did the job. Slogans of the past glories of Charlemagne, of the popes, of Western civilization were certainly heard, but they did not launch the Coal and Steel Community or the Economic Community. Converging economic goals embedded in the bureaucratic, pluralistic, and industrial life of modern Europe provided the crucial impetus. The economic technician, the planner, the innovating industrialist, and trade unionist advanced the movement—not the politician, the scholar, the poet, or the writer.

Does the argument assert the victory of economics over politics? To do so would be to oversimplify unforgivably. Politicians *were* important in the process. Economic reasoning alone was not sufficient. When the Coal and Steel Community reached the limits of the integrative action it was permitted under its treaty, it could not simply expand its powers along the lines of economic needs. Unfulfilled economic promise could not simply and painlessly give rise to new supranational economic tasks, pushing the continent closer to political unity. Politics remained imbedded in the functional logic.

How? The decline of the old national consciousness in Europe brought with it the submerging of the traditional notion of "high politics." The new national situations eliminated the possibilities of strong and independent diplomatic moves on the world stage. Those who tried them—Britain in Greece, France in Indo-China—soon recognized their error. The sharp line between the politics of economic welfare at home and the politics of national self-assertion abroad simply disappeared. Men thought in terms of realizing the welfare state—of subordinating world commitments and an independent foreign policy to the economic and fiscal demands of domestic welfare. Economics and politics became intermingled, and only a Churchill or a de Gaulle could keep the older vision of high politics alive. But the Europe of the 1950's listened to neither. However, the decision to follow the gospel of Jean Monnet rather than that of the federalists—which was "political" in a pure sense—rested on a political commitment to realize peace and welfare by way of European unification. The statesmen who wrote the treaties of the European Communities and who guided them through their national parliaments were committed to the gradual, the indirect, the functional path toward political unity. They knew, or sensed, that the imperfections of one treaty and one policy would give rise to re-evaluations that would lead to new commitments and new policies moving farther along the road to unification. No federal utopia necessarily provided the guiding beacon, but an institutionally vague "supranational" Europe did light the way. Functional integration could proceed, then, because key politicians—Schuman, Adenauer, Spaak, Beyen, de Gasperi, Van Zeeland, Fanfani—had decided to leave the game of high politics and devote themselves to the building of Europe, to achieve more modest aims. And thus the economic technician could play his role within the shelter of the politicians' support.

As the Coal and Steel Community began to run up against the legal limits of its powers to integrate the most politically sensitive sectors of the European economy after 1958, and because some of the six governments were unwilling to countenance further supranational assertion, the EEC inherited the spill-over potential of its predecessor. It displayed a five-year burst of integrative energy, launching the concrete economic policies and furthering the regional political processes described by the authors cited above (see footnote 2).

These activities came close to voiding the power of the national state in all realms other than defense, education, and foreign policy.

In the realm of decision-making by supranational institutions, the work of the EEC was particularly striking. Most major economic decisions were made by the Council of Ministers on the basis of proposals by the Commission and, after negotiations conducted by the Commission, at the level of senior civil servants. While decisions required more and more prolonged "marathon" negotiations after 1961, agreement was always eventually attained, usually resulting in increased powers for the Commission to make possible the implementation of what was decided. This was true particularly in the case of agriculture. The Commission established and cultivated direct relations with supranational interest groups of farmers, industrialists, merchants, and workers; it cemented its relations with national officials; it gave the politicians and political parties represented in the European Parliament the opportunity to study, debate, and criticize policy in considerable detail and on a continuing basis. Finally, it made crucial decisions that prompted extensive and far-reaching litigation in the European Court of Justice, resulting in the definition by that court of a European doctrine of individual rights vis-à-vis, the actions of national courts and administrative agencies, as implied by the Treaty of Rome and enforceable by the Community.

The irony of these developments from the standpoint of functionalism is that they had not all been planned or approved by the governments in 1958. This irony is underscored by the fact that the growth in the power of the Commission occurred in several instances as a result of bargains with the French Government. For instance, the defeat of the British effort to scuttle the Common Market with the "free trade area" scheme discussed in 1958 and 1959 was due to an ad hoc alliance between France and the Commission. The victory of the French-flavored policy for agriculture, prior to 1965, was mixed with the growing institutional authority of Commisson-controlled marketing committees and a policy of lower external tariff favored by the Commission. No single government or coalition controlled the decision-making process. The Commission, because of its power of initiative, was able to construct a different coalition of supporting governments on each major issue. In short, the functional logic that may lead more or less automatically from a common market to political unification seemed to be neatly illustrated by the history of the EEC. How, then, could a single charismatic Frenchman stop the process? Has the pragmatic

politics of regional negotiation for greater welfare benefits given
way once more to high politics?

De Gaulle's sentiments toward supranational institutions—as distinguished from the policies they produce—are candidly disdainful.
In the grand style of high politics it is more important to resist the
encroachment of supranational technocrats on the nation than it is
to negotiate higher prices and subsidies, even if paid by German
consumers to French farmers. We can only surmise the thoughts and
calculations that passed through the General's oracular mind. But
the results of our surmises add up to a rebirth of nationalism and
anti-functional high politics as far as France is concerned.

De Gaulle had been perfectly willing to use the Communities as
part of his design to weld Western Europe together under the confederate formula of *l'Europe des états* and under French leadership,
but his partners declined to follow his lead here as in NATO.
Hence when the economic and political spill-over logic propelled
Britain and her partners in the European Free Trade Association
to apply for membership in the Europe of the Six, de Gaulle alone
opposed it because the merger did not fit into his *Grosspolitik*. In
the process, he succeeded in stopping the Commission from asserting independent financial and economic powers and in confirming
the continuation, *de facto*, of the unanimity voting formula in the
Community Council of Ministers.

The protests and frustrations of the other five governments availed
them little. When forced by France to choose between the continued
economic benefits of a common market and dedication to the supranational method of decision-making, they preferred the former.
De Gaulle, apparently relying on the economic instincts of his partners, gave them a brutal choice by saying: "France wants a common
market as much as you; if you really want it, join me in preserving
it, but restrain supranationality." High politics may not have taken
the place of pragmatic economic calculation for all the players in
the game; but if one of them so defines the situation, the others seem
compelled to follow suit.

IV

This sequence of events suggests that something is missing in the
exploration of the integrative process presented in *The Uniting of
Europe*. The phenomenon of a de Gaulle is omitted; the superiority

of step-by-step economic decisions over crucial political choices is assumed as permanent; the determinism implicit in the picture of the European social and economic structure is almost absolute. Given all these conditions, we said, the progression from a politically inspired common market to an economic union and finally to a political union among states is automatic. The inherent logic of the functional process in a setting such as Western Europe can push no other way.

De Gaulle has proved us wrong. But how wrong? Is the theory beyond rescue? I suggest that the theory can be amended with the lessons de Gaulle has taught us and still tell us something about the logic of functional integration among nations. The chief item in this lesson is the recognition that pragmatic-interest politics, concerned with economic welfare, has its own built-in limits. Put differently, pragmatic-interest politics is its own worst enemy. The politician and the businessman who have abandoned an interest in high politics and devote themselves only to the maximization of their daily welfare are compelled by virtue of that very concern to make concessions to another actor who forces him to choose so as to sacrifice welfare. Pragmatic interests, because they are pragmatic and not reinforced with deep ideological or philosophical commitment, are ephemeral. Just because they are weakly held they can be readily scrapped. And a political process that is built and projected from pragmatic interests, therefore, is bound to be a frail process susceptible to reversal. And so integration can turn into disintegration.

With this amendment to our treatment of the logic of functionalism we can once more examine the character of political and economic decisions. Integrative decisions based on high politics and basic commitment are undoubtedly more durable than decisions based on converging pragmatic expectations. A process of integration spurred by the vision, the energy and force of a Bismarck, a Cavour, or a Disraeli is clearly more productive of permanence than an indirect process fed by the slow fuel of economic expectations. On that type of scale, a Bismarck and a de Gaulle will always be more effective than a Monnet, Hallstein, or an Erhard.

But the fact of the matter is that Europe did not have a Bismarck in 1948 or 1950. In the absence of the statesman who can weld disparate publics together with the force of his vision, his commitment, and his physical power, we have no alternative but to resort to gradualism, to indirection, to functionalism if we wish to integrate a region. Pragmatic interests may be weak, but they are real nonetheless. The reliance on high politics demands either a states- man of great caliber or a widely shared normative consensus. In most actual situations in which regional integration is desired, neither in- gredient is present in sufficient quantity.

Now the functionalist who relies on gradualism and indirection in achieving his goal must choose a strategy that will unite many people and alienate few. He can only move in small steps and with- out a clear logical plan, because if he moved in bold steps and in masterful fashion he would lose the support of many. He must make decisions "incrementally," often in a very untidy fashion. The more pluralistic the society in which he labors, the more groups there are that require satisfaction and the more disjointed and incremental the decision-making process will be. Everyone will receive a little, few groups will be deprived, few groups will receive a sudden large gift.[5] If nothing happens to interfere with the incremental process, the society or region in which this occurs will be transformed even- tually into a larger entity. Incrementalism is the decision-making style of successful functionalism if left undisturbed; in Europe, how- ever, it was disturbed by de Gaulle.

And, true to our finding above, incremental processes are always subject to reversal since they rest on pragmatic interests. Just as pragmatic-interest politics is its own worst enemy, so is the incre- mental decision-making style. While the Commission's policy re- mained within the incremental approach to political union in the summer of 1965, it began to stray far enough away from it to offer de Gaulle—given to a more heroic and direct approach—his excuse for bringing incrementalism to a halt.

This discussion of various decision-making styles brings us back to the distinction between frankly political choices and the more covert economic choices with hidden political implications that stand at the heart of the politics of common markets. Regional in- tegration can go forward smoothly if, as in the case of the heroic statesman-leader, there is a shared political commitment between him and the major elites in society in favor of union. This is pre- cisely the condition that, in a pluralistic setting, cannot be expected to occur very often. Otherwise integration can go forward gradually

---

[5] For a further explanation of the incremental decision-making style, see Charles E. Lindblom and D. Braybrook, *The Strategy of Decision* (New York, 1963).

In international organizations, the process is schematized by Haas, *Beyond the Nation-State* (Stanford, 1964), chap. 4.

and haltingly if both leaders and major elites share an incremental commitment to modest aims and pragmatic steps. The difficulty arises when the consensus between statesmen and major nongovernmental elites is elusive and temporary. An incremental commitment to economic aims among the leaders will not lead to smooth integration if the major elites are committed to dramatic political steps. More commonly, a political commitment to integration by the statesmen will rest on very shaky ground if the interests of the major elites are economic; in turn, these interests will have a very weak basis if the statesman's commitment is to national grandeur and the elites' to economic gradualism, as in the case of contemporary France. These relationships can be represented in matrix form:

		Aims of Nongovernmental Elites	
		Dramatic-Political	Incremental-Economic
Aims of Statesmen	Dramatic-Political	Integration either direct and smooth or impossible	Integration erratic and reversible
	Incremental-Economic	Integration erratic and reversible	Integration gradual but automatic

This revision of the dynamics of supranational decision-making has a number of specific implications. The incremental style of approaching the major policy choices involved in common markets and political unions depends on a certain pattern of pluralistic politics at the national level, as well as on a certain type of social and economic structure intimately related to industrialism and rational large-scale organizations. Political parties and interest groups avoiding sharp ideological conflict are essential; social units always able to unite and reunite in ever-changing coalitions are necessary at the national as well as the regional level. And the technical decisions always incorporated in the major choices must be made by technocrats; indeed, the leading role of the technocrat is indispensable in a process as close to the heart of the industrial economy as is the formation of common markets.

Hence integration is most nearly automatic when these forces are given maximal play, as is the case when both statesmen and elites entertain converging incremental-economic objectives. Until the

French veto of 1963 with respect to the entry of Britain into EEC, the supranational European decision-making style was as described by Lindberg:

> The members of the Community do not confront each other only or chiefly as diplomatic gladiators; they encounter each other at almost every level of organized society through constant interaction in the joint policy-making contexts of officials, parliamentarians, interest groups leaders, businessmen, farmers, and trade unionists. Conflicts of interest and purpose are inevitable. There is no paradox between the progress of economic integration in the Community and sharpening political disagreement; indeed, the success of economic integration can be a cause of political disagreement. The member states are engaged in the enterprise for widely different reasons, and their actions have been supported or instigated by elites seeking their own particular goals. Therefore, conflicts would seem endemic as the results of joint activity come to be felt and as the pro-integration consensus shifts.[6]

As the Community moves from a mere customs union to an economic union and a political entity, more and more difficult choices become necessary, and the propensity for conflict increases. Hence it becomes imperative that bargaining include the possibility of mutual concessions of roughly equal value, linked to a style of pragmatic moderation. Charisma and national self-assertion are clearly the worst enemies of this process. Benefits from concessions may have to involve calculated risks with respect to the future; a concession in the realm of agriculture may have to be reciprocated in the field of transport, or even in the form of a new institutional arrangement. The reintroduction of a dramatic political objective, even if by only one important member state, reveals the frailty of this process.

The strong political leader possesses an additional advantage over the functionalist when he can continue to hold out the possibility of rewards to nongovernmental elites and the people at large while rejecting the supranational method of regional economic decision-making. This de Gaulle did in 1965 and 1966 when he gave his partners the choice between no common market and a common market without supranational powers. The very fact that the attachment of many elites to a united Europe is pragmatic and rests on incremental processes makes the supranational method dispens-

[6] Leon N. Lindberg, "Decision-Making and Integration in the European Community," *International Organization*, XIX, 1 (Winter, 1965), 80.

able. As long as the benefits of the common market are more important in people's minds than the means used to achieve these benefits, institutions and procedures can be sacrificed. The very success of the incremental method becomes self-defeating as important elites recognize that welfare can be safeguarded without a strong Commission and overt political unity. Supranational union among the Six, similarly, is endangered when many elites come to the conclusion that concrete economic benefits can be gained by expanding the boundaries of the Common Market, reunifying Germany, attracting Poland and Czechoslovakia—and perhaps even the Soviet Union. And the fact of the matter is that very few important European interest groups had embraced supranationality as a principle in itself, even though they had easily accommodated themselves to it in order to safeguard specific group aims. My book describes the process of accommodation, but it failed to spell out the limits here discovered.

This brings us back to the national situation and the external environment as conditioning factors. The functional logic that leads from national frustration to economic unity and eventually to political unification presupposes that national consciousness is weak and that the national situation is perceived as gloomy and the outside world unpromising. To be sure, the situation may improve. If integration has gone very far by then, no harm is done to the union; but in Europe it had not gone far enough before the national situation improved once more, before self-confidence rose, thus making the political healing power of union once more questionable.

V

This excursion into the recent history of West European nationalism, de Gaulle, and the politics of the EEC enables us to state the necessary amendments to the functional theory of integration in reasonably brief form.

The background conditions that favored the initiation of integrative institutions and policies must continue to operate during the formative stage *and* the subsequent period of evolution. Alternatively, the new forces that are most likely to manifest themselves some time after the formative period must, at the least, not profess aims that run counter to the integrative logic or previous common economic policies. Such a reversal of objectives can be caused by a dramatic change in political leadership in one or more of the constituent nations or by a sharp change in the environmental setting. When rewards larger than those anticipated by a continuation of the common market are envisaged as possible because of a change in the international system, as compared to the system prevailing during the formative period, a new dimension is given to the functional logic. It yields a *disintegrative* thrust as compared to the system in gestation, a thrust that at the same time may be integrative as far as a different set of relationships and different units are concerned. When changes in the international system are perceived simultaneously by a new leadership and by nongovernmental elites—as, for example, benefits that might accrue to a France pursuing an active world policy at the expense of devotion to European matters —the limit of the automatic spill-over thrust has been reached. If this limit defines the boundary of positive expectations on the part of actors already in the union, it describes equally well the expectations and fears entertained by both nonmember countries anxious to join and those who resist joining the Community.

Thus we can say that: (1) positive expectations of rewards from the continuation of the union must continue to prevail after the passage of the formative period, even though the identity of the actors and their precise objectives need not remain the same; and (2) the external environment must be perceived as less rewarding than the continuation of the internal community-building process in terms of political-national gratifications as much as in purely economic welfare terms.

These amendments to functional theory imply definite assumptions concerning the role of "pure politics" and political ideology as agents of action. And these, in turn, constitute a limit on the predictive power of the theory. The type of society baptized "the new Europe" by George Lichtheim contains the major clue: a society dominated by pragmatic bargaining on the part of highly specialized groups of actors who avoid ideological confrontations. The language of "pure politics," insofar as it is garbed in the costume of Marxism, existentialism, Christian personalism, cultural nationalism, or laissez-faire liberalism, is incompatible with the processes on which the functional theory of integration rests. Therefore, we must postulate that the actors in contemporary Western Europe are generally indifferent to these doctrines. They have ceased to furnish the building blocks out of which the political actor fashions his image of reality—present and future.

The social facts of the last twenty years support this assumption. European federalism, an explicit ideology heavily indebted to Proudhon and Sorel, proved a failure largely because its language seemed so peripheral to the objectives of the great majority of active citizens. While the tolerance and unstructured sympathy for a united Europe that was one consequence of federalist agitation undoubtedly eased the manipulative tasks of the functionally and incrementally inspired actors, the specific ideological tenets nevertheless proved to be beside the point in the New Europe. We can now affirm that while it was vital for the technocrats to work in the protective shadow of sympathetic politicians aiming at "unity," there was no need for this shadow to possess a federalist lining. The lack of viability shown by federalism indicates not only that it arrived too late on a social scene that was already in a post-ideological stage, but that the successes of the integration movement owe much to the lack of concrete ideological content. "Europeanism" today, as poll after poll makes clear, is too unstructured and too permissive in terms of concrete steps to deserve the label of an ideology. It is merely a mood, an *ambiance* that remains compatible with the attenuated national consciousness that now prevails. In short, the functional theory predicts incremental integrative steps only as long as there is a dominant and accepted ideology of action or no commitment to ideology at all.

But what happens when new expectations and new leadership not wholly compatible with the initial pro-integration impulse come to the fore? Must they upset the earlier movement toward unity? Again, our discussion of the vicissitudes of EEC suggests that this need not be the case. While limits are imposed, it is not possible to affirm that they constitute firm boundaries incapable of being breached. Moreover, even if a spill-over tendency is brought to a halt by such developments, this by no means implies a return to a purely national framework of action, a spill-back. It may signify merely a more or less prolonged period of stagnation, an integrative plateau.

This formulation and the actual stage of contemporary Western Europe suggest a limit to spill-back processes as well as to the spill-over. The concept of an "integration threshold" comes to mind, describing a condition in which the beneficiaries of earlier integrative steps have achieved such vested positions in the new system as not to permit a return to an earlier mode of action. The 1966 elections in France showed that farmers and industrialists no longer were willing to consider giving up the Common Market. One "threshold" thus is determined by aroused and organized expectations of benefits that no politician dares to disappoint. But there may be a second and less tangible "threshold" beyond which a spill-back cannot flow: the actual regional enmeshment of administrative ties and practices among a myriad of national and supranational agencies that cannot perceive themselves as functioning except in terms of ongoing cooperative patterns. The next task of functional theory, now ensconced in its more modest limits, will be the exploration and operational definition of these thresholds.

Berkeley, California
  January 11, 1968

PREFACE

" UNITED EUROPE " is a phrase meaning many things to many men. To some it implies the creation of a full-fledged federation of the independent States of Western Europe, either the Six of " Schumania " or the Fifteen of the Council of Europe. To others the phrase means no more than the desirability of creating a loose concert or confederation. Some see in it the guarantee for future greatness, a political, economic and cultural renaissance for the Old Continent, about to be eclipsed by the United States, the Soviet world, and perhaps the Arab-Asians. But others identify it with the death of cherished patterns of national uniqueness. Even government policy, on both sides of the Atlantic, sometimes hesitates between endorsing the creation of a new centre of economic and political power and fearing the evolution of a high-tariff region or of institutionalised " third force " sentiments. One must add the still lively controversy over whether economic or military unification, or both, is possible without prior or simultaneous political federation. The arguments over the merits and types of unification have continued since the end of World War II; they are unlikely to be exhausted soon.

But for the political scientist the unification of Europe has a peculiar attraction quite irrespective of merits and types. He may see in it, as I do, an instance of voluntary " integration " taking place before his eyes, as it were under laboratory conditions. He will wish to study it primarily because it is one of the very few current situations in which the decomposition of old nations can be systematically analysed within the framework of the evolution of a larger polity—a polity destined, perhaps, to develop into a nation of its own. Hence, my purpose is not the evaluation of the virtues and drawbacks of a United Europe in terms of European, American, national, international, free-enterprise, or welfare-State values. Nor is it an analysis of the advantages of federation over intergovernmental co-operation, economic over military unity. My aim is merely the dissection of the actual " integration process " in order to derive propositions about its nature. Hence, I focused my analysis on selected groups, institutions and ideologies which have already been demonstrated to act as unifying agents in political systems clearly " integrated " by any applicable standard. Further, I confined the analysis to the impact of the one organisation whose powers, functions and composition make it _a priori_ capable of redirecting the loyalties and expectations of political actors: the European Coal and Steel Community. My study, then, attempts to advance generalisations about the processes by which political communities are formed among sovereign States, and my method is to select specific political groups and institutions, to study their reactions to a new species of " federal " government, and to analyse the impact of that government in terms of the reactions caused. On the assumption that " integration " is a two-way process in which the central institutions affect and are affected by the subject groups, the Coal and Steel Community is to serve as a case study illustrating the effects on the totality of interactions.

My emphasis is placed on community formation processes, implying full voluntary participation in an international agency possessing some federal powers. Hence my discussion must perforce exclude countries and groups rejecting membership and thus shielding themselves from the integrating impact of the Community. No analysis of attitudes and policies in Switzerland, Austria, and Scandinavia is therefore attempted. Britain constitutes a special case. She declined membership in the Community but agreed to a special form of " association " with it. New behaviour patterns discovered in the policies of the member governments cannot be expected to apply to Britain; but the special nature of the tie to the Continent must be discussed, if only because it is considered so vital by Europeans. Because of my inability to interview British leaders or to obtain access to the papers of relevant private groups, my discussion must be confined to official government policy and to the interpretation of published documents.

Definitions of key terms will be presented in the first chapter. But the essential conclusions may be briefly summarised. The initiation of a deliberate scheme of political unification, to be accepted by the key groups that make up a pluralistic society, does not require absolute majority support, nor need it rest on identical aims on the part of all participants. The European Coal and Steel Community was initially accepted because it offered a multitude of different advantages to different groups. Acceptance of a federal scheme is facilitated if the participating State units are already fragmented ideologically and socially. Moreover, the acceptance of such a scheme is considerably eased if among the participating industrial, political, or labour groups there is a tradition, however vague, of mutual consultation and of rudimentary value sharing. A helpful, but by no means indispensable, condition is the existence of an external threat, real or imagined.

Once established, the central institution will affect political integration meaningfully only if it is willing to follow policies giving rise to expectations and demands for more—or fewer— federal measures. In either case, the groups concerned will organise across national State boundaries in order to be able to influence policy. If the central institution, however, fails to assert itself in any way so as to cause strong positive or negative expectations, its impact on unity will be as small as the integrative role of such technically powerful international administrative unions as the Danube Commissions or the Universal Postal Union. As far as the industrial groups—business and labour—are concerned, they tend to unite beyond their former national confines in an effort to make common policy and obtain common benefits. Thus perhaps the chief finding is that group pressure will spill over into the federal sphere and thereby add to the integrative impulse. Only industries convinced that they have nothing to gain from integration will hold out against such pressures. But industrial sectors initially opposed to integration for a variety of motives do change their attitude and develop strong positive expectations if they feel that certain common problems can be more easily met by a federal authority. More commonly still, groups are likely to turn to the federal authority for help in the solution of purely national problems if the local government proves unco-operative. Groups with strong initial positive expectations do not necessarily turn against the principle of integration if their hopes are disappointed: they merely intensify their efforts to obtain the desired advantages on the federal level, thus integrating themselves into organisations less and less dependent on and identified with the national State. Political parties, if allowance is made for their varying ideologies and constituencies, tend to fall into the same pattern. National governments, operating in the nexus of all these forces, may on occasion attempt to sidestep, ignore, or sabotage the decisions of the federal authority. The study of the Coal and Steel Community shows, however, that governments also recognise a point beyond which such evasions are unprofitable, and that in the long run they tend to defer to federal decisions, lest the example of their recalcitrance set a precedent for other governments.

After five years of activity, the pattern of supranational pressure and counter-pressure has become apparent: groups, parties, and governments have reassessed and reformulated their aims in such a way that the drive for a United Europe has become the battle cry of the Left. The " sinistration " of federalism has been accomplished in the recognition of trade unions and Socialist parties that their version of the welfare State and of peace can rationally be achieved only in a federated Western Europe. Perhaps the most salient conclusion we can draw from the community-building experiment is the fact that major interest groups as well as politicians determine their support of, or opposition to, new central institutions and policies on the basis of a calculation of advantage. The " good Europeans " are not the main creators of the regional community that is growing up; the process of community formation is dominated by nationally constituted groups with specific interests and aims, willing and able to adjust their aspirations by turning to supranational means when this course appears profitable.

Our study thus substantiates the pluralistic thesis that a larger political community can be developed if the crucial expectations, ideologies, and behaviour patterns of certain key groups can be successfully refocused on a new set of central symbols and institutions. Yet this conclusion also begs the question of the generality of the process laid bare. Can larger political communities be created on this basis in all sections of the world, in all ages, irrespective of the specific powers initially given to the central authority? [1] I suggest that the value of this case study is confined to the kind of setting which reproduces in essence the physical conditions, ideologies, class structure, group relations, and political traditions and institutions of contemporary Western Europe. In short, I maintain that these findings *are* sufficiently general in terms of the socio-political context to serve as propositions concerning the formation of political communities—*provided* we are dealing with (1) an industrialised economy deeply enmeshed in international trade and finance, (2) societies in which the masses are fully mobilised politically and tend to channel their aspirations through permanent interest groups and political parties, (3) societies in which these groups are habitually led by indentifiable elites

---

[1] This very issue is dealt with somewhat differently in a recent study concerned with problems very similar to these, in Karl W. Deutsch *et al.*, *Political Community and the North Atlantic Area* (Princeton: Princeton University Press, 1957). The authors were concerned with integration by analysing past cases of successful and unsuccessful political community formation, resulting in a " no war " community, the absence or presence of violence as a means to settle disputes being considered the criterion of community. The study proceeds on the basis of ten historical cases, *none* of which satisfy the conditions held essential in my inquiry, because they were confined to pre-industrial and pre-mass mobilisation settings. The difference in socio-economic setting is well illustrated by the " appeals " to integration the authors found to be featured in their cases, *viz.* (in order of importance):

1. appeals to the defence of an actual or emerging " way of life " ;
2. appeals promising greater social and political equality ;
3. appeals promising the creation of more power as a result of unity ;
4. appeals promising more specific rights for given groups ;
5. appeals for the defence of some already established rights or privileges. (*Ibid.*, pp. 98–99.)

Clearly these appeals grew out of the constitutional struggles of the eighteenth and nineteenth centuries, featuring political liberalism, national self-determination, national power, or the defence of feudal rights. One misses the appeals heard most often in the contemporary setting: economic equality, industrial democracy, larger markets, and politico-military strength in the global struggle between two power centres external to the region.

Other categories of analysis and definitions used in Deutsch's study, however, relate more directly to the present inquiry, as explored below.

competing with one another for influence and in disagreement on many basic values, (4) societies in which relations among these elites are governed by the traditions and assumptions of parliamentary (or presidential) democracy and constitutionalism. It may well be that the specific economic conditions under which the European coal and steel industries operate act as additional factors limiting the possibility of generalising. Monopolistic competition and the prevalence of private ownership are such factors, though isolated pockets of nationalised industry exist in the total industrial complex. It may also be true that the impact of an overwhelmingly powerful external economic centre acts as a limiting condition. Economic integration in Europe might have been much slower if the governments had been compelled to come to grips with investment, currency and trade questions—decisions which were in effect spared them by the direct and indirect role of United States economic policy. Hence, I would have little hesitation in applying the technique of analysis here used to the study of integration under NATO, the Scandinavian setting, the Organisation for European Economic Co-operation, or Canadian-United States relations. I would hesitate to claim validity for it in the study of regional political integration in Latin America, the Middle East, or South-East Asia.

My list of acknowledgments must be heavy and long because my debts of gratitude to many are so considerable. Without the patient co-operation of dozens of industrialists, parliamentarians, and labour leaders in Western Europe, my work would have been impossible. They gave me freely of their time and their impressions and they indulged my most impertinent questions. To the many officials of the High Authority, the Common Assembly, and the Council of Ministers who indulged me equally I owe an even greater debt. A special word of thanks must be addressed to the librarians of the High Authority, the Common Assembly and the Court of Justice for the unfailing courtesy with which they met my many requests and for the great help they rendered. President Clark Kerr, of the University of California, contributed heavily by introducing me to key specialists in Europe. Mr. Meyer Bernstein, of the United Steelworkers of America, was most kind in his help. Professor Karl W. Deutsch, of the Massachusetts Institute of Technology, read the entire manuscript and gave me generously of his wealth of conceptual and historical insight. I owe him a considerable intellectual debt. None of these persons is in any way responsible for the interpretations I offer or the use made of the information they gave me.

This study was made possible by grants from the Social Science Research Council and the Institute of Social Sciences of the University of California, enabling me to spend the academic year 1955–1956 in Luxembourg and other national capitals. I am grateful, furthermore, to the Rockefeller Foundation and to the Department of Political Science at Berkeley for having given me the time in the spring of 1957 to complete work on the manuscript, and for having provided me with research assistance. To Dr. Fred von der Mehden, Rudolf Wagner, Kurt Vogel, and Charles Elliott I acknowledge a deep debt for research assistance rendered in Berkeley, and to Madeleine Ledivelec, Bep Cramer, and Ursula Hartte, a similar and even more profound debt for crucial help given in Luxembourg. To Peter H. Merkl I am particularly grateful for having prepared the index. Any errors committed in this study are mine and not theirs.

Ernst B. Haas.

Berkeley, California.
January, 1958.

ABBREVIATIONS

A-R	Anti-Revolutionary Party (Holland).
ARS	Action Républicaine Sociale (France).
ASSIDER	Larger of two Italian Steel Producers' Associations.
ATIC	Agence Technique d'Importation Charbonnière.
BDI	Bundesverband der Deutschen Industrie (Germany).
BHE	Bund der Heimatvertriebenen und Entrechteten (Germany).
CDU	Christlich-Demokratische Union (Germany).
CELNUCO	Centre de Liaison des Négociants et Utilisateurs de Charbon.
CEPCEO	Centre d'études des Producteurs de Charbon d'Europe Occidentale.
CFTC	Confédération Française des Travailleurs Chrétiens (France).
CGC	Confédération Générale des Cadres (France).
CGT	Confédération Générale du Travail (France).
CHU	Christian-Historical Union (Holland).
CIFE	Conseil des Fédérations des Industries de l'Europe.
CISL	Confederazione Italiana di Sindicati di Lavoro (Italy).
CNPF	Conseil National du Patronat Français (France).
COBECHAR	Comptoir Belge du Charbon.
COCOR	Co-ordinating Commission of the ECSC Council of Ministers.
COLIME	Comité de Liaison des Industries Métallurgiques.
Confidustria	Confederation of Italian Industry.
CSC	Confédération des Syndicats Chrétiens (Belgium).
CSSF	Chambre Syndicale de la Sidérurgie Française.
DGB	Deutscher Gewerkschaftsbund (Germany).
DP	Deutsche Partei (Germany).
ECE	United Nations Economic Commission for Europe.
ECSC	European Coal and Steel Community.
EDC	European Defence Community.
EEC	European Economic Community; also known as General Common Market and Euromarket.
EPC	European Political Community.
EURATOM	European Atomic Energy Community.
FBI	Federation of British Industry.
FDP	Freie Deutsche Partei (Germany).
FEDECHAR	Fédération Charbonnière Belge (Belgium).
FGTB	Fédération Générale des Travailleurs Belges (Belgium).
FIB	Fédération des Industries Belges.
FO	Confédération Générale du Travail-Force Ouvrière (France).
GATT	General Agreement on Tariffs and Trade.
GEORG	Gemeinschaftsorganisation Ruhrkohle.
ICCTU	International Confederation of Christian Trade Unions.

ICFTU .	. International Confederation of Free Trade Unions.
I. G. Bergbau .	. Industriegewerkschaft Bergbau (Germany).
I. G. Metall .	. Industriegewerkschaft Metall (Germany).
ILO . .	. International Labour Organisation.
ISA . .	. Smaller of two Italian Steel Producers' Associations.
MRP .	. Mouvement Républicain Populaire (France).
NATO .	. North Atlantic Treaty Organisation.
NEI . .	. Nouvelles Equipes Internationales (league of European Christian parties).
NVV .	. Netherlands Socialist Trade Union Federation.
OCCF .	. Office Commun des Consommateurs de Ferraille.
OEEC .	. Organisation for European Economic Co-operation.
OKU .	. Oberrheinische Kohlenunion.
PSC . .	. Parti Social Chrétien (Belgium).
RPF . .	. Rassemblement du Peuple Français.
RS . .	. Républicains-Sociaux (France).
SFIO .	. Section Française de l'Internationale Ouvrière (Socialist Party).
SPD . .	. Sozialdemokratische Partei Deutschlands (Germany).
UDSR .	. Union Démocratique et Socialiste de la Résistance (France).
UENDC .	. Union Européenne des Négociants Détaillants de Combustibles.
UIL . .	. Unione Italiana di Lavoro (Italy).
VVD .	. Volkspartij voor Vrijhijd en Democratie (Holland).
WEU .	. Western European Union.

Part One

INTEGRATION: IDEOLOGY AND INSTITUTIONS

CHAPTER 1

COMMUNITY AND INTEGRATION

Two major opposing trends have come to characterise international relations at the end of the Second World War: while some twenty new states have made their appearance since 1945, with every indication that the process will gain even more momentum, a network of international organisations has sprung up countering the full impact of this multiplication of sovereignties. Whether in the realm of political relations or specific functional tasks, whether at the universal or the regional level, contacts and associations among governments, private groups and individuals have been institutionalised as never before. Whereas the trend in Africa and Asia is toward the evolution of ever more political groupings aspiring to statehood, the process in Europe and in the Atlantic area tends toward the limitation of sovereign independence, the growth of more rather than less formal bonds among national communities and perhaps toward the substitution of a new federal organism for the present national state.

New states may grow up as the result of the splintering of an existing political community—or an empire—as well as from the merger of hitherto distinct and independent entities. In both processes the evolution of " national consciousness " is held to be the crucial factor. Loyalty to the established font of authority wanes as a feeling of separate identity takes possession of the group clamouring for new forms of political organisation. Yet we know little about the constituents of this process. While it is possible frequently to specify the content of the new doctrine of national consciousness it is far more difficult to explain who originates, propagates, expands and accepts it. More difficult still is the question of why the doctrine originates and why it gains—or fails to gain—acceptance. How and why does national loyalty tend to coincide with the territorial boundaries of the state? Is it inherent in political evolution that it must be so? Is it natural and inevitable that India, Ghana or Belgium are characterised by a sense of national identity which extends to their frontiers but not beyond?

The process of development of a political community, therefore, is but little understood in terms of the analytical standards and

criteria of observation with which the social scientist today works.
While much work is being done in the study of this process among
the nascent political entities in underdeveloped areas, much less
attention has been paid to the reverse process of community
formation through international organisation, among western
industrial states. This is true in all fields of trans-state activity,
whether intergovernmental at the level of formal diplomacy, intergovernmental at the level of informal discussion by experts,
" supranational " or federal. Each of these is a device to arrive
at collective decisions by means other than unlimited action by a
national government. Each is a means for peacefully unifying
diverse groups in common action. Yet detailed data on how—
if at all—cohesion is obtained through these processes is lacking.

International relations in contemporary western Europe provide
a living laboratory of these processes at work. The Organisation for
European Economic. Co-operation at the level of intergovernmental
contacts, the Council of Europe as an inter-parliamentary forum, the
system of Scandinavian co-operation and the Western European
Union as a mixture of the two, and the European Coal and Steel
Community as a quasi-federal government in two economic sectors,
provide landmarks in the process of substituting collective action
for decisions by governments acting in isolation. It is time that
these efforts be examined to judge if and how " political community "
results from measures of " political integration."

BASIC DEFINITIONS: POLITICAL COMMUNITY

The systematic study of the process of community formation
through organisations of this type necessitates the explicit stating
of an ideal type appropriate to the known institutional setting of
western Europe. Here, the existing national states *are* political
communities. While they seem to enjoy the unquestioning
" loyalty " of their citizens—with the exception of dedicated
Communists as distinguished from the mass of Communist voters—
they are by no means monolithic units. Pluralism of groups, values
and institutions is the hallmark of western European political life.
Nor, as past history and contemporary developments indicate,
are these existing states immutable entities. Belgium came into
existence in 1830; Germany federated in 1870; the bloody history
of boundary changes is well remembered by the present generation.
The existing political communities are neither so homogeneous

internally as to speak with one united voice on national or international issues nor preordained historically as to constitute
" natural " units.

" Loyalty " was singled out as a crucial term in this definition
and it must be specified further in operational terms. A population
may be said to be loyal to a set of symbols and institutions when it
habitually and predictably over long periods obeys the injunctions
of their authority and turns to them for the satisfaction of important expectations. In part the existence of such sentiments
can be tested by the regularity of popular compliance with
fundamental government decisions; and in part it is subject to
verification by the kind of attitude testing of perceptions of mutuality
of aspirations made familiar by post-1945 surveys.[1] *Political
community, therefore, is a condition in which specific groups and
individuals show more loyalty to their central political institutions
than to any other political authority, in a specific period of time and
in a definable geographic space.* In this study, this condition will
be the one toward which the process of " political integration "
is supposed to lead.

Group conflict is a given and expected form of conduct in the
nations under study. French, German or Italian policy emerges
as the result of this conflict. Hence a larger political community,
composed of the nations now still separate and distinct, may well
be expected to display the same traits. Hence our ideal type of
community formation will assume group conflict as given on the
level of the present national units as well as in the larger community
which may emerge. In fact, the competing activities of permanently
organised interest groups and of political parties are singled out
as the significant carriers of values and ideologies whose opposition,
identity or convergence determines the success or failure of a
transnational ideology.

---

[1] When confronted with a similar problem, the authors of *Political Community
and the North Atlantic Area* (Princeton: Princeton University Press, 1957) concluded:
" The populations of different territories might easily profess verbal attachment to
the same set of values without having a sense of community that leads to political
integration. The kind of sense of community that is relevant for integration, and therefore, for our study, turned out to be rather a matter of mutual sympathy and loyalties;
of ' we-feeling,' trust, and mutual consideration; of partial identification in terms of
self-images and interests; of mutually successful predictions of behaviour, and of
co-operative action in accordance with it—in short, a matter of a perpetual dynamic
process of mutual attention, communication, perception of needs, and responsiveness
in the process of decision-making." P. 36.

If group conflict is one central characteristic of political community so is the existence of a commonly accepted body of belief. Despite the opposition of ideologies and their adherents, consensus exists to a sufficient degree in the contemporary national units to preclude recourse to civil war and revolt. The ideal type of political community implicit in this study assumes, therefore, that the condition toward which the process of integration is expected to lead is one in which a sufficient body of general consensus imposes limitations upon the violence of group conflict. These limitations are the basic agreement on the *means* for settling differences, even if consensus as to *ends* of political action can be achieved only at such high levels of abstraction as to be irrelevant to the analysis of political conduct. Stated in constitutional terms, the agreement on the means of political action is equivalent to the acceptance of the doctrine of respect for the rule of law. Official decisions, once made according to procedural rules accepted as binding by all, are carried out.

For purposes of this discussion, the beliefs common to otherwise antagonistic groups will be labelled the " nationalism " of a given community, while the doctrines peculiar to a group will be referred to as " ideology." Nationalism is composed of values and claims acceptable to the great bulk of the population while also setting it apart from the values and claims of other political communities. At the socio-cultural level of attitudes and beliefs our political community is held together despite the internal strife of the constituent groups by the general acceptance of national identity, of nationalism, which manifests itself primarily in the consensus on the means for achieving agreement on policy.

Conflict and consensus, unity in diversity are the chief components of existing western European political communities, and of the possible larger unit imputed in this descriptive scheme. The institutions which characterise this social pattern are those standard to western national government. Decisions of the central authority are binding on the citizenry, regardless of the consent which might have been given or withheld. Consent is assumed if the legislature, by majority vote, enacts law. It is assumed also in the administrative acts of the executive in carrying out the legislative injunctions. Majoritarianism, though perhaps questioned in some political doctrines and rarely applied to its logical limits in a crisis situation approaching civil war, is nevertheless the operative principle of day-to-day political life.

This picture of political community differs in some essential respects from the kindred concept of " security community " proposed by some contemporary students of nationalism and community formation.[2] In both formulations, the absence of violence as a means of political action among the participating groups is given a central place. Deutsch's concept, however, does not insist on the presence of a specified institutional structure, contenting itself with the consecration of non-violent means of achieving social change as the major criterion differentiating " community " from ordinary international relations. The scheme here used, by contrast, makes the existence of political institutions capable of translating ideologies into law the cornerstone of the definition. While the co-existence of conflict and harmony within the same social system can no doubt be achieved without the attributes of a single statehood, the deliberate creation and per- petuation of a new national consciousness can hardly be expected to come about without the presence of formal governmental institutions and practices. Since the possession of such a con- sciousness is considered a criterion of political community, the techniques for realising and maintaining it must be posited as necessary to the ideal type.

These are the central characteristics of pluralistic nations in contemporary western Europe and at the same time the earmarks of our model of political community. In clearly positing an extreme scheme, rather than an intermediate one permitting of violence-free conduct short of the attainment of statehood by the entities under study, it is intended to furnish a precise yardstick for the analysis of governmental and group conduct in western Europe in the effort to determine now to what extent the condition of political community has been or is likely to be reached.

Political community, as here defined, need not presuppose the emergence of a federal state, though this is one possibility and certainly the aim of many contemporary European statesmen and thinkers. While a central government is essential institutionally

[2] Richard W. Van Wagenen, *Research in the International Organisation Field: Some Notes on a Possible Focus* (Princeton: Centre for Research on World Political Institutions, Publication No. 1, 1952). Karl W. Deutsch, *Political Community at the International Level* (New York: Doubleday, 1954); and by the same author, *Nationalism and Social Communication* (New York: Wiley, 1953).

and a collective national consciousness socially, the constitutional form which will qualify for the ideal type may be that of a unitary, a federal or even a confederate arrangement. No special conceptual problems are posed by the unitary or federal alternatives; the confederate possibility, however, requires a note of explanation.[3] Normally the type of confederation represented by international organisations in which only states are subjects and governments are vested with a power of veto does not approach our definition of community. A structure could emerge, however, in which a compulsory and binding judicial system is combined with a majoritarian legislative device, supervising the work of a central administration of restricted powers but with direct jurisdiction over groups and individuals, while many major decisions are still made at the level of inter-governmental negotiations. If in such a system governments negotiate and compromise so that one or several severely modify their position in the effort to arrive at a binding common agreement of profound consequence, the resulting habitual pattern of reaching consensus could well fit into the definition of political community, though representing neither the typical unitary nor federal categories of constitutions.

Hence the institutional criteria of " political community " as here defined combine the separate features posited by Deutsch and his associates. They analyse in terms of two types: " amalgamated security communities " and " pluralistic security communities." The former correspond essentially to unitary or federal states while the latter comprise relationships between sovereign states from which the possibility of recourse to force has been banished, *e.g.* in Canadian-American or inter-Scandinavian relations. While my definition would exclude " pluralistic security communities " of this type because of the absence of judicial, administrative and legislative ties and because of the scarcity of institutionalised

---

[3] Much overlapping and confusion has subsisted historically in relation to these terms, explaining in part the resistance of many Europeans to the principle of federalism. For a strong statement of this opposition, see Franz Neumann, " Federalism and Freedom: A Critique," in Arthur Macmahon (Ed.), *Federalism Mature and Emergent* (Garden City: Doubleday, 1955), pp. 44–57. For an exploration of the various meanings and their constitutional implications in western Europe, see Carl J. Friedrich, " Federal Constitutional Theory and Emergent Proposals," in *ibid.*, pp. 510–529. These differences, however, have no direct bearing on the problems implicit in our statement of a model of political community. Any kind of federal arrangement, regardless of the degree of centralisation or decentralisation implicit in it, is compatible with our scheme so long as loyalties to the central symbols overshadow attachment to local ones.

relations among private groups, our concept of "political community" is nevertheless broader than Deutsch's "amalgamated security community" because it includes the possibility of a constant flow of obedience to central decisions made by intergovernmental agencies.[4]

The co-existence of traditional national governments in Europe with institutions of a "supranational" character—like the European Coal and Steel Community—poses some terminological problems for our subsequent discussion of integration and the development of a political structure and consciousness transcending that of the existing nations. The word "national" will subsequently be reserved to refer to activities, organisations and loyalties within the framework of the existing national states, members of the "supranational" structures to be assessed. This usage will be adhered to despite the possibility that the process of political integration may result in an all-European government, in turn characterised by a larger national consciousness and loyalty. The words "federal," "central" and "supranational" will be used interchangeably and synonymously to refer to activities, organisations and loyalties transcending the existing nations, *even though* in a strict constitutional sense there are no clear "federal" powers now in existence, and legally the vague and novel term "supranational" is the only correct one in this context.

Having stated the ideal type of political community, our task is the assessment of empirical data in an effort to determine whether and why developments leading to the evolution of a community are taking place. General estimates of the existence or absence of loyalty other than to the national state do not suffice. Hence a number of indicators of community sentiment will be discussed here, applicable specifically to the study of how interest groups, political parties and governments act in a supranational setting.

Community sentiment would be considered to flourish if—

> 1. Interest groups and political parties at the national level endorse supranational action in preference to action by their national government, or if they are divided among themselves on this issue. Only the case of unanimous national opposition to supranational action could be considered incompatible with community sentiment;
> 2. Interest groups and political parties organise beyond the

---

[4] Deutsch, *et. al.*, *Political Community and the North Atlantic Area, op. cit.*, pp. 3–21.

national level in order to function more effectively as decision-makers *vis-à-vis* the separate national governments or the central authority and if they define their interests in terms larger than those of the separate national state from which they originate;

3. Interest groups and political parties, in their efforts at supranational organisation, coalesce on the basis of a common ideology, surpassing those prominent at the national level;

4. Interest groups and political parties, in confronting each other at the supranational level, succeed in evolving a body of doctrine common to all, or a new nationalism (*i.e.*, " supranationalism)."

5. Interest groups, political parties *and* governments show evidence of accepting the rule of law in faithfully carrying out supranational court decisions, administrative directives and rules even when they oppose these, instead of obstructing or ignoring such decisions; further, when opposing federal policy, they channel their objections through the legal avenues provided instead of threatening or practising secession.

6. Governments negotiate with one another in good faith and generally reach agreement, while not making themselves consistently and invariably the spokesmen of national interest groups; further, community sentiment would seem to prevail if governments give way in negotiations when they find themselves in a minority instead of insisting on a formal or informal right of veto.

Clearly, only a collection of saints could be expected to display positively all these indicators of community sentiment at the onset of a process of integration. In order to qualify as a true political community, however, all the above indicators must be positively established before the condition defined in our scheme has been met. Given a series of pluralistic assumptions, any establishment of sentiment confined to parties alone, or to interest groups, or to governments considered in isolation from their subjects, would fall short of the final condition posited.

A final word of caution should be introduced with respect to the use of ideal types in political analysis. If the desirability for neatness and clarity is met in the abstract statement of the scheme, there is nevertheless no need to assume the empirically established political processes to appear equally orderly. In Max Weber's terms, an ideal type is a heuristic device: it does not and should not guarantee a neat " falling into place " of the data analysed, thus in effect " proving " the " reality " of the scheme. The purpose of using a tight definition of political community is the easier assessment of group conduct with reference to the criteria of an ideal community. Precisely the same caveat applies to the schematic presentation of our concept of " political integration." If specific groups do not seem to behave quite as neatly as the scheme requires, the pattern of their conduct may nevertheless be studied more easily if it can be analysed within the framework of an ideal type.

BASIC DEFINITIONS: POLITICAL INTEGRATION

Our definition of political community relies not so much on " objective criteria " as on an assessment of the conduct of groups, individuals and governments. On a more abstract level, the criteria singled out as crucial to the definition result from habitual behaviour patterns: they are not superimposed by the observer upon the social scene. The same rule governs the definition of the second key term used in this study, " political integration." Conceived not as a condition but as a *process*, the conceptualisation relies on the perception of interests and values by the actors participating in the process. Integration takes place when these perceptions fall into a certain pattern and fails to take place when they do not. If pluralism is considered an inherent part of the ideal type of political community, pluralistic processes of decision-making and interest-perception, naturally, are considered equally essential attributes of the process of political integration.[5]

Before a firm definition or scheme can be stated, it must be recognised that integration in western Europe has thus far been essentially confined to economic measures. Hence it is necessary to establish the meaning of " economic integration " as that term is generally used in the nexus of European politics. Following Gehrels and Johnston, the possible general definition as " the presence of important economic links between a group of countries " must be rejected as too vague operationally.[6] The development of

---

[5] See Deutsch, *op. cit.*, for the use of " objective criteria " in the discussion of community and integration, such as the volume of economic transaction, the volume of social communication and the adequacy of the communications network to carry the " integration load." These devices are developed as indicators of the potentiality inherent in certain communities in the effort to integrate, in Deutsch, " The Growth of Nations," *World Politics*, Vol. 5, No. 2 (January 1953).

[6] Franz Gehrels and Bruce F. Johnston, " The Economic Gains of European Integration," *Journal of Political Economy* (August 1955), pp. 275–292. My definition of economic integration is taken from this article.

This definition is essentially identical with that of former ECA Administrator Paul Hoffman and was taken to represent U.S. policy during the Marshall Plan

such links can and does result from organisations, such as OEEC, which do not pretend to represent or aim at political community. Economic aspects of integration, if relevant to the evolution of community, must possess these characteristics: " (1) agreement for gradual but complete elimination of tariffs, quotas and exchange controls on trade among the member countries; (2) abandonment of the right to restore trade restrictions on a unilateral basis for the duration of the agreement, regardless of difficulties that may arise; (3) joint action to deal with problems resulting from the removal of trade barriers within the community and to promote more efficient utilisation of the resources of the area; (4) some degree of harmonisation of national policies that affect price structures and the allocation of resources (for example, social security and agricultural programmes) and of monetary and fiscal policies; and (5) free, or at least freer, movement of capital and labour."

But economic integration, however defined, may be based on political motives and frequently begets political consequences. The existence of political motives is a matter for empirical research and, in western Europe, is clearly established. More hypothetical formulations are required to deal with the problem of political consequences. Thus it may be posited that economic integration unaccompanied by the growth of central institutions and policies does *not necessarily* lead to political community since no pressure for the reformulation of expectations is exercised. Free trade, therefore, cannot be automatically equated with political integration; nor can the interpenetration of national markets be so considered. If economic integration merely implied the removal of barriers to trade and fails to be accompanied by new centrally made fiscal, labour, welfare and investment measures, the relation to political

period. It also agrees with the definition of Robert Marjolin, former Secretary-General of the OEEC, though the latter added that the achievement of these goals required the concurrent establishment of political unity. The definition here used is deliberately less sweeping than that of Gunnar Myrdal, who wrote:

an economy is integrated when labour of a given kind commands the same price, when there is one market for capital, with a single price for comparable risks, and when the price of the same kind of land has been equalised . . . The realisation of these conditions would in human terms mean the achievement of that old ideal in Western democratic thinking, equality of opportunity. Quoted by Michael T. Florinsky, *Integrated Europe?* (New York: Macmillan, 1955), pp. 27–28.

integration is not established. If, however, the integration of a specific section (*e.g.*, coal and steel), or of economics generally (*e.g.*, the " General Common Market ") goes hand in hand with the gradual extension of the scope of central decision-making to take in economic pursuits not initially " federated," the relation to the growth of political community is clear. It must be stressed, more-over, that the degree of " success " achieved as measured by purely economic standards—growth in the value and volume of trade, business earnings, wage levels, etc.—is not necessarily an index of political success. Economic dissatisfaction may go hand in hand with demands for more federal political action. Unequal dis-tribution of economic benefits may give rise to political opposition where none existed before. Hence the measure of political success inherent in economic integration lies in the demands, expectations and loyalties of the political actors affected by the process, which do not logically and necessarily follow from statistical indices of economic success.[7]

The decision to proceed with integration or to oppose it rests on the perception of interests and on the articulation of specific values on the part of existing political actors. Rather than relying on a scheme of integration which posits " altruistic " or " idealistic " motives as the conditioners of conduct, it seems more reasonable—assuming the pluralistic basis of politics here used—to focus on the interests and values defended by the major groups involved in the process, experience showing that these are far too complex to be described in such simple terms as " the desire for Franco-German peace " or the " will to a United Europe." As the process of integration proceeds, it is assumed that values will undergo change, that interests will be redefined in terms of a regional rather than a purely national orientation and that the erstwhile set of separate

---

[7] For a thoughtful exploration of the relation between political federalism and economic integration, see William Diebold, Jr., " The Relevance of Federalism to Western European Economic Integration," Macmahon, *op. cit.*, pp. 433–457. Diebold stresses that federalism does not of itself imply a specific economic policy leading to integration of separate economies. Nor is federation a *sine qua non* for the achievement of economic integration. However, the attainment of specific welfare standards in a larger market would almost automatically compel some kind of central action even if the initial plan of economic unity did not provide for it. It is demonstrative of the close link between political and economic motives in contemporary western Europe that the draft treaty for the establishment of the European Political Community also included a provision for the establishment of a General Common Market within ten years. Later developments saw the shelving of the political scheme but the resuscitation of the economic plank, with the expectation that it would lead eventually to more political centralism.

national group values will gradually be superseded by a new and geographically larger set of beliefs.

The scheme, finally, assumes that the process of integration will yield a new national consciousness of the new political community, uniting the erstwhile nations which had joined. If the content of nationalism at the level of the former nation had been posited as the overlapping and agreement on principle of the multitude of separate group ideologies, the same conception applies at the level of the new community. As the beliefs and aspirations of groups undergo change due to the necessity of working in a transnational institutional framework, mergers in values and doctrine are expected to come about, uniting groups across former frontiers. The expected overlapping of these group aspirations is finally thought to result in an accepted body of " national " doctrine, in effect heralding the advent of a new nationalism. Implied in this development, of course, is a proportional diminution of loyalty to and expectations from the former separate national governments.

Shifts in the focus of loyalty need not necessarily imply the immediate repudiation of the national state or government. Multiple loyalties have been empirically demonstrated to exist, either because no conflict is involved between various foci or because the political actor manages psychologically to ignore or sublimate a conflict even if it does exist " objectively." In fact some psychologists suggest that attachment to new foci of loyalty, such as international or supranational organisations, may come about by a threefold process in which attachments to the new centre exist side by side with continued deference to the established foci. New loyalties may come into existence as end values, *i.e.*, the new order is desired as an end in itself. Secondly, new loyalties may develop merely in response to a pressure for conformity exercised by the new centre of power. Thirdly—and most importantly for the study of political integration in a framework of consensus—new loyalties are thought to grow haphazardly in their function as intermediary means to some ultimate end, perhaps the same end also fought for in the context of the established national loyalties. Groups and individuals uncertain of their ability to realise political or economic values in the national framework may thus turn to supranational agencies and procedures, without being attracted by " Europeanism " as such. If the process of developing dual loyalties via this mechanism continues for a sufficiently protracted period, the new central institutions may ultimately acquire the symbolic significance of end values.[8]

A process of political integration, stated in these general terms, is susceptible of detailed investigation only if a set of specific indicators is provided as well. Integration being a process over time, certain identical questions can be raised for purposes of analysis at regular intervals. Care must be taken that indicators of integration are designed with specific reference to the scope of activity of the organisation studied: the reactions of groups concerned with the production, processing, manufacturing and marketing of coal and steel in the instance of the European Coal and Steel Community.

Put in terms of questions, these indicators are proposed for a periodic analysis of development toward the end of political community:

> 1. What is the position of key interest groups, political parties and governments toward the proposal to integrate a given sector or to federate, or to the treaty formalising such a step? Can the position taken be correlated with the economic expectations of the actors, their political fears or hopes, their satisfaction or dissatisfaction with the national political context, their ideologies or their notion of the national interest?

Having established the initial positions of these groups, the next step in the process of establishing indicators is to sort out the patterns of agreement, opposition and convergence. At the national level, groups may favour integration because they agree in their definition of interests on the basis of identical values: the case of identity of aspirations. They may also agree on the ends of a policy of integration, arriving at this stage, however, on the basis of different values and interests. This constitutes the case of convergence of interests. Finally, groups may oppose integration, either for identical or convergent reasons. Accurate analysis demands that we establish clearly the starting positions as the process gets under way.

> 2. After the advent of new central institutions, can shifts in position among political parties, interest groups and governments

[8] Harold Guetzkow, *Multiple Loyalties: Theoretical Approach to a Problem in International Organisation* (Princeton: Centre for Research on World Political Institutions, Publication No. 4, 1955). W. Buchanan and H. Cantril, *How Nations See Each Other* (Urbana: University of Illinois Press, 1953).

be noted? Shifts for more integration as well as in opposition thereto must, of course, be considered. The indicators would include the same range of questions posed in the effort to define the characteristics of political community. How can shifts be correlated with the ideologies and expectations listed above? Naturally, demands for the extension of the scope of supranational action are especially important here, when voiced by governments as well as by other groups. In the context of economic integration, such demands could well include the elaboration of a joint commercial policy of the participating states *vis-à-vis* third countries; or the non-discriminatory treatment of trade with colonial possessions belonging to some member country; or even their inclusion in the federal scheme.

However, the framework of analysis shifts in the second step. While positions taken at the national level still require attention, these must be contrasted with claims made at the level of the new institutions. If new patterns of identities, convergence or opposition are in evidence, the effort must be made to determine whether they originate at the national or the " supranational " levels.

3. Periodically, the basic question of whether the conditions identified with political community have been realised must be raised. The question can be answered in terms of the indicators for political community presented above.

Such conclusions can be reached only on the basis of again sorting out group values and political demands and structuring them in terms of points of identity. By relating the findings back to earlier positions defended and correlating these with political activity within the frameworks of national government and federal institutions, more definite conclusions with respect to the impact of specific measures of integration on the evolution of ideology and nationalism can be advanced.

We can now state a formal definition of political integration, as used in our ideal type. *Political integration is the process whereby political actors in several distinct national settings are persuaded to shift their loyalties, expectations and political activities toward a new centre, whose institutions possess or demand jurisdiction over the pre-existing national states.* The end result of a process of political integration is a new political community, superimposed over the pre-existing ones.

Before a formal analysis can be made, however, it is essential to specify who the political actors are. It is as impracticable as it is unnecessary to have recourse to general public opinion and attitude surveys, or even to surveys of specific interested groups, such as business or labour. It suffices to single out and define the political elites in the participating countries, to study their reactions to integration and to assess changes in attitude on their part. In our scheme of integration, " elites " are the leaders of all relevant political groups who habitually participate in the making of public decisions, whether as policy-makers in government, as lobbyists or as spokesmen of political parties. They include the officials of trade associations, the spokesmen of organised labour, higher civil servants and active politicians.

The emphasis on elites in the study of integration derives its justification from the bureaucratised nature of European organisations of long standing, in which basic decisions are made by the leadership, sometimes over the opposition and usually over the indifference of the general membership. This gives the relevant elites a manipulative role which is of course used to place the organisation in question on record for or against a proposed measure of integration.

A further important justification for the elite approach to the study of integration lies in the demonstrable difference in attitudes held at the leadership levels of significant groups, as contrasted with the mass membership. Thus a French public opinion poll, based on a representative national sample, brought to light these interesting findings [9]:

[9] *Sondages*, Vol. 17, No. 2 (1955), " La Communauté Européenne du charbon et de l'acier." From the standpoint of interest group participation, these figures are perhaps the most interesting (*ibid.*, p. 23):

ECSC has:		Workers			Industrialists		
		yes	no	don't know	yes	no	don't know
reduced steel prices	*no*	11	19	39	31	30	38
raised steel prices	*no*	10	16	43	28	43	28
taxed coal steel-producers	*yes*	10	12	47	35	19	45
increased coal production	*yes*	30	9	30	45	16	38
abolished coal-steel tariffs	*yes*	37	6	26	90	2	7
closed certain mines	*yes*	20	11	38	41	21	37
modernised certain plants	*yes*	26	5	38	59	5	35
suppressed steel trusts	*no*	7	23	39	32	39	28
floated big loans	*yes*	17	7	45	36	23	40

The " correct " answers have been indicated by the author in italics. Since 26 per cent. of *Sondages*' total sample had no information whatever concerning ECSC, neither the workers' nor the industrialists' totals add up to 100 per cent.

	%
Frenchmen ignorant of the existence of ECSC................	26
Frenchmen ignorant of the existence of the High Authority....	70
Frenchmen able to identify the six member states	10
Frenchmen believing ECSC can make binding decisions	20
Frenchmen able to specify powers of ECSC.................	2
Frenchmen unable to mention achievements of ECSC	63
Frenchmen not knowing whether ECSC will succeed..........	68

Even of the best informed professional group, the industrialists, only 21 per cent. could identify the president of the High Authority, the seat of ECSC and enumerate correctly the member states. The corresponding figure for the workers' group was 2 per cent. Assuredly, such a combination of ignorance and indifference toward the issue of integration does not hold true among the elite groups in labour, industry and politics.

Similar factual ignorance or general misunderstanding can be noted among German businessmen involved in integration. ECSC is accused of setting high steel prices, or being a government-run cartel, of discriminating against German steel sales in South Germany and in favour of French coal purchases from the Ruhr. All of these judgments are factually incorrect but do not prevent the nurturing of anti-integration attitudes at this level of group activity.[10] It must be stressed, therefore, that no such attacks or claims are made by the leadership of German industrial trade associations, thus indicating a significant difference of attitude between the two strata of interests.

Having so far focused on the perceptions and activities of politically significant groups and their elites, it remains to state the role assigned to institutions and structured belief patterns in our ideal type of political integration. Groups put forward interdependent sets of values—ideologies—in their struggle with other groups for political prominence. In a given political community, these ideologies merge and overlap to permit the existence of a set of beliefs held by almost all citizens. But since group action at all levels of political activity hinges around action by governmental institutions, the relationship assumed between beliefs and institutional conduct must be made explicit.

During the initial stages of any process of political integration,

[10] Gabriel A. Almond, "The Political Attitudes of German Business," *World Politics*, Vol. 8, No. 2 (January, 1956), p. 179.

the nationalism established in each of the participating countries is still supreme. The decision to join in or to abstain from the proposed steps of integration is defended in terms of national values by each interested group. Once the institutions associated with the step of integration are established, however, a change is likely to take place. The ideologies defended by national groups are likely to influence— and perhaps shape—the values and ideology of the officials manning the new institution. Certainly no effort will be spared to make the attempt at shaping. However, a reverse process of gradually penetrating national ideologies can also be supposed to get under way. Decision-makers in the new institutions may resist the effort to have their beliefs and policies dictated by the interested elites, and advance their own prescription. Or the heterogeneity of their origins may compel them to fashion doctrines and develop codes of conduct which represent an amalgamation of various national belief systems or group values. A two-way process is likely to result in any case: influence originating from national sources seeking to shape " federal " or " supranational " decisions and efforts to make national groups conduct themselves in accordance with doctrines originating from the new central institutions. If permitted to operate for any length of time, the national groups now compelled to funnel their aspirations through federal institutions may also be constrained to work within the ideological framework of those organs. Eventually, the transformed doctrines will again be utilised to influence the federal decision-makers, who in turn will have to react in one or both of the approaches sketched above.

It is evident, therefore, that a complex pattern of interaction between national ideologies on the one hand and the beliefs of the office-holders in the central institutions on the other will come about. The eventual changes produced at the national level will constitute one of the indicators of the degree of integration as the process continues, while the analysis of this interaction is one of the crucial problems of this study—and of any study of political integration. Hence the contemporary doctrines and institutions relating to European integration must be examined more closely.

" EUROPEANISM " AS A DOCTRINE

We have defined " nationalism " as the values and interests common to groups with distinct ideologies, as applied to the doctrine uniting the citizens of modern states. The rationality of such beliefs is as immaterial as their precise content. The only feature of relevance is the question of whether the beliefs are actively entertained by the overwhelming majority of the population and can be shown to influence the making of policy. Such doctrine performs an " integrating " function in the sense that it blunts domestic ideological conflict and permits a measure of harmony to develop in spite of a tenacious group struggle. It leaps over class barriers, it defies age differences, shows itself stronger than regional differences within nations and—most important of all—it often has an external referent against which it can be turned in justifying a proposed set of policies.

Is the movement for the unification of Europe in possession of a doctrine which performs such functions? The evidence suggests that it is not. Yet the values and doctrines of the movement's constituent groups must be explored first in the effort to discover and establish clearly the pattern of ideologies which functions at the European level—beyond frontiers and national politics. From this pattern it may then be possible to abstract the collective doctrine.

" United Europe " seems to be a remarkably resilient and adaptable symbol: individuals of Conservative, Liberal and Socialist leanings have no difficulty in embracing it. Political parties in all countries contain adherents as well as opponents of the symbol. And the heterogeneity of movements specifically devoted to the realisation of the symbol in fact is equally impressive.

Heterogeneity among individual " Europeans " runs the gamut from historicitic Conservatives to reformist Socialists. To some Conservatives the creation of a United Europe implies the salvation of an ancient civilisation cherished by them, while continued disunity is thought to spell a certain decline through fratricidal strife or some kind of annexation by East or West. In the scheme of one German scholar, unification today is the only alternative assuring survival consistent with the historically determined pattern of European life.[11] Others, like De Rougemont, attach an over-riding importance to the European cultural heritage: a unique amalgam of Greek-humanist, Roman-legal and Christian-spiritual values. Only unity can save these from the challenges of internal dissent and external danger.[12] In fairness, however, it must also be

---

[11] Heinrich Scharp, *Abschied von Europa* (Frankfurt/Main: Verl. Josef Knecht, 1953), pp. 193 *et seq.*

[12] For an American endorsement of this view, see F. S. C. Northrop, " United States Foreign Policy and Continental European Union," *Harvard Studies in International Affairs*, Vol. 4, No. 1 (February 1954).

stressed that other Conservatives hold any federal pattern of unification to be inconsistent with the equally " historically determined "
uniqueness of each European nation.

Geographic determinists have also found their way into the
heterogeneous camp of " Europeans." Gravier sees a " west
European economic space," elongated into West Africa, whose
resources must be developed by a United Europe. The six countries
of ECSC, augmented by Austria and Switzerland, are held to
constitute a natural community of agriculture, industry and trade.[13]
But François Perroux inveighs against any regional groupings and
" natural " federations on the argument that only a universal
division of labour can lead to permanent reduction of production
costs and higher standards of living. Furthermore, he disputes the
existence of any specific " European " values which can be protected
by union.[14]

Yet Giscard d'Estaing, president of the French Chamber of
Commerce, is convinced that economic progress, reduced costs of
production, higher productivity, and lower prices can result only
from the creation of a unified west European market, free of trade
restrictions. While opposing " legalistic " and " theoretical "
schemes of federation, the mechanism of a free market is held out
as a panacea.[15] Other free trade " Europeans " see in the Continental free market the means for rising from the doldrums of a
stagnant economy, with special reference to France, and the prevalent conviction of spiritual decay among European intellectuals.[16]
Yet the counter-arguments of Perroux are as applicable to this
variety of Europeans as to the geographic determinists.

Neo-liberal dogmatism which flourishes in post-world war II
Germany has also contributed its quota of Europeans. Alexander
Rüstow, for instance, has argued that the economic integration of
Europe through schemes such as ECSC is a desirable step for
maximising the natural geographic advantages of certain industries
and thus rationalise patterns of distribution—provided wages are not
raised prematurely and the federal institutions resist the temptation

[13] J.-F. Gravier, " Géographie Européenne," *Hommes et Commerce* (January-
February 1955), p. 23.
[14] F. Perroux, *Europe sans Rivages* (Paris: Presses universitaire de France, 1954).
[15] E. Giscard d'Estaing, *La France et l'unification économique de l'Europe* (Paris:
Genin, 1953).
[16] See, *e.g.*, Guy de Carmoy, *Fortune de l'Europe* (Paris: Domat, 1953).

to exercise " totalitarian dirigist " functions.[17] His ideological colleague in Bonn's Ministry of Economics, Ludwig Erhard, has been a consistent defender of the same principles in the political councils of European economic integration. A refinement is introduced into this approach by those Liberals who are dissatisfied with the continuing close connection between the state and the economy. While the trend toward public control over the economy is conceded to be all but inevitable, the state is not considered the best institution for doing this; nor is the submission of free economic forces to the ordinary processes of government held desirable. Therefore, measures of integration resulting in the setting up of federal " technocratic " or " detached expert " organs, separate from both state and economy, are welcomed. A United Europe achieved through these means would not only bring the benefits of a rationally organised free market but also introduce a new principle of political-social-economic organisation.[18]

Still other " Europeans," however, stress the complete bankruptcy of both classical and neo-liberal economic thought. Considering that factors of production are rigid and that governments are forever tied to programmes of full employment, rendering irrelevant the automatic mechanism of adjustment held out by Liberals, the only real choices are between planning and stagnation. Since existing international organisations—with the exception of ECSC—are impotent to bring about the structural changes necessitated by planning, stagnation can be avoided only through the imposition of policies by an outsider—the United States—or through voluntary federation. While *full* federation alone can assure democratic planning, the *sector* approach to integration may be temporarily justified since it is held to compel the eventual full merging of economies.[19]

Clearly, an attachment to " European " values is the monopoly of no school of thought. Equally clearly, the only real unifying factor among these proponents of a United Europe is the devotion to the symbol of Europe. Heterogeneity characterises every other aspect of their thinking.

[17] A. Rüstow, " Pour Juger le Plan Schuman," *Etudes Economiques* (November 1951), p. 167.
[18] See, *e.g.*, Raymond Racine, *Vers une Europe nouvelle par le Plan Schuman* (Neuchâtel: Editions de la Baconnière, 1954), especially Part III.
[19] See, *e.g.*, André Philip, *L'Europe unie et sa place dans l'Economie internationale* (Paris: Presses Universitaires de France, 1953), for a leading " European " socialist position.

Nor can a homogeneous devotion to Europe be deduced from the values defended by contemporary European political parties. Almost each party numbers adherents and opponents of integration among its members. What is even more significant, opposition to proposed integration measures is usually couched in terms just as " European " as the arguments of devoted federalists, with the only consistent " national " opposition to such schemes as ECSC being voiced by the various Communist parties.[20] Categories for classifying political conduct traditionally relied upon in discussions of European politics prove of little relevance in the analysis of ideologies of integration. Differentiations according to class founder on the finding that there are pro- and anti-integration Socialists, pro-European industrialists and businessmen as well as those of their colleagues who favour the " idea " of integration only to oppose each specific measure proposed to implement it. The otherwise useful distinction between clerical and anti-clerical groups of voters and politicians emerges as of little value in this context. The " clerical " *Mouvement Républicain Populaire* (MRP) in France is solidly for almost any kind of integration; the equally " clerical " *Christlich-Demokratische Union* (CDU) in West Germany is far less doctrinaire on the subject and the very " clerical " *Parti Social Chrétien* (PSC) in Belgium took its time in finally deciding to favour the Schuman Plan. If internal differences of intensity regarding enthusiasm for European unity characterise both CDU and PSC, much the same is true of their major " anti-clerical " opposition groups, the German and Belgian Socialist parties. As Goriély concludes, " the theoretical value of the European idea has today been accepted, at least in most of the western European and Continental countries, without anyone's ceasing to think and to act in national terms. It may happen that a nationalist position finds its subjective ' European ' justification and the struggle against the first serious steps toward real unification has been carried on in the name of Europe." [21]

Certainly this use of the symbol " Europe " does not necessarily imply its worthlessness as an ideological device promoting political integration. However, it is equally certain that the prevalence of the symbol alone does not guarantee the firm agreement on principle

[20] My treatment relies heavily on G. Goriély, " L'Opinion publique et le Plan Schuman," *Revue Francaise des Sciences Politiques,* Vol. 3, No. 3 (September 1953).
[21] *Ibid.*, p. 592.

of those individuals, groups and parties—at the national level—who use it in their political activity. A symbol which seems as useful to Conservatives, Liberals, Christian-Democrats and Socialists, to lawyers, economists, geographers and political scientists seems to leave something to be desired in terms of specificity. Our final test of the value of Europeanism as an integrating doctrine is its meaning to trans-national political groups of various persuasions.

Among the most unanimous and consistent advocates of European unity has been the European-wide association of Christian-Democratic parties, *Nouvelles Equipes Internationales* (NEI). Its European ideology is well represented in a resolution adopted in 1954:

> The immediate objectives of Christian-Democracy are:
> In the economic realm, increases in production and in productivity, as well as the maintenance of full employment.
> In the social realm, the equitable distribution of productive wealth, implying the growing access to property of all.
> In the realm of European economic and social policy, the Congress stresses the attitude taken for a long period by NEI. This attitude is based on the facts, considered in the light of the principles and objectives just stated. Considering the tasks demanded by modern economics and technology, our European states can no longer assure, as isolated economic entities, the continuous well-being of their populations and imitate the progress which can be realised by large economic entities which exist and do not stop developing. In order to promote the economic development and the prosperity of Europe's nations they must create a large economic area within which goods, capital and persons circulate freely. Following the opening and the functioning of the common market for coal and steel, this economic area is best established by stages. The Congress recalls that NEI demands economic integration and wishes soon to promote the freeing of trade, the harmonisation of economic, financial and social policies, and all other measures constituting progress along the road indicated.[22]

While federal institutions, both general and by sectors, are held out by some Christian-Democrats as the only way of breaking with the tradition of the self-seeking national state, great differences in

[22] 8th International Congress of NEI, Bruges, September 10 and 11, 1954. *Nouvelles de l'Europe* (November 1954), p. 25. For more information on these associations, see Alfred Grosser, " Les Internationales de Partis Politiques ", *Encyclopédie Française*, Vol. XI, Section B, Chap. 1.

emphasis are found on this point in NEI. Perhaps the essence of the Christian approach to economic progress, moreover, lies in its emphatic rejection of any notion of class or group conflict, and on the corresponding necessity for inter-group co-operation. Robert Schuman, a prominent member of NEI, characterised the scheme of integration bearing his name in these terms:

> We persist in believing that to solve the problems which face and those which will follow thereafter, co-ordination of efforts among governments will not do. If we do not wish to resign ourselves in the face of naturally separate and opposed interests, if we do not wish to resign ourselves indefinitely to compromises, we must substitute a true community of interests for this division, based on concrete foundations, on which the problems and interests which have become common are treated from an over-all point of view, without the preponderance of certain particular or national interests, but for the benefit of all.[23]

Socialists, no less than Christian-Democrats, have their European-wide association dedicated to promote a United Europe along Socialist lines. However, in their eyes, the symbol " Europe " takes on a different colour. European unity can be achieved only through the medium of a mass movement built along class lines, designed to save the stagnant European economy from the irremediable doldrums of capitalism. In fact, some reliance is placed on a European action of this kind to save France from the " immobilisme " resulting from a deadlocked class-struggle. The " class " with a stake in unification would be made up of the following groups: younger members of the industrial bourgeoisie, reconciled to doctrines of progressive labour relations, productivity and adaptability; peasants willing to break with traditions of government-subsidised price stability; independent artisans who realise their dependence on big business; the salaried professional middle class. The proletariat, in turn, must be wooed away from its political apathy—when it is not Communist—by far-reaching policies of economic democracy and democratic planning, which can be realised only on the federal level with its large common market. Europe, in short, is essential in the realisation of a Socialist better world even at the national level.[24] In contrast to the deceiving

---

[23] Speech in the National Assembly, July 25, 1950. *Journal Officiel*, No. 90, A.N., p. 5944.
[24] André Philip, *op. cit.*, pp. 326 *et seq.*

ideological homogeneity of such conceptions, it should be pointed out that within the European Socialist parties nothing approaching unanimous approval of this thought-pattern exists in day-to-day politics.

With due allowance for differences in emphasis, both the Socialist and Christian-Democratic groups advocating an integrated Europe show a measure of ideological unity, if not among each other then within each formation. Not even this much can be claimed, however, for perhaps the largest and least " confessional " pro-Europe organisation, the European Union of Federalists. Committed before 1954 to a programme of achieving the political federation of Europe through continuous contact and liaison with ministers and parliaments, the Union was confronted with the bankruptcy of this approach when the French National Assembly rejected the treaty for the European Defence Community (EDC). A new action programme was thereupon worked out by the leaders, under the sponsorship of Altiero Spinelli. With all the " sublimity " and *élan* of the Sorelian general strike doctrine, Spinelli posited the immediate need for recognising and organising the " European people," and making a " European front " of dedicated and militant federalists of them, demanding the immediate abolition of the national state. Anticipating a minority status for the " front " in European politics, he sought to give it the role of a " European opposition," confronting *en bloc* the traditional political parties, accused of not being interested in the success of federation. The battle cry of the " opposition " was to be the demand for the immediate convocation of a European constituent assembly charged with drafting a federal constitution. Yet this programme of the Union was sharply attacked by many member organisations because, among other things, it sought to impose strict majority rule and discipline upon the Union, instead of permitting wide autonomy to national member groups. Upon these procedural as well as the implied substantive questions of the future programme, the Spinelli plan went down to defeat in 1956,[25] while UEF split formally in 1957.

What conclusions as to the nature of a series of European ideologies or a European doctrine can be drawn from this examination

[25] See *Europa* (organ of the Swiss Europa-Union), February 1956, " Um was geht es in Luxemburg? "; the crucial resolutions embodying the various doctrines are found in *Informations Federalistes, UEF*, Vol. 3, No. 27–28 (January 1956).

of individual, party and continent-wide advocates of integration? Clearly, the widest variety of fundamental values and consequent reasons for advocating a united Europe are evident among individuals. It is impossible to speak either of ideology or true collective doctrine at this level of action, without depriving these concepts of analytical significance. Among national political parties, there is plainly no unity of thought and even within these parties, the wide variety of emphasis makes it difficult to isolate an accepted body of rationally connected propositions which could qualify as ideology. With the exception of the MRP in France, " Europe " is far too nebulous a symbol to act as an integrating device for developing a political doctrine. The situation is only a little more definite among the continent-wide associations of national political parties. Agreement to basic propositions does obtain among both Socialists and Christian-Democrats at this level, only to be sloughed off in the arena of national parliamentary strife. Agreement, however, does not seem to obtain within the non-party " federal " European Union of Federalists. When a comparison of the various continent-wide groups is made in the effort to discover overlapping or agreed points—the crucial aspect of isolating a national doctrine in a pluralistic setting—accord can only be found on the most general, and consequently non-controversial, propositions, as well as on a limited number of specific programmatic points. An examination of the " peak organisation " of proponents of a United Europe, the European Movement, will exemplify this finding.

The European Movement is a loose association of all the continent-wide groups favouring some kind of European unity, through which these bodies seek to develop a common programme. Thus, in its first congress at The Hague in 1948, the Movement managed to reach agreement on these points: (1) Europe constitutes a cultural and spiritual unity; (2) the essence of European politics is respect for basic human rights, to be safeguarded by a European charter and court; (3) economic progress can be achieved only through the measures of integration discussed above; (4) national sovereignty must be restricted in so far as necessary to achieve the aims of social and economic betterment. Agreement did not then prove possible on a more specific definition of human rights, on governmental institutions to result from the limitations on sovereignty, except the creation of an elected European assembly, or on the means of achieving social or economic progress.   Five years later, in the Hague Congress of 1953, the Movement practically restricted itself to endorsing such actual integration measures as had already been taken or were then proposed.   It demanded merely the continuation of economic integration, along sector lines if necessary, by more harmonisation of separate national fiscal, social and investment policies, the need for rearming Germany through EDC, and the necessity of establishing the then drafted European Political Community (EPC).[26]   Of the more specific demands and reasoning processes discernible among Christian, Liberal, Socialist and UEF member organisations, nothing made itself felt at the level of the European " doctrine."

To be useful as an indicator of political integration toward community, the concept of a collective doctrine must have a precise meaning.   Certainly it implies the acceptance of certain basic propositions, such as at the foundation of the European Movement in 1948.   It also implies a minimum of agreement on specific programmatic points, such as revealed in the 1953 resolutions.   But most important, there must be some agreement on the process of reasoning which leads from the basic principles to the points of action, such as we find in the ideologies of individuals and groups analysed above.   Instead, we merely discovered a minimum of agreement, resulting from the almost fortuitous convergence of separate and distinct strands of thought.   This convergence, while certainly of crucial importance in explaining parts of the process of integration and deserving of great attention, is not the equivalent of a more highly structured agreement, such as we identify with an ideology.   It follows, therefore, that while the nuclei of various European ideologies can be isolated in the contemporary political scene, " Europeanism " now does *not* provide a doctrine useful for the study of the integration process.   A doctrine which means all things to all men, while useful in explaining convergences, is hardly a significant tool for the study of structured social action.   In the words of Raymond Aron, a sympathetic critic of European unity efforts, " the name Europe distinguishes a continent or a civilisation,

---

[26] For the 1948 resolutions, see *Die Friedenswarte*, Vol. 48, No. 3, pp. 178 *et seq.* Also Ernst B. Haas, " The United States of Europe," *Political Science Quarterly*, Vol. 63, No. 4 (December 1948).   For the 1953 resolutions, see *Europe Today and Tomorrow* (November 1953), pp. 12–16.   For an outspoken critique of the Movement's approach to unity, as ignoring real ideological affinities and cleavages, see Raymond Rifflet, " L'Europe, est-elle un préalable à toutes les idéologies? " *Gauche Européenne* (No. 26, December 1955), pp. 12 *et seq.*

not an economic or political unit. . . . The European idea is empty; it has neither the transcendence of Messianic ideologies nor the immanence of concrete patriotism. It was created by intellectuals, and that fact accounts at once for its genuine appeal to the mind and its feeble echo in the heart." [27]

The Coal and Steel Community as a European Institution

Another picture obtains in the realm of the institutions whose interaction with beliefs and doctrines must be analysed in dealing with the process of political integration. The study is here facilitated by the fact that there exists in Europe today one organisation possessing the formal attributes necessary to make it an agent of integration —provided these attributes are exercised in the proper manner. The Coal and Steel Community is empowered to make policy binding on the governments as well as the coal and steel industries directly under its sway. It has a taxing, lending, borrowing, planning and rule-making capacity in excess of any other existing international agency. Within its framework, national trade associations, trade unions, political parties and civil servants constantly meet, debate, and seek to influence policy. The two-way flow of pressure and influence sketched in our ideal type of integration is present institutionally. Finally, the sphere of activity of ECSC—coal and steel, as well as the related fiscal, transport and labour questions— is sufficiently vital to the economic and political lives of the member countries as to remove the organisation from the category of such " technical " groups as the International Civil Aviation Organisation or the Universal Postal Union, whose considerable powers nevertheless render them peripheral to the study of political integration because of the specialised and non-controversial nature of their activities.

[27] Raymond Aron, *The Century of Total War* (Garden City: Doubleday, 1954), pp. 313 and 316. In this context, the relevance of the "take off" concept used by the authors of *Political Community and the North Atlantic Area* might be noted. They argue that up to a certain point in the cases they studied, sentiment for integration was confined to small and scattered groups, usually of intellectuals, but that after a decisive event or as a result of gradual changes over several generations, the sentiment intensified to such an extent that the movement for integration acquired a qualitatively stronger role. This change constitutes the "take off," after which the movement possesses an independent impetus. It may be suggested, therefore, that the efforts of the European Movement prior to the years 1952–1955 were of the pre- "take off" variety, and that the events ushered in by concrete steps towards integration marked the transition toward the change in kind. In such a context, the causative importance of the European Movement would be considerable. *Op. cit.*, pp. 83–85.

The relevance of ECSC to the study of political integration remains intact despite the fact that the founders of the Community thought of it merely as one side of a triangle, the other two sides planned being the EDC and the EPC. With the failure of the other two organisations and the consequent isolation of ECSC as the sole functioning quasi-federal agency in a sector artificially separated from the totality of the economies of the member states, it has been argued that ECSC is without significance and condemned to eventual atrophy. It must be countered, therefore, that regardless of the eventual importance and status of ECSC in a more or less divided or United Europe, the activities of the Community in the last five years have been such as to set into motion forces which relate to the process of political integration. And it is as such that the study of ECSC can be instructive.

What questions, then, can be raised with respect to ECSC in this context? Broadly speaking, it is essential to ask whether and to what extent the policies followed by ECSC have advanced economic and political unity, if not federation. Have the attitudes of significant groups of Europeans changed as the result of ECSC policies? If so, as the result of which policies and which codes of conduct among the officials of ECSC? If such changes have come about—at the level of simple demands, of ideology, or of a general doctrine—have they found their way back into the subsequent decisions of ECSC? Put differently, have the officials of the Community exploited such changes in outlook and political pressure as the earlier policies may have occasioned?

These questions must be raised in the specific context of the Community's scope of activity.[28] They relate to the introduction of attitudes of competition among industrialists, to notions of an expanding market, to more tightly and efficiently organised firms, to trusts and fair trading codes, to the reaction of private groups to ECSC regulatory, taxing and lending activities, to improvements in living standards among workers, to improved means of collective bargaining, to the willingness of labour to adjust more readily to

[28] For a very interesting check list of such questions, see ECSC, High Authority, " A Note on New Developments in Europe with Pointers to the Questions They Raise for Inquiry, " Doc. 6394/55 e.

technological innovation and to the willingness of governments to negotiate under the stimulus of a federal " conscience " rather than as completely free agents. The interplay of values and institutions in the process of integration can thus be studied in the nexus of concrete, day-to-day interests rather than on the plane of a doctrine so general as to be devoid of relevance.

CHAPTER 2

THE NATURE OF SUPRANATIONALITY

IF the term "federation" can boast an ancient and honourable lineage in the history of political thought, the same cannot be said of the kindred expression "supranationality." Yet this term, like political integration, is now current in discussions of regionalism and, like the notion of integration, is sadly in need of precise definition. The only existing institutions for which "supranationality" is claimed as a special criterion are the European Coal and Steel Community, and to a lesser extent Euratom and the European Economic Community; the purpose of the new term is explained by the desire of the organisation's founding fathers to set it apart from the full federation which many of them hoped to achieve by way of supranationality. It will be our task to define supranationality and the processes associated with it, not in terms of a variety of possible legal formulations, but merely by *describing* the institutions, powers, limitations, decision-making capacity and executive facilities of ECSC, as well as the powers still wielded by the member states or especially created and conferred upon the new organ.

This task is complicated by the plethora of commentators who have already tried their hand at definition. Some of them proceeded on the basis of the intentions of the treaty drafters, others by pure contextual treaty construction, and still others by means of comparing ECSC with similar international agencies. The confusion of the intellectual setting may be illustrated by the following examples. Chancellor Adenauer, former Premier Arnold of North-Rhine-Westphalia and French Deputy A. Coste-Floret see in supranationality the modern antidote to nationalism, sovereignty and egotism. A Dutch Minister of Economics saw in it " a legal body of pre-federal structure."[1] More cautiously, the German jurist K. H. Klein thought the structure *per se* inconclusive and preferred to speak of a potentially federal organisation, worthy of that name only if substantial integration in fact results from the activities of

---

[1] Henry L. Mason, *The European Coal and Steel Community* (The Hague: Nijhoff, 1955), p. 13.

ECSC.[2] An American commentator prefers to talk in terms of
" partial federation," a notion which is shared by such politicians
as Brentano and Dehousse and the jurists von der Hedte, Ophüls
and Jaenicke.[3] Schlochauer, however, goes so far as to characterise
ECSC as a " partial economic state " (partieller Wirtschaftsstaat),
in which the High Authority acts as the European Ministry of
Economics, while " supranational " merely refers to the method
of federal organisation.[4] Another team of commentators takes the
opposite point of view. To Verdross, ECSC is a " union of states "
with a federal framework, subject at all levels to the rules of international law. Wehberg sees in the new organ merely the highest
form of traditional international organisation, without authority
above the member states.[5] Similarly, Riphagen argued that " supranational " and " international " are the same thing so long as ECSC
remains an isolated example of the former, while Van Houtte argues
that ECSC is *sui generis* institutionally but in essence not much
different from international administrative organisations of the past.[6]
And an official of the United Nations' Economic Commission for
Europe notes with great satisfaction that, despite an ambitious
" supranational " structure, ECSC in practice acts exactly like an
intergovernmental organisation.[7]

In the effort to avoid the blind alleys of purely legal analysis
and formulation, these judgments will be left aside. The only
politically relevant method of giving meaning to the elusive concept
of supranationality is to examine the actual conduct of ECSC
officials, trade associations and unions and the governments influencing or responding to the dispositions of Luxembourg. The
subsequent description of ECSC powers and institutions is a simple
synthesis of the treaty establishing the Community and not an
exhaustive commentary on possible meanings. Legal expositions,

---

[2] *Ibid.*, p. 124.

[3] The American comment is William Diebold, Jr.'s, in Arthur Macmahon (ed.),
Federalism, Mature and Emergent, (Garden City: Doubleday, 1955), pp. 451 *et seq.*
The other comments in Albert Van Houtte, " La Communauté Européenne du
Charbon et de l'Acier: Communauté Supranationale," Conférence faite à l'Uni-
versité de Naples, Décembre 15, 1955, p. 5.

[4] Van Houtte, *op. cit.*, p. 6.

[5] *Ibid.*, p. 5. The Belgian jurist and senator, Henri Rolin, concurs in this formulation. Wehberg's position is described in Mason, *op. cit.*, p. 125.

[6] Van Houtte, *op. cit.*, pp. 4, 35–36.

[7] Lazare Kopelmanas, " L'exercise de leurs pouvoirs par les institutions de la
Communauté Européenne du Charbon et de l'Acier," *Droit Social*, Vol. 17, no. 9
(October, 1954), pp. 536 and 539.

however, must be cited if they come from individuals who participated in the drafting of the instrument, and who therefore may be considered as exponents of views typical of the " founding fathers." Yet even among this group a variety of conceptions and formulations can be encountered.

According to one of its French initiators, Jean Monnet, ECSC is a " supranational, in other words a federal institution." [8] An official French commentary on the then draft treaty upholds this viewpoint and Monnet himself never tired of stressing it after he became the first president of ECSC's High Authority. Yet his colleagues on the French delegation negotiating the treaty do not fully concur. Thus, Professor Reuter agreed that ECSC was endowed with " real " governmental powers, *i.e.*, powers of considerable political significance, but still held to the viewpoint that the juxtaposition of national with federal powers in ECSC made it " pre-federal." [9] Similarly, Robert Schuman himself was content to consider ECSC as " midway between ' international ' and federal organisations." [10] Professor Monaco, a member of the Italian delegation negotiating the treaty, also takes the position that ECSC is *sui generis*—neither federal nor inter-governmental—but for reasons which differ considerably from those of his French colleagues.[11] The feature common to most of the jurists who were active in the drafting of ECSC is an admission that supranationality refers to a type of integration in which more power is given to the new central agency than is customary in the case of conventional international organisations, but less than is generally yielded to an emergent federal government. Our examination of ECSC powers, therefore, will hinge around these two accepted archetypes.

INTERNATIONAL ORGANISATION *v.* FEDERATION: ARCHETYPES

Federation is commonly defined as a " form of government in which sovereignty or political power is divided between the central and local governments, so that each of them within its own sphere is independent of the other." [12] Such a skeletal formulation must be made relevant to the examination of any given process of integration

---

[8] Mason, *op. cit.*, p. 123.
[9] *Ibid.*, p. 122. Also Van Houtte, *op. cit.*, p. 5. Also see Paul Reuter, " Les institutions de la Communauté à l'epreuve," *Droit Social*, Vol. 17, no. 9 (October, 1954).
[10] Mason, *op. cit.*, p. 121.
[11] Van Houtte, *op. cit.*, pp. 4–5
[12] K. C. Wheare, *Federal Government*, 2nd ed. (New York, 1951), p. 15.

by raising additional questions with respect to the scope of the task assigned to each level of government, methods of decision-making, the independence of decision-makers, the nature of the decisions and their execution, as well as the possibilities of evolution, duration and terminability of obligations assumed.

Members and subjects

Federations as well as international organisations are made up of states and therefore do not differ in terms of the criterion of membership. The picture is otherwise, however, with respect to the subjects of each. The dominant practice in international organisations is to consider only states as subjects equipped with legal obligations and rights. While some departures from this rule may be pointed out in the realms of river commissions, human rights, national minorities and, perhaps, in the Trusteeship System, it is clear that the subjects of a federation can be private persons, physical as well as legal.

Scope of Task

No significant differences between the two archetypes can be stated with respect to their tasks. Both may be extremely restricted —such as regulation of a specific economic or communications sector—or broad enough to cover military security and foreign affairs, as is the case in the United Nations as well as in any contemporary federation. Nevertheless, the task of a federation must be intimately related to the crucial social relations and issues of its people, *e.g.*, defence, economic policy, foreign affairs or social welfare.

Methods of Decision Making

In international organisations, decisions are typically made by majority votes, either simple or qualified. Further, in certain organs decisions can be made only if certain member states concur: the principle of qualitative representation implying that the agreement of the members most important in a given task—the maintenance of security, the setting of air safety standards or of rules for labour—is indispensable to effective decision-making. The same aim is sometimes achieved by weighted voting in international organisations. In a federal legislature, by contrast, decisions are always made on the basis of a simple majority, though special devices of qualitative representation are not unknown. Yet, the members protected by them never have a veto power.

Independence of Decision-Makers

Delegates acting in international organisations are almost always the instructed representatives of member governments. They are not free agents able to vote as their personal values and interests may dictate. Consensus, if it is achieved, reflects an agreement of governments. In federal bodies, by contrast, delegates of member states may or may not be instructed; but the delegates representing population rather than governments are never subject to formal instruction by their local governments. Instead, instructions may be issued by their parties, constituents or interest groups.

Nature of Decisions

Federal decisions are binding upon both local governments and private subjects, unless explicitly formulated as advice or recommendations. Decisions of international organisations, however, are almost always recommendations without binding effect, with the power of issuing binding decisions restricted to very few organs and even fewer functions.

Execution of Decisions

While the recommendations of international organisations are implemented only through the free will of the member governments, even " decisions " which are binding technically cannot be executed without recourse to war if a member chooses to ignore a ruling. An impressive array of " economic " and " communications " sanctions featured in many treaties has been significant primarily in being totally ignored. Rulings of federal authorities are carried out regardless of the volition of the subjects by appropriate officers or through the instrumentality of the member states.

Evolution of Scope

Expanding the powers of the organs of government in response to new conditions and demands is a claim made on international as well as on federal authorities. In the case of international organisations this can be achieved only through the consensus of the membership, not through the initiative of the permanent institutions. The member governments, deciding on the basis of their perception of proper interests, make the appropriate disposition. The obvious ability of a federal legislature, judiciary or executive, to determine on an expansion of powers regardless of the consent of member governments need hardly be stressed as the opposing principle of action.

Duration and Terminability

International organisations are created by treaty and the law of treaties governs the possibility of withdrawing from them. Hence, denunciation is possible and practicable. Membership—and with it submission to obligations—can be terminated at will whether the organisation's charter permits this explicitly or not. Federations, by contrast, are intended to be permanent. The attempt at withdrawal usually occasions civil war, which in turn acts as a potent restraint on the practice of unilateral termination of membership.

Archetypes are analytical devices, generalising on a dominant pattern of behaviour on the world stage. As such they obviously violate some actual organisational and federal practices without, however, reducing themselves thereby to uselessness. One prominent departure from the archetype " international organisation " is found in the United Nations as a multi-purpose structure, whose Charter does not provide for withdrawal or termination, permitting majority decisions on some issues, and providing for binding decisions on the part of its Security Council. Hence, some commentators have argued that ECSC, featuring some other departures from the usual practices of international organisations but falling short of the criteria typically associated with a federal government, is merely a union or confederation of states.

For the concept of " federation " to be useful as an analytical device, in opposing it to that of " international organisation " or testing the meaning of " supranationality," its meaning must be established beyond doubt. Hence, it is here argued that in a true federation, *all* of the archetypical features claimed above must be present in fact, as indeed they are in the federations now existing. Further, in order to set it apart from the notion of the state, especially the unitary state, the division of powers between a central and a series of more or less autonomous local governments must also be retained. If any existing governmental structure is found to lack even one of the features claimed as federal above, the structure in question belongs in the realm of inter-governmental organisation. If it is found to possess all these features without also allowing for the division of power between two levels of territorial organisation, it is a unitary state and not a federal one. What, on the basis of this categorisation, can be said to be the meaning of supranationality in the case of ECSC?

ECSC as a Federation

No doubt as to the federal nature of ECSC can develop if we examine the criterion of membership in and subjectivity to the organisation. The members of the organisation are the states who have agreed to join: France, the Federal Republic of Germany, Italy, Belgium, the Netherlands and Luxembourg; membership is open to other states willing to accept the obligations of the Treaty. It is less simple to specify the subjects of ECSC. The member governments are clearly subjects, as are the " enterprises " concerned with coal and steel. Thus, individuals and private groups are clearly under the rule of the High Authority of ECSC, but disagreement subsists as to which " enterprises " are included.[13] Producers of coal and steel as well as their associations, it is agreed, fall under the Treaty. Whether processors, manufacturers, and wholesale and retail dealers should also be so considered, and for what purposes, is still a doubtful point. Even unattached private persons are subjects to the extent that they can be subpoenaed as witnesses before the ECSC Court and punished for refusal to appear or to testify truthfully.

Federal characteristics again earmark the scope of the task assigned to ECSC under its Treaty. The task of the ECSC system is best summarised under these headings: (1) innovations agreed to by virtue of the Treaty even without special action of ECSC organs, as well as future innovations pledged for later action by the contracting governments; (2) definition of the general purposes or doctrine of ECSC; (3) regulatory and police powers for the enforcement of decisions taken under the preceding titles; (4) economic liaison, survey and advice functions; (5) economic planning and direction in case of crisis.

The basic innovations introduced by the Treaty all hinge around

[13] On this topic see René Roblot, " Les relations privées des enterprises assujetties à la Communauté Européenne du Charbon et de l'Acier," *Droit Social*, Vol. 17, no. 9, (October, 1954) and J. P. Abraham, " Les enterprises comme sujets de droit dans la Communauté Charbon-Acier," *Cahiers de Bruges* (October 1954).

the establishment of a *common market* for coal and steel among the members, implying the abolition of all restrictions blocking the unhampered flow of these products across national frontiers according to the laws of competitive economics. Hence, all tariffs, quantitative restrictions, exchange controls and double-pricing practices were declared abolished even before the High Authority began its delicate long-term economic task. Only Italy was permitted to retain a temporary tariff for steel products (CTP, Sec. 30). Further, the governments pledged themselves to eliminate the systematically discriminatory rates charged by transport media, designed to protect the domestic producer from the competition of his foreign neighbours. Other practices inconsistent with a competitive common market, such as subsidies, compensation payments and discriminatory rebates, were declared abolished in Article 4 of the Treaty but concrete action was reserved for later rulings of the High Authority. Other engagements accepted by the contracting governments for eventual action by themselves rather than by the Community include the negotiation of an agreement permitting the free movement of qualified coal and steel labour within the ECSC countries (Art. 69), common and co-ordinated negotiations with third countries over tariffs and commercial policy (Art. 72) and overall harmonisation of ECSC policy with the general economic policies followed in the member countries (Art. 26).

Great pains were taken to outline a general philosophy for ECSC's task, an effort which proved to be full of contradictions and ambiguities. Article 2 of the Treaty proclaims the expansion of employment, economic activity and the raising of living standards through the medium of the common market as the prime goal. The Community is given the unenviable task of establishing " conditions which will *in themselves* assure the most rational distribution of production at the highest possible level of productivity, while safeguarding the continuity of employment and avoiding the creation of fundamental and persistent disturbances in the economies of the member states." [14] Particularly, the Community is to assure regularity in the supply of raw materials and coal-steel products, equal access to these of all consumers " in comparable positions," to seek the lowest possible prices without causing price increases in

---

[14] Quotations from the Treaty text are taken from the translation prepared by the British Iron and Steel Federation, in co-operation with the High Authority. The French text is the only official one.

other sectors or hindering amortisation and " normal returns on invested capital," to obtain rising living standards for workers " so as to harmonise those conditions in an upward direction," equitable prices in trade with third countries, as well as unsubsidised and unprotected expansion of production in the industries concerned.[15] Yet, Article 5 holds that this formidable task shall be accomplished " under the conditions provided for in this Treaty, with limited intervention." Specifically, though not exclusively, the means given to the Community include the collecting of information and the definition of " general objectives," providing investment funds for enterprises and assist them to " readapt " to competitive conditions, maintaining normal competition but taking " direct action with respect to production and the operation of the market only when circumstances make it absolutely necessary," the publishing of reasons for its actions and the ensuring of Treaty implementation. For this purpose, the Community is given full legal personality in each of the member states. Economic progress, in short, is to be brought about through the normal play of vigorous competition, while leaving the door open to direct " federal " intervention only in rather narrowly circumscribed cases. The obligations to assure rising living standards, lower prices, continuity of employment, fair returns on invested capital and non-discriminatory practices are not regarded as mutually antagonistic in this philosophy.

The most strikingly federal powers of the Community lie in the field of maintaining and policing the competitive common market. Summarised briefly and without reference to possible non-federal institutional limitations, these powers consist of the following provisions. ECSC is to abolish existing cartels and prevent the formation of new ones through constant supervision of price and sales practices on the market; ECSC is to pass on the permissibility of mergers among coal and steel firms and avoid the development of monopolistic combinations; non-discriminatory pricing and sales policies by the firms concerned are to be assured by the establishment of a fair trade code, the essence of which lies in continuous price publicity and the illegality of departing from published prices without due notice; inter-firm compensation mechanisms are made subject to ECSC approval while the Community can also institute such arrangements on its own initiative;

---

[15] Article 3, italics provided.

private investments necessitating special support, subsidies or other non-competitive discriminatory devices can be forbidden; the insertion of discriminatory clauses in private contracts concluded between ECSC firms and national governments is to be policed; possible interference by governments with the competitive market is to be prevented [16] and trade with third countries is to be supervised by ECSC only to the extent that it remains compatible with the principles of the common market.

A less sweeping array of functions is assigned to ECSC in the realm of economic liaison, surveys and advice. ECSC is enjoined to watch the development of market conditions continuously and to make periodic forecasts on trends. More important, it is called upon to define the " general objectives " of the Community, *i.e.*, long-term requirements and the allocation of investments needed to meet them. ECSC is empowered to borrow funds and to lend them out to the Community's enterprises to aid in the realisation of the objectives. Further, funds can be lent as well as granted in order to aid specific firms adversely affected by the introduction of the common market in modernising their plant and techniques. Similar outlays can be made for the retraining of workers—a programme known as "readaptation" in the Treaty's jargon. To assure funds for this purpose, for guaranties on loans to enterprises and for administrative expenses, ECSC was given the power to tax the enterprises under its jurisdiction. Private investments held incompatible with the general objectives but only if not financed from a firm's own resources—can be forbidden. Research considered necessary for attaining the aim of a rationally organised, efficient and competitive common market is to be encouraged and financed by ECSC. Periodic checking of the books and records of coal and steel firms is to facilitate these activities and continual consultations with producers, consumers and workers are to be the basis on which economic advice and investment directives are issued.

The final aspect of ECSC's task relates to an undefined condition labelled " manifest crisis." Subject to the injunction (Article 57) that preference shall be given to " indirect means of action,"

---

[16] Article 67 speaks of " any action by a member state which might have appreciable repercussions on the conditions of competition in the coal and steel industries." Such action is held to include measures " liable to provoke a serious disequilibrium by substantially increasing differences in costs of production otherwise than through variations in productivity." The measures envisaged include currency depreciation, tax increases, changes in contributions to social security funds, etc.

the following direct techniques of control are given to ECSC: in the event of a serious production surplus and insufficient consumer demand, production quotas can be imposed; conversely, in the event of a serious shortage, compulsory production programmes can be decreed, exports to third countries controlled and production centrally allocated; finally, price ceilings can be imposed to cope with shortages and minimum prices established to aid in limiting surplus production. A curious " crisis " power relates to the maintenance of a certain minimum wage level. Article 68 provides that " abnormally low prices " resulting from " abnormally low wages " can be corrected by Community action imposed on the firms or governments concerned. This aspect of the Community's powers fully equals that of any national state, though the initiation of the proper measures is hedged around with limitations not common at that level.

Decision-making provides the next crucial area for investigating the federal attributes of ECSC. Voting rules and the independence of decision-makers from instructions by governments furnish the significant indices in this quest, necessitating a brief description of the institutions through which ECSC functions. These are the High Authority, the Consultative Committee, the Common Assembly, the Court of Justice and the Council of Ministers.

High Authority

The High Authority is the motive force of the ECSC system, the originator of almost all decisions, plans and forecasts. In fact, the other four organs are primarily designed as checks upon the power of the High Authority rather than as initiators of action. The High Authority is composed of nine persons, no more than two of whom may possess the same nationality, and who may have no connection with the industries covered by the Treaty. They serve for six years and may not receive instructions from any government, party or interest group. The method for their selection is both complicated and highly significant of the meaning of " supranationality." Initially, eight of the nine members are designated by the common consent of *all* member governments, instead of the conventional method of simple nomination by one government and automatic acceptance by the others. The ninth member was elected by the majority vote of the eight already chosen, or " co-opted " in ECSC language. Subsequent elections will require only a five-sixths majority of the member governments as well as a simple majority of the remaining incumbent members. Since one-third of the High Authority's membership is elected every two years, the " federal " body in effect participates in its own selection on a basis of equality with national governments. The President and Vice-Presidents of the High Authority are chosen from among the Authority's members by the governments in the same manner as the initial choice of members, after consultation with the High Authority. An indefinite right of veto is expressly denied to the national governments in this electoral mechanism. After a certain number of vetoes, another member government may protest to the Community's Court of Justice and this body may declare a veto null and void if the right is considered to have been abused. Thus chosen, the High Authority is regarded as a collegial agency, collectively accountable for its decisions to the other Community organs. It makes all its decisions by a simple majority vote. In some respects, especially as regards many of its powers, independence and majority voting principle, the High Authority resembles the United States Federal Trade Commission more than the executive of a federal government.

Consultative Committee

The Consultative Committee is a quasi-corporative body designed to advise the High Authority on certain important decisions specified in the Treaty. It makes decisions by simple majority vote, but its resolutions have no binding effect on the High Authority. Its membership is equally balanced between " experts " chosen from among coal and steel producers, consumers and dealers considered as one group, and workers. Members are appointed by the Council of Ministers for two-year terms, upon nomination by " representative " trade associations and trade unions, after the Council of Ministers has determined which groups shall be considered " representative." Members of the Committee " shall be appointed in their individual capacity (and) . . . shall not be bound by any mandate or instruction from the organisations which proposed them as candidates " (Art. 18).

Common Assembly

To the extent that a parliamentary check upon the High Authority exists in this system, that role is played by the Common Assembly. Chosen either by election in the six national parliaments or by direct universal suffrage, the Assembly consists of eighteen delegates each from West Germany, France and Italy, ten each from Belgium and Holland as well as four from Luxembourg. The delegates serve as individuals and are not formally subject to any instruction. At its annual meeting, as well as in extraordinary sessions, the Assembly hears and debates the formal report of the High Authority on current policy. It may ask written and oral questions of members of the High Authority. But its sole power of control lies in its ability to compel the resignation of the High Authority *en bloc* if it passes a motion of censure. This requires a two-thirds majority, " representing a majority of the total membership." With the entry into force of the EEC and Euratom treaties the membership and functions of the Assembly were enlarged appreciably.

Court of Justice

A singularly striking innovation in this array of " supranational " innovations, the Community's Court is a mixture of arbitral tribunal, dispenser of constitutional interpretation, and—most important —an administrative court on the model of the *Conseil d'Etat*. Composed of seven independent judges, selected for six-year terms by common agreement of the governments, it chooses its own president and makes decisions by simple majority vote. Governments may sue each other or the High Authority, firms and individuals can file litigation against the High Authority, and the various organs of ECSC can seek to protect their respective prerogatives by appeal to the Court. Unlike international arbitral procedure, the consent of both parties is *not* required for judicial pronouncements. The Court is thus perhaps the most typically federal aspect of the Community.

Council of Ministers

Among the possible objections to the federal nature of the Community, the nature and functions of the Council of Ministers can well occupy the front rank. The Council is composed of national ministers, certainly entitled to receive instructions from their governments and therefore definitely not independent, at least on the prima facie evidence of the Treaty. Governmental conduct, and especially the decisions of civil servants appointed to serve as substitutes for ministers of economics or transport, suggests that the Council has *not* functioned as a conventional permanent diplomatic conference, irrespective of the legal possibility of its being just that. Some commentators, relying on Article 26 which defines the task of the Council as " harmonising the actions of the High Authority with those of the governments," have described the organ as federal second chamber, or a House of States. Others, considering a distinction without a difference the assertion that the Council usually acts as an " organ of the Community " and not as conference of governmental delegates, have concluded that " having given extensive executive powers to the High Authority, the treaty sets up a companion body to curb the exercise of these powers." [17] Neither of these interpretations can be properly assessed without an examination of the complex voting rules applying to Council decisions, as well as the situations to which they refer. Since ordinarily the Council merely approves or forbids policy measures initially proposed by the High Authority, only the functions not relating to High Authority policy will be outlined here, with the following section devoted to the more general problem of the High Authority's independence as a federal organ.

Depending on the situation, the Council decides by simple majority, two-thirds majority, five-sixths majority or unanimity. Further, in some situations votes are weighted, *i.e.*, the consent of states producing at least 20 per cent. (18 per cent. since 1957) of the Community's total value of coal and steel may be required; in short, France and West Germany may enjoy more voting strength than possible under the rule " one state, one vote." On still other occasions the Council is merely consulted without necessarily proceeding to a formal vote at all. Unanimity, two-thirds and five-sixths majorities are self-explanatory, but the simple majority requires some elaboration.[18]

An " agreement " by simple majority can be obtained (1) if any three states plus either France *or* Germany vote affirmatively or (2) if France *and* Germany plus any other member state take an affirmative position. The second alternative comes into play only if the High Authority insists on maintaining its proposition after a second reading, implying a failure to obtain the regular simple majority on the first vote. " Decision " by simple majority is

---

[17] Raymond Vernon, " The Schuman Plan," *American Journal of International Law*, Vol. 47, no. 2 (April 1953), p. 199.
[18] Article 28 of the Treaty. Following the semi-official English text, *avis conforme* is translated as " agreement " and *décision* as " decision."

identical with the first alternative and excludes the possibility of the second. It applies to the more fundamental issues which may come before the Council. In addition the Treaty on occasion speaks of *avis conforme à l'unanimité* and of *décisions unanimes* but no real difference between the two seems to exist.

These rules relate to the following fields of competence belonging exclusively to the Council, leaving purely procedural and administrative measures aside: decision by simple majority is needed to name members of the Consultative Committee and to determine the representative organisations of those members; to ask that the Court annul a decision of the High Authority or compel that body to make a decision if the Treaty seems to require it; to convoke the Common Assembly in extraordinary session and putting issues on its agenda. Unanimous decisions are required to reduce the number of High Authority members, extend the list of products subject to ECSC jurisdiction, admit new states to the Community, end or impose a rationing system if the High Authority fails to do so, declare the existence of a state of shortage and decree export restrictions to third countries in that case, as well as ask the High Authority to establish minimum or maximum prices.[19]

While majority voting dominates the decision-making processes of ECSC, the crucial question is: under what conditions are the " federal " dispositions binding on governments and individuals? In the case of the Consultative Committee and of the Common Assembly, the answer is " never." The Consultative Committee merely advises the High Authority and the Common Assembly's only true power is the capacity to unseat the High Authority. All other resolutions and activities lack binding force. The Court's decisions, on the other hand, are always binding upon organs of the Community, governments and enterprises as well as persons, without possibility of appeal.

Less categorical replies must be given in the case of the Council of Ministers and the member governments. Whenever the Treaty requires the agreement or a decision of the Council, such acts are binding upon the High Authority, while the results of simple consultations with the Council are not. In addition, the ECSC system is based on a number of governmental undertakings outside the

[19] My treatment follows closely the exhaustive and careful analysis of the Institut des Relations Internationales (Brussels), Groupe d'études presided over by Paul de Visscher, *La Communauté du Charbon et de l'Acier* (Brussels, 1953), pp. 68–71. (Hereafter referred to as IRI).

direct sphere of High Authority activity, including the agreement to abolish all barriers to the free exchange of coal and steel, the decision to harmonise transport rates (Article 70), the obligation to arrange for the free migration of skilled miners and steelworkers without discrimination as to nationality (Article 69) and the undertaking to harmonise tariff and commercial policy *vis-à-vis* third countries (Articles 71, 72, 73, 75). While " bound " to these obligations in the sense that all international law is binding, member governments recognise no authority above themselves to assure the enforcement or execution of these steps toward greater economic integration. Certainly the presumption is that the governments are bound by the decisions of the Council in these matters.

As for the High Authority itself, Article 14 clearly defines the nature of its decisions. Directives labelled " decisions " are " binding in every respect." As for directives called " recommendations," these " shall be binding with respect to the objectives which they specify but shall leave to those to whom they are directed the choice of appropriate means for attaining these objectives." Finally, the High Authority can issue " opinions," which lack any binding force. In general, " decisions " are addressed to coal and steel enterprises and refer to the regulatory and police powers of ECSC, as well as to the crisis functions. " Recommendations " are usually addressed to member governments and refer to the alteration of national legislation tending to obscure or interfere with the operation of a competitive common market. " Opinions " can be addressed to either subject of the Treaty, mainly with reference to the economic liaison, survey and advice functions of ECSC.

Decisions which are binding in principle and arrived at by way of majority voting are no unique characteristic of federal organisations. International organisations may feature them equally well, without thereby meriting the label " supranational." The crucial distinction which must be drawn at this point refers to the question of sanctions. How can decisions be implemented or enforced in case of default? The standard method available to the High Authority for compelling firms and individuals to conform to ECSC regulations consists of monetary fines. These may be imposed for violations of the fair trade code, for failure to pay the Community's tax, for non-observance of investment directives, production quotas, rationing rules and price controls or for refusal to furnish information. While the High Authority is permitted to maintain a

staff of inspectors whose rights of access to the records of enterprises is the same as those granted by national law to local revenue
agents (Article 86), it is not in a position to enforce its decisions and
fines through its own officers. According to Article 92, each member
state assumes the obligation to enforce the carrying out of High
Authority regulations, merely on receiving verification that a
decision has been made, according to the administrative practices
in force within that state. Each government must designate a
minister who is responsible for implementation and execution of
decisions.[20] Judgments of the Court are executed in exactly the
same manner if they are directed at ECSC enterprises.

Methods of enforcement are less " federal " as regards recommendations addressed to governments. " If the High Authority,"
reads Article 88, "considers that a State has failed in one of the
obligations incumbent upon it by virtue of this Treaty, it shall . . .
allow the State in question a period of time within which to provide
for the execution of its obligations," after having issued a reasoned
decision and asked for a reply. Failing compliance or a Court
judgment opposing the High Authority, that organ may suspend
the disbursement of funds owed the delinquent state or " adopt
measures or authorise the other member states to adopt measures
which would otherwise be contrary to the provisions of Article
4 . . . ," *i.e.*, authorise the reintroduction of discriminatory trade
measures. Such a step requires the agreement of the Council,
acting by two-thirds majority. " If these measures should prove
ineffective," concludes Article 88 rather hopelessly, " the High
Authority shall refer the matter to the Council."

International organisations can expand the scope of their
functions only with the consent of their member states, while
federations manage to do so through procedures inherent in the
central rather than the local seats of power. Even the formal
process of amending a federal constitution rarely requires the consent of all member states. Hence, the amendment procedure for the
ECSC Treaty as well as less formal possibilities of task expansion
must be examined.

The Treaty can be amended in three different ways. (1) Amendments may come into force as a result of a two-thirds majority in

---

[20] For an excellent treatment by the Advocate-General of the Court, see Maurice
Lagrange, *Le caractère supranational des pouvoirs et leur articulation dans le cadre
de la Communauté Européenne du Charbon et de l'Acier* (Luxembourg, Nov. 1953).

the Council of Ministers, backed by the ratification of *each* member state. This, in effect, is dependence on the principle of unanimous consent. (2) After the first five years of operation, the powers of the High Authority may be amended without affronting the basic principles stated in the Treaty's Articles 2, 3 and 4 or changing the relationship between the Community's organs. This limited but potentially vital process merely requires agreement of the High Authority, a five-sixths majority in the Council, a majority of the Court and a three-fourths majority in the Common Assembly— without any reference whatever to the member parliaments.[21] (3) Finally, amendment is possible for situations not expressly provided for in the Treaty if action appears necessary to fulfil one of the basic purposes of ECSC. Unanimous approval by the Council is then required for the proposition of the High Authority— again sidestepping the vicissitudes of parliamentary ratification in the member countries.

Among the " informal " means of task expansion, the existence of elastic clauses, leading to " implied powers " doctrines, can be a distinct help. Mason suggests that " the general clause in Article 86 under which the member states accept the obligations of the Treaty has been phrased in such a way as to give the High Authority the widest possible leeway in its interpretation of delinquency." [22] Emphasis on the need " to facilitate the accomplishment of the Community's objectives," as broadly and ambiguously defined in Articles 2, 3 and 4, could thus become an opening wedge for con- stitutional interpretation leading to an expansion of central powers. Similarly, Article 67 furnishes the possibility of informally extending the Community's scope. Under it, the High Authority may make recommendations to member governments with regard to regulations affecting the conditions of competition of their national coal and steel industries, as compared to other national industries. A " spill over " into sectors other than coal or steel may be implied if it is desired, for example, to avoid burdening an industry competing in the common market with heavy social security charges.[23] The question of currency exchange rates, taxes and wage policy suggests the incompleteness of the division of powers between central and local authorities in ECSC. Clearly, these affect the competitive

---

[21] Articles 95 and 96.
[22] Mason, *op. cit.*, pp. 39–40.
[23] *Ibid.*, p. 65; IRI, *op. cit.*, p. 119

Checks and balances there are in profusion in the ECSC system, but they hinge mostly around the High Authority, the Council and the Court. According to the Treaty, the High Authority *must* seek the advice of the Consultative Committee in every major policy decision concerning prices, production, market conditions, labour questions and investments, but the advice never binds the High Authority. Similarly, while the Common Assembly is empowered to discuss every aspect of ECSC policy, it is unable to influence this policy in the face of an unco-operative High Authority unless it is willing to bring about the resignation of that body—a most unlikely contingency. The Treaty—as distinguished from political practice—therefore, condemns both Committee and Assembly to the role of the peripheral critic.[28]

Hence, it is our task to state systematically the scope of powers which can be exercised independently by the High Authority as well as the actions subject to the approval of the Council of Ministers. Our review will close with an examination of the Court's jurisdiction. Apart from internal administrative measures, the High Authority, *acting alone*, may [29]—

> establish study groups and study commissions (Art. 16);
> take remedial measures when the Court annuls a preceding decision (Art. 34);
> take remedial measures when the Court finds that " persistent and fundamental difficulties " have been created for a member state (Art. 37);
> fine enterprises refusing to furnish information demanded (Art. 47);
> obtain loans and impose a production tax (Art. 49, 50);
> fine tax-delinquent enterprises (Art. 50);
> lend funds to enterprises and guarantee loans from other sources (Art. 51);
> negotiate to assure the transfer of currencies (Art. 52);
> prepare and publish " general objectives " as the economic " plan " of ECSC (Art. 46);
> obtain investment plans from enterprises and comment on these in terms of its own economic forecasts; discourage, encourage and notify to the governments such plans;

[28] This conclusion must stand despite Monnet's repeated pronouncements that the Treaty made the Assembly a " federal " organ. See IRI, *op. cit.*, p. 65.
[29] My discussion follows that in IRI, pp. 36–57.

forbid investments not self-financed if they violate ECSC plans; fine violators of the injunction (Art. 54);

fine violators of the production quotas (Art. 58);

establish consumption priorities in case of shortage, if the Council was unable to reach agreement, in consultation with producer associations; fine violators of the priorities system (Art. 59);

instruct governments on how to deal with systematic violations of the fair trade code (Art. 63);

compel producing enterprises to establish their price schedules so as to compel dealers and agents to abide by ECSC rules (Art. 63);

fine violators of the fair trade code (Art. 64);

determine whether given cartels are in conformance with the treaty and dissolve them if not; authorise individual agreements for specialisation, joint sales or purchases; fine violators of these rulings (Art. 65);

authorise industrial mergers and dissolve unauthorised ones; fine violators of these rulings; instruct authorised enterprises " tending to dominate " the market on prices and production policy, in co-operation with the government concerned (Art. 66).

fine enterprises violating the minimum wage clauses (Art. 68);

facilitate the negotiation by the governments concerned of an agreement permitting freedom of migration for qualified labour (Art. 69);

authorise temporary or conditional special transport rates for specific enterprises (Art. 70);

propose means for harmonising commercial relations with third countries; advise on changes in tariff rates *vis-à-vis* third countries; supervise administration of export-import licence system; propose measures to governments for joint action against third countries in case of foreign dumping (Art. 71, 72, 73, 74);

determine violations of Treaty by member governments (Art. 88);

maintain liaison on behalf of the Community with international organisations; report annually to the Common

Assembly, Committee of Ministers and Consultative
Assembly of the Council of Europe (Art. 93);

establish the rules of the fair trade code (Art. 60);

authorise inter-coal enterprise compensation systems, within
same basin (Art. 62).

The High Authority may take the following measures only after
consultations with the Council of Ministers:

establish the general conditions under which the production
tax is to be levied (Art. 50);

obtain the guarantee of governments for certain loans
(Art. 51);

define conditions constituting " control of an enterprise "
(Art. 66);

recommend measures for liberalising export-import licensing
systems (Art. 73);

authorise the creation of inter-firm compensation systems
(Art. 53);

authorise the creation or maintenance of governmental compensation systems (Art. 53);

establish maximum or minimum prices (Art. 61);

intervene to assure certain minimum wage levels (Art. 68).

The High Authority may take the following measures only if the
agreement of the Council of Ministers, voting by *simple majority*,
has been obtained:

establish the list of enterprises exempt from the requirement
of ECSC authorisation for purposes of mergers (Art. 66);

establish quantitative restrictions *vis-à-vis* third countries
(Art. 74);

establish a system of production quotas in case of " manifest
crisis " (Art. 58);

establish export restrictions *vis-à-vis* third countries in case
of " serious shortage " (Art. 59).

The High Authority may take the following measures only if the
agreement of the Council of Ministers, voting by *two-thirds majority*,
has been obtained:

pronounce sanctions against a state, declared to have been
delinquent (Art. 88);

raise the rate of the production tax above 1 per cent. of
average value of production (Art. 50);

exempt the giving of a re-adaptation grant from the requirement that the amount be matched by the government
concerned (Art. 56).

The High Authority may take the following measures only if the
agreement of the Council of Ministers, voting *unanimously*, has been
obtained:

establish ECSC compensation systems in the coal and steel
industries (Art. 53);

participate in investment programmes designed to further
production, marketing or lowering prices in ECSC
industries, but not *ipso facto* under the Treaty (Art. 54);

amend the Treaty to allow for situations not foreseen
initially (Art. 95).

The following actions of the High Authority can be *forbidden* by the
Council only if it manages to act *unanimously:*

prevent the High Authority from ending a régime of production quotas (Art. 58);

prevent the High Authority from declaring that a condition
of " serious shortage " exists, implying the use of crisis
powers of allocation, etc. (Art. 57); prevent the High
Authority from ending such a system (Art. 59).

In a last category of cases, the High Authority can act only if asked
to do so by the states concerned, requiring agreement of the Council:

make grants to workers laid off because of reorganisation of
plants occasioned by the opening of the common market,
if matching amounts are contributed by the government
concerned;

participate in the financing of industrial development other
than coal and steel in order to re-employ labour laid off
because of reorganisation of plants occasioned by the
opening of the common market (Art. 56);

recognise the existence of conditions likely to provoke
" fundamental and persistent disturbances " in the
economy of a member state and decide on remedial
measures (Art. 37).

The balance of " federal " as against " intergovernmental "
powers seems to point to the conclusion that in all matters relating
to the routine regulation of the common market, the High Authority
is independent of governments. As regards measures to be taken in
a crisis situation, however, as well as in areas not clearly part of the

coal-steel complex, the controlling capacity of the member governments remains potent if not dominant. *Hence, ECSC is a far from
federal structure with respect to the crucial criteria of executing
decisions and expanding tasks.*

Nor is the federal element necessarily strengthened by the considerable powers given to the ECSC Court. This organ is charged
in essence with protecting the rights of enterprises and member
governments against the exercise of arbitrary power by the High
Authority. As such it enjoys jurisdiction in the following circumstances and relationships.[30]

(1) Suits by one ECSC organ against another. In the main,
this possibility refers to challenges of High Authority decisions on
the part of the Council of Ministers, and can be brought on the
following grounds (Art. 33):

> (a) *Ultra vires*, or actions performed by an agent outside the
> defined limits of his legal power;
> (b) Violation of a substantial procedural requirement;
> (c) Violation of the Treaty or of any rule of law relating to
> its application;
> (d) Misapplication of power, or performance by an agent of
> an act other than intended when the power was granted
> to him (Art. 31);[31]
> (e) Failure of the High Authority to take action when the
> Treaty requires a decision (Art. 35).

(2) Suits by member government and private enterprises. Such
suits can be brought on the same grounds as above, except that
enterprises must confine their suits against the High Authority to
decisions applying specifically to themselves. Only member states
may sue to obtain the annulment of Council or Assembly deliberations (Art. 35, 38).

(3) Suits for damages, in the event that a High Authority decision
later annulled by the Court was so faultily conceived as to incur the
financial liability of the Community (Art. 34, 40).

(4) Appeals by enterprises against fines imposed by the High

---

[30] These categories follow the excellent treatment of D. G. Valentine, *The Court of
Justice of the European Coal and Steel Community,* (The Hague: Nijhoff, 1954).
They are slightly different from the classification used by P. Reuter, *La Communauté
Européenne du Charbon et de l'Acier* (Paris, 1953), the standard legal commentary
on the Treaty. See also the excellent synthesis in Mason, *op. cit.*, pp. 41 *et seq.*
[31] Following Mason, " détournement de pouvoir " is translated as " misapplication
of power."

Authority as well as by member governments against sanctions pronounced against them (Art. 36).

(5) Disputes between member states, if they involve the application of the Treaty, fall under the Court's jurisdiction, as do disputes involving the aims of the Treaty, provided the parties have also concluded an arbitration agreement (Art. 89).

(6) All cases generally involving the interpretation of the Treaty, including instances of disputes between member states or the Community and third countries (Art. 31, 40).

(7) Appeals to suspend the implementation of a decision, pending adjudication, may be heard by the Court (Art. 39).

(8) Preliminary questions. The Court has exclusive jurisdiction in confirming the validity of an ECSC organ's action if such an issue were to arise in litigation before a national court (Art. 41).

(9) The Court may remove, under specified conditions, certain officials of the Community from their posts.

(10) The jurisdiction of the Court may be enlarged by the insertion of an appropriate clause in contracts between ECSC and other parties (Art. 42), by a national legislature (Art. 43) or by an arbitration agreement (Art. 89).

(11) " Fundamental and persistent disturbances." According to Article 37, a member government may sue the High Authority if the latter's actions or failure to act have " provoked fundamental and persistent disturbances " in a national economy. Since these terms are nowhere defined in the Treaty, this provision has, not unreasonably, been considered the general escape clause from the whole common market scheme. If the claim is upheld by the Court, the High Authority must then seek to remedy the situation as best it can " while safeguarding the essential interests of the Community."

In principle the Court is a purely " legal " and never a " political " or " economic " organ. Its decisions are to be based on legal judgments and not on economic assessments. Apart from the fact that such distinctions are of little use in explaining the actual conduct of judicial bodies, the presence of Article 37 alone would suffice to indicate that the Court may be compelled to make non-legal evaluations.[32] Its decisions may have the most far-reaching

---

[32] Mason lists a number of less important instances in which the Court may also be compelled to rule on the basis of economic rather than purely legal facts. *Ibid.*, p. 48. It must also be noted that the supremacy of the Court over national tribunals in the interpretation of the Treaty is by no means clearly established. See Reuter, *op. cit.*, p. 79 and Valentine, *op. cit.*, p. 121.

effects in relation to the expansion of the Community's task and the freedom with which the High Authority will interpret its role. With respect to federalism, the powers of the Court seem to permit an extensive ambivalence. Many of its claims to jurisdiction are clearly within the federal historical tradition, especially the capacity of *de facto* judicial review so rare in European legal systems. Yet, the presence of Article 37 suggests that a high respect for national sovereignty and narrow interpretation among the judges could lead to a truncated common market and central institutions little different from their counterparts among international organisations.

Meaning of Supranationality

The examination of the structure and powers contained in the ECSC Treaty, in the analytical field defined by the archetypes of federation and international organisation, now permit us to assess the meaning of supranationality. There is, certainly, the necessary division between central and local areas of governmental power. The member states have yielded their former ability to control— actually or potentially—the production, pricing, marketing and distribution of coal and steel, as well as the forms of organisation adopted by the enterprises engaged in these pursuits. Yet, they clearly have *not* yielded their ability to control the economic conditions under which coal and steel are produced and sold: monetary, fiscal, foreign economic, wage and social welfare policy. The capacity of the High Authority to enter these areas is confined to studies and advice, as well as to the introduction of compensatory measures to preserve the existence of comparable competitive conditions for coal and steel in the event member states decide to introduce radical changes in the areas outside ECSC jurisdiction. The local power centres, therefore, continue to define the basic lines of economic policy within which coal and steel must live. Translated into political terms, the new central institutions depend on the good faith of the old power centres for the realisation of their aims, both because of the real powers retained by the national governments and because the High Authority lacks any substantial means for compelling compliance from a recalcitrant member state.

If the division of functions is heavily weighted on the side of national states, the same is true in the field of powers of control and manipulation. Clearly, ECSC possesses the necessary regulatory and planning scope under the Treaty to establish and maintain the common market—so long as national states co-operate in terms of their fiscal, monetary and wage policies. Yet even the capacity of the High Authority to rule the conduct of coal and steel enterprises, unprecedented as it is as compared to the archetype of international organisation, falls considerably short of the powers enjoyed by federal governments. In crucial cases, *e.g.*, in crises, final power of decision rests with a majority of the instructed state representatives in the Council of Ministers. The role of the Council and the manner of exercise of the right of judicial review by the Court make even the institutional aspects of ECSC fall short of a typical federation.

Supranationality in structural terms, therefore, means the existence of governmental authorities closer to the archetype of federation than any past international organisation, but not yet identical with it. While almost all the criteria point positively to federation, the remaining limits on the ability to implement decisions and to expand the scope of the system independently still suggest the characteristics of international organisation. However, supranationality in operation—as distinguished from structure—depends on the behaviour of men and groups of men. It is in this realm that the final answer to the query may be found.

CHAPTER 3

THE COMMON MARKET IN OPERATION

AFTER defining the nature of political integration and examining the legal powers of the supranational system created to further the process, it will be our task to describe the major operations of this system during the first five years of its life. No attempt at an economic assessment of success or failure will be made at this stage; nor will the degree of integration in the realm of political relations be examined in this chapter. Our purpose here is merely the description of major policy measures undertaken by the High Authority in co-operation with the Council of Ministers, the re-actions to these measures expressed in the Common Assembly and the opposition voiced by governments and private groups through the medium of suits in the Court of Justice.[1]

ESTABLISHMENT OF THE COMMON MARKET

Trade among the six countries of ECSC with respect to coal, iron ore and scrap was freed of restrictions on February 10, 1953. On this date, the six governments removed quantitative and currency restrictions from their regulations. While there had been no tariffs applicable to these commodities previously, certain transport discriminations and double pricing practices disappeared on that date, after the expiration of a six-months preparatory period during which the High Authority was established institutionally and negotiated with the governments for the removal of these trade obstacles. Originally, the common market for steel was scheduled for establishment on April 10, 1953. However, the first real crisis of the Community soon proved to be involved in this step. The inability of the French and German Governments to agree on the treatment of turnover taxes forced a rather bitter delay. The German tax charged until then was much lower than the French, a reason which prompted the German Government to argue that the

---

[1] Unless otherwise indicated, the information on which this description is based was obtained from the following sources: ECSC, High Authority, *First, Second, Third, Fourth* and *Fifth General Report on the Activities of the Community* (Luxembourg, April 1953, 1954, 1955, 1956, and 1957 respectively); ECSC, Common Assembly, *Annuaire-Manuel de l'Assemblée Commune* (Luxembourg, 1956); ECSC, High Authority, *Bulletin mensuel d'Information*, Vol. 2, Nos. 4, 5, 6, 7 (1957).

producer should be taxed on the basis of local law in the country of origin, regardless of his sales market. The French, of course, contended that the basic principle of non-discrimination in a common market implied that all producers be taxed equally on the market in which they competed. German steel sold in France, in short, would have to pay the higher French turnover tax, while French steel sold in Germany would be burdened only with the lower German rates. The High Authority appointed a commission of economists to make recommendations and that body favoured the French position. This was adopted as a provisional policy, pending detailed study of the general distortions caused by conflicting fiscal policies. With the tax issue temporarily shelved—not without a good deal of bad feeling in German steel circles—the common market for ordinary steels was opened on May 1, 1953. The preceding months had been taken up not only with harmonising the policies of six governments in simultaneously removing trade barriers, but also in identifying the firms subject to ECSC, working out new price rules, assessing the production tax as well as collecting it and making transitional arrangements with respect to certain transport questions, subsidies, rebates and temporary tariffs in the case of Italy. The statistical importance of the removal of import duties may be judged from this table:

Import Duties immediately before the Common Market
(Per cent. ad valorem)

	Benelux	Italy	France	Germany
Coal	0	0	0	0
Coke	0	5–10	0	0
Iron ore	0	0	0	0
Pig Iron	0–1	11–20	5*	12*
Crude and semi-finished products	1–2	11–15	7–10*	15–18*
Hot finished products	1–6	15–20	10–18*	15–25*
Finished steel products	6–8	15–23	16–22*	15–28*

* Temporarily suspended during the Korean war boom. Duties were subsequently enacted by all participating states for trade with non-member countries.

Source: Figures are taken from Mendershausen, H., " First Tests of the Schuman Plan," *Review of Economics and Statistics,* November 1953, p. 273.

Obvious trade barriers were thus removed except for the group of products known as " special steels," which according to the Treaty were not to be freed from trade restrictions until one year after the opening of the common market for steel.[2]   A number of reasons, however, compelled the High Authority not to take this step until August 1, 1954, after three months of arduous negotiations.   It proved extremely difficult to establish internationally valid conditions of comparability for special steels, which are not usually mass produced to standard specifications.   Hence it became necessary to exempt some producers of special steels from the price publicity rules of ECSC.   Italy was again granted the right to maintain some transitional tariff rates on its high-cost special steels industry.   It was the French producers, backed by their government, however, who caused the basic difficulty.   Enjoying under French law the right to be reimbursed for certain taxes on exported steels, the French producers were unwilling to forgo this advantage— illegal under the anti-subsidy rules of the ECSC Treaty—in the expected competitive struggle on the common market.   Hence they applied, through the French representative on the Council of Ministers, for temporary special safeguards.   Such measures, under paragraph 29 of the Convention on Transitional Provisions,[3] can be temporarily authorised to prevent production and employment dislocations occasioned by the opening of the common market, if the expected dislocations are greater than the benefits awaited.   The High Authority submitted the request to the Consultative Committee, which answered negatively, and then appointed a commission of experts to examine the French special steel industry to see whether it was really in need of special protection.   Upon receiving a negative reply from this group, the High Authority asked the Council for its advice.   Here, the spokesmen of the five other countries succeeded in prevailing upon their French colleague on July 28, 1954, to submit in good grace.   With a vague assurance that special safeguards might be authorised if found to be necessary, the unconditional opening of the common market for special steels was decreed for August 1, 1954, with the unanimous approval of the Council.

[2] The technical definition of " special steels," generally alloy steels, is contained in Annex III to the ECSC Treaty.

[3] The Convention on Transitional Provisions (CTP) is a general catalogue of temporary exceptions, valid only for the period ending February 10, 1958, to the competitive price, anti-subsidy and free trade rules of the common market.   The bulk of High Authority decisions during the first four years of operation dealt with the administration of this Convention, as described in the remainder of this chapter.

German objection to the opening of the common market for steel and French anxiety over special steels were not the only evidence of second thoughts on the desirability of free competition. In the spring of 1953, the French Government lodged a complaint in the Court of Justice against the High Authority's setting of certain low prices on Belgian coal, which the French found to compete much more vigorously against their own in northern France, after February of that year. While the High Authority complied by raising the rates on Belgian coal the French proceeded to establish a discriminatory coal barge compensation fund for canal-carried coal in northern France, in an effort to burden imported Belgian coal. Upon the High Authority's failure to remand the French, the Belgian Government proceeded to sue, and withdrew its case only when the High Authority instructed the French Government to discontinue the compensation fund.

Despite these fragmentary efforts at resistance to the Treaty, the common market has become a reality. The growing inter-penetration of formerly protected national markets is evident in these figures [4]:

Volume of Trade between ECSC Countries in Coal, Ore, Steel Products and Scrap

1952 = 100

	Iron Ore	Coal	Steel Products	Scrap
1952	100	100	100	100
1953	112	111	127	225
1954	117	125	191	434
1955	137	140	251	457

The volume of trade in ECSC products rose by 93 per cent. between 1952 and 1955, while the increase in trade in all other sectors liberalised under the OEEC code, but not under the common market, amounted to only 59 per cent. in the same period. With the exception of Italy, all ECSC countries buy more steel from each other than before 1953 while production rose by 32 per cent. during that period.

PRICE POLICY

Price publicity and non-discriminatory pricing are the twin pillars

[4] ECSC, High Authority, *Towards European Integration: First Results for Coal and Steel* (Luxembourg, June 1956), pp. 7–8. 1955 figures include first six months only.

of the ECSC doctrine of economic progress through a larger, free market. While freedom to set prices within the laws of competitive behaviour are assumed as normal in this system, emergency powers of price control and routine authority to enforce non-discrimination are the remaining important aspects of this system. What has been done in this field since 1952?

Like a national Fair Trade Commission, the High Authority speedily established a fair trade code as the basic rule of conduct for coal and steel enterprises active in the common market. Enterprises are compelled to submit price schedules to the High Authority, who then disseminates these to any interested potential purchaser. In addition, terms of sale and transport must also be specified. Normally enterprises are free to submit new price schedules at any time and steel producers possess the right to " align " their prices in specific sales areas to those practised by their competitors, so long as they do not select artificial or fictitious basing points. The code, finally, forbids a number of practices as discriminatory. The conditions stated in the price schedules must be applied uniformly by the seller and not varied as a special favour to certain customers. Price, quantity and delivery conditions must be the same for all customers, regardless of nationality or place of business within ECSC. The granting of rebates on the basis of past dealings between a given supplier and consumer is outlawed. And finally, it is forbidden to include in the sales price listed in the schedule such taxes as will be refunded to the producer.

In practice, these rules have so far been applied only to trade in ore, scrap and steel, while coal is subject to a series of transitional arrangements. But even in the field of steel, producers soon complained that the publicity and anti-discrimination rules introduced a certain rigidity into the price structure which made rapid adjustment in case of cyclical changes almost impossible. During the winter of 1953–1954, the High Authority received reports that producers were granting illegal rebates by underselling their own published schedules by as much as 20 per cent. Accordingly, on February 1, 1954, the High Authority decided to relax the code by permitting producers to vary the prices charged by 2·5 per cent. above or below published schedules without depositing new price lists. Known as the " Monnet rebate " in European steel circles ever since, this measure was immediately challenged by the French and Italian Governments as well as by the two Italian steel trade associations.

The Council of Ministers, had previously neither clearly authorised nor forbidden the relaxation of the code; the governments now argued before the Court that the Treaty did not permit this latitude of interpretation to the High Authority and that the rebate allowed for the reintroduction of discrimination. In its first—and potentially vital—decision, the Court upheld the Franco-Italian claim and annulled the Monnet rebate decisions.[5]

Rigid enforcement of the code has been the policy since. Between April of 1954 and April of 1956, about one hundred spot-checks on pricing practices were made by the High Authority's inspectors, bringing to light twenty-five violations of the code, in the form of illegal rebates. Fines were imposed on one Belgian and one Italian firm while warnings were sent to the remaining offenders. In these instances the High Authority refrained deliberately from asserting its full punitive powers. Again in October of 1955, ECSC demanded of the French steel producers that they cease granting a 3·29 per cent. rebate to their French customers either by adhering to the published prices or extending the reduction non-discriminatorily to all Community buyers. While the firms in question chose the former alternative, no punitive measures were imposed. Persuasion rather than fines characterise the ECSC policy of enforcing the fair trade code, given the legal impossibility of allowing for flexibility in applying the schedules.

During the transitional period, price competition among coal producers in ECSC is almost completely ruled out. Until 1958, the High Authority is enjoined to prevent decreases in production and instability in employment due to sudden shifts in the established pattern of coal sales (CTP, Par. 24). Feeling that unbridled competition in this sector would result in a drastic decrease in sales from French and Saar coalfields in the southern German market and would produce " price increases of damaging scope and suddenness " in Germany, the High Authority has cushioned the impact of the common market through a system of " zonal prices." In certain circumstances, coal sellers who are not ordinarily permitted to align their prices to those of their competitors are nevertheless given this privilege temporarily. In other cases, rebates may be granted on specified types of coal to avoid penalising the high-cost

[5] Decision of December 20, 1954. *Journal Officiel*, January 11, 1955, p. 547 and p. 560. Also ECSC, Cour de Justice, *Recueil de la Jurisprudence de la Cour*, Vol. I, pp. 7–121.

producers and in still other instances price zones are set up by the High Authority, in which sellers may meet the prices of their competitors and thus enjoy a measure of special protection.   While the major beneficiaries of the system are the Lorraine, Saar, Aachen, Helmstedt, and Nord/Pas-de-Calais basins, the continuation of the system was made conditional on changes in sales prices made possible by the introduction of non-discriminatory railway rates.   Hence in 1955 and 1956, the High Authority reduced the allowable rebate in some instances, redefined zones in others and abolished zonal prices completely for purely domestic French and German sales. Yet in May of 1956 the High Authority came to the conclusion that even with the elimination of the railway rate discrimination, the Lorraine/Saar basin could not compete effectively with the Ruhr on the Southern German market and therefore once again permitted zonal pricing in that area.   Even though coal wholesalers are now compelled to submit and publish price schedules, in addition to the producers, competition is far from the established policy in this sector.

Price controls furnish the most dramatic and far-reaching aspect of the ECSC effort to establish and maintain a common market. No such measures were imposed on steel and ore but a price control mechanism has been applied to scrap, to be examined below.   Coal once more furnished the crucial area of regulation.   Confronted in 1953 with unanimous national policies of holding down the price of coal, the High Authority decided, in full agreement with the Council of Ministers, to continue with controls during its first year of operation.   During the coal year 1953–1954, all basins found themselves compelled to observe price ceilings.   Not anticipating a general increase in prices if the " leaders " were held in check, ceiling prices for 1954–1955 were confined to the Ruhr and Nord/Pas-de-Calais fields, furnishing in the aggregate 62 per cent. of the Community's production.   For the year 1955–1956 only the Ruhr, accounting for roughly 50 per cent. of ECSC production, was controlled and in March of 1956 ceiling prices were abolished altogether.

Opinions on the desirability of controls were and are divided. Most of the governments favoured ceilings, even in 1956, while the High Authority in principle favours a free market and argues that needed investments in mines will be made only if the returns are promising.   Officially, the Ruhr was singled out for control—even though its prices were granted a substantial increase in 1955—because its sales were controlled by an as yet undestroyed cartel whose command over the entire ECSC market was feared in Luxembourg. Unofficially, it is believed that the German Government was glad to make Luxembourg shoulder the burden of unpopular controls. In any case, the Dutch Government on May 7, 1954, challenged in the Court the right of the High Authority to use price ceilings as means to control a cartel, arguing that a frontal attack on illegal practices was required by the Treaty. The appeal failed. Conversely, the Ruhr coal trade association on May 15, 1955, challenged the right of the High Authority to impose ceilings as not permitting a fair return on the investment. No judgment had been handed down in this case as of 1957. Mine-owners chafe under " discriminatory " regulation, consumers and governments fear spiralling prices in an economically and politically sensitive sector, while the High Authority seeks to create a free market, countered by a Common Assembly which " invited " the High Authority " to promote, in conformance with Art. 3c of the Treaty, the stabilisation of prices on Community products and to this end make use of *all* the powers conferred upon it." [6]

But what happens if free prices decreed in Luxembourg clash with controlled prices in one or more of the six national economies? As inflationary pressures throughout the ECSC area mounted during 1956 and 1957 the High Authority felt compelled to

---

[6] *Journal Officiel*, July 19, 1956, p. 231. Italics supplied.
  With or without regulation, prices have been rising slowly since 1954. However, the increase is less than on non-ECSC products.
  Ruhr coal prices increased between $3 and $4 per ton since 1952, depending on kind and grade. Average prices in the other basins remained stable or decreased in relation to Ruhr prices. The Belgian pits, despite rising labour costs and successive increases authorised in 1956 and 1957 by Luxembourg, reduced sales prices relative to the other ECSC basins. High Authority, *Annexes to the Fifth General Report* (Luxembourg, April 1957), pp. 56–59. Average prices for all types of rolled steel products stood at 109 in December of 1956 (May 1953 = 100). *Ibid.*, pp. 42–43.

ECSC Production Development

Commodity	Production 1952	Production 1955–1956	Increase, Million tons	1952–1956 per cent.
Coal	238·9	249·1	10·2	4
Coke	62·4	72·0	9·7	15
Iron Ore	65·3	79·4	14·1	22
Crude Steel	41·8	54·7	12·9	31
Scrap (domestic sources)	19·2 to 20·2	22·7	2·5 to 3·5	12 to 18

Source: ECSC, Common Assembly, *Un Témoignage sur la Communauté des Six* (Luxembourg: February, 1957), pp. 86, 91. Production figures in million tons.

admonish the French Government to refrain from seeking to freeze steel prices by informal means and to control dealers' margins which are technically not subject to ECSC regulation. Similar remonstrances were addressed to the Belgian and German Governments who seemed unwilling to permit the price freedom nationally decreed by the High Authority for the common market. With respect to Italy, Luxembourg had to invoke Article 88 of the Treaty in order to persuade the government in Rome to cease the practice of setting coal prices through the Interministerial Price Committee. On the other hand, the French Government exempted products subject to the rules of the common market from the new payments rules decreed as a result of the devaluation of the French franc in August of 1957. Confronted here with a cardinal issue posed by the principle of " partial integration," the Common Assembly in 1957 " formally insisted on the necessity of better co-operation between the High Authority and the governments and underlines the fact that the first condition of such co-operation is abstention by the governments of unilaterally using their influence in areas relating to the competence of the High Authority, particularly in price regulation." [6a]

INVESTMENT POLICY

In the realm of investment policy, the High Authority possesses a number of direct and indirect methods of intervention. Among the direct means are its power to borrow money, float loans and lend out the proceeds to Community enterprises, without itself, however, acting as a banking agent. The only other direct power available is the right to forbid investments planned by ECSC firms if these run counter to High Authority economic forecasts *and* if they are financed from borrowed funds or subsidies. Indirectly, the High Authority may seek to direct investments by periodic short-term market forecasts, by regular surveys of investments planned by firms and their compatibility with needs, and by the definition of long-term " general objectives."

A short-term survey of investment needs and activities in 1954

[6a] Resolution voted on June 28, 1957. *Journal Officiel*, July 19, 1957, p. 305. In December of 1957, the Socialist members of the Assembly formally went on record against the free coal price policy of the High Authority and demanded the inauguration of investment and price planning linked with the kind of subsidy policy already followed by several national governments and challenged by Luxembourg. *Ibid.*, December 7, 1957, pp. 571 *et seq.*

led the High Authority into its first large-scale financial venture, the $100,000,000 Export-Import Bank Loan contracted on April 24, 1954. Alarmed by the generally high interest rates on short-term capital in Europe and by the tendency of firms to resort to extensive self-financing, as well as motivated by the desire to bring down these rates by means of external capital competition, the High Authority decided to enter the investment field directly. In agreement with American authorities, it was determined to devote these funds exclusively to cheapening the production of raw materials and providing alternative uses for low-grade coal, otherwise difficult to sell. At first it was also hoped to finance an ambitious programme of worker housing but this had to be met from other sources as legal and transfer problems arose. Before any systematic surveys of investment plans had been made and before any general long-term objectives had been worked out, the High Authority proceeded to allocate this fund largely on the basis of the considerations set forth above, with these results:

(millions of dollars)

	Germany	Saar	France	Luxembourg	Belgium	Italy
Coal pit modernisation	20,94	4,20	6,30	—	—	—
Coking plant modernisation	3,00	70	—	—	—	—
Pithead power stations	18,91	5,50	7,70	—	14,00	—
Ore extraction	4,55	—	8,00	1,00	—	5,20
	47,40	10,40	22,00	1,00	14,00	5,20

No Dutch firms applied for a slice of the loan, since interest rates in Holland are very low. Requests for loans totalled $488,130,000, thus imposing a delicate burden of screening the projects on regional committees staffed with government, producer and High Authority representatives. Projects totalling $370,520,000 were approved; since only $100,000,000 of this need was met from the ECSC loan, the American funds were thus used as a catalyst for more intensive local borrowing.

In addition to the American loan, the High Authority succeeded in obtaining $17,000,000 worth of low-interest funds in Belgian, German, Luxembourg and Saar currencies, to be spent locally for

the construction of worker housing. Since the elaboration of general
objectives in mid-1955, $11,655,012 have been obtained from
Switzerland, allocated now on the basis of the long-term aims the
High Authority hopes to realise, and thereby contributing to
" steering " private investment.

The basis of the Community's financial security is provided by
the tax on production. From the opening of the common market
until June 30, 1955, it was levied at the rate of 0·9 per cent., reduced
to 0·7 per cent. until December 31, 1955, to 0·45 per cent. in 1956–
1957 and to 0·35 in 1958. Pressure for reduction has come not
only from the taxpaying firms, but also from certain governments.
The High Authority yielded without consulting the Common
Assembly despite repeated efforts made by the Common Assembly
to share in the financial power. Thus in March of 1953 the Assembly
passed an angry resolution demanding to be consulted on the
Community's draft budget and income, and in June of 1955 it came
close to censuring the High Authority for having failed to consult
the parliamentarians on the reduction of the tax, an issue of obvious
relevance both to the claimed powers of the Assembly and to the
long-term evolution of ECSC investment and welfare policy. The
following figures show the yield and incidence of the tax:

FINANCIAL YEAR

	1952–1953	1953–1954	1954–1955	1955–1956	1956	Total	%
Germany	4,896	22,282	26,867	20,256	7,657	81,958	47·2
Saar	697	3,133	3,532	2,535	959	10,856	6·3
Belgium	1,243	5,467	6,157	4,541	1,673	19,081	11·0
France........	2,581	11,243	13,024	9,414	3,500	39,762	22·9
Italy..........	452	2,580	3,346	2,798	1,129	10,305	5·9
Luxembourg ..	347	1,466	1,792	1,334	516	5,455	3·1
Netherlands ..	405	1,928	2,041	1,415	535	6,324	3·6
Total	10,621	48,099	56,759	42,293	15,969	173,741	100

Source: *Annexes, op. cit.*, p. 9. Figures in millions of dollars. 1956
    figures include only six months.

The levy is assessed on the basis of production reported by firms
as verified by ECSC auditors. It is collected by banking agents
appointed by the High Authority in each member country and tax

delinquent firms are subject to fines. After four years of indecision, the High Authority in May of 1956 finally determined to tax and fine nine German, French and Italian enterprises which had hitherto refused to pay.

Apart from the administrative expenses of running the Community's institutions, these funds are largely allocated to subsidising technical research, contributing to the re-adaptation of workers and guaranteeing loans obtained from other sources. The Guarantee Fund absorbs by far the largest share of this money, having risen to $100,000,000 in December of 1956. Deposited in various national banks, it is used as a basis for additional credits granted only to Community firms, amounting to a total of $42,000,000 by mid-1956. The High Authority, however, has no control over the direction of these disbursals, which thus may or may not fit into ECSC general objectives.

The omnipresent issue of central planning as against investment risks independently assumed by each producer is, of course, inherent in the definition of general objectives. In this area, the cautious policy of restraint followed by the High Authority during the first years of its life clashed sharply with continuous pressure exercised by the Common Assembly for a vigorous ECSC investment policy. In 1953 the Assembly confined itself to asserting its right to be consulted on all investment forecasts and planning *prior* to the publication of High Authority statements and reports and to comment on such plans. By 1954 ECSC parliamentarians were demanding that the High Authority follow an energetic programme of reducing steel costs and assuring a higher level of coal production, while systematically seeking to coordinate the overall investment and expansion programmes of the six member countries. Co-ordination of investments has been the battle cry since, in an effort to give a far more centrally directed character to the aim of assuring a " rational distribution " of new productive resources than a free enterprise orientation can sanction.

Yet the High Authority did respond to Assembly pressure. During 1954 it issued its first medium-term market and production forecasts, stipulating a need for a fifty-million ton steel capacity by 1958. Coal policy occupied first place in the effort to direct investments. A market and policy memorandum was submitted to other ECSC organs which provided the first tentative steps in the direction of long-term coal policy. Assuming a slowly increasing demand for coal despite an ever-growing dependence on liquid fuels, the central problem was one of obtaining greater production, reducing prices, meeting sharper competition with new sources of energy in the face of increasing extraction costs. While endorsing the kind of investment programme in mines, cokeries and pithead power stations which was already implicit in the administration of the American loan, the High Authority also suggested flexible rather than rigid coal prices, to allow for variations in demand, and a planned policy of alternating between the use of solid and liquid fuels, depending on the supply and price picture. The memorandum received a markedly cool reception from all sides and remains largely unimplemented.

In 1957, the High Authority submitted a more detailed and considerably less free-enterprise oriented statement on coal policy, drawing on the fuel shortage, the Suez crisis, intergovernmental discussion for more economic integration and the admonitions of the Common Assembly for an integrated energy policy which had occurred since the first memorandum. First and foremost, the High Authority insisted that the problems of coal can only be solved in the framework of a supranational plan for all sources of energy and demanded a mandate from the governments for elaborating such a plan. Further, it proposed that price and supply stability be enhanced through measures of systematic stockpiling, control over the quantity and price of imports from third countries, internal price predictability and a reduction of tax and social security burdens weighing on the mining industry to be introduced uniformly in all six countries. Instead of letting the free market assume risks the High Authority now declared that it " has decided to work in co-operation with the Governments with a view to finding ways and means of lightening the financial burden and reducing the risks on investments in the coalmining industry, since the whole future of the Community's economic expansion depends on these investments."[6b]

Slow at first in producing an overall body of general objectives, the High Authority once again responded to the lively pressure of the Common Assembly to interest itself in this aspect of ECSC policy with the publication of its first objectives in July of 1955. Apart from stressing the need for new steel investments minimising dependence on scarce scrap, the " objectives " were largely confined to outlining probable demand in the near future and assessing the

[6b] ECSC, High Authority, *Fifth General Report* (Luxembourg, April 1957), p. 318.

current rate of investment with respect to its meeting anticipated needs. Almost no concrete policy recommendations or directives were made. These measures were confided to a series of advisory committees composed of representatives of producers, governments and workers, whose task was the application of the objectives to specific industrial sectors.

By 1957, a far more detailed set of objectives emerged. Consumer demand patterns were projected to 1975 and elaborate requirements for the production of all materials needed and the machinery necessary for their processing were outlined, including a steel production capacity of 105,000,000 tons per year in 1975. Productivity needs were postulated in all sectors and manpower needs thrown into focus. Most important, detailed suggestions were made for a sweeping re-orientation of demand for various grades of coal and for changes in coal production methods. Inactivity had given way to a plethora of concrete proposals.

The implementation of the general objectives, so far, is thus left squarely in the hands of ECSC firms on whose agreement with High Authority forecasts the emergence of a " co-ordinated " investment programme depends. Only the distribution of loan funds obtained by the High Authority can be directly used in steering investments, a policy which was inaugurated in summer of 1956 with the allocation of a $11,500,000 loan floated through the medium of a Swiss banking consortium. Two German, three Italian and one Saar steel firm received these credits, earmarked clearly for investments designed to reduce dependence on scrap and economising on the consumption of scarce coke supplies.

The only other avenue of direct control open to the High Authority lies in commenting on the investment plans which firms are compelled to submit to Luxembourg, and forbidding non-self-financed investments considered unadvisable. The High Authority waited until July, 1955, to require the compulsory submission of investment plans and even then it exempted schemes of modernisation which would cost less than $1,000,000 and new installations costing less than $500,000.[7] Details of these plans are not generally divulged by Luxembourg and only the aggregate statistics are made public; but the information received finds its way into the definition and implementation of general objectives

---

[7] This requirement was tightened somewhat for certain categories of steel by High Authority decision 26–56, *Journal Officiel*, July 19, 1956, p. 209.

by the committees created for that purpose. By November of 1957 over two hundred investment programmes had been submitted to High Authority comment, but not all were answered with detailed opinions. Still, an increasing number of opinions critical of certain phases of investments planned by Community firms were handed down, and several plans were discouraged because they tended to bid up already scarce raw materials. No investment scheme submitted, however, was forbidden by the High Authority. Instead the Luxembourg officials expressed satisfaction with the voluntary co-operation given them in the co-ordination of investments by private firms in the steel sector, noting gratefully that due to ECSC investment guidance less steel-making equipment dependent on scarce scrap is being planned while the steel-pig iron ratio is developing favourably in line with earlier High Authority suggestions. Investments already executed and planned between 1955 and 1958 total $2,630,000,000, considered ample to achieve the steel production capacity of 73·5 million metric tons per year projected by the general objectives for 1960.

In the coal sector, on the other hand, the High Authority is dissatisfied with the record of voluntary investment co-ordination under the programme of submitting company plans to High Authority comment. Mine investments averaged $250,000,000 per year between 1952 and 1956. Plans for 1957–1958 amount only to $694,000,000, considered insufficient to achieve the increases in coal production held out as essential by the High Authority's forecasts. The Common Assembly already expressed its dissatisfaction with investment co-ordination in 1956 by declaring that " the application made by the High Authority of Article 54 is insufficient " and demanding " that more efficient use be made of the obligation to declare investment programmes through High Authority opinions." [8] In 1957 it still deplored the absence of rigorous investment planning in the energy sector and again called upon the High Authority and the six governments to establish clear investment schedules designed to rationalise and increase coal production. Further it encouraged the High Authority to pursue a policy of cyclical stability through buffer stocks and long-term coal import contracts.[8a]

[8] *Ibid.*, pp. 232 *et seq.*
[8a] *Ibid.*, March 11, 1957, p. 107; July 19, 1957, p. 311.

CARTEL POLICY

With the possible exception of ECSC policy in the fields of labour and welfare measures, no area has aroused as much controversy as the question of cartels. According to the Treaty, the High Authority is under obligation to forbid and destroy cartels—if necessary by means of very heavy fines—unless they can prove to contribute to increased efficiency while not preventing competition. Yet the practices of joint sales organisation, non-competitive pricing, compensation payments by low-cost firms to their less fortunate colleagues and the like have a long and honourable history in ECSC countries. They derive support not only from industrialists, but from labour anxious to maintain stable employment conditions and governments eager for constant production and regular supply at stable prices. It is, therefore, hardly surprising that few radical anti-cartel decisions were made in the first few years of the High Authority's life. The Common Assembly expressed itself with restraint on the topic, encouraging the High Authority to implement the Treaty as early as possible, while bearing in mind the possible social upheavals occasioned by too drastic a policy. Only certain Dutch members strongly criticised the High Authority for waiting until November of 1955 in attacking the German coal cartel while the Dutch Government sued the High Authority, unsuccessfully, for failing to act sooner.

The first actions were taken in July of 1953 when Luxembourg demanded that all existing cartels register and apply for permission to continue in existence. Seventy-one applications for authorisation were received at that time. Over the next two years, action was taken with respect to most of these without as yet tackling the large organisations, GEORG, OKU, COBECHAR and ATIC. All national scrap purchase and distribution cartels were dissolved immediately though the French agency only complied in 1956 and the German cartel had to be redissolved by a new order in 1955. Many joint sales agreements among secondary coal basins were approved, as were joint sales agreements among some Belgian steel producers and accords for production specialisation for several Italian steel-makers. None of these involved more than 3 per cent. of the production volume of the common market. Other national cartels, such as the Dutch State Coal Office, dissolved voluntarily. The German steel industry's compensation scheme for imported American coal was approved by Luxembourg and in the field of scrap supply the High Authority itself assumed a number of cartel-like functions. A bitter case arose with respect to the Luxembourg Government's Office Commerciale de Ravitaillement, a state coal import monopoly. Repeated demands by the High Authority for dissolution went unheeded, until the Luxembourg steel industry—the major coal importer—sued the High Authority for failure to act. While the case was pending, the government complied but insisted on a vague licensing of imports, which was promptly used in winter of 1955 for refusing a licence on German coal. Again after some wrangling, the High Authority's protests resulted in the licence being granted, while the Luxembourg steel industry lodged a second—and unsuccessful—suit in the Community's Court for having in the past been compelled by its own government to contribute to a compensation fund for imported coal.

While spotty success and much direct and indirect resistance thus marked the first two years of ECSC anti-cartel policy, plain failure accompanied the effort to control steel export prices. During the recession of 1953, the German, French, Belgian and Luxembourg steel producers concluded an export entente—known as the Brussels Cartel—designed to fix prices on steel exported to third countries. Protests from the United States and Denmark induced the High Authority to consult the Council of Ministers and the Consultative Committee on whether price ceilings were appropriate to curb this practice. The answer from both bodies was a firm negative, motivated in part by the fragmentary powers conferred upon ECSC organs in questions concerning trade with third countries. Thus nothing was done, even though the cartel soon proved its ineffectiveness in controlling its own members from underselling one another.[9] It is likely that the cartel's inability to impose production quotas and fines against offending members contributed to the lack of success, departures from past steel cartel practices made necessary by the rules of the ECSC Treaty and the punitive powers of the High Authority.

Action against the Community's largest and most tenaciously defended cartels came only in 1956. The simplest case was that of the Comptoir belge des Charbons (COBECHAR), which did not

[9] See British Iron and Steel Federation, " The European Export Entente," *Monthly Statistical Bulletin* (February 1954), and ECSC, High Authority, " The High Authority and the Trusts," Information Documents No. 2 (Luxembourg, September 1955).

resist reorganisation once measures against its German and French sister organisations were sketched out.   COBECHAR is the joint sales office of the Belgian coal industry, monopolising sales to the main industrial coal consumers on the Belgian market.   Whether coal is sold through the cartel or directly, the cartel-fixed prices were observed by all.   While the Belgians agreed to alter the monopolistic characteristics of this system, they received the agreement of the High Authority, supported by the Council of Ministers, to continue the practice of inter-firm compensation payments for the equalisation of transport costs and protection against declining demand in other ECSC countries.

A similar compromise solution was used for dealing with the Oberrheinische Kohlenunion (OKU).   OKU is a Franco-Saar-German coal cartel, monopolising the sale of Ruhr, Aachen, Saar and Lorraine coal on the Southern German market.   A request of authorisation for the arrangement was refused by the High Authority.   But Luxembourg admitted that the cartel fulfilled desirable functions to the extent that it assures equitable distribution in time of shortage, especially through the coordination of transport facilities.   To achieve these aims, Luxembourg decreed the re-organisation of OKU making it a voluntary union of coal wholesalers, entitled to deal jointly with the former cartellised producers and transport media.

However, compared to the problem of reorganising the Gemeinschaftsorganisation Ruhrkohle (GEORG), all these measures may well appear trivial.   GEORG furnished at once the symbol for advocates of supranational policy and power and the rallying point for the defenders of a " sane " policy of competition. GEORG was merely the most recent form of non-competitive sales practices in the Community's dominant coal field, inheriting over fifty years of successful cartel activity.   Matters were made more complicated because of almost unanimous support in Germany for the necessity of continuing these practices.   GEORG was the central office of six weak separate coal sales groups, to which all of the Ruhr's fifty-one mining companies belonged.   Its *raison d'étre* lay in the policy of equalising prices among high- and low-cost producers, thereby assuring—according to its and generally prevalent German claims—stability of production for high-cost mines, employment stability, and guaranteed access for unpopular grades of coal.   The transformation of GEORG was viewed as a danger to living standards and the needs of regular supply. Luxembourg received an initial request in 1953 for authorisation without change of the six sales agencies, with continuing strong discipline to be exercised by the central office. The High Authority refused this request and began two years of arduous negotiations, aiming first at setting the six agencies up as completely independent competing groups, but finally settling for a milder compromise which took effect in spring of 1956.

Three independent sales agencies were authorised, each representing from fourteen to nineteen mining companies, and each marketing about fifteen million tons of coal and five million tons of coke annually. Within each sales agency firms can fix prices and delivery conditions, but the powers of the central agency, now called Joint Office, were severely restricted. It is permitted to monopolise sales to a few bulk consumers and to third countries. Further it is given an " operational reserve " of coal, whose size is subject to supervision and veto of the High Authority, to equalise prices in case production and employment seem threatened by cyclical trends—thus retaining a shadow of its former main power. Competition is limited further by providing fixed sales areas for the entire ECSC realm, in which wholesalers are permitted to handle Ruhr coal only if they have sold certain minimum quantities in past years. Continuing ECSC-wide control over the activities of the new Joint Office is facilitated through a Consultative Committee, composed in equal numbers of representatives of German coal producers, German mineworkers, as well as consumers and dealers in all Community countries. Further, a High Authority representative is a member of the Committee. Nobody seemed elated with the results of the compromise, and the association of independent Italian cokeries in 1956 proceeded to lodge a suit against the High Authority in the Court of Justice, alleging failure to carry out the meaning of Article 65. While this suit was eventually withdrawn, one of the Ruhr sales agencies sought— unsuccessfully—to obtain a judgment strengthening the remaining centralised sales features.

Since the decartellised system went into effect, the High Authority has conscientiously checked and supervised every decision of the three agencies and the Joint Office. It has investigated complaints, especially from Dutch purchasers, that non-competitive practices still prevail and has adjusted its original re-organisation decision so as to ease direct access of non-German dealers to the Ruhr. Despite the complaints of producers, therefore, the new system is working to the satisfaction of Luxembourg.

In France, a government-controlled agency called Association Technique de l'Importation Charbonnière (ATIC) had the power to issue licences for all coal imports. Further, additional anti-competitive practices and groupings were associated with ATIC. A compulsory association of steel producers centralised the purchases and distribution of coal consumed in steelmaking. Other consumers were compelled to apply for their supplies of imported coal to a trade association of recognised coal importers and wholesalers, whose membership was regulated by ATIC. The purpose of all these restrictive arrangements was to compel coal consumers to purchase a certain minimum supply of French coal before turning to foreign suppliers.

Two years of negotiations with ATIC and the French Government were needed before satisfactory results were obtained. The most the French were initially willing to concede was the abolition of discriminatory practices against imported tonnages, the dis-solution of the steelmakers' import group and the admission of all coal dealers to the privileged group of recognised importers. They continued to refuse to abolish the major weapon of ATIC, the right to license—and restrict—the importation of ECSC coal. Losing patience on June 22 of 1956, the High Authority ordered the trans-formation of ATIC, calling upon the French Government under Article 88 of the Treaty to lodge objections to the order within the allowable three-months' period. Paris at first retaliated with a suit against the ruling, but eventually withdrew it while ordering a partial reorganisation of ATIC. Remaining issues regarding the future role of ATIC continue to be under negotiation.

Despite this array of measures against cartel practices in the Community, price competition is far from established. In the steel sector, the boom conditions prevailing in 1955 and 1956 would have prevented price cutting in any event, even if it were not for the fact that the price alignment and non-discrimination provisions of the fair-trade code tend to limit competitive pricing. The scrap trade is regulated by the High Authority itself and various equalisation and compensation arrangements for coal imported from third countries are tolerated. As regards coal produced and sold in ECSC, competition is not the practice now nor is it likely to come about in the near future. The arguments in favour of guaranteed access, stable production and sustained employment are far too strong to permit the intrusion of such permanent " disturbing " factors as effective competition within and among coal basins.

INDUSTRIAL CONCENTRATION

The basic economic fact underlying both the production of coal and of steel in ECSC—as in other countries—is that production is concentrated in a few enterprises. Thus twenty-eight groups of enterprises control 82·1 per cent. of ECSC coal production. This includes the totally nationalised coal of France, the state-administered Saar production, the 60 per cent. of Dutch coal mined by state-owned firms, as well as the highly concentrated private firms of Belgium and Germany. It must be added that despite private ownership and control in Belgium, coal prices and investments are in fact completely determined by the Belgian Government acting in co-operation with the High Authority.

In steel the picture is the same. Twenty-one trusts account for 80·8 per cent. of pig iron production, and twenty-two for 76·2 per cent. of crude steel. The breakdown by countries shows these results for the twenty-four trusts responsible for 80 per cent. of Community production in all kinds of steel products.[10]

[10] Statistics on concentration were obtained from the High .Authority's services. Figures on the number of ECSC firms in Wolf-Rodé (Ed.), *Handbuch für den gemeinsamen Markt*, Montan- und Wirtschaftsverlag (Frankfurt am Main, 1955), pp. 407–462. The total number of firms is as follows:

	Coal mines	Iron mines	Iron and steel mills	Total companies per country
Germany	247	14	100	361
Belgium	79	1	38	118
France	60	59	100	219
Italy	21	5	134	160
Luxembourg	0	26	3	29
Netherlands	8	0	3	11
Saar	14	0	6	20
	429	105	384	918

Country	Total number of steel enterprises	Number of trusts
Germany	100	11
France..............	100	6
Belgium	38	3
Saar	6	1
Italy...............	134	1
Netherlands	3	1
Luxembourg	3	1
	384	24

A merger movement in the steel industry was well under way even before the entry into force of the ECSC Treaty, but it is admitted on all sides that the logic of the common market has accelerated the trend further. The need for efficient production methods can be met in part by large-scale financing and pooling of resources.

What has been High Authority policy toward mergers and concentrations? Article 66 of the ECSC Treaty announces a general philosophy under which mergers—as opposed to cartels— are presumed as beneficial and to be encouraged unless they lead to monopoly. Hence while the High Authority is called upon to review and approve proposed mergers, its consent must be given unless the proposal is thought fatal to competition. Mergers completed before 1953 are not reviewable by the High Authority, which automatically exempted the massive concentrations in France achieved since 1945. However, the reconcentration movement in the decartellised German coal and steel industry is definitely subject to continuing control from Luxembourg. Criteria of approval were defined by the High Authority in May of 1954 in three regulations setting up the conditions under which an enterprise can be said to be " controlled " by another, exempting firms producing less than specified amounts from the need to have mergers approved, and detailing the kind of information stock or bond-holders normally outside ECSC jurisdiction must give when the ownership of a firm is under review. " Control " of an enterprise is defined so broadly as to include every conceivable kind of influence which can be exercised. Firms which after a merger would produce less than 1·2 million tons of steel, pig iron or coke, 4 million tons of ore, 900,000 tons of rolled products or 100,000 of special steels are exempt from the authorisation requirement. These figures were agreed on only after bitter debate in the Council of Ministers since the High Authority initially wanted to fix the limits at a much lower level.   In principle, ownership of securities must be declared, though no effective means for compelling banks and trustees to violate rules of confidence has yet been found.

On the basis of these rules, the High Authority has approved *every* request for mergers put before it.   In fact, convinced that concentrations are beneficial to productivity, mergers are actually encouraged.   Thus few objections accompanied the merger of the two largest Belgian steel producers, the purchase by the French combine Sidélor of a large German mine, the acquisition of the biggest Ruhr steel firm by the Dutch Hoogovens, and the purchase of another large German plant by the Swedish financier Axel Wenner Gren.   Most significant, however, is the degree of recon-centration among German steel producers authorised by Luxem-bourg since 1954.[11]   Twenty-four major steel firms emerged from the lengthy and confused decartellisation measures undertaken by the Allied occupation authorities.   Of these, however, eight have already merged with German or foreign interests, leaving

[11] For details, see Daniel Cois, " La renaissance de la siderurgie allemande," *L'Economie*, No. 518 (December 8, 1955).   On the refusal of the High Authority to countenance reconcentration of the Vereinigte Stahlwerke see its Press Release of October 1, 1957.

AUTHORISED MERGERS AS OF DECEMBER 31, 1956

| | Coal/Coal | | | Coal/Steel | | | Steel/Steel | | |
| | Cases | % of Production | | Cases | % of Production | | Cases | % of Production | |
		Region	ECSC		Region	ECSC		Region	ECSC
West Germany	2	15	7·5	4	16 coal 38·5 steel	7·9 13	1	11	3·8
France		none			none		2 1 1	64 13 —	0·8 5·5 19
Belgium		none			none		1	34	4

Source: Reply of the High Authority, May 16, 1957, to written question no. 38 by M. De Smet, Member of the Common Assembly; *Journal Officiel*, June 3, 1957, pp. 232–33.   The German cases all represent instances of reconcen-tration, both vertical and horizontal.   Percentages of production figures are based on 1955 statistics.

only sixteen separate large enterprises. Even this figure is not wholly reliable, however, since much of the share capital is held by banks refusing to divulge the names of the real owners, while exercising effective control as trustees. Further, significant coal-steel mergers have been authorised as well. Some of the more spectacular cases of reconcentration have been the mergers of the erstwhile separate Mannesmann interests, the emergence of a large holding company called Rheinstahl, and the *de facto* reconcentration of many of the former Thyssen interests. Still, no combination approaching in size the once dominant Vereinigte Stahlwerke has yet emerged or is likely to be authorised by the High Authority.

CONTROLS IN THE COMMON MARKET

Despite the heavy emphasis on free enterprise doctrine, as evidenced in the price, investment and merger policy of the High Authority, the Luxembourg officials have been compelled to impose certain central regulations on the common market. With the exception of the allocation of ECSC-subsidised Belgian coal exports, these measures have been concentrated in the regulation of the Community's scrap market.

Scrap is normally a highly speculative commodity, with variable supply and very variable price conditions. The problem is compounded further by the fact that the newer steel installations of the Community, particularly in Italy, feature the electric and Siemens-Martin processes over the older Bessemer process. The former require far more scrap, thus leading to an ever increasing demand for this already scarce commodity. As early as 1953 the High Authority moved to meet this problem by authorising a voluntary scrap import compensation system among ECSC steelmakers, under which the higher price of non-ECSC scrap was equalised for all consumers by requiring each consumer to pay a tax proportional to his total purchases of scrap. The system, though self-governing, was accompanied by scrap ceiling prices imposed by Luxembourg. The need for unanimity among the members of the system soon wrought its downfall. Failing agreed consumer policy, the scrap crisis worsened. In March of 1954, the High Authority abolished price ceilings, made membership in the system compulsory for all steelmakers wishing to purchase scrap, and reserved for itself the right to make decisions on scrap imports and compensation payments in the event of consumer disagreement. It became, in fact, a public scrap-import and distribution cartel. As a corollary, the French authorities in 1956 gave way to Luxembourg's pressure and dissolved their national scrap sales cartel.

With minor modifications this system has been continued in force ever since, even though steelmakers are dissatisfied with it and the Council of Ministers by no means unanimous in its approval. But failing a clear majority for an alternative system, the Council has approved High Authority policy on a short-term basis from year to year. Studies in 1955 convinced the High Authority that the crisis would continue indefinitely despite central regulation unless significant economies in the consumption of scrap were encouraged. The compensation system was changed, therefore, in such a manner as to entitle firms using a certain percentage of pig iron instead of scrap to a bonus, while continuing the compensation for imported scrap as well. The net effect of the device was to reduce the tax charged to the German steelmakers, who had already begun to use pig iron instead of scrap, and to burden the Italian firms who continued to rely heavily on scrap. Reactions set in speedily. Assider and Isa, the Italian steel trade associations, sued the High Authority on September 12, 1955, in protest against the bonus system, while the Italian Government followed in 1956 by filing a complaint in the ECSC Court against the setting of the compensation price for imported scrap. Further tightening of the system in 1957 resulted in the deposition of additional suits by all ECSC steel associations protesting against increased surcharges on scrap consumption.

A further instance of High Authority regulation over the common market has gone unchallenged. In return for a subsidy paid by Dutch and German mines, the Belgian coal enterprises are obligated by Luxembourg to export certain minima of coal to other ECSC countries at prices fixed by the High Authority. While the export quotas have rarely been met, no overt instances of dissatisfaction with this policy have arisen.

Nor has the continuing inadequacy of ECSC coal and coke production led to steps for central regulation. Imports of American coal have risen steeply in 1955 and 1956, without measures of allocation or equalisation of the cost of importation being considered seriously in High Authority circles. Certain misgivings about the shortage have been expressed by the Common Assembly and by the coal-poor Italian firms. The High Authority has preferred to let trade associations make their own arrangements, and has approved *ex post facto*, with the consent of the Council of Ministers, a compensation system among German steelmakers by which these share the cost of imported American coal, while not passing on the savings realised to ECSC purchasers of Ruhr coal thus freed for export. However, long-term import contracts have been considered since 1957.

ELIMINATION AND REDUCTION OF SUBSIDIES

The basic rule of the Treaty makes all subsidies and special charges in the coal and steel sectors factors distorting the normal play of competition and therefore illegal. However, during the transitional period, the High Authority may temporarily authorise the continuation of certain national subsidies and permit inter-coal basin compensation systems in order to avoid unemployment and production dislocation (CTP, Paragraphs 11 and 24). What has been the policy of ECSC in the area of subsidies, firmly rooted in the marketing and production of coal as they were prior to 1952?

Thus in Germany, the High Authority early ordered the abolition of certain subsidies paid to special classes of consumers. The German Government complied despite abortive efforts of the Federation of German Shipowners—one of the groups adversely affected—to challenge the decision in the ECSC court. A more complex case arose in 1956. Wishing to avoid a steep wage increase for miners while meeting demands of the miners' union, the German Government undertook to pay certain production bonuses. The High Authority at first retorted by forbidding this practice as a *de facto* subsidy of wages, but later gave the German Government a longer period for officially defending the bonuses, as the Council of Ministers decided that special measures might be necessary in order to encourage recruitment and productivity of miners. Upon continuation of the bonus, the Dutch mines proceeded to sue the High Authority for permitting the subsidy.

In Holland and Luxembourg the anti-subsidy rule applied particularly to the compensation systems for coal earlier practised in these countries. The Dutch Government in 1954 voluntarily abolished its system, while considerable pressure was necessary to induce the Government of Luxembourg to follow suit, as told in the section on cartels. In Italy, apart from the ECSC subsidy accorded to coal, the High Authority allowed the continuation of a

subsidy on coke but forbade the Italian Government to continue
the subsidisation of shipyards.

France presents by far the most complex case because of the
wide range of subsidies in vogue prior to 1953 and the conviction
of many French producers that they could never compete with
their ECSC rivals. The High Authority followed the policy of
authorising, but gradually reducing, these subsidies, with a view
toward their complete abolition by 1958. The progress of the
programme is shown in these figures:

Subsidy	Authorised in 1953	Authorised in 1954	Authorised in 1955	Authorised in 1956
Briquette plants ..	4,654	3,302	2,091	2,920
Coking coal for steel (imports only)	3,930	3,244	3,201	2,002
Coke for steel (imports only) ..	1,253	182	170	189
Saar-Lorraine coal sold in South Germany	3,486	3,344	1,804	—
Totals	13,323	10,072	7,266	5,111

(amounts in millions of French francs)

Rounding of figures accounts for the difference between the totals
and items.

Further, the French Government announced in March of 1956
that its subsidy on imported coking coal had been abolished completely, while receiving approval to raise once more two other
subsidies. On the other hand, the Charbonnages de France has
sought to equalise the losses regularly suffered by certain of its
coal fields with the profits earned by others through a nation-wide
compensation system, in fact an indirect subsidy for marginal
producers. The High Authority has regularly approved this practice
and its abolition does not seem contemplated, as the Charbonnages
are considered as one enterprise.

The Belgian and Italian coal-mining industries constitute a
situation different from their German, Dutch and French colleagues. Both have been in financial difficulties for decades, their
extraction techniques are antiquated and their remaining deposits
limited. They have lived under direct subsidies accompanied by

government controls for many years, and the Belgian Government made its participation in ECSC conditional on a special transitional régime for its collieries. This régime compels the High Authority to pay an annual subsidy to both the Belgian and Italian coal enterprises, covering half the difference between actual production costs plus a profit margin and the ceiling price at which the coal is sold. The other half is contributed by the government concerned. A further subsidy on coal exported to other ECSC countries is also allowable (CTP, paragraphs 25, 26, 27). The proceeds of this support must be used by the recipients for modernising and re-equipping their plant as well as reorganising corporate structure and pit holdings. The support ends in 1958, at which time the recipients are expected to be able to compete on the common market.

This supranational compensation system is financed from a " compensation levy " assessed against the coal producers whose costs are below the ECSC average. In practice this has meant the German and Dutch coalfields, who since 1953 have contributed $46,500,000 and $4,215,000 respectively. The rate of this levy has been consistently reduced by the High Authority from a high of 1·1 per cent. to a low of 0·3 per cent. of receipts per ton of coal sold.

Until June of 1955, all Belgian collieries shared in the subsidy without distinction as to productivity or special position, receiving a total of $33,619,000 at the end of that year, matched by an equal amount from the Belgian Government. In summer of 1955, however, a joint decision of the High Authority and the Belgian Government introduced drastic alterations. The subsidy payments allowable to the most antiquated mining region—the Borinage—were stepped up, together with a mandatory scheme for reorganising the more productive enterprises while gradually closing down the oldest. At the same time, the most modern region—the Campine— was taken out of the subsidy system altogether as being no longer in need of special assistance, while a third category of producers continued to receive help at the same rate as before. Concurrently, the Belgian Government was authorised to make special credits available to the Borinage while the High Authority agreed to advance special grants for the retraining of workers laid off in the closing of pits. Help by the High Authority was once more made conditional on Belgian governmental special measures, directives with which

Brussels had complied fully by 1956. At the same time, the subsidy for coal exported to ECSC countries was stopped.

Opposition from Belgian coal interests to the change in the system has been intense. Campine collieries have filed suit against the High Authority for withdrawing their compensation payments and the Belgian coal trade association has challenged in court the right of the Belgian Government to reduce price ceilings, in line of modernisation of equipment, even though this change was made in agreement with the High Authority. Both cases were decided in favour of Luxembourg.

As regards the Sardinian high-cost mines—the sole Italian enterprise—$6,000,000 had been made available through 1955, matched once more by the Italian Government. This aid has been accompanied by a joint Italian-High Authority investigation of the Sardinian potential, resulting in a mandatory decision to re-organise the enterprise and close down certain of its mining activities. An ECSC-financed technical assistance programme is to bring about the necessary improvement in worker skills, while additional special subsidies have been granted by the Italian Government. Reorganisation of the mines is under way.

LABOUR POLICY

In December of 1955, the jurisdiction of ECSC extended over 1,615,400 workers, of whom 1,112,700 were miners and the rest metalworkers. Yet the Treaty seems to give the High Authority only truncated powers over labour policy while the Common Assembly, accompanied by trade unions in all ECSC countries, has set up an unceasing clamour for an active wage and welfare policy, interpreting the Treaty very liberally indeed. Generally, of course, ECSC is committed to bring about rising living conditions, but specific powers over wages, working conditions and collective bargaining are denied it, with the exception of the marginal situations involving a falsification of competitive conditions. Positive powers are limited to the collection and dissemination of statistical information relating to these areas, preventing wage cuts as a means to improve competitive power, facilitating the free movement of workers in the coal and steel trades throughout the Community, and contributing to the retraining of workers laid off because of technological or financial adjustment to the common market.

Early High Authority policy had remained rigorously within these limits. Prior to fall of 1955, demands for a wide interpretation of powers were invariably ignored, with the exception of the housing programme explained below. Efforts were then concentrated on getting the member states to agree to free labour mobility, undertaking systematic research on manpower problems, comparative living standards and wage/social security scales, making suggestions for vocational training and studies in the field of industrial hygiene and morale.

The impetus for a more ambitious policy came from trade unionists, strongly supported by a barrage of Common Assembly resolutions and the articulate criticism of its Socialist Group. In 1953, that body still confined itself to encouraging the High Authority to make maximum use of the powers clearly given it. By 1954, the Assembly already wanted the High Authority to go beyond the language of the Treaty in making readaptation grants and urged the entry of ECSC into the area of collective bargaining. In 1955, impatience with delays in the ratification of the Convention on Labour Mobility was voiced, extension of the agreement was urged, the inadequacy of readaptation measures chided, the role of a progressive labour policy held out as part of the need for more co-ordination of economic policies, and—most importantly—clear demands were made for immediate harmonisation of living conditions by means of commonly determined standards on overtime, holiday and vacation pay. When the High Authority, thereupon, cautiously moved into the area of harmonising working-time standards in the steel sector, the Assembly followed this up by demanding the same policy for coal. In May of 1956, all these past complaints were voiced once more and an even more strongly worded resolution passed, while the Socialist Group overtly attacked the member governments for interpreting the Treaty too restrictively.[12]

These and other efforts brought about a distinct change in policy on the part of the High Authority by the latter part of 1955. While nothing could be done about labour mobility, a less cautious attitude became apparent in the field of readaptation, as explained below. More important still, the apparently innocuous research-and-advice function in the field of wage and working condition statistics began

[12] Statement of G. M. Nederhorst, Common Assembly, *Débats*, compte rendu *in extenso*, May 9, 1956, pp. 422–426.

to acquire a different face. On December 20, 1954, the Consultative Committee unanimously passed a resolution urging the calling of a general conference of governments, workers and employers to undertake measures " bringing about progressive harmonisation " of working conditions, with respect to working hours, overtime, holiday and vacation pay. The conference was to lay the ground-work for ECSC-wide model contracts to be used eventually in ECSC-wide collective bargaining. The High Authority declined to take action on the resolution and confined itself to continuing its pioneering studies in comparative real wages and consumer purchasing power. It reiterated its legal confinement to studies, but agreed to extend its surveys to cover the six national systems of social security and the practices singled out for " harmonisation " by the Consultative Committee.

Another jolt came with the introduction of the 45-hour week in the Belgian steel industry in the summer of 1955. Afraid that Belgian steel producers would henceforth suffer from a competitive disadvantage, the Belgian representative on the Council of Ministers asked that body to authorise the High Authority to undertake measures along the line suggested by the Consultative Committee. Opposition developed and the Council on November 15, 1955, instructed the High Authority to undertake a factual study of ECSC steel industries with respect to actual hours worked, without mentioning policy recommendations or collective bar-gaining. The High Authority has complied not only with the request for studies, but has called ECSC-wide meetings of employers and unionists to discuss the feasibility of establishing model contracts on the basis of the studies. In all fairness, however, it must be stressed that the High Authority's factual findings tended to weaken the argument for the need for harmonisation, since they uncovered more differences in working conditions within than among the six countries. Further, they pointed to a definite trend toward an automatic harmonisation of conditions, without need for special legislation or ECSC-wide collective bargaining. In any event, a more active labour policy developed, with demands for more and more action certain in the future. Among the positive steps taken by the High Authority in response to these pressures were its efforts to persuade national governments to relax their immigration laws and make up for manpower shortages in the mines with liberalised rules for the recruitment of Italian workers.

Further, in response to the serious manpower problem, overall coal policy and trade union pressure for harmonisation efforts, the High Authority has lent its support to private efforts to arrive at a " Miners' Charter " for all ECSC countries, defining in detail the wage, hour, health, safety and retirement benefits of this painful occupation.

The development in the realm of assuring free labour mobility is less striking. Article 69 of the Treaty imposed the obligation to assure freedom of movement on the six member governments, who negotiated an agreement to that effect in the Council of Ministers. The High Authority had previously suggested to the six governments that the agreement define the qualifications necessary to entitle workers to employment elsewhere, that a standard labour card be issued to all qualified, that governments circulate lists of vacant positions, with a placement office in Luxembourg to assign foreign workers, and that a standard social security convention be concluded for the personnel so qualified.

The resultant agreement defined professional qualifications so narrowly as to assure free mobility for only 20 to 25 per cent. of ECSC labour, and excluded the inflow of unskilled surplus Italian labour completely. While providing for the standard labour permit, the Convention denied the High Authority any real role in the placement of migrants and left this power in the hands of national employment offices. Its terms, in many respects, are more rigid than a similar agreement applied under the auspices of OEEC.[13] The relaxation of national obstacles to the free mobility of labour envisaged here seems to have been largely achieved already in the informal co-operation among employment offices practised under the Brussels Treaty Organisation.[14] In December of 1957 the Common Assembly expressed its disappointment with progress and called upon the High Authority to study means for assuring the non-discriminatory treatment of foreign workers.

Negotiations for standard social security coverage for migrant coal and steel workers have been conducted jointly with the International Labour Organisation, under an ECSC-ILO Agreement on Consultation, providing not only for the giving of technical advice by ILO on labour questions, but for continuing liaison on

[13] A. Delpérée, *Politique Sociale et Intégration Européenne* (Liège: Thone, 1956), pp. 93 *et seq.*
[14] J. Schregle, *Europäische Sozialpolitik* (Cologne: Bund-Verlag, 1954), pp. 33-3 ;

all common interests generally.[15]   It took two years of intergovernmental and inter-organisational negotiations to compromise the rival social security principles of " personality " and
" territoriality " and to secure agreement on the kinds of coverages
to be offered as well as over the means of financing them.   Particularly, countries who do not normally offer " family allowance "
payments were at first unwilling to make them available to migrant
workers entitled to them in their home countries.   Compromise
proved possible only by splitting the costs unequally, depending
on the kind of coverage, and by including *all* types of migrant
workers, not merely miners and metalworkers.   A comprehensive
convention, taking the place of all previous bilateral and multilateral instruments, and including all kinds of coverage was approved
by the six ministers of labour in December of 1957.   It characterises
the inability of governments to limit measures of economic
integration to the sectors initially selected.

Readaptation policy, by contrast, has provided ECSC with the
possibilities of considerable extension of scope as regards labour
problems in general.   The Treaty (Art. 56 and CTP, par. 23)
insists that readaptation payments may be made only on application
by the government concerned, only if the ECSC contribution is
matched by the requesting government (unless this is waived by
the Council), and only for situations in which the difficulties of the
enterprise and its personnel are due to the opening of the common
market.   If these contingencies are met, the High Authority may
contribute to unemployment compensation, subsidise wages by
supporting the enterprise, pay resettlement allowances and retraining costs, even for skills outside coal and steel if necessary.
During the first two years of operation, the High Authority therefore
turned down a number of French and one sizeable Italian application
for help since the common market was not held responsible for the
difficulties encountered.   Nor did the Luxembourg authorities
consider waiving the requirement for matching contributions by
the Italian Government.[16]   Since that time, policy was liberalised.
The matching requirement has been waived in a number of instances,
less complete evidence that the common market was the cause of
difficulty was demanded, and in the case of a massive Italian steel

[15] Text of agreement in *Journal Officiel*, August 14, 1953.
[16] See *Annales des Mines*, Vol. 143, Numéro spécial 1954, " Le Fonctionnement de la
Communauté Européenne du Charbon et de l'Acier au cours de l'Année 1954,"
p. 60.

readaptation grant, the High Authority agreed to finance new skills in productive pursuits other than metallurgy. The same broad attitude was displayed in the retraining and resettlement of the miners laid off in Sardinia.

Readaptation activities are best summarised in these figures: [17]

Country	Requests Received	Requests Granted	Funds Allocated	Number of Workers Benefited
France	12	8	$2,450,000	about 2,000
Italy	2	2	$5,990,000	about 10,000
Belgium	1	1	$1,400,000	1,100
	15	11	$9,840,000	13,100

One of the most daring supranational efforts of ECSC has been the ambitious housing programme, undertaken without special Treaty authorisation, but with the full support of the Common Assembly, Council of Ministers and Consultative Committee. The programme consists of two parts: a project designed to experiment in cheaper construction methods permitting standardisation later, for which $1,000,000 has been allocated, $1,000 for each house to be built; and High Authority participation in large-scale construction, either through direct loans to builders or future owners or by means of guarantees to banking institutions underwriting the loans. The full scope of the first plan and the degree of implementation are shown below [18]:

Country	Number of Houses Planned	Amount of ECSC Loan	Number of Houses Completed October 1957
Germany	10,400	$12,000,000	6,422
France........	2,750	$7,150,000	266
Saar	400	$1,000,000	—
Belgium	1,750	$4,000,000	546
Italy.........	468	$800,000	68
Luxembourg	75	$500,000	50
Netherlands [18]	54	—	54
Totals	15,897	$25,450,000	7,406

For Footnotes, see following page.

Encouraged by the results of this effort, the High Authority began a second programme of financing worker housing in the coal and steel industries by setting aside $30,000,000 for loans to builders and banks, to be spent in 1957 and 1958. The Council of Ministers approved this step in May of 1956,[19] expected to yield 20,000 more housing units. It also planned to set aside $4,000,000 for a second experimental housing programme.

The remaining work of ECSC in the labour field is confined to the undertaking and financing of studies in the fields of industrial hygiene and morale, manpower availabilities and trends, with increasing attention being paid to the problems of vocational training for miners. The mining disaster at Marcinelle, Belgium, in summer of 1956, has compelled the High Authority to interest itself actively in mine safety and to mediate between the Italian and Belgian Governments over the issue of the future encouragement of the migration of Italian miners to Belgium. Due to its efforts, a supranational mine rescue organisation was set up in 1957.

Far more important than any one single programme in the High Authority's labour policy is the growing conviction that ECSC, despite the silence of the Treaty on the subject, *should* have social and welfare objectives in addition to supervising a common market. The High Authority's acceptance of the Common Assembly's oft-repeated admonitions in this realm came in 1957; its *Fifth General Report*, instead of taking refuge behind a Treaty which did not make ample provision for powers in the labour and welfare field, defines the social mission of ECSC as the aggregate of the separate programmes already pursued. Further, " the High Authority intends to pursue and intensify its endeavours to bring

[17] Details in Answer No. 29 of the High Authority to written question No. 29, M. Alain Poher, Member of the Common Assembly. *Journal Officiel*, March 29, 1956, pp. 117 *et seq.* In 1957, the German Government applied for aid in retraining 2,100 miners about to be laid off while the Italian and French Governments submitted new requests affecting some 1,700 steelworkers.

[18] High Authority, *Bulletin mensuel d'Information* (November 1957). The Dutch housing programme was entirely under the experimental construction scheme and therefore required no loans.

[19] Housing loans were facilitated after 1956 through an agreement between ECSC and the Bank for International Settlements, liberalising the collateral to be accepted by the High Authority. The earlier ECSC–BIS agreement had severely restricted the financial independence of Luxembourg and contributed to the difficulties encountered in financing the first housing programme.

about a *levelling-up in working conditions*. It hopes that its first steps in this field will prove fruitful, that consultations between representatives of the workers' and employers' organisations will continue on an increasing scale, and that it will ultimately be possible not merely to pinpoint disparities in the conditions at present prevailing, but in some cases to do something about them." [19a] In its session of June 1957, the Common Assembly welcomed this declaration as a " first step " in the evolution of a long-term European social policy, but urged the High Authority to put pressure on the six governments to persuade certain of their economic interest groups to participate in good faith in the mixed commissions.[19b]

INTEGRATION OF TRANSPORT MEDIA

The common market would have been a façade for further trade discrimination if the prevalent practices of charging differential transport rates, depending on the foreign or domestic origin or destination of merchandise, had not been declared illegal. The actual measures for eliminating transport discriminations, however, were left to the member governments, acting upon the suggestions of the High Authority. Systematic rate discrimination by the six state-owned railway systems—each fearing a considerable loss of revenue if the practices were changed—provided the first field of effort.

By 1954 agreement had been reached in the Council of Ministers to abolish discrimination as well as introducing a tapered through-rate system which operates regardless of frontiers and does away with the " rupture de charge," a device which had compelled the recomputation of rates at each frontier as if the train had to be unloaded. The resulting reductions in rail transport charges are set out overleaf:

[19a] *Fifth General Report, op. cit.,* p. 235. Italics in original.
[19b] *Journal Officiel,* July 19, 1957, p. 307.

Reductions in International Foreign Rates
Since the Advent of the Common Market
(French francs)

	Before common market	After suppression of discrimination	After introduction of direct tariffs	
			May 1, 1955	May 1, 1956
Coke				
Germany–France (Gelsenkirchen-Homecourt)	2,331	1,992	1,694	1,599
Germany–Luxembourg (Gelsenkirchen-Esch)	2,603	2,546	2,128	1,962
Belgium–France (Zeebrugge-Thionville)	1,706	1,640	1,661	1,579
Coking Coal				
Germany–Saar (Alsdorf-Saarbrücken)	2,157	1,959	1,668	1,599
Coal				
Saar–Germany (Reden-Grube-Regensburg)	3,187	2,633	2,419	2,341
Iron Ore				
France–Belgium (Sancy-Ougrée)	850	784	674	606
Luxembourg–Germany (Tétange–Duisburg)	1,243	1,067	973	912

Source: These figures are presented in greater detail in the High Authority's *Third General Report*, April 10, 1955, pp. 108–109.

The system went into effect gradually, and the tapers were so computed as to protect certain jealously guarded preserves of railway systems, as a result of top-level compromise. Work on the standardisation of techniques of computing rates is continuing. The Common Assembly was so encouraged by the results of rate harmonisation that it recommended in 1955 the extension of this system to all merchandise, calling on the Council of Ministers to enlarge its own competence in this respect. High Authority negotiations with the Swiss and Austrian Governments resulted in the same principles of non-discrimination being applied by these railways for coal and steel shipments through Switzerland and Austria from one ECSC country to another.

Less concrete results have been attained in the field of inland waterways. The problem here is not systematic discrimination, but a cyclical disparity between the higher rates charged for shipments within national boundaries (subject to cabotage rights) and the highly competitive rates prevalent on inter-state shipments. The High Authority therefore proposed a general rate standardisation agreement to the six governments, which the Council sidestepped by deferring to the concurrent activities of the European Conference of Transport Ministers. Since the activities of this body resulted in nothing concrete, the High Authority renewed its proposals, only to have the governments favour a solution tending to perpetuate the centralised allocation of shipping space without touching rate differentials. A Convention of June 1957, adopted by the Council of Ministers, promises to harmonise rates on the basis of " representative levels freely established " under the watchful eye of the High Authority. In the meantime, a controversy developed between the High Authority and the Belgian Government, over the latter's practice of requiring special licences for Ruhr coal shipped on Belgian waterways. As of mid-1956, Belgium had refused to alter the system.

Even though goaded in 1956 to undertake measures for the regulation of both water and road transport by the Common Assembly, nothing had been done in the field of trucking by the High Authority. No uniform loading or pricing rules exist and price publicity is not the practice among truckers. A first step was taken in 1955 with a request that member governments issue a uniform lading document on a compulsory basis, a request with which certain states have complied. In 1956 the High Authority has proposed a procedure for the publication and supervision of rates charged, but the system is not yet in effect. In 1957 the Common Assembly congratulated the High Authority on its proposals in all transport fields and urged the six governments to adopt them forthwith.

RELATIONS WITH THIRD COUNTRIES

Since ECSC is obviously neither a state nor a conventional international organisation the nature of its " international " relations provides much interesting material as to its real status. Thus the High Authority negotiates with foreign governments, represents the member states for certain purposes and maintains its own diplomatic relations—but not without some supervision from the Council of Ministers.

ECSC's position in international economic organisations of which the six governments are also members provided the first test of status. Thus OEEC early granted the six governments a waiver from the extension of free trade rules on the common market to the members of OEEC, an obligation which would normally have been applied under the Code of Trade Liberalisation. Further, the High Authority is recognised as an observer in meetings of the OEEC Council and on its technical commissions. Finally, the six governments have agreed to designate the High Authority as their spokesman in OEEC on all matters concerning coal and steel.

Relations with the members of the General Agreement on Tariffs and Trade (GATT) have been more complex. GATT agreed on November 10, 1952, to regard ECSC " as if the European territories of these states constituted the territory of a single contracting party as concerns coal and steel." Waivers from the application of the most-favoured-nation clause to third countries as regards the free trade rules of the common market were granted as well. As in OEEC the six governments instruct the High Authority to represent them in GATT meetings, and to submit an annual report on ECSC operations, on which GATT has insisted. Despite frequent and lively complaints from GATT members of alleged discrimination practised by ECSC, the Six and the High Authority have steadfastly insisted on the supremacy of ECSC obligations and have jointly resisted the attacks of GATT. Since 1956 the High Authority acts as the negotiator for the Community in GATT tariff bargaining.

The position of the High Authority as an international person seems to have been cemented by the accreditation of permanent foreign missions in Luxembourg. The following countries maintain diplomatic relations with ECSC: Great Britain, the United States, Switzerland, Austria, Norway, Denmark, Sweden and Japan. So far the High Authority has accredited a representative only to the United Kingdom.

As a negotiating agent, the High Authority has been active in the dual capacity of seeking tariff concessions from third countries and attempting to extend the common market by the conclusion of treaties of association. In both capacities, the High Authority acts under instructions from the Council of Ministers, which must enjoy unanimous consent (CTP, par. 14). Council supervision is assured, furthermore, by its right to appoint observers to negotiating sessions with third countries. On this basis, reciprocal tariff concessions were negotiated in 1956–57 with the United States and especially with Austria. The Austrian agreement not only provides for joint anti-dumping measures but also extends to non-Treaty products.

Extending the common market by agreements with non-member states constitutes the crucial area of ECSC activity as a negotiator. Such agreements have been sought and concluded with Britain and Switzerland. The Swiss agreement dates from the summer of 1956 and merely provides for regular consultation between the High Authority and the Swiss Government, especially if ECSC intends to declare a " serious shortage," limit exports, or impose price controls on exports. It was rumoured that the negotiation of the Swiss loan for ECSC enterprises was eased by the High Authority's willingness to take on this obligation toward a major consumer of ECSC products. Consultations take place in the framework of a " Joint Committee," composed of an equal number of High Authority and Swiss Federal Council members. This Agreement did not require the ratification of the six member governments, a distinct recognition of ECSC independence.

Ever since 1950 it had been one of the prime ambitions of Jean Monnet and many Continental federalists to overcome the aloofness of Britain toward the " Community of the Six " by the conclusion of some kind of agreement between London and ECSC. The British Government itself had expressed the hope for " an intimate and enduring association with the Community " in 1952, and had dispatched a diplomatic mission to Luxembourg as soon as the High Authority was established. This mission was headed by Sir Cecil Weir and consulted informally with the ECSC executive in the form of another " Joint Committee " until the formal Agreement on Association went into effect on September 23, 1955.[20]

---

[20] ECSC, High Authority, *Agreement Concerning the Relations between the European Coal and Steel Community and the United Kingdom of Great Britain and Northern Ireland and Connected Documents* (London, December 21, 1954). ECSC, High Authority, "*Joint Committee*" *entre le Gouvernement du Royaume-Uni et la Haute Autorité*, (Luxembourg, mimeo., st. 1283). ECSC High Authority,

Negotiations for this agreement were initiated by a letter from Luxembourg late in 1953. The High Authority, after the approval of the Council of Ministers, proposed to London the establishment of permanent consultative machinery, able to discuss and agree on joint policy with respect to investments, tariffs, trade practices, quantitative restrictions and research. An additional aim of Monnet was to persuade Britain to abolish double pricing on coal exports, and thus stimulate ECSC coal producers to lower their prices to meet British competition. One year of negotiations saw not only the cutting down of the topics proposed for consultation, but also a growing desire of the Council of Ministers to control the High Authority's freedom of action. The agreement which went into effect, after ratification of the seven parliaments concerned, provides: (1) the parties will consult on the possibilities for the reduction of trade barriers between them; (2) the parties undertake to consult one another *before* either contemplates the introduction of additional restrictions on trade between them; (3) the parties agree to exchange information " on matters of common interest concerning coal and steel, and, where appropriate, in regard to the co-ordination of action on these matters." These matters include all major aspects of policy. For purposes of carrying out consultations, a standing Council of Association is set up, composed of four representatives each from the High Authority and the British Government, equipped with a special Secretariat. Further, special sessions of the Council of Ministers are envisaged, to be attended by the British minister concerned. Members of the Council, of course, are entitled to attend meetings of the Council of Association and the Council has the power to instruct the High Authority on its attitude in the sessions.

From the viewpoint of integration the work of the Council of Association has been far from spectacular. It does demonstrate two key trends, however: London is willing to negotiate as an equal with a quasi-federal entity by-passing the national governments and thus has come to recognise ECSC as a permanent reality; further, the work demonstrates that a supranational organisation can

Information Service, " First Report of the Council of Association," Luxembourg, April 1, 1957, Doc. No. 2522/57e. (Also published as Cmd. 116 in Great Britain). For an authoritative assessment of association, see Sir Cecil Weir, " The First Step in European Integration," published by the Federal Educational and Research Trust (London, 1957). Weir concludes that the positive experience of ECSC-British relations should encourage the closest possible association between the United Kingdom and EEC.

establish and maintain relations with the government of a major outside power on a basis identical with dealings typical in standard inter-governmental agencies. The Council of Association met six times between November of 1955 and October 1957. It created committees on coal, steel and trade relations, in which the spadework is done, and whose activities provide an excellent survey of the record of " association." Thus the Steel Committee's work was dominated by the discussion of price and market trends and by the exchange of information on how scarce scrap supplies might be economised. The level and rate of investment in both markets was also discussed. The Trade Relations Committee busied itself with exchanging factual information on export and import regulations; but more significantly, it negotiated a tariff agreement under which British steel duties on ECSC exports were reduced from a range of 15 to $33\frac{1}{3}\%$ to 10%, while ECSC rates would vary between 3 and 12%. The most concrete measures were taken in the Coal Committee. Mere exchanges of information—typical of the Council in general— were supplemented by a concrete undertaking on Britain's part not to cut down its exports of coal to the ECSC countries, despite the general British fuel shortage and the decision of the National Coal Board to curtail exports. Assessments of long-term supply trends and the impact of nuclear energy on coal demand were made as well. Further, the principle of " association " facilitated the participation of Britain in the ECSC Conference on Mine Safety, called after the Marcinelle disaster of 1956. No other foreign government participated.

Clearly, the Agreement on Association, while by no stretch of the imagination making Britain a member of ECSC, nevertheless establishes closer relations between London and Luxembourg than between ECSC and any other third country. By and large, the consultations have not gone beyond the submission and examination of statistics and experiences typical of other international organisations. There is no evidence yet of any kind of " co-ordination " of separate policies or of concrete undertakings to act jointly. It was no doubt because of this restricted meaning of " association " that all parties in Britain welcomed the conclusion of the Agreement while many Continental circles tended to be disappointed over the modest scope of the work.

The Common Assembly, while contenting itself with the results achieved, had nevertheless hoped for a tighter system of association.

In 1953 it had urged the High Authority to obtain the suppression of double pricing from Britain. In 1954 it expressed the hope that the High Authority's original proposals to Britain be crowned with success and in 1956 it urged the Council of Association to " influence favourably the close and constant nature of association." At the same time the Assembly proposed the creation of an inter-parliamentary commission, composed of nine British members of Parliament and nine members of the Assembly, to be connected in an undefined manner with the work of the Council of Association. In 1957 the Assembly insisted on more drastic steps by proposing the elimination of all duties on Treaty products between ECSC and all members of OEEC.[21]

INTERNAL TARIFF QUESTIONS

An ECSC doctrine of free competition tempered by concern over structural unemployment carried the logical consequence of permitting transitional tariff arrangements in cases where severe differences in cost of production prevail. Section 27 of the Convention on Transitional Provisions permits the High Authority to authorise the Italian Government to retain import duties on ECSC coke, within rigidly defined limits and with the obligation to reduce the rates each year. The same system applies with respect to steel (CTP, Section 30). The upper limits of the Italian tariff are fixed by the Annecy Convention rates. Once again the High Authority is under obligation to reduce the duties at an increasing rate each year, with their final abolition scheduled for 1958.

Proceeding on this basis, the steel tariff had been reduced from an average of 19 per cent. to 5·7 per cent. by 1957, and the rates on special steels from 17 per cent. to 5·7 per cent. Agreement between the Italian Government and the High Authority could not always be reached, in which case the High Authority set the rates unilaterally. As regards the provisional tariff on the importation of ECSC pig iron, a special situation developed. As part of its programme of scrap conservation, the High Authority asked the Italian Government to suspend the duty on pig iron indefinitely. Rome complied only to the extent of suspending the tariff provisionally, a decision which Luxembourg considered inadequate and insists on overruling if agreement cannot be reached. The main trend

[21] *Journal Officiel*, July 19, 1956, p. 229; July 19, 1957, p. 301.

is plainly in the direction of the full inclusion of Italy in the common market, despite these minor delaying tactics.

A final internal tariff problem is raised by the different rates applied by the six member states in their steel trade with third countries. Article 72 makes possible the determination of uniform tariff ceilings and floors by unanimous decision of the Council and Article 74 permits the High Authority to intervene in tariff practices in case of dumping. The High Authority may compel member states to adjust tariff obligations incurred prior to 1952 in the light of ECSC obligations (CTP, Par. 16) and the same is true of new trade agreements to be concluded (CTP, Par. 17). With the exception of tariff harmonisation on special steels between France and Germany —prior to the negotiations with Austria—the intra-ECSC alignment of tariff rates *vis-à-vis* third countries has not been completed, though the British tariff agreement assumes its success. Germany raised her low rates and France decreased her higher ones in the Austrian case, while Italy remains outside the system and the Benelux countries preferred to retain their very low rates. In order to prevent the re-exportation of imports from third countries via the low-tariff Benelux area, these countries have agreed, in co-operation with the High Authority, to charge a special countervailing rate in addition to their standard rates, on goods destined to other ECSC countries (CTP, Par. 15).

Beyond Coal and Steel

Friends and critics of ECSC alike were agreed on one point: economic integration in the long run cannot rest on supranational rules and institutions for one economic sector alone, no matter how vital that sector may be in the total scheme of life. Opponents of ECSC used this argument to prevent acceptance of the Treaty, while federalists utilised it to support their demand for later, additional steps toward integration. But even apart from the doctrinal implications of sector integration, a number of practical problems were raised by ECSC which called for action beyond the scope of coal and steel. How would six different tax systems affect the conditions of competition? Could investments in coal be considered apart from investment in other energy sectors? How much distortion in prices can be attributed to six different wage and social security systems? Must economic forecasts be made for coal and steel alone, or for the entire range of industrial and financial activity? And in the realm of politics the fundamental question of the future of ECSC in an integrated or unintegrated Europe had to be considered.

The political questions of ECSC will be considered last in this chapter. As concerns the economic defects of sector integration, the Council of Ministers attempted to come to grips with them in its basic resolution of October 13, 1953, which has become the reference point for all subsequent activity. Worried by a slump in consumer demand late in 1953, the Council instructed the High Authority to undertake periodic economic surveys and make suggestions jointly with the six governments in order to stimulate a general policy of economic expansion, by no means confined to coal and steel. The surveying and possible co-ordination of investments seemed to have been uppermost in the Council's mind. With the onset of boom conditions, the interest in joint economic studies beyond coal and steel increased rather than diminished. Justified by the 1953 resolution, the Council decided on long-range studies concerning the influence of fiscal, wage and social security systems on the price structure of the common market, in addition to investment surveys. The need for these studies and for co-ordinated national policies resulting from them was re-affirmed in connection with the Messina Conference of June 1955, during which far-reaching decisions for further integration were made.

Implementation of the resolution of October 13, 1953, has lagged behind Council intentions. The High Authority, on behalf of the six governments has made periodic economic reports, hinging around the development and breakdown of the Community's gross national product. It has stressed general inflationary or deflationary trends, but has restrained itself from making any significant recommendations on the basis of these findings. It was the Council rather which has asked for more frequent and more detailed reports of this kind. With respect to investment co-ordinated with general cyclical developments, it was the Council once more which has asked for suggestions on the use of counter-cyclical public service spending techniques.

Long-range implementation of the resolution is achieved through the work of a Mixed Committee, composed of representatives of the High Authority and of the member governments, functioning through appropriate expert sub-committees staffed largely, by national civil servants. These efforts have resulted in a standard questionnaire used to ascertain the level and rate of investments, reliable data on total energy consumption and need patterns, apart from coal, and joint efforts to determine the incidence of differing tax systems—including social security contributions—on the structure of enterprises and the rate of investments. However, it cannot be said that any effective and active harmonisation of general governmental economic and fiscal policy had resulted from these studies by 1957. With the onset of serious inflationary conditions in several ECSC countries, several governments proceeded to influence directly or indirectly the price structure of the coal and steel industries over which they had ceded jurisdiction to Luxembourg. The High Authority, while admitting its failure to influence fundamental cyclical trends, then openly called for the harmonisation of wage and social security policies and for co-ordinated fiscal measures designed to stem the tide of inflation and extra-legal national controls since the unequal incidence of such measures in the member states threatened to undermine the very structure of the common market. Sector integration had run up against its own logical boundaries, a conclusion recognised by the Council of Ministers in its directive to the Mixed Committee, issued in June of 1957, to intensify its efforts to make suggestions for a co-ordinated supranational policy of dealing with the business cycle.

Thus the Council and the Common Assembly have openly admitted the " spill-over " of sector integration into other fields. The Council on several occasions authorised High Authority spending in areas not normally falling under ECSC jurisdiction. The Assembly in 1953 urged the High Authority to maximise its " co-ordinating " role with a view toward general economic integration and in 1955 it called on the Council of Ministers to take the same view. Finally, it expressed impatience with the delays in implementing the resolution of October 13, 1953, and requested immediate action in this field, a position reiterated forcefully in 1957.

The mounting fuel crisis of Europe has offered ECSC a dramatic possibility of enlarging its sphere of competence since 1954. While the need for increasing quantities of coal in the near future is admitted by all, estimates have varied sharply as to the relative position of coal *vis-à-vis* oil, natural gas and nuclear power a generation hence, with investment policies in the mining sector governed by these long-run speculations. It was unfortunate that early High Authority suggestions for the elaboration of an integrated European energy policy were linked with the political federalism of its first President, Jean Monnet, who was to make this issue the partial cause for his dramatic resignation. While task expansion seemed indicated by the facts and by the inability to plan for coal in the absence of jurisdiction over other fuels, the political issue of supranational powers prevented any sustained governmental interest in these proposals until after the fundamental decisions to proceed with economic integration had been made. Hence the energy studies of the Mixed Committee proceeded at a leisurely pace and the Council of Ministers confined itself during 1955 and 1956 to instructing the High Authority to participate in the energy discussions of the appropriate commissions of OEEC. However, the spill-over became an immediate reality in 1957. The aftermath of Suez, combined with the decision to establish Euratom and EEC, resulted in a formal mandate from the Council of Ministers to the High Authority to proceed to the presentation of precisely the kind of energy policy Monnet had urged in 1954. To be formulated on the basis of the studies already completed by the Mixed Committee and with its co-operation, the plan is to include estimates of immediate and long-term needs and recommendations as to the most efficient means for meeting them. Task expansion has come in the wake of demonstrated economic weakness, clashing national economic policies and the determined pressure of both High Authority and the Common Assembly.

ECSC AND EUROPEAN INTEGRATION

The Council of Ministers, under the chairmanship of Adenauer, held its first session in Luxembourg on September 8, 1952, and as its initial measure authorised the Common Assembly to transform itself into an " ad hoc " Assembly by co-opting some additional, members, and proceed to the drafting of a *political* constitution for the six member states. Clearly, the first measure of the economic ECSC was the initiation of the political federation of Western Europe.

After six months of deliberations the draft constitution of the European Political Community (EPC) was presented to the six governments for action. The Common Assembly, transposed into a Constitutional Convention, had produced a document describing a governmental system patterned essentially after the institutions of coal and steel, with jurisdiction over defence, military procurement, coal, steel and any other segments of Western European public life that might later be ceded to it. Immediately only the powers of the ECSC and the proposed EDC would become the province of EPC. The crucial difference between the political community and its two functional sub-divisions was to be clear ministerial responsibility to a bicameral supranational parliament. Federalism seemed to have come into its own in 1953, via the efforts of the Common Assembly.

This impression seemed confirmed by the declaration of the Council of Ministers on May 4, 1954, that an Assembly based on universal suffrage and direct elections would take the place of the Common Assembly as soon as the EDC Treaty went into effect. But time after time active consideration of the EPC draft by the six governments was postponed as cabinet after cabinet in France recoiled from the test of presenting the treaty for parliamentary ratification. While EDC was being negotiated to death—even before its final demise in the National Assembly on August 30, 1954—interest in EPC lagged proportionately. With the end of EDC the effort to build a European federation via EPC was given up.

It was in this context that Monnet, in the late months of 1954 and early 1955, sought to bring about a direct expansion of the powers of ECSC. Taking the European fuel crisis—especially in its long-range implications—as his major argument he proposed that ECSC be given jurisdiction over all sources of energy. He coupled his proposal with a declaration that he intended to resign as President of the High Authority in February of 1955. The Common Assembly, for its part, backed Monnet, urged him to remain in office, but also stridently demanded the right to be consulted by the Council of Ministers in the choice of the next President.

If Monnet had counted on using his announced intention to resign as a means for exerting pressure on the six governments for expanding the scope of ECSC, his calculation misfired badly. The proposal received a sympathetic response in most of the six countries —at least in governmental circles—except in France. The governments of Mendès-France and Edgar Faure proved delighted with Monnet's resignation, indicated their hostility to new supranational powers, and made their disagreement with the President so obvious that the latter finally decided to resign his seat on the High Authority

as well as the presidency in order to devote himself more actively
as a private citizen to the fight for federation.

Yet the desire of the other governments for progress along the
road of integration had to be met. Hence the Council of Ministers,
in the form of the six foreign ministers, met in Messina on June 1,
1955, and agreed on a " new start " for economic integration, since
dubbed the " Relance Européenne." The ministers refused to
commit themselves either to an intergovernmental or supranational approach. They determined that a concurrent effort be
made to establish a Western European atomic energy agency
(Euratom) and to abolish trade obstacles for *all* commodities, or
the so-called " General Common Market." To this end a committee
of experts appointed by governments was convened, under the chairmanship of an " eminent European personality," Belgium's Paul-
Henri Spaak, and instructed to lay the groundwork for treaties in
each of the two fields of endeavour singled out for the " new start."
At the same time, however, the Conference ignored the demand of
the Common Assembly that the powers of ECSC be explicitly
widened and that the Assembly participate in the selection of the
next President of the High Authority. Seeking their own counsel
exclusively, the ministers unanimously elected former French
prime minister René Mayer to this position, after it turned out that
France's first choice, former prime minister Ramadier, was unacceptable to the other five governments.

The labours of the intergovernmental expert committee were
completed in the spring of 1956 in the form of two reports concerning
Euratom and the General Common Market, committed to treaty
form, signed at Rome in March 1957, ratified, and the resulting
institutions began operations on January 1, 1958. The High
Authority as well as the Council of Ministers were directly associated
with this work in the form of permanent delegations to the Brussels
conference which drafted the reports. Four years of experience
with sector integration were thus brought to bear on future plans
and the conclusions of ECSC personnel found a wide hearing in
the proposals before the six governments. For its part, the High
Authority under Mayer's presidency has preferred to funnel its
advocacy of further integration through these intergovernmental
channels instead of insisting on any immediate increase in the sphere
of competence of ECSC. Thus the period of a lonely and isolated
supranational ECSC came to an end, an end symbolised by the

resignation of René Mayer and the election of Paul Finet in 1958. The High Authority warmly welcomed the creation of EEC and Euratom; far from harbouring jealousy toward the new instruments of integration, it expects its own task to be facilitated. Sector integration has yielded to general economic unity.

Attitudes were more formally federal in the Common Assembly. Expressing great disappointment over the failure of the Council to consider any immediate change in the institutional powers of ECSC, the parliamentarians on June 24, 1955, decided to launch their own programme of task expansion, designed to prove the necessity for political and democratic controls over whatever new Western European agencies the expert conference would recommend. The fact that the first public report on the work of the experts was presented to the Assembly by M. Spaak was not considered enough. In the so-called Poher Report, it was recommended that henceforth the High Authority indicate clearly which of the Assembly's resolutions have been implemented, that the Council formally report to the Assembly on its efforts in co-ordinating general economic policy and that ministers submit to questioning as well as attend meetings of the Assembly's commissions. Further, the Assembly should share in naming High Authority presidents and vice-presidents and be notified of any failure of member governments in carrying out their obligations. Finally, joint action by the six parliaments should be promoted by the preparation of parallel programmes for debates and joint meetings of the *bureaux* of the national parliaments with that of the Assembly.[22]

With respect to the Euratom and EEC, the Assembly had demanded that *it* be the democratic organ charged with supervising these schemes and was gratified in having the wish met in the final outcome.[23] At the same time, reports were made demonstrating that the High Authority had not yet used its powers under the Treaty as fully as possible for the realisation of economic integration, and suggesting specific ways in the realms of finance, readaptation, and investment for doing so even without amending

[22] ECSC, Assemblée Commune, Rapport sur l'organisation à donner à l'Assemblée Commune pour rendre plus efficace son action dans le cadre des dispositions actuelles du Traité, par Alain Poher. Doc. No. 2 (1955–1956), November, 1955.

[23] See ECSC, Assemblée Commune, Rapport préliminaire sur le développement de l'intégration economique de l'Europe, parts I and II, by van der Goes van Naters. Doc. No. 7 (1955–1956) March, 1956. Also ECSC, Assemblée Commune, Rapport sur le marché commun et l'Euratom, by P. Wigny and van der Goes van Naters, Doc. No. 14 (1955–1956).

the Treaty.[24] While asserting its own role, the Assembly also called on the member governments to enact speedily the recommendations for a general common market, if possible by securing adherence of states not members of ECSC.[25] At the same time it cautioned the governments not to repeat the " mistakes " of the ECSC Treaty in its subordination of labour and welfare policy to free trade and economic expansion, and to be ready for supranational planning measures in easing the adjustment to competitive conditions. Agreement was almost impossible to reach concerning Euratom because of the conflict between pacifists and those who wished to facilitate a military role for the organisations, between those committed to economic planning and the advocates of free enterprise. By way of compromise the Common Assembly in 1956 underwrote without significant comment, the recommendations of the expert commission, criticising only the inadequate powers foreseen for parliamentary control over the new agency.[26]

Having failed in achieving the status of a genuine European parliament in the defeat of EDC and in the peripheral role accorded to their opinions in the intergovernmental deliberations during the " new start," federalists in the Common Assembly now hope for an extended scope under Euratom and the general common market. After five years of activity, ECSC clearly had not brought with it a general enthusiasm for supranational institutions and federal powers in limited spheres. Yet it gave an undoubted impetus to further integration.

---

[24] ECSC, Assemblée Commune, Rapport sur (1) les mesures susceptibles d'assurer la pleine application des dispositions du Traité sans modification de celui-ci; (2) l'extension des attributions de la Communauté, en matière de charbon et d'acier, nécessaires pour la pleine réalisation des objectifs assignés par le Traité, by Gerhard Kreyssig, Doc. No. 1 (1955–1956), October, 1955.
[25] *Journal Officiel*, March 29, 1956, p. 116.
[26] *Ibid.*, May 26, 1956, pp. 145–146.

Part Two

PROCESSES OF INTEGRATION AT THE NATIONAL LEVEL

CHAPTER 4

POLITICAL PARTIES: 1952 AND 1957

FIVE years of intensive supranational activity in two economic sectors vital to the standard of life of the six member countries of ECSC may well be expected to arouse controversy among the parliamentarians normally charged with the business of ruling. Given the rigid party structure of Western European politics, with its concomitant tendency toward discipline (except in France and Italy) and ideological commitment, changes in party positions toward ECSC can be highly significant indicators of a process of political integration. What features of party conduct should be singled out for attention in testing integration in this realm?

The first step in such an analysis must be a pinpointing of party atitudes toward the ratification of the ECSC Treaty in the years 1951 and 1952. What reasons were advanced for favouring or opposing the step? Is there evidence of a homogeneous *national* position in the six parliaments on the basis of French or German or Italian nationalism? Or does the pattern of conduct point to a distinct set of party ideologies explaining majorities for ratification on the basis of a convergence of positions rather than agreement on principle? Such an effort must come to grips with the role of the " European myth " in party doctrine and conduct and assess its causative role.[1]

Following the analysis of conduct during the ratification debates, it becomes necessary to examine the activities of parties in national parliaments in terms of their efforts to support, oppose or criticise ECSC and additional steps toward unity. Do these efforts follow from the positions taken in 1951 and 1952 or do they indicate a shift

[1] The following secondary works treat the ratification process in fragmentary form: Mason, *The European Coal and Steel Community*, Chap. 1; J. Goormaghtigh, " European Coal and Steel Community," *International Conciliation*, no. 503, May 1955; R. Racine, *Vers Une Europe Nouvelle par le Plan Schuman* (Neuchâtel: Baconnière, 1954), pp. 102–114; G. Goriély, "L'opinion public et le Plan Schuman," *Revue Française des Sciences Politiques* (July–September 1953); *Chronique de Politique Etrangère*, May 1953.

in outlook, either for or against ECSC?   Once more the question of the role of party ideology as opposed to national doctrine arises, as in the context of the ratification debates.

If it can be shown that national cohesion is absent or unimportant in accounting for party conduct, some meaningful generalisations of supranationally shared party values may be ventured.   It may then become possible to speak of European ideologies and a " European majority " for integration.   It will be our task to state and analyse a scheme of such a majority on the basis of party conduct, and to deduce from it such principles of political integration as seem defensible.

In the discussion which follows, no attention will be paid to the activities of the Western European Communist Parties during and after the ratification debates.   The Communist position was uniformly " national " from parliament to parliament and continued so since.   Unanimous opposition to ECSC and all other forms of integration was justified in terms of its alleged harm to French, Belgian, Italian or Luxembourg workers, the decay of national industries, the inevitable growth of international monopoly capitalism and of American imperialism, and the concomitant rebirth of an aggressive and armed Germany.   The Schuman Plan was dubbed the " Truman Plan " and equated with the conspiracy against the Soviet Union.

The French Parliament and Parties

The Communists were not the only solid *bloc* of opposition to ECSC in France.   The Gaullist RPF (Rassemblement du Peuple Français) tended to take a similar position.   While it denied any opposition in principle to European unity, the RPF insisted, nevertheless, on a successful " Franco-German dialogue "—after France had once more grown strong—to precede any federation with Germany.   Yet the conditions and qualifications voiced in connection with ECSC were so sweeping as to demonstrate a clear opposition of principle despite the attempt to evade the issue.

The following juxtaposition of claims, though expressed outside the National Assembly, should make the point clear.[2]   Thus, all

---

[2] These views were expressed consistently in the writings of B. Lavergne. See, *e.g.*, " Le Plan Schuman," *Nouvelle Revue de l'Economie Contemporaine* (no. 16–17, 1951), edited by Lavergne. Flandin's contribution appears on pp. 5–10. See also Lavergne, " La petite Europe pangermaniste et cléricale," *L'Année Politique et Economique*, Vol. 28 (No. 126–127, July–September 1955).

federation with the culturally different Germans was held unnatural; the common market principle is a naïve rebirth of Manchesterian economics, doomed to ruin French industry and to create " legions of unemployed "; alternatively, a planned European economy would subject France to the iron yoke of the " nine dictators " on the High Authority, and institutionalise supranationally extra-parliamentary and unconstitutional economic direction; Monnet was accused of being the " grey eminence " of the Fourth Republic anxious to achieve regional economic direction " after the advantages of this system are exhausted in the national realm." In any event, without British membership, Germany is bound to gain most:

> Bismarck said: " He who possesses the Bohemian quadrangle possesses Europe." We shall say with more truth: the nation which dominates the High Authority and which enjoys the lowest price structure will annex Western Europe.

Former premier P.-E. Flandin, on behalf of the RPF, urged that all the advantages of post-1945 control over the Ruhr would be yielded in ECSC. Constitutionally and ideologically, all the virtues and achievements of the nation as a cultural unit would be submerged in a German-dominated supranationalism. Said Flandin: " We are offering to defeated Germany what victorious Germany imposed on us. Why did we fight the war? "

If faith in the nation constitutes the bedrock of RPF thinking, doctrinal rejection of this very notion is the basis of thinking in the Christian-Democratic MRP (Mouvement Républicain Populaire), the only French party for which European federation is the unanimously accepted first principle of modern politics. Favoured by the long incumbency of its leader, Robert Schuman, in the Quai d'Orsay, the MRP was enabled to press for general Franco-German rapprochement on the basis of the natural unity of Western European Christian (*i.e.*, Catholic) values. In addition, union would prevent German political and economic hegemony. Catholic theory reinforces this political penchant. Human associations are pictured as a natural hierarchy, rising from the family unit to the universality of mankind. Hence, the nation as the major claimant for loyalty is considered a usurper, to be overcome by supranational federation of the like-minded. While this doctrine would logically lead to world federation, in the immediate future Western European unity is actually predominant in MRP thought. Finally, the Catholic doctrine of pluralism with its emphasis on co-operation and harmony among distinct social groups further favours and conditions a political orientation toward permanent union with erstwhile rivals and competitors. Hence, union with Germany is all-important, while the inclusion of Protestant Britain in such a grouping is not a major concern to the MRP. Conviction on these points not only made possible the Schuman proposal for ECSC, but solid MRP support for its adoption and consistent activity for its expansion since.

No such solidarity has characterised the French Socialist Party (SFIO). In May of 1950 Guy Mollet saw in the Schuman proposal little more than a scheme to shore up a decadent German and French capitalism and affront the British Labour Party.[3] Ultimately, the SFIO came to support the Treaty, but not without serious misgivings and reservations. Gouin, Lacoste, Philip and Naegelen, among others, fulsomely supported the general " European " doctrine of free association with Germany, rising living standards through a common market and progressive industrial practices, and the need to counter the Soviet appeal by rousing a new Europe against economic stagnation, especially that of a new cartel system.[4] Yet the deep-seated national preoccupation of many Socialists was equally patent. ECSC would be good only if French coal and steel can successfully compete with their German rivals. Hence, modernisation and investments—*not* subject to High Authority direction—must be continued, argued Robert Lacoste. Everything must be done to protect marginal enterprises and cushion the working class against unemployment due to ECSC. Everything must be done to interpret the ECSC Treaty so as to permit special protection for French coal production during the transitional period.[5] The absence of Britain from ECSC was deplored by all Socialists and not considered final. If commitment to " Europe " was present, so was a determination not to allow a European rationale to interfere with the claims of French workers.

Ambivalence toward Europe and ECSC was the chief attitude of the Centre political formations—various Radical groupings and

[3] Racine, *op. cit.*, p. 52.
[4] See the German Socialist pamphlets, " Der Schuman Plan," Berlin, June 28, 1950: " Sozialisten über den Schuman Plan."
[5] *Journal Officiel de la Republique Française*, Débats parlementaires, Assemblée Nationale, no. 150 (December 6, 1951), pp. 8870–73; no. 151 (December 7, 1951), pp. 8918–8921, 8926–8928; no. 152 (December 11, 1951), pp. 9008–9009, 9000–9001. Conseil de la République, no. 29 (March 25, 1952), pp. 712–719; no. 30, (March 27, 1952), pp. 773–775, 758–760).

the Union Démocratique et Sociale de la Résistance (UDSR). ECSC was defended because it promised coke supplies for French steelmakers and freed France from the fear of future German commercial discrimination, in addition to opening a new market for French exports. Yet some Radicals attacked ECSC because France would be unable to compete with Germans, and because a full-scale Franco-German political rapprochement was undesirable. Others granted that relations with the United States might be complicated by non-ratification and favoured ECSC because it promised to guarantee German industrial deconcentration after the demise of the International Ruhr Authority. René Mayer, later to become President of the High Authority, while endorsing the principles of European unity, dwelt most lengthily on all these specifically pro-French points: control over German enterprises, access to coke, new market for steel, exemption from ECSC control over French investments in Lorraine and protection of French coal production. Opportunist arguments relating to immediate French political and industrial aims characterised the Centre. Of commitment to principle—for or against integration—there was little evidence.[6]

The inchoate non-Gaullist Right—Independent Republicans and several Peasant Parties—proved not only devoid of ideological commitment, but badly divided into the bargain. One portion, including Pinay, Paul Reynaud and André Mutter, favoured ECSC for the usual general reasons: economic benefits of the large market, protection against the Soviet threat, Franco-German rapprochement. Another portion, however, strenuously opposed the Treaty as harmful to specific French industries, playing into the hands of German imperialism politically and rapacious German industry economically. These opponents either represented certain French steelmakers and ore enterprises directly, or else came from nationalist lineage, such as M. Boivin-Champeaux who exclaimed: "faites l'Europe, parvenez-y, mais ne défaites pas la France." The bulk of the Independents favoured the Treaty because of its assurance of coke supplies, but did so with a great many hesitations and reservations. Assurances were demanded of the Government that German industrial expansion be checked, that the Saar remain firmly under French control because of ECSC—an autonomous Saar being

[6] *Ibid.*, Assemblée Nationale, no. 150, pp. 8865–8866; no. 151, pp. 8969–8972, 8956–8958, 8939–8944; no. 152, p. 9028, 9002–9004, 9011–9012. Conseil de la République, no. 29, pp. 723–726; no. 30, pp. 760–762, 762–764, 804–810, 819–820; no. 31, pp. 798–799.

suspect of voting with the German representatives in ECSC organs and outvoting France—that the Moselle canal be built to assure water transport of Ruhr coal and coke to Lorraine, and that taxes and social security payments be equalised everywhere in ECSC in order to remove the handicap of higher costs from French producers.[7] Expediential considerations motivated the bulk of the Independents and Peasants, commitment to " Europe " very few indeed.

It is hardly surprising, therefore, that the Treaty was ratified only because it was accompanied by a set of special conditions, which Parliament considered as interpretative resolutions because the Government refused to consider formal amendments. The Government was enjoined to continue its subsidisation of the massive investment programmes in coal and steel, to negotiate an agreement to build the Moselle Canal *before* the advent of ECSC, to consult the Assembly on the progress of modernisation in industry and not to discriminate against French workers under ECSC jurisdiction as compared to those solely subject to French law. The Council of the Republic insisted that French steel be assured of a guaranteed profit margin equal to other producers in ECSC and a fair share in the distribution of raw materials in the event of shortage. France should insist on postponement of the opening of the common market and assure survival to marginal firms, as well as insist on the equalisation of taxes and social charges. Even so, approval in the various commissions of the Assembly was hardly overwhelming:

	In Favour	Opposed	Abstained
Foreign Affairs	26	18	0
Industrial Production	23	8	12
Labour	21	20	1
Economic Affairs	18	21	0
Military Affairs	15	21	1

The National Assembly, on the question of confidence, upheld the government by a vote of 376 to 240, with 11 abstentions. The Council of the Republic approved by a vote of 177 to 3, with 92 abstentions.[8]

---

[7] *Ibid.*, Assemblée Nationale, no. 150, pp. 8873–8875, 8876–8881, 8888–8891, 8870; no. 151, pp. 8937–8939; no. 152, pp. 9001–9002, 9004–9006; no. 154, pp. 9113–9115. Conseil de la République, no. 29, pp. 738–740, 731–733, 719–722, 727–731; no. 30, pp. 756–758, 755–756; no. 31, pp. 822–825, 833–834, 804, 838, 803–804.

[8] The best discussion of ratification in the French Parliament, with emphasis on the methods used to assure passage by the " Europeans," is H. Ehrmann, " The French Trade Associations and the Ratification of the Schuman Plan," *World Politics*, (July 1954).

In the five years following ratification, neither chamber of the French Parliament has held a full-dress debate on ECSC, no resolutions were passed, and no legislation infringing on ECSC was enacted. However, enough was said in questions and interpellations, commission meetings and reports, as well as in connection with the kindred issues of EDC and Euratom to permit an assessment of changes in party position.

Thus, it is clear that the Gaullist opposition to supranational integration has not diminished. Between July 1953 and April of 1956, thirty-two hostile questions concerning ECSC were asked in Parliament, twenty-one of them by Gaullist spokesmen.[9] The points made in the questions are revealing: France pays too much of the ECSC tax and has insufficient control over the ECSC budget; ECSC employees vote themselves exorbitant salaries and pensions; ECSC permits the reconcentration of Ruhr industry and the flooding of the French labour market by foreigners and deprecates the dignity of the French language by permitting the publication of the U.S. loan agreement in English exclusively; the agreement on association with Britain was held inconsistent with France's right to conduct her own diplomatic relations while Monnet was castigated for negotiating on behalf of " France " in his talks with American leaders. The high-point of the Gaullist attack was the introduction of a resolution by Deputy Vendroux in the National Assembly inviting the government to sue for the annulment of Common Assembly actions tending to extend the scope of ECSC by Treaty interpretation. The resolution was defeated in the Foreign Affairs Commission by the uncomfortable vote of 18 to 16, with 3 abstentions.[10] Again during the discussion of Euratom in 1956, Gaullist deputies and senators concentrated their attack on the supranational features proposed and especially on the loss by France of her ability to make her own atomic weapons policy.

---

[9] Eight questions were raised by Radical-Socialists and three by Independent-Republicans. For detailed information concerning questions and ministerial answers, see *Annales des Mines*, Vols. 144 and 143, numéro spécial 1954 and 1955, " Le Fonctionnement de la Communauté Européenne du Charbon et de l'Acier." The standard source for parliamentary activity in all the member states is Assemblée Commune, Division des Etudes et de la Documentation, *Informations Bimensuelles* (1954 and 1955) and *Informations Mensuelles* (since January 1956).

[10] Assemblée Nationale, (2e Legislature, session de 1955), Doc. 11,096 annexe au procès-verbal de Juillet 5, 1955. Another favourite Gaullist objection concerns the Saar, whose unification with Germany was held to make France's position in ECSC untenable.

How, it was urged, could great power status be preserved without the H-bomb?

Socialist attitudes are far more subtle and difficult to categorise clearly. Reservations and doubts entertained in 1952 continue to plague the SFIO, though in principle the party is firmly committed to further integration. But principle and political practice are sometimes hard to reconcile, as evidenced by the stand of Robert Lacoste, until 1956 president of the National Assembly's quite inactive Co-ordinating Commission for ECSC Problems. Even though he favoured ECSC in 1952, Lacoste warned of the difficulties for French miners involved in permitting the importation of greater amounts of German coal, feared unemployment and stagnation in the Centre-Midi mining area, and counselled the postponement of the opening of the common market for special steels. Most Socialists, including Guy Mollet and Christian Pineau, have re-iterated their opposition to a federal Europe without Britain. Said Pineau: " What we call ' Europe of the Six ' is not and will never be Europe; it can only be bait for the greater co-operation which we wish to achieve." [11] Uneasiness over a federation with Germany, without the British counterpoise, was expressed in the ratification debates and contributed heavily to the SFIO's division over the EDC issue. Enthusiasm for further supranational efforts or even for the full implementation of the common market logic of ECSC is confined to those socialists—almost certainly a minority—who see in Western European unity the means for organising a new type of society.

Nevertheless, during the election campaign of 1956, SFIO leaders defended Euratom and even purged a candidate for the Assembly for failure to toe the line. Confronted later with the argument of rightist deputies that Euratom should make possible the manufacture of atomic weapons, the Mollet Government had a hard choice. In principle it was committed, in view of the Pacifist-Socialist tradition, to exclusive dedication to the peaceful application of atomic energy. It yielded to the compromise proposal of its Belgian colleague Spaak by shelving the question at the European level until Euratom will

---

[11] Speech in the Consultative Assembly, Council of Europe, April 1956. *Informations Mensuelles* (April 1956), p. 28. But compare these positions with the whole-hearted cooperation of French Socialist deputies with their colleagues from other ECSC countries in the Common Assembly, tending toward the demand for more and more supranational powers and activity, *within* the framework of the Six. " Déclaration de M. G. Mollet," *Nouvelles de l'Europe* (July 1955), p. 3.

have been in operation for four years. But Mollet and Pineau also courted rightist support for their position by giving assurances that in the interim France would go ahead with its own atomic weapons programme. In terms of Socialist doctrinal purity nothing was gained even though the resolution authorising the Government to pursue Euratom negotiations was passed.[12]

None of these considerations have bothered the MRP. Despite the EDC setback, its National Committee in 1955 urged the extension of ECSC powers to other sectors. New supranational communities have been advocated as well, and regardless of the argument over pacific as against military aspects of Euratom, that plan has been defended. A European investment fund was demanded and the extension of ECSC to the area of labour and welfare held a desirable next step. During the elections of 1956, the party staunchly defended its European outlook, though it lost votes.

A definite deterioration of Europeanism is the trend among the Radicals, here including the Radical-Socialist, UDSR and Rassemblement des Gauches Républicains parties. A solid vote for ECSC characterised this *bloc* in 1952 while it split into equal halves on the EDC issue. Yet many Radicals had voted for ECSC for such patently anti-German reasons that their defection from the integrationist camp is hardly surprising when one of their leaders, M. Mendès-France, took the initiative in 1954 in working for a modernised, strong French economy *first*, with integration to take place *after* a position of industrial " equality " with Germany had been attained. Mendesist Radicals took up the cudgels in blaming ECSC for French unemployment in 1954 and for the difficulty encountered by marginal steel firms in the Midi. Violent attacks were levelled against Monnet personally while more energetic measures for increasing French power and representation in ECSC organs were demanded. The alienation from the European Movement, on ideological grounds, of the Mendesist wing of the Radicals is thus patent.[13]

[12] *Ibid.*, p. 40 and *Informations Mensuelles* (June–July 1956), pp. 59 *et seq.*
[13] See *Annales des Mines*, Vol. 144, *op. cit.*, p. 118. Also articles against Monnet in the Mendesist *Express*, June 13, 1953. But contrast these statements with the uncompromisingly pro-ECSC declaration of M. Claudius-Petit, UDSR deputy for an area forced to lay off labour and shut down plants, partly because of the common market, in *Bulletin of the European Coal and Steel Community*, (January 1955). Said Mendès-France to the Radicals' congress in Bordeaux, in October of 1952: " I do not forget the anxieties which were revealed in Parliament when the Coal and Steel Pool Treaty was ratified. We ratified it only on condition that in the little time which remains for us, important investments in coal and steel be

At the same time, such Radicals as René Mayer, Pléven, and Maurice Faure continued to defend integration, even though they admitted that the addition of other European countries to " the Six " was essential. Yet Edgar Faure, though the bitter opponent of Mendès-France, joined those who wished to prevent ECSC from acquiring new tasks and took a strong hand in ousting Jean Monnet—while verbally remaining pro-European in outlook.

Among the rightist Independent Republicans and Peasants, by contrast, a permanent pro-integration majority seems to have developed, largely as a *result* of the common market. To be sure, those who opposed ECSC bitterly in 1952 continue to oppose. Some continue to hold out the spectre of inevitable German hegemony and insisted until 1956 on the building of the Moselle Canal as a precondition for any Franco-German peace. Others fear the delegation of too much atomic development control to Euratom. But speaking for the bulk of this group, Pinay could say during the election campaign of 1955-1956: " Let us wish that Frenchmen will vote on January 2 [1956] for men determined, without reservation or afterthought, to return to France the role which she should never have lost: to lead the organisation of Europe." [14]

The overtones of this statement convey concern for France rather than for Europe and the correct assessment of Independent Republican " Europeanism," indeed, is support for integration motivated by French industrial fear. The case of Senator Armengaud is revealing, since he typifies those political spokesmen for heavy industry opposed to ECSC in 1952, but who have been compelled by their own basic motives to champion further integration measures. The fundamental fear—in 1952 as well as in 1956—was that a common market would result in German industry's satisfying the bulk of the increasing European demand for coal and steel, because of its lower production costs and higher investment rate, with the anarchic French economic system condemned to further stagnation, if not decline. However, while the remedy suggested in 1952 was a weak ECSC, the demand among these politicians today

immediately undertaken so that our industries are not crushed by German competition. . . . The policy of European unification would be criminal if we undertook it without putting ourselves into condition to meet the competition of our future associates." Quoted in Rieben, *Des Ententes de Maitres de Forges au Plan Schuman* (Lausanne, 1954), pp. 384–385.

[14] *Le Figaro*, December 31, 1955, p. 11.

is the opposite: the High Authority should *control* the level of investments to avoid " duplication " and " multiplication " of production facilities; the High Authority should *allocate* surplus labour and *adjust* supply to demand in periods of declining economic activity. Finally, the High Authority should initiate ECSC-wide collective bargaining—anathema to French Conservatives otherwise—in order to compel the equalisation of wages and social security contributions, *i.e.*, force an increase in the German and Dutch rates. For free-enterprise minded parliamentarians the conversion to supranational " dirigisme " could hardly be expressed more strongly:

> The High Authority must, we think, undertake concerted planning of investments as well as their co-ordination, and harmonise fiscal, financial and social charges burdening production costs.[15]

At the same time, the French Government is to be compelled through ECSC to modernise its tax structure and social security system and encourage further concentration of French steel. Naturally, the Moselle Canal was a *sine qua non* here too.

Clearly, there was no " majority " for integration among the French parties in 1951–1952: there was only an *ad hoc* alliance in which the separate converging party motives were far more important than either commonly held principles of French or European politics. The defeat of EDC merely underscored the ephemeral nature of the earlier majority; it did not initiate a new trend in party outlook and activity.

Yet it was on the basis of impressions and opinions derived from four years of experience with supranational integration that the National Assembly in its debate on the Economic Community endorsed this major step toward European unity. Convergence of separate party opinions and fears was again very much in evidence, but it sufficed to assemble the majority which was lacking in the case of EDC. Procedurally too a crucial innovation was in evidence: all the French members of European parliamentary assemblies united in the French Section of the Parliamentary Council of the European Movement, thus making themselves into a pro-integration pressure group within the French Parliament—an

---

[15] These opinions are expressed with the greatest forthrightness in two reports of the Council of the Republic. Conseil de la République, Doc. 171 (1954) and Doc. 259 (1955). Both reports are entitled " Rapport d'Information sur la Communauté Européenne du Charbon et de l'Acier," par MM. Amengaud et Coudé du Foresto. The quotation is from p. 58 of the 1954 Report.

imitation of similar steps which had already been taken in the Bundestag in an effort to mobilise opinion for EEC and Euratom on a cross-party basis. On January 22, 1957, the National Assembly adopted the following resolution, which had been presented by the group: the draft treaty for EEC was considered to meet the essential interests of the French economy, *provided* the Government would insist, before signature, that (1) social security payments would be harmonised if found to be distorting competition; (2) EEC-wide agricultural marketing and price support machinery be created to take the place of the national protective and anti-competitive practices now in force; (3) overseas territories be associated with the common market so as to induce other European countries to contribute to their development; (4) that concurrent negotiations with Britain be carried on " with determination " to realise the Free Trade Area; and (5) that the Government follow a national investment policy designed to strengthen and prepare France for participation in the common market.[16]   While supporting the principle of EEC, the French politicians nevertheless managed to link with the agreement the special protective devices to which they remain attached: like the Independent Republicans, they merely transferred them from the national to the European level.   Why, then, was it impossible to construct a European majority in the case of EDC?

ECSC was passed in the National Assembly by a vote of 376 to 240, while EDC was defeated by a vote of 264 to 319.   Who defected in 1954 from the earlier majority to doom the second major effort at supranational integration?   Since the right- and left-wing anti-parliamentary parties stood firm in their opposition to integration, most defections came from the third-force *bloc* of roughly 400 deputies.[17]   SFIO had voted for ECSC; it split into opposing

---

[16] This resolution does not bind the Government.   As in the case of the ECSC Treaty, the Government refused to entertain amendments and the resolution is merely " interpretive " of the Assembly's will.   *Informations Mensuelles* (January 1957), pp. 13–16, and (February 1957), pp. 73–74.

[17] Actually sixteen Gaullists voted *for* EDC, while the number *for* ECSC had been only two.   The reason is to be found in the already accomplished split by 1954 between a radical reforming wing, consistently nationalistic, later called Social Republican Group, and the so-called Action Republicaine Sociale; this latter group consisted essentially of Conservatives similar in outlook to the Independent Republicans, with whom it merged in 1956.

While SFIO support for Euratom had to be bought with a compromise on the atomic arms question, Independent-Republican and Gaullist support could be obtained only by keeping the questions of Euratom and EEC distinct, given the opposition of these groups to further supranational economic integration in sectors

halves over EDC, for reasons which could have been deduced from the reservations expressed during the ECSC debates. Socialists were afraid of German hegemony and being federated with an ascendant Germany—unless they were assured of the counter-poise of British participation in the supranational effort. Some Socialists further opposed German rearmament on pacifist grounds, or because they felt that rearmament would endanger German democracy, just as they opposed an Euratom able to manufacture atomic weapons in 1956—while again insisting on a Europe larger than that of the " Six." In addition, the Radical centre—by 1954 divided into pro- and anti-Mendesists—also split into two opposing halves. Some opponents of EDC took their stand because they too feared a Franco-German federation in which France was considered the handicapped partner from the start. Others granted the need for rearmament but preferred the non-federal NATO-WEU solution. Integration was accepted by the Mendesists only if it conduced to control over Germany—as was already implicit in the motives for ECSC expressed by many Radicals. Hence, inter-governmental institutions in 1954 were preferred over federal ones in the military sphere. In the discussions concerning Euratom, the same point was made again and half the Radicals opposed that proposal for supranationalism. Finally, more Independent Republicans opposed EDC than ECSC, though majorities for both supranational schemes were furnished by this party. Among these Conservatives the implication, not of a German army, but of abolishing the glory and traditions of the French army by merging it with a " traditionless " European force seemed to be the main reason for opposition. Reasons of national preoccupation clearly swayed most of those who opposed EDC, while equally clear considerations of national preoccupation have made this party a champion of further supranational integration for coal and steel. At the same time, these groups harbour reservations against EEC for precisely the same reasons as posed against ECSC in 1951. Thus,

other than coal and steel. Further, the vote on Euratom was not a wholly reliable index of sentiment, since many deputies were under the misapprehension that the vote involved the question of confidence. Even so, enemies of further supra-nationalism extracted a statement from Mollet—subsequently ignored by the Government—that if Euratom is established, its institutions will be kept distinct from ECSC's, in order *not* to strengthen the institutional forces of supranationalism, despite the fact that the recommendations of the Brussels Intergovernmental Committee called for joint institutions. See Klaus Knorr, *Nuclear Energy in Western Europe and United States Policy* (Princeton: Centre of International Studies, 1956), pp. 9–10, 22.

the difference in conduct over three vitally related issues of integration makes plain that Independent Republican support for " Europe " is far from reliable.

The EDC vote has been contrasted with the behaviour of French parties on other issues involving the principle of supranationality despite the fact that extremely complex and complicating factors were present in the issue over German rearmament. EDC brought to the fore passions in French political life whose demonstration had seen no precedent since the Dreyfus Affair. It pitted advocates of direct negotiations with the Soviet Union against supporters of NATO and against third forcists. It opened up the Pandora's Box of the role of Germany in East-West relations. And it forced dedicated " Europeans " to come to grips with politicians merely concerned about the least dangerous way of rearming Germany.[18] Compared to this maelstrom, the debate over ECSC had been quiet and rational. The only valid point of comparison, therefore, is the question: to what extent did the principle of supranationality and commitment to federal integration account for the larger anti-European vote in the EDC case? The studies of Lerner and Aron seem to support the contention that this was a minor issue in a total picture, taken seriously only by the groups who had already voted against ECSC, plus some Mendesist Radicals.[19]

The conclusion is obvious: there is no ideologically homogeneous European majority in the French parliament and party spectrum, a dictum which remains true despite French ratification of EEC. This point is driven home by a survey conducted on behalf of the European Movement of the newly elected French deputies in

[18] See the material adduced by Stanley Hoffmann in D. Lerner and R. Aron, *France Defeats EDC* (New York: Praeger, 1957), pp. 173–196.

[19] D. Lerner and R. Aron, *France Defeats EDC.* See especially the section by Alfred Grosser, pp. 54–71. Elsewhere, Lerner has argued that the long time permitted to elapse between the original proposal of the Pleven Plan and the parliamentary debate gave anti-German passions an opportunity to develop and thus assured defeat of EDC. " Franco-German Political Relations: Politics, Public and the Press," *Journal of International Affairs*, Vol. X, no. 2 (1956), pp. 138–152. N. Leites and Christian de la Malène argue that the principle of supranationality should bear most the burden for defeat because it enabled the " anti-cédistes " to pose as the defenders of the most potent symbol of French independence and national tradition—the Army. WEU, avoiding the merger of the French with the new German army, was free from this stigma. " Paris from EDC to WEU," *World Politics*, Vol. 9, no. 2 (January 1957), pp. 193–219. In view of the arguments presented above, neither of these explanations seems valid.

January of 1956.[20]   All were asked whether they would support
(1) Euratom confined to *pacific* uses, (2) a general common market
for all ECSC countries *and* others willing to join, (3) a European
Political Community, (4) direct elections to the ECSC Common
Assembly, (5) transfers of national sovereignty and (6) national
parliamentary action expediting the achievement of the foregoing.
The following results were obtained from the 204 non-Communist
deputies replying to the questionnaire:

Party	Replying " yes " to all questions	Replying " yes " to all except (3), (4) and (6)
MRP	72	0
SFIO	43	13 [21]
Radicals & UDSR ..	26	4
Ind. Republicans	35	8
Gaullists	1	0
Poujadists	2	0

This total of 204 pro-integration deputies, replying to a questionnaire already heavily weighted in favour of the SFIO and Radical
reservations to integration along ECSC lines, thus falls short of an
arithmetical majority based even on the tenuous bond of separate
and converging party motivations.

The West German Parliament and Parties

Support for the ECSC Treaty was obtained in the Bonn Parliament from all parties except the Socialists and Communists.
Analysis of the reasons for this support, however, will show that
a variety of motives was at play here as in France and that a convergence of separate aspirations explains the victory of ECSC in
Germany, not unanimous endorsement of supranational principles.
This generalisation holds true even in the dominant Christian-
Democratic Union (CDU), the most " European " of the German
parties until 1955.

In leading circles of the CDU, the triptych of self-conscious
anti-Nazism, Christian values and dedication to European unity
as a means of redemption for past German sins has played a crucial
ideological role.   Exhortations to support ECSC were pitched by

[20] " L'Europe et les Nouveaux Elus à l'Assemblée Nationale," *Nouvelles de l'Europe*,
January-February 1956, p. 34.
[21] This number, significantly, includes MM. Mollet, Pineau, Lapie and D. Mayer.

Adenauer and many of his lieutenants on the theme of anti-nationalism, sacrifice for a higher aim of permanent European peace and faith in France. Allegations that ECSC would merely serve the French interests of obtaining cheap Ruhr coke and controlling the level of German industry were indignantly rejected by Adenauer. State Secretary Hallstein patiently explained that Germany would not be outvoted in ECSC, that the government hoped instead for the evolution of supranational political parties in the Common Assembly, that there would be no question of discrimination against German industry. Surprisingly, he found that a mass base for further European action already existed.[22] In the interest of these aims, the CDU was prepared not to push the issue of German reunification, which agitated the other parties. Adenauer praised the French for not insisting on making a Saar settlement a pre-condition for ECSC and expressed the hope that the logic of integration would make the economic aspects of control over the Saar meaningless in the long run.[23] As Hallstein urged:

> Don't do it [support ECSC] because it would be a tactical device to gain freedom for Germany from the fetters from which we still suffer, or because it may be profitable in terms of dividends, but only because it is one of those efforts through which mankind can progress.[24]

To be sure, dedication to European union and the fear that the failure of ECSC would end the integration process was not the only reason in the mind of the CDU. The Schuman Plan also offered an excellent opportunity to remove some of the " fetters " of which Hallstein spoke. Equality with the other five member states, specifically, implied the abolition of the International Ruhr Authority which allocated German coal exports. It spelled the end of the Allied controls on the level of steel production, and—most importantly—offered an opportunity for reopening the deconcentration and decartellisation issue. Even Adenauer, let alone the bulk of the CDU, had never accepted Allied Law No. 27, " imposed on the German people by the victorious powers," under which the steel trusts were deconcentrated and coal mining partially removed from control by steelmakers. " After the full implementation of . . .

---

[22] Interview with Walter Hallstein, in *Neue Zeitung*, January 6, 1952.
[23] Adenauer's declaration to the Bundestag, January 9, 1952. *Ibid*, January 10, 1952.
[24] Walter Hallstein, " Der Schuman Plan," *Frankfurter Universitätsreden*, Heft 5, (1951), p. 52.

law 27," declared the Chancellor, " the coal and steel industry of Germany will be subject to no limiting conditions other than the provisions of the Schuman Plan Treaty . . ."[25] And Article 66 of that instrument permitted concentrations if economically justified. The non-discrimination provisions of the Treaty, finally, tended to establish a uniform standard of concentration of industrial power, giving the German industrialists hope to be permitted to reconcentrate to reach the level of their French competitors.

If the political advantage of full equality was a potent reason for CDU support of ECSC, economic doctrine and industrial advantage were by no means absent. ECSC would make possible the victory of free enterprise over state planning and cartels, asserted Ludwig Erhard, otherwise very cool toward the Schuman Plan and unwilling to defend it in the Bundestag despite his position as Minister of Economics:

> The Schuman Plan has two implications. . . . One incorporates the principles of supranational . . . dirigisme under the scope of power of the High Authority. We also and simultaneously find in it the other principle, the preparation for free competition in a common market. . . . We in Germany will certainly attempt to send people to the Schuman Plan organisation who will stress the spirit of freedom—of the common market—and who will trust more to competition than to planning.[26]

CDU adherents of the neo-liberal Freiburg school of economists could thus equate ECSC with their doctrine, if only cartels could be controlled under the Treaty. Other German industrial interests— identified with CDU by means of deputies designated by trade associations—rallied to the Plan because its rationale dovetailed with their desire to achieve more " economic " production units, or to reconcentrate the plants just separated by the Allies and especially regain steel control over coal—the famous *Verbund-wirtschaft* held out as " inevitable " and " natural " by industry spokesmen.[27] Europeanism was curiously mingled with the political desire for equality and the economic aim of undoing parts of the

[25] Declaration to Bundestag, January 9, 1952. *Neue Zeitung*, January 10, 1952.
[26] Speech in Zurich, February 6, 1952. *Schweizer Monatshefte*, Vol. 32, No. 1 (April 1952).
[27] See the arguments of CDU deputy Günther Henle, " Der Schumanplan vor seine Verwirklichung," Sonderveröffentlichung des Rheinisch-Westfälichen Institut für Wirtschaftsforschung (Essen, 1951).

occupation policy. The convergence of these factors goes a long way in explaining CDU enthusiasm for ECSC.

In the smaller parties of the governing coalition, an equal enthusiasm was lacking. The Refugee Party (BHE) abstained during the first and second reading of the ratification bill, and voted for ratification only on the third reading. While endorsing the political and economic objectives of ECSC, the BHE wanted definite assurances on the return of the Saar to Germany and a dismantling of allied controls over German industry *before* entry into force of ECSC. Last-minute assurances of the immediate disappearance of these controls persuaded the BHE.[28] The German Party (DP) identified itself with the CDU position, if possible going beyond that group's pro-European statements in stressing the need for unity in the West and the mission of opposing Communism. However, it also made clear that it saw in ECSC a way for bringing East Germany—and even unspecified other Eastern European countries—eventually into the framework of a European *Raum*. The DP thus forged a link between integration and reunification demands which was avoided by the CDU.[29]

Opposition to ECSC until four weeks prior to the opening of the ratification debate characterised the right-wing, pro-free enterprise Free Democratic Party (FDP). Identified with industrialists, Protestant—and, therefore, anti-Adenauer—middle class elements as well as former Nazis, the FDP initially was concerned only with the " German " interests involved in ECSC. Worried privately especially about the vigorous anti-cartel provisions of the Treaty, FDP speakers publicly tended to criticise only the insufficiently " European " or inadequately free market aspects of the plan. While some elements in the party tended to see in ECSC a French conspiracy to open up a wide new market for excess steel production capacity, others saw in it a welcome means to re-establish German equality, underpinning European peace and enabling German industry to compete, if the necessary domestic investments were realised.[30] By the time the ratification debate came to its end,

---

[28] *Deutscher Bundestag, Sitzungsberichte*, 161. Sitzung (July 12, 1951), pp. 6552–6553; 184. Sitzung (January 11, 1952), p. 7827.

[29] *Ibid.*, 161. Sitzung, pp. 6539–6542; 183. Sitzung (January 11, 1952), pp. 7734–7739, 7813–7814, 7705–7706.

[30] For an industrial-liberal viewpoint, see F. Haussmann, *Der Schumanplan im Europäischen Zwielicht* (Munich: C. H. Beck, 1952). Bundestag, *Sitzungsberichte*, 161. Sitzung, pp. 6545–6547, 6521–6525; 184. Sitzung, pp. 7810–7812, 7827, 7769–7771, 7697–7702, 7720–7721.

the pro-European declarations of the FDP were almost as sweeping as those of the CDU, demanding especially that ECSC be used as the initial stepping stone toward political federalism. As might be expected, these sentiments did not preclude the expression of satisfaction with ECSC because it would stop and reverse deconcentration proceedings, abolish the Ruhr Authority and Allied controls on the level of production. This mixture of expediential with ideological argumentation leads to the conclusion, as in the case of the French centre parties, that the *Europasehnsucht* of the FDP was perhaps an acquired taste.

The opposition of the Social Democratic Party (SPD) was exactly as sweeping—and self-contradictory—as that of the RPF in France. Every facet of the Treaty was subjected to bitter criticism. Ruinous competition would destroy an already handicapped German industry, or cartels would find shelter under the protection of the dictatorial and capitalist-dominated High Authority. ECSC would institutionalise French hegemony over Germany and mulct an already overstrained Ruhr of all coal and coke. German representatives would invariably be outvoted in ECSC organs, German sovereignty was being given away in violation of the Constitution. While the need for a true federal European union was trumpeted, ECSC was held far short of this ideal because of its concentration on " clerical and capitalist Little Europe " and the continued inequality of Germany. Finally, the reunification of Germany was made impossible by this overly close tie with the West while the Saar was being handed to France on a silver platter.[31]

Inconsistent as these arguments were, they represented a domestic political opportunism rather than ideological conviction. Principles of socialism were rarely invoked in opposition to ECSC, while national German claims were featured consistently instead. Individual SPD members, as in West Berlin, supported the Treaty

---

[31] These arguments have been summarised from the following SPD pamphlets: Kurt Schumacher, " Deutschlands Forderung: Gleiches Risiko, gleiches Opfer, gleiche Chancen! "; " Der richtige Weg? Eine sachliche Würdigung des Schuman-Plans " ; " Was weisst Du vom Schumanplan ? "; " 50 Jahre mit gebundenen Händen ? " All these were published by the Vorstand of the SPD in Bonn, in 1950 and 1951. The parliamentary activities of the SPD are conveniently summarised in " Der Schumanplan führt nicht nach Europa ! " (Bonn, January 1952). Note especially the violent anti-ECSC arguments of deputies Schöne, Imig, Birkelbach, Kreyssig, Henssler, and Wehner, all of whom later took the initiative in criticising the High Authority for insufficiently energetic supranational action !

and opposition was in some measure artificial even in Bonn.[32] In May of 1950 Schumacher had stated certain conditions for SPD approval of ECSC—including worker representation on the delegation negotiating the Treaty, suppression of all Allied economic controls still in force, emphasis on the political and federal aspects of the Plan and nationalisation of German heavy industry. In effect, all but the last of these were granted before the Treaty went into effect, while ECSC explicitly left the property status of industry to national legislation and German labour obtained codetermination almost simultaneously with the entry into force of the Treaty. More stringent conditions were put forward later, all seeking to end Allied supervisory and control measures immediately, but were voted down in the Bundestag. SPD opposition, therefore, boils down to purely national German demands, stressing domestic prosperity, reunification and the Saar issues, while demanding purity of motives on the part of the French. Said Ollenhauer:

> We want to cover up finally the ditch which separates the German people from the French people. It is wide and deep. We know our responsibility. But if we want to put an end to this tragic chapter in the history of our two peoples, then we have to face each other as free people in the solution to this problem, and there should not exist two completely different reasons in Bonn and in Paris for entrance into this union.[33]

ECSC passed the Bundestag without amendment on January 11, 1952 by a vote of 232 to 143. Simultaneously, however, the Chamber passed resolutions urging the Government to take measures to enable German industry to compete with its ECSC rivals and to work for the liberation of the Saar. The Upper House, before ratifying the Treaty by a unanimous vote (including SPD members), had insisted that the Government give assurances that all Allied control mechanisms over coal and steel cease functioning before entry into force, that continued heavy investments take place in coal and steel, that the centralised sales agency for coal be retained

---

[32] Racine, *op. cit.*, p. 56. *Der Telegraf*, January 9, 1952. Verbal information received from participants in the ratification process indicates that SPD leaders consulted previously with the Government to see how far they could go in criticising the Treaty, and that they would have voted for the Treaty if passage had not been assured.

[33] *Chronique de Politique Etrangère*, Vol. 6, no. 1 (January 1953), p. 26.

and that the High Authority refrain from hampering reform of the social security system.[34]

The evolution of opinion in Germany since has been dramatic and continuous, with the rightist groups showing less and the SPD far more interest in integration than was true during the ratification debates. Discussion, however, has rarely been solely in terms of ECSC: the issue of economic integration in the Europe of the Six has inevitably been tied up with the larger preoccupation of German unity, relations with the West, and especially the future of the Saar. Further, inevitable internal questions relating to the oppositional tactics of the SPD—and later the FDP—have come to the fore in this context. This nexus of problems has given rise to full-fledged debate in the Bundestag on several occasions, most dramatically in connection with the ratification of EDC, the London and Paris Agreements of 1954, the Saar Statute connected therewith, and Euratom.

Discussion of the Saar issue will illustrate the connections accepted by German politicians. Before the plebiscite of December 1955, the CDU and DP pressed for the outright acceptance of EDC—despite the renunciation of German " rights " in the Saar demanded by France as part of her ratification—and after the defeat of EDC in France, pressed for the adoption of the Saar Statute drafted on the basis of the Van Naters Report and incorporated into the London and Paris Agreements, giving the Saarlanders the option between the pro-French *status quo* or Europeanisation under WEU. SPD and FDP speakers, however, urged the establishment of a *quid pro quo* relation: acceptance of WEU to be contingent on the prior return of the Saar to Germany. In the final vote on the Statute, the FDP defected from the coalition and voted in opposition with the SPD.

Naturally, all spokesmen tied up the desire for all-German reunification with the pro- or anti-integration measures under discussion. For the SPD, and increasingly the FDP, reunification on the basis of four-power talks was made impossible by Adenauer's policy of integration-at-all-cost. By raising reunification to the role of the first German necessity, SPD and FDP appeals for voter

---

[34] The text of these resolutions is found in Belgium, *Documents parlementaires*, Chambre des Représentants, Doc. 410 (Session 1951/52), " Projet de loi portant approbation du Traité instituant la Communauté Européenne du Charbon et de l'Acier," Rapport fait . . . par M. Bertrand, May 14, 1952, pp. 41–45.

support became the crucial consideration, with ECSC discussions the necessary butt for general attacks on the Government's neglect of reunification, though no great criticism of ECSC *per se* was necessarily intended.

The continuum of anti-CDU tactics with concern over German unity prompted the creation in 1954 of a special Bundestag Commission to explore desirable changes in the ECSC Treaty, from the viewpoint of German economic development. While attacks on ECSC policy sparked the SPD demand, the real reason lay in the desire to achieve a position independent of the influence of the Foreign Office for members of parliament habitually delegated to go to Common Assembly and Council of Europe meetings.[35] The Commission was created, but its activities since have been minimal.

What, within this setting of inter-connected issues, has been the pattern of evolution among the German parties concerning ECSC? Both the CDU and DP have stood firm in adhering to the positions they defended in 1951 and 1952. Reunification demands a position of strength, which calls for integration as completely as possible—economic, military, cultural and political—with the West in general and the " Six " in particular. Still, within the DP more voices have been raised supporting integration only if it is to take in all of Europe, including the East. Nor has continued CDU support for the bases of Adenauer's policy implied the absence of criticism from big business-oriented members. Thus, a spokesman for this group, Deputy Wolfgang Pohle, has attacked the High Authority for keeping coal prices too low, for permitting France to subsidise imports of Ruhr coke, for making German industry pay too much of the ECSC tax while not giving it enough investment funds to make up for the alleged initial German industrial handicap when the common market was established. Anguished cries were raised against High Authority " dirigisme " and discrimination in favour of France and Italy was frequently charged even in CDU ranks. Yet the same speakers never fail to endorse the principle of integration and to demand more of it.[36]

[35] See Deputy Kreyssig's statement, 2. Bundestag, 26. Sitzung, 29 April 1954, p. 1136.
[36] Pohle's statement in 2. Bundestag, 26. Sitzung, April 29, 1954, pp. 1127 *et seq.* See same debate for statements of other major CDU and DP leaders. Also Furler, *Nouvelles de l'Europe*, (April–May 1956) pp. 12 *et seq.* DP opinions in H. J. von Merkatz, " Europa in den Sattel heben !," *Europa* (September 1955), and " Unity of Spirit—Europe's Greatest Strength," *The Bulletin* (Press and Information Office, German Federal Government), April 12, 1956.

Despite the declining leadership of Adenauer, therefore, there is no evidence to suggest a major trend away from " Europeanism."

The same cannot be said of the FDP, however. Since the accomplishment of ECSC ratification, consented to only hesitantly by the FDP, reservations have again come to the fore, fitting in with the party's general trend away from the Adenauer coalition and its demand for German reunification before everything else. Unlike the CDU, these Conservatives were not willing to join EDC and EPC without first being reassured about French plans. While critical of the anti-cartel policy of the High Authority, of the alleged discrimination against the Ruhr as concerns investments in steel modernisation, no general opposition to the principles of integration has been put forward. Thus, former FDP leader V. E. Preusker, called for a revision of the ECSC Treaty which would (1) do away with remaining national protectionist measures, (2) limit the power of the High Authority to intervene in the market through price and production controls, but (3) enlarge High Authority powers with respect to the co-ordination of national fiscal and investment policies.[37] As long as " dirigisme " is avoided in Luxembourg, FDP members will not oppose further European economic integration—provided such measures do not conflict with the all-German platform on which the party has capitalised since its move into the opposition. All these generalisations apply equally to the diminutive Refugee Party, which also left the CDU-led coalition over the reunification issue.

Yet the FDP attitude toward the twin issues of Euratom and the General Common Market was ambiguous. On ideological free enterprise grounds, it opposed a Euratom equipped with sweeping control powers, but favoured a large free market since it expects German Industry to dominate it. But, convinced that a freer market will come sooner or later, it was not adverse to connecting Euratom with the common market legislatively in order to assure the defeat of both in the French National Assembly. It must be added that the FDP, as well as many members of the CDU— including Erhard—oppose a General Common Market equipped with supranational institutions. Erhard has not been very enthusiastic about Euratom either, despite the firm position of his chief.[38]

[37] See Bundestag, *op. cit.*, pp. 1092, 1110, 1115, 1139. Also *Informations Bimensuelles*, December 1, 1954, p. 3.
[38] Knorr, *op. cit.*, pp. 6–8. *Informations Mensuelles*, (April 1957), pp. 29–30.

The case of the SPD is by far the most striking and the most significant in demonstrating the logic of sector integration in shaping new attitudes, if the ideology of the group question fits the demands of the situation. Far from changing its initial attitude of national opposition to ECSC after ratification, the SPD through 1953 continued to voice the same arguments as before, taking pleasure in the recession of that year to " prove " the accuracy of its predictions.[39] It pointed to pro-French discrimination in investment policy and especially in the issue over the turnover tax refund. The Bundestag, on SPD initiative, passed a law which would strike imported French steel with a " compensatory " 6 per cent. tax. Predictions that ECSC would result in mass unemployment, falling production, rising prices and German inequality in relation to the other member countries continued to be made.

A subtle change crept into SPD thinking during 1954. In attacking the Adenauer Government, the old arguments showed up again, but the remedy for the evils prophesied was now found in more energetic and consistent *supranational* policy: joint business cycle analysis and co-ordinated counter-cyclical spending were demanded, as well as the co-ordination of investments by Luxembourg.[40] In sharp contradiction to statements made the year before, SPD speakers accused Adenauer of not using his influence in the Council of Ministers to achieve these aims, while they claimed to have acted consistently with their demands in the Common Assembly. In this process, the thinking of Heinrich Deist—SPD specialist for steel and ECSC questions—is crucial.[41] Thus, Deist could argue in one speech that EDC had failed—fortunately, from his viewpoint—because " the history of the last four years has shown that the assumptions for [supranational integration] have not been met, that the time is not yet ripe for such far-reaching integration measures." [42] In principle, such organs as ECSC were therefore not appropriate for the solution of current problems. Yet in the context of the very same speech, Deist maintained that full employment—a basic demand—could be attained only in a

[39] See the SPD pamphlet " Götterdämmerung beim Schumanplan " (*ca.* July 1953) for a summary of the party's position then.
[40] Bundestag, *op. cit.*, pp. 1062, 1076, 1130.
[41] Deist was initially proposed for appointment to the High Authority by the West German Trade Union Federation. His appointment was rejected because of his alleged Nazi record. His speech is contained in Protokoll über den 3. *Ordentlichen Gewerkschaftstag der Industriegewerkschaft Metall* (Hanover, September 18, 1954).
[42] *Ibid.*, p. 178.

large common market, that centrally directed investment in such a scheme was essential and that the High Authority must engage in more consistent planning! He reiterated the old SPD complaint that supranationalism was a new means for keeping Germany down while at the same time calling for more supranationalism to meet some of the fundamental SPD economic objectives.

By 1955 the change-about was complete. SPD foreign affairs specialist, Herbert Wehner, proclaimed that what Europe needed was a unified and co-ordinated policy of investment, modernisation, business-cycle control and full employment, and that ECSC had not gone *far enough* along this road. Yet in welcoming the association of Britain with ECSC, the SPD also reiterated that it was not satisfied with " Little Europe " and would insist on the expansion of the Community to the other European countries.[43] At the same time, the party welcomed the Messina meeting of the foreign ministers and called for rapid and energetic measures for achieving full economic integration along every relevant institutional path, provided only that sufficient democratic parliamentary control over new central agencies be provided.

How can this change of heart be explained? The doctrine of the SPD and the environment in which the party seeks to achieve its programme furnish the answer. In its 1952 programme, the SPD castigated supranationalism as " a conservative and capitalist federation of the miniature Europe," inimical to the achievement of peace, stability and overall European unity. In the same programme, the party voiced its opposition to uncontrolled autonomous investment policies by major firms, unsupervised cartels and the impairment of competition. It called for nationalisation of basic industries and state-supervised investment policies.[41] Nationalisation of steel and coal, especially, was singled out in order to enable these industries to escape the ECSC. In its 1954 programme, however, we find a different tune. While EDC and rearmament are rejected, the very economic planks of the 1952 programme are cited as justification for now demanding the large-scale Europe-wide initiation of full employment policies, with a common market. " In so far as sovereign powers are transferred to international agencies these must be subject to a genuine democratic-parliamentary

[43] 2. Bundestag, 96. Sitzung (July 8, 1955), pp. 5415 *et seq.*
[44] *Action Programme of the Social Democratic Party of Germany*, Dortmund, September 28, 1952.

control." [45] Thus, while not endorsing ECSC or any other specific type of integration, readiness for integration is made manifest, provided only that full German equality was maintained. Consistent with this attitude, anti-French statements ceased after the pro-German results of the Saar plebiscite became known and the Saar was readied for transfer to Germany.

Yet the conversion to European economic integration is not explainable solely on these grounds. Many SPD members seemed convinced that if Socialists did not follow a united policy in ECSC, the organisation would be dominated by industry and become a cartel. Since the defeat of EDC, further, the party was no longer compelled, on grounds of consistency, to oppose all supranationalism because it led to militarism and alliances. Hence, its all-German policy could remain intact and pure while economic integration could be supported as well. But all these reasons do not add up to the complete ideological commitment typical of many Christian-Democrats. In its Munich Convention in 1956, while saying nothing directly on ECSC, Euratom or the General Common Market, the SPD were resolved:

> The federal Republic should participate in all attempts to free European and world-wide economic co-operation from the fetters of fruitless ideological and regional integrationalism [sic] and to base such co-operation on considerations of the common weal. She [sic] should give her support to the developing peoples and countries of former colonial empires now in a state of disintegration and transition.[46]

Economic specialist Joachim Schöne expressed his conviction that supranationalism was not an appropriate means to achieve integration, implying that intergovernmental co-operation—thus including the Britain the SPD wishes to woo so ardently—was preferable. Yet he too spelled out a number of specific policy fields in which the supranational ECSC High Authority should take more direct action while calling for democratic and parliamentary organs of control.[47]

But by the time the SPD had to decide on whether to support the establishment of the General Common Market and of Euratom,

[45] *Aktionsprogram der SPD, as amended in the Berlin Convention,* July 24, 1954, p. 16.
[46] SPD *News from Germany* (August–September 1956).
[47] Joachim Schöne, " Liquidierung oder Fortführung der Integration," *Jugend Europas,* November 24, 1955, p. 3.

the hopes of using supranational authorities for the implementation of planned economic policies carried the day over any other consideration.   Thus Heinrich Deist, in supporting ratification of the EEC Treaty in the Bundestag, presented arguments which are a direct translation of SPD experience with ECSC into the realm of general integration.   Retroactively justifying Socialist opposition to ECSC in 1952, Deist urged that the pooling of the coal and steel industries had been a failure because it had not resulted in joint counter-cyclical policy planning and increasing living standards. But, provided that EEC and Euratom did not lead to a mere joining by Germany of one of the military *blocs*, the General Common Market would make up for these shortcomings and compel the German Government to raise wages to the level obtaining in some partner countries.   Its economic logic had led the party once more to the supranational lobby, even though it barely managed to cover its switch of position and despite the remaining political worries experienced by it.[48]

It appears, therefore, that the " conversion " of the SPD is not yet complete.   In economic policy demands, supranational action is lauded.   In political statements, supranationalism in the Europe of the Six is avoided and sidestepped.   Euratom is supported because it will facilitate planning in a technologically revolutionary situation and control private enterprise, but membership in it must be open to all European countries, not merely the Six. And if the German unification issue were to arise in such a fashion as to clash with integration, the political reservations might easily carry the day once more, as they did in the case of the ECSC and EDC ratifications.   In fact, in the SPD's endorsement of the Euratom and EEC Treaties, Adolf Arndt also urged that the party would support the agreements only on the assumption that they would not make more difficult German reunification.   Europe was to be neither a symbol nor a substitute for the unity of all Germans.[49]

---

[48] *Die Debatte*, March 1957, " Gemeinsamer Markt—Fortschritt oder Belastung? " The SPD's endorsement of EEC and Euratom was subject to these conditions, all but the third of which were met in the agreements: (1) Germany should assume no responsibility for the colonial policies of the countries whose overseas territories were to be under EEC; (2) No tariff barrier to be erected at the West German— East German border; (3) The new level of customs duties should not be higher than the German level in 1957; (4) The common market should be open to all countries, thus facilitating British and Scandinavian participation; (5) Euratom should be dedicated exclusively to the peaceful utilisation of atomic energy and retain title to all fissionable materials.

[49] *Ibid.*

Clearly, there is a German majority for Europe, though the Right is less sure than in 1952 and the Left more so. Ideological homogeneity does not explain this majority any more than it did France's shifting alignment of votes. Christian-Democrats, now as in 1951, favour Europe on principle and because they feel German industry and commerce will benefit. Conservatives, insofar as they favour integration, do so largely for the second reason. Socialists oppose the notion of a federated Little Europe, but in fact favour all energetic means of achieving economic integration which will give them a controllable, stable, large market. Further, their commitment to democratic control compels them to favour ECSC-wide parliamentary institutions even though in principle they oppose supranationalism. While the ideology of each party certainly clarifies the reasons underlying its European policy, there is no all-German body of doctrine which explains this majority. Fragmentation exists here as elsewhere, but despite it, overwhelming majorities in all parties—each for its own reasons, to be sure—voted for the ratification of Euratom and the General Common Market.

THE ITALIAN PARLIAMENT AND PARTIES

Acceptance of the Treaty in Italy was complicated by the fact that industry was opposed to it while the ruling coalition of centre parties was in principle in favour of any step toward integration. Industrial spokesmen feared a ruinous competition from the other ECSC countries because of the higher raw materials costs of Italian steelmakers, who lack a significant domestic source of both ore and coal, though they were attracted by the idea of having their supplies of scrap and coke augmented from ECSC resources. Some industrial spokesmen within the Liberal, Republican and Christian-Democratic parties expressed reserve and opposition to ratification. Communist, Nenni-Socialist, Monarchist and Neo-fascist support was not available in any case. Consequently, De Gasperi had to make some efforts to solidify the support of his coalition parties for the Treaty. He did so by agreeing in the Senate to take the initiative for obtaining a modification of the Treaty if experience showed unfavourable developments for the Italian steel industry, to work toward the harmonisation within ECSC of tax and social security burdens and to have the Community assume responsibility for coal or steel surpluses in the event of declining demand for

Italian products. These concessions were made at the demand of Senator Falck, himself one of the largest Italian steel manufacturers. Additional demands that Italian representation in ECSC organs be increased and that the agreement with France for supplying North African ore to Italy be made part of the Treaty, however, were rejected by De Gasperi.[50] In the Chamber of Deputies, the Treaty aroused little interest and was adopted after considerable delay on March 17, 1952, by a vote of 275 to 98, with 201 abstentions and absences.[51]

Clearly, business-influenced deputies in the centre parties yielded to party discipline in approving ratification, but essentially opposed the Treaty. Yet the basic doctrine of the Christian-Democratic, Liberal, Republican and Social Democratic Parties is unflinchingly committed to the principles of economic integration and political federation in Europe. Almost two hundred members of Parliament are members of the European Union of Federalists—by far the highest number in any European country.[52] Catholic doctrine supports Christian-Democratic thinking in this field, while the more mundane considerations of the expanded market doctrine appeal to the smaller parties. Even though spokesmen for specific industries will object to particular steps toward integration—as in the case of ECSC—near unanimous agreement reigns in the centre that Italy's economic future, her unemployment problem, her need for capital and her military weakness can be solved only by participation in an organised European framework.

In the five years following ratification no step of the Italian parliament and parties can be interpreted as having wrought a change in these positions. Systematic and co-ordinated debate and action with respect to ECSC and integration is rare in Italian

---

[50] *Chronique de Politique Etrangère*, Vol. 6, no. 1 (January 1, 1953), pp. 30–31. The agreement in question is the Santa Margherita Convention of 1951, under which France agreed to supply Algerian ore at "reasonable" prices. This undertaking is not part of the ECSC system, which lacks jurisdiction over non-metropolitan areas.

[51] A party breakdown of this vote is impossible since it was secret. The large number of abstentions cannot, therefore, be completely explained. Clearly, both supporters and opponents of ECSC abstained massively, indicating that (1) passage seemed assured and (2) that little interest was aroused by the actual vote.

[52] Many Socialist parliamentarians belong to the Socialist Movement for the United States of Europe and many Christian-Democrats to the Nouvelles Equipes Internationales. Parliamentary membership in the "non-denominational" European Union of Federalists is as follows: Italy 196, Germany 30, France 24, Luxembourg 15, Belgium 8. See Union Européenne des Fédéralistes, Secrétariat-Général, "U. E. F. en 1956" (Paris, 1956).

parliamentary circles. No appropriate parliamentary commission exists, no debates have been held and EDC did not come up for a vote. The sole dramatic exception was furnished by the Marcinelle mining disaster, which led to numerous interpellations aiming at greater security and protection for Italian migrant miners. But the centre parties have periodically reaffirmed their faith in integration and ECSC in their conventions. Christian-Democrats and Social Democrats still demand general economic integration, the setting up of a European investment and labour allocation machinery and insist on the creation of political institutions to assure democratic control over these economic sectors. Yet after the demise of EDC, even Christian-Democratic spokesmen, including foreign minister Gaetano Martino, have made plain that they too prefer a Europe larger than the ECSC countries, and consider supranational integration among the " Six " merely as a prod for general unification for all Europe.[53] Hence, the coexistence of supranational with intergovernmental organisations is defended.

In the Senate, Government spokesmen and centre party legislators have resisted efforts by the Communist and Nenni-Socialist parties to discredit ECSC and integration. Questions designed to embarrass the government over the Sulcis mine reorganisation issue and the layoffs connected with it were rejected. Demands for the nationalisation of all steel plants in order to escape " discriminatory " ECSC investment policy fell on deaf ears. But Conservative senators also admitted that the introduction of the full logic of competition to Italian industry had its drawbacks, though they have made no effort since 1952 to limit the application of that logic through restrictive legislation.[54] As far as EEC was concerned, Italian parliamentary discussion was confined to insisting on institutional consolidation among supranational agencies. Some members questioned the privileged position yielded to France and complained about inadequate measures for the liberalisation of migration rights. But no fundamental debate took place. The same mixture of motives which explained the ratification of ECSC in Italy, therefore, can be expected to make possible majorities for additional measures of integration.

[53] See, *e.g.*, Martino's statement in the Consultative Assembly, Council of Europe, April 1956. *Informations Mensuelles*, (April 1956), p. 75.
[54] *Informations Bimensuelles*, (July 1, 1954), p. 25; *ibid.*, (March 15, 1955), p. 41; *ibid.*, (April 30, 1955), p. 54; *ibid.*, (August 1, 1955), p. 65.

Russia's destalinisation campaign, the resulting discomfiture and weakness of the Italian Communist Party and the efforts of Nenni to re-establish relations with the pro-Western Social Democratic Party may even have brought with it a trend toward European integration on the part of the Left.[55] Thus, leaders of the Communist-controlled General Confederation of Italian Labour went on record as welcoming the positive contributions of ECSC and asking for a pro-ESCS orientation by their organisation. Leaders of the Socialist Party almost immediately followed suit, hoping perhaps to gain respectability if they succeeded in obtaining representation on the Italian parliamentary delegation to the Common Assembly from which they had thus far been excluded.[56]

THE BELGIAN PARLIAMENT AND PARTIES

Both chambers of the Belgian Parliament approved ECSC by large majorities. Yet severe reservations and outright opposition were manifest in all three major Belgian parties just the same—reservations and opposition stemming essentially from expediential considerations of the consequences of ECSC on the high-cost and antiquated Belgian coal industry, on the relatively high Belgian wage standards and plain reluctance to yield sovereign powers to a group of " foreigners."

Pro-ECSC feeling in the Christian-Democratic Party (PSC) was in part derived from the general Catholic ideological impetus toward European unity, as in all the other Community nations. These leanings, however, were by no means the only ones. PSC speakers and ministers pointed out that the Belgian steel industry would acquire a larger market and assured sources of coke and ore. With Belgian pressure for the progressive equalisation of wages and social security rates, Belgium would cease to be the highest-cost producer in ECSC. Most important, only ECSC support can finally lead to the modernisation and reorganisation of the sick mining industry, for which no adequate consistent measures had been taken in thirty years. Yet other PSC members dissented from this combination of pro-European and expediential arguments. They expressed fear of German hegemony in ECSC, concern over

[55] *Informations Mensuelles* (April 1957), pp. 24–27.
[56] See the statements of MM. Foa and Di Vittorio as quoted by *Agence Europe*, July 5, 1956.

the closing of marginal mines, unemployment and foreign competition. Perversely, but typically, they tended to argue simultaneously that the yielding of sovereign powers over Belgian citizens and property on Belgian soil was unconstitutional and that ECSC did not go far enough in assuring defence against Russia and European federal strength.[57]

The Belgian Socialist Party abstained *en bloc* in the Senate vote on ECSC and split in the Chamber. Spaak and his friends defended the Treaty on " European " grounds, extolling the necessity of taking a step toward federation, praising the expanded market doctrine, pointing out increased economic stability, while insisting that everything must be done to keep Belgian industry competitive and to modernise the mines immediately, thus preventing closings and unemployment. Even the pro-European wing of the Socialist Party made support for ECSC conditional on the preservation of the advanced wage standards of Belgian workers. Yet many Socialists were unconvinced by Spaak's efforts. Achille Van Acker, subsequently Prime Minister, voted against ratification because he felt that wage standards and mining employment were not sufficiently safeguarded. Senator Rolin opposed ECSC because he was unwilling to yield sovereignty to any supranational organisation. Still other Socialists felt that the Schuman Plan was not Socialism and therefore a step back rather than evidence of progress. Feelings were not soothed by the failure of Parliament to consider the Socialist-sponsored amendments designed to meet these worries.[58]

Within the smaller Liberal Party the dissident strain was more muted. All spokesmen urged ratification and praised the free market and competition principles of ECSC, as well as extolling the Franco-German rapprochement implied. Caveats were expressed only with respect to the necessity of soon raising foreign wage rates to the level of Belgium's, pushing the modernisation of Belgian

[57] Belgium, *Annales Parlementaires*, Chambre des Représentants, no. 70 (June 3, 1952), pp. 3–8, 12–14; no. 71 (June 4, 1952), pp. 13–18, 6–9; no. 74 (June 11, 1952), pp. 2–3, 4–6; no. 75 (June 12, 1952), pp. 11–12. *Ibid.*, Sénat, no. 16 (January 30, 1952), pp. 316–319; no. 17 (January 31, 1952), pp. 348–349, 359–360, 341–345, 334–341; no. 18 (February 5, 1952), p. 366, 373–374.

[58] *Annales Parlementaires*, Chambre des Représentants, Doc. no. 361 (1951–1952), p. 1; no. 70, pp. 9–10; no. 71, pp. 2–6, 18–22; no. 74, pp. 3, 8–10; no. 75, p. 11. The Socialist-sponsored amendments aiming at watering down and postponing ECSC, are contained in Sénat de Belgique, Session de 1951–1952 (meeting of January 9, 1952), Doc. 84, Annex I and II, pp. 77–82. Also *Ibid.*, Senat, no. 16, pp. 305–315, 319–324; no. 17, pp. 349–354, 355–358; no. 18, pp. 365–366.

waterways more energetically, hoping for co-ordinated tax and monetary policies and minimising any " undemocratic " and " technocratic " tendency on the part of the High Authority to direct the common market.[59] It was made perfectly clear by Liberals, as well as by many Catholics and Socialists, that Belgium *could not* stay out of ECSC even if it wished, simply because its economy depended too heavily on the dispositions of its neighbours.

Reservations entertained by all parties were fully expressed in the careful and voluminous reports prepared by the Senate and the Chamber commissions charged with studying the Plan. In these documents, Europeanism went begging as concrete economic and social advantages and disadvantages were soberly examined. In the Senate, a declaration was adopted concurrently with the Treaty, demanding that: ECSC be followed up by negotiations establishing convertibility and common deflationary monetary measures; emphasis be placed on the equalisation of wages and living conditions in all ECSC countries; measures to avoid funda- mental and persistent disturbances in national economies be taken before the need arises; the High Authority's investment policy refrain from interfering with national credit policy and that direct ECSC intervention in the common market be minimised.[60] A stronger Court was also demanded, thus meeting the objection of Rolin and his friends that this organ was too weak, too much confined to making purely legal judgments and likely to represent capitalist interests.[61]

Similar action was taken in the Chamber. Former Prime Minister Eyskens submitted a resolution urging the same measures, adding his desire that negotiations for the establishment of a general European common market be opened soon after the opening of the common market for coal and steel.[62] To continued worries that the living standards of Belgian workers would be undermined by ECSC, the Government gave the same assurances as did Prime Minister Bech of Luxembourg in a parallel situation:

[59] *Annales Parlementaires*, Chambre des Représentants, no. 70, pp. 10–12. *Ibid.*, Sénat, no. 16, pp. 309–310; no. 17, pp. 358–359, 345–347; No. 18, pp. 371–373, 366–368, 375–376.
[60] *Documents parlementaires*, Sénat de Belgique, no. 107 (Session 1951/52), pp. 1–3.
[61] Valentine, *op. cit.*, p. 14.
[62] *Documents parlementaires*, Chambre des Représentants, no. 457 (Session 1951/52), June 3, 1952. Also *ibid.*, Doc. 410, " Rapport fait au nom de la Commission speciale pour l'approbation du Traité instituant la Communauté Européene du Charbon et de l'Acier."

Articles 33 and 35 of the Treaty give a right of appeal to the Court every time the interests of the workers are adversely affected by a decision of the High Authority.[63]

Thus, with doubt and trepidation, the Schuman Plan was accepted by all Belgian parties, subject clearly to a number of preconditions and qualifications, including the firm promise of the Government to intensify its efforts to modernise the coal mines with suitable subsidy and tax measures.

In the years since ratification, the central issue of Belgian coal has provided almost the only occasion for systematic parliamentary discussion of ECSC problems. And it reflects less a dissatisfaction with Luxembourg's declared policy of reorganising and closing the marginal mines in the Borinage than the normal effort to discredit the majority parties. Thus, in 1953 and 1954, it was the Socialists who asked leading questions in Parliament, designed to demonstrate that the Borinage miners were being thrown out of work by an over-enthusiastic pro-ECSC government; later, by contrast, it was the PSC which asked the same questions of the Van Acker government, when its Minister of Economics, Jean Rey, proceeded to cut coal prices in line with increasing productivity, while backing the High Authority decision to refuse further subsidies to the Campine mines and concentrate on the Borinage instead. It did not help the parliamentary situation that the Campine happens to be Flemish and the Borinage Walloon; discrimination was, of course, charged by the PSC. Party politics provided the chief theme of the PSC attack on Government coal policy after the Marcinelle disaster. Catholic speakers sought to link the catastrophe to inadequate investment and modernisation measures, again without in any way attacking the High Authority. Coal is Belgium's political football, and the bitterness of the charges did not imply criticism of supranational integration as such.[64]

In terms of doctrine, party positions have not changed significantly since 1951. The Liberals still favour economic integration, a maximum of common market and a minimum of institutional control over such a market. If they are cool toward political

[63] Valentine, *op. cit.*, p. 15.
[64] See debates in Chamber of Representatives, January 21, 1954, and December 22, 1954. *Informations Bimensuelles*, January 15, 1955, and March 1, 1954. Also the Senate debate of June 7, 1955, Sénat, *Compte Rendu Analytique*, pp. 638 *et seq.* As well as Chamber of Representatives, *Annales Parlementaires* (1954–1955), no. 105, June 14, 1955.

federalism, they have never swerved in supporting actual measures of integration, even when involving supranational institutions. In the PSC, the majority, led by firmly federalist Théo Lefèvre, has supported all measures of integration. Federalists among the Christian-Democrats have criticised the High Authority for timidity and called for the extension of its powers. PSC leaders have taken the initiative in proposing, as early as 1954, the extension of the Benelux system to a general ECSC-wide customs union, a plan realised through EEC in 1957.[65] Even conservative PSC members, not necessarily federalist in outlook, have called for the evolution of a coordinated ECSC economic and anti-depression policy, for a minimum ECSC-wide wage and social security system and for the common market. Still, the party includes a wing of anti-integrationists who voted against EDC and Euratom, and who use Belgium's membership in ECSC to discredit that effort. Senator Struye, leader of this minority of the PSC, has been consistently held in check by the party bureaucracy.

But a continued division of opinion is equally typical of the Socialist Party. Its leading " European," P.-H. Spaak, might declare that " Europe will only survive in unity! The period of small markets has ended and it is necessary to create a common market in Europe. No European country is able to assure its liberty and existence alone; together we can do it, but it is necessary to begin today." [66] Such opinions are backed by a majority which calls for the drastic extension of ECSC powers to the field of labour and welfare policy as well as for the creation of new European agencies democratically controlled by real parliaments. But the party continues to include a minority of leaders who see in supranationalism the way to undermine Belgian living standards and habits. As one of their spokesmen, Senator Rolin, put it:

> I am surprised when some of our colleagues consider it imperative that the ECSC acquire greater powers in the welfare field. Maybe. But which powers in the welfare field? Shall we transfer our [national] competence to the High Authority? And after we have done that, no doubt, we will have to transfer powers relating to production costs, and then we'll have to yield the taxing power.

[65] 10th National Congress of PSC, December 1954. *Informations Bimensuelles,* January 15, 1955, p. 35.
[66] *Informations Bimensuelles*, February 15, 1955, p. 33.

> When we have transferred our powers over economic, welfare and
> tax policy, which powers will remain for our national parliaments?[67]

Five years of experience with the common market seem to have
done nothing to shake these convictions on the part of the minorities
in both major Belgian parties.

The same beliefs came to the fore in the Euratom debate held
in Parliament in the spring of 1956. By a large majority, the
following resolution was passed: Euratom was supported, provided
it was open to all states and democratically controlled, that co-operation with the OEEC plan was possible, that rigorous control over
private production and use of fissionable materials be enforced,
that only peaceful uses for atomic energy be envisaged and that
the common market be established soon. Further, it was the
desire of Parliament to exclude the Congo from the system.

Speaking for the PSC, M. Lefèvre supported the resolution
because a maximum of control powers—even if they infringed on
property rights—would make integration a reality. For M. Struye,
however, the plan was acceptable only because it made possible
British membership eventually and would function within the framework of the non-supranational OEEC scheme of co-operation.
Socialist Buset agreed with Lefèvre and backed Spaak, who saw
in a large control power the possibility of eliminating Europe's
time handicap as concerns nuclear development. But Socialist
Rolin was for Euratom only on condition that it be separated from
the common market scheme, since the latter does not and should
not call for the creation of new supranational institutions. Liberal
Motz, by contrast, was for Euratom only because he saw in it a
means for simultaneously achieving the common market to which
his principles attached him far more rigorously.[68] As in France and
Germany, the solid majority for integration, therefore, does not in
the least imply inter-party unity on ideology or aims. A convergence
of separate aims still explains the nature of support for integration
in Belgium.

THE DUTCH PARLIAMENT AND PARTIES

After some hesitation during the negotiation of the Treaty, near-
unanimous support for integration developed in Holland. Despite

[67] Sénat, *Annales Parlementaires* (July 5, 1955), no. 83, p. 1510.
[68] *Informations Mensuelles*, April 1956, pp. 23, 33, 37, 43, 45, 88.

the fact that Dutch politics is dominated by ideologically very articulate and most disparate Protestant, Catholic, Socialist and Liberal parties, no one objected in principle to ECSC or political federation for Europe. This amazing feature is explained by Goriély as the result of the loss of Indonesia, causing Netherlanders to turn from overseas preoccupations to Europe and their involvement with the European economy.[69] In any event, all the major parties accepted the Treaty without demand for amendment, interpretation or pre-conditions, by a vote in the Lower Chamber of 62 to 6. In the Upper House, the vote was 36 to 2.

Agreement in principle, however, did not rule out objections to details. The absence of Britain was universally deplored. The fear that ECSC subsidies to Belgian mines would lead to their superiority over Dutch mines was explained away by the Government—inaccurately—by saying that only inefficient mines would be aided. Many Catholics and Socialists praised the " pre-federal " supranational features of ECSC and a leader of the Liberal Party (VVD) regretted the overly strong role of the Council of Ministers, while voicing fears of being too closely associated with politically unstable France and Italy. Whatever fears for Dutch interests were entertained, however, tended to be overcome by a strong reliance on the Court, which was frequently likened to the United States Supreme Court in its potential role. Holland offers the only example in which the separate doctrines of Socialist, Calvinist, lay liberal and Catholic groups were merged in a common " European " outlook, here made to equate, in effect, the Dutch national interest.

No systematic debate on ECSC issues has been held in the Dutch parliament since that time. In five years of operation, only one hostile question has been asked in the Second Chamber, while both EDC and Euratom were approved by majorities larger than the one obtained for ECSC. The pro-integration consensus among Dutch politicians makes itself felt particularly significantly in the consistent effort made by Dutch members of the Common Assembly to hammer home the Luxembourg viewpoint in purely national legislative discussions. Even specific criticisms of High Authority policy have enjoyed a broad inter-party base. Socialist Deputy Nederhorst's attacks on the slow anti-cartel policy of Luxembourg was backed by support from Economics Minister Zijlstra and the unsuccessful

[69] Goriély, *op. cit.*, p. 604.

Dutch complaint in the ECSC Court of Justice. The High Authority's temporary authorisation of the German Government's policy of subsidising the coal purchases of the German high seas fisheries fleet was sharply challenged as discriminatory against Dutch fishermen.[70]

Still, the annual debate on the Government's draft budget has elicited demands and statements which permit the construction of a rough spectrum of enthusiasm for supranationalism. Thus, representatives of the Labour and Catholic Parties have been the ones to call regularly for extending the scope of power of ECSC to other sectors—notably energy and transportation—and for publicly discussed, ECSC-wide measures of counter-cyclical investment and spending. It was the Catholic People's Party which praised the Messina Conference most extravagantly and demanded that its conclusions be implemented exclusively through supranational institutions. It is these parties which see in economic integration a precursor to political federation. The same is true to a far lesser extent of the small parties of the right, Anti-Revolutionaries, Christian-Historical Union and VVD. Significantly represented in most post-1945 Dutch Cabinets, these parties certainly favour the kind of economic integration that will lead to a unified common market. However, they are suspicious of supranational institutions, though willing to grant the need for them during the transitional period. In no sense of the term can these people be considered federalists.

Even though the Second Chamber approved the Euratom resolution in 1956, it did so with the admonition to the Government that it was hostile to further sector integration and favoured the simultaneous establishment of the General Common Market. Only if this would hinder ratification would a separation of the two issues be in order. Some politicians expressed opposition to the extensive ownership and control features over fissionable materials claimed for Euratom as unnecessarily burdensome for private enterprise. But others, notably former Foreign Minister Beyen, strongly came out for the supranational approach to all these issues, even if it excludes British membership.

THE LUXEMBOURG PARLIAMENT AND PARTIES

With the exception of the Communist deputies, approval of ECSC

[70] For this controversy, see *Journal Officiel*, June 27, 1953.

in the unicameral Luxembourg Parliament was unanimous. Agreement was reached painlessly despite the strong ideological cleavages among the three parties—Christian-Democratic (PCS), Socialist and Liberal. As in France and Italy, the Luxembourg PCS is committed to integration on doctrinaire Christian grounds as well as on the basis of expediency. Liberals and Socialists lack a similar motivation, both being more consistently concerned with purely domestic economic aspirations. Yet they too agree that Luxembourg—dependent almost entirely on the exportation of steel for its foreign exchange earnings—cannot remain outside any close economic or political union decided upon by its neighbours, especially Belgium, with whom it has been joined in a full economic union since 1922. Considerations of expediency, not an initially developed ideological commitment, determined Luxembourg's position.

However, objections and worries were heard here too. Prior to ratification, the Conseil d'Etat pointed out that special safeguards for Luxembourg's steel production and its higher-than-average living standards might be necessary, but recommended in favour of ratification and even proposed a change in the Constitution to facilitate adherence to future federal arrangements. In defence of its desire to join ECSC, the Government pointed out to the deputies that the Treaty contained a special safeguarding clause for Luxembourg steel (never invoked thus far in practice) and that the Treaty's Article 37 (fundamental and persistent disturbances in a national economy) was inserted especially for the benefit of Luxembourg.[71] Thereafter, ratification was voted without further objection.

Fundamental debates on integration have been lacking since, apart from the ratification of EDC and the approval of Euratom negotiations by the same unanimous non-Communist votes marshalled in the case of ECSC. Progress on the road to integration via supranationalism has been the demand of Christian-Democrats and Socialists alike. The resolution favouring Euratom was introduced jointly by all three parties and passed without reservation or amendment. Socialists, like their colleagues in Germany and France, insisted on the exclusively peaceful role of Euratom, and therefore endorsed the draft resolution prepared by Monnet's

---

[71] See Valentine, *op. cit.* The same claim was made on behalf of their national economies in other ECSC countries. Prime Minister Bech's assertion is almost certainly erroneous in point of fact.

Action Committee for the United States of Europe. But the other parties, unlike their counterparts in other ECSC countries, had no objection.

Few specific issues regarding ECSC have come to the fore in Luxembourg politics. All the parties expressed themselves in opposition to the canalisation of the Moselle—for fear of financial loss to the already heavily subsidised Luxembourg state railways. Since the common market for coal and steel has not affected the country adversely, there is support now for the General Common Market—with the exception of the agricultural sector. The Christian-Democrats, dependent on the rural vote, have hedged on the in-clusion of Luxembourg in an agrarian pool and have insisted on " special safeguards." Governmental coolness toward the free migration of ECSC labour was overcome as late as 1957 with the ratification of the ECSC convention. With respect to transport, taxes, and long-range financial and investment policy, however, all the parties again have supported and demanded that the ECSC scope of powers be expanded. Clearly, in Luxembourg the majority for further integration along economic lines continues to be unanimous. While overt enthusiasm for political federation is absent, support for such measures would nevertheless be com-pletely consistent with the ideologies of all the parties and therefore not meet serious opposition, should it be decided by the Grand-Duchy's neighbours.

THE " EUROPEAN MAJORITY ": WHY WAS ECSC RATIFIED?

That a unified dedication to the common good was not the chief feature which explained European parliamentary support for ECSC has become obvious. But what kind of collective thinking did characterise the ratification process? Were decisions reached on the basis of consensus within each parliament based upon an agreed version of the national interest? Conversely, did parlia-mentarians in their national settings respond to a common version of the European doctrine? In the first case, the accidental con-vergence of six distinct national interests would explain acceptance, while in the second instance, trans-national solidarity of some kind would be central. Or again, is ratification to be explained on the basis of ideological solidarity among like-minded parties co-operat-ing across national frontiers, such as the Christian-Democrats or Socialists? Perhaps none of these explains as much as the expediential thinking of a multiplicity of groups, each finding some advantage in voting for the Treaty.

The possibility of agreement on the basis of the national doctrine seems to explain ratification only in the case of Holland and Luxembourg. In both parliaments, ratification was almost unanimous. In both the future of the national economies was considered inevitably tied up with ECSC, with the nation responding in concert to the new scheme. Wide divergences of opinion were typical of the other four countries. Further, not even the majority found in each parliament for ratification offered homogeneous reasons for its action, some stressing one feature and some another. Negatively speaking, it could only be said that all pro-ECSC German parties took their stand, in part, because the Treaty offered release from some allied controls.

Nor can a common dedication to European principles be isolated as a unifying element. Clearly this was absent as a characteristic applying to all parties in five of the six parliaments. Only in Holland was the essence of " Europeanism " accepted without dissent, thus becoming actually part of the content of Dutch nationalism. No such conclusion, however, can be drawn from Luxembourg's ratification, unanimous though it was. While a common definition of the national interest was found there, this did not include an equally striking commitment to European principles among all the parties.

More can be made of the pattern of agreement and co-operation of certain national parties with their ideological counterparts across the frontier. Certainly the groups of the extreme right and the liberal parties exhibited no such traits. Agreement even among the traditionally " internationalist " socialist parties was too tenuous to explain much in this context. Vague pro-ECSC declarations on the part of the Socialist International in 1951 must here be contrasted with the actual opposition of the SPD, the hesitations of the SFIO and Luxembourg Socialists, as well as the continued doubts of the Belgians. In the case of the Christian-Democrats, however, the case is otherwise. On the level of doctrine there was commitment to a united peaceful Europe, commonly shared by all six parties and cemented with Church teaching. Further, it must be stressed that in 1950-1952 in all six countries, Christian parties were represented in the cabinets, with Christian-Democratic prime ministers presiding in all but Holland and France. Convinced that Europe's ills demanded a new approach and unpalatable steps these men were hesitant to take within the national framework, they tacitly agreed to shift the burden to a supranational agency:

> It will relieve these men of difficult decisions while they are in office and perhaps help to keep them in office. It will provide them with a joint source of prestige and patronage as long as they stick together, and strengthen them against their opponents of the right and left. . . . This group of leaders recognised in the project an instrument for prolonging the political advantages that time and circumstances had played into their hands.[72]

Christian doctrine and opportunity combined to suggest the creation of a new type of " pre-federal " organisation to solve problems considered economically too difficult and politically too dangerous to tackle in the national setting.

But Christian-Democratic votes, after all, did not suffice to establish ECSC. The only generally valid explanation of the success of the Treaty lies in the convergence, not of six separate national interests, but of a sufficiently large number of separate national party positions to push the Treaty over the top. In France, the SFIO was favourable because it accepted the principles of the free competitive market and Franco-German peace; the Liberals of the centre and right concurred because it gave them German coke and the hope for continuing control—via Luxembourg—over German heavy industry; MRP was favourable for the doctrinal and expediential reasons summarised above. In Germany, all parties except the SPD were favourably inclined because of common anti-Allied motives, with the CDU impelled also by Europeanism, but the FDP largely for industrial and business reasons—in essence for precisely the opposite reasons which motivated many French politicians. Italian adherence was based on a mixture of doctrine, the promise of financial aid and the assurance of raw materials and larger markets. Belgian support was derived from free market motives as well as from the boon of foreign assistance to outdated mines. The very ambiguity of the Treaty, of course, made this pattern of convergence possible. Something seemed to be " in it " for everybody and a large enough body of otherwise quarrelling

[72] Mendershausen, " First Tests of the Schuman Plan," *Review of Economics and Statistics,* (November 1953), p. 270. See also in this connection the excellent treatment of political motivation in W. N. Parker, " The Schuman Plan—A Preliminary Prediction," *International Organisation* (August 1952).

politicians was persuaded to launch the first experiment in deliberate integration.

Is There a " European Majority "?

The elusiveness of a majority based on convergent rather than homogeneous motives and ideologies was demonstrated in the debacle over EDC. In Germany the old mixture of European with anti-Allied motives again sufficed to pass the Treaty, but not so in France. If the device of supranationalism seemed acceptable to Socialists and Radicals in 1951 in order to assure peaceful Franco-German relations without clear German hegemony, the feeling was otherwise when it came to putting guns into the hands of the *boches*. The dispute over Euratom merely implies the same problem once more. German Conservatives seek a minimum of supranational nuclear control, for nationalistic as well as free enterprise reasons. French Socialists as well as Conservatives prefer tight supranational controls: the former for pacifist and economic planning reasons, the latter because they hope to be able to enforce the ban on German atomic equipment in this fashion.

Hence, the following statistics on the European majority, as measured by votes on the three supranational issues so far before the national parliaments, must be understood in terms of a possibly temporary convergence of party motives and ideologies, and most emphatically not in terms of a clear, permanent and united majority. Europeanism, even after five years of successful ECSC operations, continues to be a mixture of frequently opposing aspirations. Certainly it is significant that a *homogeneous* movement combating such steps has also failed to materialise. The lack of opposition is attributable to the fact that no group or nation has suffered economic or political damage as a result of the common market, whereas the conversion to integration among certain parties stems from their realisation that their long-range aims may be met more effectively through expanded supranational action. But the dominant fragmentation of ideologies and groups also explains why support for integration must continue to rely on convergence and cannot go forward on the basis of generally accepted propositions. The nature of pluralism militates against their ever being accepted by all simultaneously.

THE EUROPEAN MAJORITY: 1951 to 1956

	ECSC[1]				EDC[1]				Euratom[2]			
	Tot.[3]	Yes	No	Ab.[4]	Tot.	Yes	No	Abs.	Tot.	Yes	No	Abs.
France:												
Gaullists	121	2	116	—	121	16	83	2	22	19	3	—
Independents & Peasants	91	73	20	—	91	45	22	?	95	73	2	20
Radicals, RGR, UDSR & RDA	91	85	1	5	91	41	44	3	91	64	27	—
MRP	85	87	—	—	85	80	2	4	73	73	—	—
SFIO	107	105	—	1	107	50	53	1	95	95	—	—
Communists & Progressives	103	—	101	—	103	—	99	—	150	—	148	—
Others[5]	28	21	2	5	28	32	16	1	70	8	1	61
Total	626	376	240	11	626	264	319	12	596	332	181	81
Germany:												
German P.	24	22	—	—	24	20	—	—	15	unanimous		
Others[6]	37	21	6	3	37	15	22	2	24	approval	by	
FDP	51	48	—	—	51	46	1	—	48	show	of hands	
CDU	145	141	—	—	145	143	1	—	224			
SPD	131	—	123	—	131	—	128	—	151			
Communists	14	—	13	—	14	—	14	—	—			
Total	402	232	142	3	402	224	166	2	467			
Italy:												
Neo-Fascists	6	No figures available			29	No vote taken			29	No vote taken		
Monarchists	14				40				40			
Christian-Democrats	306				262				262			
Republicans	9				5				5			
Soc.-Democ.	33				19				19			
Communists & Socialists	183				218				218			
Others[7]	23				17				17			
Total	574	265	98	201	590				590			
Belgium:												
PSC	108	108	—	—	108	all other	10	1	95	23	?	?
Socialists	77	37	6	13	77	mem-	29	1	86	86	—	—
Liberals	20	20	—	—	20	bers	3	1	25	25	—	—
Communists	7	—	7	—	7	pre-	7	—	4	—	4	—
Independ.	—	—	—	—	—	sent	—	—	2	—	—	2
Total	212	165	13	13	212	148	49	3	212	134	?	28

For footnotes—see p. 157.

	ECSC[1]				EDC[1]				Euratom[2]			
	Tot.	Yes	No	Abs.	Tot.	Yes	No	Abs.	Tot.	Yes	No	Abs.
Netherlands:												
Liberals (VVD)	8	all members present			9	all other members present 1			9	all other members present 2		
Anti-Revolutionary tionary	13				12				12			
Christ.-Hist.	9				9				9			
Catholics	32				30				30			
Labour P.	27				30				30			
Communists	8		6		6		6		6		6	
Others[8]	3				4		4		4		4	
Total	100	62	6	32	100	75	11	14	100	64	12	24
Luxembourg:												
Christian-Democrats	21	All other members present			21	21			21	all members present		
Socialists	19				19	17	—	2	19			
Liberals	8		—		8	8	—	—	8			
Communists	4	—	4		4	—	4	—	4		4	
Total	52	47	4	1	52	46	4	2	52	48	4	—

[1] The ECSC and EDC votes refer to the ratifications in the lower house of the two treaties in question.

[2] The Euratom votes refer to the resolutions passed in the lower houses of five parliaments in spring and summer of 1956, authorising the governments to pursue negotiations leading toward the establishment of Euratom. See the text of this chapter for reservations and amendments to the draft resolution voted in some chambers, departing from the draft prepared by the Action Committee for the United States of Europe and submitted to the parliaments on its initiative.

[3] The "total" column lists the parliamentary strength of each party or group of parties as of the election preceding the vote. Since it does not take account of deaths, resignations or switches in party identification, the sum of the "yes" "no" and "abstention" columns does not always correspond to the parliamentary party total.

[4] The figure given for "abstentions" does not in all cases correspond to the figure officially recorded in the parliamentary documents. In many cases there were absences and vacancies in addition to strictly "voluntary abstentions," though frequently such absences reflected a desire to abstain without being so recorded. Wherever possible I have identified these unofficial abstainers. Failure of the "yes" "no" and "abstention" columns to add to the "total" listed for each party, therefore, may also reflect an inability on my part to identify completely all those who abstained or who were physically absent.

[5] "Others" in the French parliament include members without party affiliation, Overseas Independents and, since 1956, the Poujadists (52 elected).

[6] "Others" in the West German parliament include the Refugee Party and an assortment of neo-Nazi groups which failed to be re-elected in the 1953 balloting, as well as independents.

[7] "Others" in the Italian parliament include members without party affiliation, South Tyrol Autonomists, and the diminutive Liberal Party.

[8] "Others" in the Dutch parliament includes the Staatskundig Gereformeerede and National Catholic Parties.

Paradoxically, a theory of transnational integration can derive considerable comfort from this finding. In the absence of the initial agreement of all parties to integration on the precise motives for working toward political community, the fact that a variety of motives are dominant in each national unit actually facilitates the emergence of supranational ideologies at a later stage, as will be demonstrated in the chapter on ECSC political parties. If a uniform consensus within each national unit had existed at the onset of the integration step, ideological realignments would be made more difficult because of the pre-existing rigidities in outlook and expectations, some of which are bound to be disappointed as integration goes forward.

This conclusion, to be sure, rests on two assumptions, both of which have been met in the ECSC framework. The dominance of pluralism in each unit and the inability to agree nationally on basic propositions must be accompanied by the kind of ideological predisposition which will make possible a realignment of loyalties at the supranational level. Groups in each country must be partisan of thought patterns having their parallels in groups across the border. Socialism as well as Christian-Democracy, and to a much lesser extent Liberalism, furnish precisely the necessary ideological predisposition. The emergence of a Socialist and a Christian doctrine of European economic integration is no more than the necessary result of these social forces. The second assumption is the existence of supranational institutions capable of channelling convergence into merging ideological patterns. Congresses and conventions without the power or desire to legislate cannot approximate this condition. A Common Assembly, potentially, at least, capable of moulding the policy of a federal High Authority does provide this opportunity. Small wonder then that the very fragmentation of beliefs in five of the six member states has found its supranational answer through the instrumentalities of ECSC institutions.

The political community which may result from this trend— and its emergence is by no means assured merely because the trends have been set into motion—is, of course, bound to be equally pluralistic and perhaps unable easily to define a general consensus. Nevertheless, in the effort to give a Socialist, Christian or Liberal stamp to the emerging pattern of interdependence, the political actor is compelled to work through the medium of new central symbols. And his doing so may suffice to make these symbols the equal of a new regional " national " doctrine.

In the meantime, however, this end result is by no means at hand. Supranational realignments are under way, but convergences of motives continue to dominate now. But they have already achieved the next step in integration: Euratom and the European Economic Community.

British Parties and Continental Unity

This survey of trends among political parties would hardly be complete without an examination of opinion in British ranks. Certainly, membership in ECSC or in any supranational system was never entertained as a serious possibility. This, however, does not preclude the probability that the evolution from OEEC to the General Common Market brought with it some serious soul-searching in Westminster.

The ruling Labour Party's position in 1950 permitted of no doubt. In *European Unity*, an official party pamphlet published in May of that year, it was argued that close economic cooperation with Europe was unnecessary because the economies concerned are not complementary. Further, the very logic of the common market was challenged: far from leading to a more rational distribution of the factors of production it was likely to result in chaos. More specifically—and probably more honestly—the pamphlet declared that Socialists would be in a permanent minority in a federated Europe, that Britain could sacrifice neither her newly won social welfare benefits nor her sovereign power to plan her economy, that the Commonwealth and Atlantic unity took precedence over European ties—an argument to which no Tory could take exception. Supranationalism, in short, was ruled out and intergovernmental co-operation described as adequate.

The opposition Conservative Party did not basically challenge the Labour position; in fact, it shared the essence of it. However, it attacked the stubborn unwillingness of the Government even to attend the conference called to draft the ECSC Treaty and insisted that British isolation should have been avoided by participation in it. To this, Aneurin Bevan answered that " those who do not wish to confide our steel and coal to the popularly elected at

Westminster, would hand British coal and steel workers over to a group of international capitalists on the Continent." [73]

Did the parties react differently when Monnet offered to conclude an agreement on association in December of 1953? During the long months of negotiation, many polite statements on the desirability of closer ties—always safeguarding British freedom to act—were made. When the agreement was before the House for ratification, approval was general and criticism confined to deploring excessive diplomatic immunities to be granted to ECSC agents in Britain. A number of members of all parties expressed doubts about the feasibility of supranationalism while Labour speakers merely wished to compel the Government to consult the trade unions before making commitments in the Council of Association. To fears that in the absence of the association agreement, the steel groups would form a cartel, Mr. Anthony Nutting replied that the Government had deliberately insisted on purely intergovernmental organs, but would consult all interested groups before committing the country.[74] Approval of the agreement was obtained without controversy or dissent.

Did the evident success of supranationalism and the European " New Start " make a difference in British party opinion? Apparently it did. Clement Davies told the Liberal Party conference of 1956 that duties toward the Commonwealth—the argument always heard when European integration is discussed—did not justify a " superior snobbery " toward the Six. As the common market plan of the Brussels Intergovernmental Committee became known, a cross-party group of fifty prominent Britons signed a declaration demanding more cooperation with EEC. Harold Macmillan told the Conservative conference in October 1956 that while ties with the Commonwealth would always take priority, they did not preclude ties with EEC via the Free Trade Area. In the House of Commons, the Brussels plan elicited statements from Conservatives and Labourites deploring an eventual British economic isolation and praising the obvious advantages of a common market.[75]

---

[73] This statement was made during the House of Commons debate on Labour's ECSC policy, June 26, 1950. Racine, *op. cit.*, p. 70.

[74] *The Times*, February 22, 1955.

[75] *The Times*, October 8, 1956. *Weekly Hansard*, no. 361, on the debate of July 5, 1956. The reasons underlying the British change in attitude are analysed in detail in Chaps. 5 and 8.

As late as 1956, Denis Healey repeated the standard British objections to federation, but insisted that Britain, in military plans, favoured closer unity for the six

Provided the issue of supranationality was not raised, all British parties by 1957 showed not only interest, but a definite eagerness to be associated with the Continent. Nothing further was heard of the arguments featured in *European Unity*. A common market, implying the possibility of discrimination against British trade in search of increasing Continental rather than Commonwealth outlets, proved to be a potent centre of attraction.

Continental countries. H. Field Haviland, Jr. (ed.), *The United States and the Western Community* (Haverford: Haverford College Press, 1957), pp. 31–52.

CHAPTER 5

TRADE ASSOCIATIONS: 1952 AND 1957

INDUSTRIALISTS are the private parties most consistently and continually under the direction of supranational institutions, and therefore directly concerned with the process of integration. However, it would violate the logic of pluralism to assume that firm " national industrial " attitudes prevailed in any of the ECSC countries in 1950 or at any time thereafter. Positions toward the ratification, implementation and extension of coal and steel integration differed in each country with the perception of interests of the trade association concerned. Opinions expressed by steel producers tended to differ from those of coal interests, consumers diverged from producers. Fragmentation was and is typical. Hence, the data on which the following conclusions are based was drawn from the statements and aspirations of the chief national trade associations in each of these fields, with a national consensus being deducible in exceptional cases only.[1]

GERMAN INDUSTRY AND EUROPEAN INTEGRATION

To judge by the glowing statements issued shortly after the French announcement of May 9, 1950, German heavy industry was delighted with the Schuman Plan and eager to participate. A respected German business economist wrote feelingly of the need for *Grossraumwirtschaft* and the possibility of achieving it through ECSC.[2] Speaking for the Wirtschaftsvereinigung Eisen- und Stahlindustrie as well as for the coal producers, Hermann Schenck declared in 1950:

---

[1] Unless otherwise specified, the following conclusions are based on a number of standard sources. For German industrial attitudes, the trade journals *Stahl und Eisen* (steel) and *Glückauf* (coal) are central. French industrial opinions are regularly expressed in *Usine Nouvelle* and the *Bulletin* of the Conseil National du Patronat Français. Other professional and press comments are carefully reprinted in ECSC, Assemblée Commune, Service des Etudes et de la Documentation, *Informations Bimensuelles* (bi-weekly in 1954 and 1955) and *Informations Mensuelles* (monthly since January 1956). Note especially the issues of January and November 1956, since they contain summaries of company reports to stockholders for the years 1954 and 1955. Other central sources not specifically cited hereafter include the daily press service reports of *Agence Europe* and the issues of *Chronique de Politique Etrangère* for January 1953 and September 1955.

[2] Günther Henle, *Der Schumanplan vor seiner Verwirklichung, op. cit.*

The basic industries Coal and Steel firmly and without reservation support the idea of the Schuman Plan. We must realise the Schuman Plan because it will finally end the rivalries between our Western neighbours and ourselves, even if this, as we know, will demand sacrifices from all. However, we believe that the complete equality of the industrial partners is a self-evident presumption for the frictionless functioning of the plan. But granting this we shall enter the scheme with complete conviction. It is not necessary to imagine that the issue of the Schuman Plan must be linked with remilitarisation, which does not tempt us.[3]

Even during the early stages of ECSC discussion, spokesmen for the trade associations made it plain that they expected their representatives to assist the official government delegations in the drafting of a definitive text.

The reservations implied in Schenck's " unconditional " acceptance were soon expressed by industry leaders. Delighted to substitute ECSC for the highly unpopular Allied Ruhr Authority—which allocated German coal exports over the dissent of the German representative—fears of French hegemony were voiced just the same. " It cannot be denied that the Ruhr, despite everything still the strongest potential within ECSC, has had to make the greatest sacrifices for the sake of the European Community." [4] Germany is certain to be outvoted on the High Authority and made the pawn of the politico-economic interests of France, especially since ECSC is likely to be " dirigist " in outlook. It was widely feared in Germany that France would seek to throttle German steel production and seek to flood the German market with the surplus French steel for which Monnet—in his capacity as the architect of France's post-1945 industrial modernisation programme—could find no other outlet. Objections were raised against the anti-cartel features of the draft Treaty, which were derided as one more instance of the post-war mania to remake the European economy in the American image.[5] German weakness due to war losses, damage and reparations were mentioned incessantly in order to buttress the argument of sacrifice; but hopes were also expressed by industry spokesmen for ECSC investment funds. In fact, this hope

---

[3] *Stahl und Eisen*, Vol. 70, no. 27 (November 23, 1950), p. 1096.

[4] K. H. Herchenröder, Joh. Schäfer, Manfred Zapp, *Die Nachfolger der Ruhrkonzerne* (Düsseldorf: Econ Verlag, 1954), pp. 44 *et seq.*

[5] Haussmann, *op. cit.*, provides lengthy examples of these arguments, which he seems to accept as valid.

was one of the major attractions of Schuman's proposal, despite the other objections raised.[6]

One of the chief criticisms and simultaneously a major attraction of ECSC was the issue of deconcentration and mergers. German industry backed the CDU's interpretation of Article 66 of the Treaty as permitting, subject to High Authority approval, the *reconcentration* of the pre-war German coal and steel combines to levels corresponding to the size of French combines— while French industry and politicians argued that Article 66 would serve to freeze the conditions created by Allied Law 27. ECSC Treaty negotiations were accompanied by German efforts to raise the size of industrial units permitted under Law 27 and the announcement of the final wording of this law—coinciding in time with the completion of the ECSC Treaty drafting—disappointed those who were fearful of entering the common market but gave hope to others who saw in Article 66 the legal means for circumventing Law 27.[7]

While by no means as enthusiastic about the Schuman Plan, as finally ratified, as implied in early statements, the bulk of the German coal and steel industries, nevertheless, saw in the scheme more virtues than drawbacks. Other segments of industrial opinion did not share this feeling. It was argued that German ratification should have been accompanied by reservations insisting on a weaker High Authority, abolition of Law 27, and continuation of coal sales organisations. Said the influential *Wirtschaftszeitung:*

> Everyone in Germany favours Europe and conciliation with France, even with sacrifices, but of course only sacrifices which can be justified in terms of the basic interests of the German people. And therefore the question is posed more and more often how the Coal and Steel Community could have been changed and improved.[8]

---

[6] The figures and arguments are given in Horst Carl Hahn, *Der Schuman Plan* (Munich: Richard Pflaum Verlag, 1953).

[7] The history of these concurrent negotiations is told by H. Rieben, *Des Ententes de Maitres de Forges au Plan Schuman* (Lausanne, 1954), pp. 426 *et seq.* Disagreement on the future size of German industrial combinations held up the completion of ECSC Treaty drafting. It is widely supposed that only the last-minute intervention with Monnet of U.S. High Commissioner John J. McCloy made possible the " compromise " under which a fairly stringent Law 27 would go into effect with the common market, to be modified later in terms of the developments of mergers in the ECSC area. Thus, the future German units would be comparable in size to those developing in other ECSC countries, creating some " countervailing power." See *Industriekurier*, March 7, 1951, for such suggestions.

[8] *Wirtschaftszeitung*, June 27, 1951.

Improvement, in the opinion of these reluctant Europeans, would have included stripping ECSC of all powers of control and the achievement of a common market through the cooperation of interested industries. " Pro-European " sentiment was widely mingled with anti-supranational demands, indicating that for many businessmen integration meant little more than the removal of Allied controls.

The enthusiasm of German steelmakers for integration was subjected to a severe test at the very time when the common market was to open. They considered as discriminatory the High Authority's endorsement of the French position on the question of whether the exporter's or the importer's sales tax ought to be refunded.[9] As was argued heatedly by the Steel Association:

> A common market excludes the concepts of " imports " and " exports." Each buyer, regardless of the country in which he resides, must be enabled to obtain conditions and prices from a seller identical with his other buyers.[10]

Different sales taxes on " imported " steel would therefore clearly discriminate against the then higher-priced, *i.e.*, German, products.

Luxembourg's decision evoked loud German demands that the Government sue in the ECSC Court to obtain redress against this " obvious pro-French discrimination." The Government, through State Secretary Westrick, however, refused to sue or to apply the compensatory special sales tax measure against French steel passed by the Bundestag, while French steel obligingly raised its prices. A compromise thus eased the situation, causing the *Frankfurter Allgemeine* to comment:

> M. Monnet, who undoubtedly had something to do with the raising of French steel prices, has shown himself to be an " obliging " European, but State Secretary Westrick has greatly outdistanced him in obligingness by refusing to speak of a tax war.[11]

While outraged feelings in the steel industry were assuaged with respect to the tax issue, the question of coal sales organisations— the one dominant cartel issue—has led to a permanent and bitter criticism of ECSC in almost all German circles concerned. Joint

[9] For the extremely complex figures and cost implications, see Mendershausen, *op. cit.*, pp. 279–282. *Etudes et Documents* (May 1953), pp. B13–15. The details of the *Steuerstreit* are discussed in Chap. 3.
[10] Radio address of E. W. Mommsen (Klöckner Works), printed in *Stahl und Eisen*, (February 26, 1953), pp. 318–319.
[11] June 24, 1953.

non-competitive sales at prices fixed by GEORG are considered essential by the Coal Association, coal wholesalers and dealers, the Steel Association, the Bundesverband der Deutschen Industrie (BDI), as well as by trade unions and many Government officials. Competition would force marginal mines to close, introduce sharp fluctuations in supply and make the marketing of poor grades impossible. Virtually nobody in Germany—with the significant exception of the Federal Ministry of Economics—challenged this reasoning, thus initiating two years of bitter resistance to the High Authority's efforts to transform GEORG and OKU, and loud objections to the decision announced in fall of 1955. The virtually unanimous opposition to Luxembourg's policy has brought with it scepticism as to its enforceability and predictions of national cartel practices even under the three competitive sales organisations authorised. And in some cases, it has brought forth threats which betray little loyalty to supranationalism:

> Our solid front [of opposition to ECSC cartel policy] in favour of centralism and against anti-economic experiments should be a sufficient basis to prepare seriously for changes in the Treaty once the transitional period is over.... We must confidently hope that the German [*sic*] representatives on the High Authority will not ignore these voices from the German economy and relevant German government agencies.... In a decision of I. G. Bergbau it was held that if Luxembourg insists on a decentralisation of joint sales, coal mining must be nationalised.... Did the creators of the Schuman Plan wish for this kind of result....? When the High Authority makes false decisions of this magnitude the entire fabric of the Treaty could collapse. And it is not only a question of ECSC.... Reverses for ECSC must affect the whole European idea negatively.... Let the members of the High Authority and all those possessed of the theory of free competition who loudly demand that cartel ghosts must be hunted in the coal sector, recognise their mistake in the last hour and be wise enough to draw the consequences from their recognition.[12]

The opposite is true of the industrial response to the reconcentration

---

[12] Leading editorial in *Kohlenwirtschaftszeitung*, " Montan-Union und Gemein-schaftsverkauf," no. 17 (September 18, 1955), pp. 4 *et seq.* This journal is the organ of German coal wholesalers. For similar opinions, coupled with strong attacks on High Authority Vice-President Franz Etzel, the man who negotiated with the Unternehmensverband Ruhrbergbau for changes in GEORG, see *ibid.*, October 15, 1955, p. 3. Also the statement of Grosse at the convention of German coal wholesalers, *Informations Bimensuelles*, September 15, 1955, p. 15.

issue. Those who favoured ECSC because it seemed to permit both vertical and horizontal mergers were amply rewarded by the policies authorised in Luxembourg. In 1953 there was an initial period of strident demand for permission to reconcentrate, justified not only by a quasi-religious insistence on the naturalness of vertical coal-steel-engineering plant combinations but also by the need to achieve intra-firm capacity to compensate for fluctuations in demand for specific steel products. While the High Authority laboured over the implementation of Article 66 in working out the maximum allowable mergers exempt from the authorisation requirement, German steelmakers argued that Luxembourg should take Law 27 into account and not insist on a rigorous application of whatever rules were determined. Apparently satisfied with ECSC reluctance to enforce Law 27, Hans-Günther Sohl, president of August Thyssen-Hütte, conceded:

> If the High Authority acts so as to make the European steel industry internationally competitive through an active investment policy and the encouragement of organic mergers. . . . the aim of the economic integration in Europe may be attained despite all initial difficulties.[13]

By 1955 it was evident that in the field of mergers, at least, the positive expectations entertained in 1951 had been met. While one series of complaints against supranationalism was thus dropped, the fulfilment of the expectation did not demonstrably lead to an increase in loyalty to that form of integration.

A markedly national preoccupation in German business circles subsists with respect to the acquisition of coal and steel properties by foreign financial interests. About 25 per cent. of German coal production is owned by French, Dutch, Belgian, Italian, Luxembourg and American firms, while three of the largest steel corporations are Dutch and Swedish controlled. The sale of these properties has aroused resentment and the absence of proportional German investments in the industries of these countries is by many considered another " discrimination." Four years of supranationalism seem to have done little to alter this attitude.

On the crucial question of price stability, flexibility and price fixing, the German interest groups show the characteristic split between producer and consumer interests. Coal producers have

[13] *Stahl und Eisen*, June 17, 1954, p. 861.

argued without break since 1952 that the policy of rigid price ceilings is wrong, discriminatory against the Ruhr and dirigistic. Mounting production costs, intensive capital requirements and constantly rising wage demands compel a gradual upward adjustment of prices, they argue, punctuating their periodic claims for increases in the ECSC ceilings with voluminous cost studies designed to prove their claims. Steelmakers have supported these claims—they own about 20 per cent. of Germany's mines—and coal wholesalers have also inveighed against High Authority " planning " in the coal price field. Only the major organised coal consumers, supported by Erhard, have urged Luxembourg to set limits to price freedom. Suggestions that the ECSC-wide coal shortage be met by planned imports and intra-ECSC compensation payments have been met with charges of " supranational dirigisme."

Nor have the steelmakers been completely satisfied with the fair trade code which governs their sales. Especially during the recession of 1954 they complained of rigidities and centralised planning, expressing their preference for " direct " and " friendly " understandings with their French and Belgian competitors. As boom conditions developed in 1955 these complaints diminished; but organised steel consumers began then to argue for price flexibility. While generally very satisfied with the common market and anxious for more competition, they nevertheless argue that " we should like to see a proper balance kept between dirigisme and freedom." Price controls are opposed by the consumers, but measures of relaxation, like the ill-fated Monnet Rebate, were warmly greeted as a constructive step.[14] Coal and steel producers think of supranationalism in terms of a potential controller over price policy, to be resisted at all cost, but consumers find in the system a forum sympathetic for their long-range demands for a multiplicity of choice. Yet as regards the pricing and allocation of scarce scrap supplies, even the German steelmakers welcomed supranational and national cartel-like practices—without complaining of any dirigisme. When their national cartel was dissolved by Luxembourg in the summer of 1955, they agreed cheerfully to an ECSC scheme of allocation and control, providing also for bonuses paid to steel producers who save scrap in favour of pig iron.

Transport harmonisation and development also split the ranks

---

[14] Eberhard Jung, representative of German steel consumers on the Consultative Committee, in ECSC *Bulletin* (January 1956), pp. 7 *et seq.*

of German industry. Steelmakers expressed grave reserve on the introduction of uniform tapered railway rates in the Community, fearing to lose an existing transport advantage on the southern German market and arguing for a maximum of intergovernmental negotiation at the expense of High Authority action. Coal producers shared this fear with respect to the German market, but favoured the measures as far as sales to France and Belgium were concerned. The question of the Moselle Canal arose to split attitudes further in this context. Steelmakers, of course, protested violently against the construction of the canal and urged that ECSC remain aloof from the issue, while coal producers were favourably inclined. The fact that decisions running directly counter to steel interests were made in both the railway and Moselle questions did not engender any demonstrable new antagonism to supranationalism.

The issue of investments served at once as a source of lively expectation for benefits not otherwise available and a stimulus for disappointment. Coal producers, using as their argument the antiquated nature of their installations compared to other ECSC countries and the fact that they provided half of the Community's production, demanded the lion's share of the American loan. Four-fifths of the $100,000,000 was mentioned as an appropriate sum, justified thus:

> The true " parity " of which it is spoken in ECSC circles must not be based on specific national desires and aims. It must be based on the interest of European steel production and economy, keeping in mind a careful assessment of the most favourable natural preconditions. These exist exclusively in the Ruhr. Investment in coal and steel here is the proof of the truly European attitude of the ECSC.[15]

While scoring their need for funds, the mine owners were nevertheless reluctant to apply for a share of the loan because they objected to the " dirigistic " elements connected with its administration. Despite all these criticisms, however, they gladly took their share of the funds and admitted that no discrimination was practised in the distribution.[16]

[15] *Schnelldienst des Deutschen Industrieinstituts*, June 16, 1953, p. 4. The demand continued in 1955. See *Informations Mensuelles* (November 1956), p. 76.
[16] Unternehmensverband Ruhrbergbau, *Jahresbericht*, 1953/1954 (Essen, 1955), pp. 34, 37.

In the steel industry, the remarkable increases in production achieved since 1952 have very largely been the result of massive programmes of self-financing. This, however, did not keep the Steel Association from demanding investment aid from ECSC in 1953 and 1954. On the contrary, the priority of investment in coal and ore mining was criticised and a share of the American loan for German steel claimed as essential, while industry spokesmen denied that they possessed sufficient means for self-financing. It was in this context that consistent attacks at the rate of the ECSC production tax were heard, a rate accused of being a disincentive to investment and a great burden for German industry. As self-financing showed striking results by 1955, despite the earlier calls of woe, the Steel Association turned to attack the investment supervision powers of the High Authority. No longer interested in ECSC aid, the producers were concerned with eliminating their duty to report investments to Luxembourg and obtain authorisation for outlays beyond the amounts fixed by the High Authority under the Treaty's Article 54. And in this regard they found a High Authority not disposed to challenge their preferences.[17]

German industrial and financial circles outside coal and steel have been extremely reserved toward the prospects of supranational investments and investment supervision. Disappointed over the " small " share of the American loan given to German coal and coke interests, many businessmen nevertheless welcomed outside aid of any kind for enabling German collieries to bring their equipment up to date, especially in relation to recent French modernisation measures. German bankers were on the whole extremely hostile to the loan, not because they denied the need for investments, but because they resented the High Authority control powers. Hermann J. Abs, head of the Kreditanstalt für Wiederaufbau and executive of several Ruhr collieries, had taken the lead in demanding outside aid for German industries, said to lag behind their French competitors, coupling the call with objections to the rate of the ECSC production tax as making self-financing even more difficult. But he wanted his bank to administer the loan funds, not Luxembourg:

> In the future, national governments or public agencies controlled by them cannot be the centres for making decisions on investments

---

[17] See the figures in Daniel Cois, " La renaissance de la sidérurgie allemande," *L'Economie* (December 15, 1955), pp. 14 *et seq.*

and credit. Nor should these questions be handled by a supra-national authority, which has even less contact with individual firms.[18]

Any notion of competition between High Authority loan operations and the activities of national banking establishments was sharply attacked by Abs and others, who feared the ECSC programme of forcing down Continental interest rates. While the mining enterprises were generally satisfied with ECSC activity in the investment field, neither bankers nor steelmakers look favourably to supra-nationalism in this area.

Clearly, German industrial opinion is far from unanimous on the issue of loyalty or opposition to supranational measures of integration. Even positions within a given trade association vary, according to the issue. However, it is clear that specific grievances are entertained and have not diminished over time, though fears of " discrimination " have tended to disappear and expectations of economic chaos have evaporated. Price, cartel, transport and investment questions continue to arouse critical comment in some German industrial circles, even though open rebellion against supranational control is seldom voiced. When it is heard it is sharply criticised and rebuked by leading industrialists.[19] The key to the evolution is the business attitude to questions of expanding the task of ECSC or of creating new institutions for integration: the common market, integrated fuel policy, the harmonisation of labour and welfare measures and Euratom.

How did the coal and steel industries react to the common market and the need to compete once more? As for the collieries, no hardships of any kind were involved since, with the exception of certain months, there was always more demand for German coal than could be delivered. In the steel sector, the picture was more complex. The common market opened in the spring of 1953

---

[18] Abs, as quoted in *Stahl und Eisen*, May 21, 1953, p. 752.
[19] In this connection, see the frequent statements of principle in favour of ECSC—mingled with specific items of criticism—of former Steel Association heads Karl Barich (*Stahl und Eisen*, May 21, 1953, pp. 747–751) and Gerhard Schröder, as well as the sharp statement of Mannesmann head Wilhelm Zangen to one of his stockholders, reported in *Agence Europe*, July 4, 1956. For a concise summary of industrial viewpoints, see Deutsches Industrieinstitut, *Material zum Zeitgeschehen*, " Zwei Jahre Montan-Union," no. 21, August 16, 1954. The conclusion is revealing: " In general, the High Authority encounters great resistance from governments and interest groups when it seeks to propose coordinating measures in the fields of commercial policy, transport and welfare which go beyond what is foreseen in the Treaty." (p. 13).

amidst German expectations of losses in some sectors and gains in others: the steelmakers seemed content to let the logic of free trade, expanded sales and new patterns of specialisation take its course. By the winter of 1953–1954, however, the general recession in Europe had caught up with the steel trade and cries of anguish against the " disturbing " influence of the common market were heard.   Complaints against the imports of cheaper French steel, resentment against the cutting of prices compelled by these imports, and suggestions for " understandings " with French steel producers were heard more and more.   While individual firms thus clearly objected to the common market and regretted the growing inter-penetration of trade, Steel Association President Gerhard Schröder emphatically restated his faith in the Treaty and welcomed the competition thereby introduced.   In any event, with the onset of boom conditions late in 1954, the estimates once more changed to optimism and approval for market interpenetration.   Stable prices, increased production and easier sales resulted in tributes to the common market—and in demands for extending it.   Only remaining pockets of protectionism, the prevalence of exchange controls and the absence of valid exchange rates were said to prevent real economic integration, the creation of a general free market.   With heavy emphasis on the need for the dominance of private enterprise, the head of the Gutehoffnungshütte noted in 1955:

> German industry has supported the goal of European economic unity.   Unfortunately, our expectations have been disappointed in certain respects and the aims to be realised by ECSC have recently become problematical once more.   We must emphatically warn against the inclusion of new sectors, *e.g.*, fuels, in the jurisdiction of the High Authority.[20]

The common market for coal and steel, clearly, has whetted the German appetite for a General Common Market among those producers who expect to profit therefrom, *provided* that it will be a common market free from supranational controls of the kind opposed in the ECSC framework.   Increasingly, German steelmakers and financiers—as distinct from coal interests—have criticised any kind of directives and control from Luxembourg as " dirigisme " and " falsification of competitive conditions," unless they themselves favoured the controls initially, as in the case of

---

[20] Hermann Reusch, January 11, 1955, as reported in *Stahl und Eisen*, January 27, 1955, p. 121.

scrap. The primacy of private property and free enterprise have been singled out as the precondition under which Germany entered ECSC. Professional competence of industrialists as alone capable of managing the common market has been opposed to the bungling of the " politicians " in Luxembourg. Revision of the Treaty has been demanded to expunge implications of dirigisme from it and such industry leaders as Schröder and Abs haye warned that the common market is not to be considered a German sacrifice for the benefit of the French and Belgians, who alone have profited from the " dirigistic " measures of readaptation, special subsidies, and the " rigid " fair trade price lists. Not supranational direction but a healthy and continuous understanding among industrialists across national frontiers is going to integrate the European economy. And with this judgment, the head of the Bundesverband der Deutschen Industrie, Fritz Berg, has often and vociferously associated himself, in attacking the High Authority for failure to " understand " industry, to " establish confidence in industry." [21]

The coal people, however, have been far less sweeping in their attacks on any semblance of supranational planning. Worried increasingly by rising costs and the competition of fuel oil, natural gas and potentially atomic energy, mine owners seem not at all averse to the kind of supranational direction which will protect their position. Thus, ECSC measures for minimising cyclical fluctuations have been welcomed, as well as suggestions to discriminate against the sale of fuel oil by the imposition of a supranational " compensatory " tax. At the same time, coal producers have praised the various international studies which tend to stress the continued need for coal, while sharply attacking the OEEC report of Louis Armand for suggesting that coal is doomed in the long run and advocating the immediate exhaustion of remaining coal reserves so that atomic energy will have a clear field a generation hence.[22]

This juxtaposition of worries and defences has led to the demand

[21] Fritz Berg's quarrel with the High Authority and his withdrawal from the Consultative Committee as a result are reported in *Agence Europe*, May 19, 1954. Berg is frequently at odds with the Steel Association over this issue since he takes a far more anti-ECSC position than the steelmakers, having led to considerations of withdrawal from the BDI on the part of the Wirtschaftsvereinigung Eisen- und Stahlindustrie.

[22] The international studies in question are: United Nations, Economic Commission for Europe, *Relationship between Coal and Black Oils in the West European Fuel Market* (Geneva, 1954) and Organisation for European Economic Cooperation, *Quelques Aspects du problème Européen de l'Energie* (Paris, June 1955).

for an integrated European "coal-energy policy." The task of such a policy is the reduction of production costs, the stabilisation of prices and markets and the planning of secure new investments in the pits—precluding a régime of free competition. The means for achieving these aims lie in ECSC-wide controls over the ratio of coal–oil consumption and controls over the ratio of imported coal–ECSC coal consumption. If the Treaty withholds the appropriate powers from the High Authority and commands more competition than seems warranted by the needs of the coal industry, the Treaty should be changed or reinterpreted accordingly.[23] Clearly, a commitment to free enterprise and opposition to nationalisation does not preclude a dedication to appropriate supranational " dirigistic " measures protecting the coal producers.

The future of integration, therefore, includes expectations of appropriate " planning " for the coal industry and opposition to such activities, if carried out by supranational public agencies, as far as the bulk of German industry is concerned. In the demand for the harmonisation of labour and welfare policies pro-integration attitudes are put to their most severe test. With great unanimity German industrialists have rejected notions of harmonising living standards by way of High Authority decrees or ECSC-wide collective bargaining. They have gleefully pointed to the ECSC real wage studies as indicating that German wages are not very much below those in comparable French industries, and have therefore objected to the suggestions of Mendès-France and others that a systematic harmonisation of living standards (*i.e.*, wages and social security contributions) must precede further integration. While " in principle " favourable to the forty-hour week in Germany, according to Fritz Berg, German industrialists have warned against the sudden introduction of such measures and prefer " direct talks between representatives of German and French industries " rather than supranational action.[24] And to specific requests for harmonising new sectors, such as labour conditions, German industrialists answer that the introduction of general convertibility and valid exchange rates should take first place, together with the

---

[23] Helmut Burckhardt, " Gründe und Aufgaben einer Kohlenwirtschaftspolitik," *Bergfreiheit* (July 1955). J. Schaefer, " Zum Thema Kohlenpolitik," *Glückauf* (January 1, 1955), pp. 53 *et seq.*

[24] The consistent opposition of German industry generally to extending the task of ECSC, especially in questions of living standards, is reported in *Schnelldienst des Deutschen Industrieinstituts*, February 10, 1955, February 8, 1955 and July 18, 1955. Also BDI, *Jahresbericht, op. cit.*, pp. 56–57.

suppression of subsidies, tariffs and quantitative restrictions. Not even the complaints of manpower shortages in the mines change this picture. The Ruhr collieries have supported Bonn's efforts to increase incentives and productivity through the governmental subsidisation of wages. High Authority directives calling attention to the illegality of the practice have resulted merely in the Ruhr's encouraging the German authorities to hold out against Luxembourg's pressure. The majority of industrial leaders thus clearly oppose the extension of powers of ECSC, while concentrating their efforts on limiting even the exercise of the powers given the High Authority under the Treaty.

Sector integration under supranational auspices enjoying less support in 1956 than in 1951, proposals for Euratom have been greeted with indifference or hostility in German industrial circles. While favouring the international sharing of nuclear information and the establishment of a common market for fissionable materials, German industrialists reject supranational powers of purchasing, selling, importing, leasing and controlling the use of nuclear energy materials. They feel that if left unrestricted they will soon develop an atomic industry of their own, free from possible limitations imposed by a suspicious supranational authority. Conversely, the principle of a General Common Market has a great deal of appeal—if left free from supranational investment, harmonisation and coordination powers, especially with respect to labour costs. As Hermann Abs pointed out in his negative comment on the Messina Conference, German industry wants a general world-wide elimination of all trade barriers, not a vertical integration of the West European economy alone. For this, simple inter-government cooperation on the model of the OEEC suffices and the creation of new " dirigistic " supranational organs can be avoided.[25]

Compared with the attitudes prevalent in 1951, then, enthusiasm for the kind of integration which would conduce to the growth

---

[25] Within the BDI, the French demand for the harmonisation of labour cost factors prior to the inauguration of the General Common Market was greeted with the most lively opposition. On Euratom, the BDI *Jahresbericht* for 1955/1956 remarked:

> It goes without saying that all energy policy must be a liberal policy. International cooperation, especially in the nuclear energy field, cannot result in giving supranational authorities control powers which have fortunately been denied to the State.

Informations Mensuelles, (January 1957), pp. 22–23, 80–81.

of a political community has weakened considerably. The positive expectations entertained with respect to supranational powers and institutions have been realised: German inequalities have been removed, mergers have been left unrestricted, sales have expanded, and investment autonomy is unimpaired. No new demands have developed, so that current orientations toward ECSC hinge around the negative expectation of hindering supranational action. The General Common Market is favoured only on the assumption that it would give rise to no new federal institutions. From the position of the defeated enemy, associated with war guilt, the German industrialist has again emerged as the leader of the European economy, for whom it is no longer necessary to make sentimental political concessions, as in 1951. Hence, lukewarm support for the European idea in its federal form has turned to indifference.[26]

Most significantly, however, those branches of industry, such as coal, which equate supranational action with their own survival differ from this pattern. And, on the basis of demands heard during the recession of 1954, it may well be hazarded that a new crisis will once again lead to expectations of supranational counter-cyclical measures, and thereby build up a demand pattern looking to powerful central institutions for the realisation of immediate aims.

FRENCH INDUSTRY AND EUROPEAN INTEGRATION

To judge by the opinions and demands expressed by significant sectors of French industry during the Schuman Plan ratification and drafting period, there was no likelihood of French industrialists ever turning to the support of any doctrine of integration. Opinion was overwhelmingly critical of sector integration, rule by " technocrats " far removed from the realities of the business world, relaxation of protective measures for French industry and especially the possibility of supranational anti-cartel and general regulatory measures.

On the political level, the French Steel Association—Chambre Syndicale de la Sidérurgie Française—manufactured and disseminated the very arguments which were later used in the National

---

[26] See, for instance, the sentiments of K. P. Harten, president of the Verein Deutscher Eisenhüttenleute, as described in his " Kohle und Eisen unter der Sicht der europäischen Integration," *Glückauf*, March 28, 1953, pp. 330 *et seq.* Also the conclusions of G. Almond, " The Political Attitudes of German Business," *World Politics* (January 1956), pp. 157–186. In general, it is accurate to say that the opinions encountered in the leadership levels of trade associations are much more consistently pro-integration oriented than the more unstructured attitudes encountered among rank-and-file businessmen.

Assembly and the press by rightist opponents of ECSC.[27]   The
Association went so far as to subsidise Communist mass propaganda
against the Treaty, emphasising the decay of French industry,
unemployment and inevitable servitude to Germany.   Among
strictly economic objections to the plan, the steelmakers admitted
their preference for the private cartel-like approach to industrial
integration which their then vice-president, Pierre Ricard, had
proposed at the Westminster Conference of the European Movement
in 1949.   Throughout the pre-ratification debate they complained
about having been ignored and shut out from the negotiations by
Monnet, and that they could not support a long-range plan which
would deny them participation in decision-making.[28]   Sector integration would perpetuate the practices of German discrimination
in the unintegrated but vitally related sectors and also conduce to
the premature exhaustion of Lorraine iron ore deposits.   At the
same time, the higher French social security and indirect tax charges
would make successful competition with Germany an impossibility.
Investment would be necessary, but who would furnish the necessary funds?   A French steel economist answered:

> Can the solution to certain problems be found through the
> good will of the other countries of the Community?   Truly, it is
> difficult to imagine that foreign steel industries and the governments
> which support them will gladly accept the suppression of the real
> advantages they enjoy in international competition, which the
> French Government has been awkward enough to give them without
> insisting on counter-concessions. . . . We must not delude ourselves.
> Let us not expect that foreign countries and competitors will make
> gratuitous gestures of good will.   Each country says it is European,
> but " European sentiment," supposing it exists elsewhere than in
> official utopias, is compelled to make peace with the bitter law of
> economic competition.[29]

[27] See Chap. 4 for the details. See, above all, H. Ehrmann, " The French Trade
Associations and the Ratification of the Schuman Plan," *World Politics* (July
1954), pp. 458–463, pp. 465 *et seq.*

[28] On great sympathy for cartels as an approach to integration, see the frank statement
of Jacques Ferry and René Chatel (both steel executives), *L'Acier* (Paris: Presses
Universitaires de France, 1953), pp. 90, 107, 117.   Position of the French steel
industry toward ratification in Louis Charvet, " La Sidérurgie française devant
le Pool," *Nouvelle Revue de l'Economie Contemporaine, op. cit.,* pp. 42 *et seq.* For
the ore mines (mostly controlled by steel firms), see Louis Lacoste, " Notre Fer en
Peril," *ibid.,* pp. 49 *et seq.*

[29] Jean Chardonnet, *La Sidérurgie française: Progrès ou Décadence?* (Paris: Armand
Colin, 1954), pp. 229–230.

This bitter opposition to integration on the part of steelmakers did not stem only from the fear of being undersold by Germany and directed by supranational technocrats. Opposition was inherent in the conservative and family-dominated nature of the industry. While massive concentrations have reduced the number of firms and obscured family control, few of the mergers are actually complete amalgamations of assets. Instead " groups " of enterprises are formed in which new plants are set up jointly by existing firms, or shares in established properties exchanged.[30] Independence is the watchword of the steelmaker, whether with regard to foreign suppliers or domestic competitors. Symptomatic of this spirit is the plan to produce 14·3 million tons of crude steel by 1957, as demanded both by the producers and the Government, and the scheme to develop sufficient coke-oven capacity in Lorraine by 1960 so as to make the local steel industry largely independent of Ruhr coke purchases. New coking processes developed are to render the Lorraine-Saar coal useable for cokification, with production scheduled to reach 8,200,000 tons per year.[31] Pride in independent family operations and the refusal to alter them, then, is a large factor in resistance to any expanded market doctrine, specifically one which would eliminate cartels as the means to protect families. Integration, finally, would mean giving up the separate national existence of this complex, including its claims in the Saar. Pierre Ricard neatly joined the issue of national French steel power with owners' claims in the Saar at the onset of ECSC operations:

> I ask you to remember three figures: our actual production is a little more [1952] than 11 million tons per year in France, the Saar produces 3 million tons. I stress the three figures: 11, 3, 15·5 [German steel output in 1952]. . . . If the Saar is within the French economic system, that gives us 11 millions plus 3 millions, 14 million tons of steel, or 90 per cent. of 15·5 million, and that is about even. Considering our investment efforts, we are in the position of equal competitive strength. If the Saar is removed from the French system, to join the German side, that would give us 11 millions against 18·5 millions, a little less than 60 per cent. One can fight

---

[30] Fritz Hellwig, " Die Unternehmerorganisation in der westeuropäischen Eisen- und Stahlindustrie," *Stahl und Eisen*, Vol. 71, no. 7, March 29, 1951.

[31] *Etudes et Documents* (May 1953), pp. 24, 31. British Iron and Steel Federation, " Steel Developments in France," *Monthly Statistical Bulletin*, Vol. 30, no. 8, August 1955.

when the chances are even, when strength is approximately equally matched, but nobody can fight when he is about one against two.[32]

Critical voices by far overshadowed pro-integration sentiment in other segments of the business world. The Charbonnages de France, despite their status as a public monopoly subject to Government direction, clearly opposed ratification of the ECSC Treaty. In a reaction hardly differing from that of private managers, the Charbonnages leaders feared the competition of cheaper German and subsidised Belgian coal, and foresaw nothing but disposal problems for their own low-grade production, especially in the Centre-Midi mines. In the steel-consuming industries the picture was more complex. A schism developed in the association of steel processing and engineering industries — Syndicat Général des Industries Mécaniques et Transformatrices des Metaux — with André Métral, the president, strongly opposing ratification and the secretary-general, Jean Constant, favouring it. Each had behind him a segment of the industry. Métral spoke for those who objected to the " technocracy of international super-planners, uncontrolled and eternal," feeling that ECSC implied the death of politically powerful employers' associations.[33] Constant, on the other hand, led those firms who welcomed the common market because it seemed to free them from the price and quality dictation of the steelmakers, thus showing as early as 1951 that " national trade association interests " could be split by the demonstration of economic advantage through supranationalism. Constant, receiving the support of Monnet, succeeded in building up a rival association of steel consumers favourable to ECSC, and ended up by becoming its president.

It was the steelmakers' position, however, which triumphed in the official position of the French Employers' Association, the Conseil National du Patronat Français. Its president, Georges Villiers, as well as its pre-war leader, Gignoux, repeated in essence the Steel Association's arguments, thus creating the impression that French industry in its totality opposed supranational integration and obscuring the voices of dissent within it. Hardly anyone attacked the principle of integration or of a united Europe: the

---

[32] Statement to the French press July 4, 1952, quoted in Rieben, *op. cit.*, p. 383.
[33] A. Métral, " Le Plan Schuman constitue un Saut dans l'Inconnu," *Nouvelle Revue de l'Economie Contemporaine, op. cit.*, p. 39.

charges concentrated on the powerful High Authority, on the over-ambitious institutional structure, on the absence of trade association representation in top echelons, and especially on the anti-cartel powers of ECSC, as going far beyond powers possessed by national governments.   As Giscard d'Estaing, an "internationalist" industrialist, noted:

> Just because we are profoundly attached to the unification of Europe we do not want to see it serve the pretext of doing at the European level what nobody dares do at the national level.[34]

The French Economic Council, on November 30, 1951, passed a resolution favouring ratification by a vote of 111 to 15, with 29 abstentions.   The negative votes came from the Communist-dominated trade unions, while the abstainers included all indus-trialists associated with the CNPF, the middle class organisation, and the Charbonnages de France.   In order not to be confused with the Communists, these opponents of ECSC preferred to abstain.

Once the Treaty was ratified, despite all these efforts, a new attitude was almost immediately adopted—at least outwardly—by the trade associations.   Villiers told the CNPF General Con-ference that a supranational Europe was a reality and that industry should concentrate its efforts on making it a free enterprise Europe, by organising supranationally.   Steelmakers conceded that, with energy, they might be able to compete with German imports after all and they demanded elimination of French Government price ceilings with the inauguration of the common market.   Pierre Ricard, advanced to the presidency of the Steel Association after the success of ECSC in the National Assembly, congratulated himself on the appointment of steelmaker Léon Daum to the High Authority and free enterprise-minded economist Jacques Rueff to the Court of Justice.   " I may say that the High Authority . . . can really count on the loyal cooperation of the French steel industry.   I ask you to consider as an act of faith in the permanence of the Community the important step we took recently . . . the radical reform of the Comptoir Sidérurgique [the former steel sales cartel].[35]   Naturally, M. Ricard coupled these declarations

[34] E. Giscard d'Estaing, *La France et l'Unification Economique de l'Europe* (Paris: Editions Genin, 1953), p. 187.

[35] Announcement to the press, December 10, 1952. *Bulletin du Conseil National du Patronat Français* (hereafter cited as CNPF Bulletin), January 5, 1953, p. 15.

of resignation to ECSC with redoubled demands for the immediate canalisation of the Moselle, more investment aid and relief from French taxation. These claims were to form the substance of French industrial activity at the national level for years to come.

At the onset of the common market, it seems safe to conclude, negative expectations among French industrialists outweighed positive ones. While anxious to obtain reduced transportation costs and an " equalisation " of social security contributions by way of ECSC, their primary preoccupation was the limitation of the common market principle so as to have as little interference as possible with their past production and sales practices. In view of this concern, the evolution of industrial attitudes with respect to market interpenetration, prices and sales practices under ECSC rules provides an interesting index.

Among steelmakers the inflow of foreign steel was greeted with cries of anguish and dismay. While welcoming the pro-French decision of the High Authority in the controversy with Germany over the sales taxes, Pierre Ricard in May of 1953 foresaw stiff competition from Belgian and German steel imports on the hitherto protected French market. But Ricard also expected greater French sales on the southern German market and reaffirmed the steelmakers' will to adhere to the spirit of the Treaty. With the onset of the 1953–1954 recession, this willingness seemed to undergo some subtle changes. Sharp attacks were directed against the High Authority for having opposed the Brussels Export Entente and a suit in the Court threatened in case of Luxembourg's formal dis-approval. Vigorous protests were heard against the importation of Belgian steel, especially from steel firms near the Belgian frontier. The system of price lists, initially opposed by French industrialists, was suddenly found to possess the virtue of stabilising prices and preventing competitive price cutting. When, therefore, the High Authority permitted the 2·5 per cent. departure from list prices, in response to consumer pressure, the French Steel Association was among the most important groups to challenge this decision as permitting " discrimination."

If in the matter of steel prices the industry turned toward the ECSC Treaty for protection against competition, and thus made it fulfil some of the functions of a cartel, such positive expectations were much slower in developing in the field of scrap. French steelmakers at first preferred a purely national arrangement, under which French industrialists would not be compelled to contribute to the ECSC-wide compensation fund, from which they derived no advantage. The logic of the common market, in short, was resisted and denied. Only in 1955 were demands for the firm central allocation of scrap heard, with the request that the High Authority declare a state of shortage. And so it went with the common market for special steels, whose establishment was successfully postponed—though not prevented—by the concerted hue and cry of French manufacturers, alleging higher costs and inability to compete. Objections were still heard a year later, but as 1955 drew to a close, it was generally admitted that catastrophe had failed to overtake this sector.

On balance, the French steelmakers are restive toward the interpenetration of markets and by no means reconciled to economic integration by way of intensified sales competition. Complaining especially of the " difficult " position of the steelmakers in the North of France, special tax and tariff concessions are demanded of the French Government to enable this sector to survive in the ECSC common market. And as one spokesman for the region put it, in the context of the General Common Market plan:

> ... Nothing has been done to counter the disparities which the Schuman Plan compels the steel industry of France to endure, and especially that of the North, for the benefit of foreign competitors to whom our frontiers have been thrown open without precaution. Those who have thrown us into the ECSC adventure, while deliberately neglecting French interests to obtain the signatures of our partners, have taken on a crushing responsibility.[36]

The opposite picture obtains in the ranks of steel consumers in France. Even the initially hostile association of steel consuming industries headed by André Métral, while continuing to protest against " supranational technocratic dirigisme," turned to lobbying and arguing in Luxembourg in order to compel French steelmakers to lower their prices and to encourage the importation of more German steel into France. It was Métral's organisation which led the battle for the Monnet Rebate, though it was highly dissatisfied with the solution adopted in Luxembourg and disappointed with the Court's decision. It demonstrated, however, that doctrinal

---

[36] Statement of René Damien, of USINOR, in *Agence Economique et Financière*, January 17, 1956. See also Joseph de Beco in *Usine Nouvelle*, November 18, 1954, p. 2.

opposition does not suffice to prevent the development of supranational expectations when it is a question of cheaper prices.[37]

Much the same is true of Jean Constant's Association des Utilisateurs de Produits Sidérurgiques, composed mostly of small enterprises initially attracted to ECSC because of the promise of active price competition and freedom from cartel rule. Constant has argued from 1953 until the summer of 1956 that the High Authority should take the responsibility for encouraging and enforcing the lowest possible steel prices, even though this may indeed imply " supranational dirigisme." In particular, Constant demanded more stringent anti-cartel action in the steel sector than the High Authority has been prepared to undertake. For this group, nevertheless, the common market has been a success and its continuation a positive expectation:

> All the French consumers rejoice over the common market and it has benefited the French economy greatly. Of course, we do not yet see the bulldozers taking on the canalisation of the Moselle and the railway rates are still somewhat discriminatory. We must direct our efforts to these concrete tasks and have them take the place of words. However, our national steel industry has made more progress in the last twenty months than in the forty years preceding. Some more remains to be made and it will be made much more spontaneously if we do not permit it to fall back once more into the anaesthesia of cartelisation.[38]

Among the economists and the managers of the Charbonnages de France, scarcely any evidence of a change of heart over 1951 can be discovered. Since the opening of the common market for coal, the complaint against increased German and Belgian competition, artificially low prices, unjustly high production costs has been the same. The staid *Annales des Mines* blamed the common market for unsaleable stocks in 1954. The ECSC subsidy to Belgium is considered discriminatory if it permits Belgian coal to undersell French production in the Nord/Pas-de-Calais region. Ruhr price ceilings, and before 1954 the ceilings applicable in France, are said to keep all ECSC coal prices too low and " rigid," while according to the Blanzy Basin collieries:

[37] A. R. Métral, " Les espoirs et les angoisses engendrés par le Traité de la Communauté du Charbon et de l'Acier," *Bulletin de la Société Belge d'Etudes et d'Expansion*, May–June–July 1954, pp. 638 *et seq.*

[38] Jean Constant, " Ce que demande le consommateur," *Hommes et Commerce* (January–February 1955), p. 78. See the similar statement in *ECSC Bulletin* (January 1956).

> This organisation [ECSC] has not brought us any advantage
> equal to the payment of 90 million [French francs, production tax]
> which we had to give it in 1954. A reduction of these payments
> seems very desirable to us.[39]

To the extent that market interpenetration is said to have resulted
in unemployment and disposal problems, the common market is
attacked without mercy; but to the extent that the anti-subsidy
rules of the Treaty will militate against the importation of German
coke and coking coal, the common market is welcomed. As will
be shown below, the Charbonnages de France express their
opposition to the common market in ways designed to lead to
more integration, rather than to a return to a completely protected
national economy. In the meantime, however, politically sensitive
groups have rallied to the negative position of the Charbonnages
if they fear the closing of mines and the lay-off of workers.

The anti-cartel rules of the Treaty had been uniformly opposed
in French industrial circles, with the exception of the small steel
consumers. Five years of common market have done little to
change this distribution of attitudes. Formally, the practice of
joint sales by the steelmakers and ore mines has been discontinued,
though the institutions earlier created for this effort have merely
been redesigned as " statistical " centres. Yet, the insistence of
steelmakers on the non-discrimination rules of Article 60, especially
during the Monnet Rebate crisis, indicates that French industry
prefers to rely on this new legal device to minimise price competition perhaps because the formal use of cartels is no longer easy.
As far as coal is concerned, no French industrial group has attached
much importance to the ECSC reorganisation of German and
Belgian sales organisations. The Charbonnages de France, as a
member of OKU and as the *de facto* national coal sales cartel of
France, has opposed anti-cartel measures as stringently as any
private producer, especially since it practises inter-basin compensation of gains and losses through fixed prices, much as did
GEORG in the Ruhr. Hence, all industrial groups have defended
the semi-public ATIC coal import monopoly. Much as in Germany,
most of the groups see in ATIC a means to protect industrial coal
consumers, wholesale dealers and mines which would have to close

[39] *Informations Mensuelles*, January 1956, p. 67. *Annales des Mines*, numéro spécial
1954, *op. cit.*, p. 28. Charbonnages de France, *Rapport de Gestion pour l'Exercise*
1954, p. 32.

if fully exposed to foreign competition. It is only natural, therefore, that the organisation of retail coal dealers should be the only
interest group to attack ATIC and to rally in support of stringent
ECSC anti-cartel measures.[40]

Nor has supranationalism gained many friends in French
industrial circles as a result of activity in the field of mergers. Like
their German colleagues, French industrialists—consumer and
producer alike—have attacked the High Authority's rules as too
stringent and dirigistic. At the same time it is urged most illogically
that the Luxembourg officials are not sufficiently alive to the spirit
of the Treaty in permitting the massive German reconcentration
process. What is wanted, in short, is freedom for French firms
to merge as they please coupled with careful supervision over the
parallel German process.[41]

In contrast to these negative expectations with respect to the
desirability of an integrated community, the French steel industry
entertains the strongest possible hopes in the area of transportation.
The hope for cheaper German coal and reduced freight costs on the
southern German market was crucial in obtaining some industrial
acquiescence—if not support—for ECSC in 1952, especially when
coupled with the demand for the Moselle Canal. Steel Association
leaders have kept up an unbroken stream of demands and threats
in this realm. First and foremost, they concentrated their attack
on the harmonisation of railway rates and the abolition of the
rupture de charge. Satisfied in their demands with the introduction
of ECSC-wide tapered through-rates in 1956, the problem of the
Moselle Canal received attention. Arguing that France had ratified
the Treaty only on condition that the canal be built immediately,
Pierre Ricard as well as André Métral constantly urged their own
government to press for its construction; and failing German and
Luxembourg agreement, they demanded of the High Authority

---

[40] Mendershausen (*op. cit.*, p. 277) strongly suspects collusion nationally and supranationally in the deposition of largely identical price schedules in Luxembourg,
permitted by the " price alignment " rule of Article 60. In interviews, spokesmen
for ATIC confirmed that their reasoning was hardly " European " but that the
issues and consequences were much too delicate to permit a sentimental approach.

[41] See " Déconcentration et reconcentration de la sidérurgie allemande," *Perspectives* (December 14, 1955). *Agence Europe*, May 24, 1954. Métral, *Bulletin, op.
cit.*, p. 639. Interviews confirm the impression that French steelmakers would
love to have the High Authority apply Law 27 rigorously to German industry,
on political as well as economic grounds, and fear deeply falling under the politico-
industrial hegemony of Germany. For convictions that German industry has
merely used ECSC as a device to regain autonomy, without in the least " merging "
with Western Europe, see *Usine Nouvelle*, January 5, 1956, p. 13.

that it take the plan in hand.   Success came only with the con-current negotiations over the future of the Saar, after the victory of the pro-German parties in the plebiscite of 1955, and only after Ricard had threatened his industry's boycott of ECSC if the High Authority persisted in its refusal to enter the controversy.   With the Moselle issue out of the way, the only remaining major transport expectation of French steel producers and consumers is the reduction and non-discriminatory regulation of rates on inland waterways, which ECSC has so far failed to achieve.

The Charbonnages de France has reasoned otherwise.   Strongly opposed to the tapered through-rate system, its spokesmen have blamed ECSC transport policy for unemployment in the mines and have demanded—and received—exemptions from the obli-gation to pay the new uniform freight rates in some localities. More importantly, the discrimination against Belgian barge-carried coal on French canals was introduced at the demand of the Charbonnages.   For the same reason the nationalised coal industry has—unsuccessfully—fought the initiation of the Moselle Canal project, even though it agrees with the steel people on the desir-ability of improving and cheapening inland waterways.   Demands for transport integration by steel, however, have led to bitter counter-attacks of a coalition of groups, including the French Rhine shippers, the French National Railways, and the Chambers of Commerce of ports expecting to lose shipping as a result.   These groups, apart from invoking the inevitable charge of supranational dirigisme, have preferred purely national measures of cheapening costs, improving facilities and—on the Rhine—stabilising rates through a new cartel.   They have succeeded in persuading the Conseil National du Patronat Français to go on record against extending the High Authority's jurisdiction to transport questions generally and argued for a purely inter-governmental approach to these problems, on the basis of participation by all European countries.   On this, as on other issues, the immediate economic benefits and drawbacks of the integration measure under con-sideration determine positive and negative expectations.   While steel interests are here " pro-European," other French business circles clearly are not.   And with the fulfilment of its aims in this area, no net gain for future general measures of integration among French steelmakers can be expected, while the voices of opposition are unmistakably plain.

What does French industry expect of supranationalism in the investment realm? Steel spokesmen have, ever since the recession of 1953-1954, talked of the need to " co-ordinate " investments on an ECSC-wide basis. They have not, however, meant by this the rigorous central planning of investments on the basis of Article 54. " Co-ordination " has meant simply the sharing of information, through the High Authority, on what new installations are planned so that firms acting individually may avoid duplication and overlapping. Only to the extent that French steelmakers object to the construction of competing continuous strip mills in the Ruhr do they invoke the latent power of the High Authority to forbid certain investments. As for High Authority financing, no strident claims for funds have been made and the rate of the production tax was uniformly denounced. Investment co-operation is strongly advocated on a private inter-industry basis: Pierre Ricard and André Métral have spoken of the need for joint German-French investment in the ore deposits of North Africa and other gigantic means for joint economic development abroad, as well as friendly specialisation agreements between Lorraine and Ruhr for the ECSC market.

As for the Charbonnages de France, they wish above all to retain their *de facto* " special position " in the ECSC investment picture. Supported by a gigantic investment and modernisation effort, largely financed from government subsidies since 1946, the collieries wish to continue this effort without High Authority interference.[42] Despite the fact that some of the funds used are probably a subsidy subject to Luxembourg's special authorisation, the approval has always been given automatically, thus confirming the extra-Treaty position of the Charbonnages.

While immediate negative expectations dominate the thinking of French industry in the field of investments, an immediate positive aim characterises one of their crucial price demands: the abolition of French ceiling prices for processed steel and steel products. While crude and semi-finished steel is subject only to Luxembourg's rules, the other products remain part of the French price control system, thus cutting into the profit margin of steelmakers. Much " European " sentiment has therefore been expressed on this score

[42] The statistics and surrounding circumstances are given in Charbonnages de France, *op. cit.* Only about 25 per cent. of the funds invested clearly came from the collieries' own savings. The rest came from subsidies and loans.

by the Steel Association as well as Métral's Steel Consuming Group. Ricard, finding his lobbying activities in Paris unavailing, has on several occasions asked the High Authority to intercede on behalf of French steel industry against his own government. Under the heading " Doesn't the Government know the ECSC exists? " one French steel journal said:

> These rules have the effect of creating unacceptable discrimination between French and foreign steel, preventing French steelmakers, unlike their competitors, from having a price policy dictated by the logic of the common market.[43]

Attachment to independence and reluctance about the common market is not carried to the extreme of neglecting the supranational levers of ECSC to gain an advantage *vis-à-vis* the national government. And to this extent the French steel industry in 1956 certainly is not as exclusivist minded as its stand toward Treaty ratification seemed to imply.

None of these demands, however, indicates any *permanent* growth of loyalty to supranational institutions and rules. Some of them reflect disloyalty and others are short-range in nature and therefore neutral with respect to the creation of abiding sentiments. The question of an ECSC-wide labour and welfare policy provides an entirely different kind of aspiration: the permanent levelling-up of wage and social security standards through continuous supranational action. In this context nothing is heard of technocracy, dirigisme and the evils of sector integration. The conviction that lower German, Dutch and Italian taxes and social charges weighing on industry make possible the successful competition of these ECSC partners with " heavily burdened " French industry has persuaded industrialists—as well as their parliamentary spokesmen in the Independent group—that supranationalism should be given the task of " equalising " these charges. Their efforts at obtaining the extension of ECSC powers in this realm is their notable step towards *more*, rather than less, integration.

No group has been more bitter on this issue than the Charbonnages de France, which blames its domestic problems not only on unwanted imports of coal but also on the high wage and social security payments imposed on it by Parliament:

---

[43] *Actualités Industrielles Lorraines* (July/August 1955), p. 7. The same is true of the Charbonnages de France in objecting to Paris pressure on coal prices. *Informations Mensuelles*, November 1956, pp. 85 *et seq.*

While the other ECSC countries have had scarcely any unemployment, France possessed this regrettable privilege. Why this situation, so disturbing for various reasons? An analysis of the reasons makes clear that the situation can be considerably improved. It is not due to a given unfavourable technical picture in France. Thanks to modernisation and to the work of its personnel, the French mines take first place among European pits as regards productivity. This slowness in the upswing [from the slump of 1953–1954] is explained by the existence of handicaps which we have many times denounced and whose removal would suffice to establish a just equilibrium. . . . It is indispensable that a long-term energy policy be worked out, meeting two problems: co-ordination of energy sources, capable of preserving balance and security in our economy; constant research aiming at a reduction of fuel prices, not only by increases in productivity but also *through a better distribution of social and financial charges which now burden the producing enterprises.*[44]

Favourable in principle to the statistical studies of real wages and income undertaken by High Authority, the collieries as well as the steelmakers have been quick to criticise the validity and accuracy of the findings when these seemed to weaken the claim for equalisation of charges. In fact, the widest variety of statistics are flourished in the debate, all designed to prove the French handicap, but none reliable if judged by the limited comparable international figures available.[45] Thus, French industrial groups are solidly

---

[44] Charbonnages de France, *op. cit.*, pp. 7–8. Italics mine. *Ibid.*, p. 65 with figures to prove the French mine burden. P. Gardent, " Harmonisation des charges salariales et élévation des niveaux de vie des ouvriers de la C. E. C. A.," *Bulletin du Centre International d'Informations* (December 5, 1955).

[45] This, perhaps, explains the opposition—as " technocratic "—to further statistical studies by the High Authority of the Conseil National du Patronat Francais, even though this group supports the harmonisation effort. See *CNPF Bulletin* (June 1955), pp. 46 et seq. *Usine Nouvelle*, July 1, 1955, p. 11, for the harmonisation demands of E. de Mitry (de Wendel group): *Usine Nouvelle*, in protesting against the High Authority's real wage studies, gives these " true " figures:

Total average manpower costs per hour, French francs

		High Authority	Usine Nouvelle
coal	France	347	347
	Germany	311·40	290
steel	France	262	326
	Germany	284	284

Informations Mensuelles, August 1956, pp. 15–16. According to French claims, the higher French costs are due to the "social charges " the employer is compelled to pay either by law or his contract with the union. These charges include: social security, family allowances, paid vacations, apprentice tax, industrial accident insurance, recreation tax, bonuses, vocational training, rent assistance tax, " miscellaneous." Source: Rapport Nathan in *Etudes et Conjoncture*, 1954, p. 768.

behind this effort at task expansion for ECSC, though by no means in favour of ECSC-wide collective bargaining.

Task expansion and positive expectations towards supranationalism are evident also in the demands for an integrated European fuel policy, as urged by French as well as German collieries. Afraid of the same long-term adverse developmental steps in the coal sector as the Germans, the Charbonnages de France have urged discriminatory restrictions on coal imports from third countries and systematic measures to limit the consumption of fuel oil. Successful in these demands in France, they have turned to the whole common market for the achievement of the same aims. Unlike the steel industry, the Charbonnages deny the existence of a coal shortage and oppose High Authority rationing. Pierre Ricard and M. Thedrel for the Saar steelmakers, by contrast, have urged the stepping up of imports from third countries and demanded High Authority allocation of priorities to satisfy the coke needs of the steel industry, in the face of the " unofficial " European coal shortage existing since 1955. Fuel worries, in both cases, have led to lively expectations of basic supranational action though the conditions are mutually exclusive in their implications, despite the fact that spokesmen of the same nation are formulating the demands.

In view of these conflicting aspirations—not only among groups but within the same group, as regards different issues—can French industry really be considered opposed to " supranational dirigisme " in terms of the protests voiced consistently in 1951 and intermittently in the years following? The record would seem to indicate that dirigisme—national or otherwise—is opposed when the interests of a given industry are affected adversely and favoured when benefits are expected from it. Not principle but expediency determines industrial positions. Thus, in addition to the instances explored above, French industry continues to denounce supranational direction if the activities of a cartel are preferred in a specific situation. Ricard's bitter and highly personal campaign against the continuation in office of Jean Monnet was due to the latter's continued efforts on behalf of EDC. And this supranational venture was opposed because it would have put the French armaments and military supplies industries under further " dirigistic " controls. But in making his political anti-integration points, Ricard far overstated his own negative assessment of ECSC, in which—

as we saw—French steel found a number of advantages after 1952.
To round out the picture it must be stated that "dirigisme" was
no obstacle to demands for new supranational action, not only
in the case of fuel oil and social security burdens, but in urging
common measures against the importation of coal and steel from
third countries or in bringing additional industries under ECSC
control when this was thought to stimulate sales. French industry,
in short, has no hesitation to denounce supranational Government
—when appropriate—or to press for its expansion—when appropriate. And does its attitude toward supranationalism differ from
its conduct with respect to its national government?

Has there been an evolution of French industrial attitudes for
or against integration? Opinion surveys suggest that, at least,
opinion is by no means clearly negative. Asked "which of these
changes will come about as a result of ECSC?" industrialists
answered as follows:

ECSC:	yes	no	don't know
Will make for higher living standards for all Europe	44	25	30
Will make for unemployment	27	55	17
Will reduce risk of European wars	64	18	17
Will make for more independence against the U.S.	58	24	17
Will facilitate the rapid recovery of Germany	41	37	21
Is the first step towards United States of Europe	84	7	8
Means more American control over Europe	20	61	18
Means the loss of French independence	28	52	19

80 per cent. of the industrialists wished ECSC success.[46] In view
of the fuel situation in France, Euratom is generally favoured since
it is hoped that export prices can be reduced with lower fuel costs.
The definitely "dirigistic" elements of the scheme did not
cause the same sort of difficulty in 1956 as corresponding portions
of ECSC created in 1951—indicating a slight change in attitude
on this score.

As far as the General Common Market is concerned, the coal
and steel industries are far from hostile toward it. The bulk of
French industry, however, is as opposed to this integrative step
as coal and steel were to ECSC in 1951. Freedom of competition

[46] *Sondages:* "La Communauté Européenne du Charbon et de l'Acier," Vol. 17,
no. 2 (1955), pp. 45–47.

is feared because of higher French export prices, held to be due to higher wages and social charges. While some economists have pointed to the success of the common market for coal and steel in having kept French prices stable, rationalised production and expanded sales, spokesmen for trade associations prefer to foretell chaos and suffering if France is compelled to eliminate her tariffs without having first obtained the equalisation of taxes and social charges. Demanding a basic forty-hour week and equal pay for men and women (both standard in France) as a pre-condition for the General Common Market, *Usine Nouvelle* declared:

> Before undertaking the next step, we must first make sure that all the partners begin from the same starting position, which is far from being the case. Otherwise, we risk the impairment of the vitality of the [socially] most advanced countries.[47]

The principle of economic integration was, of course, never attacked head-on in the debate over EEC and Euratom. The Economic Council during 1956 confined itself to stressing the need for safeguarding clauses, exceptions to the common market rules in favour of France, preservation of the *status quo* as concerns the subsidisation of agriculture. It insisted that EEC contribute to steady economic growth, but on condition that regional economic concentrations be reduced and that the massive readaptation of industries crucial to a specific locality be avoided. While the French overseas territories were to be included in EEC, the Economic Council also wants to have the best of both possible worlds by retaining the unilateral right for France to maintain economic ties with the franc zone countries. As for the CNPF, it came out in favour of Euratom but attached such far-reaching restrictions to its endorsement as to make that agency little more than an international research centre. Employer approval of EEC was confined to vague generalities: in the crucial and concrete details, the CNPF stressed only the need for safeguarding clauses, exceptions for France and the " duty " of the other members to contribute to the economic development of the French colonies while being deprived of any kind of political control over the areas concerned. The Chambers of Commerce stressed the prior harmonisation of labour costs, the machine-building industry

---

[47] July 28, 1955. For leading steelmakers' opinions in favour of the General Common Market, see Ferry and Chatel, *op. cit.*, p. 131. Métral in *Journal de Genève*, January 1, 1955. Also Jacques Tessier in *Informations Mensuelles*, June–July 1956, p. 42.

urged its members to prepare for the common market by establishing contacts with foreign firms, while the builders of public works inveighed against the investment powers of EEC and reaffirmed their desire to deal only with national governments. In view of these hostile judgments and negative expectations among industrialists, it is interesting to note that three different associations of agricultural interests came out in favour of EEC on the assumption that an integrated policy of protection and subsidisation would maintain their prices intact while reducing the cost of manufactured goods.[48]

French arguments about the " greatest sacrifice " and the " greatest danger " in 1957 are strangely reminiscent of identical German arguments in 1951. Yet, experience with the common market for coal and steel has demonstrated that predictions of catastrophe may be mistaken, if not hypocritical. The compromise on the question of social charges will induce French industry to accept the common market as it accepted ECSC. In the process, however, it will demand that Germany grant equalisation of taxes and employers' contributions as proof of its " faith in Europe," much as it clamoured for the Moselle Canal on identical grounds, until success rendered the argument pointless. A tactical conversion to " Europe " there has been, even if no major ideological change has occurred. Expediential considerations, especially since they have already split French business into a heterogeneous congeries of opposing groups on the issue of integration, may well suffice to make EEC acceptable to industrialists. If this occurs, the " spill over " effect of the common market for coal and steel will have had the result of bringing about crucial and permanent realignments among the industrial elite.

BELGIAN INDUSTRY AND EUROPEAN INTEGRATION

The proposals of Robert Schuman were greeted by the arch-Conservative foreign minister Paul van Zeeland as a " leap into the unknown." Belgian industrialists reacted strictly in accordance with the perception of economic interest typical of each sector: steel consumers welcomed the idea, steel producers were reserved but not opposed, while coal producers were adamantly hostile. What were the reasons for these positions?

---

[48] See *Informations Mensuelles*, September–October 1956, p. 43; January 1957, pp. 25–31, 33–35, 36–38, 61–64.

" The Schuman Plan is an attempt for Belgium to solve at the international level the difficulties which we have failed to solve nationally," declared the Association of Steel Consuming Industries.[49] Blaming the government and the decadent coal industry for artificially high fuel prices and collective subsidisation of the collieries, the steel consumers welcomed with great relief the expected era of competition on the coal market. Far from fearing High Authority dictation, new investment funds, free access to raw materials, expanded sales outlets—apart from cheaper coal— were all confidently expected through ECSC. In castigating the Federation of Industries for attacking ECSC, the steel consumers found that " the projected Community is a life-saver for us."

Fears of central direction and under-representation of industrial interests were expressed at length by the Steel Association, through its influential head, Pierre Van der Rest. If free competition is to be the principle of ECSC, the plan would be welcomed by Belgian steelmakers; but the expectation was one of continuous High Authority interference in private decisions, made worse by anticipated " meddling " of consumers and workers representatives. And perhaps the largest reservation was expressed with respect to wage and labour conditions: ECSC should have been given larger powers to compel the " equalisation " of these components of the cost production, thus protecting the high-cost Belgian export industries.[50] As long as ECSC contained these shortcomings, " Belgian steelmakers can neither approve nor reject this great experiment."

Mine owners faced no such difficulty. They rejected ECSC in the strongest possible terms. Accustomed to government subsidies for a generation and not compelled to compete, the collieries were convinced that their high wage and extraction costs would destine them to ruin and shut-downs, despite the special compensation payments and the readaptation system provided for the transitional period. Prices would be fixed by Luxembourg (instead of Brussels), thus imposing an unprecedented measure of dictation, with the result that German coal would surely carry the day. " In submitting to this apparatus, Belgium will forever give up all the virtues which hitherto have made it great and prosperous: courage

[49] Paul Romus, " Les Industries Transformatrices Belges et le Plan Schuman," *Etudes Economiques*, no. 81–82, November 1951, pp. 109 and 110–129.
[50] Pierre Van der Rest, " L'Incidence du Plan Schuman sur l'Industrie Sidérurgique Belge," *ibid.*, pp. 94–104.

and the spirit of initiative of its industries, the extraordinary flexibility of its economy." [51] Unemployment was, of course, predicted, as well as the influx of hordes of foreign miners. " Shall we compromise the flower of our prosperity for some billions in Community aid? " asked another mine owner. The collieries, in short preferred their national dirigisme, which assured their survival, to the supranational system into which they were being forced, over whose workings they would have less control and whose doctrine of free competition they distrusted.

Spokesmen for the Federation of Belgian Industries officially went along with these condemnations, but certain member industries—such as the steel processors and the chemical sector—strongly dissented from this position in favouring ratification. [52] The Flemish section of the country tended to distrust ECSC while the Walloon section extravagantly favoured the plan because it was thought to reinforce ties with France, with the Walloon Economic Council voting in favour, and the Central (mixed) Economic Council unable to make a decision. As in parliamentary circles, then, wide divergences and rival assessments prevailed among industrialists.

Despite a large number of specific criticisms of supranational policy, the Belgian steel industry has overcome its initial ambivalence and is now firmly in favour of more economic integration, having been persuaded to this position through its experience with five years of common market for coal and steel. One company report found that " we are hopeful that despite many problems which remain to be solved, the enlargement of the domestic market represents great progress." Uniformly satisfactory comments are made about market interpenetration and the development of ECSC-wide sales while greater ease in obtaining French ore and scrap are gratefully noted. Annoyed with Luxembourg during 1954 over the price list system and the attendant " rigidities " and outraged over the Court decision outlawing the Monnet Rebate, the 1954 report of John Cockerill still noted that " in all fairness, the Community must be credited with stabilising prices."

The Steel Association criticises Luxembourg " dirigisme " with respect to investments, cartels, mergers and coal prices. The

[51] Pierre Delville, " L'Industrie Charbonnière devant le Plan Schuman," *ibid.*, pp. 75–83. G. Delarge, " Le Plan Schuman et l'Industrie Houillière du Borinage," *ibid.*, pp. 86–91.
[52] Max Meeus, " Le Plan Schuman," *ibid.*, p. 135.

American loan was considered too small and too onerous in terms of transfer burdens and no new supranational funds are wanted in Belgium. The coordination of investments is " dirigistic," unnecessary and undesired in Belgian steel circles and the High Authority is praised for not pushing the implementation of Article 54 farther than it has. Cartels—including GEORG—are considered necessary and ECSC interference with them unrealistic and to be opposed. As for mergers, the steel people oppose all High Authority examination of requests—except for Germans—and argue that mergers should be encouraged on principle. Annoyance was especially vociferous over the delay encountered in the approval of the merger in 1955 of the two biggest steelmakers, Ougrée-Marihaye and John Cockerill. Finally, steel expected a drastic reduction of coal prices under ECSC and has criticised the administration of the Belgian compensation system for having failed to achieve this.

More significant than these expressions of opposition to supranationalism are the arguments for more ECSC-wide policy. These have been featured in the realm of labour policy and the extension of the common market to new sectors. Confronted in its labour relations with strong demand for the forty-five-hour week without loss of pay, the Steel Association was compelled to yield in fall of 1955—and promptly sought to pass on the increased cost to its ECSC competitors, in seeking to standardise the forty-five-hour week and thus raise costs in Germany and Holland. Despite steel opposition to the welfare programme of the High Authority and ECSC-wide collective bargaining as advocated by labour and the distinct fear of increasing the role of trade unions by way of a supranational emphasis, the Steel Association has been constrained to seek its immediate commercial advantage through ECSC task expansion. Van der Rest, further, has since 1955 argued for the extension of the common market to certain finished steel products as well as to the production of electric energy. His reasoning is clear:

> There is danger in placing the production and the consumption of the same commodity under two different systems. This can only lead to conflict and disequilibrium, *i.e.*, to crises of overproduction or to bottlenecks. This is one reason leading the industrialists of the Community to thinking that one of the principal problems to be

solved is the creation of a common European market, progressively including all economic sectors.[53]

But while the general common market is being created, the immediate extension of ECSC's common market is also demanded in the effort to enlarge the circle of steel consumers and submit them to the same rules applying to the producers.

It follows, of course, that the Steel Association favours the General Common Market without reservation—provided " dirigisme " is kept to a minimum. Yet the existence of outstanding adjustment problems is also granted and, hence, the need for a supranational institution to deal with them is posited as well—in contrast to industrialists elsewhere. Less enthusiasm is manifest for Euratom and for an ECSC-wide investment fund. But the needs of assuring uniform treatment for consumers and producers alike has led the Association to a supranational position in excess of its stand in 1951, despite continued objections to central direction.

If the Steel Association's development followed from its initial ambivalence, evolution of thought in the Fédération Charbonnière de Belgique (Fédéchar) marks a complete reversal. From die-hard opposition to supranationalism, the coal association developed into a warm advocacy of ECSC and further integration. The common market resulted in greatly increased sales abroad, coupled with price stability generally and slowly rising prices in the Ruhr—ardently desired by Belgian collieries. The special compensation payments enabled Belgian coal to compete and modernise, resulting in reductions of the difference in production costs between the Ruhr and Belgium. Per ton of coal this difference had been 250 Belgian francs in 1950, as compared to 85 francs in 1955. While thirty-six pits were closed, productivity increased by 37·5 per cent.[54] Fédéchar no longer complains of discrimination by Luxembourg but praises the High Authority for its impartiality and judiciousness, while defending the need for supranational institutions with real powers to achieve and maintain a large competitive market, clearly preferring this road to integration over mere inter-governmental cooperation. And when presented with opportunities to blame ECSC for Belgian coal problems, Fédéchar has resisted the temptation and attacked general economic conditions or the

[53] P. Van der Rest, " L'Industrie Sidérurgique Belge et le Marché Commun," *Nouvelles de l'Europe* (April–May 1956), p. 21.
[54] M. Dessart in *La Libre Belgique*, December 11, 1955.

Belgian Government instead.[55] The reasons for this turn-about are largely political. Fédéchar sees in supranationalism an anti-dote to continued direction, if not dictation, by a national government more sympathetic to consuming interests than to the sick coal industry. Supranationalism provides a temporary refuge, at least, against threats of formal or indirect nationalisation in Belgium, and a means to obtain higher price ceilings than would be granted by Brussels, given that competitive price determination is out of the question. If there has to be dirigisme, Luxembourg's is considered the more benevolent.

It is in this context that the coal price crisis of 1955-1956 acquires its full significance. Belgian protests against the modification of the ECSC compensation system and the reduction in ceiling prices were officially directed against the High Authority, in two separate suits alleging violation of the Treaty. Luxembourg's Court rejected both appeals as groundless.[56] Company reports, however, make it quite clear that the initiation of legal proceedings was intended as an appeal to supranational institutions to oppose and nullify a policy of the national government tending to lower prices and compel modernisation. Further, it is the price and compensation question which concerns the collieries almost to the exclusion of other ECSC policy issues. Fédéchar takes little interest in them and favours a High Authority policy of inactivity with respect to the bulk of the Treaty.

In concert with other European coal people, Fédéchar is worried about the competition of fuel oil and nuclear energy and therefore favours a common ECSC fuel policy, dirigistic though it may be. The General Common Market is fervently desired now, and the need for supranational regulation is clearly spelled out, especially with respect to planned market splitting between coal and other sources of energy. The general reasoning, identical with Van der

[55] This conclusion is based on an unpublished questionnaire circulated by the Federation of Belgian Industries, June 1955. The questionnaire was phrased most tendentiously, designed to present supranationalism in the worst possible light from the point of view of free enterprise thinking and the national Belgian industrial interest. Fédéchar's replies were consistently critical of the F. I. B.'s bias and uniformly laudatory of ECSC, both on institutional and economic questions.

[56] For the details, see chapters 3 and 7, and *Chronique de Politique Etrangère*, Vol. 8, no. 5 (September 1955), pp. 554–559. It is significant that the attorneys who unsuccessfully represented the coal interests in the suits include two of the most consistent enemies of supranationalism, MM. Rolin and Mertens de Wilmars. For the text of the Court judgments see *Journal Officiel*, January 23, 1957. Arrêt de la Cour dans l'affaire no. 8–55, pp. 25–38; Arrêt de la Cour dans l'affaire, no. 9–55, pp. 39–58.

Rest's, clings to the desirability of subjecting consumers of commodities already integrated to the same general rules.

That neither coal nor steel have succeeded completely in persuading all Belgian industrialists to their position is manifest in the continued opposition within the Federation of Belgian Industries to Euratom and the General Common Market, if these measures are to be accompanied by standing institutions possessing " dirigistic " powers. The notion of a European investment fund is particularly repugnant to Belgian financial interests, making for constant internal dissent within the Federation. Yet the Federation of Belgian Catholic Employers strongly endorsed EEC, objecting only to the extensive special privileges granted to France. The Central Economic Council—in sharp contrast to its reserve toward ECSC in 1951—unanimously approved the EEC project, stressing the need for strong central political institutions and adequate powers to deal with economic crises and monetary problems. It also took exception to the special position granted to France as undermining the spirit of a true common market, while expressing its hope that the common tariff toward third countries would not result in a system of protection and would facilitate the association of Britain with EEC.[57] The story of attitude changes in Belgium, demonstrates the general rule that once an industry is forcibly " integrated," it adjusts to the situation, sees advantages in the new system and works hard for the extension of the principle in those areas considered beneficial to it, thereby putting pressure on unintegrated sectors to be included as well.

ITALIAN INDUSTRY AND EUROPEAN INTEGRATION

In contrast to the overwhelming political support for economic integration in Italy, most industrial interest groups remain opposed to it, despite five years of experience with a common market. Reaction to the Schuman Plan is understandable only if certain peculiarities of heavy industry in Italy are kept in mind. Firstly, the steel industry was recently created, is subject to extremely high costs; it was in 1950-1951 undergoing a process of modernisation

---

[57] With respect to Euratom, the Federation of Belgian Industry has put forward a plan of its own which would minimise supranational institutions, investment and control over production. It would concentrate instead on research, on procurement of fissionable materials in case of crisis, on controls over illicit uses of these materials and the financing of installations too costly for private industry. See *Informations Mensuelles*, April 1956, pp. 13–18; January 1957, pp. 23–25; April 1957, pp. 10–13.

and concentration known as the Sinigaglia Plan. Hence, it was feared that removal of protective devices would strangle growth and reorganisation. Secondly, the bulk of Italian steel is made with open hearth or electric equipment, requiring a 79 per cent. consumption of scrap in relation to crude steel produced, as compared to an ECSC average of 36 per cent., thus making a successful steel economy dependent not only on coal but also on heavy scrap imports. Thirdly, 50 per cent. of Italian steel capacity is financially controlled or directly owned by the Italian state, thus making protests of the industry unavailing in the face of a determined government policy.[58]

Confronted with the ECSC Treaty in 1951, the attitude of both steel associations (Assider and Isa, including the Government-controlled enterprises) and of the Federation of Industrialists to ratification was wholly negative. Politically, Italy was considered under-represented in ECSC organs, supranational dictation was expected, and cartels were outlawed, despite Assider desire for a " Franco-Italian understanding." Scrap and ore supplies were not assured, taxes and social security charges were left unharmonised and the removal of protection—despite the five-year transitional period allowed for a continuation of Italian tariffs in ECSC—considered to wreck the Sinigaglia Plan.[59] In the Senate, the efforts of Signor Falck, the largest independent Italian steelmaker, to have the Treaty amended to meet these points was defeated, though the government agreed to press for an early revision to take care of the purely economic grievances of the industry.

Even though Italy four years later was far from being fully integrated into the common market and relatively unaffected by the process of market interpenetration, Assider was already trying to prolong the transitional period and retain the Italian steel tariff, arguing that a " true " common market for coal and scrap, free of cartels, should precede full Italian integration. The associations opposed the tapering railway rates and the price alignment principle for steel as easing the access of Belgian exporters to the Italian market. When the High Authority relaxed the price publicity rule through the Monnet Rebate, Assider and Isa were among those

[58] Franco Peco, " Progress of the Italian Steel Industry," *Review of Economic Conditions in Italy* (Banco di Roma), March 1954, pp. 154 *et seq.*
[59] Italicus, " L'Industrie Italienne face au Plan Schuman," *Nouvelle Revue de l'Economie Contemporaine, op. cit.*, pp. 63 *et seq.*

who challenged the decision in Court, in order to hamper competition.

While seeking to avoid introduction of the common market for steel, no effort is spared to force its full advent as concerns coal and scrap. Italian purchases of scrap from other ECSC countries jumped from 270,000 tons in 1952 to 1,340,000 tons in 1954, with a reduction of purchases from third countries of 300,000 tons during that period,[60] incidentally, of course, bidding up scrap prices in France and Germany and creating the speculative shortage conditions partly responsible for the introduction of the compulsory ECSC perequation, import control and bonus-for-savings systems. Assider and Isa complain, however, that the forced perequation and bonus arrangements discriminate against them and violate the logic of a completely free common market, and they lodged their suit against the bonus decision on these grounds. As for coal, Italy as an importing country has favoured the lowest possible prices and the most stringent possible anti-cartel action, even if dirigistic means were used to realise them. Independent coke producers have especially been dissatisfied with the Ruhr price ceiling measures, which allegedly made prices higher than they would otherwise have been. And the conviction that GEORG will continue under the new dispensation was made manifest in the coke industry's suit against the High Authority for inadequate anti-cartel measures. The complaint was withdrawn only when the Ruhr sales office agreed to set aside specific amounts of coking coal for Italian needs. As concerns transportation, the steel and coke associations want High Authority action to reduce ocean freight rates. According to the coke people, the coal shortage even calls for ECSC-wide rationing, though they would resist bitterly a compulsory compensation fund to reduce the price of coal imported from third countries.

Disappointment of positive expectations obtains in other areas as well. Steelmakers oppose the coordination of investments as a French device to control German and other competitors and want full freedom to make their own. They are disappointed in the meagreness of ECSC finance and naturally complain that they do not derive full value from their payment of the production tax. In the absence of huge investment funds to modernise the large

[60] See H. Jürgensen, " Die Montanunion in den Funktionsgrenzen der Teilintegration," *Wirtschaftsdienst*, Vol. 35, no. 11 (November 1955), p. 626.

number of tiny Italian steel producers, massive concentration and specialisation is recognised as the only alternative. The upward harmonisation of living and wage standards, for obvious reasons, does not rank high among Italian industrialist expectations from supranationalism. Yet they are keenly disappointed over the slow implementation of the rules for the free movement of labour and feel that ECSC has not shown " faith in Europe " by thus neglecting the permanent Italian unemployment crisis. On balance, the industries directly concerned with supranationalism—steel and coke—have found more to oppose than to favour. While steel consuming industries, here as elsewhere in Europe, have come to support the common market and integration as beneficial to them, no such change in attitude over 1951 has taken place among those already integrated. They look forward with fear and opposition to the end of the transitional period.[61]

Yet certain demands suggest that more, rather than less, common market would satisfy some of the Italian claims. Coke producers argue that a consistently free market-oriented High Authority would benefit them; or alternatively no common market at all would be preferable. It is the intermediate position which they find intolerable. Steelmakers, equally, argue that small firms who have somehow escaped High Authority jurisdiction should be compelled to join and publish price lists and that a maximum effort should be made to subject special steel producers to the rigour of the fair trade code. Clearly, when it suits their interests, industrialists have no objection to the extension of supranational powers. But of doctrinal conversion to such principles, there is no trace, as emphasised by Confidustria's reasoned rejection of the idea of a General Common Market.[62]

[61] Mario Vaglio, " The European Coal and Steel Pool and the Italian Economy," *Review of Economic Conditions in Italy* (Banco di Roma), March 1954.

[62] As in Belgium, however, the rejection of EEC by the central federation of employers does not mean that all trade associations agree with this judgment. A survey conducted by an Italian research group in 1956 indicates that with the exception of the following industries, all others are either favourable or indifferent to the General Common Market. The dissenters include almost all heavy industries, some of whom have been most conspicuous in their success on export markets, *viz.*: the metallurgical industry, the machine building industry (including manufacturers of bicycles, motor cycles and sewing machines), railroad equipment and electrical equipment manufacturers, portions of the chemical industry, makers of paper, canned fish and dairy goods, as well as the distillers, who are usually found among the most protection-minded. It appears that the makers of Necchi sewing machines and Vespa motor-scooters are confident of retaining their command over export markets even without EEC, while being unwilling to open the Italian market to competing products. *Informations Mensuelles*, January 1957, pp. 39–42.

DUTCH INDUSTRY AND EUROPEAN INTEGRATION

Ratification of ECSC caused no serious soul-searching or cries of anguish in Dutch industrial circles: the industries concerned were fully in favour of the plan, though they insisted on changes during the drafting stage favouring the powers of small countries. The nature of the steel industry provides the major reason for this attitude. Dutch steel is concentrated in one giant firm, Koninklijke Nederlandse Hoogovens en Staalfabrieken, N. V., and its subsidiaries, including the Ruhr's Dortmund Hörder Hüttenunion. Hoogovens, in turn, is indirectly controlled by the Dutch state and the municipality of Amsterdam as the major stockholders. Equipped with a modern plant, enjoying low wage and price costs, and having doubled its output between 1938 and 1952, Hoogovens had nothing to fear and everything to gain from a larger market, especially since Holland expected to be a net steel importer.[63] And so it went in the coal industry. Over half of the Limburg coalfield is state-owned, extraction costs are relatively low and coal imports are required beyond the national production. The Dutch collieries favoured ECSC despite their share in the special Belgian subsidy payments.

Opinion toward integration has remained entirely favourable since ratification. Market interpenetration has benefited the coal mines, whose sole complaint against the common market has been their opposition to price ceilings, national and supranational. Further, they formally objected to the German Government's subsidization of miners' wages by suing the High Authority in 1957 for failure to stop this practice. Steelmakers, after some initial doubts, adjusted quickly to the fair trade code, though they worked for its relaxation through the Monnet Rebate and were very disappointed with its outlawry. Used to controlled prices through the informal direction of the Dutch Government, price stability in ECSC was nothing new. But they gladly avail themselves of price freedom and have supported the Dutch mines in opposing coal price ceilings. Used to fending for themselves, the steelmakers see no need for an elaborate ECSC scrap control or coal compensation system, and favour letting the common market take its logical course.

Steel consumers have been equally pleased with the common

---

[63] British Iron and Steel Federation, " The Dutch Iron and Steel Industry," *Monthly Statistical Bulletin*, November 1951.

market. The supply situation has been eased and access facilitated for purchases in other Community countries. Like the steelmakers, however, consumers have long argued for a relaxation in the price schedule system to allow limited flexibility without reintroducing discriminatory practices. Undismayed by the rejection of the Monnet Rebate, the Dutch consumers have been suggesting alternative formulas for obtaining price flexibility.[64] In any case, their expectations have been met and their loyalty to supranationalism as practised in Luxembourg is unshaken.

ECSC investment activity finds no favour with Dutch industry since interest rates in Holland are below the Community's. Consequently industrialists object strongly to the production tax, from which they claim to derive no benefits, and they see little purpose even in the mild coordination of investments carried on through the research-and-advice function of the High Authority. Nor are the industrialists interested in extending the scope of ECSC in the transport realm or the labour field. Enjoying low wages and no stringent demands for change, the programme for the harmonisation of taxes, wages and social charges is quietly opposed by Dutch industry.

No single ECSC issue has so aroused Dutch opinion as the question of cartels. Parliament and the Government were determined to compel the High Authority to live up to the letter of the Treaty in dissolving GEORG and ATIC and this pressure was a major reason for eventual ECSC action, even though the attempt to have the High Authority condemned by the Court failed. While Dutch opinion generally agreed with the government position, the steel industry opposed the suit and found the joint sales organisation for Ruhr coal an entirely natural device. Consistent with their general position, Dutch industrialists have been among the most reticent in Europe in condemning the High Authority for " dirigisme."

Dutch industry generally can thus be expected to favour more integration and especially the creation of the General Common Market, the initiative for which came from the Dutch Government. Yet, reservations are attached to this commitment: no direction of any kind which would interfere with the natural Dutch advantage in the realm of costs is to be suffered. Hence, any suggestion of stringent supranational powers over the General Common Market

[64] See the interview with M. Van der Pols, in *ECSC Bulletin*, January 1956.

and any extension of the direct powers of the High Authority of ECSC has been resisted by the as yet unintegrated sectors of the economy.

In no situation has this been expressed more succinctly than in the field of inland shipping. Dutch shippers own the largest fleet on the Rhine and are active on other inland waterways in western Europe. Their costs are the lowest in Europe and thus they benefit from the fact that international rates are below national charges, even though the distance covered may be longer. Efforts of ECSC to equalise this disparity, which is considered a discrimination in violation of the Treaty, have been consistently opposed by shippers, ports and Chambers of Commerce in Holland. Suggestions for strengthening the hand of the High Authority were greeted with cries of " dirigisme." What is demanded instead is a European solution to the waterways problem along inter-governmental lines, banning national subsidies and establishing the principles of free user's choice and uncontrolled rates. In industrial circles, therefore, the commitment to integration presumes a dedication to competition not shared in all European industrial circles, and an insistence on conditions distinctly favourable to Dutch commercial interests. If the attitude of shippers is to be taken as typical, no integration at all is preferred to an institutionally strong supranationalism in the Europe of the future.

It could easily have been predicted on the basis of these perceptions of interest that the EEC Treaty, as signed in March of 1957, would arouse a great deal of opposition in Dutch industrial and commercial circles. Such was indeed the case. The objections held that the common market planned was not free enough: it excluded agriculture and continued uneconomic protection in that sector; the transitional provisions and escape clauses permit too large a residue of national exclusion; monetary integration is ignored; the common tariff toward third countries might make the association of the Free Trade Area (and therefore of Britain) with EEC too difficult and too protectionist; far too many concessions were made to France in permitting her some continuing rights to discriminate against her EEC partners. Along with these maximalist free market demands came a number of objections based specifically on Dutch industrial needs. Thus nearly every interest group—including some labour leaders—opposed the harmonisation of social and wage legislation and every aspect of EEC which could be branded as " inflationary," *i.e.*, likely to raise Dutch costs. The common tariff against third countries is deeply suspected of raising all Dutch prices because it is bound to be higher than the current Benelux rates. Agricultural producers, so deeply averse to integration in other European countries, complained loudly of the exclusion of agriculture from the free market rules because they feel thus deprived of export outlets.[65] It must be noted, however, that contrary to Belgian, French and Italian objections to further economic integration, these Dutch protests stem primarily from the feeling that *not enough* common market is being introduced. Hence it can be ventured without difficulty that these Dutch interests will not only support EEC initially, but adjust very speedily in seeking to give the new institutions a maximal free market policy orientation.

Luxembourg Industry and European Integration

Industrial reactions in the tiny Grand-Duchy not only tend to duplicate those prevalent in Belgian circles because of the almost complete Belgo-Luxembourg Economic Union which has linked the two economies since 1922, but are also heavily influenced by the dominant role exercised by steel in Luxembourg's foreign trade. According to L. Bouvier, head of the Groupement des Industries Sidérurgiques Luxembourgeoises, almost 50 per cent. of the country's population makes its living in the industry, while the steel payroll accounts for 73 per cent. of the nation's. Steel production encompasses 75 per cent. of Luxembourg's total output in terms of value, 98 per cent. of which is exported and tends to pay for the large imports necessitated by the country's limited resources.[66] Small wonder then that the Steel Association had considerable misgivings about joining ECSC and insisted on the insertion of paragraph 31 into the Convention on Transitional Provisions, designed to exempt Luxembourg from the rules of the common market in case of serious hardship. Doubts were increased by the high wage levels and considerable tax and social security burdens weighing on the industry's cost structure. Some critics insisted on their upward harmonisation as a condition for Luxembourg's joining and others demanded a reduction in domestic wages as an essential precondition. Commented an industry organ:

[65] *Informations Mensuelles*, January 1957, pp. 42–49, 65–66.
[66] L. Bouvier, " La Sidérurgie Luxembourgeoise dans l'Economie du Grand-Duché," distributed by the Luxembourg Steel Association, October 1954.

> This Treaty, as it will be submitted to the vote of our Chamber, contains basic provisions and details which cannot but give rise to severe fears for the future of our industry and which could compromise it dangerously. . . . One is entitled to ask if we do not find ourselves at the threshold of an adventure.[67]

Once ratification was accomplished, M. Bouvier was constrained to note that " for us, national prosperity and the living standard of our population are intimately related, henceforth, to the policies, the successes or the failures of ECSC."[68]

Events since that time have made the industry more optimistic. The common market has facilitated sales and eased access to French iron ore. While hostile to the " inflexible " price list system, the principle of price alignment is considered a boon to steel exports at stable prices, especially if supplemented by a stiff High Authority enforcement policy to " discipline the consumers." Steel opposes any kind of ECSC control over the coal market and has fought the centralised scrap purchase and distribution system as a discriminatory subsidisation of the Italian producers from which Luxembourg industry—concentrating exclusively on basic Bessemer steel—derives nothing but disadvantages. The logic is clear: industrialists favour the competitive common market under circumstances considered favourable to them but oppose the inclusion of commodities to which they are indifferent, *e.g.*, scrap. Within these confines, the annual reports of the largest firm, ARBED, make clear that the common market has had no revolutionary effects on the industry and that the High Authority's policies, on balance, are acceptable.

As concerns investments, the industry welcomes the inactivity of ECSC organs and has no particular enthusiasm for " dirigistic " co-ordination measures. Nor is the industry interested in supranational financing; it emphasises self-reliance as a strong argument for the elimination of the production tax. Elimination of transport discriminations was greeted with great satisfaction while the issue of free migration of labour is regarded with indifference. The industry is satisfied with the High Authority's automatic approval of merger applications but a tightening of the rules is regarded as

---

[67] L'Echo de l'Industrie, May 19, 1951. See also Leon Metzler, *Le Plan Schuman dans la Perspective Luxembourgeoise* (1951), pp. 58–61.

[68] L. Bouvier, " La Sidérurgie Luxembourgeoise dans la Communauté du Charbon et de l'Acier," distributed by the Luxembourg Steel Association, October 1954.

" dirigistic." With respect to cartels, the industry had profited from the International Steel Cartel of the inter-war period and foresees circumstances under which such an arrangement might again be useful. This, however, has not prevented it from appealing to the High Authority against its own government in the effort to obtain the elimination of the national coal import monopoly, which was linked to a compulsory compensation system to subsidise the price of domestic fuel. While defending GEORG and condemning the High Authority's anti-cartel decisions in that case, the industry went to the Court to compel ECSC action against the national coal import and compensation system.

These activities reflect short-run aims and expectations, easily satisfiable by supranational decisions or inaction, but implying no permanent identification with ECSC policy or activity. Demands for expanding the supranational scope of action would provide such expectations but these have been slow to develop. In principle, industry favours the equalisation of working conditions and wages since this would increase German and Dutch costs. But it hesitates to endorse ECSC-wide collective bargaining under supranational auspices as the means to this end because this would strengthen the position of trade unions. Hence, while favouring the High Authority's real wage studies, it opposes the use of ECSC for the achievement of harmonisation in fact.[69]

Attitudes toward the continuation of economic integration are thus ambivalent, much like in Holland and Belgium. The restriction of the common market to coal and steel is considered an anomaly which cannot last. Desire for the success of this venture compels the industry, as well as steel processing groups, to endorse extension of the principle to other sectors, but using " less formal methods, less useless paperwork, and therefore more flexible, efficient and less costly." In short, the General Common Market is indeed favoured, provided it is free from supranational institutions with directing, taxing and lending powers. The expansion of integration is made dependent upon the mere elimination of trade barriers giving maximum scope to private enterprise to profit from this freedom and certainly permitting the use of cartels to cushion undesired consequences of competition. To the extent, however,

[69] *Ibid.*, October 1, 1955. See the leading article of Carlo Hemmer, " Wo steht unsere Wirtschaft? " in *D'Letzeburger Land*, June 17, 1955. *Echo de l'Industrie*, October 15, 1955.

that satisfaction with the common market for coal and steel has overcome premonitions of disaster with respect to the principle of integration, a change in attitude toward a new focus has certainly come about as a result of ECSC.

ECSC IMPACT ON BRITISH INDUSTRIAL ATTITUDES

The opening of the common market for coal and steel did not go unnoticed on the other side of the Channel. A number of reasons combined to make British industrial reactions in 1952 and 1953 somewhat less than cordial. The steel sector had just undergone denationalisation even though Whitehall continued to have a considerable say in the fundamental policies of the industry. Nevertheless, it is understandable that British steelmakers, having just escaped the direct rule of their own government, were in no mood to trade in their relative freedom for the authority of Luxembourg's supranational system. Furthermore, the industry was confident of its competitive position on world and domestic markets. Its costs were lower than the continental steelmakers', an extensive investment and modernisation programme had been completed and the mills did not suffer from the indirect taxation featured in most ECSC countries. Finally, 60 per cent. of its exports was destined for Commonwealth countries and only 6 per cent. to the ECSC area. As for coal, the National Coal Board, even though an agency of the government, tended to react very much like a private firm despite the fact of nationalisation. It was far from eager to sacrifice revenues and pricing policies found satisfactory for its purposes to the rules of the supranational system. Least of all was it willing to give up double pricing, despite the wishes of Jean Monnet.[70]

It is therefore hardly surprising that the High Authority's initiative for the negotiation of an agreement of association fell on quite unsympathetic ears in Britain. There seemed to be no need for any special tie with ECSC. However, by spring of 1954 a recession was upon Europe, overproduction loomed once more and the continental steelmakers were accused of dumping on export markets. The British Iron and Steel Federation announced that it would welcome the kind of agreement which would recognise

[70] See the article of Sir Ellis Hunter, former president of British Iron and Steel Federation, in *National Provincial Bank Review*, February 1954, and *Continental Iron and Steel Trade Reports*, March 4, 1954.

the inevitable impact which the two production areas would have upon one another, to be concerned with tariffs, exports and investments. At the same time the Federation expressed its fear of governmental domination over any kind of British-ECSC tie and expressed its preference for a direct understanding with the steelmakers on the Continent, *i.e.*, a cartel. And it must be added that even during the earlier period of indifference to association, some spokesmen had qualified their position by noting the need for special arrangements in the event of abnormal conditions and overproduction. Hence it is not surprising that when the Agreement on Association was finally completed, the British steel industry was disappointed. The absence of any kind of definite economic or commercial content was greeted with dismay.[71]

The National Coal Board, to judge by published reports, seems to have taken no particular interest in the establishment of association. Even after the establishment of the Council of Association, one of its British members, Mr. D. J. Ezra, who is also a member of the National Coal Board, once more expressed the customary British argument that no extensive trade ties existed between ECSC and the United Kingdom, that the Commonwealth took first place in British thinking and that the domestic market could absorb all the coal mined in England. But he also urged that association with ECSC be pushed beyond the mere exchange of technical information and be given the task of exploring the degree of full co-operation possible and desirable for both parties. What kind of co-operation was meant? Perhaps the National Coal Board intended no more than the creation of a favourable climate of opinion on the Continent, an appreciation for the growing British fuel shortage, and thus lay the groundwork for the eventual decision to curtail coal exports. Other evidence suggests that the National Coal Board is genuinely interested in the techniques and problems of Luxembourg and is anxious to maintain the best public relations with it, therefore giving way on its desire to cut down on coal shipments to the Continent in the interest of political harmony.[72] There is no evidence yet that the National Coal Board is adopting the reasoning pattern of the ECSC collieries, private as well as nationalised: the need for

[71] British Iron and Steel Federation, *Monthly Statistical Bulletin*, (March 1954). *The Metal Bulletin* (April 2, 1954), *Financial Times* (April 2, 1954), *Economist* (April 3, 1954). *Iron and Coal Trades Review* (December 31, 1954).
[72] *Colliery Guardian*, October 6, 1955; November 24, 1955.

gradual adaptation of the coal industry to the challenge of non-conventional energy sources, rising costs, and manpower shortage by means of a supranational planned energy policy involving ECSC subsidies, centrally planned investments and high tariff protection against third countries.   But *The Economist* suggested that Britain's new position as a net importer of coal and a growing consumer of increasingly scarce steel imposed an entirely new set of needs on the Council of Association, that of making common policy, and especially coal policy.[73]

Analyses of this kind have not succeeded in infusing the machinery of ECSC-British association with a spirit of bold policy-making.   But they were straws in the wind of the vigorous re-examination of European economic integration which was catalysed in Britain by the Messina Conference and the subsequent work of the Brussels Intergovernmental Committee.   Quality journals now began to present and argue the need for a more definite British interest in Continental integration, and above all stressed the necessity for taking seriously the budding union of the Six.[74]   It was then that the fears and hopes connected with the Free Trade Area—as an adjunct or counterpoise to the General Common Market—began to be voiced openly in British industrial circles. Those who favoured freer trade on principle saw in it the best opportunity in decades to break into the protectionist preserve; but those who merely feared exclusion and discrimination by a newly powerful European *bloc* were equally forced to consider their future relationship to the Continent in more direct terms than had been necessitated by the role of ECSC.

Consulted by the government as to the attitudes of organised business, the Federation of British Industries, on November 1, 1956, announced the results of a survey it had conducted.   The Federation asked all of its affiliated trade associations and many individual firms whether the government should directly participate in negotiations with the members of EEC in order to establish the Free Trade Area.   The replies were as follows:

---

[73] *The Economist*, November 19, 1955.
[74] *Informations Mensuelles* (September–October 1956), p. 30   See especially the series of articles which appeared during October 1956 in *The Spectator*, *The Times*, and *The Economist*.   Mr. Peter Thorneycroft made similar public statements.

Trade associations circularised by the F.B.I.   287
Trade associations submitting answers   128
1. answer favourable, provided special safeguarding clauses
    can be written into the agreement   52
2. answer favourable, assuming that special protection is
    already provided for industries in difficulty   15
3. answer unfavourable, unless strict assurances of special
    protective safeguarding clauses are given   9
4. unqualified unfavourable answer   18
5. answer arrived too late to be counted   22
6. membership of association too divided for clear answer. .   12

Of the individual firms which answered the questionnaire, 479
were favourable, 147 opposed and 38 were indifferent to the government's announced plan.   Associations favouring the Free Trade
Area, subject to various safeguarding clauses, include the steel,
cement, construction, electronic, aviation, textile, shipbuilding and
metal processing industries.   Opponents of the plan counted among
their number the railway engine builders and paper producers.
After the government had announced its intention of excluding
agriculture from the Free Trade Area, the major agricultural associations approved this decision while the Cocoa, Chocolate and
Confectionery Alliance, the Scotch Whisky Association and the
National Association of Soft Drink Manufacturers urged that
some segments of the food industry might well be included.
   These results are hardly unexpected.   Industries which are
confident of their competitive strength share the general fear of
British isolation and exclusion from a newly strong Continental
market, accompanied by a less and less attractive export picture
in the Commonwealth.   Consequently they prefer active competition in Europe to discrimination, dumping and stagnation.   In
fact, a number of industries went so far as to express fears that the
new low tariff duties which would apply in EEC-British relations
would force a reduction of the duties applied by the United Kingdom
against Commonwealth countries.   Confronted with the possibility
of different and unbalanced tariff structures in the increasingly
complicated relationships which would result, these industries
failed to express any particular preference for the imperial tie.
As for those who oppose the Free Trade Area, the arguments invoked could easily have been predicted: the British market will be
flooded with Continental goods without a reciprocal flow taking

place; the Continental producers enjoy natural advantages which Britain cannot match; any possible safeguarding clauses would not suffice to protect British interests.[75]

Can it be hazarded that the expectations and attitudes here expressed reproduce the pattern extracted from the ECSC experience? Low-cost and efficient producers, at the onset of a common market, are easily reconciled to integration if they do not actively favour it; high-cost producers oppose it and predict national catastrophe. If the ECSC pattern were to be reproduced, the next step would involve insistence on the part of the low-cost producers that the governments refrain from any institutional integration which would result in " dirigisme " and permit business to run its own affairs, after obstacles to " comparable competitive conditions " are eliminated—a step which would of course involve the spill-over of the Free Trade Area into the field of wages and taxes. But it would also involve loud demands for protection on the part of high-cost producers, for discriminatory duties against third countries, for compensation payments, if not for centrally administered subsidies. And in terms of political integration, it would then be the erstwhile opponents of the common market who would be the carriers of the expectations and attitudes most favourable to the growth of strong political institutions.

[75] The report of the Federation of British Industries is given in the form of a letter from Sir Graham Hayman to Mr. Peter Thorneycroft. *Informations Mensuelles* (January 1957), pp. 90–93.

CHAPTER 6

TRADE UNIONS: 1952 AND 1957

EUROPEAN TRADE UNIONISM: STRENGTH AND DOCTRINE

The attitude of labour toward integration depends on the economic and political conditions under which the unions of the ECSC countries live and operate. The very differentials have acted as catalysts for those who suffer from poor organisation to seek power through co-operation with those who are strong. Wide varieties in wage and hour benefits have induced those who enjoy little to work together with unions whose attainments are envied.

The trade union movement in each of the six countries is split. Rival Catholic and Socialist-dominated federations exist in all ECSC countries, with Communist organisations complicating the picture in France, Italy and Holland, not to mention the Dutch Protestant federation. Even in Germany, where until 1955 a united federation, the German Federation of Trade Unions (DGB), held sway, a Catholic dissident wing seceded in that year. In addition there are unaffiliated foremen's and white-collar workers' unions, as well as the small Gaullist federation in France and the Neo-Fascist organisation in Italy.

Because of their unswerving opposition to integration between 1950 and 1957, the Communist-dominated unions are of no direct interest to this study, though there are suggestions of a pro-ECSC trend in Italy since 1956. However, since Communist unions in two ECSC countries dominate the labour field, it must constantly be borne in mind that the General Confederations of Labour in both France and Italy, because of their attitude, condition the positions adopted and defended by their smaller Socialist and Christian rivals. These are simultaneously compelled to seek strength through alliance with other ECSC unions while defending themselves at home against the Communist charges of selling the French and Italian working-class to foreign capitalist interests. The membership figures, speculative though some of them are, of ECSC unions are instructive in this respect [1]:

	Communist-dominated	Socialist-dominated	Catholic	Protestant	Other
Germany	—	6,104,872	8,600	—	870,000
France	1,500,000	500,000	600,000	—	300,000
Italy	4,561,214	560,000	2,045,542	—	900,000
Belgium	—	681,709	645,000	—	—
Netherlands	40,000	463,300	374,085	204,084	—
Luxembourg	3,000	22,285	8,549	—	—
Totals	6,104,214	8,332,166	3,681,776	204,084	2,070,000

These figures, moreover, tend to understate the weakness of the non-Communist unions in France and Italy in the mining and metallurgical branches which are of most direct interest to this study.[2]

Differentials in membership, of course, beget differences in financial power and self-confidence. The German, Belgian, Dutch and Luxembourg unions are wealthy, well organised and confident of their bargaining positions in industry, even though they do suffer from marked inferiority feelings in the political realm and in social relations. The French and Italian unions, by contrast, are unable to collect membership dues, hold their members, speak with a united voice, or assert themselves consistently and meaningfully in politics. While this generalisation applies less to the Communist-led groups, even they suffer from member apathy and financial strain.

The collective bargaining practices and laws in force in each of the ECSC countries provide a further guide to the variations in

[1] French figures from Val R. Lorwin, *The French Labour Movement* (Cambridge: Harvard University Press 1954), p. 177. All other figures from U.S. Department of Labour. Office of International Labour Affairs, *Directory of Labour Organisations*, 2 vols. (Washington, 1956). These figures are of variable reliability. With the exception of the French, which are based on reliable outside estimates, the figures comprise the membership *claimed* by each union. German, Dutch and Luxembourg claims are probably accurate, while Italian claims for all unions are grossly exaggerated. The Socialist Belgian claim seems accurate, while the Catholic Belgian figure is probably too high. The heading " other " includes the German white-collar workers and civil servants' unions, the Italian Confederazione Italiane Sindicati Nazionale Lavoratori, and the French Gaullist federation and Confederation Générale des Cadres. Generally, see Walter Galenson (ed.), *Comparative Labour Movements*, (New York: Prentice-Hall, 1952), Chaps. 4, 5 and 6 Lorwin, *op. cit.*, pp. 179 *et seq.*

power and influence enjoyed by the rival labour movements. In Germany, trade associations and trade unions are legally competent to bargain collectively and do so in practice. The agreements concluded, however, merely fix minimum standards for wages, hours and working conditions, to be adjusted upward in direct talks between given firms and the union. It is widely reported, moreover, that the Ministry of Economics intervenes in the negotiating sessions by calling on both parties to moderate their demands, and especially on labour to " hold the line " with respect to prices and maintain productivity with respect to export and reconstruction needs. Until 1955, the unions were very responsive to such appeals, and have refrained from calling for drastic wage increases or a reduction of hours. In Holland, the same practices prevail, even though the law limits collective bargaining by making all contracts negotiated subject to the formal approval of the government. An appropriate inter-ministerial commission examines contracts for their compatibility with general economic policy, particularly price policy.

Belgian and Luxembourg unions bargain collectively with trade associations on a nation-wide basis, without government intercession. However, the contracts agreed upon can be extended to plants and workers not represented in the negotiations only by means of governmental decrees, which are usually issued without difficulty. In practice, furthermore, Christian and Socialist unions have had little difficulty in striking and bargaining jointly. In France and Italy the same formal pattern prevails, with quite different consequences, however. There the fragmentation and internal hostilities of the unions hamper co-ordinated or joint striking and bargaining, while the weakness of single unions makes them very ineffectual bargaining parties indeed. The unions enjoy no closed shop, no check-off, no definite membership; what is more, they carry out no welfare functions of their own, leaving these to the firm or the Government. Consequently, only ideology and social reasons prompt workers to join the union in the first place. There is no definite obligation to bargain collectively for the employers' associations, who furthermore are better organised and united on points of doctrine. As a result, French and Italian practice knows little nation-wide bargaining, with local and regional agreements flourishing instead, introducing wide variations in standards within these countries, including even the removal of wage questions from the negotiations. The Government, in principle, is to extend the content of agreements to firms and workers not represented in the bargaining, but in fact usually fails to do so. The consequence has been worker apathy, union weakness, and a universal reliance on the state to realise wage and hour benefits by means of legislation instead of trusting to collective bargaining.[3]

A final characteristic difference in power is revealed by the varying union activities with respect to controlling their respective industries. In France, after the achievement of nationalisation of the coal mines, the trade union movement has been content with peripheral participation in management, without asking for control. Unions are represented—as a minority—on the " independent " boards in charge of administering the nationalised coal, gas and electric industries. They participate in the management of social security funds financed from employer and state contributions, and they deal with local plant problems through works councils. No consistent effort is made to participate in the overall planning and management of the non-nationalised bulk of industry. Even the development of joint labour-management productivity teams came as an innovation in 1950–1952, which was by no means universally welcome in labour ranks.

In the German coal and steel industries, by contrast, the system of co-determination has been in effect since 1947 (on the basis of German law since 1951). It provides for the nomination by the relevant trade union of one-half of the membership of the firm's supervisory council (Aufsichtsrat) and for the appointment of the " labour director " member of the management (Vorstand). German unions hoped to be able to control the basic policy of the chief industries through this technique, without having to achieve formal nationalisation. Experience indicates that unions have succeeded in obtaining higher wage and hour benefits through this system, without succeeding in controlling the management of the industry. In part, this is due to the tendency of operating coal and steel firms to fall into the hands of holding companies not subject to co-determination. But in part, the failure to achieve control is due to a tacit division of labour among the supervisory council members, leaving labour relations, wages and hours to the union delegates,

[3] Lorwin, *op. cit.*, concluding chapter. Kirchheimer, Otto, " West German Trade Unions," *World Politics*, Vol. 8, no. 4, (July 1956). Much of the material on which these summary statements are based was collected on the basis of interviews with union officials.

while the business members concentrate on managerial issues.[4] In any event, both the miners' and metalworkers' union officials are pleased with the system—in the face of rank-and-file indifference— and now demand extension of the technique to holding companies. The system certainly demonstrates an aggressiveness of union leadership and a concern for overall economic policy which is lacking in the other ECSC countries.

The crucial test of trade union relevance to the study of integration is the doctrinal position defended. What is the relationship of union activity to politics? In principle, all the unions claim to be " neutral " toward national politics, *i.e.*, they are not formally associated with political parties. In practice, of course, the opposite is the case. The leadership of the Force Ouvrière and UIL in France and Italy, having split off from the Communist-dominated General Confederations of Labour in both countries at the onset of the cold war, are in fact Socialists and defend Socialist principles even when not formally co-operating with the national socialist parties. The NVV in Holland, FGTB in Belgium and CGT in Luxembourg are Socialist-led and part of the general national socialist constituency. The German DGB is dominated by Socialists, but has until 1956 attempted to preserve a neutral position toward the Government and provided for representation of Christian unionists. Further, it has not always seen eye to eye with the Social Democratic Party. In 1956, however, some Catholic unionists split off to form their own federation and the DGB then openly took its place with the SPD in opposing the Adenauer Government. All the ECSC Socialist unions are affiliated with the International Confederation of Free Trade Unions (ICFTU), whose European Regional Organisation, in turn, is Socialist in orientation.

Less categorical statements are possible of the Christian unions. The Dutch Catholic KAB and Protestant CNV espouse a Christian ideology, but hardly differ from one another or the NVV on points of labour policy. The Belgian CSC and Luxembourg CLSC are certainly Catholic organisations and devoted to papal social doctrine, but in practice their activities do not differ from those of their Socialist rivals. The French CFTC, however, has formally dissociated itself from papal encyclicals and the MRP, and minimises

[4] See W. Michael Blumenthal, *Co-determination in the German Steel Industry*, Industrial Relations Section, Princeton University (Princeton, 1956).

its " Christian " nature, while the Italian CISL has refused to join the International Confederation of Christian Trade Unions (ICCTU)—of which all the other Christian groups are members— and remains affiliated with the ICFTU. With the exception of the CFTC all these unions are politically allied with the respective Christian-Democratic parties and press for a pro-labour, pro-planning, pro-welfare policy within these parties.

In Germany, the white-collar workers' federation (DAG) and the civil servants' union stridently retain their autonomy *vis-à-vis* the DGB, but do not differ in concrete policy from it without, how-ever, being Socialist. To underline its autonomy, the DAG is affiliated with the ICCTU. While the Socialist and Christian federations, nationally and supranationally, have become the striking force of pro-integration sentiment, these unions remain relatively uninterested in the process.

GERMAN UNIONISM AND INTEGRATION

In view of their overwhelming numerical and organisational pre-ponderance among the ECSC non-Communist unions, the German miners, metalworkers and the DGB must take first place in any analysis of attitudes toward integration. Unlike the German Socialist Party, with which the majority of DGB leaders maintain close personal and ideological relations, the unions favoured ratifi-cation of ECSC in 1951. Not only did they welcome the removal of Allied controls on German production, but they feared the ascendancy of producer organisations over the Schuman Plan unless checked by trade union opposition, thus carrying the men-tality of the German co-determination struggle over into the supranational arena. In contrast to SPD efforts, DGB lobbying was moderate, factual and restrained, rejoicing over the elimination of discriminatory measures against Germany and looking forward to political equality for labour as well as for their country as a major boon.[5]

However, opinion was far from unanimous. A minority in all unions concerned opposed ratification on the same grounds as the SPD. Viktor Agartz, former director of the DGB Economic Institute, predicted the ruin of the German steel industry because

---

[5] See Memorandum No. IV–19/51 to DGB officials, May 15, 1951. Approval of ECSC, incidentally, by no means implied that demands for the nationalisation of basic German industries were abandoned. It did imply, however, that as ECSC became operative and co-determination was established in the coal and steel sectors, less and less emphasis was given to the formal demand for nationalisation.

of the initial investment disadvantage, deconcentration and coal compensation payments to Belgium.[6] At the end of the debate, ratification was favoured only on the understanding that Allied controls would cease immediately and that reconcentration be permitted proportional to mergers in other ECSC countries.

The evolution of German trade union attitudes toward economic integration has shown the same ambivalence which characterises other interest groups. Among the concrete issues which have arisen, opposition to integration has been manifest whenever a cherished national claim has been challenged by a supranational decision or lack of decision: the question of GEORG and cartellised coal sales, price controls, free migration of labour, the Moselle Canal and the overall issue of German foreign policy.

The need for a coal sales cartel has been defended by almost all Germans but no group fought harder for it than the miners' union, I. G. Bergbau. Without centrally determined non-competitive prices, it was feared, the marginal mines would be forced to close, unemployment would set in and the wages of the remaining active miners forced down. " It is possible that a new and better organisation can be created, more compatible with the [ECSC] Treaty," commented the union, " but we can in no event agree to unlimited competition in the coal sector, which would lead to unpredictable social, economic and political consequences." [7] Alternatives to GEORG were proposed, and disappointment was keen when they were rejected by Luxembourg.

Integration has come in for its share of criticism on the price issue. All unions have opposed the consecutive coal price increases granted by the High Authority and the removal of ceilings in 1956. Wage demands—put forward regularly each spring by the unions— could be met exclusively out of company earnings, it was urged, and did not require price increases. And for once the unions praised Erhard for opposing the inflationary wage-price spiral implied in the policies of raising German coal and steel prices.[8]

---

[6] DGB pamphlet *Das Steht im Schumanplan* (Cologne, 1951) and *Industriekurier*, June 19, 1951. Agartz was dismissed in 1956, apparently over differences of opinion with the DGB leadership; Agartz repeatedly took stridently nationalistic and doctrinaire Socialist positions, especially on the nationalisation issue. See Kirchheimer, pp. 493–494.

[7] *Bergbauindustrie*, May 29, 1954, p. 1. *Bergbau und Wirtschaft*, June 15, 1954, p. 376.

[8] *Der Gewerkschaftler*, no. 4 (1955). *Bergbauindustrie*, May 7, 1955; March 26, 1955; May 15, 1954; March 27, 1954. *DGB Nachrichtendienst*, June 7, 1955. *Metall*, April 20, 1955.

Even though rebuffed, the unions went out of their way to declare that their disappointment did not imply opposition to integration, as falsely urged by " reactionary " business interests.

German foreign policy is not normally discussed by the politically " neutral " unions; yet when occasion arose they aligned themselves with the SPD on the general issue and took pains to criticise the French arrangements for the Saar. To repeated French claims for the canalisation of the Moselle—that perennial issue of " an act of faith for Europe "—the unions responded by asking why they should show their good faith first and pointed to loss in railway revenues and jobs if the plan were adopted.[9] The most consistent opposition to measures of integration, however, was patent in the issue of permitting the free movement of qualified coal and steel labour from other ECSC countries. It was the German unions who insisted on such rigorous standards of professional competence as to reduce to a trickle the number of workers eligible for the European labour card. " We shall resist to the utmost the use of foreign labour in the mines," declared Heinrich Imig, the late head of I. G. Bergbau.[10] Other leaders echoed these sentiments in un- compromising language, even though paying lip-service to the unity of labour aspirations everywhere. This position, it must be stressed, is not unique to German labour and is not a specific criticism of European integration: it is merely a restatement of the deep-seated fear of organised labour everywhere that unorganised foreign workers will depress wage standards and make for unemployment.

Criticism of integration is far less important than a wholesale turning to supranational institutions as devices for more effectively realising demands at the national level. The metalworkers— I. G. Metall—fear the unbridled reconcentration of German steel, coal and processing industries as uncontrollable centres of economic power, likely to circumvent the co-determination law. They look increasingly to Luxembourg to curb this trend. All the unions fear private cartels in Germany and hope that ECSC will force them into the open. As Socialists, they abhor the unplanned placing of investments and call for their co-ordination by the High Authority, over the unwillingness of German industry. The unions complained bitterly over the early reluctance of German mines to interest themselves in a share of the American loan and urged

[9] *DGB Nachrichtendienst*, October 4, 1955. *Bergbau und Wirtschaft*, Nov. 7, 1955.
[10] *Welt der Arbeit*, July 1, 1955.

submission to supranational planning. They praised the High Authority's plans for furthering the efficient utilisation of low-grade coal and argue for a long-term European fuel policy. When declining demand threatened lay-offs in the inefficient German ore mines, I. G. Bergbau demanded the granting of readaptation payments by Luxembourg, even though this was initially opposed by the German Government. Most important, I. G. Metall, after dire predictions of economic fiasco, admitted as early as 1953 that the common market was a success and highly beneficial for production, employment and living standards. One of its leaders, Hans Brümmer, went so far as to demand a more consistent ECSC policy of raising production through competition and a forward-looking welfare policy.[11]

In no field is the reliance of German labour on supranationalism more evident now than in the area of wage and hour demands. Until 1954, the dominant concern of union leaders was the reconstruction of German industry. They shared the Government's and industry's eagerness to rationalise production, reduce costs, contain inflation and capture export markets. Hence, they moderated their wage demands and did not consistently challenge the fifty-four-hour work week then typical of the industries under study. In 1954 a new attitude developed. More strident wage demands were heard, accusing fingers pointed to high dividend payments, and the German export surplus was characterised as a burden on the balances of payments of other European countries. Most important, a strong campaign for the introduction of the forty-hour week without loss of pay was launched by all unions and the DGB, a demand which by 1956 was central to the trade union programme.[12] One consequence of the new emphasis in the national programme of the DGB was enthusiasm over the High Authority's comparative wage, hour and purchasing power studies, which were promptly cited to support the domestic claims of the unions.

In terms of integration, the consequence has been increasing reliance on Luxembourg for the achievement of the programme of

---

[11] *Die Quelle* (August 1954), p. 338, *Bergbau und Wirtschaft*, August 1, 1954, pp. 267 *et seq.*; May 15, 1954, pp. 299 *et seq.*; *Bergbauindustrie*, May 21, 1955; September 4, 1954; August 20, 1955; January 1, 1955; *Der Gewerkschaftler*, July and August 4, 1953. *Welt der Arbeit*, February 11, 1955.

[12] DGB, *Aktionsprogramm*, 1954. (Sonderdruck für die Delegierten des 3. Ordentlichen Bundeskongress, 1954). DGB *Auslandsdienst*, May 1955, "Aktionsprogramm des Deutschen Gewerkschaftbundes, 1955." *Bergbau und Wirtshcaft*. September 1, 1955, p. 434.

improvement. While not sharing the enthusiasm of some unions for ECSC-wide collective bargaining, the German labour leaders have strongly supported the effort to introduce the forty-hour week, uniform overtime, vacation and holiday pay via the Schuman Plan. Their major criticism has been the insufficiently active welfare policy of the High Authority and the appointment of René Mayer to the presidency was greeted with derision and scepticism because it was feared the new president would be indifferent to these claims.[13] Yet the national desire for higher wage and hour benefits has not led the German unions to the position of their French and Belgian colleagues in striving for the harmonisation of social security benefits. A much more cautious attitude is typical of the Germans—

> A certain amount of confusion is engendered by the demands of trade union conventions for a uniform European social security system. This creates the impression that unions in principle demand the harmonisation of social security contributions. In reality, these efforts aim at something quite different, namely the reorganisation of social security in all European countries to attain the highest level already achieved in one of the participating states, and to design this system in the most rational and meaningful manner in the interests of workers as well as of the economy. The standardisation of the systems is in no way intended. . . . The rationalisation of production and means of production would result in much greater adaptation to the payment ability achieved in the most highly developed European country than the attempt to introduce the harmonisation of social security contributions. Harmonisation can never be achieved in terms of payments and must fail because it assumes a break with old customs and habits which are firmly anchored in the mentality of the European nations.[14]

Activities of the powerful I. G. Metall illustrate most strikingly this trend toward supranational activity as a means to achieve national benefits. Thus, Heinrich Straeter has expressed his conviction that ECSC, through the co-ordination of investments, control of prices, construction of worker housing and industrial hygiene research would go far toward meeting labour's aims. He has criticised ECSC for insufficient joint policy-making in the fields of taxes and business cycles. In the face of opposition in his own

[13] *Bergbauindustrie*, April 16, 1955. *Bergbau und Wirtschaft*, July 1, 1955, p. 297.

[14] Arthur Riess, " Harmonisierung der Europäischen Soziallasten? " *Gewerkschaftliche Monatshefte*, Vol. 6, no. 2 (February 1955), pp. 105 and 107. See also the much more enthusiastically pro-integration outlook on welfare questions of Albert Müller, *ibid.* (January 1954), p. 35.

union, Straeter counselled that ECSC and EDC be sharply separated and that German labour be patient and make maximum use of the principle of economic supranationalism.[15]

In the 1954 convention of I. G. Metall this attitude was put to the test. The union leadership submitted a resolution expressing faith in ECSC and the need for further economic integration through a more powerful supranationalism, side-stepping the issue of nationalisation of the steel industry, dear to many union members. Many rank-and-filers contested the resolution and demanded a new draft condemning supranationalism and advocating I. G. Metall withdrawal from participation in ECSC. They were defeated by a vote of 142 to 86 with 9 abstentions.[16]

Perhaps the most significant reason which attracts German labour to supranationalism lies in the political doctrine of the movement and is closely associated with the rationale of co-determination and labour's search for social respectability and equality. German unionists argue that parliamentary institutions characterised by strong parties and influential employers' groups are insufficient to achieve and maintain true democracy. Parties other than the SPD are suspected of plotting with employers' associations, who in turn are thought of primarily as an anti-consumer and anti-union conspiracy. Without continuous control over industrial power groups, considered to tend towards monopoly because of the " inevitable " development of large-scale industrial organisation, parliamentary democracy is likely to give way before rightist authoritarian groups at the first sign of crisis. " Economic democracy," functioning through a network of regional and national commissions representing labour, the public and the employers and thus controlling business, is considered a means to perfect parliamentary institutions.[17]

Co-determination—in the absence of nationalisation—is one facet of this approach. " It is a mistake to consider co-determination as the partnership of capital and labour," said Viktor Agartz. " Co-determination attempts to *regulate anew* the relationship of

[15] ECSC *Bulletin*, November 1954. *Protokoll über den 3. Ordentlichen Gewerk-schaftstag der I. G. Metall* (September 14, 1954), pp. 83 *et seq.*
[16] *Protokoll* (September 14, 1954), pp. 208–211, 506–507.
[17] V. Agartz, " Wirtschafts- und Steuerpolitik," *Die Quelle*, Sondernummer 1954, pp. 37 *et seq.* Hans Rehhahn, " Zum Problem der Kontrolle privater Macht-positionen," *Gewerkschaftliche Monatshefte*, Vol. 5, no. 5 (May 1954), pp. 268 *et seq.* Also see the identical argument of the Catholic trade union theorist Oswald von Nell-Breuning in *ibid.*, (Feb. 1954), pp. 65 *et seq.*

organised economic power and solidly organised labour in the sense of democratic control, by way of the delegates of the trade unions." [18] It follows that any extension of this principle, nationally or supranationally, is likely to be favoured by German unionists.

In the nexus of further integration, German labour has not been slow to make use of the possibilities thus offered. Apart from the hope of controlling the power of industrialists, the unionists also see in organs like the ECSC Consultative Committee a means for achieving supranationally the respectability and equality with business denied them in the national framework. These sentiments have found expression in uncompromising demands for trade union participation in the planning and implementation of new steps toward integration, including the steps envisaged by the Messina Conference. Said DGB executive Willi Richter:

> European organisations must, in much larger measure than heretofore, call on trade unions for consultations and decisions, since the unions are solely competent and specifically created to represent workers and all those who produce. The tremendous and responsible tasks of trade unions make clear that mere occasional consultations can no longer be considered adequate. Trade unions must demand that they be admitted as voting participants in all European organs charged with questions affecting or interesting labour and welfare. Only thus can trade unions help carry the common responsibility for shaping the future of Europe along lines of social progress for the working-man, in harmony with the demands of personal freedom and economic and social security.[19]

On this assumption—which would give labour a position of power supranationally which it has never enjoyed nationally in Germany— even the fragmentary pro-integration measures planned at Messina and Brussels were welcomed by the DGB, always provided that the new organs would possess greater powers for initiating a common welfare policy for Europe than is wielded by ECSC.

French Labour and European Integration

In the economic realm, the French unions—whether Communist, Socialist or Catholic-dominated—have been waging an identical desperate fight for basic working-class benefits since 1945. Emphasis has been less on an increase in living standards than on a defence

---

[18] Agartz, *op. cit.*, p. 40. *Das Mitbestimmungsgespräch*, (July/August 1955), p. 11. Italics mine.
[19] *Welt der Arbeit*, October 1, 1954. Ludwig Rosenberg, *ibid.*, September 2, 1955.

of collective bargaining rights and wage-and-hour standards previously achieved.   Confronted with mounting inflation and deterioration of bargaining power due to government regulation and union fragmentation, French working-class standards have tended to remain stationary, or to decline.   The battle cry of all the unions since 1948 has been the *preservation* of living standards through successive cost-of-living adjustments, increases in social security benefits and family allowances, and a guaranteed minimum wage standard likely to survive further inflation.   In the face of this preoccupation, differences in doctrine have been of peripheral significance: all the unions claim to protect the working-man against the evils of unchecked liberal competition and the process of proletarianisation.[20]

Politically, however, this identity of aims has by no means led to working-class unity.   On the contrary, the Christian Confederation (CFTC) prides itself on its independent role and demands " trade union freedom against the possibility of various totalitarianisms, with the logical consequence of [union] pluralism, but safeguarding unity of action." [21]   The Socialist-oriented Force Ouvrière (FO) defends its institutional independence equally ferociously, claiming to preserve democracy through pluralism in the trade union movement, by opposing the dominance of political parties over union activities.   In the face of these statements, the Communist-controlled CGT claims to stand for working-class unity, while of course being the object of those non-Communist charges which protest against party dominance over labour.   CFTC and FO are thus forced into a dual defensive role: economically they fight against a further deterioration of living standards while politically they seek to stave off Communist attacks of breaking union solidarity and fragmenting the working class.[22]

One important reaction to this doubly defensive position has been the favourable attitude of the non-Communist unions to foreign economic ties of all kinds for France.   FO and CFTC welcomed the Marshall Plan—in the face of CGT charges of American imperialism and French subordination to Wall Street.   They have advocated strong international ties among Socialist and Christian unions, respectively, and have stressed the global mission

[20] J.-L. Guglielmi and M. Perrot, *Salaires et Revendications Sociales en France,* 1944–1952, (Paris: Armand Colin, 1953), pp. 99–129.
[21] Guglielmi and Perrot, *op. cit.,* p. 141.
[22] *Ibid.,* pp. 85–96.

of the trade union movement, in under-developed areas as well as on the European Continent. And as if to seek supranational support for domestic weakness, they embraced the Schuman Plan proposals from the first. " Without wishing to reiterate the [pro-European] thesis defended for decades by trade unions," noted the FO Central Committee on May 12, 1950, " we wish to remind that since the end of the war the free trade unions have advocated the thought of a European agreement on coal." Said FO president, Robert Bothereau, of the ECSC in 1951: " Co-operation is substituted for competition, order takes over from anarchy, planning takes the place of improvisation." For the CFTC, President Gaston Tessier expressed enthusiasm for the Plan, but he added:

> It goes without saying that the rights and interests of the working class must be guaranteed in this new structure. Therefore it is essential that the labour movement be represented on the High Authority . . . whose role in labour and welfare matters must be as great as its economic power.

Both FO and CFTC agreed that the ECSC must conduce to full employment and the creation of new industries able to absorb those unemployed in the readaptation process, in addition to providing for the direct representation of trade unions.[23]

In the years which followed, positive identification with ECSC aims and activities has far outweighed occasions of criticism and opposition. The miners have complained about inadequate social security coverage, but their dissatisfaction was directed against their own Government in even greater measure than against the High Authority. Insufficient pensions, lagging public housing programmes, long working hours and low salaries have regularly figured in the list of union complaints. Again, however, miners and metalworkers have blamed Paris and Luxembourg indiscriminately, without initial loyalty to supranationalism being undermined by these grievances.[24]

For the FO Miners, however, the problem of the future of French coal production has been by far the most serious grievance against ECSC. As succinctly put by their president, Noel Sinot, the High Authority is accused of neglecting the establishment of ECSC buffer stocks to equalise and compensate for price movements,

[23] Georges LeFranc, " Les Syndicats ouvriers face au Plan Schuman," *Nouvelle Revue de l'Economie contemporaine*, no. 16–17, November 1951, pp. 55–57.
[24] *Informations Bimensuelles*, August 1, 1954, p. 18; September 15, 1954, p. 13.

of declining to interest itself in employment stability for the mines by arranging long-term regional coal trading patterns and for being eager to import Polish and American fuels while French mines have difficulties in disposing of their excess stock of low-grade coal.[25] It is in this connection that the issue of national coal sales organisations comes into prominence in the French as in the German context. FO as well as CFTC unions had no quarrel with GEORG in the Ruhr, if only because they hoped that France's ATIC would also be permitted to function if joint sales were permitted in Germany. Joint sales, fixed prices and restrictions on imports—even on the common market—are defended as essential, with only the " legalism " of the ECSC Treaty opposed to this " economic necessity." [26] Opposition to large-scale labour migration is as typical of the French unions as of their German colleagues. Strikingly then, on the cartel and manpower issues, purely *national* group interests militate against loyalty to the integration movement on both sides of the Rhine.

Yet the remedies for the problems here implied are found almost invariably in demands for additional *supranational* powers and activities. FO demands that social security contributions be equalised in all ECSC states, though its motives are nationally derived and identical with the claims of the Charbonnages de France. More ECSC investment through supranational lending, a higher ECSC production levy and, above all, a joint ECSC policy for the protection of coal against the competition of fuel oil are demanded. In short, an extension of ECSC powers is urged in those aspects of labour policy in which the total cost bill of other ECSC countries is *below* the French cost structure, implying a movement of wages, hours and social security factors *upward* to the French standard. Further, the unions demand more supranationalism in the economic sector of greatest concern to them: the slow decay of the French mining industry, unable to compete with newer fuels and German coal. Here they see an answer in a co-ordinated and planned energy policy (designed to protect coal) which national French planning can no longer give them because of the common market.[27]

---

[25] Questions put to High Authority in Consultative Committee, July 8, 1955.
[26] J. Grandier and A. Williame, " La question des Cartels dans la CECA," *Bulletin du Centre International d'Informations*, no. 64, December 5, 1955.
[27] *Informations Mensuelles*, May 1956, p. 43; September 15, 1954, p. 13. CFTC Mineworkers' statement in ECSC *Bulletin*, November 1954. CFTC Mineworkers' 19th National Congress (July 1956), in *Informations Mensuelles*, August 1956, p. 24.

Loyalty to supranationalism was aroused, more than in any other context, by the High Authority's re-adaptation programme, of which France has so far been the major beneficiary. The common market compelled a series of mergers and corporate re-organisations which entailed lay-offs in the steel industry.[28] Without the use of unemployment, retraining and tide-over allowances paid jointly by the High Authority and the French Government, the CGT predictions of economic disaster for labour might have been realised, at least locally. FO and CFTC therefore exerted themselves for expediting the payment of these sums and frequently sharply attacked their own Government for slowness and indifference, using Luxembourg as their major support. CFTC pressure on Paris was largely responsible for the creation of bipartite labour-management commissions to examine and process demands for re-adaptation aid. CFTC insists that the payments be administered jointly, and thereby gains equality with management in at least one facet of French industrial relations.[29]

Nevertheless, in the crucial coal sector not even the re-adaptation factor has been able to overcome some rank-and-file opposition to integration. In the Centre-Midi mining centre of Alès, coal mining is becoming increasingly inefficient, with gradual closing of the mines planned. Some 5,000 miners were offered tide-over allowances, removal expenses and new housing in Lorraine, if they consented to transfer to that bustling mining region. By 1956 only 648 had agreed to move, however, with the remainder insisting that the Alès mine be kept open, cost what may. Part of the opposition to re-adaptation stemmed from the fact that many of the miners were part-time farmers, domiciled in the region for centuries, but others insisted on the bad climate, alien customs and typically industrial conditions prevailing in Lorraine. In any case, the CGT presented the removal programme as " deportation," leading to slave labour in Germany, and organised resistance among the already reluctant miners. The net result was not only

[28] The classical example of this development is found in the formation of the Compagnie des Ateliers et Forges de la Loire, from four pre-existing small and inefficient firms. See the description of the merger and readaptation mechanism in High Authority, Information Service, " New Deal for French Steel," July 6, 1955. Doc. 2684/55e.

[29] Paul Brayet, " L'avis du syndicaliste," *Hommes et Commerce*, no. 25, January–February, 1955, p. 70. René Puiraveau, " Mécanisme des reconversions de la CECA," *ibid.*, pp. 64 *et seq.* Employer enthusiasm about the system has been equally pronounced with industrialists joining the union in castigating the government for not taking greater interest in the possibilities of readaptation.

the economic defeat of FO and CFTC unions anxious to adapt to the common market, but their crushing political defeat in subsequent works council elections.[30]   Having learned their lesson, French unionists since have demanded that re-adaptation aid be used to re-employ surplus labour locally instead of seeking to encourage removal to another region.   The consequence has been the demand that ECSC investment and similar activities under additional integration measures be geared to the creation of new industries in the regions where structural unemployment is likely. Extension of ECSC powers is thus implied once more.

Loyalty to supranational institutions on the part of the non-Communist French union leadership thus dates from the domestic weakness of the unions, but has since been immeasurably reinforced by the recognition that the difficulties and shortcomings of the common market can be solved only by more supranationalism, and not by a return to the closed national market.   Certainly, purely national economic fears are at the base of these claims, but a strengthening of supranational loyalties follows just the same, since only Luxembourg is considered to possess the means for allaying the fears.   This mediation of aims by way of the High Authority is facilitated in the case of FO and CFTC by their already deeply developed dependence on state action to realise wage demands, given the limitations of French collective bargaining.   Dependence on the French Government has simply been transferred to the supranational authority, with the nature of the claims essentially unchanged.   Hence, it is hardly surprising to find French unions

---

[30] See the complete treatment of J.-M. Albertini, " Problèmes humains et aménagement du territoire? Les mineurs d'Alès," *Economie et Humanisme*, Vol. 13, no. 88, Nov.–Dec. 1954, pp. 18–26. *Informations Mensuelles* (November 1956), p. 84.

That rank-and-file enthusiasm for integration is far less pronounced is clear from this opinion survey (*Sondages, op. cit.*, pp. 45 *et seq.*). The question asked was: which of these changes will come about as a result of ECSC?

ECSC:	*yes*	*no*	*don't know*
Will make for higher living standards for all Europe	15	24	30
Will make for unemployment	23	18	28
Will reduce risk of European wars	29	18	22
Will make for more independence against the U.S...	22	20	27
Will facilitate the rapid recovery of Germany	32	9	28
Is the first step toward the United States of Europe..	36	10	23
Means more American control over Europe........	19	20	30
Means the loss of French independence	23	19	27

The total is less than 100 per cent. because 31 per cent. of the workers' sample was unaware of the existence of ECSC. 27 per cent. of the workers wanted ECSC to succeed, 10 per cent. did not, with the rest opinionless. The combined influence of apathy and CGT influence is thus clearly demonstrated.

calling for the harmonisation of ECSC-wide labour standards through the medium of ECSC-wide collective bargaining under High Authority auspices.[31]

For the CFTC, Catholic social doctrine provides yet another strong motive for increasing supranational loyalty. The federation is opposed to nationalisation of industries if this process merely entails state management. Its notions of industrial harmony include a corporatist, anti-class struggle and social harmony component, which it seeks to achieve in practice through tripartite commissions in all major phases of the economy, representing labour, industry and the public. As with the DGB, but for different reasons, economic democracy is held out as the answer to the problems of modern industrialism. And as in the case of the German unions, the institutions of ECSC and of the future organs of integration provide for far more representation of trade union leaders in responsible positions of equality than do the institutions prevalent within the national framework. Supranationalism once more becomes the means for achieving social and economic respectability.[32]

ITALIAN LABOUR AND EUROPEAN INTEGRATION

As in France, the non-Communist Italian unions greeted the Schuman Plan with enthusiasm while their Communist rivals predicted the death of the Italian coal and steel industries. With the exception of the key issues of migration and re-adaptation, however, Italian labour has followed Italian attitudes in arguing for integration generally without taking a sustained interest in ECSC developments since 1952. Certainly no opposition to ECSC has developed, while the Social-Democratic labour leader Italo Viglianesi expressed the sentiment of most European trade unionists in demanding more supranational action in the welfare field.[33]

---

[31] It is equally natural that FO, while generally endorsing the EEC Treaty as well as Euratom, has again gone out of its way to demand a maximal representation of trade unionists on supranational organs and the association of labour leaders with the delegations negotiating the treaties. Contrast this position with the attitude of the nationally identified CGC, which took position against EEC and Euratom in 1956 because the integrated European economy would destroy the French Union, militate against French control over industries crucial for national defence, make France dependent on rule by a Commission in which she would be in a minority, and because the immediate harmonisation of social legislation was not obtained. *Informations Mensuelles* (January 1957), pp. 38 and 109.

[32] Guglielmi and Perrot, *op. cit.*, Chap. 2 and pp. 52–53.

[33] *Informations Bimensuelles* (March 31, 1955), p. 13.

Migration has been the chief interest of Italians in all aspects of integration because they see in it a means for facilitating industrialisation without being burdened by an excess labour force and permanent unemployment, which might—if unchecked— result in negating the benefits of industrialisation. The restrictive interpretation given to Article 69 of the ECSC Treaty and the hostile attitudes toward migration typical of the other ECSC countries have given rise to disappointment in Italian labour circles. With respect to re-adaptation payments to steelworkers threatened with loss of jobs due to the forced reorganisation of the fragmented Italian steel industry, both the UIL and CISL have been critical of their own government far more than of the High Authority. Reconciled to the necessity for mergers and concentrations if Italian steel is to compete successfully with other ECSC countries after the expiration of the transitional period, they have argued for the creation of new industries with ECSC funds. Administrative inefficiency as well as a certain reserve toward the creation of a group of " privileged unemployed " in an economy already burdened with two million jobless workers have combined to produce an extreme slowness on the part of the Italian Government in requesting aid from Luxembourg—and without governmental request the High Authority cannot act.

The unions, in this situation, have tended to sidestep Rome and approached the High Authority directly, while Luxembourg has used union demands to put pressure upon the Italian Government for filing requests for aid. The result has been a reinforcement of loyalties to the supranational centre, despite the disappointment on the issue of free migration rights.

The Italian unions being weak, they cannot afford to forgo the support they may receive from ECSC and stronger unions to the north. Aid and pressure from the International Confederation of Free Trade Unions have been instrumental in inducing UIL and CISL to agree to a gradual merger. Encouragement has been received from striking electoral victories over the Communist unions in the works councils of the giant Fiat plants, followed up by indications of a pro-ECSC *volte face* by Communist union leaders. Hopes for increasing benefits under the ten-year Vanoni industrialisation plan have spurred efforts for gaining wage benefits now, especially with the reinforcement of supranational institution and measures.[34]

DUTCH LABOUR AND EUROPEAN INTEGRATION

Dutch labour, like the bulk of Dutch opinion, welcomed all integration proposals at all times and almost under all circumstances. While unswervingly supporting ECSC since its inception, the paradoxical feature about Dutch unions has been their relative indifference to the demands and preoccupations of other ECSC labour groups against the High Authority. Wedded to a " no conflict " doctrine in domestic Dutch economic affairs, the unions have been unwilling to upset the internal price-wage-cost equilibrium and have therefore refrained from taking their grievances to the supranational forum. To the agitation for the forty-hour week they have continued indifferent, with the Socialist-oriented NVV claiming that other considerations are more important. Only the Catholic Miners' Union has taken up the general European cry for a reduction of the work week.[35] The overall programme of harmonising overtime and vacation pay as well as the length of vacations in the ECSC industries has failed to interest the Dutch, though they have not opposed it overtly. Nor have they made a special point of common counter-cyclical policy-making or investment planning.

The reasons are obvious. Under the actual economic conditions which have prevailed in the Netherlands since 1946, industry has flourished, prices have been kept down and exports have boomed. No group in Holland, including labour, wishes to interfere with this happy state of affairs even if drastic increases in living standards are not immediately obtained. With more economic integration and a General Common Market, exports would develop further. Hence, labour is not interested in now changing the future competitive position of Dutch industry by burdening producers with a higher bill. Yet it is quite conceivable that the example of unions in other ECSC countries—especially in Belgium—seeking to generalise their domestic wage and hour gains throughout the ECSC area will ultimately fall on receptive ground in Holland. Already the Catholic KAB is restive under the restrictions governing

[34] *Auslandsnachrichten des DGB* (May–June 1955), pp. 14 *et seq.* (July 1955), pp. 7 *et seq.*
[35] *Informations Bimensuelles*, October 15, 1954, p. 8; November 15, 1955, p. 23; May 1956, p. 44.

collective bargaining, though the NVV is quite satisfied with them. Under the well-developed stimulus for joint union action through the Federation of Christian Trade Unions in ECSC, it is quite conceivable that some of the Dutch unions will sooner or later be drawn into the general pattern of claims and counterclaims.

BELGIAN LABOUR AND EUROPEAN INTEGRATION

Under the leadership of André Renard, the Socialist-oriented FGTB in Belgium can well be considered the most important single stimulus to the evolution of a common ECSC labour policy. The joint effort for " harmonisation of living conditions " is largely the work of this organisation, if not of Renard personally.

FGTB as well as the Catholic CSC approved the Schuman Plan wholeheartedly in 1951. However, they made the specific request that welfare policy and labour standards be considered among the major purposes of the Treaty, and not merely an adjunct of economic policy, and to this position both federations have adhered ever since, giving rise to frequent outbursts of impatience and dissatisfaction. Further, both unions demanded that they be consulted in the drafting and the implementation of the Treaty, thus demonstrating once more the appeal of supranationalism to Continental trade unionists anxious to achieve positions of equality with industry and government. The fears of unemployment, mine shut-downs and deterioration of Belgian living standards voiced by some Socialists in Parliament found little support in union circles.

FGTB as well as CSC took their pro-integration positions because they accepted the common market rationale, the aim of Franco-German amity and hoped for increases in living standards enforced by federal authority. The CSC, moreover, found in Catholic labour doctrine further reasons for supporting ECSC. " We have the duty to make understood, alongside with other viewpoints, the Christian socio-economic programme at the international level. This is of first importance for the Schuman Plan because we are part of a group of countries strongly characterised by Christian doctrine." [36] Further cogency is given to this outlook if it be recalled that Belgian Catholic trade unionists, unlike their French colleagues, claim a mission of combating the effects of

[36] Louis Dereau, " Les Syndicats chrétiens et le Plan Schuman," *Etudes Economiques*, no. 81–82, November 1951, p. 137.

industrial capitalism while opposing the Socialist " materialist " programme of coping with these.[37] CSC Metalworkers, while somewhat apprehensive about the possible influx of foreign labour under ECSC, fully subscribed to the common market doctrine, while CSC Miners saw in the Treaty a technique for " equalising " living standards throughout the area.

Specific criticism and opposition to High Authority policy has been rare, so that no evidence is at hand to indicate a diminution of early loyalty to the idea of integration. The bulk of opposition occurred with reference to the ever-present issue of Belgian coal mining. Naturally, the unions oppose any policy—national or supranational—which would result in the closing of mines and unemployment. Efforts at modernising the Borinage pits are considered inadequate and the rate of concentrating and re-distributing the strips too slow and modest. Nationalisation of the whole industry or the setting up of a single firm in the Borinage are demanded. Conversely, the unions fear price competition among economically unequal coal fields and have opposed the High Authority's anti-cartel programme, arguing the need for sales organisations exactly as do the Ruhr miners. Housing construction is considered inadequate and the recurrent disasters in Belgian pits have led to complaints that Luxembourg does too little in the field of safety. At the same time, however, FGTB Miner leader, Nichol Dethier, has given the High Authority credit for efforts which were undertaken along these lines and has called for " an ECSC spirit, and beyond that, a European spirit " among young miners.

An expanded supranational labour and welfare policy is the chief demand of Belgian miners, both Socialist and Catholic. They are committed to the attainment of the forty-hour week, to higher salaries and improved working conditions, despite rising extraction costs. Since the future of Belgian coal depends on the common market and joint Belgo-High Authority aid measures until 1958, the miners are turning increasingly to Luxembourg for support in their demands, only to be told that the ECSC organs lack jurisdiction over welfare questions. " The Community possesses complete authority for regulating economic problems," answers Dethier. " But when labour issues come up, it withdraws into an

[37] Msgr. A. Brys, *The Principles and Organisation of the Christian Labour Movement of Belgium* (mimeographed CSC pamphlet, *ca.* 1952).

ivory tower and, like Pilate, washes its hands of the matter! . . . That we can never admit." [38]

The claim of the miners, in microcosm, is the general demand of the FGTB. Its overall economic doctrine and programme forces the Socialist federation into a firm supranational position, in which it must in sheer self-defence seek solutions through ECSC action. The FGTB is committed to a Belgian policy of democratic economic planning, combining the nationalisation of energy-producing industries with the setting of production targets for the private sector. Central steering of investments is considered essential, as is a lowering of prices and a stimulation of exports. Concurrently, however, the FGTB demands full employment, a shorter work week and a guaranteed weekly wage. Economic democracy on the model of the German unions also figures among its claims— though stopping short of co-determination—while a vigorous Government policy for the public control of the gigantic and strategic Belgian holding companies is advocated. And with this programme the CSC agrees as regards the details, though not in the reasons advanced for it.[39]

This juxtaposition of claims has led directly to Luxembourg for action. Throughout the year 1954 the FGTB's demands for a five-day week without loss of pay had been rejected by Belgian industry and Government spokesmen as ruinous to Belgian exports since it would increase production costs. As far as the steel industry was concerned, any increase in Belgian worker benefits would have to be matched by competitors in Germany and France, thus keeping the cost ratio unchanged. The Belgian Government, finally, opined that it lacked the powers to act and referred the unions to the High Authority. " Yes, we have to take the question to the international level," answered the FGTB metalworkers.[40]

The economic logic of the situation is clear. Unable to achieve a purely nationally planned economy with rising worker benefits without at the same time undermining Belgium's foreign and intra-ECSC trade prospects, the answer could be found only in " harmonisation of social conditions " throughout the ECSC area. Pre-existing enthusiasm for economic integration thus combined with compelling national trade union tactics to result in the

---

[38] N. Dethier, " La C. E. C. A.," *L'Ouvrier Mineur* (September 1955).
[39] FGTB, Information à la Presse, March 8, 1955. *Syndicats*, November 13, 1954; May 15, 1954; June 5, 1954. *Informations Bimensuelles*, November 1, 1954, p. 24.
[40] *Syndicats*, November 13, 1954.

programme of André Renard to give ECSC sweeping powers in the labour and welfare fields. In July of 1954, the Metalworkers passed this revealing resolution: the workers

> appreciate the results already obtained by the Coal and Steel Community in the economic realm, but will support all action likely to prevent capitalist cartels from taking the place of the High Authority and imposing their dirigist practices, which are well known. Considering that Europe cannot be created except on the condition that the living standards of workers are raised first, demand of sister organisations in other European countries that they establish among themselves the closest possible ties in order to bring about finally the creation of true European trade union power; wish for the conclusion *within the framework of international bipartite commissions, of collective agreements, freely negotiated among producers' and workers' representatives under the aegis of the High Authority.* Consider that the time has come to demand . . . a meeting of employers and workers of the six countries, in order to draw up a bill of basic rights for European workers.[41]

The programme is nothing short of ECSC-wide collective bargaining. André Renard, following up with his cry for action in the Consultative Committee in December of 1954, noted that these demands " would make for a true welfare community by progressively eliminating the causes of economic friction " and thus truly establish the common market.[42] " The European Idea will have taken a great step ahead the day on which the workers of the Community will decree of their common accord a general strike, if only for twenty-four hours, to attain a common objective." [43]

The CSC, though not in the forefront of groups seeking to extend the authority and scope of supranationalism, nevertheless has identified itself with the FGTB. CSC metalworkers joined the FGTB union in asking for the five-day week without loss of pay and CSC circles share fully the impatience of Socialist unionists with the slow and peripheral quality of ECSC welfare policy. Both unions, immediately upon the conclusion of the Messina Conference, demanded of their Government that they participate in the work of the Inter-governmental Commission to report on the common market and Euratom schemes; further, they stressed that the common market provide for the harmonisation of living standards as well as for free movement of goods, capital and manpower.

[41] *Ibid.*, July 10, 1954. Italics supplied.   [42] *Syndicats*, April 3, 1954.
[43] *Ibid.,* January 8, 1955.

A threefold causative process explains the motivation of the FGTB toward European integration. Initially, this federation, like almost all other European trade unions, was in principle " internationalist " and committed to the co-operative global raising of living and working standards, through the activities of the ILO and of the International Confederation of Free Trade Unions. Reassured on specific national sources of concern—the mines, re-adaptation, protection of high living standards—espousal of ECSC was perfectly consistent with ideology and safe with respect to national economic tactics. Once part of the common market, however, the internationalist dedication was strongly reinforced by purely *national* economic issues: the inability to realise a planned economy and rising worker benefits without generalising such policies throughout the ECSC area, thus perforce necessitating an extension of supranational powers. Pre-existing loyalty to supranational symbols was strengthened by essentially expediential economic considerations at the national level.

The third and final element is introduced into this process of reinforcing loyalties to supranational symbols by the tendency to justify the demand for more federal powers with arguments derived from Socialist—international—ideology. FGTB protested strongly against the tendency to exclude from the General Common Market the colonial territories of the six member states, characterising such efforts as leading to " native revolts against exploitation by the metropolitan country, ending in political and economic disaster for all interested parties."[44] The effort to exclude the Belgian Congo, for instance, from the common market was regarded as a reactionary capitalist device to prevent rational economic planning for the common benefit of Europeans and Africans. Further, the view of the integrated market held by the unionists is Socialist-tinted:

> In foreseeing a transitional period of adaptation, we must certainly also suppress the obstacles barring the free circulation of men, goods, services and even capital. But if we wish to avoid that this progressive suppression of protectionism within this integrated zone produce grave economic and social upheavals, engender unemployment and lowering of salaries, it is essential that the supranational institutions dispose of means of aiding in structural transformation, to direct adequate investments to underdeveloped zones,

[44] Rapport du Congrès extraordinaire de la F. G. T. B. (October 1954), p. 254.

to stimulate consumption in case of recession, to harmonise economic, welfare, fiscal and financial policies of the member states.[45]

Thus, clearly visions of international labour harmony lead to a predisposition for integration—provided specific fears are allayed. Expansion of institutions and practices of the integrated sectors is demanded as the result of national tactics and needs, but the vision of the larger integrated economy, finally, is again that dictated by labour ideology. Ideological and institutional pressures thus neatly reinforce one another in producing a drive for additional integration, once the process has been set under way.[46]

This conclusion can serve as an accurate summary of the total attitude toward integration typical of the trade union movements in the six countries. Original support for ECSC is explained by the convergence, in each country, of general ideological support—whether Catholic or Socialist—and specific material advantage expected. Realisation that the advantage cannot be fully reaped without a stronger ECSC gave rise to demands in all six countries for a stronger High Authority and more economic integration. Convergence of aspiration in six separate national compartments thus continues to explain the drive for federation. Yet this convergence nationally results in most significant *supranational* efforts at joint trade union thinking and action, to be explored in a later chapter.

---

[45] *Ibid.* (October 1954), pp. 256–257.

[46] Even the British Trade Unions Council, after considerable hesitation to take any interest in the efforts at economic integration and support for the Labour Party's erstwhile sense of aloofness, decided in November of 1956 to support the General Common Market in principle by expressing its approval for the Macmillan Government's Free Trade Area proposal. Over the dissent of the representatives of the Amalgamated Engineering Union and the pottery workers, the T.U.C. General Council approved the government's policy, provided the following safeguarding measures were insisted upon: special assistance to industries adversely affected by the common market and special efforts to obviate structural unemployment; Britain is to retain fiscal autonomy and the right to plan for its industries; balance of payments reasons may be invoked to suspend the free trade aspects of the common market; dumping is to be illegal and minimum standard of living rules for workers must be inserted into the agreement; explicit provisions for maintaining full employment must be stated; cartels are to be combated; Britain is to remain free to conclude agreements on raw materials with the Commonwealth and with third countries: *Financial Times*, November 20, 1956. In view of these reservations, it can hardly be argued that British trade unions embraced the idea of economic integration with any great enthusiasm. On the other hand, their very protectionism is such that it would logically lead them to demand of future international or supranational agencies the same sweeping welfare programmes and protection against instability through planning as have come to characterise the attitudes of their Continental colleagues.

CHAPTER 7

THE CONDUCT OF MEMBER GOVERNMENTS

IF the countries partaking in the European integration movement were habitually ruled by single parties possessing an absolute parliamentary majority, there would be relatively little need to analyse the conduct of the member governments in addition to discussing the evolution of party doctrine. The beliefs of the ruling political formation would be identical with government policy. Obviously, however, this precondition is not met in any of the six states in question. Coalitions of parties habitually rule in all of them and government policy is invariably a compromise among the partners, a compromise which by no means necessarily implies the carry-over into policy of the attitudes toward integration held by the largest constituent. Further, multi-party government—especially in France —depends far more heavily for consistency and expert guidance on participation by the higher civil service than is true in some other democratic settings. Policy toward integration, consequently, reflects much more than the attitude of single parties: it includes judgments held in the bureaucratic hierarchy as well as the compromises which accompany coalition government. Hence a separate analysis of governments is imperative.

The discussion of parties, trade associations and trade unions was confined to tracing changes in attitudes and ideology expressed in the setting of the national state and reflecting aspirations growing out of that setting. It left aside the equally relevant and highly important index of changes in attitude due to continued interaction with kindred groups in the other ECSC countries as well as the pattern of that interaction. The next portion of this work is explicitly devoted to this index. Our discussion of governmental conduct, however, cannot be based on that same division of labour. Interaction among the six governments is continual and direct. National administrative decisions in the setting of the common market necessarily beget positive or negative reactions from other member governments. Hence the organisation by national groups followed heretofore will be abandoned in favour of a threefold approach: negotiation, implementation and expansion of the ECSC Treaty as dealt with by each government, in response to stimuli by

the other governments.   Nevertheless, no attention will be given
in this chapter to the processes of joint governmental decision-
making and conferences will not be systematically analysed.   While
the consequences of such meetings will, of course, be relevant here,
the process of ECSC inter-governmental decision-making is reserved
for a later chapter.

How can we measure the degree of loyalty or opposition shown
to ECSC by the member governments, as distinguished from
parties or private groups?   Four sets of questions appear relevant:

1. Has there been resistance to supranational rules and decisions?
If so, is the undesired decision (a) ignored, (b) administratively
sabotaged, (c) accepted after legal appeals provided for in the Treaty
are exhausted, or (d) loyally accepted and implemented?

2. Do national governments make specific demands and claims
of the High Authority in obedience to national policy?   If so, do
they yield to the opinion of the High Authority or the Council of
Ministers if the claims fail to be accepted or met?

3. Do national governments freely make themselves the mouthpiece of the kind of national trade association and trade union
demands sketched in the preceding chapters?   Especially anti-
supranational demands?

4. Do governments advance and/or oppose arguments for
extending the powers and scope of supranational institutions in the
integration process, or do they hew closely to the preservation of
national sovereignty in favouring inter-governmental techniques
of co-operation?

The conduct of the six member governments from 1950 until 1957
will be analysed in terms of these questions.

Negotiating the ECSC Treaty

For France, at any rate, the purely economic aims intended by the
proponents of the Community are easily spelled out.   Informing
the cabinet of their intention of suggesting a supranational plan of
integration only five days before making the announcement and
keeping Parliament entirely in the dark, Robert Schuman and Jean
Monnet were the true architects of French policy.   Since they
guarded the monopoly of participating in the negotiations until

the very last stages of the eleven-months process, their aims were then the true aims of France.[1]

Economically, the plan was a multi-purpose project. Unwilling to create an all-embracing customs or economic union immediately because of the difficulties it would offer to small producers, a start toward economic unification seemed most promising in two industries responsive to internationally identical investment, rationalisation and organisational principles, accounting for relatively few firms and including a labour force not more than 1·5 per cent. of the total ECSC population.[2] Moreover, these industries were particularly liable to fears of oversupply and falling prices. Such fears had led to tentative steps toward a revived European steel cartel by 1950.[3] The common market would open for France a new outlet for her vastly expanded steel production, thus safeguarding the planning and investment for steel carried on in the four previous years by Monnet's Commissariat du Plan, then beset by fears of having overinvested. The common market, finally, would assure a French coke supply from the Ruhr, all previous French efforts for international control of that area, compulsory deliveries of coal or transplantation of German equipment to Lorraine having been blocked by Britain and the United States.[4] Finally, tied to a common market, the danger of German hegemony seemed susceptible of control. As Monnet said, " without the Schuman Plan . . . without the unified market, Germany will dictate the rate of development of the French steel industry." And Schuman added:

[1] Robert Schuman, " Origines et élaboration du Plan Schuman," *Cahiers de Bruges* (December, 1953), pp. 13–14. This article is a remarkably frank statement by Schuman, three years after the event, of his motives and methods. No formal instructions were ever issued to the French delegation. The motives of all the governments, but especially those of the French Government, are fully discussed in Pierre Gerbet, " La Genèse du Plan Schuman," *Revue Française de Science Politique*, Vol. 6, no. 3 (1956), pp. 525–553. Gerbet's discussion includes a summary of the private, semi-public and public schemes and suggestions for the internationalisation of basic industries current in western Europe between 1948 and 1950. See also the excellent study by G. Goriély, " Naissance de la Communauté Européenne du Charbon et de l'Acier," circulated as High Authority Doc. 7889/56f (mimeo.).
[2] Schuman, *op. cit.*, pp. 7–8.
[3] Gerbet, *op. cit.*, pp. 529 *et seq.*
[4] Racine, *op. cit.*, p. 37. Paul Reuter, *La Communauté Européenne du Charbon et de l'Acier*, (Paris: Librairie Générale de Droit et de Jurisprudence, 1953), pp. 129 *et seq.* This is the most authoritative French legal interpretation by a member of the French delegation. For inferential, but completely convincing, evidence of fears of over-investment in French steel as a major French motive, see Hahn, *op. cit.*, pp. 11, 17, 26–33, 45–47. The coke argument was widely used by the Government in parliamentary discussions.

If French industry rejects this effort—which is out of the question —then we really have to fear the hegemony of those who have given evidence of the greatest dynamism and who are quick in making up for lost time. But this danger exists also if the Treaty is not applied. The whiplash which will thus be given will be a salutary one, not only for industry but for the whole nation.[5]

But economics played a very secondary handmaiden to politics in the priority of French governmental aims. Economics provided the attraction to make the political pill palatable to certain groups. Only to the extent that ECSC was to serve the rejuvenation of French industrial society did economic aims occupy an important part. Politically, ECSC was to serve simultaneously the aim of a federated Europe and the national needs of French security against German growth. Franco-German peace—the central aim of Schuman and his friends—was to be achieved by means of a "solidarity of facts," of creative measures to develop industrial resources in common, thus to achieve "a fusion of interests" in a "community of nations," subject to federal authorities which would make any new war physically impossible and spiritually unthinkable. At the same time, the supranational institutions and powers would act as a stimulus to further integration and ultimately result in a federation just because the separation of coal and steel from the bulk of the economy was artificial. The "spill-over" effect of the sector approach was explicitly understood and deliberately planned by the French initiators of ECSC. Specific French interests, however, were by no means forgotten in this array of federal aims. ECSC would make possible the removal of the most irritating Allied controls over the German economy, while being a "Community" agent for the supervision of remaining controls instead of a purely alien overseer. Hence the French insisted on continued German decartellisation and deconcentration— albeit in a new framework—which Monnet originally carried to the extreme of wishing to forbid all mergers which would give an individual shareholder stock in excess of 10 per cent. Finally, as far as Schuman, at least, was concerned, ECSC would provide a step toward the solution of the Saar problem by rendering the question of control over Saar coal and steel irrelevant: submersion in ECSC would give French and Germans equal access at market

[5] Rieben, *op. cit.*, p. 455 for the Monnet statement, and *Journal Officiel* (French), no. 150, A. N., December 7, 1951, p. 8896, for the Schuman statement.

prices to these commodities, while leaving formally untouched the eventual political future of the area.[6]

Because of this dual bedrock of political objectives, Schuman and Monnet refused to depart from the principle of supranationality all through the negotiations. Insisting that these pre-federal features were the essential element of the plan, they alienated British interest in the early stages of discussion in a direct and uncompromising manner. Said Schuman:

> The essential thing is the creation of a supranational authority which will be the expression of solidarity among the countries, and which will exercise a part of the powers of each of these countries. . . . A common and independent authority must be installed. The treaty which we want to write will determine its composition, purpose and powers. . . . We persist in thinking that the simple co-ordination of governmental efforts [as demanded by Britain at that time] is insufficient. We must create communities of interest on concrete foundations without the preponderance of certain countries, for the advantage of all.[7]

But the initial French formula had foreseen even more " pre-federalism " than was ultimately admitted by the other five governments. Monnet had wanted to make the High Authority responsible only to the Common Assembly, exactly as in the parliamentary

---

[6] Schuman, *op. cit.*, pp. 8–10. Reuter, *op. cit.*, pp. 3–5. Schuman's political aims are clearly summarised in his declaration of May 9, 1950, given in full in Racine, *op. cit.*, pp. 29–30. R. Evely, " Les cartels et la Communauté Européenne du Charbon et de l'Acier," *Cartel*, (July 1954), p. 88. Schuman's argument on the Saar was sharply challenged by French High Commissioner in Saarbrücken, Gilbert Grandval, who argued in June of 1951 that ECSC made the Franco-Saar economic union even more vital to France in order to maintain " equilibrium " with dynamic Germany. Racine, *op. cit.*, p. 97.

[7] In the National Assembly, July 25, 1950. Racine, *op. cit.*, p. 41 The tenor of the diplomatic correspondence which crossed the Channel between May 10 and June 3, 1950, leaves no doubt that the issue of supranationality was the hurdle Britain refused to jump. London, despite rather unconvincing French disclaimers and Monnet's personal efforts to convince the Foreign Office, insisted that Schuman's proposal made the acceptance of the supranational principle a prior condition for participating in the treaty-drafting conference. Paris replied that without reaching some agreement on basic principles even before undertaking the talks there was little hope of success. But London answered that while it wished the effort well and hoped for speedy Franco-German reconciliation, it was quite unable to accept a definite scheme based on a sovereign High Authority as a point of departure. British suggestions for the convening of a preliminary conference of ministers to work out the procedure to be adopted by the eventual treaty-drafting conference went unheeded. A Foreign Office counterplan was actually prepared but never submitted. Under it, OEEC-type committees would have sought to " co-ordinate " coal and steel problems, reduce trade barriers, control investment, split markets and stabilise prices; the principle of the common market was not clearly put forward and the essence of ECSC—supranationality—was scrupulously left out. Details in Racine, *op. cit.*, pp. 62–75.

system generally, and thus institute an embryo European legislature. Further, the initial plan had made no mention of a Council of Ministers, provided the High Authority with more direct powers over planning and investment than the final Treaty, and foreseen the formation of producers' organisations along regional rather than national lines.[8] On all these points, the French view did not prevail. The supranational formula was accepted in sufficient measure to exclude British participation—though it was hoped that this would be only temporary—but not to the extent of shutting the member governments out from key ECSC decisions.

Preoccupation with federation and Franco-German peace, however, did not imply the neglect of French economic aspirations in the details of the Treaty. Monnet's specific proposals on market rules, prices, access to raw materials, non-discrimination, subsidies, re-adaptation, and exemptions during the transitional period were accepted in essence in the final version of the Treaty, including the rigorous interpretation of Article 60 which made " non-discrimination " almost the equivalent of " no price competition," a deliberate device to limit the flow of German steel to the French market. If Monnet was successful to this extent, he failed to achieve two additional aims, vital to French motives. The rigorous deconcentration formula planned for German enterprises was not accepted and hopes for an immediate " equalisation " of production costs among the six countries were dashed. The French negotiators had insisted on equalisation from the first and suggested that member countries be given four months for coal and eight months for steel to achieve it in fact, after the opening of the common market. German and Dutch production costs—wages, taxes and social security contributions, in particular—would thus have been forced up, easing competition for France. The compromise adopted—a statement of principle in favour of equalisation unaccompanied by any supranational powers to achieve it—was a severe concession extracted from the fathers of ECSC.[9]

---

[8] Monnet's extreme proposals on the legislature were made at the second day of the conference, causing sufficient consternation to provoke an immediate adjournment. June 21, 1950. The more modest proposals which became, without major change, the terms of the Treaty, were contained in the French working paper of June 24, 1950, on which all subsequent negotiations were based. Racine, *op. cit.,* pp. 83–87, for the text.

[9] See the argument in the Declaration of May 9, 1950 and the Working Paper, *infra.* For the French interpretation of Article 60, see *Rapport de la Délégation Française sur le Traité* ... cited in Institut des Relations Internationales, *op. cit.,* p. 141.

Despite the concessions, the official French commentary on the Treaty retains a good many of the initial aims in the interpretation offered. The High Authority is characterised a supranational collegiate entity, fully independent of national governments, and marking a complete break with inter-governmental techniques. The competence of the Council of Ministers is restricted, according to the commentary, to matters of general economic interest, external to coal and steel. While the economic principle of the Treaty is liberalism and competition with a maximum of scope for free enterprise, in regard to the functions of the High Authority crises and transitional planning are stressed equally.[10] And the fact that the French Parliament was not led by the Treaty to renounce its claims for the Moselle Canal, cost equalisation, nationally-subsidised investments and German deconcentration was made evident in the resolutions attached to the act of ratification.[11] The French Government gained the bulk of its points in 1951, not without a good deal of compromise, despite the "fusion of interests" and the "solidarity" of which M. Schuman spoke so fondly.

With the striking exception of the cost equalisation and deconcentration issues, the French position during the treaty negotiations was strongly supported by the German delegation. Some months before Schuman's proposal, Adenauer had already offered France "economic union within a European Framework" and Karl Arnold had suggested an ECSC-like entity in place of the Interallied Ruhr Authority. Furthermore, Schuman made his suggestion only after previous consultations with Bonn and encouragement from that quarter as to the acceptability of the supranational principle.[12] Once the negotiations were begun, the delegation led by Hallstein and Blankenhorn, both senior civil servants, was able to function with almost the same autonomy as its French counterpart.

Politics carried the day over economics in the minds of the German negotiators. Economically, they stressed and supported the same convictions as to the merits of larger markets, Franco-German economic co-operation and a common investment approach which were featured by Monnet. Consequently the specific economic clauses of the Treaty encountered objection from the German side only to the extent that they would force cost increases on German

[10] *Ibid.*, pp. 57, 54, 70, 87.
[11] Discussed in Chap. 4, above. See Belgium, Chambre des Représentants, *Annales Parlementaires* (1951–52, Doc. 410), pp. 40–41, for text of the resolution.
[12] Reuter, *op. cit.*, p. 23.

producers or restrain competition. Politically they shared the French federalist position and favoured a small High Authority responsible to a European legislature. Defeated in this approach, Hallstein still felt satisfied with the powers of the Common Assembly as permitting the evolution of a true federal legislature, facilitating the formation of political parties and participation in the revision of the Treaty. He declared that the High Authority

> is to be a federal agency, a unitary central authority in which the particularistic national interests of the member states shall not be expressed. . . . Nor should this be influenced by our creation of the Council of Ministers since the Council . . . corresponds to a federal upper house [Bundesrat]. . . . This European community is really a union of states . . . or if you wish . . . a merger of ministries of economics.[13]

Dedication to the political and federal implications of ECSC, however, implied no neglect for essential German demands here any more than in the French case. Absolute equality for Germany, cessation of Allied economic controls and strict non-discrimination were demanded and granted without difficulty. Federalist enthusiasm did not prevent the restatement of the German thesis that deconcentration of industry should respond to identical principles throughout ECSC, irrespective of special rules for Germany, and thereby facilitate reconcentration. Unwillingness on the French side proved to be the single most difficult issue in the negotiations and held up completion of the Treaty until a compromise formula had been agreed upon at the inter-Allied level, a compromise which, in the German interpretation, included the possibility of upward revision by the High Authority of the concentration limits.[14] The free enterprise features of the common market were, perhaps, stressed more on the German side than on the French, though Hallstein freely admitted that the régime envisaged was one of " regulated competition " with necessary central crisis planning powers. More important, the logic of the common market was so

---

[13] Walter Hallstein, " Probleme des Schuman-Plans," *Kieler Vorträge* (Neue Folge, no. 2, Kiel 1951), pp. 10, 15. See also Walter Hallstein, " Der Schuman-Plan *Frankfurter Universitätsreden* (Frankfurt: Klostermann, 1951), esp. pp. 10–11 These two articles are remarkably frank statements by the head of the German delegation concerning interests defended and attained. Hallstein was chosen to head the Commission of EEC on January 1, 1958.

[4] Reuter admits that the German Government never agreed to the French interpretation—freezing the *status quo* under Law 27—of the Treaty's Article 66. See Rieben, *op. cit.*, for the details underlying my conclusion, pp. 426 *et seq.*

readily accepted partly because the Ruhr was expected to be the greatest beneficiary. Enjoying a natural cost advantage because of the presence of high-grade coking coal, the German negotiators resisted unflinchingly all French efforts at " equalising " wages and taxes in order not to jeopardise the advantage considered to be within their grasp. In Hallstein's words—

> I shall illustrate what this means; it means that the High Authority in principle has no power to intervene in the labour and wage policies of the member countries. Labour and wage questions are part of the social geography of production. A limitation of this principle can be derived only from the rule *pacta sunt servanda*. No state may . . . change the competitive conditions of its producers to their benefit.[15]

Finally, no amount of federalist good will was able to extract a concession from the German delegation or the Chancellor on the subject of the Saar. While admitting that a final solution would be eased considerably by ECSC, the Germans insisted on anchoring in diplomatic correspondence between Adenauer and Schuman their determination not to recognise the *status quo* as final. The two leaders agreed that ECSC implied nothing with respect to the claims of either side for an eventual settlement. This conclusion, Hallstein considered eminently fair and he therefore agreed to the inclusion of the Saar parliamentarians in the French delegation to the Common Assembly.[16] The concessions made by the German Government, therefore, were largely in the realm of federalism, while in terms of national economic advantage nothing was given up and a good deal gained.

For Italy, Count Sforza accepted the principles announced by Schuman without condition, one day after the French declaration. In subsequent weeks, however, the Government added that ECSC would be expected to guarantee Italy the successful completion of the Sinigaglia steel reorganisation plan, *i.e.*, temporary exemption from the common market principle. It further demanded complete equality of access to all sources of raw materials, including the ore

---

15 Report of the German delegation to Parliament, as cited in Institut des Relations Internationales, *op. cit.*, p. 87. The Hallstein statement in " Der Schuman-Plan," *op. cit.*, p. 12.

16 *Ibid.*, pp. 25–26. The exchange of letters on the Saar is annexed formally to the ECSC Treaty and printed in the British Iron and Steel Federation's English-language edition, pp. 93–95. See Chap. 4 above for the Saar resolution voted by the Bundesrat in connection with the ratification of the Treaty.

deposits of French North Africa on which the Sinigaglia Plan partly depended. The exclusion of these areas from the Treaty almost resulted in Italian withdrawal from the negotiations and only a bilateral accord with France saved the situation. Assured of the right to retain tariffs on steel and coke for five years, assuaged in their concern over unemployment by the migration provisions of the Treaty, the Italian demands were then confined to whittling away at the Franco-German idea of an all-powerful High Authority composed of five members. Joined by the Benelux countries, the nine-member formula finally adopted was successfully opposed to this extreme supranational programme, whereupon the Italian Government rejected all further Italian private demands for increased representation.[17]

The three Benelux Governments defended a common position in the negotiations to a far greater degree than was to be true in later years. It was they who took almost immediate exception to the deliberate vagueness of Monnet's proposals. Economically, they insisted on the determination of commercial policy rules and tariff limits toward third countries in the Treaty while Monnet apparently wished to reserve this power for his High Authority. Politically, the three governments found that in the absence of political federation it would be dangerous indeed to permit a small High Authority full latitude for making policy for coal and steel, as well as for the related economic sectors not clearly under its jurisdiction. Hence it was they who insisted on the enlargement of the High Authority and on the creation of the Council of Ministers, in which they saw a protection of the aims of the small member states. Further, as the delegations' reports to their parliaments indicated, it was felt that the High Authority must limit itself to indirect means to achieve the basic aims of the Community and therefore intervene as little as possible with the decisions of firms and governments.[18] Unwilling to raise their already unified low tariffs toward third countries to the rates prevailing in France, Germany or Italy, the Benelux delegations obtained the right to retain their rates, but undertook to levy a countervailing duty to prevent re-exportation of steel to the other ECSC countries.[19]

[17] Racine, *op. cit.*, pp. 59–60, 99–100. *Die Welt*, January 9, 1951.
[18] Racine, *op. cit.*, pp. 88, 99–100. Institut des Relations Internationales, *op. cit.*, pp. 86 *et seq.*
[19] Details in High Authority, *Establishment of the Common Market* (Luxembourg, April 1953), p. 26.

Once their special demands were satisfied, spokesmen for the three countries agreed in speaking of ECSC as a " real political entity " with full sovereign powers in its restricted realm and the Luxembourg Council of State went so far as to declare that while the Treaty was fully consistent with the needs of the times, it was the Grand Duchy's Constitution which was outmoded and needed revision.[20]

For Belgium especially, the problem of the sick coal industry provided additional worries. Her delegation at first wanted full inclusion in the common market, with the differences between Belgian and German production costs to be met in full by German subsidies. This the Germans refused, and countered with a demand for exclusion of Belgian coal from the common market. The compromise finally embodied in the Convention on Transitional Provisions (Par. 26) met the positions of both countries. Yet the emphasis placed by Parliament on the modernisation of the collieries as a condition for ratifying the Treaty indicates that not all Belgians were reassured by the text of the Treaty.[21] The Dutch Government felt that only a rigorous judicial limit on supranational powers would guarantee the protection of legitimate national industrial fears against arbitrary decisions, and hence stressed the powers of the Court over the High Authority's and foresaw full indemnity payments to private firms in the event of a wrongful decision.[22] For Luxembourg, Premier Joseph Bech insisted on the insertion of a special safeguarding clause in the Convention on Transitional Provisions and on a very wide interpretation of the Court's powers. Said Bech—

> Articles 33 and 35 of the Treaty give a right of appeal to the Court every time the interests of the workers are adversely affected by a decision of the High Authority.

In company with other Benelux spokesmen, the Luxemburgers held that the clause protecting a national economy against " fundamental and persistent disturbances " was inserted especially for their benefit.[23]

---

[20] Mason, *op. cit.*, pp. 13–14, 16–17. The Benelux delegations were all headed by senior civil servants: Max Suetens (Belgium), Dirk Spierenburg (Netherlands), Albert Wehrer (Luxembourg). Spierenburg and Wehrer ultimately became members of the High Authority, whose powers they sought to define carefully and limit, and co-ordinate with those of the Council of Ministers.

[21] Racine, *op. cit.*, p. 93. Also see *Annales Parlementaires, op. cit.*, pp. 5–9.

[22] Valentine, *op. cit.*, p. 18.

[23] *Ibid.*, pp. 15–16, 24, 27–28. As the negotiations proceeded, the initially guarded and sceptical statements of Benelux statesmen became more and more positive. See Metzler, *op. cit.*, p. 22, p. 40.

Despite the evident dilution of Monnet's initial federal proposals, these negotiations still represent a remarkable degree of compromise, but also agreement on basic principles. The unprecedented techniques used by the drafting conference provide the explanation. Agreement to the principle of supranationalism was made a precondition for participation. The Franco-German delegations indicated the limits within which they were willing to depart from this principle and adhered to them. The talks were carried out by expert civil servants, not by diplomats or ministers. Instructions from governments were lacking or general in nature. Technical ministers—*e.g.*, economics, transport, foreign trade—were deliberately excluded and the talks were handled in absolute secrecy from national parliaments, the press and the public. All technical questions were solved at the expert level, with only the political issues of representation and voting rules left to secret sessions of the foreign ministers, meeting rarely and only when agreement among the experts seemed slow in coming. As a result, the hard bargaining was kept to a minimum while the delegations in a real sense sought to elaborate a common scheme based on accepted first principles.[24] These techniques were to be used again with consummate success in the preparation of the EEC and Euratom Treaties.

IMPLEMENTING THE ECSC TREATY

The Italian public authorities, after having succeeded in diluting supranationalism and postponing the full inclusion of Italy in the common market, have shown some reluctance in implementing all the rules of the Treaty or acting in the spirit of the common market. Even though Italy agreed to the High Authority's reduction of the transitional tariff on steel imports at a rate faster than had been originally hoped, some major administrative measures contrary to Treaty rules were removed only after continued protests from Luxembourg. Illegal steel subsidies to the shipbuilding industry were abolished as late as 1957, a 0·5 per cent. *ad valorem* " administrative tax " continues to be charged on steel coming from other ECSC countries, in addition to the modified Annécy rates approved by the High Authority. The Interministerial Price Committee has ceased to fix coal prices in violation of the schedules set up by the High Authority under the perequation scheme for Sulcis coal on September 1, 1956. To all requests for compliance

[24] Schuman, *op. cit.*, pp. 13–18.

with Treaty rules, the Government initially replied that these measures were determined by Act of Parliament and could not be changed without formal repeal, a plain denial of federal logic.[25]   Yet eventually compliance came about after patient refutation by Luxembourg of Rome's reasoning.

In addition to these measures of administrative obstruction, the Italian Government has directly attacked the High Authority by demanding the annulment of the Monnet Rebate ruling in the ECSC Court, in full conformity with the consistent policy of limiting the competition of ECSC steel on the Italian market.   The Government has verbally supported Italian industrialists in their efforts to challenge the scrap bonus scheme and the transformation of GEORG.   Scrap, it was argued, should be available without restriction to all ECSC consumers and the coal sales cartel should be completely destroyed instead of being split into three cartels. Unlike other governments in ECSC, the Rome authorities have made themselves the loyal defenders of national industrial claims on all issues.   While their record of co-operation with Luxembourg is poor, it must nevertheless be granted that in crucial cases, the legal avenues of redress are fully respected.   Further, the marginal importance of Italy to the common market makes efforts of obstruction of relatively little overall concern, though French exporters have complained against them bitterly.

The reluctance of the Italian Government to make use of the Treaty is especially striking in the case of re-adaptation aid.   About 8,000 steelworkers were laid off as a result of modernisation.   But even though the trade unions and the High Authority encouraged Rome to submit requests for re-adaptation aid, none was forthcoming for a two-year period, largely because the Government did not wish to create a group of " privileged unemployed," entitled to more public aid than the bulk of Italy's jobless.   When requests were finally submitted they had to be returned because the share of the Government in the financing was left vague and the future of the workers affected not clearly planned.   And even after these administrative difficulties were ironed out, the failure of Parliament to enact the appropriations required further delayed the operation of re-adaptation.   The nation-wide consultative committee of

[25] High Authority, *Fourth General Report*, (Luxembourg, April 1956), pp. 129, 132. These cases are also discussed in High Authority, *Service d'Information*, " La Haute Autorité, Les Entreprises et les Gouvernements," January 10, 1957, Doc. No. 265/57 (mimeo.).

workers and employers required by Article 48 of the Treaty for countries requesting aid was not established until January of 1956.

Dutch authorities, by contrast, have scrupulously observed the terms of the Treaty and the rulings of the High Authority even when these resulted in increased prices and the abolition of special measures to protect coal consumers, and even if they might lead to an increase in inland waterway freight rates, a most delicate issue in Holland.[26-27] On the other hand, the caution observed by the High Authority in " co-ordinating " and " harmonising " the fiscal and investment policies of the member governments has made it unnecessary for Holland to justify or explain its indirect controls over the coal and steel sectors, or their planned development.

While anxious and willing to implement the Treaty, the Dutch authorities are not slow to take advantage of the supranational institutions to press their advantage when they feel others have acted less loyally, always confining themselves to the strictly legal means of redress provided by ECSC. Thus their quarrel with the High Authority over the use of price ceilings to control the Ruhr coal cartel was taken to the Court; and upon being defeated in that forum, discussion of the grievance was stopped.[28] Further, the government insisted on a literal interpretation of the common market rules when it complained that the French and German Governments have interfered with the legal re-exportation of Russian pig iron, even though the goods in question were apparently priced discriminatorily. In company with the Belgian and Luxembourg Governments, The Hague has protested against French discrimination with respect to exports to Morocco, alleged to violate Article 79 of the Treaty. Unwilling to envisage the " harmonisation of living conditions " as a device to increase national production costs, Economics Minister Jelle Zijlstra has not been slow to find that the Treaty requires no such step.[29]

Yet Zijlstra and Minister of Transport Algera have gone further, perhaps, in resisting the demands of Dutch interest groups and hostile politicians, in deference to supranational solidarity,

---

[26-27] *Usine Nouvelle*, October 6, 1955, p. 5. For the subsidy and price rules see High Authority, *First* and *Second General Reports* (Luxembourg, April 1953 and 1954, respectively) pp. 81–84, 70–71 and pp. 79 *et seq.*

[28] *Government of the Netherlands* v. *The High Authority*, requesting annulment of decisions 18/54, 19/54, 20/54. Valentine, *op. cit.*, pp. 192–194.

[29] *Usine Nouvelle*, October 6, 1955, p. 5. *Informations Bimensuelles*, December 20, 1954, p 11; December 20, 1955, p. 50.

than any other government. Allegations of hardships suffered by Dutch consumers because of the common market were voiced in Parliament; they have been judiciously but firmly rejected, even though the fact that coal price increases were occasioned by supra-nationalism was openly admitted. Trade relations with third countries were not entirely satisfactory in the Dutch view; yet Zijlstra was unwilling to jeopardise the relations of confidence in the Council of Ministers by making an open issue of this. And risking the wrath of Dutch shippers, Algera stated in Parliament that the ECSC organs had every right to deal with the inland water-ways problem and that integration in this realm should be pushed forward.[30]

As for the Grand Duchy of Luxembourg, its Government has complied with all legal obligations imposed on it, though not always gladly or expeditiously. The crucial issue was that of the government coal import monopoly, the Office Commerciale de Ravitaillement. Successive requests for negotiation and delay were used by the Government to stave off the High Authority's order to modify the monopoly as contrary to the common market principle. These steps, plus a complaint in the Community's Court, were exhausted during a year's time, after which the changes ordered were under-taken. Nevertheless, a licence to import coal from Germany was denied a Luxembourg firm, followed by renewed recriminations in 1956, resulting eventually in the compliance of the Government with a High Authority order to issue the licence.[31] Luxembourg Government spokesmen were displeased with the decision to unify railway rates and protested against it, but they complied with ECSC arrangements just the same. For years the Government vociferously opposed the building of the Moselle Canal as harmful to Luxem-bourg's railway system, but it dropped its complaints in the face of the Franco-German agreement of 1956, apparently unwilling to interfere with the peaceful solution of the Saar issue. Its tactics in postponing ratification of the ECSC labour migration convention delayed entry into force for almost three years.[32]

[30] *Ibid.*, April 30, 1955, pp. 56–57; October 15, 1955, pp. 49–50, p. 24; June 1, 1955 pp. 48–49; May 1956, p. 68.

[31] *Agence Europe*, October 16, 1954, September 19, 1955, October 12, 1955. High Authority, *Third* and *Fourth General Reports*, p. 92, p. 135.

[32] *Informations Bimensuelles*, April 30, 1955, p. 58; November 1, 1955, p. 30, February 1, 1955, p. 21, for the statements of Victor Bodson, Minister of Transport; June–July 1956, p. 56, for Bech's statement on labour migration. On the question of subsidies, a decision of the ECSC Court on April 23, 1956, upheld certain

In view of the Belgian Government's delicate coal situation, the degree of loyalty to supranational commitments demonstrated by Brussels is striking. Still, at least two discriminatory administrative practices have been noted by the High Authority, followed by orders to modify or discontinue them, without having been immediately implemented. Thus Belgium continues to require certain licence formalities for Ruhr coal shipped on Belgian waterways. A 3 per cent. sales tax was charged against all steel, but refunded to Belgian sellers furnishing Government agencies. After High Authority protests, the refund right was extended eventually to all ECSC sellers in Belgium. Yet when government economists, in 1954, urged High Authority encouragement of sales cartels to cushion the recession, no cries of anguish were heard when the suggestion was rejected.[33]

Willingness to abide by supranational decisions even when they are disliked is equally apparent in the protracted dispute with France over the imposition of a compensation fund on Northern French canals, designed to make the importation of Belgian coal more expensive. Brussels was annoyed by French efforts to compel the High Authority to raise the sales price of ECSC-subsidised Belgian coal. France had even initiated proceedings in the Court to this effect, but the case was withdrawn when the High Authority succumbed and adjusted the price upward. Brussels, thereupon followed up by suing the High Authority for failure to suppress the canal compensation system, but this case too was withdrawn when Luxembourg ordered the system abolished. Since France has not yet—1957—completely complied, while Belgian prices have been forced up, it is evident that Brussels chose to accept, without causing further bad feeling, an adverse decision.[34]

significant State powers, specifically growing out of a measure of the Grand-Ducal Government. The Court held compatible with the Treaty the policy of charging industrial coal consumers a special tax then used to reduce the price of domestic coal. The meaning of " special charge," as outlawed in Article 4c of the Treaty, was construed so narrowly as to permit this form of national subsidisation of certain consumers. *Journal Officiel*, July 10, 1956, for text of judgment.

[33] *Informations Bimensuelles*, January 15, 1954, pp. 11, 18. *Usine Nouvelle*, October 20, 1955, p. 5. *Fourth General Report, op. cit*, p. 130. High Authority Doc. 265/57. *op. cit.*

[34] Government of the French Republic *v.* the High Authority, April 1953, requesting annulment of Decision 24/53 (March 13, 1953). Government of H.M. the King of Belgium *v.* The High Authority, August 1953, requesting annulment of " implicit decision " to refuse action against the French Government's decrees of March 30, 1953. Valentine, *op. cit.*, pp. 185–186. Detail in Bok, *op. cit.*, pp. 17–18.

Long-range coal policy and the modernisation of the Borinage collieries provide the crucial test of Belgian co-operation with ECSC. Despite continued domestic pressure against the closing of any mines, Brussels has agreed with the High Authority on a gradual integrated programme of closing the least productive pits, making heavy investments in the ones that can be saved, retraining the workers who will lose their jobs in the reorganisation and building pit-head steam plants for the utilisation of low-grade coal. Disagreements have come to the fore on the pace of closing mines and the share to be financed by ECSC, but the principle of joint planning with ultimate power of decision residing in Luxembourg has not been questioned in Brussels.[35]

Further, the Belgian Government has refused to associate itself with the protests of its mining industry against this programme. A re-allocation of subsidies and a reduction of price ceilings were among the measures imposed in 1955, after joint deliberations between Brussels and Luxembourg. When the collieries, in two separate suits, challenged these decisions, the action was as much directed against their own Government as against the supra-national " technocrats."[36] While the Government has supported the aims of its steel industry in demands for extending the task of ECSC, on the central issue of coal policy great resistance to domestic pressure groups has been shown, implying complete loyalty to the terms of the Treaty.

Perhaps because of its doctrinaire dedication to free market principles, the Government of West Germany has an excellent record of deferring to ECSC decisions. Thus a series of special coal subsidies—including domestic consumers, utilities, deep sea fisheries, inland waterways, the federal railways, etc.—were removed by ECSC directive almost immediately after the opening of the common market, without giving rise to any evidence of opposition or resentment in government circles. On other issues, however, matters did not go this smoothly. The Ministry of Economics was in complete sympathy with the steel industry on the question of refunding sales taxes on exported (or imported) steel. It questioned

---

[35] *ECSC Bulletin*, June 1955, for details on the plan, and *Usine Nouvelle*, September 22, 1955, p. 5, for Belgian counter-proposals to postpone the closing of mines.

[36] See Chap. 5 for the details on these suits. An earlier suit, *Société Anonyme de Charbonnages Réunis de la Minerie* v. *The High Authority* (April, 1954), which also sought to compel an adjustment in ceiling prices, similarly failed to enlist the support of the Belgian authorities. The suit was dropped when Luxembourg made the adjustment demanded. Valentine, *op. cit.*, p. 192.

the compatibility of the High Authority's decision with the Treaty, and the Tinbergen Commission's Report with respect to the asserted need for the removal of all distortions in the tax field. Despite the fact that possible grounds for legal action existed, and that such action was urged by the steel industry, and in the face of the fact that the Bundestag enacted discriminatory tax legislation capable of blocking imports of French steel, the Ministry refused to take advantage of these measures and abided by the supranational decision.[37]

Railways rates and tariffs provide additional fields in which the German officials consented to central direction only after considerable opposition. The elimination of rate discrimination against coal shipped to Lorraine and in favour of southern Germany called forth sharp protests from federal railway officials and from the Minister of Transport, Seebohm. Negotiations in Luxembourg over harmonisation measures seemed doomed to failure until the Federal Government overruled its transport minister and agreed to the compromise finally adopted.[38] If conviction of the benefits of economic integration were here strong enough to defeat the aims of a specific ministry who considered its immediate interests threatened, much the same development took place in the realm of tariff harmonisation. Apparently anxious to liberalise as much trade as possible at the onset of the common market for steel, the Government in 1953 sharply reduced the duty on steel imported from third countries, a unilateral step taken without consulting Luxembourg. The protests of the French Government were accompanied by an admonition of the High Authority that such a measure, while entirely legal under the Treaty, would nevertheless jeopardise eventual intra-ECSC negotiations for tariff harmonisation against third countries. Economics Minister Erhard thereupon emphasised the "temporary" nature of the measure and agreed to negotiate with France for a common tariff, under High Authority auspices. This was ultimately fixed at a compromise point mid-way between the French and German rates.[39]

---

[37] *Die Welt*, June 1, 1953. *Handelsblatt*, May 20, 1953. *Frankfurter Allgemeine Zeitung*, June 24, 1953. Mendershausen, *op. cit.*, pp. 279 *et seq. Usine Nouvelle*, May 14, 1953, p. 11 and especially T. C. Clark, " Inaugurating the Coal and Steel Community," in A. Macmahon (ed.), *Federalism, Mature and Emergent* (New York: Doubleday, 1955), pp. 485 *et seq.*

[38] *Informations Bimensuelles*, September 1, 1954, p. 24. *Usine Nouvelle*, December 30, 1954, p. 5.

[39] *Agence Europe*, July 14, 1953. *Annales des Mines, op. cit.*, pp. 14, 24–25. Such

In the early years of the common market, therefore, the German Government consistently deferred to central decisions even when its initial wishes departed from those of other ECSC countries or the High Authority's. It is not yet clear whether the same will be true if fundamental governmental decisions regarding the long-term trends desired of the German economy are involved. Thus the Federal Government has made no move to eliminate various direct and indirect subsidies it affords to miners. Its decision in 1956 to bolster miners' pay with a special productivity bonus was condemned by Luxembourg as a hidden subsidy; but the Bonn officials have challenged this decision and postponed compliance.

Germany's positive record of deferring to central decisions and observing the letter and spirit of the common market rules is in large part due to its success in having Luxembourg adopt policies approved by Bonn. This is true especially of the pro-*laissez-faire* attitude of the High Authority, which meets entirely with Erhard's approval. It is equally true of the encouragement of reconcentration. These words of High Authority Vice-President Coppé, spoken in Duisburg, could have been those of the Ministry of Economics:

> We at the High Authority are persuaded that the structure of enterprises must be slowly modified. The road toward this modification lies in the concentration of several enterprises into a single one. . . . We are persuaded that some concentrations serve the producer and consumer equally well. The High Authority will support every concentration which will conduce to stronger enterprises and dynamic initiative. We want a progressive economy.[40]

ECSC scrap policy measures, unpopular with the French and Italian Governments, are in perfect accord with German preferences. High Authority reluctance to enter the field of tax, wage and social security equalisation finds its support in Bonn, while the decision to lower the rate of the ECSC production tax took shape partly as a result of German insistence.

Yet it would be a mistake to conclude that the government

agreements on the part of the government are subject to parliamentary approval. Yet Franco-German common measures have gone into effect. *Informations Bimensuelles*, June 1, 1955, p. 47; January 1956, pp. 27–51.

[40] *Agence Europe*, July 29, 1954. Fearing ECSC interference with free enterprise, the head of the Government's Bureau of Mines advised collieries against seeking financial aid from Luxembourg. *Usine Nouvelle*, March 12, 1953, p. 7.

merely makes itself the mouthpiece of industrial demands. While it did so in the case of the levy reduction and in insisting that the common market for special steels be opened on schedule despite the bitter opposition of the French Government, on the crucial issues of Ruhr coal the Government opposed the collieries.[41] It aided the High Authority in compelling the transformation of GEORG, largely because Erhard is a bitter foe of all cartels. It lent no support to coal consumers who initiated legal proceedings against the High Authority when their subsidies were eliminated.[42] And most important, it took an active role in retaining price controls because it feared an inflationary spiral if the mines were free to fix their own levels—despite the fact that the free market economy is the bedrock of Erhard's thinking.

Much as the Belgian and French Governments, the German officials have no hesitation in encouraging the High Authority to make politically and economically unpopular decisions, for which the national regimes prefer not to take public responsibility. Of this the coal price ceiling discussions of 1955 and 1956 offer striking examples. Luxembourg, in principle, wanted to abolish the ceilings in 1955 and was legally free to do so. But Erhard, anxious to prevent a possible inflation without seeming to subscribe to dirigistic controls, wanted the High Authority to make the necessary decision and put pressure on Luxembourg to that effect. He succeeded in obtaining the retention of ceilings for another year, though he was defeated in his simultaneous effort to prevent the granting of a price increase.

When the issue arose again in 1956, the High Authority wanted to compel Bonn to shoulder the burden of unpopular controls if prices were to be held down, arguing that prices should be either free or controlled in all sectors, not only for coal. Bonn, meanwhile, was embarrassed by the twin demands of the Ruhr for higher prices and of the miners' union for a raise, while seeking to maintain price stability. Convinced that Luxembourg would insist on the abolition of ceilings, Bonn, unilaterally and before a High Authority decision had been made, announced a DM. 2 per ton increase in prices, coupled with indirect wage benefits in the form

---

[41] *Agence Europe*, October 7 and 10, 1955; July 20, 1954.

[42] *Verband Deutscher Reeder et al.* v. *The High Authority*, and *Bunkerfirmen-Vereinigung* v. *The High Authority* (March, 1953), seeking annulment of decision 25/53. Both cases were withdrawn before a decision was handed down. Valentine, *op. cit.*, 182–185.

of tax refunds and the special productivity bonus. Eventually, the ceilings were abolished despite Bonn's *fait accompli* and the bonus scheme challenged as a disguised subsidy. Defeated in their efforts to use supranationalism as the mechanism for maintaining unpopular controls at home, the German officials then showed great reluctance in carrying out the High Authority's decision against the bonus.[43] Deference to supranational decisions and rules seems easier when the obligations imposed fit in with national policy and values.

But the obverse of this proposition may once more lead to a forced reliance on supranational powers, as illustrated by Erhard's troubles with the German collieries in 1957. No longer troubled by ECSC ceilings, the Ruhr in October of that year announced the largest price increase since the war, followed almost immediately by threatened price increases in related sectors and the demand of I. G. Metall for a ten per cent. increase in wages. The inflationary spiral so dreaded by Erhard was now a reality, a situation compounded politically by the promises of price stability made during the CDU election campaign which had just ended. Erhard's answer was to turn to Luxembourg and to call on the High Authority to step in with new price controls, despite his disgust with "dirigisme." But he also prepared to reduce the cost of non-ECSC fuels and thus force the Ruhr to compete with cheaper imports. While the aims of a purely national policy thus lead back to supranationalism when implementation in the narrow framework is impossible they also beget a further undermining of the common market rationale when import policies in one member state conflict with those prevalent in others or with the central policy.

If loyalty to supranationalism is made relatively simple for Germany by the coincidence of the bulk of national policy with ECSC objectives, the opposite is true for France. Special protective measures, tax refund rights, subsidies, compensation systems and cartels so honeycombed the French industrial and commercial structure at the opening of the common market that a full compliance with all the rules of the Treaty would certainly have caused chaos. While no doubt the extent of administrative obstruction to ECSC measures is greater in France than in any other member

---

[43] Bonn's decision and State Secretary Westrick's announcement to the Bundestag in *Financial Times*, February 14, 1956. The bulk of the above information was obtained by interviews in Luxembourg.

state, outright and insistent violations are absent. The flavour of the French situation, however, is perhaps symbolised by the fact that of all ECSC countries France alone has so far declined to abolish export and import licences on coal and steel, though their granting is automatic. The simplification of these formalities is now " under study." [44]

While Government subsidisation of investments are to be avoided in ECSC, the French steel industry evidently continues to rely on financial assistance from Paris and expected to be aided by its Government in the massive outlays disbursed in 1957.[45] Even though the conditions of competition are to be identical in ECSC, the French Government continued to subsidise steel exports by granting tax refunds on sales to third countries, without having so notified the High Authority.[46] In the coal sector, the net reduction in the subsidies long granted to certain operations has been very significant. Yet the French Government felt compelled to request an increase for certain plants in 1956, while the Charbonnages de France have been authorised to engage in inter-basin compensation operations indefinitely, an indirect means of subsidising the weaker basins.[47] Government experts foresee the need of subsidising coal production, discriminating against imports even from ECSC countries, developing autarky and paying export bounties, even though these steps would—regrettably—violate the common market rules.[48]

Enough has been said in other contexts about the compensation system for inland waterways to stress once more the discriminatory nature of this hidden subsidy. Yet so determined were successive ministers of commerce and industry to protect the sales of the Northern French coal basins as to refuse absolutely repeated High Authority requests for the abolition of the system, demanding instead an overall regulation of waterway rates in order to equalise the higher domestic levels with low international freight costs. In the absence of Council of Ministers agreement on such equalisation,

[44] High Authority, *Third General Report, op. cit.*, p. 102.
[45] *Usine Nouvelle*, December 29, 1955, p. 3; February 2, 1956, p. 7.
[46] See the questions asked in the Common Assembly, July 9, 1954. *Journal Officiel*, August 1, 1954.
[47] *Usine Nouvelle*, February 9, 1956, p. 9.
[48] Thus J. Desrousseaux, Director of the Government's Bureau of Mines and Steel, and Government representative to the Charbonnages de France, in " Réflections sur la Politique Charbonnière," *Revue Française de l'Energie* (Vol. 7, no. 68, October, 1955), pp. 3–14.

the Government insisted on holding out against Luxembourg.[49] Obliged under the common market rules to discontinue the mono-polistic control over scrap exports, the Government refused until 1956 to abolish altogether its control agency, insisting it only fulfils a " statistical " function. In accordance with the wishes of its industrial consumers, the Government in fact seeks to prevent the large-scale buying up of scrap by Italian steelmakers.[50] Further, in violation at least of the free enterprise spirit of ECSC, the French Government has sought to maintain pressure on its steel companies to keep prices low. It threatened to curtail investment aid in 1954, permitted a discriminatory rebate in 1955 and kept prices in the steel consuming industries under rigid public controls. While the Mollet Government in spring of 1956 plainly exempted coal and steel from its general price-freezing order, later measures saw a return of national price pressure on Treaty products.[51] With regard to re-adaptation, the authorities in Paris have been slow to request assistance because they are afraid of being confronted with similar demands from industries other than coal and steel, and therefore not entitled to supranational aid. And to cap things off, several French requests for re-adaptation aid have been turned down in Luxembourg because the hardships alleged could not be proved to be due to the establishment of the common market.

Reluctance to accept the full logic of the common market made itself felt particularly strongly in the effort of the High Authority to remove trade obstacles in the special steels sector. Defending the complaints of French producers of special steels that their pro-duction and raw materials costs were higher than those of their German competitors, the Minister of Commerce and Industry, Bourgès-Maunoury tried his best to stave off the opening of the common market in the summer of 1954 and sought to obtain ECSC approval for the continuation of special tax benefits to French producers. Suggestions that, pending the authorisation of special safeguarding measures for the French producers, a 15 per cent. tariff against special steel imports should remain intact were

[49] *Agence Europe*, July 6, July 10, August 2, October 22, 1954. *Annales des Mines*, *op. cit.*, p. 24.
[50] In 1953, following the establishment of the common market for steel, the Govern-ment did abolish the Comptoir français de la ferraille, only to substitute for it the Union des consommateurs de ferraille en France. *Usine Nouvelle*, April 16, 1953. *Agence Europe*, June 3, 1953, July 16, 1954, September 6, 1954.
[51] *Usine Nouvelle*, November 10, 1955. Bok, *op. cit.*, p. 41. High Authority, *Fifth General Report*, pp. 106–108.

rejected by the High Authority and the other ECSC Governments. Despite domestic pressure and the outcry in business circles and despite attacks in the French Cabinet on Bourgès-Maunoury's insufficiently " national " stand, France gave way in the end.[52]

The test case of France's willingness to abide by the rules it proposed in 1950 is the controversy over ATIC. The agency itself is semi-public in character: its Governing Board is composed of representatives of the steel industry, Gaz, Electricité and Charbonnages de France, French National Railways, as well as of five separate cartels of coal importers and wholesalers. Its president, M. Jean Picard, is a coal wholesaler, but all decisions of ATIC are subject to the suspensive veto of the " commissaire du gouvernement," M. Jacques Desrousseaux, who is also Director of the Government's Bureau of Mines and Steel, and " commissaire " of the Charbonnages de France. It is far from clear whether ATIC is a private cartel shaping Government policy, or the Government's technique for controlling coal imports and assuring a market for its nationalised mines. In any case, ATIC performed the following tasks: (1) it fixed the amount of coal to be imported on the basis of a given ratio to the production of the Nord/Pas-de-Calais mines; (2) it placed the orders for coal to be purchased abroad and resells it to private wholesalers or bulk consumers, such as the utilities, railways and steelmakers; (3) it computed and paid the subsidy designed to equalise the cost of domestic and imported coal. In its totality, ATIC was clearly a monopoly which sought to limit the competitive impact of non-French coal. Its usefulness in this task is defended by importers, wholesalers, trade unionists and government officials, common market or not.[53]

In its efforts to transform ATIC, the High Authority was thus facing not merely a private cartel—as in the case of GEORG— but an agency which enjoys the full support of the French Government, if it is not its creature. Hence a compromise was held out as possible, if ATIC would only renounce its power to licence and control in a compulsory manner all coal imports. Apart from that,

---

[52] British Iron and Steel Federation, " Special Steels in the ECSC," *Monthly Statistical Bulletin*, August 1954. *Agence Europe*, June 15, 21, 24, 26, 1954; June 30, July 2, 19, 28, 31, 1954.

[53] Details in Association Technique de l'Importation Charbonnière, *Rapport du Conseil d'Administration* (1954). *Etudes et Documents* (January 1953) pp. 31 *et seq.* ATIC also maintains close relations with the ECSC-wide Committee of Coal Consumers and Dealers, occupying joint office space with this group in Paris.

Luxembourg was willing that the production of French mines be protected by some kind of import formula and that centralised purchasing arrangements continue. ATIC, however, agreed only to free the steel industry from the compulsory import control rule and to open the tight circle of recognised coal importers to all additional dealers interested. It adamantly refused to give up its licensing power, whereupon the High Authority *ordered* the agency transformed under Article 88 of the Treaty. The decision was promptly appealed by the French Government to the ECSC Court. As in the case of the Italian Government's decision to yield on coal price fixing, the invocation of Article 88 seemed to work wonders. Paris in December of 1956 dropped its suit and on January 14, 1957, reorganised ATIC so as to deprive it of a veto power over coal imports,[54] after receiving assurances from Luxembourg that ATIC might continue to act as the " authorised agent " of all French importers of ECSC coal. Paris and Luxembourg continue to negotiate since they are agreed that this formula does not fully guarantee the rights of access of French dealers to non-French coal suppliers.

That the French Government has made itself a more consistent defender of interest group demands than any other ECSC Government is evident from its stand on these issues. The point is reinforced when additional French claims and demands in Luxembourg are examined. Thus Jean-Marie Louvel, Minister of Industry in the Laniel Government, argued heatedly for the retention of coal price ceilings and the institution of effective central controls for scrap procurement and allocation, thus clearly meeting the demands of the French steel industry as well as buttressing his Government's price stability programme. Louvel and his successors sought to insulate the French price structure from free market fluctuations by urging the imposition of price ceilings for steel on the one hand, and on the other hand taking their bitter opposition to the " flexibility " implied in the Monnet Rebate programme to the ECSC Court. At the same time, the position of the coal and steel industries was defended in consistent demands on ECSC organs to harmonise indirect taxes, or alternatively to prepare special tax

---

[54] Picard in 1954 warned of ECSC liberalism and the dangers of uncontrolled trade, calling on his colleagues to be ready to reorganise their structure even if the outward form would have to be changed. *Agence Europe,* June 9, 1954. News of French compliance in High Authority, *Bulletin Mensuel de l'Information* (January 1957), p. 29.

exemptions for the French ECSC sectors to enable them to compete. Advocacy of steel association interests is underlined by the vitriolic government demands for the Moselle Canal. Bourgès-Maunoury went so far, in calling on the High Authority to undertake this project, as describing it as of the same importance to Europe as the piercing of the Isthmus of Suez. Chaban-Delmas, when he was Minister of Transport, acted in a like manner by making himself the fervent defender of steel interests in insisting on the speedy elimination by Germany of rail discrimination.[55]

It must be stressed nevertheless that advocacy of interest group and government policy in ECSC organs has remained strictly within the framework of legal obligations contained in the Treaty. Temptations to depart from these strictures have been consistently rejected by Cabinet members in their tussles with parliamentary interpellations. Gaullists thus have demanded that the French Government assert itself in controlling directly the budgetary dispositions of ECSC organs and that French power in ECSC be used to enforce unflinchingly the continued deconcentration of Ruhr industries. Radical and Conservative deputies have urged the compulsory co-ordination of investments to hinder the development of German continuous strip mills, as well as demanding exemptions for specific French plants from common market rules and blaming the recession of 1954 on the High Authority. All these demands were firmly rejected by the Minister of Industry as contrary to the obligations assumed by France under the Treaty.[56]

Those aspects of supranationalism which have affected the French ability to conduct foreign policy independently have been the hardest to accept without protest. This is patent from the French reactions to the alteration of the relationship with the Saar as well as to the association arrangements with Britain. Prior to the plebiscite of 1955 and the Franco-German agreement of 1956, French control over the Saar economy was perhaps veiled, but real nevertheless. Under the terms of the Franco-Saar agreements on

---

[55] *Usine Nouvelle*, January 22, 1953, p. 5; March 5, 1953, p. 5; April 23, 1953, p. 11; December 2, 1953, p. 5. Conseil de la République, *Rapport d'Information par MM. Armengaud et Coudé du Foresto* (1954), *op. cit.* pp. 14 *et seq.* This report also contains strong strictures against efforts to circumvent the Treaty and to exploit it solely for national advantage. *Agence Europe*, October 21, 1953, July 19, 1954, August 5, 1955, October 15, 1954.

[56] Questions of Michel Debré, de Léotard, J. Soustelle and Paquet, December 28, 1953, March 26, 1954, August 28, 1954. *Annales des Mines*, Vol. 144, Numéro Special 1955, pp. 116–125, for text of questions and answers.

economic union, all French price and foreign exchange regulations applied to the Saar.　Saar banking was entirely under French control, as were the railways.　The mines, considered crucial by Lorraine steelmakers, were administered by an autonomous body, Saarbergwerke A. G., whose governing board of eighteen members included nine Frenchmen.　The active managerial posts were monopolised by the French members who included a high official of the Charbonnages de France, the president of ATIC and a managing director of SIDELOR.　The board had the power to lease portions of the seams, and did so by handing over to the Charbonnages de France the much desired Warndt deposits.　Of the six steel plants on Saar territory, French firms controlled two and the French Government, through its sequestration administration, a third, the Völklingen properties of the Röchling family. In ECSC questions, Saar demands were forwarded through the French Inter-ministerial Co-ordinating Commission for Coal and Steel questions.[57]　It is thus hardly surprising that French steelmakers, coal interests and parliamentarians anxious to preserve the economic advantages provided by the economic union were determined not to yield control to Germany or to ECSC organs, and insisted on equating success in the common market with the continuation in force of Franco-Saar arrangements.　The fact that a settlement with Germany was reached with a minimum of difficulty and bitterness, even though the bulk of these advantages had to be given up, testifies to the will of French ministers to make sacrifices within the framework of economic integration.

The Saar negotiations, even though they resulted in a diminution of French national influence, were still based on the formally reassuring basis of bipartite talks.　It is the absence of bipartite diplomatic equality in negotiations conducted under ECSC auspices

---

[57] Details on French controls under successive economic conventions in W. Bosch *Die Saarfrage: eine Wirtschaftliche Analyse* (Veröffentlichungen des Forschungs-Instituts für Wirtschaftspolitik an der Universität Mainz, Vol. 4, 1954). Especially pp. 17–38, 54–60, 70–75, 119–150.　The remaining three steel mills are owned by the Luxembourg ARBED and HADIR firms, and by the German Stumm and Wolff families.　This state of affairs has led Saar economists to complain that the Saar occupies a " colonial " status since the overwhelmingly foreign ownership of the steel mills and *de facto* foreign control over coal means that the foreign interests use Saar capacity merely for reserve purposes and consequently fail to invest sufficiently in their Saar properties.　Even the Hoffmann Government complained bitterly about a reported Paris–Bonn deal to divide ownership over the Röchling plant evenly between French and German interests, though the plan apparently failed of adoption.　The future status of the Völklingen plant is still unsettled, since it is claimed by France as reparations.

which concerns some French politicians. With respect to the key case of British association with ECSC, Gaullist Senator Michel Debré put the matter in these words: " Is it in accordance with French interests that an organisation be set up for ECSC and Great Britain which will result in France's obtaining a lesser position than Great Britain? " [58]

Debré was referring to those aspects of the agreement with Britain which made all diplomatic contacts with London a collective ECSC effort rather than preserving the formal independence of the member governments. This agreement was the result of a compromise, reflecting the fears of the French Government of Pierre Mendès-France. Monnet's initial proposals had made no provision for participation by the Council of Ministers but had suggested that Britain and ECSC go so far as to define joint production and investment aims, and include Britain in the common market to the maximum degree possible.[59] Of Monnet's marked emphasis regarding the supranational aspects of the agreement, Mendès-France's Minister of Industry, Henri Ulver (Gaullist), remarked bitterly:

> The definitive text of the agreement could have been completed sooner and more easily if the president of the High Authority had not formally opposed the demand of the British Government to send one of its representatives to establish contact with the Council of Ministers of ECSC.[60]

The French Government, explained Ulver, was extremely interested in obtaining British participation in the work of " Little Europe," and " even a weakened participation by Britain in the work of the Community would contribute a balancing element into the Franco-German relationship." But the Government opposed Monnet's formula of giving Britain representation equal to that of all six of the Continental states combined. In fact, the Government denied the power of the High Authority to negotiate permanently on behalf of the six governments, or at least of France. Said Ulver, " to the extent that she has not given a special mandate to the High Authority, France remains mistress over her commercial policy with the United Kingdom." Mendès-France's counter-proposal was to deprive the High Authority of negotiating power by providing for

[58] Oral Question no. 571, by Michel Debré, Conseil de la République, December 14, 1954. *Annales des Mines, op. cit.*, pp. 125–126.
[59] *Chronique de Politique Etrangère*, (September 1955), pp. 561–574.
[60] *Annales des Mines, op. cit.*, p. 126.

full British participation in the Council of Ministers, in which the French Government could influence matters directly. The compromise agreed upon made the Paris Authorities far from happy, as indicated by Ulver's expression of regret in answering Debré's question, that some of France's independent negotiating powers had been yielded after all.[61]

Paris, after protesting and seeking the implementation of the French viewpoint, always yielded in the final analysis. With the fall of Mendès-France, no further nationalist obstacles of this kind have been inserted into the work of the Standing Council of Association, while no meetings of the enlarged Council of Ministers took place in 1955, 1956 and 1957. Looking over the five years of common market and the extent of necessary French adjustment to the new rules, in terms of the divergence of French economic practices from the norms laid down in the Treaty, the degree of loyalty to supranationalism is far greater than a catalogue of initial protests and obstruction would show.

EXTENDING THE ECSC TREATY AND INTEGRATING FURTHER

Given the pattern of governmental co-operation with supranational institutions and the differences in enthusiasm exhibited toward promptly carrying out decisions at variance with nationally desired measures, what is the policy of the six governments toward an enlarged ECSC, toward more economic integration and toward the retention of the supranational principle in such efforts?

As far as the Governments of Holland, Belgium and Luxembourg are concerned the answer is clear: preference for more integration at the earliest possible moment. Thus Jelle Zijlstra has on numerous occasions called for the suppression of the sector approach and the need for a General Common Market. Dutch spokesmen have minimised legal and institutional considerations in saying " we would rather be alive with a limited sovereignty, co-operating with other friendly nations, than be dead on account of full sovereignty." [62] Sidestepping the question of formal federation in Western Europe and the bothersome issue of whether the " Six " should go it alone, successive Dutch ministers have stressed the need for an open community—free to British accession, in particular —with a minimum of centralised direction; but they have also

[61] *Ibid.*, pp. 126–127.
[62] Minister A. B. Speekenbrink in a Washington, D.C., speech, summer, 1955.

admitted the need for a sufficient amount of supranationalism to give planned cohesion to the whole and to ease the transitional period.[63] Unlike their Benelux colleagues in Brussels, however, the Dutch advocates of further integration oppose any planned equalisation of production costs or any publicly sanctioned " super cartel," to quote Zijlstra once more.[64]

Belgian support for further integration is based far less on this enthusiasm for free competition and the virtues of specialisation due to cost differentials. Thus Jean Rey was led to request the Council of Ministers to study the introduction of the five-day week in all ECSC steel plants because he did not wish to have the Belgian steel industry alone so burdened.[65] A high civil servant, and a frequent participant in ECSC inter-governmental negotiations, has noted that the primary task of successful further integration lies in the joint regulation of general economic policies, wages, labour conditions and taxes, necessary in order to solidify the benefits which already have accrued from ECSC in the areas of trade development and diminution of cyclical fluctuations. Yet the same participant-observer also notes that in the short run, at least, supranational and intergovernmental organisations achieve broadly the same kinds of result, while the superiority of supranationalism for the achievement of full economic and political integration can become evident only in the future.[66] Politician and civil servant alike, however, share the conviction of the need for additional steps toward a European political community.

Political factors combined with these economic reasons early in 1955 to persuade Dutch Foreign Minister Beyen to present the " Beyen Plan " for further integration: the competence of ECSC was to be extended to transportation, oil and atomic energy. The political motive implicit in the scheme, supported by Spaak and Bech, was a test of French willingness to continue the work of the " Six," then seemingly jeopardised by the Mendès-France régime. With the fall from power of that Government, there seemed less

---

[63] See Zijlstra's statements in *Informations Bimensuelles*, April 30, 1955, p. 42; October 15, 1955, p. 24. Statements of Foreign Minister Luns in *ibid.*, April 1, 1954, pp. 38–39; April 15, 1954, pp. 32–33.

[64] Tweede Kamer, *Vaststelling Hoofdstuk X* (Economische Zaken), 1955. 16de Vergadering (November 18, 1954), pp. 3076–3090; 17de Vergadering (November 19, 1954), pp. 3111–3115.

[65] *Agence Europe*, September 22, 1955.

[66] J. Van der Meulen, " L'Intégration Economique Européenne: Essai de Synthèse," *Annales des Sciences Economiques Appliquées*, (August 1955), pp. 246 *et seq.* The author is *directeur-general* in the Ministry of Economics.

reason to stress the supranational features of the Beyen Plan, whose modified version became the so-called Benelux Memorandum put before the Messina Conference of June 1955.

This " new step along the road of European integration " specifically proposed: (1) a European transport development plan and central equipment fund; (2) a European fuel development and investment plan; (3) the creation of a new supranational authority to undertake the development of atomic energy for peaceful uses; (4) a gradual and centrally supervised system of abolishing all trade obstacles, or the initiation by stages of the General Common Market; (5) the progressive harmonisation of all national legislation relating to working conditions and wages, *other* than the basic hourly wage itself.[67]   New supranational organs were thus foreseen for atomic energy (Euratom) and for administering the General Common Market (EEC), and a conference was to be convoked immediately to draft appropriate treaties.   All states which had concluded treaties of association with ECSC were to be invited, while other OEEC members might also be considered. Britain, clearly, was to have the place of honour among the guests.

That France, despite recalcitrance with respect to numerous supranational decisions, has by no means been opposed to all measures of further integration is clear from the preceding discussion.   Even Mendès-France, the most consistent and articulate middle-of-the-road critic of integration leading to the formation of a political community among the " Six," proposed his supranational Arms Pool immediately after the creation of the Western European Union.   New tasks for supranational agencies, thus, are not opposed as such and on principle: Mendès-France was quite prepared to have such an agency for controlling German armaments and allocate orders for war materials on a basis other than rewarding the cheapest and most efficient producer.   French Governments since 1952 have argued for conferring new tasks on ECSC when they considered such an extension of authority to be in their national interest.   The most striking instance of this trend is in the field of equalising wage burdens throughout ECSC by means of harmonising social security contributions of all kinds.[68]

[67] *Chronique de Politique Etrangère, op. cit.*, pp. 524–526 for text.
[68] See Louvel's argument in *Usine Nouvelle*, April 2, 1953, p. 5. The Government argued in the ECSC Council of Ministers that pure wages were between 15 and

On other occasions French ministers have been very interested in extending the powers of the High Authority in the investment field, as in fall of 1953 when they sought to stimulate demand for steel by pushing investment in the processing industries which are not under ECSC sway.[69] Conversely, they have bitterly opposed or quietly sabotaged supranationalism when it was not thought to be in the immediate national interest, as in the case of EDC and the European Political Community. But the instance of the common market for special steels shows that once a basic commitment has been undertaken, even a government frightened by the possible consequences of supranationalism can be induced to go along with its partners.

This conclusion is illustrated once more by the tortuous moves and counter-moves which led to the Benelux initiative for continuing economic integration, tied to the resignation of Jean Monnet as that suggestion was. Monnet announced his decision to resign his ECSC position in November of 1954 in direct reaction to the anti-supranational policy of the Mendès-France Government, which he hoped to counter by independent political activity in France. He reconsidered, however, in February of 1955 when Mendès-France fell, enlisting the support of Schuman and Pinay in urging Edgar Faure to advance his name once more for the ECSC position. At the same time he made his continuation in office contingent on the acceptance of the Benelux Plan by the six governments.[70]

Mendès-France, meanwhile, had put forward the name of Paul Ramadier as his candidate for president of the High Authority.

20 per cent. higher in France than in Germany, and that with respect to fringe benefits the figures were as follows:

	France	Germany
	Social costs as % of pure wages	
Totals of all kinds of aid	79%	53%
Family allowances	18%	2%
Worker housing	16%	5%

Etudes et Documents (January 1953), pp. 52–54. These figures were naturally disputed by German public and private sources and they are by no means to be taken as factually established.

[69] See Louvel's statement in *Usine Nouvelle*, October 22, 1953, p. 1.

[70] It is rumoured that it was Monnet who drafted the Benelux Plan and then persuaded Spaak and Beyen to present it to the six governments. The juxtaposition of steps at this time is certainly suggestive—if inferential—evidence of such a connection. For French Governments who had been quietly delaying and changing the proposals for a European Political Community, whose draft Constitution had been ready since 1953, Monnet's insistence on political unification could not but be obnoxious. Monnet is reported to have acted on the following formula during his tenure with ECSC: " je me f . . . du charbon et de l'acier. C'est l'Europe qui m'intéresse." *Chronique de Politique Etrangère, op. cit.*, p. 513.

Ramadier was unacceptable to the five other governments partly because he is a Socialist and partly because he had a consistent record of opposing supranational steps toward European unity as harmful to French interests. Confronted with the negative attitude of the others, Faure dropped Ramadier's candidacy, but also refused to put forward Monnet once more since the latter was *persona non grata* to French industry and the Gaullists. Compelled to find a candidate acceptable to Bonn especially—the other governments having indicated that France could not count on the permanent right to choose the president of the High Authority—the name of René Mayer was put forward in May of 1955. This former premier, temporarily in political difficulty in Paris because of his role in having brought down the Mendès-France Government, had a consistent pro-European record, though less messianic in tone than Monnet's; in exchange for being permitted to retain the presidency of ECSC, Faure put forward a " European " acceptable to his partners but not very popular with French critics of supranationalism.[71]

The decision to appoint Mayer was formally made at Messina on June 1, 1955. As part of the same pattern of decisions, France agreed to the essence of the Benelux proposals for continuing integration, even if this would involve more supranational institutions, though this question was explicitly reserved for later study.

After the obstruction of Mendès-France and the indecisiveness of Edgar Faure, the position of the Mollet Government, which took office in February of 1956, marked an important change. Taking the bull by the horns, Guy Mollet asked Parliament: " My Cabinet is supposedly European, an unatonable sin, as everyone knows. What exactly does this mean? " And he answered—

> There are some who voted for EDC without being especially interested in Europe. There are some who voted against it because

---

[71] *Ibid.*, pp. 505–519. René Mayer himself seems to have accepted the evolving rule of national rotation in key supranational offices. He offered his resignation on September 18, 1957, explaining his step thus: " now that the Rome Treaties are signed and their ratification is under way in the six countries a new era in the construction of Europe is here. It appears to me that by making available my present functions to the disposition of the Governments, I shall facilitate their task in distributing the positions of members and presidents of the three European institutions and at the same time launch them together and in harmony." (Mayer to Pineau, High Authority Doc. 6325/57f.) The six governments took the hint in naming Louis Armand (France) to head Euratom, considered by many in France more vital than ECSC. Mayer himself accepted a key private financial position in connection with " Eurafrican " plans to develop jointly the French Sahara.

they were sincerely convinced that it would hinder the construction of Europe. Are we all going to behave as if France's international activity had suddenly stopped on that day? Could we be incapable of overcoming past differences in order to devote ourselves to the future? I solemnly entreat the Assembly to stop regarding the European idea as a subject of disagreement, but to consider it rather as a great bond between us.[72]

But in order to make it a " bond " among France's quarrelling parties, Mollet and Pineau had to emphasise clearly, as they did, that the Europe of the Six was not an acceptable solution and that British association with new integration measures was essential. They insisted further that in any General Common Market, the French colonial empire and not merely metropolitan France— as in ECSC—would have to be a member. At the same time the Socialist government sought to take a " progressive " step in colonial relations by insisting that one of the obligations of a united Europe should be collective participation in a new global scheme for economic development.[73] Following the British example, French statesmen sought to compensate for weakness in Europe by enlisting the numerical and ideological support of their imperial responsibilities in bolstering their voting position in new European institutions. Conversely, they linked the " Eurafrica " investment scheme to the General Common Market because their national colonial problems would thereby become the collective responsibility of Europe. And these aspirations naturally aroused some dismay among the other governments seeking to implement the Messina resolutions, contributing to the slow pace of the negotiations in 1956. A significant note of caution with respect to unbounded enthusiasm for supranationalism as a road to federation was sounded by Pineau at the Council of Europe:

It would be an error to believe that Europe will be built in our circles of the initiated, if we do not know how to create a great tide of popular sentiment in its favour. If, from an intellectual standpoint, we are right in asserting that our ancestral nationalisms are now outdated, we must not for all that neglect the emotional and legitimate aspect of the concept of country. We must make clear to our people that none of us intend to relinquish our traditions, our patterns of thought, our way of life. We are sacrificing neither

[72] Statement of Policy of Premier-Designate Guy Mollet to Parliament, January 31, 1956. Ambassade de France (U.S.), Service de Presse et d'Information, Speeches and Conferences, no. 55 (February 1956), p. 5.
[73] *Ibid.*, no. 64 (April 1956), especially p. 3. *Ibid.*, no. 67 (June 1956), pp. 9 *et seq.*

the land nor the legacy of our ancestors, but the isolation and loss of strength which may jeopardize their very existence. We must explain to our people that Europe is our final hope for saving our threatened values and that the term " supra-national," often used exaggeratedly, is not synonymous with " anti-national." [74]

Guided by this intellectual context, the Mollet Government associated itself with the Messina Programme of " relaunching Europe." It favoured a Euratom which is open to the membership of all OEEC countries, especially Britain, devoted exclusively to peaceful pursuits and able to plan a long-term European fuel policy. Similarly, the Government favoured the establishment of the General Common Market, under these conditions—

> Organising a General Common Market in Europe is a long-term job. The Government is resolved to set up such a market in a way that will ensure the necessary transitions and adaptations and prevent competition from being corrupted by disparities in the various taxation and social security systems. Of course measures will have to be taken to protect the worker from all the risks which might result from the elimination of frontiers.[75]

Thus the attitude differs hardly from past French claims with respect to specific measures advocated in the ECSC framework. Yet the courage of Pineau in defending ECSC against continuing criticism in France is considerable. To an interpellation of Michel Debré, alleging the bankruptcy of France's role in ECSC because of the Saar plebiscite, the delays in building the Moselle Canal, Ruhr re-concentration, price increases for coal and continued German rail discrimination, Pineau answered as follows. The Saar dispute is on its way to a fully amicable settlement; the High Authority had no jurisdiction over the Moselle Canal and should not be blamed for any delays; and the High Authority, finally, can be blamed neither for German re-concentration nor coal price increases and that the last minor transport discriminations are on their way out. France intends to stand by the ECSC Treaty unflinchingly.[76]

Italy's basic policy toward extending the scope of supranationalism and achieving a European political community has not been

---

[74] Pineau, before the Consultative Assembly in Strasbourg, April 18, 1956; *ibid.*, no. 64, p. 2.
[75] Mollet's speech to the National Assembly, *op. cit.*, p. 5. It should be recalled in this context that the " bond " which was to be forged among all parties by means of the European idea demanded concrete concessions on the issue of Euratom's peaceful or warlike uses. See Chap. 4 above for details.
[76] *Informations Mensuelles*, August 1956, pp. 33–34.

changed since Giuseppe Pella made his proposal for a General Common Market to the OEEC in 1950. The government's reaction to the Benelux initiative was entirely favourable in principle, though different conceptions were advanced with respect to the question of further sector integration. While the Euratom idea was accepted, the Italian Government argued for the greatest possible measure of general economic integration, with a de-emphasis on special work in the sectors singled out by Spaak and Beyen, fuel and transportation. The General Common Market, insisted Rome, was to include a positive European labour policy, a European re-adaptation fund, a European investment fund to aid such schemes as the Italian Vanoni Development Plan, full convertibility and freedom of movement for manpower. Paradoxically, in view of Italy's indifferent record in promptly heeding ECSC decisions, it was urged that " it would be useful if the six governments were to re-affirm solemnly the intention of co-operating fully with the High Authority and to make easier its task in the great supranational effort which it has been assigned." [77]

Expanding the task of ECSC or creating new supranational economic organisations aiming at the political unification of Europe is an issue on which the German Government has been increasingly divided since 1952. Committed federalists favour either or both approaches without deeply questioning the economic logic implicit in them. Indeed, they favour any institutional programme whatever which would seek to advance their cause. Of this trend, Chancellor Adenauer and the cabinet members close to him are the living symbol. Before the rejection of EDC by the French National Assembly, Adenauer pinned his hopes for the attainment of a united Europe on military integration, crowned by the immediate establishment of the European Political Community, whose legislators were to be popularly elected. After the defeat of EDC, Adenauer continued to affirm his faith in ultimate federation, urged the creation of any substitute scheme which would please France and keep her in the movement toward integration, and—most important—refused to make an issue of the Saar crisis when under

[77] *Chronique de Politique Etrangère, op. cit.,* pp. 529–533. Foreign Minister Martino later indicated that his government had no firm position on the question of whether Euratom should be limited to peaceful uses of atomic energy. He brushed aside as irrelevant suggestions that the common market would entail new limitations on national sovereignty. *Agence Europe,* May 3, 1956.

strong pressure from all parties to do so.[78] To these members of the Government, then, post-EDC schemes for continued economic integration were welcome.

The minister responsible for specific measures of economic co-operation or merging with other nations, however, is Ludwig Erhard. While by no means hostile to a united Europe on principle, Erhard has opposed the idea of European regional economic union in general and the sector-cum-supranationalism approach in particular, without having departed from this position one iota since the debut of ECSC. In his words:

> We must have trade relations with all countries. We cannot be satisfied with even the most extensive regionalism. Even the smallest and farthest market is an indispensable part of our foreign economic policy.... Unconditional most-favoured-nation treatment, full convertibility, abolition of quantitative restrictions and distorted exchange rates, these are the intellectual and practical fundamentals of a global commercial policy necessitated by a highly specialised industrial and export-oriented country like Germany.[79]

Hence the Havana Charter, GATT and OEEC are singled out as the institutional centres of German attachment, since they alone can make possible a sufficiently large trading zone to overcome balance of payments crises and bilateralism. While willing to support ECSC because it might lead to a general economic pattern of integration, Erhard was always sceptical about the sequence implied, preferring to abolish first the commercial practices which falsify competition and block trade. The General Common Market, in short, was preferred to sector integration if there had to be regionalism.

> What is the true economic significance of European integration? Certainly it would be the creation of a large common market, which would facilitate growing mass production, accompanied by free labour and capital movement and location of production at optimum points (günstigsten Standorte). Simultaneously, such a common market would open up the possibility of co-ordinated employment and cyclical policies, as well as the rationalisation of costs of production. Economic processes would thus be converted more easily to the common denominator of one currency. Such a currency could then, supported by the potential of a large common market, be made convertible in relation to the dollar and third countries.[80]

[78] *German Bulletin*, May 6, September 9, September 16, 1954.
[79] Ludwig Erhard, *Deutschlands Rückkehr zum Weltmarkt* (Düsseldorf: Econ Verlag, 1954), p. 9.   [80] *Ibid.*, Chap. 8.

But sector integration which neglects to co-ordinate fiscal, financial, and budgetary policy would violate the logic of this process and therefore not lead to the general free trade area Erhard wishes to establish. In practice, therefore, he is convinced that the problems created by such ventures as ECSC outweigh possible long-term advantages.

It follows that Erhardian Liberalism is constrained to oppose any increase in ECSC activity if this entails a growth in institutional powers. Erhard has supported such measures as the extension of the common market to special steels and has strongly argued for the removal of discriminatory national taxes through ECSC. But these demands follow from the attachment to simple free trade rules and the preference for competition based on considerations of comparative cost—thus favouring the German export drive. Conversely, he has vigorously fought against the initiation of an ECSC labour and welfare policy and castigated the High Authority's study of comparative real wages as leading to comparative cost studies, preparatory to efforts at " harmonising " costs in an upward direction. Equalising costs is held to violate every rule of sound economic policy and therefore implies disintegration rather than unity.[81] Planning, whether national or international, is anathema:—

> Where is the institution which is called upon to do the right thing, the rational thing, from a European social welfare viewpoint? Such an institution is an impossibility, if we do not wish to construct a supranational centralising dirigisme. If we did this, we would do on a larger plane exactly the same thing which we did in our national economies, but the tragedy would even be greater. The larger the plane, the more difficult to grasp the total economic structure, and the less the possibility of managing the co-operation and harmonising of economic communities, and the more tragic will be the results of a planned European economy.[82]

Given the dominance of this ideology in the Ministry of Economics, the German reaction to the Benelux proposals in June of 1955 could not but be reserved. Even though Hallstein,

---

[81] *Informations Bimensuelles*, June 1, 1955, pp. 19–20. Erhard's announcement coincided with the discussion of extending the jurisdiction of ECSC initiated by the Monnet resignation.

[82] Ludwig Erhard, " Die Wirtschaftlichen Aspekte," in G. Bally and G. Thürer (eds.), *Die Integration des Europäischen Westens* (Zurich and St. Gallen: Polygraphischer Verlag, 1954. Reihe B in Veröffentlichungen der Handels-Hochschule St. Gallen), p. 120.

representing Chancellor Adenauer at Messina, made no difficulty about agreeing to the choice of René Mayer as head of the High Authority, critical comments abounded in the German press about the " French monopoly " on the office and the need for Germany to occupy the post in view of her dominant role in the Community. Concerning further steps toward an integrated Europe, the German memorandum emphasised the General Common Market and scarcely mentioned Euratom.   It is nevertheless significant that the principle of an atomic authority was not challenged even though this would represent yet another " sector " to be unified, in violation of Erhardian economics. In its demands for a generally unified European market, the German proposals featured the removal of all the standard obstacles to trade, praised the efforts of OEEC and GATT, conceded that the effort must be a gradual one and admitted that " measures of transition and adaptation may be necessary."

It is in the institutional realm that the decline of Adenauer's federalist conceptions became most apparent. Emphasis in the German rejoinder to the Benelux Memorandum was uniformly placed on inter-governmental co-operation. The ECSC Council of Ministers—not special supranational authorities—was to be charged with transport rationalisation. The co-ordination of national fuel policies was to be achieved by the same body. Finally, " a permanent consultative organ under the responsibility of the ECSC Council of Ministers " was to work out trading rules between third countries and the General Common Market *bloc* and to make proposals for additional steps toward unity. A European university should be founded also " to give evidence of the will toward European unity," added the German proposal.[83]

The ultimate decision of the Messina Conference reflected a good deal more supranationalism than Germany favoured and therefore represents a distinct compromise between Spaakian maximalism and Erhardian minimalist conceptions, supported at the institutional level by French preferences, though for quite different reasons. Speaking for Adenauer, Walter Hallstein at the opening of the Brussels Expert conference convoked after the Messina decisions, could thus declare:

---

[83] *Chronique de Politique Etrangère, op. cit.*, pp. 526–529, for the text of the German Memorandum. For the details concerning post-Messina negotiations, see Chaps. 8 and 13.

Our policy is not merely an unconditional acceptance of the Messina resolutions. It is continually expressed in our will to give our preference, wherever possible, to European solutions whenever an alternative is present. The Federal Government believes that we must take a decisive step now. This is much more a political than an economic necessity. A balance between East and West is only possible if there is European unity. We believe that the purely economic activities of GATT and OEEC must have a political counterpart. This political aspect will give us the criteria for judging the details which the experts will work out, who will always have to consider which will contribute most to the political unification of Europe.[84]

Once more, " der Alte " had carried the day over Erhard, who then sought to defend his reputation by publishing an article entitled " Who is a good European? " In this effort the Minister of Economics restated all his past arguments and added that the more modest successes of such intergovernmental ventures as OEEC and GATT cannot be explained on the basis of their lacking federal administrative powers. " Not my escape from Europe, but my search for it makes me fear that this kind of addition (more sector integration on the ECSC model) will further neither the economic nor the political aim." [85] Only sound economics can lead to sound politics, and therefore to Europe: the rapid achievement of a free and competitive European market including all countries and dedicated to free private enterprise.

Our past discussion of German party and interest group attitudes indicates, of course, that Erhard's position is by no means generally accepted in Germany. It has not triumphed in the negotiations on the Euratom and General Common Market treaties, though former Minister of Atomic Affairs, Franz Josef Strauss, has defended the Erhardian position by insisting on a minimum of supranational control powers over national atomic developments. But compromises among the clashing governmental positions have characterised the entire negotiating process since the summer of 1955, indicating again that the West German Government is by no means so wedded to its economic ideology as to preclude a meeting of the minds with its five ECSC partners. Like their French colleagues, then, the German officials seek to enforce a maximum of their position on

[84] *Ibid.*, pp. 547–548.
[85] Ludwig Erhard, " Wer ist ein guter Europäer? " *Bulletin des Presse- und Informations-amtes der Bundesregierung* (August 6, 1955), p. 1221.

the emerging structure. But they have not so far carried their zeal to the extent of obstructing the evolution of consensus and have thereby joined the other ECSC governments in making possible the evolution of *more* integrated decision-making over time. The processes explaining this evolution will be examined in a later chapter.

Part Three

PROCESSES OF INTEGRATION AT THE
SUPRANATIONAL LEVEL

CHAPTER 8

THE EXPANSIVE LOGIC OF SECTOR INTEGRATION

THE effort contrasting sector integration with general economic
integration is a vain one. The common market for coal and steel
by itself contributes decisively to the producers and consumers
of coal and steel. But at the same time it offers the opportunity
for stating and effectively solving the problems of creating an
integrated European economy suitable to the modern world.[1]

THUS wrote Pierre Uri, chief economic analyst for ECSC and a
participant in the effort to draft a General Common Market treaty.
In his view, sector integration is merely a first step toward full
integration and a living laboratory of the measures necessary for
achieving it. The " spill-over " effect in sector integration is believed
to lead inevitably to full economic unity. If this causal juxtaposition seems self-evident to the economist, the political study of
changes in attitude would seem to give support to his conclusions.
Yet it is very doubtful indeed whether a direct beam of insight into
the merits of the larger market and increased production was
operative in persuading the bulk of European industrialists and
trade unionists to favour a General Common Market. It will be
our task in this chapter to summarise and categorise the evolutions
in attitude which have occurred and to project them. The essential
preliminary question, however, is: has " integration " really taken
place in ECSC Europe since 1952?

METHODS OF ASSESSING INTEGRATION

The most inviting index of integration—because it can be
verified statistically—is the economic one. Such an approach was
developed specifically for studies of ECSC by Harald Jürgensen.
Defining integration as the creation of a free market for goods,
capital and labour, the author assumes productive conditions in
which an equal input of capital and labour will yield a greater final
output and in which no marked institutional differences between
international and interregional trade prevail. Measures undertaken
in the integrated sector must tend toward the perfection of that

[1] Pierre Uri, " Ce qui se réalise," *Hommes et Commerce* (January-February 1955),
p. 82.

sector but not hinder the realisation of a general free market later. Measures in the integrated sector must also be made to harmonise with national policies not yet subject to central rules.   The High Authority is credited with achieving this triple order, without limiting production, encouraging ECSC autarky or interfering with optimum cost considerations.   Trade statistics support Jürgensen's conclusion that market interpenetration along optimum cost and price lines is taking place in ECSC without discrimination in trade with third countries.[2]   The economic criteria of integration seem satisfied.

Jürgensen's scheme, however, does not by itself answer the basic political question whether the unified economy meets with the satisfaction of people active within it, whether it leads to expectations of hope and progress or fears of doom and decay.   It permits, in short, of no assessment and projection of changing attitudes, values and ideologies and therefore is of no help in the study of political integration even when it takes place in an economic setting.

Communications theory, in the work of Karl Deutsch, would open up another series of criteria for judging the success and future prospects of integration.[3]   Integration is identified, following the analogy of physics and electronics, with the capacity of the total communications network of society to accommodate the burden of social, political, cultural and economic transactions.   If the balance of capacity and load is upset, disintegration may set in. Deutsch would measure the total bulk of transactions between political units about to integrate or in the process of integration, assess the range of social transactions and determine the compatibility of transactions in terms of the perceptions of the actors.   Integration can then presumably be advanced by perfecting the network— institutionally as well as psychologically—where it seems incapable of accommodating the load.

A rigorous statistical application of Deutsch's concepts would no doubt reveal a positive adjustment of capacity to load, or net

---

[2] H. Jürgensen, *Die Westeuropäische Montanindustrie und ihr gemeinsamer Markt*, Göttingen: Vandenhoeck & Ruprecht, 1955.   Also " Die Montanunion in den Funktionsgrenzen der Teilintegration," *op. cit.*   He demonstrates statistically that market interpenetration is strongest in trade between the main industrial centre of an exporting country and sections of the importing country farthest removed from its own national industrial nexus, *e.g.*, steel trade between Lorraine and southern Germany.   Economically, this is also the most rational pattern. *Ibid.*, pp. 624–625.

[3] See Chap. 1 for bibliography on Deutsch.

progress in the direction of successful integration. As in the case of purely economic criteria, however, it is most doubtful that the demonstration of the process proves anything with respect to its causes. Integration is the result of specific decisions made by governments acting in conjunction with politically relevant, organised groups. Unless it is suggested that these actors deliberately seek to improve communication, Deutsch's concepts do not contribute directly to the study and projection of motives and expectations responsible for decisions to integrate.[4]

In the work of F. S. C. Northrop, emphasis is thrown on still a third set of criteria: the " political living law " of states.[5] Northrop argues that if political conduct flows from social norms, the total socio-cultural context of a country must be outlined in order to assess the progress and prospects of integration. He selects the nominal religious affiliations of citizens as well as their secular

[4] Deutsch does not claim that his approach is concerned with the study of motives. He argues, however, that political actors anxious to advance integration can usefully apply the lessons presented by his studies in improving deliberately the communications capacity in crucial areas.

The following revealing Indices of Relative Acceptance of trade among ECSC countries were kindly supplied by Karl W. Deutsch to the author.

$$\text{Index of Acceptance} \quad = \quad \frac{\text{Actual trade} - \text{Expected trade}}{\text{Expected trade}}$$

Indices of Relative Trade Acceptance

1913

	Ger.	Fran.	Belg.	Neth.	Italy	Total Countries
Germany.........	—	−·09	·007	·08	·17	·01
France...........	−·27	—	2·33	−·79	·50	·12
Belgium	·50	1·72	—	·54	−·29	·72
Netherlands	1·82	−·87	1·29	—	−·76	·87
Italy............	−·17	·25	−·51	−·89	—	−·24
Total Countries	·58	·007	·78	−·17	−·003	·30

1954

	Ger.	Fran.	Belg.	Neth.	Italy	Total Countries
Germany	—	·30	1·16	1·22	·94	·85
France..........	·46	—	1·17	−·39	·30	·36
Belgium	·66	·93	—	4·06	−·09	1·39
Netherlands	1·75	−·16	3·37	—	−·34	1·13
Italy............	1·02	·24	−·24	−·44	—	·25
Total Countries ..	·88	·32	1·39	1·01	·37	·79

[5] F. S. C. Northrop, *European Union and United States Foreign Policy*, New York: Macmillan, 1954; " United States Foreign Policy and Continental European Union," *Harvard Studies in International Affairs*, Vol. 5, no. 1 (February, 1954).

values—in terms of Communism, Socialism, Liberalism, Authoritarianism and Christian-Democracy—for this structure. His conclusion is that the combined spiritual-secular norms of the six ECSC countries are mutually compatible and likely to yield a consensus in favour of pluralistic democracy. But he also concludes that the inclusion of some other European countries, *e.g.*, East Germany, would destroy this emergent pattern by introducing too large a share of right- or left-wing authoritarian norms. Northrop explains the failure of EDC on these grounds: French democrats were dissuaded from joining EDC because they feared the victory of non-democratic norms if European military integration were tied to the reunification of Germany.

There can be little doubt that broad similarities in the social values entertained by the dominant elites of the ECSC countries explain in large part why the Treaty was accepted and successfully implemented. Such reasoning, further, goes a long way in explaining why certain groups see in supranational institutions a technique for systematically realising their specific values. However, the literal application of this scheme would impute far more ideological cohesion to groups only nominally united by religious or secular norms than seems warranted by the facts of political behaviour. It would permit projections of pro-integration sentiment merely on the basis of religious or party affiliation, without raising questions about the qualifications and special demands voiced constantly in the integration framework. Hence Northrop's scheme of national " living laws " must be rejected in this assessment as insufficiently precise.

Integration there has been in Europe since 1950 even if it cannot be meaningfully delineated with a few central concepts. To do justice to the multiplicity of aspirations involved in the pluralistic setting provided, we must return to the ideal type stated in Chapter 1. There is no circumventing the need for stating the initial demands and expectations of relevant elites, and to sort them with respect to identities, opposition and convergence. Our basic finding was that the acceptance of ECSC is best explained by the convergence of demands within and among the nations concerned, not by a pattern of identical demands and hopes. Further, there is no circumventing the need for exploring the changes in demands and expectations which developed after the supranational institutions began their work, and there is no avoiding the task of projecting the future pattern of integration in terms of the hopes and demands set free by unification of the coal-steel sector. The success of integration must thus be assessed in terms of the perceptions of the crucial actors. To what overall identities did the common market give rise? To what convergences of group and national aspirations? If there is a spill-over, is it explained by identical hopes or by another accidental convergence of separate aspirations? And, finally, have the identities given rise to a pattern of unified ideologies cutting across national boundaries or has the common market resulted merely in *ad hoc* group alliances along supranational lines, devoid of ideological unity? If the latter is the central finding, the basic conclusion must then be that continuing integration can well rest on progressive convergences of expectations without any significant central ideological underpinnings.

TYPES OF POLITICAL EXPECTATIONS

The evolution of the hopes characteristic of the chief political groups active in the ECSC setting, nationally and supranationally, has been described in detail in Part II of this study. If it seemed extremely difficult to state any general proposition summarising the pattern of evolution, it became evident, nevertheless, that crucial changes did take place: opponents of integration became supporters, initial supporters became neutral or disinterested, while still other initial supporters developed even stronger motives for continuing integration. It is now our task to state four categories of evolution under which all these developing aspirations can be subsumed. After identifying the ideological component in each, it may then be possible to state some further propositions about expanding the scope of integration to sectors other than coal and steel.

Long-run positive expectations

A system of demands may develop in the programme of a national elite, seeking the support of kindred elites in other ECSC countries, designed to establish a far-reaching series of policies realisable only in the framework of supranational institutions. Further, the successful realisation of such a programme depends on continuing supranational activity; it cannot be terminated with the publication of a single decree or ruling. Any programme of long-range economic planning would fall into this category, as would a policy of permanent harmonisation of social welfare benefits. In the political realm, the asserted need for continuing parliamentary supervision over the activities of supranational administrative bodies would also constitute a long-run positive expectation.

Short-run positive expectations

Whenever a national or supranational elite wishes to make use of supranational institutions for the establishment of a single condition, or a series of unconnected individual measures, positive action is indeed expected, but the element of continuity is absent. The desire to establish conditions of free trade by abolishing quantitative restrictions, exchange controls and tariffs is such an expectation. After the achievement of these steps, no further far-reaching action is expected from supranational authorities, except perhaps the routine steps of policing the free market. The same is true of demands to curb cartels, do away with rail discrimination or permit free labour migration. Whenever the expectations in question involve in fact some kind of continuing administrative measures, however, an initially short-run expectation may develop into a long-run demand. This, for instance, would be true of the desire to regulate the scrap market or to permit a regulated price flexibility.

Short-run negative expectations

Elites may, singly and collectively, seek to prevent the supranational institutions from undertaking a specific policy, *e.g.*, regulate prices or break up a cartel. The process of combining and pooling their political power may reflect no permanent desire whatever to work together. It may merely be an *ad hoc* alliance designed to block a specific policy. If successful, the alliance may then disintegrate and give rise to no permanent pattern of interelite integration. If not immediately successful, however, the negative combination of groups may, in self-defence, become a permanent institution with a common—albeit negative—body of expectations.

Long-run negative expectations

Elites opposed to integration at the onset of supranational activity and continuing in their opposition thereafter are irreconcilable with a unification pattern either in the short or the long run.

Their demand pattern not only seeks to direct the policies of their national government away from supranationalism or federation, but it continues to block and oppose central policy after it has been active for some years. Unlike groups opposed to supranationalism in essence but reconciled to work with it if only to block its progress, elites possessing negative long-range expectations will use their influence with national authorities to bring about withdrawal from supranational bodies and block the creation of new ones.

IDEOLOGY AND POLITICAL EXPECTATIONS

Intensities of ideological convictions associated with each of these types of expectations vary distinctly. We are here concerned not with the committed " European," be he Liberal, Conservative or Socialist, but with permanently functioning elites for whom " Europe " is one of several important symbols, but not necessarily the dominant one. Groups with long-range expectations, for example, are likely to possess well-developed bodies of doctrine, whose implementation is closely associated with the positions taken toward further integration. Those with positive expectations look to supranationalism to achieve their goal, having decided that the national framework is not up to the task. The " spill-over " is real for them, since basic ideological tenets even in the coal-steel sector seemingly cannot be attained without expanding the supranational task to additional fields. The demand pattern of ECSC labour and of the Socialist Parties is the most striking case in point. Conversely, groups marked by clearly negative long-range expectations, notably the Communists and small businessmen in high-cost countries, have an equally well-structured and staunchly defended body of ideology at their disposal, whose very firmness commits them against integration.

Those who entertain short-range expectations, whether negative or positive, are less likely to be sharply motivated by ideology. ECSC, Euratom, the General Common Market or the European Political Community are programmes affecting a part of their total aspirations; but they do not represent a depository for the bulk of their values and hopes. Immediate expediential considerations are far more likely to shape the pattern of expectations toward integration. Ideology, in fact, may be so vague as to permit a given group to pose as pro-integration on one range of issues while countering further unification on others. This is typically true of the belief patterns of trade associations whose dedication even to the free enterprise principle is far from consistent or convincing. Hence ideological tenets are of little relevance here in projecting a pattern of expectation with respect to future issues of integration, especially when the group in question firmly opposed ECSC in 1951 on some point of doctrine but subsequently made its peace with the common market.

In fact, the entire evolution of the common market for coal and steel and its extension to additional economic areas in 1957 is largely attributable to the weakness of national ideological commitments and to the fragmentation of opinion in four of the six countries concerned. The very fact that firm national attitudes prevailed in 1950–1952 only in Holland and Luxembourg in large part explains the acceptance of the ECSC Treaty and the accommodation of initially hostile groups to its scope. One important conclusion must certainly be that additional measures tending toward political unity could be introduced as a result of the same fragmentation: a new treaty need merely be so constructed as to contain a large variety of otherwise unrelated provisions and thus appeal to a large enough constituency to establish another converging pattern of support. Ideological diversity becomes a distinct help to further integration and doctrinal vagueness facilitates the conversion to " Europe " of those who are initially cool.

However, even ideological fragmentation would hardly have sufficed to make a success of integration if another series of conditions had not also been present. Most important perhaps, there were in the Western Europe of the post-1950 era no outstanding political issues sharply setting nations against one another. The Franco-German relationship even had become sufficiently amicable to permit the unspectacular and speedy solution of the Saar dispute, while German politicians have shown far more sensitivity about the fears of their French ally with respect to problems of re-unification and relations with the Soviet Union than ever before. The stated policies of governments, unlike any period before in European history, were no longer mutually exclusive.

Further, no issues of cultural diversity arose to plague the integrating units, and to that extent Northrop's thesis is relevant to this study. Legal and economic systems were already sufficiently alike as not to pose big initial problems of adjustment and compromise between rival practices and habits. Political institutions and practices are identical in all six countries as regards the basic lines. Cultural and religious values accepted in one are typical equally of, at least, a large portion of the population of the others. Finally, some identity in political programmes prevailed across national boundaries even before the *douaniers* stopped checking the coal wagons. Not only did the European Movement exercise its unifying influence here but the broad similarities in outlook and programme among the Continental Christian-Democratic and Socialist Parties made possible almost immediately the initiation of joint economic policy-making. It is unlikely that in the absence of these conditions even the most cleverly drafted treaty would have brought with it such rapid progress in political integration.

Non-ideological factors go a long way in explaining the pattern of co-operation typical of negotiations within ECSC among instructed government delegates.[6] The conventional pattern of hard bargaining based on the initially stated national positions has undergone considerable change because over long periods of time the same persons habitually negotiate with one another. In conventional negotiations the final agreement is almost invariably a compromise between the differing initial positions of the parties, without changes in opinion or instructions being part of the compromise pattern. In inter-governmental ECSC negotiations, the long familiarity of the negotiators with each other's habits and viewpoints enables them to differentiate almost immediately between argument based on bargaining points and positions defended because of technically sound information and relevant conditions. As a result, discussion for the sake of bargaining diminishes in importance and attention is paid more and more to the technical needs in question. Issues which seem imbued with vital interests and strong doctrine in the national capital lose this aura as they are discussed by high civil servants in the council chambers of Luxembourg. Ideology, already weak with respect to a myriad of economic issues, tends to shed the importance it seems to have in the debates of parties and movements.

THE " SPILL-OVER " AND POLITICAL EXPECTATIONS

Only the convinced " European " possessed long-run positive expectations with respect to ECSC in 1950, and among the elites directly concerned with coal and steel there were few such persons.

[6] This information is based on the impressions of negotiators in Luxembourg who were interviewed by the author.

The crucial evolution of such expectations among the bulk of ECSC labour leaders—both Socialist and Christian—is one of the clearest demonstrations of the role of a combined social welfare-economic democracy ideology, seeking realisation through the medium of new central institutions. These groups as well as the Socialist and left-wing segments of Christian-Democratic Parties associated with them are now in the vanguard of more integration—through ECSC as well as in the form of Euratom and the General Common Market—because they see in supranational rules and organs the means to establish a regulated large-scale industrial economy permitting the development of permanent worker influence over industry. Thus a " spill-over " into new economic and political sectors certainly occurred in terms of expectations developing purely in the *national* contexts of the elites involved. Yet these expectations were reinforced along supranational lines not only because action was demanded of the High Authority but because continuous joint lobbying with labour leaders from other countries became both necessary and possible. The same, of course, is true of the Socialist Parties, whose national aims found supranational support in the formation of the Socialist political group in the Common Assembly. Hence the true impact of integration can be appreciated only after a study of joint supranational activity on the part of these groups.[7]

[7] Classification of ECSC group expectations, 1956-1957.
  (1) Long-run positive: all Socialist parties, all Socialist trade unions, all Christian trade unions, welfare-oriented wings of Christian-Democratic Parties (particularly in Italy and France), coal trade associations (with respect to coal-oil competition and investment nexus), CDU leadership with respect to political integration, French small-scale Steel Consumers.
  (2) Short-run positive: all free trade-oriented parties, *e.g.*, FDP, part of CDU, DP, Belgian, Dutch and Italian Liberal Parties: free trade-oriented industry groups, *e.g.*, BDI, FIB, Dutch Employers' Associations, Dutch Steel Association, Belgian and French Steel Associations (with respect to social security harmonisation), Charbonnages de France (as above), Italian Coke and Steel Associations (with respect to coal prices and cartels and transport), all Steel Consumers' Associations (with respect to prices and cartels), Fédéchar, most coal consuming groups.
  (3) Short-run negative: Conseil National du Patronat Français, Confidustria, French and Italian Steel Associations (on most issues), German Steel Association, Dutch and Luxembourg Steel Associations, steel consuming groups (on price rigidity and investment co-ordination), Ruhr Coal Association, Charbonnages de France (on most issues). Radical-Socialist and Independent Republican Parties.
  4) Long-run negative: Associations of Small Business in France, Italy, Belgium; Inland Waterway Shippers, trucking firms (all ECSC countries), all Communist Parties, all Communist-dominated trade unions, Gaullists and Poujadists, Neo-Fascists and Monarchists (Italy); agricultural groups everywhere except in Holland.

The evolution of industrial attitudes and of parties sympathetic to business interests is much more difficult to classify. Not only is the ideological component far less consistently represented, but the common picture is one of a given group simultaneously exhibiting short-range positive *and* negative expectations, depending on the issue, thus introducing a thoroughly expediential ambivalence. A general summary of the evolution of business attitudes is the simplest way to sketch the situation.

Certainly there have been sweeping changes in industrial attitudes since 1951. But it is most doubtful that these reflect a solidification of opinion toward the desirability of an integrated European economy—not to mention a political community—on doctrinal grounds. Trade association activity in the six countries fails to support any hypothesis of the evolution of a prevalent and unified industrial ideology in favour of a common market under the direction of central public authorities. Instead, there developed a series of opportunistic and frequently anti-competitive demands for specific measures of integration designed to benefit a specific national industry, though supranational action is commonly invoked for such purposes. Conversion to " Europe " is therefore short-range, limited and " tactical " in nature.

Yet it is of the greatest significance for a study of integration processes to isolate even these instances of changed attitudes, because permanent loyalties may still develop from these initial faltering steps, if long-range expectations are identified with them. Viewed from this vantage point, considerable changes can be noted if the question is raised in terms of conversion to " integration " merely in the sense of abolishing trade restrictions and introducing free movement of capital and manpower. With the weighty exception of the Italian steelmakers, *all* groups now subject to ECSC jurisdiction favour the extension of the common market principle to new sectors, for the reasons spelled out clearly by Pierre Van der Rest. This, certainly, had not been true in 1950 and 1951. Even the industrial sectors not now subject to unprotected competition appear much less reluctant about the introduction of a common market than was true at the debut of ECSC. While coal and steel consuming industries were ready to welcome ECSC even then, many others were not. The endorsement of the General Common Market, if free from " dirigisme," by four of the six national associations of industries is a significant index in this respect.

The more important index, however, is the readiness of industrial groups to accept integration if accompanied by supranational institutions possessing powers of direction and control, potentially " dirigistic " in nature.   In 1951, all groups without exception opposed such an approach and were compelled by national legislative action to accept the ECSC rules.   Four years later this unqualified opposition had changed to a demand for *more* supranational powers and control if specific benefits were expected from this.   Such a conversion is true for almost all the coal associations in Europe if it is a question of limiting the competitive impact of other fuels and rationalising investment in collieries.   It is equally true for the French and Belgian steel associations with respect to the harmonisation of wages, taxes and social security rules.   On the other hand, groups who already have succeeded in obtaining all they had expected in 1951 from supranationalism just as consistently oppose any extension of this principle of control. This conclusion applies to the German, Dutch and Luxembourg steel associations who admire the principle of the common market and favour its extension, without supranational features.   Finally, the industrial groups not yet integrated are agreed in their opposition to any kind of European public authority with powers to direct them, unless, of course, they consider such a power necessary to impose conditions limiting competition on their future partners, as in the case of some French associations.   In each case, however, individual short-range calculations of benefits and drawbacks determine attitudes.   Of a general doctrine or ideology there is no trace.

Outspoken statements by industry leaders underscore this tactical conversion with its remaining negative expectations. While opposing supranationalism, Pierre Van der Rest nevertheless argued with reference to the adoption of the forty-five-hour week in Belgian steel that:

> we think that the introduction of such reforms in Belgium alone, without certainty that the other member countries will follow our example in the near future, would constitute a terribly dangerous step, which will be regretted some day.[8]

[8] As quoted in *La Métropole*, January 25, 1956. Note also that a spokesman for the Belgian Federation of Chemical Industries argued strongly that the benefits of increased production can be realised only in an integrated European market. Yet M. Sermon, for the giant Brufina investment trust, came out merely for a

André Métral opposed not only ECSC in 1951, but objected strongly to EDC and EPC as well, as permitting low-cost German and Dutch steel-consuming firms to acquire the bulk of the projected European armaments procurement programme. Yet he also used the High Authority to put pressure on the French Government to relax its price-control system, citing supranational obligations in this context.[9] And the uneasy mixture of negative with positive expectations is well expressed in Jean Raty's speech to the stockholders' meeting of the Hauts Fourneaux de Saulnes—

> The powers of the High Authority, if unfortunately they do not extend to consumption [*sic*], extend very rigorously to production in all its forms, including investments. We must consequently realise that we shall be forced to follow precisely everything which goes on in Luxembourg, where I have already spent much time. . . . Will salaries increase generally in Europe or rise variably in each country? Will taxes increase uniformly in Europe or in each country? Will transport costs, so unfavourable for us at the moment, be changed? I know nothing about all this and I must tell you honestly that I am completely unable to tell you anything about the situation of our firm three months from now. I know nothing about it. I know even less about another basic element that is never mentioned: exchange rates. Six currencies are in competition. Will they remain in the same relationship? I know nothing about this. If the exchange rates are going to change for one or several of our countries, it is evident that the future of the industries subject to the pool will change at the same time, in those countries at least. We are completely in the dark on this point. . . . Despite everything, in a country which is not yet part of an integrated Europe, some weapons must be retained, notably a steel industry as strong as possible.[10]

That the definition of political objectives and their underlying ideologies go hand in hand with long-range negative expectations regarding supranationalism in the case of the Communists and rightist authoritarians—Gaullists, Monarchists and Neo-Fascists—

completely free European capital market, without any supranational " undemocratic " and " technocratic " agencies to interpret and apply the rules of such a market. He opposed Euratom, and the European investment fund and advocated the abolition of ECSC after the establishment of the General Common Market. *Agence Economique et Financière*, February 28 and 29, 1956.

[9] See the discussion by Bernard Jarrier, " L'Etat investi par les intérêt," *Esprit* (June 1953), pp. 878–902; *Usine Nouvelle*, February 26, 1953. A. Métral, " Le Comité Consultatif: cheville ouvrière de la C. E. C. A.," *Annales des Mines*, Vol. 144 (June 1955).

[10] As quoted in the press digest of the Chambre Syndicale de la Sidérurgie Française, June 23, 1953.

has become perfectly clear from our earlier discussion of political parties. However, these groups are by no means the only ones finding it difficult if not impossible to reconcile their aims with the supranational economic and political organisation of Europe. Spokesmen for agricultural associations, for example, stress that a common market for agricultural commodities would ruin the tariff-protected and nationally subsidised peasantry in most ECSC countries. And they invoke arguments of a " blood and soil " nature to justify a rigorously national agricultural policy. Small businessmen, put on the defensive everywhere, take much the same position, justifying their own survival as a socio-economic entity in terms of their contribution to national strength and diversity. As put by the head of the French *classes moyennes* movement, M. Gingembre—

> In freeing trade, it is admitted that the economic changes which will result therefrom will bring with them the transformation or closing of a certain number of enterprises. We are not hostile in principle to the European idea; we have no inferiority complex on the problems of European integration, or about free trade. But we assert that we are not ready to disappear; but on the contrary know the place which our enterprises occupy in the national economy, and we know also the contribution which we can make to the recovery of the French economy and the unification of Europe. . . . It is essential that at the beginning our country has the same opportunities as the others and that the European idea does not become the pretext for the policy of the strongest against the weakest, the latter being sacrificed because he has first been placed in an inferior position. . . . It is not possible to build Europe on the ruins of small and medium-sized business. . . .[11]

But even the consistently negative-minded may be persuaded to adjust. Independent French shipping firms on inland waterways strenuously opposed integration and specifically the extension of ECSC powers to the Rhine and connected canals, invoking the usual arguments of " technocracy." But responsive to the threat of the Council of Ministers' approving the High Authority programme of freight-rate equalisation, the shippers adjusted to

[11] President of the French Confédération Générale des Petites et Moyennes Entreprises, as quoted in *Agence Europe*, June 14, 1954.

the extent of admitting the principle of non-discriminatory, competitive and public pricing of all hauls—provided the actual administration of the system were left to voluntary international arrangements among shippers, subject to supervision by intergovernmental organs like the Central Rhine Commission.[12] This, certainly, is far from welcoming supranationalism. But it implies tentative adjustments toward an integrated economy in order to head off supranational " dirigisme." Similar opinions and expectations may be found among Dutch and German shipping interests. The "spill-over" thus takes place despite long-term negative expectations.

Sector integration, however, begets its own impetus toward extension to the entire economy even in the absence of specific group demands and their attendant ideologies. Thus, ECSC civil servants speaking for national governments have constantly found it necessary to " harmonise " their separate policies in order to make it possible for the integrated sectors to function, without necessarily implying any ideological commitment to the European idea. This is illustrated by the German reluctance to impose a sales tax corresponding to the French practice, and in the French reluctance to devalue the overpriced franc. While not in principle favouring the control of the scrap trade with third countries, civil servants in the Council of Ministers decided on such supranational administrative measures just the same, merely in order to make the common market for steel a reality. Since the rate of investment bears a direct relation to inflationary pressures, the member governments have recognised that their over-all investment and monetary policies be harmonised in order to assure unity of action in this general economic sector with investment recommendations issued for coal and steel by the High Authority, even though serious steps in this realm were taken as late as 1957.

The practical need for co-operation in other international economic organisations is especially striking. The six countries had to act in unison in being recognised as a single contracting party in GATT and in being exempted from extending liberalisation requirements in OEEC. Had GATT permission been denied, the six countries would automatically have been compelled to pass on their tariff relaxation to third countries under the most-favoured-nation clause, thus possibly eliminating any special benefit to the

[12] Pierre Brousse, " La France et l'organisation des transports fluviaux internationaux," *La Vie Française*, December 16, 1955.

integrated sectors. If OEEC had not exempted them from the obligation to pass on the complete liberalisation of coal and steel, the six governments would have been forced to compensate for their failure to do so by liberalising a proportionate quantity among other items in their inter-European trade. To prevent such developments, constant intergovernmental decisions passing far beyond the integrated sectors are being made, even in the absence of any overt desire to be a " good European."

It was only in 1956 that Jean Monnet's doctrine of a strong, united Europe, revitalised by a progressive industrial economy resting on a large common market, came into its own. Among the early supporters of ECSC and general economic integration there had always been individuals who saw in economic unity the only means of survival in a global setting of Soviet-American dominance and rising Asian and African nations. The lesson was driven home in a much more direct fashion by the Suez Canal crisis and the isolation of a weak Europe in the face of Afro-Asian, Soviet and American opposition. Economic integration—with its evident political implications and causes—then became almost a universal battlecry, making complete the " spill-over " from ECSC to Euratom and its promise of independence from oil imports, from sector common markets to the General Common Market.[13] Certainly the process of extending the integrated sector had been under way since the recession of 1953–1954 when the first industrial demands for supranational market regulation were heard. It came into its own with the patent demonstration of political weakness and the desire to unite economically to constitute a power centre

---

[13] Yet even this kind of consensus may still contain strictly national demands and ideological advocacy directed *against* one of the units in the integration process. Wrote the Conservative *Wirtschaftszeitung* about France: " What is usually called ' European integration ' is not only political and military, but equally the economic duty, a task which must be urgently realised. The road toward sector integration which is represented by the European Coal and Steel Community is not passable. We must realise that we must now take the good road, the road of the single market. . . . We know that the economic weakness of France is the main reason for her hesitancy toward integration. The first necessity is that France liberate herself from this weakness, which is evident in that her production today does not surpass that of 1929. . . . But how could France liberate herself from this weakness? Her only possibility consists in defeating the four bad ' isms ' which she so lightly adopted in the last decades: protectionism, unionism, cartellism and inflationism. . . . The prescription is to recommend to France the principle of the ' social market economy,' the creation of internal and external competition, and the creation of a large market for buyers. Europe will see the Gallic miracle if France accepts this prescription. . . . It is time that France set her clocks to the hour which strikes in the rest of the world." Cited in *Agence Europe*, June 9, 1954.

independent of both Moscow and Washington. This consciousness now seems to form part of the expectations of most European elites, though supranationalism is not necessarily the technique universally agreed upon to realise unity.

ECSC POLICY AND INTEGRATION BEYOND COAL AND STEEL

A supranational High Authority anxious to draw on popular support for a policy of profiting from the spill-over tendency would do best to rely on groups with long-run positive expectations. Socialists, trade unionists and coal interests eager to protect their future all demand strong central institutions able and willing to make and implement federal policy. Social welfare, housing, planned investments, price controls, worker training and buffer stocks for ore and coal constitute only some of the demands which, if fully met, would call for a large, permanent federal administration. This institutional logic would lead naturally to an increase of supranational responsibilities and thereby to the increasing importance of ECSC as a focus of loyalty or opposition. Political pressure for parliamentary supervision over High Authority policy, for task expansion within or beyond the Treaty—as repeatedly urged by the Common Assembly—would clearly lead to an increase in the responsibility of that body and thereby to stronger federal institutions. Planning, and especially democratic planning, would be the simplest way to insure an ever increasing scope to the new agencies.

If the groups showing short-run positive or negative expectations were consistent champions of free trade and free enterprise, no institutional future whatever would accrue to a High Authority looking to these groups for support. Once cartels were abolished, railway discrimination eliminated, subsidies removed and prices made competitive, the task of the central authority would be confined to policing the free market. No practical or doctrinal support for an active supranational policy could then be expected. But with the possible exception of Dutch industrialists, few business interests and their political friends take this extreme position. They recognise the disparities in economic conditions which call for almost permanent administrative adjustments. They fear depressions and hence gladly avail themselves of rationing or price control measures when necessary. They seek the equalisation of taxes and welfare contributions in some instances, and lobby to block such steps in others. And they have no hesitation in favouring strong federal policies whenever they disagree with their national governments. Hence, even these groups see a continuing interest in the maintenance of supranational institutions, and often in their expansion; an active High Authority policy can in many instances count on their support. Yet a High Authority which self-consciously defines its own task as merely the establishment and policing of a free market argues itself out of a permanent institutional role in assisting the spill-over process. If the classical liberal state was a night-watchman's agency, the application of this formula to European economic integration cannot, in the nature of political institutions, lead to political community formation.[14]

The institutional framework of ECSC, the rules under which it operates, the planning and directing powers it enjoys, and the manner in which these provisions have been applied, were all described in Part I of this study. What remains to be done is to analyse the policy-making process of the High Authority in the interplay of group, political party and governmental pressures. Has the planning approach or the liberal conception carried the day? Which groups and governments seemed most successful in persuading the nine men in charge of ECSC? Has High Authority policy, in short, contributed to the acceleration of the spill-over process? The answers may suggest how the measures of existing supranational agencies can influence the formation of political communities.

But our discussion of non-ideological pressures for expanding the task of supranational organisations has shown that the simple concern for the proper functioning of the integrated sector may also lead to a spill-over effect. The " harmonisation " of general economic policy in the ECSC framework must therefore be analysed, necessitating a decision-making study of the Council of Ministers. Here we are likely to find not only direct concern over making the

---

[14] In this connection it is important to note the support for a vigorous High Authority policy expressed in spring of 1955 by the business-oriented press and the predictions of decay outlined in the event of inactivity. See ECSC, High Authority, *Revue de Presse*, May 16, 1955. Note also that the Belgian Central Economic Council, negative toward ECSC in 1951, called for more active steps looking toward full economic integration, accompanied by supranational efforts to ease the transitional problems and equalise cost conditions, as well as work out a general European economic policy. Charles Roger, " Les attributions économiques et sociales de la Communauté Politique Européenne," *Bulletin de la Société Belge d'Etudes et d'Expansion* (May–June–July 1954) pp. 629 *et seq.*

Treaty work, but an institutionalised code for dealing with recalcitrant members and a test of ministerial responsiveness at the intergovernmental level to interest group pressure for task expansion or task reduction.[15] If conflicts in national interests are reconciled merely in accordance with conventional diplomatic methods, supranationalism would seem to offer no uniquely valuable road toward the goal of political community. If, on the other hand, processes different from standard diplomatic conferences prevail at this level, the juxtaposition of supranational with intergovernmental institutions might prove to be the most crucial innovation of the ECSC system.

EURATOM, THE GENERAL COMMON MARKET AND INSTITUTIONAL INTEGRATION

One obvious demonstration of a spill-over effect from sector integration is the successful conclusion of two additional treaties seeking to integrate the European economies further. Our preceding discussion has shown that there was a direct causal connection between the negotiation of the Euratom and General Common Market treaties and the crisis over the extension of ECSC powers. The crucial question regarding these new institutions is this: will they, in line with liberal and short-run expectations, merely create new conditions without leading to permanent new institutions possessing political power, or will they serve such positive expectations that the growth of a political community can be safely projected from their work? An answer will here be attempted.

In October of 1955, Jean Monnet punctuated his desire to accelerate the spill-over process within the framework of the Messina Conference resolutions on nuclear integration by the formation of his " Action Committee for the United States of Europe." This organisation is altogether different from the European Movement and its constituent groups. It is composed exclusively of representatives of political parties and trade unions agreed on the desirability to fashion a federal Europe. It is supranational, composed solely of members of existing elites, and ideologically unified on one major point: to tie the political federation of Europe

---

[15] An example would be the consistent pressure of French industry to persuade its Government *not* to consent to any further integration before French costs are reduced or Germany's raised. See the editorials of Georges Villiers, president of the Conseil National du Patronat Français, *CNPF Bulletin*, October 1954, December 1954/January 1955.

to an immediate programme of raising the living standard of the working population, relying on the rapid and joint utilisation of atomic energy for this task.[16] The Committee sidesteps industrial interests and thus gives a decided left-wing, social welfare and economic democracy tone to the spill-over process. As such its membership and aspirations overlap with groups in the Common Assembly anxious to push ECSC into new fields and with the Consultative Committee's efforts to force ECSC into the welfare and collective bargaining field.[17]

Monnet's purpose was evidently the elaboration of an atomic plan designed to appeal to a large audience but so fashioned as to require a maximum of supranational powers and institutions. His primary tactical aim was the active mobilisation of party and trade union opinion behind the plan *before* the treaty was drafted and submitted to parliamentary ratification, thus reversing the process used in the ECSC and EDC situations. The practical measures of the Action Committee have included the drafting of an Euratom scheme, whose adoption Monnet urged continuously on the Brussels Intergovernmental Committee seeking to implement the Messina Resolution. Further, an identical resolution authorising each government to negotiate such a treaty was introduced by the Committee's parliamentary members in each national legislature.[18] And finally, the Committee late in 1956 seized on the European

[16] The Committee is composed as follows: Dutch Labour Party, Belgian Socialist Party, Luxembourg Socialist Party, Italian Social-Democrat Party, C.D.U. M.R.P., Anti-Revolutionary Party, Belgian Christian-Social Party, Luxembourg Social-Christian Party, Dutch Catholic People's Party, German Free Democratic Party, German Party, Radical-Socialist Party, Independent-Republican Party (with affiliates), U.D.S.R., Italian Liberal Party, Italian Republican Party, Belgian Liberal Party.

Parties not participating: Luxembourg Liberal Party, Christian-Historical Union, Dutch Liberal Party, German Refugee Party, Gaullists, Poujadists, Italian Monarchists and Neo-Fascists, Italian Socialist Party, all Communist Parties.

Trade Unions: Dutch Federation of Workers, Force Ouvrière, German Federation of Labour, German Mineworkers, Luxembourg Federation of Workers, General Federation of Belgian Labour, German Metalworkers, Italian Union of Labour; French Confederation of Christian Workers, Confederation of Belgian Christian Trade Unions, Italian Confederation of Trade Unions, Federation of Dutch Trade Unions (Protestant), Dutch Christian Trade Unions (Catholic).

Unions not participating: all Communist organisations, German Employees' Union, Gaullist Federation, Confédération Générale des Cadres. *Nouvelles de l'Europe*, January–February 1956, p. 36. As a rule, all organisations are represented by their presidents or their parliamentary floor leaders.

[17] A. Williame, " L'experience doit servir," *ibid.*, April–May 1956, p. 26. *ECSC Bulletin*, June 1956, p. 1.

[18] See Chap. 4 above for the outcome of the various parliamentary debates on this resolution.

fuel crisis to call for the implementation of the nuclear scheme even before the treaty drafting was completed, demanding the creation of a group of " three wise men " to explore the setting of production targets for the speedy manufacture of nuclear fuel. Monnet's efforts were rewarded by the appointment of such a group—including the High Authority's Franz Etzel—which promptly went to Washington to seek aid for the European atomic programme whose treaty had not even been signed at that time.

Monnet's Euratom scheme was clearly designed to assure a maximum of political institutional growth and hence stresses positive long-run economic hopes. The central argument is the need to avoid any diversion of atomic facilities into the production of armaments. Hence, Euratom must have (1) a monopoly over the procurement of fissionable materials, (2) retain ownership over such materials even after they have been released to private users and (3) engage in continuous control and inspection to assure peaceful application. Joint research activities and financing of reactors at the public supranational level are demanded as well. The institutions would include a fully independent federal Commission to carry out all these tasks, flanked by the ECSC Council of Ministers, Common Assembly, Court of Justice and Consultative Committee, whose functions would be the same as under the ECSC Treaty.[19] Apparently using the security reasoning of the ill-fated Baruch Plan, Monnet merged the ECSC-wide Socialist opposition to atomic arms with the desire for economic planning, meeting French centre and right-wing aims for controlling German re-armament with German industrial hopes for rapid nuclear progress, while providing an institutional mechanism for the rapid expansion of supranational political activity dear to federalist parliamentarians.

A minimalist scheme for atomic co-operation was almost immediately opposed to this approach in an effort to shape the work of the Brussels Intergovernmental Committee. It originated with the OEEC and had the support of governments hostile to supranationalism, *i.e.*, Great Britain, as well as many industrial interests in the ECSC countries. This plan is open to all OEEC countries. All nuclear installations would remain under national control and

[19] Details in *Informations Mensuelles*, Numéro spécial (March 1956), " Energie-Marché Commun, Projets et Opinions," pp. 36–40.

all central decisions would be issued by a conventional inter-governmental body. Control of industrial activity to keep production from being channelled into the military realm would be subject to this limitation. The primary function of the central organisation would be the co-ordination of information, the encouragement of research, with the creation of public or private firms interested in reactor and fuel development left to governments and private initiative and finance. All measures of international co-operation would thus be purely voluntary. The Council of Ministers of OEEC, meeting on February 28, 1956, approved this plan with the proviso that it was fully consistent with any scheme of closer supranational organisation agreed upon by some of its members. A committee was appointed to work out the necessary details.[20] While perhaps intended as a device to block the progress of Euratom, the OEEC Plan was thus reformulated at the insistence of the six ECSC governments, making possible the eventual co-operation of Euratom with the eleven other European states in a non-federal setting.

The Euratom Treaty worked out in Brussels by the experts of the six governments and signed in Rome by their foreign ministers in March of 1957 bears the heavy imprint of the Action Committee rather than of OEEC. The negotiations, analysed in detail elsewhere, show the influence of Paul-Henri Spaak, who acted as the eminent representative of the " European New Start," without being formally responsible to any government or group, but solely to the laws of political opportunity. What are Euratom's political and institutional implications with respect to community formation?

One set of conclusions may be drawn from the functions entrusted to the atomic community, as they impinge on the expectations of groups and elites. Unlike ECSC and EEC, Euratom will start with an almost clean slate in terms of the prior commitment of trade unions and trade associations since there are as yet no established atomic interests in Western Europe, at least in the private sector. Hence the policy of the Community can go a long way toward shaping expectations and attitudes without being subjected to their already articulate buffeting from the onset. Euratom

[20] *Ibid.*, pp. 28–35, 44–45. Also see, Organisation for European Economic Co-operation, *Possibilities of Action in the Field of Nuclear Energy* (Paris: January 1956).

will have the power to establish research centres for reactor development and schools for training technicians; it is to co-ordinate private research, undertake costly research of its own, and keep itself informed of patent development. More significant for purposes of integration, Euratom is to develop its own patents and license them out to private interests; it is to work out a code of health and security norms and constantly inspect the users of fissile materials to prevent the illicit employment of atomic energy. More important still, Euratom has a purchase priority on domestic and world markets on all ores suitable for nuclear energy application, continues to enjoy title to such materials after they are released to private or public interests, has the power to fix prices and to ration supplies, encourage private investment and itself establish installations too costly for single firms or countries, either alone or in partnership with governments or firms.[21]

While going far beyond the attributes suggested in the OEEC plan, Euratom's powers nevertheless remain ambiguous with respect to their integrative impact. The research, advice, training, norm-setting and inspecting powers will probably have little effect on the expectations of groups. Functions relating to any kind of economic planning—procurement of ores, licensing of patents, prices, agreements with third countries and participation in investment—can conceivably influence the politics of industrial interests. Much will depend on the manner in which these powers are actually exercised by the Community's organs. If they are asserted to the maximum degree permitted by a wide interpretation of the Treaty, the future pattern of interest group activity could be forced into a European rather than a multitude of national patterns. A word must therefore be said about the institutional structure of Euratom.

Unlike ECSC, the main repository of power is the intergovernmental Council of Ministers. It makes all important decisions, usually by a qualified majority and sometimes by unanimity,[22] especially in the fields of investment, prices, the European tax, rationing, and the creation of European " common enterprises." A five-member independent executive is provided in the

[21] This discussion is based on the unofficial and provisional translation of the *Treaty Establishing the European Atomic Energy Community* prepared and published by the Information Service of the High Authority (Washington, D.C., April 22, 1957).

[22] See the table on p. 310 for the Council's non-unanimous voting rules.

form of the European Atomic Commission. Routinely, its functions comprise the execution of whatever programme has been approved by the Council. But in addition the Commission is to make proposals to the Council on all policy questions relating to Euratom, and thus, by implication at least, fulfil a mediating function among the six governments. Finally, the Commission enjoys considerable autonomy as regards the co-ordination and conduct of research, the procurement of ores and the inspection of industrial establishments for violations of Euratom's security code.

Euratom's Court of Justice and Assembly are identical with EEC's and ECSC's, but their powers are considerably enlarged under the new Treaty. The Court is now empowered to issue search warrants to the Commission to facilitate its inspection functions, in addition to enjoying a wide variety of new opportunities to protect the rights of individuals, firms and governments against arbitrary action by Euratom. Conversely, the Court is the major medium for action against the member states in the event of violations of the Treaty since the Council and Commission enjoy very few powers of sanction. As for the Assembly, it is given the power to unseat the Commission by way of a censure motion, a capacity devoid of political meaning since the Commission's own independent decision-making powers are so restricted. What is far more vital to political integration, however, is the Assembly's expanded task in the preparation of the operational and the research and investment budgets of Euratom, in the approval of security norms, the eventual establishment of a Euratom taxing power, and the amendment of the Treaty as concerns the rules governing prices, property relations, and the inspection system. On all these questions the Assembly *must* be consulted, thus giving it *as of right* a truer legislative function than that enjoyed by the precursor ECSC Common Assembly. Clearly the truncated powers of the supranational Commission and the uncertainty which must govern the implementation of the rules most relevant to political integration may raise doubts about the political impact of Euratom on the re-alignment of group expectations. But the enlarged powers of the Assembly and of the Court make safe the prediction that a political spill-over among parties and lawyers is certain to result from the operations of Euratom.

If the integrating influence of Euratom is still subject to doubt, a much more positive statement can be made of the companion measure elaborated in Brussels under the "New Start": the European Economic Community. The basic principles of the draft treaty are as follows: During a transitional period lasting from twelve to fifteen years, all tariffs, exchange controls, currency restrictions, limits on the movement of labour and capital, subsidies, import and export monopolies, and market-splitting agreements will be abolished among the six member states. This will be accomplished by stages, for each of which the percentage of liberalisation is specified, though flexible. During this period, a common tariff toward third countries will be worked out. Tax and welfare payment differentials allegedly distorting free competition will be studied, and if found to hinder competition, eliminated. National fiscal and wage legislation is to be harmonised. Agriculture is exempted from the rules regarding competition, but common policies on controlled sales and subsidies must be worked out wherever real competition is rejected as a final solution. A general fair trade code is to be elaborated to eliminate discrimination. To aid industries adversely affected, a central European Social Fund will be set up, while an autonomous European Investment Fund will finance integrated and national public works as well as spur economic growth in European and overseas underdeveloped areas. Funds will be subscribed by governments and by private investors, with minimum contributions specified for large-scale development in overseas territories. Nothing is said of a common currency, common central banking, or of joint balance of payments arrangements, except that the rule on the removal of exchange controls can be relaxed temporarily. Transitional subsidies may be authorised and France is given the right to continue temporarily discriminatory taxes against imports from the other five countries, and to subsidise exports. It may be surmised that the issues here opened up will concern almost every conceivable group to such an extent that central institutional development is inevitable—if the institutions provided have sufficient power.[23]

[23] This summary is based on the unofficial and provisional translation prepared by the Information Service of the High Authority, Washington D. C., May 6, 1957, *Treaty Establishing the European Economic Community;* including *Annexes I* through *IV* (lists of tariff headings); *Annexe V, Protocol on the Statutes of the European Investment Bank; Protocol Relating to German Internal Trade and Kindred Problems; Protocol Relating to Certain Provisions of Concern to France; Protocol Concerning Italy; Protocol Concerning the Grand Duchy of Luxembourg; Protocol relating to Goods Originating and Coming from Certain Countries; Protocol relating to the Treatment to be Applied to Products Controlled by the European Coal and Steel Community in Respect of Algeria and the Overseas Departments of the French*

Before the institutions are examined in some detail, certain vital features of this treaty must be noted with respect to the likelihood of its contribution to political integration. Legal instruments which transfer crucial powers to new central institutions may nevertheless be prevented from creating a spill-over effect if the language of the instrument, coupled with the timidity of its interpreters, permits no adaptation to new conditions without formal amendment. The EEC Treaty is one of the rare federative agreements which leaves its own central organs—as distinguished from the member states acting singly—a tremendous degree of discretionary power. Witness Article 235:

> If action by the Community appears necessary to achieve one of the aims of the Community, in the operation of the common market, and if the present Treaty has not provided the powers of action required for this purpose, the Council, voting unanimously on a proposal by the Commission, and after consulting the Assembly, shall take the appropriate steps.

Escape clauses abound in this agreement: balance of payments difficulties may be invoked to re-impose exchange controls, passage from the first to the second stage of liberalisation may be blocked temporarily, the free migration of labour may be opposed, restrictive agricultural practices can be demanded by states unwilling to adapt, the non-colonial member states are free to demand a withdrawal from their participation in the development of overseas territories after a five-year trial period. However, in none of these situations is the state alleging a hardship the sole judge of its case! Escape clauses are uniformly subject to review by the Council voting by the " prescribed majority " and not unanimously and their use must be continuously justified to the Commission. This is true even of the temporary right given to France for the retention of discriminatory taxes.

Republic; Protocol concerning Mineral Oils and Certain of Their Derivatives; Protocol of Signature concerning the Non-European Parts of the Kingdom of the Netherlands; Convention relating to the Association of the Overseas Countries and Territories with the Community (with Annexes A and B); *Protocol concerning the Tariff Quota for Imports of Unroasted Coffee; Convention relating to Certain Institutions Common to the European Communities.*

For a succinct summary of the economic aspects of these agreements, see Raymond Bertrand, " The European Common Market Proposal," *International Organisation*, Vol. 10, no. 4 (November 1956). The background and institutional problems are discussed more satisfactorily by Miriam Camps, *The European Common Market and American Policy* (Princeton: Centre of International Studies, November 1956).

Almost all the rules spelled out in the Treaty may be changed by the Council, aided by the Commission and compelled to submit its desires to the consultative deliberation of the parliamentary Assembly. Formal amendment seems unnecessary. In many instances, the drafters contented themselves with stating only the general principle of liberalisation they wished to introduce, leaving to the subsequent action of all the Community's organs the task of spelling out the detailed rules to be applied to governments and enterprises. Thus the Assembly is given the opportunity to participate in the drafting of rules concerning the general right of establishment regardless of nationality, for the equivalence of national professional qualifications, the determination of non-discriminatory transport rules, the fair trade code, the revision of the original schedule governing tariff reductions, the establishment of general European agricultural pricing and marketing arrangements and the rules governing the granting of re-adaptation payments. Crucial definitions regarding the conditions and contingencies under which rules or exceptions are to prevail are left extremely vague: again it is the duty of the Commission and the Council to work them out. Temporary exceptions may be granted to a great many of the rules stated; but it is the supranational nine-member Commission which administers them and not the national government anxious to escape an obligation.

Industrial objections to supranational " dirigisme " combined with the fears of the French and German Governments to result in a central administrative authority—the European Commission—far less powerful than its ECSC colleague. The Commission has the duty to *study*, *suggest* and *propose* measures in these situations: changes in the liberalisation schedule, tariff negotiations with third countries, fair trade code, removal and control of export and import monopolies, harmonisation of national legislation dealing with trade in agriculture and services, transport rate harmonisation, joint commercial policy, anti-competitive effects of varying national wage, social security, tax and credit legislation, temporary authorisation of exchange controls, freeing of capital movements. It can make *decisions* only in relatively few areas, *e.g.*, in granting re-adaptation aid, disbursing funds for investment, ruling on the admissibility of national subsidies and permitting exemptions from the rules governing the freedom of labour to migrate. Though composed of independent persons and voting by simple majority, the Commission is more a technical study group than an autonomous federal executive.

Real power is lodged firmly in the Council of Ministers, making binding decisions almost entirely by unanimity during the first four years of operation, and changing to a weighted majority voting system thereafter. The Council approves Commission studies and recommendations in all the areas mentioned above, with the exception of the few fields in which the Commission is " sovereign." Clearly, the framers of the treaty expected a continuous pattern of intergovernmental compromise to dominate the decision-making process.

COUNCIL OF THE EUROPEAN ECONOMIC COMMUNITY AND OF EURATOM
Non-Unanimous Voting Rules

	Minimum Vote Required for a Decision	Ger.	France	Italy	Neth.	Bel.	Lux.
Council of European Economic Community							
" prescribed majority "	12	4	4	4	2	2	1
qualified " prescribed majority "	12 by at least four members	4	4	4	2	2	1
Social Fund budget	67	32	32	20	7	8	1
Development Fund administration	67	33	33	11	11	11	1
Council of Euratom							
" prescribed majority "	12	4	4	4	2	2	1
qualified " prescribed majority "	12 by at least four members	4	4	4	2	2	1
Research and Investment budget	67	30	30	23	7	9	1

If the reduced role of the Commission and the enlarged scope of decisions requiring unanimous consent seem to represent a defeat for supranationalism, the enhanced powers of the Common Assembly argue the opposite. Unlike ECSC, the new Assembly has the power to approve the budgets of all institutions as well as censure the Commission. Some of the most explosive political issues are under federal parliamentary scrutiny, with the possibility emerging that the Council of Ministers will in effect become a collegiate executive, responsible to the Assembly if a vigorous supranational party system dominates in that body. As in the case of Euratom, the power of censuring the Commission is somewhat platonic in view of the restricted decision-making capacity of that " executive." As for the Court of Justice, the EEC Treaty extends the ability of that organ to shape Western European commercial and economic legal principles by widening the scope of appeals possible. For some purposes, the drafters seem to have foreseen the emergence of the Court to the status of a European supreme tribunal for economic questions by explicitly subordinating decisions of national tribunals to its judgments in matters concerning the Treaty. As in ECSC, individuals and corporations can be parties to suits as well as governments. Unlike ECSC, the Commission cannot impose direct sanctions but must go before the Court to obtain a judgment. In fact the only sanction explicitly provided by the EEC Treaty is the authorisation by the Council of retaliatory economic measures against a delinquent government.

Projecting the spill-over effect observed in the case of ECSC, an acceleration of this process under the new treaty can safely be predicted. Even though the parliamentarians will not have the power to dismiss the ministers, it is difficult to imagine that the entire scope of economic relations, even those which went unmentioned in the treaty, will not be reflected in their debates and votes. The Assembly is bound to be a more faithful prototype of a federal parliament than the ECSC " legislature." As for the Council of Ministers, it is inconceivable that the liberalisation not only of trade, but of the conditions governing trade, can go on for long without " harmonisation of general economic policies " spilling over into the fields of currency and credit, investment planning and business cycle control. The actual functions then regularly carried out by the Council will be those of a ministry of economics. The spill-over may make a political community of Europe in fact even before the end of the transitional period.

One of the experts who participated in the drafting of the Brussels report which led to the Euratom and EEC Treaties summarised the spill-over thus. In economic terms, the formula of supranational integration of sectors is just as irrational as the competing formula of entrusting an intergovernmental organisation with the task of removing all obstacles to trade; the one cannot succeed because the separation of coal and steel from the economy is impossible but the other is doomed to failure since it lacks jurisdiction over some trade obstacles and cannot compel government compliance in others. Despite these irrationalities, however, the interplay of the two formulas has resulted in a spill-over since each effort at greater supranational integration was immediately accompanied by steps toward increasing the scope of joint governmental measures. Further, in their concrete programmes, ECSC and OEEC depended heavily on each other's success. However, neither can now proceed without being invested with new powers or allowed to function in a new setting resting on basic ministerial decisions—the decisions made at Messina, Brussels, Venice and Rome—and any new departure, the expert argues, demands a greater scope for central decisions on basic economic policy in all sectors. Do Euratom and EEC make this possible? " To tell the truth," answers the expert, " in the Brussels report the powers given to the European Commission have been camouflaged, minimised in words. In actual fact . . . I can assure you that the European Commission . . . would have some extremely interesting attributes and extraordinarily wide powers." [23a] Clearly, it is expected that the intergovernmental Council of Ministers would not in fact make any decisions without following the studies and recommendations of the Commission.

In the pluralistic Europe of our time the acceptance of measures of economic integration by political institutions is possible because of the sharp fragmentation of interests and beliefs within each nation. This fragmentation, in the case of coal and steel, was increased by the policies followed by supranational institutions, and there is no reason for thinking that the same will not happen on a larger scale in the General Common Market. It remains to be demonstrated in the following chapters to what extent groups have re-aligned supranationally under the impulse of ECSC rules and policy after being fragmented in the national context. The picture of unity and disunity, federal versus national confrontation

[23a] Paul Delouvrier, " Economic Integration: Problems and Possibilities," in C. Grove Haines, *European Integration*, (Baltimore: The John Hopkins Press, 1957), p. 122. M. Delouvrier is head of the Financial Division of the High Authority. For the concurring opinion of another High Authority expert who participated in the Brussels negotiations, see Pierre Uri, in H. Field Haviland (ed.), *The United States and the Western Community*, (Haverford: Haverford College Press, 1957), pp. 81–91.

of interests and values here unearthed, may serve as the true key for projecting the institutional significance of the General Common Market.

Thus, the negotiation, the acceptance by the parliaments, and the clearly predictable institutional and procedural impact of Euratom and EEC on political integration vindicate strikingly the expansive logic inherent in the sector integration principle. From the initially merged sectors, a demonstrable process of expanding group expectations among industrialists, dealers, and trade unions emerges. A spill-over into as yet unintegrated economic areas and a concern over political techniques appropriate for the control of new and larger problems is manifest. And in the process of reformulating expectations and demands, the interest groups in question approach one another supranationally while their erstwhile ties with national friends undergo deterioration. At the level of political parties a similar phenomenon takes place. Here the spill-over makes itself felt by the desire to control the new administrative organs—whether federal or intergovernmental—which are mushrooming. But in addition the larger field of legislative action opens up opportunities for the realisation of party programmes heretofore stymied in the *immobilisme* of tightly-partitioned economies. This is true for the welfare state-minded Socialists as for the free trade-oriented Liberals. Both think they stand to gain from the new dispensation. Finally, the spill-over process asserts itself in the relations among civil servants, national government offices, central banks and technical advisers. As the lesson of the ECSC Council of Ministers shows, a commitment to the realisation of agreed upon economic goals permits of no indefinite sabotaging of collective decisions: hence the logic of intergovernmental relations within the framework of the EEC-Euratom-ECSC Council of Ministers, its associated committees of national experts, working under the prodding of supranational Commissions, can lead only to more collective decision-making in the effort to overcome the inevitable crises and unforeseen contingencies.

The Spill-Over, Britain, and the Free Trade Area

Yet is there not a fourth area in which a spill-over process is discernible? Granted that interest groups, political parties and governments of the countries committed to further integration display the pattern of behaviour just sketched, is there not evidence that countries not initially members of the regional grouping find it desirable to deepen their ties with the integrating *bloc*? Is there evidence, in short, that the geographical as well as the functional dimensions of integration tend to expand as new sectors are added? The evolving attitude of Great Britain toward Euratom and the General Common Market provides some interesting speculative material on this aspect.

It is, of course, a commonplace that the attitude of British groups and governments toward the principle of Continental supranationalism and federalism has been extremely hesitating. Britain not only emphatically rejected membership in any federal or quasi-federal grouping, but her policy at times has led Continental observers to believe that London was interested in preventing, or at least delaying, the process of integration among the Six. The conclusion of the Agreement of Association with ECSC, though it seemed to imply a desire for close co-operation without full membership, was also claimed to be a device for asserting control when put into the institutional context of the " Grand Design," the OEEC Plan for atomic co-operation and the Free Trade Area proposal, which could once more replace a quasi-federal arrangement with intensified intergovernmental ties.

If it were true that these British overtures were solely motivated by a desire to delay, or to control, integration on the Continent, no good case for a geographical spill-over effect could be advanced. Such an interpretation, however, is simplistic. Granted that little British enthusiasm for supranationalism on the Continent could be discovered, it is equally true that the example of successful integration gave rise to serious reconsiderations of previous opinion in Britain. Successful integration of economies implied a threat to Britain's future possibilities of access, and the danger of discrimination; but it also implied the utilisation of new techniques, notably in the field of nuclear energy, which could be of direct benefit to Britain. Both the negative and the positive aspects of Britain's future relations with the nascent community of the Six seemed bridgeable by means of the formula of " association." And to the extent that realisations of this kind seemed to compel closer ties than previously planned, a spill-over has taken place.

Symptomatic of this train of thought were the repeated admonitions heard from *The Economist* since 1954 that Britain's economic future is inevitably tied to the Continent rather than to the Commonwealth. And *The Times* noted during the negotiation of the common market treaty that it was better for Britain to be associated with a united Europe than to remain isolated, in view of the likelihood of increasing economic nationalism on the part of the member countries of the Sterling Area. Future trading patterns demanded a closer tie between Britain and the Continent, provided Britain were not forced into a common tariff system toward third countries— thus making the imperial preference system an impossibility— and provided the harmonisation of social legislation and of fair trade rules were kept to a minimum.[24] Again during the EEC negotiations, Conservative and Labour speakers in the House of Commons pointed out that the Government should participate in the talks in order to assure some kind of British association in the event that the projects were to succeed.[25] Fear of isolation thus became a potent catalyst to the spill-over process as the feeling gained ground that supranational integration was here to stay.

Put into this context, the British position toward Euratom and EEC which emerged in 1956 is perfectly clear and quite consistent with the thesis of expanding sector integration here argued. Even if Britain's endorsement of the OEEC atomic energy plan was initially designed to take the wind out of the supranational sails of Euratom, by mid-1956 it was quite evident that London was reconciled to the tight atomic community about to grow up across the Channel; on June 13, 1956, Mr. Anthony Nutting declared in the House of Commons that the Government had the intention of seeking " association " with Euratom through the medium of the OEEC Plan, while admitting that any scheme for pooling nuclear information and spurring atomic development for peaceful purposes was of the utmost importance to the United Kingdom.[26] The history of association with ECSC indicates that the formula adopted is sufficiently flexible to permit the growth of integrative relations of some magnitude if the authorities in question feel sufficiently strongly impelled to seek them.

But the potential impact of EEC on Britain's trade is of far

---

[24] See *The Economist*, February 18, 1956; May 14, 1955; June 25, 1955; October 15, 1955; *The Times*, October 19, 1956; February 10, 1956; May 10, 1955; *Financial Times*, June 23, 1955; February 6, 1956.

[25] House of Commons debate of July 5, 1956. *Weekly Hansard*, no. 361, (June 29—July 5, 1956, pp. 1677–1689).

[26] *Ibid.*, no. 358 (June 8–14, 1956), p. 561. See also *The Economist* (February 12, 1956) for arguments underlining the need for Britain to be associated with Euratom.

more immediate concern to policy and equally to attitudes and expectations relating to integration. As Mr. Harold Macmillan has said on numerous occasions, his proposal for a Free Trade Area—the formula of association with EEC—would save London the need for an agonising re-appraisal on whether ties with a uniting Europe or with the Commonwealth should take precedence: by scrapping trade barriers with the Continent, Britain could share in the common market but by staying aloof from the common tariff toward third countries the imperial preference system might remain intact also, a feature to be reinforced further by excluding any possible British participation in the agricultural aspects of the General Common Market. The Prime Minister declared firmly that it was impossible for Britain to stay aloof from EEC or to bring about its failure; hence qualified association with it remains the only practical alternative.[27]

The integrative impact of the Free Trade Area scheme was spelled out plainly in the United Kingdom's memorandum to the OEEC. Britain expects to bring about the participation of all OEEC member states, and perhaps of the Commonwealth countries, in some aspects of the plan. While less anxious than the EEC countries, to provide immediately for joint investment, productivity, wage and social security harmonisation and re-adaptation schemes, London admits that more and more intensive measures of economic co-operation are inevitable, either through deliberate planning or spontaneous development. Continuous intergovernmental consultations on all related fiscal and monetary questions are held out as essential, even though the OEEC machinery is considered quite adequate for this purpose. While the prior harmonisation of wages and working conditions is considered unnecessary, their eventual re-alignment is conceded as likely by London. As for the methods for reducing internal trade barriers of all kinds the British scheme declares itself in agreement with the ideas of the EEC planners, arguing only that in the event of serious balance of payments difficulties each government should be free to re-impose exchange controls immediately, subject to the kind of collective review already provided for by EEC. In fact, the British memorandum agreed with the Continental planners on the need for restricting severely the use of escape clauses. While arguing again and again that the

[27] Statement in the House of Commons, November 26, 1956. *Weekly Hansard*, no. 372.

OEEC machinery would be quite adequate for the institutional realisation of the Free Trade Area, London also conceded that the unanimity rule might have to be renounced for certain kinds of decisions.[28]

A geographical spill-over is clearly taking place. In its unique British form it rigorously rejects any federal trimmings and continues to rely on intergovernmental " association." But it grants not only the need for more and more intimate economic contacts in areas of activity until recently considered the sacrosanct preserve of national governments, but even the necessity for decision by majority vote among ministerial delegates. All other things being equal, it is as inconceivable that this form of co-operation should not result in new patterns of profound interdependence as it is unlikely that the General Common Market can avoid a species of political federalism in order to function as an economic organ.

---

[28] *A European Free Trade Area,* United Kingdom Memorandum to the Organisation for European Economic Co-operation, February 1957. Summarised in *Informations Mensuelles* (April 1957), pp. 64–72.

CHAPTER 9

SUPRANATIONAL TRADE ASSOCIATIONS

IN February of 1953 the International Chamber of Commerce authorised the creation of a European Council of Merchants' Associations. Such an organisation was considered necessary, the Chamber explained, to defend *jointly* the interests of merchants, to study the impact of common markets on the retail and wholesale trade, and to represent the interests of the " commercial profession " at the level of European regional organisations. Almost all European national and international specialised merchants' associations joined the Council. Fearing that different national policies of taxation would handicap certain branches and countries in a common market, the merchants were determined to study and influence the drafting of new treaties tending toward integration. What is more, the Council warned them that a rigorous supranational organisation was necessary if common action in the future was to be attained.[1] Regional economic organisation among governments clearly led to the defensive grouping of commercial interests fearful of no longer being able to lobby effectively at the national level.

In varying degrees of intensity, this pattern has become a general one in Europe. Since 1949, no less than fifty-eight private international organisations have been founded. This number includes only organisations of manufacturers, wholesalers, retail merchants, exporters and importers, and excludes associations whose membership is not solely Western European. The great bulk of these organisations draws its members from the six countries of Little Europe, with a sprinkling of participation from Britain, Switzerland,

---

[1] Conseil National du Patronat Français, *Bulletin*, May 20, 1953, p. 29; December 20, 1953, p. 34; November 1954, p. 58. For the positive attitudes toward EEC of the International Chamber of Commerce and of the European Council of Merchants' Associations see *Informations Mensuelles*, January 1957, pp. 17–19. Both organisations accompanied their endorsement of the treaties with admonitions against supranational direction and objected to discretionary powers to be vested in the European Commission. Even though agriculture is not immediately included in the General Common Market, representatives of all agricultural organisations of the Six met in December of 1956 to demand corporate representation in the institutions of EEC, deciding at the same time to organise themselves into a supranational interest group. *Nieuwe Rotterdamse Courant*, December 22, 1956.

Austria, Spain, Portugal and Scandinavia. If we exclude organisations dedicated in large part to the improvement of quality, productivity, sales methods and professional standards, and concentrate on associations whose primary purpose is lobbying—
and only these are politically relevant—the number is still twenty-
nine.[2]

Typically, these associations are loose groupings of the
recognised national trade associations in the particular field of
interest. Sometimes they also include international specialised
associations. They rarely possess binding powers of decision-
making and are thus not federations in the technical sense even if
they use this term. Their avowed purpose is always " better
liaison " among national bodies with a common regional interest,
a conception which may or may not include cartelist aims. But
they leave no doubt that one factor which led to their formation
is the fear that the successful functioning of OEEC, ECSC and the
United Nations Economic Commission for Europe will ignore their
special needs and desires. Anxious at first merely to learn of the
plans and practices of their colleagues in other countries, the members
of these associations almost invariably try, at least, to agree on
common policies to be offered to regional economic agencies.
Finally, the fact that OEEC and ECE deliberately encouraged
the formation of supranational or international associations in
order to have regional rather than national partners for negotiation
and study provided an impetus of considerable moment.

IDEOLOGY AND INTEREST GROUP FORMATION

While sharing all these aspirations, groups functioning specifically
in the context of ECSC institutions are impelled by the additional
desire of shaping the *policy* of the High Authority with respect to
the implementation of Treaty rules impinging directly on their

[2] *Yearbook of International Organisations*, (Brussels: Union of International
Associations, 1955), pp. 605–699. The number of all types of organisations of
similar membership functioning before 1948 was fifteen. If agricultural groups
are included, the number of organisations created for lobbying purposes since
the advent of regional organs is considerably greater. The organisations in question
range from such comprehensive ones as the Council of European Industrial
Federations to the International Association of Soapmakers. Their purpose
may be the specific advocacy of economic integration, as in the European League
for Economic Co-operation, or a medley of functions mostly concerned with
advancing internal standards, market surveys and incidentally involving lobbying
at the international level. The second pattern is the more common one. Overwhelmingly these organisations have their headquarters in Paris, with a lesser
number in Brussels and Switzerland.

business methods. The Consultative Committee gives them the institutional opportunity for exerting organised pressure; and trade association leaders are only too fully conscious of the fact that industrial opinions—unless harmonised somehow—tend to neutralise one another when presented to the federal executive. These forces, however, should not obscure for a moment the fact that supranational trade association activity in ECSC functions through the medium of old and established national associations, possessing values and ideologies of considerable rigidity, harbouring old fears and animosities going back to a national focus of thinking. It remains to be seen in the subsequent analysis whether these factors making for discontinuities tend to be replaced by conceptions of value and interest based on a common, ECSC-wide " consumer," " producer," " steel " or " coal " mentality. Before undertaking such a study, however, it is necessary to spell out in some detail demonstrable national ideologies among the associations related to ECSC.

In France, significant differences prevail between small and medium enterprises as compared to large firms, especially in the heavy industries. Small businessmen, as a rule, are opposed to public dirigisme—since this implies paying taxes and opening the books to the government—and fully in favour of industrial autonomy. This makes itself felt in the demand for special " dirigistic " legislation whose administration is entrusted to the trade associations! Small as well as large industrialists of the pre-World War II generation see in stability, moderation, restraint and order the peculiar Latin contribution to modern capitalism, mitigating cyclical forces but also opposing productivity and aggressive sales methods. The saving of a colleague in difficulties is fundamental to their code and hence the cartel is a natural economic institution. It is this group which dominates numerically in almost all trade associations and in the Conseil National du Patronat Français.

It is opposed by some key leaders in associations of heavy industry. These men favour more competition, larger markets, gradual relaxation of French protectionism and, especially, productivity programmes. They have made their peace with the nationalised sector of French industry, unlike their stability-minded colleagues. Nor do they oppose all government planning on principle; several of their leaders have co-operated with Monnet's

Commissariat du Plan. Yet in the field of labour relations, they still see eye to eye with the older group. Collective bargaining takes place only under extreme pressure. Negotiations with trade unions are confined to immediate contract questions. All postwar efforts to obtain major structural changes in the nature of labour-management relations have resulted in the employers' withdrawing from the bargaining sessions and in the government's imposing the measures. Paternalism continues to be a principle enjoying a good deal of vogue; alternatively, the Catholic concept of " community " at the plant level—as advocated by Simone Weil, for instance—is accepted by many employers. But permanent bargaining at the national level is rejected as a principle.[3] The consequence, of course, is a continuing distrust of the common market principle and a lively fear of the disciplined and aggressive German competitor. These sentiments, incidentally, are in large part shared by important sectors of Italian industry.

German industry represents the opposite side of the coin. Trusting to modern equipment, Americanised sales methods and capacity for hard work, the modern German businessman's ideology exudes a mixture of self-reliance and faith in private enterprise. Like his French colleague the German industrialist opposes dirigisme and favours the discipline of autonomous industrial sectors organised in tight trade associations; but he is less likely to clamour in Bonn for special protection and therefore does not stand in fear of the common market and more active competition. " Our common goal is a united Europe. Industrial and economic problems have long grown beyond national boundaries. A European, a Western economy must take the place of national economies." [4]

But " since competition is a natural phenomenon, governments may not interfere with its normal development." Competition is a central creed which has had its supranational repercussions in German industry's much more honest opposition to any kind of

[3] The outstanding treatment of this subject is Henry Ehrmann, *Organised Business in France* (Princeton: Princeton University Press, 1957), on which these summary statements are based. It is of the highest significance that the " modern " wing of the French employers' movement has included such men as Ricard, Constant, and Villiers who have been instrumental in adjusting French trade associations to the common market principle.

[4] Statement by Fritz Berg, president of the Federation of German Industries. Cited in Bundesverband der Deutschen Industrie, *Fünf Jahre Bundesverband der Deutschen Industrie* (Bergisch-Gladbach, 1954), p. 174. For an excellent exposition of the ideology of leading German businessmen in politics see G. Stein (ed.). *Unternehmer in der Politik* (Düsseldorf: Econ Verlag, 1954).

High Authority with planning or directing powers.[5]   Any move by Luxembourg to use these powers was met with cries that industry was able to take care of itself and that the federal executive lacked confidence in it.   In labour relations the German industrialists are far less fearful of their recognised " social partner," the DGB, and quickly adapted themselves to the system of co-determination. While Germany is certainly endowed with a strong cartel tradition of its own, the cartel does not fulfil the permanent stabilising function which it has in the French mentality.   Domestic cartels are introduced when a specific crisis situation calls for " order " and " regularity "; but they are not an article of faith and certainly do not preclude normally the utilisation of productivity programmes. In large measure, the attitudes of Dutch, Belgian and Luxembourg heavy industry are identical with the German picture.   Small industry in Belgium, however, is very similar in outlook to its French neighbour.

Opposed to these rather severely different national ideological traits is the equally marked international cartel tradition of European heavy industry.   The European Steel Cartel of the thirties was a most successful undertaking, irrespective of the different political systems and attitudes represented by its members.   In a common crisis, it simply facilitated the survival of all through continuous consultation, exchange of production and sales information, and the splitting of sales territories strengthened by a system of fines.[6] The tradition still subsists.   Thus, in opposing the immediate establishment of a General Common Market, the CNPF noted that national industrial associations should be free to organise with their sister groups across the frontier, to " establish preliminary ties which alone will permit progressive adaptation to the common market." [7]   Such " ties " are assiduously cultivated through the Franco-German and Franco-Italian industrial commissions initiated by the CNPF and heartily received across the Rhine and the Alps.   " Understanding " with fellow industrialists is still held

[5] Bundesverband, *op. cit.*, p. 196. This volume contains many explicit statements of ideological relevance.   It must be added that the Steel association has not always agreed with the anti-ECSC statements of the BDI and has taken a far more tolerant attitude towards the High Authority.

[6] The classic statement on this score by Aloyse Meyer, director of the European Steel Cartel, is printed in Rieben, *op. cit.*, pp. 242–243.   See Hexner, *op. cit.*, for an excellent discussion and evaluation of the cartel.

[7] *Usine Nouvelle*, February 23, 1956.

out as the crucial technique of achieving integration by German as well as French businessmen. Said Karl Barich—

> If our organisation has recently had constant relations with the sister groups of the ECSC countries, this by no means implies a conspiracy against the High Authority, nor does it mean that internal agreements were reached which would violate the ECSC Treaty. Our co-operation with sister organisations has decisively contributed to increase mutual understanding beyond national boundaries. . . . We believe that the High Authority can insure its supranational character by supporting such co-operation. . . . But it must have confidence in such groups. . . .[8]

Whether actual cartel agreements are concluded—and this is not established—is beside the point. The important fact is that "direct understanding" is preferred to "bureaucratic" supranationalism and, in any event, inevitably accompanies public regulation.

Given the differences in national ideology and the common commitment to joint industrial action with or against ECSC, what sort of impulses can be expected to force industrialists and businessmen in the direction of supranational trade associations? It is reasonable to raise the hypothesis that interests fearful of their economic future—*e.g.*, collieries—might combine supranationally in order to force ECSC into protectionist and dirigist channels as against third countries and rival fuels. Self-reliant industries with experience in international cartel operations, such as steel, might equally well be expected to organise supranationally in order to block ECSC dirigisme and to assert industrial autonomy. Both alternatives, though mutually exclusive in the aims sought, would logically tend toward ECSC-wide group formation. Yet one must also raise the possibility of a given national association refusing close affiliation with sister organisations in other member states in order to prevent " ideological contamination," whether on protectionist or dirigist lines. The following discussion will seek to demonstrate that despite ideological differences, the institutional and political logic of supranationalism has brought with it the formation of trade association in *all* relevant fields of endeavour: ECSC resulted in the formation of one peak association, two producers' groups, three consumers' groups and one organisation of dealers.[9]

---

[8] *Stahl und Eisen*, May 21, 1953, p. 747.
[9] Two organisations of dealers already existed when ECSC went into effect, but subsequently restructured their activities in order to maximise their role in the common market.

ECSC TRADE ASSOCIATIONS: STRUCTURE AND FUNCTIONS

Council of European Industrial Federations (CIFE)

The Council of European Industrial Federations is a peak organisation of the federations of industries of all countries which are members of OEEC. The Council was organised in 1949 under French initiative, with Georges Villiers assuming the presidency. In principle, it is to work out an agreed policy of all manufacturers to be pressed in OEEC commissions. In fact, it lacks firm powers and has served as a device for creating " understanding " among industrialists and to raise the prestige of French employers among their European colleagues.[10]

Probably the most significant decision made by the Council was the creation, again on French initiative, of a " Union of Industrialists of the Six ECSC Countries." This body was called into being as the ECSC Treaty went into effect. It groups the peak associations of the six countries into a tight body, meeting far more frequently than the parent organisation, largely independent of it, and determined to gain recognition as the sole ECSC employer organisation. In ECSC, the Union seeks to assure a common position of all its members in the Consultative Committee and to obtain agreement among its members in specific demands presented to the High Authority, the Common Assembly and the Council of Ministers. While success has been spotty, the Union claims credit for having persuaded the Council to alter drastically the plan presented by the High Authority for the control of mergers. The German members have been interested in discussing a common managerial ideology while the French are more concerned in using the Union to prevent the creation of new supranational bodies.

While the Union makes continual studies of the implications to its members of further economic integration, especially in terms of manpower, capital mobility, convertibility and administrative problems, its most serious common work has been its insistence on participation in the drafting of new treaties tending toward integration. Thus it sought access to the *ad hoc* Assembly drafting the EPC Constitution and co-ordinated the work of its members in opposing drastic supranational allocation powers for EDC's armaments procurement section. It even called on its members to attend meetings of the European Movement to channel those

[10] Ehrmann, *op. cit.*, Bundesverband der Deutschen Industrie, *op. cit.*, pp. 183 *et seq.*

efforts into pro-industry ways. It took position on the armaments allocation machinery suggested for WEU in such a way as to limit competitive bidding.[11] Convinced, apparently, that " bureaucratic supranationalism " is here to stay, the industrialists have adjusted to the prospect by organising, debating and acting accordingly. In principle, they seek to limit all " bureaucratic " planning; but in practice, they are content to seek access to the bureaucrats and to press their commonly agreed aims. A survey of discussion in the Consultative Committee, however, will show that such aims do not always emerge.

ECSC Steelmakers Club

The seven national steel associations of ECSC have not so far organised a formal trade association. With the exception of the Italians they function as a " Club," completely informal, without officers, staff or statutes. Usually they meet in Brussels under the chairmanship of Belgium's Van de Rest. Little is known of their activities. It is generally assumed that the so-called Brussels Export Entente was organised by the Club and largely identical with it. If this is true, it shows that the Club is unable to discipline its members as soon as they conclude that their interests diverge. The Entente broke down with the deterioration of world steel prices in 1954 and active competition among the members was resumed on world and ECSC markets.[12] However, the Club was successful in persuading the Consultative Committee and the Council of Ministers to oppose the High Authority's plan to proceed against the Entente in 1953 and in insisting on a reduction

[11] Details are reported in Conseil National to Patronat Français, *Bulletin*, January 20, 1953, February 5, 1953, July 20, 1953, February 5, 1954, August 1954, December 1954/ January 1955, February 1955, August 1955. Contrast the functionally highly specific efforts of the Union—attempting to shape or influence given items of supranational legislation—with the much more diffuse and general efforts of the European League for Economic Co-operation, of which most of the Union's participants are also members. The League merely seeks economic integration in line with industrial and financial demands, maximising free enterprise, managerial initiative and " understanding " among industrialists. Raymond Rifflet, " La 'droite' et la ' gauche ' à l'échelle de l'Europe," *Gauche Européenne* (December, 1955), pp. 12 *et seq.*

[12] In 1953 the Entente sought to function merely by fixing the export price of steel, but drastic cuts in the British steel export price rendered this approach useless. It is believed that in April of 1954 the Entente proceeded to assign export quotas but that these were never observed by the member groups. See Richard Evely, " Les Cartels et la Communauté Européenne du Charbon et de l'Acier," *Cartel*, Vol. VI, no. 3 (July 1954), pp. 94–95.

of the ECSC tax rate.[13]   But our previous discussion shows that despite their " Club," the ECSC steelmakers frequently disagree among each other and lobby in mutually antagonistic directions in Luxembourg.

West European Coal Producers' Study Committee (CEPCEO)

The Coal producers found it desirable to establish a much more formal organisation.   CEPCEO groups the German, Dutch, and Belgian associations with the Charbonnages de France.   It functions through a general assembly, executive committee and permanent secretariat in Brussels, the ultimate purpose being the definition of common policy to be defended in Luxembourg and the national capitals.   No binding decisions are ever made.   If concensus emerges the national associations are expected to act accordingly afterward but are not formally bound to do so.   If no consensus is possible— as happens frequently—no common position is taken.   Studies are undertaken with a view to the evolution of consensus even if some of the members oppose such action initially.   If the dissent remains unchanged, the opposing group will not endorse the findings.   The Charbonnages de France and Fédéchar have, of course, sought to work on the harmonisation of fringe benefits through CEPCEO, but these efforts have been coolly received by their Dutch and German colleagues.   In terms of effective decision-making, the preponderance of the Ruhr is manifest in CEPCEO, a factor which has contributed heavily to its spotty success.

Significantly, the one important agreement reached among the coal producers is the need for a long-term ECSC coal policy. They are determined to obtain a commitment to the priority of ECSC coal over other fuels and over imported coal.   Hence they unanimously advocate discrimination against oil and American coal imports and a rational policy of more efficient utilisation of European coal production.   In CEPCEO'S words, and they smack heavily of " supranational dirigisme ":

> We can only conclude that there is a necessity for a coherent coal policy, to be applied immediately.   It is indispensable that such a policy not be based on short-term decisions, but that it realise

[13] *Agence Europe*, June 2, November 13, November 16, December 2, 1953; July 20, 1954.

long-term views. All the points comprised under it must be part of a general fuel policy.[14]

It is of the highest significance with respect to CEPCEO's ability to restructure the expectations of its member organisations that H. H. Wemmers, president of the Dutch State Mines, endorsed these demands of the organisation in 1956. Despite the extremely favourable cost structure of his own enterprises and the general Dutch resistance to co-ordinated economic planning for all ECSC countries, Wemmers associated himself in the strongest terms with the programme worked out under the stimulus of the high-cost collieries.[15]

Liaison Committee of European Metallurgical Industries (COLIME)

Since the advent of OEEC, the European steel consuming industries have sought to act jointly through the framework of a loose organisation called ORGALIM. The moving spirit in the organisation was André Métral, head of the French association of engineering industries. In February of 1953, Métral and his Belgian counterpart, M. Velter, took the initiative in forming a similar group solely composed of the steel consumers of the six ECSC countries, to function autonomously within the larger body. The need for such a special group was defended as an adaptation to the common market. Economic integration was a fact and an irreversible one at that. But it could not be left to politicians and " demagogues "; hence the industrial elite of all countries affected must take a direct hand in it. Further, the association of industrialists would be essential for jointly choosing delegates to the Consultative Committee—even though these are in principle national experts—and for training businessmen to share manufacturing and price information hitherto kept strictly secret. The common market clearly required a new approach to relations among competing national associations of engineering industries.

COLIME functions informally. No votes are taken at the frequent meetings and no effort is made to bind members and their national associations. Successful compromise is common on relatively minor points, but very difficult to achieve on questions of basic policy rooted in the structure of the national industries.

[14] Comité d'Etudes des Producteurs de Charbon d'Europe Occidentale, *Charbon et Politique de l'Energie* (Brussels, July 1955), p. 29.
[15] *Informations Mensuelles*, February 1957, pp. 53–54.

Hence no effort is made to insist on consensus when rigidly held opinions prevail. National trade associations thus retain their freedom of action, and make use of it.

Other Steel Consuming Associations

A number of specialised associations of steel consuming industries have felt the need for their own organisations, despite the existence of COLIME and of the Steelmakers' Club. Thus an Association of Galvanised Sheet Producers came into being, with the primary purpose of persuading ECSC organs to take a special interest in stimulating demand for its products.[16] The same is true of the European Committee of Foundry Associations, which seeks to operate supranationally, in co-operation with COLIME, even though its products are not subject to ECSC rules.

An ideologically fascinating group is the Federation of Iron and Steel Rerollers of the European Community (FEDEREL). It represents the small and independent rolling mills of ECSC, who depend on the large steelmakers for their supply of semi-finished steel, from which they in turn manufacture special shapes in relatively small quantities.[17] FEDEREL conceives of itself as the champion of small private enterprise, " the witness who, merely because of his existence, hinders monopolies and their abuses."[18] The reroller's major enemy is not government but the large steel-maker who can withhold supplies, control prices and drive him to the wall.

When the common market was opened in 1953, the rerollers feared that their last hour had struck because of the disappearance of national price controls and rationing. They federated supra-nationally almost immediately, with the frank purpose of seeking the protection of the High Authority against the " monopolists." They invoke the need to retain full employment, guarantee sources of supply and maintain the fair trade code. And when these normal measures do not suffice, they call on the High Authority. Thus they demanded High Authority financial participation in the construction of a new mill; in 1957 they obtained the support of the High Authority in negotiating with the major steelmakers

---

[16] *Usine Nouvelle*, June 15, 1955, p. 3.
[17] FEDEREL claims that its members operate 130 factories, employ 60,000 workers and produce about 18 per cent. of the Community's total of rolled steel.
[18] Chambre Syndicale Générale des Lamineurs Transformateurs, " Une profession qu'il faut connaitre: les Lamineurs-Transformateurs " (Paris, n. d.), p. 6.

in an effort to obtain additional tonnages of semi-finished steel at reasonable prices.[18a]   FEDEREL, because it is supranational, has been denied membership on the Consultative Committee but has had no difficulty whatever in gaining access to the High Authority through its lobbyist in Luxembourg.

No doubt, the precarious economic position of the rerollers was responsible for the far more federal nature of their organisation. A general assembly composed of three delegates each from the four participating national associations (Belgian, French, German and Italian) meets once a year.   An executive committee of two members from each association meets every four months.   Majority voting prevails in principle and decisions are binding.   In fact, no vote is ever taken and agreement is reached " à l'amicale " as a regular procedure.   While the presidency is supposed to rotate by nationality, the French representative, M. J. A. de Beco, has in fact been re-elected each year.   Fear of extinction was a potent stimulus in embracing supranationalism with enthusiasm.

Common Office of Scrap Consumers (OCCF)

In 1952, the leading steel firms of ECSC concluded a cartel agreement whereby they agreed to survey continuously their scrap needs, determine the amount of scrap to be imported from third countries, jointly import and distribute scrap, and establish a fund for equalising the price of imported and domestic scrap. Confronted with a *fait accompli* and determined to regularise the chaotic scrap situation in ECSC, the High Authority in effect authorised this arrangement through the establishment of OCCF and the related Compensation Fund.   In form, OCCF is a corporation under Belgian law, in which twenty-two leading steel firms are shareholders, though eventually 96 per cent. of all ECSC steelmakers chose to participate in the compensation system.   It is organised like any corporation and its decisions are binding on its members.   However, decisions must be made by unanimous vote of the executive committee.   In 1954, as a result of one of the recurrent crises of OCCF, the High Authority ruled that participation in the compensation system was henceforth to be compulsory for all scrap consumers.   In January of 1957, the scrap compensation

---

[18a] High Authority, *Bulletin Mensuel d'Information*, (July 1957), p. 9.   One Belgian rerolling firm shut down completely, while the German rerollers arrived at a separate solution with their steelmakers.

system was tightened still further and new formulas for determining the scrap needs of firms and the rate of contribution to the system established. The High Authority itself, thus, undertook once more to define narrowly the scope within which OCCF was able to function. In the absence of unanimity, the High Authority can decree action; and in any event, Luxembourg retains a veto power over all OCCF decisions and participates in all discussions.[19] OCCF functions are actually dependent administratively on the six national governments because of their rationing and licensing powers, and it is not always clear whether national or supranational directives are locally predominant. In any case, OCCF is less an autonomous group of industrialists than a publicly supervised cartel. High Authority directives and willingness to approve OCCF decisions in fact determine the arrangements made by the Brussels group.

European Liaison Committee of Coal Dealers and Consumers (CELNUCO)

No single interest group demonstrates the political spill-over effect of supranational economic institutions more clearly than CELNUCO. In 1956, fifty national trade associations were members of the group, including all associations of heavy industry consuming coal, and all associations of wholesale coal dealers. It also included public utilities and state railways, national federations of industry and general employers' associations. Only seventeen of the member organisations are directly subject to ECSC jurisdiction, while about twenty have enjoyed direct representation on the Consultative Committee since 1952.[20]

---

[19] See Mendershausen, *op. cit.*, pp. 284–286, for the cartel analysis. Also Office Commun des Consommateurs de Ferraille, *Statuts-Satzungen.*

[20] Breakdown of CELNUCO membership, according to information received from its secretary :

	National Total	Coal-consuming Industries	Public & Private Utilities	Feder. of Indust.	Employer Associat.	Wholesale Coal Dealers
Germany	12	7	3	1	—	1
France	11	4	3	1	1	3
Italy	2	—	—	1*	—	1
Belgium	13	9	1	—	—	3
Netherlands	8	1	2	—	3	2
Luxembourg	4	1	1	1	—	1
Totals	50	22	10	3	4	11

* for Italy, the general federation of industry (CONFIDUSTRIA) represents all industrial coal consumers.

The creation of CELNUCO therefore demonstrates that even industries not part of the common market feel compelled to organise and lobby supranationally in order to advance their interests once a sector concerning them no longer is subject to purely national political activity. Indeed, CELNUCO makes no secret of the reasons for its creation. The superior cohesion and lobbying ability of coal producers and trade unions was felt to be a distinct danger to consuming interests which had to be met by appropriate counter-measures. Effective activity on the Consultative Committee requires agreement among all consuming interests and unity as to the delegates who should be chosen to represent them. The standard pattern of pluralism at the national level is accurately projected here into the supranational realm.

Yet the heterogeneity of the membership is such that no effort at statutory organisation has ever been made. Member organisations in each country have their national secretariat which seeks to arrange for consensus. CELNUCO's central secretariat in Paris, then, attempts to harmonise the separate national positions into a common stand. On occasion, however, the process is reversed, with the centre taking the initiative in seeking the agreement of the national secretariats and their constituents. Meetings take place before every session of the Consultative Committee and it is here that a common position is debated if consensus has not already been achieved. At no level of activity are votes taken or binding decisions made. Member organisations retain complete freedom of action, and what is more, use it readily. Consumer and dealer interests diverge too drastically on many issues to permit easy agreement; net coal importing countries define their needs differently from surplus coal producers, and dealers closely associated with the collieries take a different position from independent importers and wholesalers. Yet the striking fact remains that trade associations not subject to ECSC and not represented in its Consultative Committee should demand participation in supranational policy-making and that the industries who do enjoy representation should share access with them.

In its one significant policy statement, CELNUCO took strident position against the viewpoint of CEPCEO. Instead of favouring a long-term coal policy designed to benefit ECSC collieries, it demanded price stability regardless of cyclical conditions, regularity of supply through unrestricted imports from third countries, and adaptation to cheaper fuels by continued and increasing reliance on other sources of energy.[21]   While coal consuming interests clearly got the better of the coal dealers in this definition of " common " interests, it rounds out the pattern of the transposition of national group demands to the supranational plane through the medium of ECSC-wide trade associations.

European Union of Retail Fuel Dealers (UENDC)

Founded in 1953, UENDC claims to represent some 80,000 retail coal dealers in ECSC countries as well as in Britain, Austria and Switzerland.[22]   It is a union of the dominant national coal merchants' associations, representing their collective interests against wholesalers, collieries and international organisations. Decisions can be made by majority vote.[23]

Specifically, the organisation was created to assure non-discrimination by wholesalers, to defend coal sales by stimulating the use of more modern heating apparatus, to prevent price cutting and rebates among members and persuade collieries to permit a reasonable retail profit margin.   With respect to ECSC, UENDC is determined to win official recognition and representation on the Consultative Committee, which it has been denied.[24]   It is directly concerned with making the fair trade code, price publicity and non-discrimination rules applicable to wholesalers—in short, with reaping the benefits of the Treaty in a setting in which retailers claim their interests are neglected in favour of producers and

[21] Comité Européen de Liaison des Négociants et Utilisateurs de Combustibles, *Consommation d'Energie et Politique Charbonnière* (Paris, May 1956).
ECSC public utilities—nationalised and private—also function jointly as a special sub-division of the European Association of Gas Producers.   As such they have lobbied separately from CELNUCO in Luxembourg in order to obtain price stability, warning that their operations were no longer profitable if coal price increases were to continue.   *Usine Nouvelle*, January 20, 1955, p. 9.

[22] UENDC is predominantly composed of dealers depending on coal sales, though it includes some oil dealers as well.   The Italian federation has not joined, but the British and Spanish associations participate under a special statute.

[23] UENDC, *Statuts*, November 26, 1953; *Rapport Annuel*, 1954 (Lausanne, November 8, 1955); " Aims and Plans of the European Union of Retail Coal Merchants " (Lausanne, September 6, 1954).

[24] Since nominations to the Consultative Committee are made by the Council of Ministers on the basis of " representative *national* organisations " these supra-national associations are not eligible for membership even if they could persuade the Council of their representative nature.   Supranational trade associations determined on influencing the choice of the Council are therefore compelled to persuade their national affiliates to propose centrally-agreed-upon candidates to the national ministries ultimately called upon to make the selection in Luxembourg.

wholesalers. Once more, the pattern of demand and expectations is identical with group activity and formation at the national level.

International Federation of Steel, Tube and Metal Dealers

Like the coal merchants, the association of steel dealers includes national groupings in non-ECSC countries. But as in the case of UENDC, it has increasingly concentrated on ECSC issues in seeking recognition and an interpretation of the Treaty favourable to its interests. Thus it has been concerned especially with lobbying at Luxembourg in order to compel downward adjustments of steel prices, and a rigorous application of the fair trade code. Specifically, it worked in support of the Monnet Rebate and continues to advocate " price flexibility." However, it also has been denied admission to the Consultative Committee.

Clearly, the mere fact that an impressive number of supranational trade associations has emerged in every field related to ECSC and that agreement on functions obtains does not prove that the ideological and structural differences dividing national associations have been overcome. The true test of the importance of the common market in restructuring relations between industrialists lies in the consistency of attaining a meaningful supranational consensus toward the High Authority, and toward rival associations. Does majority opinion imply deference by the minority? Is there a regular pattern of compromise permitting joint action? Are decision-making codes approaching the national pattern discernible? In order to obtain answers to these queries, decision-making in three of our organisations will be examined in detail and the solidarity of all groups in Consultative Committee discussions analysed.

Decision-Making in Supranational Trade Associations

In view of structural differences among these associations it might be hypothesised that a corporately organised body would more readily achieve agreement than an informal conference or a confederation. Hence, our discussion will seek to isolate differences in decision-making behaviour between (1) the corporately organised cartel represented by OCCF, (2) the quasi-federally organised UENDC and (3) the completely unstructured COLIME which functions merely as an *ad hoc* committee.

Differing national scrap needs, of course, go back to the structure of the steel industry as well as to commercial habits and conditions. Thus Italy is the country heavily dependent on scrap imports, France and Germany were approximately self-sufficient, Holland was a net exporter, while Belgium and Luxembourg were relatively disinterested because their steel industries feature the basic Bessemer process. These differences have been at the basis of almost all deliberations and decisions of the OCCF. Agreement among national steel associations could not be reached on the amounts of national scrap to be liberated for export to Italy, on the amount of the national contributions to the equalisation fund, and on the volume of scrap to be imported from third countries. The Italians asked for a maximum common market internally, while the Germans and French were far more interested in retaining their scrap at home. Agreement was reached, not through negotiations and friendly compromise among the associations, but through repeated unilateral rulings by OCCF president Fritz Aurel Goergen, backed up by the High Authority.[25]

This state of affairs led to a demand by the French and Italian associations that the equalisation system be made obligatory. All the other associations, feeling that this would merely mean an ECSC subsidy for Italian scrap imports, opposed the transformation into a compulsory organisation. However, in the absence of any unanimity on this or any other formula, the High Authority in agreement with the Council of Ministers adopted the French solution.[26] When despite these changes and a large increase in OCCF-financed scrap imports from third countries, Italian scrap purchases in France and Germany kept on rising steeply, the French steelmakers demanded the introduction of rationing and the declaration of a state of shortage. The Dutch representatives agreed, the Italians opposed this solution, and the Germans preferred a purely private national cartel solution to the shortage problem—a step which in 1955 led to anti-monopoly measures against them on the part of the High Authority. There being

[25] F. A. Goergen, *Tätigkeitsbericht des Präsidenten des Office Commun des Consommateurs de Ferraille und der Caisse de Peréquation des Ferrailles Importées, 1953–1955* (Brussels, 1955).
Goergen is the head of Phoenix A. G. He resigned his presidency of OCCF in 1956 in apparent disagreement with his colleagues over their continuing inability to reach consensus and his reluctance to permit the High Authority to run the organisation in the absence of consumer agreement. See his statement in *Usine Nouvelle*, February 9, 1956, p. 14. He was succeeded by Bentz van den Berg of Hoogovens.
[26] Goergen, *op. cit.*, pp. 10–11.

again no unanimity, while Luxembourg was unwilling to introduce rationing, nothing was done except to prolong the OCCF system for another year and to reward steelmakers who economised in their use of scrap.[27] When penalties against heavy scrap consumers were sharply increased in 1957, OCCF in a rare show of near-unity reacted in separate but identical suits against the bonus formula by all the national steel associations, with the notable exception of the Italians. But Luxembourg's voice was supreme still, as evidenced in relations with the United States. Heavy purchases by OCCF in 1956–57 had given rise to official American charges that ECSC imports were causing a scrap shortage in the United States and that OCCF dealings with one American scrap exporter were monopolistic and discriminatory in nature. The High Authority reacted by handling the negotiations for export tonnages directly with Washington and by imposing on OCCF a strict code for non-discriminatory dealing in Europe and abroad.[27a]

The conclusion is obvious. Despite a corporate structure and wide powers, there is no deference to majority opinion. Nor is there a regular pattern of friendly compromise among opposing views. The decision-making " code " is one of formal negotiation —almost on the diplomatic model—between instructed representatives of national steel associations generally unwilling to yield an inch of their position. This has naturally led to the preponderance of the High Authority in the decision-making process, a fact which is bitterly resented by Goergen as " dirigistic." But he also warns:

> Permit me to direct an urgent appeal to all member firms to do everything to prevent this evolution which is irreconcilable with our task as industrialists and entrepreneurs. Do not request your representatives in the committees of OCCF and CPFI to gain for you the ultimate in direct advantages. Give them the freedom to negotiate which is essential to reach compromises which are bearable for all steel industries.[28]

In COLIME, decision-making proceeds exclusively on the basis of informal discussions among the representatives of the national associations of engineering industries, usually held immediately prior to the meetings of the Consultative Committee, or when a

[27] *Ibid.*, pp. 16–17.
[27a] High Authority, *Bulletin mensuel d'Information*, (July 1957), pp. 7–9. Texts of the complaints before the ECSC Court in *Journal Officiel*, March 30, 1957.
[28] *Ibid.*, p. 18.

special appeal to the High Authority is being considered. One such situation was connected with the deterioration of the steel market in 1953, and the demand of steel consumers that the fair trade rules be relaxed to permit rebates.[29] COLIME members agreed that rebates should vary with the national situation, and that uniform ECSC-wide departures from price lists would be " discriminatory " on the part of the steelmakers. They also agreed that indirect exports should be exempt from the fair trade code in order to enable ECSC manufacturers to compete with British exporters without having to worry about price lists. Beyond these points, however, consensus never developed. The French and Dutch members were in favour of strict High Authority supervision over steelmakers' pricing practices; the Germans opposed this as interference with the autonomy of the businessman. No agreement was ever reached on the amount of the allowable rebate to be requested of the High Authority; some members, such as the Germans, preferred negotiations between steel-consuming and producing industries for lower prices at each national level; others preferred an ECSC-wide approach. Métral's efforts to persuade his colleagues to the French position failed. Despite the constant and intense presentation of demands for price flexibility to the High Authority, the members never advocated identical positions and preserved their right to vote independently in the Consultative Committee discussion of the Monnet Rebate.

Unanimous agreement was worked out, however, on the issue of relations with third countries. Being consuming industries, all six associations had no difficulty in agreeing that no obstacle should be imposed by ECSC to the free importation of any materials needed by the members in their manufacturing processes, especially coal and finished steel. They agreed, further, that the common ECSC tariff should be kept as low as possible on finished and semi-finished steel and that the High Authority obtain strict anti-dumping guarantees from Britain and Austria. While being quick to brand as " discriminatory " any suspicion of collusion among steelmakers, COLIME members insisted on their right to harmonise sales conditions and access rules while limiting imports of competing products from third countries.

Consensus evaporated once again on the issue of expanding the supranational structure and task. The Belgian and French

[29] My information on COLIME is based on unpublished internal sources.

members are fully in favour of the ECSC-wide labour harmonisation programme; the Germans and Dutch oppose it bitterly.
All insist on their opposition to restrictive practices by producers;
but they are sharply split on the issue of whether rigorous High
Authority anti-cartel measures are "dirigistic." In principle,
COLIME has gone on record as opposing the placing of any new
products under ECSC jurisdiction, extending the scope of powers
of the High Authority in any way or creating new supranational
agencies. At the same time, however, the majority of the member
organisations are in favour of the General Common Market and
privately grant the need for some supranational controls over it.
The agreement on principle, therefore, has produced neither a
true meeting of the minds nor consistently harmonised policy on
the part of the members.

On balance, it is evident that sharply divergent national
industrial viewpoints are not successfully compromised in COLIME.
When positions happen to converge—as on the question of coal
and steel imports from third countries—agreement is easily achieved.
But when positions differ in line with national ideological and
structural factors, no amount of discussion in Luxembourg has
succeeded in persuading the members to a new and common view.
Thus, for instance, all the members readily grant that as long as
steel prices rise, the consuming industries do not derive a real
benefit from the common market. For the French members this
implies vigorous protests and threats of withdrawal; but for the
Dutch and Germans it merely calls for more intensive negotiations
with national steel associations. It is not surprising, therefore,
that the members consider themselves bound to joint action only
when there is unanimous agreement. Their relations, in short,
are very similar to diplomatic negotiations between sovereign
states.

Efforts of the European Union of Retail Fuel Dealers contrast
sharply with COLIME and OCCF in that much more delegation
of power to the centre has taken place. National member
associations deliberately instructed their supranational staff to
stand above national differences, to mediate, and to represent
UENDC as a totality, regardless of differences of opinion within it.
Further, the organisation has been quite successful in having national
affiliates adopt the policy line recommended at the centre. In fact,
the directors of UENDC have become the full-time supranational

lobbyists for the national member organisational to a far more consistent degree than is true of similar organisations in ECSC.[30]

To what can this trend be attributed? In principle, coal dealers are no closer friends of federalism or European unity than are steelmakers or processors. Like the rerollers, however, they are a threatened profession whose future is beclouded and to whom supranationalism may hold out a hope already abandoned at the national level. The Western European coal dealer considers himself threatened by two forces: fuel oil and the restrictively organised wholesaler and colliery. Like the reroller, the coal merchant stresses the fact that he is a small, independent business-man. His mission is to supply domestic users of coal and other small businessmen and artisans. His interest is not with industry and large-scale consumers: those are the concern of other " mono-polists." But the mission also includes " the defence of coal " against new and cheaper fuels, a defence which he feels is losing ground day by day for lack of encouragement received from national governments. The answer worked out by UENDC is the simultaneous " defence " of coal and the coal merchant by restricting access to the profession and safeguarding the estab-lished dealer's exclusive right to satisfy the needs of households and small industry. But the significant aspect of this programme is the dominant role which supranational institutions were given. Fear and uncertainty, and the conviction that the small businessman is the underdog unless his organisation is superior to the " mono-polist's, " have provided the stimulants leading to a supranational trade association, functioning far more effectively than is true of the other groups treated.

The crucial decisions made by UENDC, even though they have failed completely in persuading the High Authority, bear out this pattern. Among the specific proposals made are suggestions for tightening the restrictions governing admission to the field, for increasing the standards of competence required of coal dealers. This argument is only in part due to a monopolistic motivation. While it would no doubt limit the number of competing firms, it also has as its objective the adaptation of the profession to new

---

[30] " UENDC -Bulletin," (January, 1955, November, 1955, December, 1955, January, 1956). See also Union Européenne des Négociants Détaillants en Com-bustibles, " Memorandum sur l'Approvisionnement des foyers domestiques dans les pays-membres de la CECA en ce qui concerne le charbon," July 1, 1955. Also *Journal des Charbonnages*, December 17, 1955.

requirements. If fuel oil is to be resisted, the design and servicing of coal stoves must be improved in order to make homes less dependent on specific grades of coal which are becoming more and more difficult to procure. Hence the coal dealer must be well enough trained and progressively enough minded to service stoves. But he must also insist that collieries and wholesalers make available enough of the grades required for domestic use. If this cannot be done, stoves must be converted to the use of other grades and the adjustment must be supervised from above. It is precisely this which UENDC asked of the High Authority, only to be told that domestic grades were not scarce and that ECSC lacked jurisdiction over the retail trade. Undaunted by Luxembourg's failure to take seriously its suggestions for long-term adjustment, UENDC also suggested that the High Authority encourage the granting of special summer rebates by collieries in order to spread coal sales more evenly over the entire year, and to give regularity to the market by having retailers assume the responsibility for carrying buffer stocks. This suggestion, as well as the demand that the fair trade rules of the common market be applied to retailers, may be falling on receptive ears. While the federal executive has thus been scarcely affected by the spill-over process, the coal merchants have certainly not been slow to grasp the economic and institutional logic of the developments. They have not only organised themselves supranationally but asked to be considered a true " European " group even though required to do so neither by the rules of the common market nor by political pressure in their home countries.

Thus our survey of the structure and activities of ECSC-wide trade associations shows that the groups most fearful of the consequences of a large common market dominated by big business are the ones who most consistently look to supranational action for their future welfare. Far from fearing dirigisme, they seem to welcome it with open arms. Yet clearly this " conversion " implies no basic change of attitude over 1953; it merely signifies a change in focus for lobbying purposes. Whether any of the national trade associations active in these groups have forgone any of their pre-ECSC ideological tenets, however, can be ascertained only on the basis of an examination of their work in the Consultative Committee.

SUPRANATIONAL TRADE ASSOCIATIONS IN THE CONSULTATIVE COMMITTEE

The Consultative Committee began its task in the spring of 1953 before most of the associations in question were formally organised. Yet initially the business representatives were dominated by a desire of regarding their Committee as an economic parliament which would consistently guide the policy of the High Authority. Hence efforts were made to discuss policy issues on the floor and in commission sessions, to endow the Consultative Committee with a statute enabling it to act like an economic and social council and to gain the attention of the federal executive. By 1955, this pattern had changed. Instead of bitter debate and careful votes, the bulk of the Committee's resolutions were being adopted by unanimity even though nothing like complete agreement prevailed in reality. Reports were unclear, resolutions tended to skirt the issue and absenteeism was rife. Interest lagged in direct proportion as the business representatives realised that they could gain access to the High Authority through orthodox lobbying channels and that the High Authority was not disposed to pay close attention to their deliberations in any case.

The growing sentiment of regarding the Committee merely as a lobbying arena is demonstrated not only by the practices cited. While less and less attention is being paid to collective decisions, the strictest secrecy is demanded for the actual deliberations. Votes are no longer recorded and the names of speakers are removed from the minutes. Attendance at meetings is denied not only to the press and the public, but also to members of the Common Assembly. As if unwilling to attract notice to their increasingly peripheral discussions, the business members of the Committee invoke the " club " atmosphere which so many of them maintain in the setting of their national trade associations. The chief remaining exception to these conclusions was the annual debate (until 1956) over the continuation of coal price ceilings. This situation has continued to evoke lively and bitter debate, formal votes and rigid positions; it will be used as the basis of the subsequent voting analysis.[31]

Have national interests given way to supranational ways of

---

[31] It follows, of course, that no published information in primary source form exists on decision-making in the Consultative Committee. My findings and conclusions are based on interviews and unpublished documents, not all of which can be cited hereafter.

thinking? Are aims defined in larger terms than before 1953? Does discussion of an ECSC-wide investment or labour policy imply identical or converging positions among nationally separate interest groups, giving rise to a permanent pattern of joint decision-making? Has fear of High Authority dirigisme compelled employer planning and action on a joint basis? An examination of key issues discussed in the Consultative Committee can hardly fail to give a negative answer.

Thus on the question of a long-range coal policy, the Committee rejected anything resembling a structural adaptation to new conditions on the part of the collieries. It dismissed the use of fuel oil as a regulator of coal prices, coal price flexibility, buffer stocks being held by wholesalers, and reliance on imported American coal to make up ECSC deficiencies. Coal imports, accompanied by equalisation provisions for costs differentials, must be strictly temporary; marginal mines should not be closed; and a general investment policy must take account of labour's welfare demands. On the positive side, however, the businessmen confined themselves to endorsing the ECSC-wide planning approach outlined by CEPCEO, while blaming the High Authority for merely recommending palliatives which they had already exhausted. It should be noted that this position was defended by the Consultative Committee even though a good many of the coal-consuming industries differed basically with the essence of the recommendations. They merely chose not to fight it out in the Committee framework.[32] On other questions regarding coal policy, CEPCEO members have a good record in defending each other's requests for price increases, even though the steelmakers have not always gone along with them. French and German coal producers agreed to minimise imports, but all Italian groups emphatically declined to rely essentially on ECSC coal. And on the question of central direction of coal consumption patterns, the German and Dutch groups clearly refused to countenance the kind of allocation defended by the French as " reasonable."

Committee activity in the investment field proved to be equally disappointing. Coal producers and consumers were found to differ widely on proper demand forecasts, with the collieries demanding more investment planning on the part of the High

[32] See the report of the sub-commission on coal policy to the Committee, High Authority Doc. 2800/55f (April 27, 1955).

Authority, a step sharply challenged by steel groups. Yet the steelmakers disagreed with the engineering industries and with each other over proper forecasts of steel demand, with many fearing that the High Authority's target figures were much too high and likely to lead to overproduction. All praised the housing programme for coal and steel workers, but many disputed the ECSC aim of wishing to bring down interest rates. As for High Authority-sponsored research into better production methods, most of the industrialists felt that this was their private domain and that the tax money of collieries should not be spent to do research for steelmakers.[33]

In a general way, the twin issues of general objectives and coal policy do reflect a crystallisation of positions in which coal consumers line up against coal producers, and steel producers against coal producers to the extent that rival claims for funds and opposing interpretations of dirigisme are involved, with the collieries taking a much more consistent view in favour of High Authority planning and direction. And this once more confirms the general finding that industries fearing serious structural problems will not hesitate to embrace supranational dirigisme with some ardour. On the other hand, the pattern certainly shows no willingness to compromise a restrictive, stability-minded ideology with an aggressive, adaptive and expanding one.

On the scrap issue, moreover, even the fraternal steel industries are unwilling to make concessions to one another. The Italian associations, as might be expected, have held out in the Consultative Committee against any kind of compulsory or voluntary cost-sharing for imported scrap, have opposed the declaration of a state of shortage and have insisted on their freedom to purchase all the scrap they want in ECSC. The Germans, by contrast, have argued in favour of intra-industry cost sharing for imports, price controls but no High Authority rationing. The French, equally consistently, have favoured price controls, cost sharing for imports *and* High Authority allocation measures to muzzle the scrap-hungry Italians. Each group clearly remained loyal to its national tradition and definition of need.

Labour-management relations in the Consultative Committee provide a fascinating index for gaining insight into the question

---

[33] Report of the sub-commission on general objectives to the Committee, **High** Authority Doc. 2730/1/55f (April 27, 1955).

of whether ECSC has tended to harmonise the rival national industrial outlooks. In December of 1954 the delegates voted unanimously, after a short and empty debate, to request the High Authority to undertake studies of comparative labour conditions, preparatory to an effort at harmonising such fringe benefits as vacations, holiday and overtime pay. During the following year, labour efforts to implement this resolution directly were met with one delaying device after another. And while the whole issue of an ECSC welfare policy was consistently raised in connection with coal policy and the definition of general objectives, no consensus ever emerged and no systematic recommendations were made by the Committee. All business organisations were unanimous in blocking the labour initiative, with the CEPCEO organisations taking the lead in heading off an energetic ECSC labour policy.

Even French business countered the labour manoeuvre, not because it opposes the harmonisation of fringe benefits but because it has no wish to aid in the establishment of an ECSC-wide collective bargaining pattern—which is the basic issue involved. Responding to relentless labour pressure, the High Authority late in 1956 called a bipartite conference of steel unions and producers in order to persuade them to negotiate collectively on some harmonisation measures clearly corresponding to obvious differentials in conditions. Even though some steel unions would have preferred an ECSC-wide contract, the conference merely agreed to collective bargaining in each national setting on categories of benefits where harmonisation seemed in order. Employer opposition to ECSC-wide collective bargaining remains intense; but at least the steel groups were willing to take up the points at issue, thus agreeing to set the framework for collective bargaining at the supranational level.

The collieries, however, declined to grant even this much. They were confronted, in a bipartite conference called by the High Authority in March of 1957, with a unanimous labour demand for a standard, ECSC-wide, miners' " bill of rights," including the harmonisation of fringe benefits. After consultations and agreement in CEPCEO, the collieries unanimously refused to negotiate even though the Belgian and French associations would welcome an upward revision of labour costs for their German and Dutch competitors. Thus, the principle of collective bargaining is considered sufficiently objectionable by these employer groups to persuade them to bury their national economic differences in order to make common front on a procedural, but ideologically charged, issue. Clearly, supranational collective bargaining has not yet resulted from these developments; but the logic of the common market has nevertheless forced a closer coalescence among employer organisations than has ever prevailed, despite the fact that the compromise once more took place at the level of minimal co-operation with labour typical of France and Italy.

Still, it is evident that the advent of supranational trade associations has not brought with it a centralised and articulated adjustment to the structural changes brought by the common market. Such adjustments, to be sure, have been made at the national level in Germany, Belgium, Holland and even in France. But at the ECSC level the organisational effort has featured either a defence against High Authority direction or a consistent effort by actual or potential marginal groups to seek cushioning *against* the common market from Luxembourg. To this extent, certainly, positive long-range expectations have led to the formation of supranational interest groups functioning in common for certain purposes. But they are not the groups on which an expanding and self-confident common market is supposed to depend.

Does nationality, supranational affiliation, or national trade association thinking determine voting in the Consultative Committee on the rare occasions when meaningful votes are taken? It is the conclusion of most observers that the business delegates vote only in accordance with the short-range perception of interests of their *national trade association*, not primarily in obedience to nationality as such or to supranational affiliations. Hence there should be no voting blocs, national or otherwise. Each issue should call for a different pattern of responses. The vote is determined by the particular immediate conditions—at home and on the common market—under which the group in question feels it must do business.

Rather than merely accept this conclusion on the basis of observations and debates, a statistical study of certain crucial votes was made in the effort to verify it. The results are as follows: [34-35]

[34-35] In these tabulations, the labour vote was excluded altogether. The votes never add up to the 34 non-labour representatives who should be present because of absenteeism or unrecorded abstentions; totals are therefore meaningless. The heading " consumers " includes the few dealers who are represented. Since our focus

TABLE 1

Consultative Committee Votes on Coal Price Ceilings

	For	Against	Abstained
Germans			
1953*	—	5	3
1954†	—	5	—
1954‡	—	3	2
1955§	7	—	—
1955**	—	7	—
French			
1953*	6	1	—
1954†	2	4	—
1954‡	5	—	1
1955§	1	3	2
1955**	—	4	2
Saar			
1953*	3	—	—
1954†	—	1	—
1954‡	2	—	—
1955§	1	2	—
1955**	2	1	—
Belgians			
1953*	—	4	—
1954†	—	4	—
1954‡	3	—	1
1955§	3	—	—
1955**	—	3	—
Dutch			
1953*	2	1	1
1954†	—	2	—
1954‡	2	—	1
1955§	3	—	—
1955**	—	3	1

is on trade associations rather than on individuals, organisations which are represented by more than one delegate (*e.g.*, the Ruhr collieries), are nevertheless counted
only once. In any event, such delegates never vote against one another. In the
computation of supranational trade association solidarity, no effort was made
to assess the solidarity of dealers since there are only two steel dealers on the
Committee and no representatives of retail coal dealers.

	For	Against	Abstained
Italians			
1953*	3	1	—
1954†	—	3	—
1954‡	2	—	1
1955§	1	3	—
1955**........	—	1	1
Luxembourgers			
1953*	2	1	—
1954†	1	1	—
1954‡	—	—	1
1955§	1	—	1
1955**........	—	1	1
Producers			
1953*	8	9	—
1954†	—	12	—
1954‡	8	2	3
1955§	10	2	2
1955**........	1	9	5
Consumers			
1953*	7	6	4
1954†	3	8	—
1954‡	6	1	4
1955§	7	6	1
1955**........	1	11	—
Steel Club			
1953*	5	2	—
1954†	—	7	—
1954‡	5	—	1
1955§	3	2	2
1955**........	1	2	4
CEPCEO			
1953*	2	5	—
1954†	—	4	—
1954‡	2	2	2
1955§	7	—	—
1955**........	—	7	—

	For	Against	Abstained
COLIME			
1953*	2	3	2
1954†	—	2	--
1954‡	2	—	—
1955§	2	3	—
1955**........	1	3	—
CELNUCO			
1953*	12	8	2
1954†	3	13	—
1954‡	9	1	4
1955§	8	8	2
1955**........	2	12	4

* 2nd Session, February 5 and 6, 1953. The question involved simply the choice of the establishment of coal price ceilings for all ECSC basins or not.

† 10th Session, March 11 and 12, 1954. The question involved the choice of whether " on the basis of existing market conditions " ceilings should be maintained for all ECSC basins.

‡ 10th Session. The question involved was whether " equal treatment for coal and steel " should be followed, *i.e.*, whether steel prices should also be controlled.

§ 19th Session, March 11, 1955. The vote was on the question " It is not appropriate to adopt a ceiling price system for the entire common market."

**19th Session. The vote was on the question " It is appropriate that a ceiling price system be established for the entire common market."

TABLE 2
CONSULTATIVE COMMITTEE VOTES ON COAL PRICE CEILINGS

	On grounds of general economic stability, ceilings are:*			If ceilings are maintained, they should be applied:†			Ceilings should be retained and/or prices raised:‡		
	necessary	possible	in-admissible	to all basins	flexibly	abstained	Unable to say	If ceilings, then higher prices	Abstained
Germans	2	3	—	4	1	—	1	6	—
French	4	2	—	—	5	—	—	1	2
Saar	1	1	—	—	2	—	—	3	—
Belgians	1	—	3	1	3	—	1	3	1
Dutch	—	—	3	—	2	1	1	1	—
Italians	—	—	3	—	2	—	3	—	—
Luxembourgers	1	—	—	—	2	—	—	1	—
Producers	5	4	4	3	11	—	2	11	—
Consumers	4	2	5	2	7	1	4	4	3
Steel Club	2	1	3	1	5	—	1	4	—
CEPCEO	2	3	1	2	4	—	1	7	—
COLIME	—	—	1	—	2	—	1	3	2
CELNUCO	5	2	8	2	12	1	5	8	3

* 10th Session, March 11, 1954.
† 10th Session, March 11, 1954.
‡ 26th Session, February 23, 1956.

TABLE 3

Fair Trade Price Issues

	For	Against	Abstained
Germans			
1953*	—	7	—
1955†	—	8	—
French			
1953*	4	—	—
1955†	4	—	1
Italians			
1953* .	1	—	1
1955†	1	1	2
Saar			
1953*	2	—	—
1955†	2	—	1
Belgians			
1953*	—	1	2
1955†	—	4	1
Dutch			
1953*	2	—	—
1955†	—	2	1
Luxembourgers			
1953*	—	2	—
1955†	—	1	1
Producers			
1953*	4	5	1
1955†	5	8	2
Consumers			
1953*	5	5	2
1955†	2	8	5
Steel Club			
1953*	2	2	1
1955†	3	2	1

	For	Against	Abstained
CEPCEO			
1953*	2	3	—
1955†	2	6	1
COLIME			
1953*	1	1	2
1955†	—	2	4
CELNUCO			
1953*	5	6	3
1955†	5	10	6

* 3rd Session, February 19, 1953. The Committee voted on the question of whether, pending the report of the Tinbergen Commission on the turnover tax issue, the High Authority should forbid sellers to include in their price lists taxes which would ultimately be refunded to them.
† 23rd Session, November 29, 1955. The Committee voted on the question of whether the High Authority should order coal wholesalers to publish regular price lists and thus abide by the fair trade code.

The single most important conclusion which emerges from these statistics is: *no consistent and striking correlation for voting solidarity can be established for national groups, categories of representation or supranational associations.* Some groups are more or less solid, depending on the issue, but none show a consistent tendency to vote together in the sense of forming a distinct *bloc.* And if no dominant pattern for any of the three possible aggregates clearly emerges, one is forced to adopt the conclusion that the logic of the common market has not gone far enough to dictate a sense of overriding common interest to supranational associations. On the other hand, on many issues it also demonstrates that the principle of nationality no longer enjoys sufficient support to act as a cohesive agent. Fragmentation is the order of the day: delegates tend to vote in accordance with perceptions of interest derived from the needs and assessments of their national trade association, as shaped by the specific issue before the Committee.

If the principle of national voting solidarity is examined, it becomes apparent that on the coal price ceiling issue, only the Germans and the Belgians display anything resembling national cohesion. Yet even they failed to vote together in 1954. Still the tendency does support the contention that German businessmen are more disciplined than their ECSC colleagues and are likely to take common positions derived from joint assessments of German business needs. The Belgians gain some homogeneity from their overwhelming dedication to free enterprise and opposition to any kind of controls which would limit natural price movements— especially since the cost structure of Belgian industry gives them an interest in an upward price trend. On the issue of the fair trade code, once more the Germans display excellent national solidarity, as did the French in 1953. The reason, however, was not " nationalism " in the everyday sense of that term so much as a conception of common interests derived from the fact that tax systems and refunds are by definition national in scope. The parties to the *Steuerstreit* of 1953 were thus compelled to take national positions by the nature of the quarrel. Hence no sweeping generalisation can be drawn from these trends.

Nationality, thus, yields no consistent correlation with voting trends. Yet neither does the principle of representation which governs the composition of the Committee: division into " producers " of coal and steel as against " industrial consumers and dealers " interested in coal and steel. On no issue do the voting statistics support any contention that a definition of interests based on these categories enjoys any meaning or recognition in the Consultative Committee. The debates show that coal producers sometimes line up against steel producers and they also indicate that a common industrial front against labour's demands does exist. But no cleavage between producers on the one hand and consumers and dealers on the other can be established.

Nor do the supranational trade associations, regardless of their organisational and structural qualities, display an impressive homogeneity. The Steel Club has a most indifferent record of solidarity on the coal price issue; only in 1954 did anything resembling unanimity prevail. Complete fragmentation was the order of the day on the fair trade code votes. COLIME and CELNUCO, as organisations of consumers, failed to hold together on a single issue involving more than two delegates present. Furthermore, absenteeism is especially striking in the case of the COLIME delegation. CEPCEO shows a much better record. The collieries were almost unanimous in 1956 in voting for higher prices if ceilings were retained; they voted solidly against ceilings in 1955, but they split in 1953 and 1954. Not even their common defensive complex and dedication to the protection of ECSC coal has sufficed to create an absolute supranational voting solidarity. The picture here at least supports the conclusion that the branch of industry most fearful of its future has made the most far-reaching efforts to ally supranationally on a permanent basis, as supported by the increasing trend toward unity over time.

Thus, the national trade association emerges as the supreme focus of interest and loyalty after five years of supranationalism. Yet, in gauging pluralistic processes toward community formation, it is at least equally significant that the national association allies itself as readily with groups across the frontier as with its own nationals. " Europe " may not yet be the focus of common industrial action; but the nation has ceased to be the dominant referent which it formerly was.

ECSC Trade Associations and Tactical Supranationalism

National trade associations rarely possess true sanctions for disciplining their members even when they operate on a majoritarian principle of voting. Yet it is true that the membership tends to bury its differences after a decision on a given issue and to lobby as a unit in its relations with the government, with the minority reserving its right to pose its preferences again in the future. In the event of unbridgeable gaps in outlook, the dissident organisations usually secede.

The organisational pattern here implied is much closer to the model of a true " community " than the actual picture presented by supranational trade associations in ECSC. Majority voting either does not exist or is not used even when permitted by the statutes. Unbridgeable gaps never lead to secession for the simple reason that serious points of difference are evaded by the organisations, who reserve for themselves full freedom of action at the national or the ECSC levels. CEPCEO, the Steelmakers Club and CELNUCO are, in effect, permanent conferences of sovereign members. In their mutual dealings, diplomatic negotiation is the central technique for achieving consensus, not imposition and voting.

It follows that the type of agreement reached very seldom relates to a commonly held ideology or to fundamentally shared values. Consensus is " tactical " in the sense that it relates to specific policy issues confronting the associations in question, giving rise to one pattern co-operation in one instance and quite a different pattern in the next. Certainly this implies a high degree of functionally specific orientation on the part of the members. Not *Weltanschauung* but price " extras " on wire rods or Grade 3 anthracite are focal issues. But it also means that no effort is made *a priori* to work out the kind of profound agreement on first principles on which sustained group action tends to be based normally.

Granted that the similar socio-economic *milieu* of all western European businessmen already predisposes them toward thought along identical or parallel lines, the institutional impact of ECSC has nevertheless so far avoided the evolution of an industrial ideology transcending national frontiers. National values remain intact. The logic of the common market has not, after five years, resulted in Dutch industrial aggressiveness seeping into French consciousness, or the French penchant for cartel-cemented stability persuading industrialists in Holland. Even the marked convergence of national demands in the " defence of coal " or the avoidance of ECSC-wide collective bargaining remains " tactical ": it involves neither an articulate ideology nor an impressive effort at general agreement. The focus remains a specific and urgent issue posed in common to the interested organisations by an outside irritant. And when the issue involves values and interests defined differently by the national affiliates of a COLIME or a CELNUCO, action follows the path typical in relations among governments united in international organisations—unilateralism.

Yet these conclusions must be put in the context of the all but unanimous opposition of coal and steel groups to the common market, which prevailed in 1951. Strikingly, no supranational association and very few national affiliates today oppose or challenge the principle of the common market or its extension to other sectors. Steelmen inveighing against supranational " bureaucracy " and " dirigisme " are far from advocating the *status quo ante*. And collieries which foretold their own doom in 1951 today transfer their cries for special protection to the supranational forum. There is no doubt, therefore, that the supranational trade associations have heavily contributed to eliminating opposition to integration. While they have not made homogeneous groups of their affiliates, they nevertheless represent the political adjustment to a regional governmental agency which is accepted as given, from whom favours must be asked and advantages extracted, or whose policies must be opposed *en bloc*.

This operational conclusion may be hazarded from the experience of ECSC trade associations: because of their functional specificity and preoccupation with immediate issues, regionally organised employer groups in a pluralistic setting will outgrow dependence on and loyalty to the national state *before* they develop a regionally defined body of values. They will band together supranationally and co-operate " tactically " on issues on which their interests naturally converge, and they will organise accordingly. But they will not immediately outgrow their separate national ideological experiences and habits. No doubt a much longer period of " tactical co-operation " is required and a much more intense series of stimuli must be injected into the scene before any marked ideological cohesion will develop.

CHAPTER 10

SUPRANATIONAL TRADE UNIONS

IF trade associations have, after five years of common market, established mutual patterns of tactical unity without achieving full federation, trade unions have gone a good deal further. Common fears and opportunities for advancing claims in a new forum of public action have resulted in a more rigid organisation for ECSC labour as well as in more unity of action. The marked differences in national strength and self-confidence have been noted before.[1] But as in the case of employers, patterns of divergent national thoughts must be balanced against old habits of international co-operation in assessing the gaps between national groups, which a successful supranational logic must overcome in order to result in the formation of new groups with larger foci of loyalty.

TRADE UNION INTERNATIONALS AND EUROPEAN INTEGRATION
Strikingly, European trade unions in their day-to-day economic thinking until recently resembled their national employer associations almost on every vital point. FO and CFTC were interested, not only in maintaining working class benefits, but in defending French industry against competition, cyclical fluctuations and higher costs. Equalising social security contributions throughout ECSC was more important to them than productivity. UIL and CISL agreed with their employers in advocating a large common market for capital, goods, and especially manpower, but were equally determined to protect Italian marginal firms against lower-priced imports from other ECSC countries. The DGB has been more interested in bettering the external competitive position of German industry than in exploiting supranationalism for the benefit of higher wages or better working conditions. The three Dutch federations, far from challenging the reasoning of their industrialists, were more concerned with price and cost stability, industrial peace and greater productivity, than in anything smacking of class struggle. Nor did Belgium's FGTB and CSC challenge the fundamental national business objectives of their employers:

---

[1] See Chap. 6. Note especially the particular *national* conditions which have led certain unions to look to supranational action for relief.

but because they had already attained the highest living standards on the Continent by purely national bargaining, they were compelled to seek further progress by way of supranational or international arrangements, given the refusal of Belgian industry to handicap itself further on export markets. Whether Socialist or Christian, ECSC trade unionists cannot be assumed automatically to be " international " or " European " in outlook because of the ecumenical principles on which their basic ideology is founded.

Yet if the principle of the cartel introduced a transnational quality into relations among trade associations, labour possesses a more consistent tradition of international awareness and co-operation because of the long history of labour Internationals and the ideological premises on which these are based. Cartels are conceived as temporary defensive devices; trade union Internationals were set up as permanent centres of working-class defence against the " international " character of aggressive capitalism. Labour was thus forced into the international arena because it wished to oppose the very dynamics of a capitalism whose local development would be subject to the laws of optimum cost conditions, cheap wages, social security differentials and trade union weakness. The nexus of related considerations perforce gave a permanent character to the Internationals which is lacking on the employer side.

Still, the International Confederation of Free Trade Unions, even though it is the largest non-Communist International, functions more like a permanent conference of sovereign members than ideologically unified interest group. ICFTU resolutions do not usually bind the member federations to any specific course of action. They merely seek to harmonise the policies of the national affiliates with respect to common problems of union freedom, economic development, political and economic democracy, and world peace. As such they tend to compromise competing national viewpoints in the interest of international labour unity. But such compromises may well be as ephemeral as those of other private or public international organisations. The overt commitment of ICFTU to the fight against Communism as the primary aim is not considered of first importance by many European affiliates who are more attached to the protection of existing working-class benefits through a controlled international economy. The welfare state—national, regional, or international—is a more vital symbol than the aggressive anti-Communism or dynamic modern industrialism preached by the American members of ICFTU. While the majority of affiliated unions is at least nominally Socialist in outlook, little ideological cohesion is gained from this fact. The unions differ too fundamentally on the kind of national welfare state they desire, on the intensity of their Marxism and on the stress to be given to national and international anti-Communist measures. A further discordant note is introduced by the existence of International Trade Secretariats affiliated with ICFTU, organisations not necessarily in agreement with national federations or with the bulk of ICFTU. On questions of European integration there have been differences in emphasis and timing, though not on basic principles.[2]

For purposes of European unity there exists within ICFTU a European Regional Organisation, through which the bulk of co-ordinated trade union relations with OEEC, ECSC and NATO are channelled. With the exception of CISL—a Catholic federation —all the affiliated groups are essentially Socialist, though the DGB officially denies any Socialist commitment in order to appease the minority of Christian unionists in its ranks. The degree of consensus prevailing among the western European unions with respect to economic integration can well be gauged from the European Regional Organisation's stand on the " New Start," worked out at a conference held in August of 1955.

In principle, the Monnet ideal of a large common market as a spur to higher production and lower prices is accepted. But, " the free trade unions demand that each stage toward economic co-operation and integration be traversed in the framework of a policy of full employment and general social progress, including the harmonisation of living conditions in an upward direction."[3]

---

[2] Thus on questions of European integration, the International Federation of Miners in 1954 came out for a general five-day week, nationalisation of mines and a more active welfare policy by ECSC. *Informations Bimensuelles,* September 15, 1954, p. 29. The International Federation of Transport Workers agreed with the last demand, but also demanded direct worker participation in the process of drafting the Euratom and General Common Market treaties. *Ibid.,* October 1, 1955, p. 44. This demand was echoed in the European Regional Organisation's endorsement of the Messina Resolutions.

[3] Organisation Régionale Européenne de la C. I. S. L., " Conférence Syndicale pour la Relance Européenne, 25–27 août 1955, Déclaration pour la Relance Européenne," Doc. No. 6593/55f, ERO/Sp.Cnf. 55/2.

For general discussions of trade union Internationals and affinities among national federations in Europe see Lewis L. Lorwin, *The International Labor Movement* (New York: Harper & Bros., 1953); Adolf Sturmthal, *Unity and Diversity in European Labor* (Glencoe: Free Press, 1953).

Thus the defensive mentality reasserts itself despite the support for the rationale of the large market. It made itself felt also in the demand for investment aid, in an unambiguous and clearly worded European obligation to accompany overall economic policy with supranational welfare measures, and in the reiteration that worker delegates must sit in all new supranational or international organs to be created. While endorsing a supranational Euratom, these unions did not at first come out in favour of federal rather than intergovernmental economic agencies and they insisted on the standardisation of social legislation as a means to limit the production and distribution displacements normally attendant on the introduction of greater competition. While CISL's Giulio Pastore continued to press for ICFTU endorsement of a maximal right to free labour migration, the Regional Organisation's statement was silent on the subject. But by 1956, the federal emphasis in the ICFTU programme had grown considerably. Declared the European Regional Organisation :

> Convinced that Europe cannot maintain its actual standing, develop its economic power or constantly increase the living standards of its people if a close collaboration among its states is not assured and that the creation of the Common Market and Euratom are an important step . . . the Conference appeals to all national affiliates to strengthen their measures among workers and in public opinion . . . to mobilise the forces necessary . . . so that these projects may be realised as soon as possible.[4]

While repeating the earlier demands for gradualism, readaptation, welfare measures and investment aid, the ICFTU unions in 1956 went out of their way to demand supranational powers and institutions to assure the success of these programmes, fearing that dependence on intergovernmentalism would exaggerate the strength of national trade associations opposed to integration. Hence the planning and directing powers claimed for Euratom were absolute and extreme, and the demand for union participation in supranational decision-making did not diminish a bit.

The consensus in ICFTU, then, may be described as a commitment to economic integration provided the logic of a freer market is not given an opportunity to work itself out along classical economic lines. This formula succeeds in placing the ICFTU unions

---

[4] Conference of the European Regional Organisation, May 22–24, 1956, Frankfurt/Main, final resolution. *Informations Mensuelles*, January 1957, pp. 19–21.

clearly in the integrationist camp without compelling national affiliates to depart appreciably from the positions they hold dear. Each is free to defend and approach integration in terms of its own preoccupations.

A second organisational focus of European labour is provided by the International Confederation of Christian Trade Unions, which includes Catholic, Protestant and non-confessional national federations, claiming about 2,300,000 members in Western Europe. Despite its early dedication to " spiritual " defences against modern capitalism and its protest against the purely " materialistic " struggle put up by Marxist-inspired trade unions, the ICCTU today possesses no more ideological cohesion than the ICFTU. Its emphasis on Christian Social doctrine—Catholic or Protestant —is minimal at the international level and its concern with anti-Communism and the welfare state no different from the ICFTU's. Small wonder then that intermittent merger negotiations between the two Internationals have been going on since 1950, and that on questions of joint action in European international economic institutions, the two confederations consult constantly and generally arrive at identical positions.

With respect to European unity, the task of the ICCTU has been simpler than that of the ICFTU, since there is within it no major *bloc* of unions indifferent or, at times, hostile to integration. Partly because of their identification with Christian parties in the national setting, the specifically Christian national federations have always favoured European unity and have demanded appropriate policy before the ICFTU had clearly committed itself to such a course. ICCTU speaks of the " duty " of workers to participate in integration and asserts their " right " to be represented on all new organs. Like ICFTU, the primacy of welfare questions is stressed over the purely economic aspects of integration, thereby introducing the same equivocation with respect to the benefits of a competitive common market. Unlike ICFTU, the Christian unions endorsed the " New Start " by insisting clearly on the creation of new institutions of a federal type. Harmonisation of living standards, of co-determination rules, labour's right to migrate under supranational auspices and protection, and investment aid to Italy are equally demanded.[5] While the

---

[5] "Intégration Européenne: Politique générale des Syndicats Chrétiens," *Labor* (September 1955), pp. 43 *et seq.* for the ICCTU programme details. See also

Christian unions exhibit consensus with respect to the same economic issues covered by ICFTU, their political demands are more specific, in that they include a federal Europe, equipped with a popularly elected Assembly, a full-fledged Economic and Social Council, and a sovereign European Commission for EEC.

Trade union Internationals, being centres for the harmonisation of policy among sovereign member affiliates, strongly resemble public international organisations. Very rarely do they " make policy "; far more commonly they merely register the opinions of their members and compromise these along the lines of the minimum common denominator. But despite this limiting factor on supranational solidarity, and despite the well developed national differences in emphasis and position, there clearly is a basic consensus among European trade unions on questions of integration. Further, this consensus enjoys more uniform ideological underpinnings— though neither particularly Socialist nor Christian in nature— and agreement on detailed demands than is true of ECSC–wide employer associations. Long before 1950, the labour movement had equated survival, acceptance as " respectable," and ultimate victory at home with a modicum of international solidarity. It was very sympathetic to the growth of a unified, democratic Western Europe as a defence against Communism. The continuity of this sentiment gave labour in ECSC a minimum common denominator in terms of articulating fears of " international capitalism " and spelling out demands for protection against it, while also motivated by specific national demands which were in large measure identical with those of the national trade associations. Without suggesting any pre-existing deep sense of unity of mission and doctrine cutting across national frontiers, it is still accurate to conclude that a sufficient body of shared values

specific demands pressed by President Gaston Tessier with Spaak, *Agence Europe*, October 8, 1955. Apparently losing patience with the slow pace of harmonisation of working conditions, the Congress of ICCTU in 1955 authorised its national federations to fight for the attainment immediately of the forty-hour week, even though it continued to assert that the struggle for the harmonisation of working conditions was a collective aim of the organisation. *Informations Mensuelies*, January 1956, pp. 23–24.

In January of 1957, the ICCTU sought to influence the content of the EEC Treaty, then about to be signed, by restating its insistence on the importance of supranational powers and a free hand for the organisation to formulate an overall economic policy for the common market, assisted by representatives from the trade unions as an " essential prior condition." The ICCTU stand on Euratom, repeated at the same time, is identical with that of the ICFTU. *Ibid.*, January 1957, pp. 21–22, 80, 105.

prevailed at the debut of ECSC to facilitate the later evolution of a closer pattern of common action.

FORMATION OF ECSC–WIDE TRADE UNIONS

Almost as soon as Robert Schuman launched his appeal for drafting a supranational coal and steel community, ICFTU and ICCTU took position on the Plan and asserted labour's internationally shared fears and aspirations. Both organisations stressed then their desire to use the establishment of a competitive European market as a lever to achieve the progressive harmonisation of living standards. They claimed all the special protective devices later put forward again in connection with the Messina Conference and the New Start. ICFTU further demanded that nationalised industries should never be considered as cartels and that coal sales organisations—under whatever name—should essentially be left intact. It endorsed the fears of the DGB and met the German Socialists half-way by stressing the need for removing all discrimination from German coal and steel production.[6]

ICFTU and ICCTU almost immediately seized upon the new supranational institutions as a mechanism for gaining policy-making equality with organised business, thus giving direct expression to labour's internationally shared fear of being once more merely the dupe of cartelised industry hiding behind the façade of the new High Authority. In order to prevent the delegation of regulatory powers to national and ECSC–wide trade associations, the unions not only demanded the strictest public supervision over business, but asserted the right to share in this effort by gaining a maximum of direct representation in the institutions concerned. It is vital to note here that the unions as early as 1950 were agreed that their future representatives would be responsible to and appointed by the Internationals and *not* the national federations. ICFTU and ICCTU agreed that the former should nominate a candidate for the High Authority, with the approval of the latter, and that the Christians would nominate " their " candidate for one of the positions on the Court of Justice. Further, the two Internationals agreed to split the seventeen-member labour

[6] ICFTU, Press Release, April 26, 1951 and May 24, 1951, Brussels. Also see Georges Lefranc, " Les Syndicats Ouvriers Face au Plan Schuman " *Nouvelle Revue de l'Economie Contemporaine* (No. 16–17, 1951), pp. 55–57.

delegation to the Consultative Committee, with eleven members coming from the free unions and four from the Christians.[7]

No doubt the unions in 1950 grossly overstated their claims for a direct share of control over the new institutions. But they co-operated in a remarkable manner during the negotiations in Paris leading to the final Treaty. All delegations included national trade union representatives, either as full members or as advisers. Despite their national status, these men met once a week as European trade unionists in the Paris office of FO in the attempt to work out common positions. Characteristically, they avoided issues deeply dividing the national movements involved, such as cartels, with a representative of the ICFTU always present to act as go-between. These consultations were largely responsible for the provisions of the Treaty defining the situations in which the High Authority must call on the Consultative Committee, minimising the situations permitting delegation of power to trade associations, and the unwritten agreement governing the selection of " trade union representatives." The consultations failed then to yield labour consensus on the question of a supranational welfare policy, with the Dutch and German members in 1950 holding out for a minimal High Authority role.

As soon as ECSC institutions began to function, the trade unionists realised that they needed permanent organisations to safeguard the interests they had formulated during the negotiating period. For the ICFTU unions, André Renard formulated the case for a permanent ECSC-wide labour organisation in these terms—

> The High Authority, the Community, confronts these choices: either it carries out the provisions of the Treaty, free competition, free migration, the largest possible price freedom; or it will develop into a group of cartels, which under the façade of the Community will merely serve international capitalism. We must work with the High Authority to destroy these cartels. We have no interest in participating in the revival of the powerful international steel cartel, or tomorrow perhaps the mighty international coal syndicate. We

---

[7] The results of the agreement were strikingly supranational. The Council of Ministers chose, as the " trade union " member of the Court, P. S. J. Serrarens, Dutch trade union leader and politician, and former Secretary-General of the ICCTU. The High Authority co-opted as its ninth member, as the joint candidate of both Internationals, Paul Finet, Belgian trade union leader, a former President of the ICFTU, and since 1958 President of the High Authority. For the sequel on the agreement concerning the Consultative Committee, see Chapter 13.

are the underdogs in this struggle, which is unequal. Colleagues, the international trade associations have taken shape already. It is so much easier to agree among a few, as with steel, as among many, as is the case with us. The steel cartel has been revived and we still debate the creation of our trade union international at the ECSC level ! I greatly fear that we will never attain a sufficiently integrated organisation which can deal with these trade associations.[8]

Yet all the ICFTU unionists would agree to was the creation of a permanent committee of sovereign equals, ultimately equipped with a standing liaison bureau lacking all powers of policy–making and functioning essentially as a lobbying centre in Luxembourg and as a communications hub for the members of the committee. Despite the demands of Renard and Luxembourg's Antoine Krier, the French and German unions countered that a sufficient number of labour Internationals existed already and that no new federation was needed. The reasons for this negative attitude were the French fear of being overwhelmed by the German membership and the Germans' reluctance to have foreign unions lean on them for collective strength.

The structure which emerged from the early conflict subsists as the Committee of Twenty-One.[9] Each organisation is represented by one delegate and one vote, but in fact Germans account for over half of the affiliated rank-and-file membership and for an equally large share of the financial contribution. Much of the time of the Committee has been taken up with bitter procedural wrangles over the future of the organisation, the powers of the

[8] Internationaler Bund Freier Gewerkschaften—Europäische Gemeinschaft für Kohle und Stahl, *Bericht über die Intergewerkschaftliche Konferenz*, 16. 17. 18. März, 1954, p. 29. Cited hereafter as " Report."

[9] The Committee of Twenty-One is composed as follows : International Confederation of Free Trade Unions; International Federation of Miners; International Federation of Metalworkers; National Metalworkers Unions from Germany, Belgium (FGTB), Holland (NVV), France (FO), Italy (UIL and CISL), Luxembourg (LAV); National Mineworkers Unions from Germany, Belgium (FGTB), Holland (NVV), France (FO); DGB, FGTB, FO, NVV, LAV, UIL and CISL.

Its budget amounted to B.frs. 2,163,020 in 1955. The German preponderance is here magnified by the fact that the French and Italian metalworkers, FO, UIL, CISL and the International Federation of Metalworkers are delinquent in their dues. The membership of the Committee overlaps with that of the Consultative Committee and with the Common Assembly, a factor naturally facilitating lobbying efforts. In 1955 it was decided to solicit the participation of British trade unionists as observers in the deliberations of the Committee. The Austrian workers, as well as a representative of the United Steelworkers (AFL–CIO), also participate as observers. The affiliated miners' and metalworkers' unions claim a membership of 2,600,000, not all of whom work in plants subject to ECSC jurisdiction. Significantly, the by-laws of the Committee contain no reference to voting rules.

liaison bureau, and the financial contribution to be borne by the ICFTU and the International Federations of Miners and Metalworkers, a large share of whose members have no interest in ECSC. The Secretary-General of ICFTU, M. Oldenbroek, held out for an active pro-integration and anti-Communist campaign as the primary field of action for the Committee; this was turned down by the bulk of the members who were more concerned with extracting a pro-labour welfare policy from the High Authority, gaining more seats on the Consultative Committee, expelling the " class enemy " delegate of the Confédération Générale des Cadres from the trade union delegation, and lobbying with Socialist members of the Common Assembly. Certainly the Committee considers its task as including the definition of a common labour policy toward ECSC and forcing admission to the charmed circle of High Authority policy–makers. But its techniques for attaining these goals are of a diplomatic character: the delegates negotiate with each other as equals and avoid formal voting, with a majority resisting the creation of a federal union structure.

Partly in response to their greater commitment to a politically federated Europe, the ICCTU unions responded much more vigorously to the challenge of supranational institutions by establishing a full-fledged federation. Until 1955, they contented themselves with a special ECSC section in the ICCTU secretariat. In that year, however, they concluded that only an independent federal structure would give them the collective strength to influence the High Authority and national employer associations. Further, they found that without a federal structure it was far too difficult to arrive at a truly uniform Christian labour position in ECSC, especially for purposes of cementing labour power in the Consultative Committee.[10]   Fundamental to the ICCTU pre-occupation

---

[10] For an explicit discussion of the motives leading to the formation of the Federation, see the statement of the Secretary-General, A. C. de Bruyn, in *ECSC Bulletin*, May 1955.

The following unions are members of the Federation: National unions of metalworkers: Netherlands (Catholic and Protestant), Belgium (CSC), Luxembourg (Christian), France (CFTC), Saar (Catholic); national unions of mine workers: Netherlands (Catholic and Protestant), Belgium (CSC), France (CFTC), Luxembourg (Christian), Saar (Catholic); white collar workers' unions: Netherlands (Catholic Employees), Belgium (Christian Employees), Germany (two non-confessional employees' federations, DHV and VWA); national federations of trade unions: France (CFTC), Belgium (CSC), Saar. Netherlands (KAB-Catholic and CNV-Protestant), Luxembourg (Catholic). A total of 135,000 miners, metalworkers and employees are represented by the Federation as working in plants subject to ECSC jurisdiction.

is the express desire to compel employers and the High Authority to inaugurate ECSC–wide collective bargaining, a task obviously requiring maximum labour cohesion.

The result was the creation in mid-1955 of the Federation of Christian Trade Unions of the ECSC. Member organisations enjoy parity of representation and voting power regardless of size. A two-thirds vote of its General Conference and Executive Committee is binding on national affiliates and the central structure is given the power to define common policy positions for the collectivity. However, " a unanimous vote is required for all decisions concerning questions of principle, relating to the religious convictions of the delegates." [11] Unlike the ICFTU group, the Christian Federation has a permanent Secretary-General with considerable powers of initiative and recommendation, and permitted great latitude in lobbying on behalf of the Federation in Luxembourg. In the event of sharp disagreement between the delegates, the Executive Committee of the ICCTU may be called upon to arbitrate; this link, however, is the only structural tie remaining between the regional and the world organisation. Neither the ICCTU as such nor the Christian International Trade Secretariats are members. The unanimity rule on religious questions, in effect, assures that such matters cannot be discussed meaningfully by the Federation because of its highly heterogeneous confessional make-up.

Regardless of structural differences, the two ECSC–wide unions are agreed on this ideological premise: ECSC provides the opportunity for gaining equality with management and with governments in the formulation of basic policy; ECSC is the ideal vehicle for achieving labour respectability, for driving home the point that organised labour is a permanent and valid collective component of the social scene, deserving of direct participation in decision-making. It is of the highest importance, in isolating social processes contributing to transnational integration, to pinpoint the analysis on this widely shared aspiration and to give it its true importance in partly explaining why labour should embrace supranationalism

---

[11] " Statuts de la Fédération des Syndicats Chrétiens dans la Communauté Européenne du Charbon et de l'Acier," Art. 16, pars 1. and 3. The only known instance in which religious issues seemed to intrude was in the Federation's resolution (May 10, 1957) protesting against the introduction of the sliding working week— as interfering with Sunday as a universal day of rest, culture and dedication to family—in certain ECSC plants.

with so much more ardour than is true of organised business. The efforts to use ECSC institutions for this purpose—partly unsuccessful though they have been so far—provide an instructive illustration of this process.

One obvious approach is offered by the opportunity to transfer legislative lobbying to the supranational forum of the Common Assembly. The free unions have not been slow to attempt this manoeuvre by organising repeatedly joint consultations with Socialist members of the Assembly in the effort to persuade them to offer resolutions meeting labour demands for housing, re-adaptation and harmonisation benefits. Yet, as both parties freely admit, these efforts have been somewhat less than successful because the legislators are far more interested in a planned economic policy looking towards public cartels, price controls, investment co-ordination and counter-cyclical measures. The trade unionists, by contrast, tended to echo to economic fears of their national employer associations and found great difficulty in agreeing with one another on basic economic policy questions. Hence they insisted merely on the demands traditional to organised labour: improvement in wages, hours, and working conditions, in the ECSC case through " harmonisation in an upward direction." This is the essence of the cry for a supranational welfare policy, endorsed in generalities by the parliamentarians but not in detail. As for the Christian unions, their natural political tie to Christian-Democratic Assembly members is somewhat less than meaningful because of the severe ideological schisms in that group with respect to labour questions. Hence legislative access has not yielded far-reaching endorsement of the Christian Federation's demands.

Labour equality has been pressed vigorously in relations with the High Authority. In 1953, the Committee of Twenty-One asked Monnet to create a labour secretariat in the High Authority to serve as a research agency for the unions and to be staffed with loyal trade unionists! Undaunted by Monnet's refusal, the Committee insisted that the High Authority use its facilities to give labour statistical information on costs and earnings of firms under ECSC jurisdiction in order to improve union bargaining positions at the national level. Repeatedly the cry went up that without such help, the unions could not make meaningful supra-national decisions. Seeking to compensate for weakness and isolation at the national level, the Committee and the Federation continuously press the High Authority for admission to all technical expert committees created to study ECSC problems, a task in which they have largely succeeded. More significantly still, the trade unionists argue that it is the duty of the High Authority to compel employers to bargain supranationally, or at least to submit to High Authority directives on labour questions, because increasingly, national firms and trade associations evade relations with their workers at the national level by referring to the existence of supranational rules and authorities. In line with the trade union tradition common in Europe of relying on government action rather than on direct relations with employers, the unions maintain in effect that it is the duty of the High Authority to meet this challenge by imposing—with union participation—a supranational labour policy.

Most significant in this effort is the conception of both labour groups that MM. Finet and Potthoff are " union men," who ought to be responsive to union demands in their capacity as members of the High Authority. As Arthur Gailly, chairman of the Committee of Twenty-One, insisted—

> The labour movement saw in ECSC the opportunity to introduce orderly economic relations in place of anarchy, disorder and speculation, to create a large common market, to eliminate the harmful consequences of uncontrolled competition, to stop crises, unemployment . . . , to lower prices, to raise the living standards of workers . . . , to harmonise working conditions in the six member states . . . , to plan investments. . . . Our demands, our noblest aims, even the reasons which persuaded us to participate in this work do not seem to occupy the role in the work of the High Authority which they deserve.[12]

While constantly seeking a special position and special protection from the High Authority, disappointment with the results prompted Walter Freitag, former head of the DGB, to assert that " we must show a certain distrust with respect to the High Authority. . . . We must not accept as clearly established everything the High Authority maintains." But he followed up this expression of non-confidence by again demanding that Luxembourg furnish the statistical studies which alone would enable labour to bargain effectively.[13]

[12] *Report, op. cit.*, p. 6.
[13] *Ibid.*, pp. 109–110.

To such accusations and demands, Finet and Potthoff reply that while Europe requires a unified labour movement to oppose cartels and restrictively minded employers organisations, the ECSC Treaty does not permit a stringent labour policy. While calling on labour to federate and put forward common demands, they resolutely refuse to bind themselves to the implementation of claims going beyond the Treaty. Yet it was Finet who sought to persuade the Committee of Twenty-One to accept a liberal ECSC migration policy, only to find himself opposed and isolated by French, German and Belgian unionists determined to limit the inflow of Italian labour. Offers by Finet to aid in the establishment of national or regional consultative committees giving the unions greater local representation were greeted coolly by his " colleagues." In short, the drive to use " their " candidates on the High Authority as a channel of permanent and successful access to supranational control has been a failure. As Finet explained:

> I have often expressed the thought that we need a welfare policy to compel the economic sector to adapt to social needs; we [trade unions] must be the midwives who, with forceps and if need be prematurely, will bring about the birth of extensive social reforms. But do not expect this of the High Authority. It can only help you.[14]

Union disappointment with High Authority energy led to a joint ICFTU-ICCTU threat to boycott the Consultative Committee in the autumn of 1955. Delays over the implementation of the resolution to harmonise fringe benefits, inconclusive and vague discussion over the welfare measures that should accompany a systematic coal policy and the definition of general objectives for ECSC, persuaded the labour members of the Committee to demand of the High Authority a list of pressing social problems with indications of priorities and means for solving them. The successful effort of President Mayer and of the employer members to evade this demand, resulted in threats of withdrawal.[15] The Consultative Committee, all but ignored by the business representatives, by

---

[14] *Report, op. cit.*, p. 86. Other revealing statements on pp. 9–11, 13, 15, 75–77, 80–85. Significantly, the Committee of Twenty-One in 1955 supported the candidacy of Paul Ramadier for the vacancy created by Monnet's resignation, despite his known anti-European sentiments. The Committee merely wished for another Socialist on the High Authority.

[15] Details in ICFTU, Verbindungsbüro-Luxembourg, *Mitteilungsblatt*, October–December, 1955, pp. 7–10. The boycott threat, took the form of a letter from Walter Freitag to René Mayer, announcing the intention of the seventeen labour members to withdraw from the Committee.

1955 had become the major arena for labour in its fight for recognition and respectability. Supranational institutions and rules, possibilities of access not available nationally, and a set of common fears facilitated the emergence of a doctrinaire minimum labour programme, for whose realisation the Consultative Committee and supranational union organisations became the primary vehicle.

Extent of Labour Consensus in ECSC

It took the unions three years to minimise their attempts to " penetrate " the High Authority and to rely instead on their own collective power in the Consultative Committee and other commissions. But given the differing national economic viewpoints functioning side by side with the agreed basic principles to which both the Christian Federation and the Committee of Twenty-One owe their origin, how deep is the ECSC labour consensus? To what extent has the collective need taken on priority over national differences? To what extent has the necessity of supranational lobbying forced a compromise among divergent national orientations? If a blunting of national differences has occurred, does the pattern of consensus include a positive ideology uniting the trade unions of the six countries more firmly than is true of the Internationals?

André Renard, the champion of an integrated ECSC–wide trade union movement possessing a clear and doctrinaire programme, admits that the unions find it far easier to agree to immediate welfare objectives than to achieve a meeting of the minds on economic policy. While he stands strongly for a union commitment to High Authority planning as regards investments, buffer stocks, trade with third countries and price stability, the early work of the Committee of Twenty-One did not encourage the conclusion that unity had been achieved in this field. Thus the Belgian miners demanded ECSC–wide wage equalisation, *i.e.*, raise mining costs in Holland and Germany to the Belgian level; Dutch Socialist labour was concerned primarily with the elimination of cartels and price ceilings. French labour argued the need for " equalising " social security contributions. The German miners held out for the continuation of cartel-like bodies for coal and for rigid price controls; only the German metalworkers evinced more interest in the kind of general economic planning advocated by Renard. Italian labour, by contrast, is almost exclusively concerned with alleviating structural unemployment and hence " doubts the good faith of other [labour] organisations with respect to the easing of labour migration " in ECSC.[16]

Experience shows that in order to bind the national unions to a common position in the Consultative Committee, a preliminary vote of the Committee of Twenty-One must be unanimous. On most crucial ECSC issues, no unanimity could ever be obtained. On scrap policy, only the French and German unions came out in full support of stringent High Authority regulation of the market. When the Monnet Rebate was taken up, the German unions showed more concern about the competitive position of German steel than about ECSC, whereas the Belgians advocated the protection of consuming industries and the need for rigorous High Authority controls over pricing practices. Coal price ceilings, for labour as for industry, provide the crucial index of consensus. The French and Dutch unionists regularly voted against ceilings and for higher Ruhr prices, while the bulk of the labour delegation voted in favour of ceilings. In 1955, a unanimous union statement attacking the logic of the High Authority in tying coal prices to wage increases was indeed made; but in the Committee of Twenty-One the German members sought in vain to persuade the bulk of the others to the indefinite need for price ceilings and price regulation of the collieries, linked to the preservation of GEORG. Coal prices and the intimately related issue of cartels pose a typical " economic " issue on which the unions find it so difficult to agree.[17]

It follows that no supranational labour position on cartels, investments, long-range price trends, labour mobility and even social security had been worked out in the ranks of the ICFTU–affiliated organisations by 1956. Sporadic efforts at promoting studies by unionists expert in these matters have led to little. Unanimous or near-unanimous votes occur neither in the Committee of Twenty-One nor in the Consultative Committee. The

[16] *Report, op. cit.*, p. 125: Statement of A. Chiari to his colleagues on the Committee of Twenty-One during the pioneering union conference of March 1954. The opinions summarised above were all expressed at the same meeting as well as in subsequent discussions of the Committee. The vigorous advocacy of a common Socialist economic—as opposed to labour welfare—policy was made on behalf of I. G. Metall by Heinrich Deist, who is primarily a Socialist politician rather than a trade unionist. His appeal found little support. *Report, op. cit.*, pp. 60–66.
[17] The bulk of my information was obtained through access to internal papers and documents of the Committee of Twenty-One. A part of the story is told in ICFTU, *Mitteilungen*, May 1955.

definition of interests based on a perception of *national* economic needs continued to prevail through 1956, bolstered by a *de facto* unanimity rule in labour's consultative organ.

Has there been no evolution of consensus over time, given the common fears of Socialist labour? The activities of three major trade union conferences—1954, 1955, 1956—should provide an answer.

In 1954, labour's defensive posture and commonly shared fears provided the bedrock of supranational agreement, bolstered by previous decades of similar sentiments inspiring the Internationals and the labour delegations to the ILO: economic progress, higher productivity, lower prices and increased consumption could not and should not be achieved on the basis of differentials in labour costs. While not necessarily attacking frontally the logic of a competitive common market, the anti-trade bias of the unions was sufficiently pervasive to cause them to insist that market inter-penetration and specialisation should not be permitted to develop in ECSC on the basis of significant structural employment dis-placement. The consensus could thus logically hinge around one single significant point: the harmonisation of living and working conditions throughout ECSC so as to avoid production, trade and employment shifts due to labour cost differentials. It was on the harmonisation issue that the Socialist unions agreed to a detailed programme in their 1954 conference. On all other ECSC issues—especially on investment, price and cartel policy—they managed merely to announce general platitudes, sufficiently vague to cover effectively the outstanding differences between national organisations.[18]

Events compelled the Socialist as well as the Christian unions to take a more specific position in mid-1955, as the six Governments were launching their " New Start." The Internationals announced their strong endorsement of accelerated economic integration, which we discussed above. In a trade union, Socialist and left-wing Christian-Democratic meeting at Strasbourg, Alfred Williame for ICCTU and Arthur Gailly for ICFTU proclaimed that the Europe of the *Relance* would be a workers' Europe, dedicated to peace and increasing welfare on the basis of planning, and made vital to labour through the medium of ECSC–wide collective bargaining. " We shall be the vanguard of those who today fight

[18] *Report, op. cit.*, pp. 173–176 for the resolutions adopted at the March 1954 meeting.

for a new Europe, Democratic and Socialist." [19]   While Guy Mollet added a demand for a European guaranteed annual wage, the 1955 meeting nevertheless refused to proclaim any detailed scheme for an anti-capitalist united Europe. Apart from echoing the general sentiments of the Internationals, the hard core of consensus continued to be the demand for harmonisation of working and living conditions.

By 1956, an important change was manifested in the deliberations of ECSC labour.   ECSC–wide collective bargaining under the auspices of the High Authority was thrown into specific relief by the unanimous demand for the introduction of the forty-hour week.   While the unions agreed to push their separate claims at the national level, they also agreed to co-ordinate their programmes supranationally and to insist on the High Authority's compelling the employers to do likewise.   But for the first time, the consensus on welfare questions began to " spill over " into the realm of general economic policy to a much more meaningful degree than had been possible in previous conferences and meetings of the Committee of Twenty-One.   Full employment, counter-cyclical investment and production planning and price control were demanded; the High Authority was called upon to make full use of its powers to steer investments and the unions for the first time evinced a collective interest in the control of mergers.[20]   The logic of spill-over process, in the context of labour's defensive economic and social complex, has given rise to the evolution of a consensus much broader than had obtained in 1951.   It is therefore symbolic of the deeper consensus and indicative of the reality of the spill-over process that the Committee of Twenty-One, before the debut of EEC, took the initiative in co-ordinating trade union positions and proposing a labour policy for the General Common Market. FO's Robert Bothereau was given the mandate as spokesman for the Committee in the work of the EEC Interim Organisation.

In the case of the mineworkers, the defensive ideological posture assumed by collieries all over Europe has been imitated by the unions.   While on general economic policy questions the workers differ with each other on national grounds, coal issues in particular have given rise to the same kind of supranational defence complex

[19] European trade union conference, held at Strasbourg on June 21, 1955.   *Gauche Européenne*, " L'Europe en construction," July/August 1955.
[20] Trade Union Conference, held in Paris on May 24, 25 and 26, 1956.   *Informations Mensuelles* (May 1956), pp. 26–27, 42, for the final resolutions.

of which CEPCEO is the institutional result on the employer side. Because the future of coal as a primary source of energy is doubtful, the miners insist that they retain the ECSC–wide position of the highest paid worker *regardless* of productivity increases in other sectors and relative rigidity in coal. They deplore the shortage of skilled young miners but object loudly that a manpower deficit be invoked as the justification for higher wages, since this might imply lower wages once the supply increases. Like their employers, they object to dependence on imported coal and agree that the special hazards and rising costs of mining be borne by the " collectivity "—the nation or ECSC—and not by the industry. Not readaptation to new jobs, but stability of employment as miners is their fundamental demand. Characterised by the same inflexibility and insecurity as the collieries, the mineworkers have embraced supranational dirigisme as the remedy for their troubles, without necessarily being any better " Europeans " in principle than the unions generally.

In the Christian Federation, consensus evolved earlier and penetrated more deeply. Like the Socialists, the Christian workers found more in common on the question of harmonisation than on issues of fundamental economic alternatives.[21] The greater supranational *élan* of the Christians makes itself felt in their political demands, in their insistence on an expanded task for ECSC in 1954, their endorsement of a federally organised Euratom and common market in 1955, and their much more insistent clamour for European—not national—trade union representation in the conferences drafting the treaties and the institutions appointed to implement them. Christian corporative doctrine is probably the single most important reason explaining this claim. Already put forward at the national level, it is but the natural extension of the doctrine to the supranational realm once the possibility of regionally controlling economic institutions is provided.

[21] Fédération des Syndicats Chrétiens dans la CECA, Resolution adopted on September 3, 1955. Confédération Internationale des Syndicats Chrétiens, " Manifeste Européen," September 14, 1955; " Note Concernant les Décisions de la Conférence de Messine." In these documents, the Christian unions established a programme for the institutional and economic unification of Europe which, even though in full harmony with the parallel programme of the ICFTU, goes much beyond the consensus announced by the free unions in 1955. Detailed proposals for the pace, degree, and control of economic integration are made, which are in large measure identical with the actual content of the Euratom and General Common Market Treaties, even though ICCTU representatives were not admitted to the negotiations.

Thus, five years of common market, the determination to integrate further and the " New Start " have combined to persuade trade unionists beginning primarily with a common defensive posture, to deepen their consensus and to make serious efforts to arrive at supranational political and economic positions going far beyond the parallel efforts of employers.   But the centre of the effort remains the desire to minimise the anti-labour competitive consequences of the common market and to counter what is, in labour's ideology, a " capitalist conspiracy " to run the integrated Europe of the future.   Programmatically, therefore, the harmonisation of living and working conditions has remained the symbolic and tactical centre around which union activity has clustered, as represented in ECSC by the efforts of André Renard to persuade his colleagues, the High Authority and ultimately the employers to bargain collectively for the equalisation of fringe benefits.

THE RENARD PROGRAMME IN ECSC

The almost incredible complexity of the " harmonisation " aim is revealed by a rapid survey over the various national rules in force and the fragmentary character of existing international agreements.   Thus in the realm of social security, no uniform rules governing the rights of aliens existed before 1957.   Some ECSC countries base their system on the principle of territoriality, while others prefer the rival principle of personality of rights.   Reciprocal rights to non-discriminatory treatment of alien workers are neither clear nor uniform, while the rate structure, of course, varies from country to country.   A network of bilateral conventions has grown up since 1945 to deal with this jungle, but it has tended to multiply the heterogeneity.   Nor have efforts at the conclusion of multilateral conventions " harmonising " the bilateral efforts brought much order.   One such attempt, the Social Security Convention (1949) of the Brussels Treaty Organisation, does not include Germany and Italy.   Another, Convention no. 102 of the ILO seeking to standardise the basic norms of social security systems, has not been ratified by most of the ECSC member states and is too general in its provisions to be of much help in the European context.   Attempts by the Council of Europe to write a European social security code have not yet been completed, and go beyond the confines of ECSC in any event.   Only the 1950 Convention on social security rights of Rhine bargemen cuts across the confusion somewhat by establishing absolutely equal rights and rates in all categories of security for all workers concerned, regardless of nationality, as well as providing a central administrative system for the implementation of the rules.[22]

ECSC efforts to give meaning to the right of qualified workers to migrate through the conclusion of an adequate general social security agreement have been inspired by the Rhine example. All forms of aid are included, even the controversial family allowances. Granting that absolute harmonisation of rates would be unachievable, the High Authority, Council of Ministers and the ILO have agreed to provide for the creation of a supranational compensation fund, to indemnify a national ministry for net losses suffered in payments to aliens, and a central administrative system. The vicissitudes surrounding the negotiation of this agreement have been related elsewhere.[22a] Suffice it to say here that not even the stimulus of the common market proved able to persuade the member governments to agree to standard rates in the various categories of aid. National structures remain intact; the harmonisation effort desired by the trade unions has merely standardised the rights of aliens. Significantly, however, a system originally intended for coal and steel workers was made general in the process of negotiation, as the ILO experts found that a special coal/steel system would be administratively unworkable.[23]

Varying family allowance systems have not only plagued the conclusion of a social security convention for ECSC, but constitute the hard core of the more basic demand for the " harmonisation " of living conditions. The difficulty is obvious from these statistics, representing the compulsory contribution of employers to national family allowance funds, expressed as a percentage of wages paid [24]:

Germany	none
France.................	16·75
Belgium	7·5
Netherlands	4·25
Luxembourg	4·5
Italy...................	11·65

[22] Details on these conventions and their implications are in Delpérée, *op. cit.*, pp. 164–170, 173–175, 182–188. Schregle, *op. cit.*

[22a] See Chapters 3 and 13.

[23] Details in Delpérée, *op. cit.*, pp. 177–180.

[24] Wilhelm Langwieler, *Die Sozialpolitische Problematik der Montanunion*, (Frankfurt: Verlag Lutzeyers Fortsetzungswerke, 1953), p. 46.

Variations in wage and fringe benefits enjoyed by ECSC labour are most clearly demonstrated by these tables:

TABLE 1

Steel Industry: Comparative Wage and Working Conditions

	Germany	Belgium	France	Saar	Italy	Luxembourg	Netherlands
Hourly direct wages and bonuses*	·67	·76	·66	·68	·50	·84	·55
Hourly social security and related benefits paid by employer*	·17	·13	·23	·23	·19	·18	·19
Workingtime hours, per day per week†	8 42-45	8 45	40–42	8 48	8 48‡	8 48	8·30 48
Overtime pay rate, applicable thereafter†	25%– 150%	25%– 100%	25%– 100%	25%– 100%	20%– 75%	30%– 100%	25%– 200%
Paid holidays per year†	11	10	7–12	6	16	10	6
Paid vacations, basic rate, days per year†	12–18	30	12	12	23	24–34	15

* High Authority, *Informations Statistiques*, Vol. 3, no. 4 (July–August 1956), p. 5. National currencies converted into U.S. dollars at the official rate of exchange.

† Information taken from Wilhelm Langwieler, *Die Sozialpolitische Problematik der Montanunion* (Frankfurt: Lutzeyers Fortsetzungswerke, 1953), Chart 2, as corrected by increases reported in High Authority, *Fifth General Report* (April 1957), pp. 191–194.

‡ Fiat introduced an average 43-hour week in 1956.

TABLE 2

Mining Industry: Comparative Wage and Working Conditions

	Germany	Belgium	France	Saar	Italy	Luxembourg	Netherlands
Hourly direct wages and bonuses*	·73	·71	·77	·76	·38	·99	·57
Hourly social security and related benefits paid by employer*	·20	·16	·28	·31	·17	·31	·22
Workingtime hours, per day	7·30	8	7·45	7·45	8	8	8
per week†	45	45	38·40	38·40	48	48	46
Overtime pay rate applicable thereafter†	25%	25%	25%	25%	22%	30%	25%
Paid holidays per year†	11	10	7	7	16	10	9
Paid vacations, days per year, basic rate†	12–21	30	12	15	23	24–34	12–20

* High Authority, *Informations Statistiques*, Vol. 3, no. 4 (July–August 1956), p. 5. National currencies converted into U.S. dollars at the official rate of exchange. Coal mines used for all countries except Luxembourg, where ore mines were used instead.

† Information taken from Wilhelm Langwieler, *Die Sozialpolitische Problematik der Montanunion op. cit.*, Chart 1, as corrected by increases reported in High Authority, *Fifth General Report* (April 1957), pp. 191–194.

Wage increases obtained in 1956–1957 do not substantially change this comparative picture. Expressed in percentages of the previously applicable base pay, the increases were distributed as follows:

TABLE 3

Basic Wage Increases, 1956–1957*

	Germany	Belgium	France	Saar	Italy	Luxembourg	Netherlands
Coal/Ore	6†	10	3	8†	—	4·5	6†
Steel	4	5	—	—	4	4·5	6

* High Authority, *Fifth General Report* (April 1957), pp. 198–200.
† Exclusive of certain special bonuses paid to certain types of miners. While a comparison of working time, paid holidays and paid vacations applicable in 1953 with the standards prevailing in 1957 shows a certain tendency toward harmonisation even in the absence of formal measures to achieve it, no such trend is apparent from a comparison of wage statistics. The differentials in the percentage increases scored have not resulted in closing the gap between national standards. In mining they still range from 38 cents (U.S.) per hour in Italy to $1·05 (U.S.) per hour in Luxembourg; among steelworkers Italy's low of 52 cents compares with 88 cents in Luxembourg and 80 cents in Belgium.

On the basis of these differentials, a united trade union movement could claim the highest benefits in each category as the norm which ought to govern the ECSC-wide level of wages and working conditions. German labour could claim the French family allowance rates, the forty-hour week as well as various tax refunds. French workers, by contrast, might demand the higher basic Belgian and Luxembourg hourly wage, more paid holidays and an unemployment insurance system. The opportunities for new claims on the basis of benefits enjoyed by the neighbouring country's workingmen are almost unlimited, and all can neatly be subsumed under the ECSC formula of "harmonisation of working and living conditions." The same is even more true under the treaty establishing the General Common Market.[25]

Independently of the harmonisation rationale of ECSC, the unions had carried on an international campaign for the reduction of the working week ever since the Great Depression, not only to

[25] *Ibid.*, pp. 62–63.

minimise overproduction and unemployment, but also for fundamental reasons of social welfare and leisure time. Yet an ILO-
forty-hour convention was fully implemented only in France, and
even there the real working week tended to run between forty-six
and fifty-six hours, with overtime pay for the time worked beyond
forty hours. Employers everywhere opposed reduction of the
working week and the Dutch, as well as the German, unions were so
absorbed in the reconstruction ideology of their nations as not
to be interested in the forty-hour week struggle. By 1950, however,
the claim of the Belgian unions for a reduction of the working week
had reached crescendo proportions. But the effort, sparked by the
Christian unions in particular, was met by the uniform employer
answer that a unilateral Belgian reduction would do irreparable
harm to the competitive position of Belgian industry on world
markets. Harmonised international measures were therefore
necessary in order to make possible national Belgian reforms.
After 1954, the Socialist-Liberal Government in Brussels took
a similar position. While it used its influence to bring about the
introduction of the forty-five-hour week in the Belgian steel industry,
it accompanied this step with the request for similar measures in
all ECSC countries.

The Belgian national scene thus compelled a spill-over of the
working week issue into the supranational scene, while parallel
efforts in the ILO were defeated. In February of 1955, the CSC
presented a petition signed by 573,000 persons to the ILO European
Regional Conference requesting the uniform introduction of the
forty-hour week. Yet the Conference voted the proposal down,
with the FGTB and DGB delegates joining business and government representatives in the negative majority.[26] ECSC thus
remained the only non-national forum promising some kind of
general formula. Hence it was no accident that Belgium's André
Renard took the initiative in using the Consultative Committee,
the High Authority, as well as the Committee of Twenty-One in

---

[26] Fédération des Syndicats Chrétiens dans la CECA, " Les Syndicats Chrétiens
et la diminution de la durée de travail " (Luxembourg, October 10, 1955). In
the same month, the international nature of the effort was underlined once more
by resolutions demanding the introduction of the forty-hour week, adopted by
both the International Federation of Miners (ICFTU) and the International
Federation of Metalworkers (ICFTU). DGB and FGTB voted against the resolution because it tied increases in productivity to the reduction of the working
week.

an effort not only to reduce the working week, but to harmonise all benefits other than wages.

Renard had the initial support of the Christian Federation, and of the ICFTU-affiliated unions in high-cost countries: France, Belgium, Luxembourg. The Dutch unions were less than enthusiastic but offered no opposition. Because of drastically different production conditions, the Italian unions were not directly interested in the effort, leaving the DGB—the most powerful Continental labour organisation—as the crucial lukewarm factor. Until the beginning of 1955, the Germans resisted harmonisation efforts because they were more concerned with reconstruction and co-determination than with welfare policies; furthermore, they felt confident of their own bargaining strength in Germany, having no wish to tie themselves down by acting as the protector of weaker unions in ECSC. The initiation of the Renard programme, however, coincided with a period of reappraisal for the DGB, resulting in a return to militancy. The rank-and-file was growing restive; apathetic toward the political issue of co-determination, it sought higher benefits as the German economy fully recovered and as prices began to increase. Confronted also with a dissident Catholic movement in its midst, the DGB leadership realised that it was time to " produce " for its followers. The response was the general demand for the introduction of the forty-hour week, now neatly tied to the already formulated and parallel claim of the other ECSC unions, and merged with the overall programme of harmonising all fringe benefits. Supranational organisation and the rules of the common market now made it easier to achieve a national demand without giving up a competitive advantage if wages and social security rules were left unaffected.

In the Consultative Committee session of December 1954, therefore, all labour delegates unanimously supported the Renard resolution enjoining the High Authority to undertake comparative statistical studies preparatory to the calling of supranational bipartite commissions of employers and labour with the task of harmonising the working week, vacations, overtime and holiday pay. Unlike the issues of prices, cartels and rebates on which the unions were split, the harmonisation issue demonstrated the area in which they were capable of joint action. While Renard and the Christian Federation made no secret of their desire to use the resolution merely as a first step in forcing permanent ECSC-wide collective bargaining, other unions—including the DGB — were not yet convinced of the desirability of this practice.[27]

A year of employer sabotage, an unco-operative and thoroughly unenthusiastic High Authority and a divided Council of Ministers produced increasing cohesion among the members of the Committee of Twenty-One, supported officially now by the Belgian Government. The Committee agreed to posit the ECSC-wide achievement of the forty-hour week as a central aim, even though national action was considered most effective for this purpose. It authorised its liaison bureau in October of 1955 to make specific proposals on how best to achieve the harmonisation of fringe benefits and demanded the immediate creation of bipartite commissions at the ECSC level to carry the demands of labour into the area of negotiation.[28] Pressure was also to be put on the Socialist members of the Common Assembly and on the Council of Ministers. As the Committee's newsletter argued:

> We should like to develop our thesis concerning the Treaty. Naturally it is not the thesis of outstanding jurists, but texts exist in order to be interpreted. The High Authority can act on labour questions *if it wants to. . . . Its jurisdiction over social issues is not a legal question but a political one. It is a problem of initiative and responsibility. . . .* Could not the High Authority, as it has done already, invoke the raising of productivity in order to justify a reduction of working time?[29]

This show of unanimity, punctuated by the threats discussed above, brought results. The Common Assembly debated and passed a resolution strongly backing the request to create bipartite commissions for collective bargaining purposes, even though in doing so it also talked of the harmonisation of wages which the DGB continued to oppose. Sufficient coolness toward the general use

---

[27] For the essence of Renard's reasoning and his programme, see Delpérée, *op. cit.*, p. 220, and *ECSC Bulletin* (January 1956), p. 2, as well as Chap. 6.

[28] Resolution of the Committee of Twenty-One, Frankfurt/Main, October 15, 1955. International Bund Freier Gewerkschaften—EGKS, *Mitteilungen*, October 17, 1955. Resolution of the Committee of Twenty-One, Brussels, November 19, 1955, IBFG–EGKS, *Mitteilungsblatt* (October–December, 1955), pp. 26–27. These resolutions were not adopted without some difficulty. Initially, the German members were quite cool toward Renard's proposal to take energetic action after the rebuff suffered in the Consultative Committee and countered the demand for the establishment of bipartite commissions with a request for an ECSC-wide twenty-four-hour strike, so unrealistic a suggestion as to be tantamount to opposing Renard. However, events in the Consultative Committee persuaded them to join their colleagues without reservation in fighting for the Renard formula.

[29] *Mitteilungsblatt, op. cit.*, pp. 1–3. Italics in original.

of supranational collective bargaining subsisted among the Socialist unions to persuade them to leave open the possibility of seeking government participation in future negotiations and to use ILO-type labour conventions rather than labour-management contracts. The Christian Federation, however, took a clear and emphatic position in favour of supranational labour contracts negotiated by employer-union teams. The High Authority speeded up the process of compiling comparative statistics on labour conditions and expressed its willingness to call bipartite commissions to Luxembourg to discuss the findings, without undertaking to compel these bodies actually to engage in collective bargaining.

When the commissions met early in 1957, it was the mineworkers who displayed the greater amount of supranational cohesion. Their demand for an ECSC–wide bill of rights for miners would in effect be a publicly-guaranteed contract providing equal benefits. Small wonder, then, that the collieries in an equally unanimous display of supranational solidarity, refused to bargain. Resentment in labour ranks was sufficiently strong to call for preparations to launch a twenty-four-hour ECSC–wide protest strike in order to compel the employers to bargain. Among the metalworkers, the Germans continued to display some uneasiness with respect to supranational contracts, especially since concurrent national negotiations were then underway. They were relieved when the commission agreed that future contracts should be concluded at the national level, though in conformity with the disparities in conditions revealed by the High Authority's survey. The Dutch unions were delighted to use the supranational meeting as a device for escaping their national price-wage straitjacket, whereas the remaining organisations took some comfort from the steel-makers' agreement in principle to harmonise fringe benefits, without gaining any additional bargaining strength in the national negotiations undertaken in 1957. Labour's consensus was sufficient to make meaningful the harmonisation formula to the extent that it enabled the unions to agree among themselves on details and to the extent that it compelled both the High Authority and the employers to take the first faltering steps toward ECSC–wide bargaining. But it is unlikely that labour will reap its full benefits from these developments until the General Common Market structure comes to grips with the principle of distortions.

DECISION-MAKING IN ECSC TRADE UNIONS

In 1950 and 1951, European trade unions were gripped by a fundamental ambivalence with respect to the common market: on the one hand they granted the principle of higher living standards through greater productivity and specialisation resulting from competition on a larger market; further, they saw in the creation of this system the possibility for introducing the regional welfare state which their international ideology dictated to them, and in strengthening their hand against communism. On the other hand, the fear of the consequences to labour of increased flexibility and competition was equally striking since it seemed to conjure up the picture of rapid industrial adjustments for which labour would pay the bill in the form of structural unemployment and lower wages. Continuous co-operation among unions and direct participation in supranational policy were thus essential operational consequences for labour even if the drive to achieve respectability and corporatist principles had not also manifested themselves.

Since, however, the national unions continued to disagree over the proper regional economic policies to be followed, the harmonisation of living and working conditions emerged as the minimum common denominator on which all could more or less agree, especially because of its tendency to take the anti-labour sting out of the common market. Only in 1956 did the tendency of achieving consensus on economic, as well as social, questions make itself manifest. And with the inauguration of this trend, a truly unified regional movement with its own ideology came into being, as proved by its overt espousal of the specific European doctrine of supranational planning represented by Monnet's Action Committee, of which the trade unions are the core.

What is labour's technique for making decisions? Decision-making must be analysed in order to find an explanation of why and how it was possible for this consensus to emerge. Certainly the prior existence of the Internationals provided a basic frame of reference and established channels of communication facilitating the creation of more restricted labour organs at the ECSC level. But the pattern of consensus in these Internationals is not such as to explain fully the emergence of a much more detailed and forceful central doctrine at the European level.

In the Committee of Twenty-One, the decision-making code hinges around the principle of tacit unanimity. Unions are not bound to common action unless they agree to the proposal before them. Once they agree, however, it is the general presumption that they will do nothing to violate the common position nationally or supranationally. Going back on agreement once reached is considered a betrayal of working class solidarity. Thus, diplomatic negotiation of a particularly intensive and sustained variety dominates the decision-making code; but the observance of agreement is assured by the pre-existence of commonly shared anti-capitalist values. It was on the basis of this thought pattern that the Italian unions chose not to make an issue of the opposition to free labour migration expressed by their colleagues. It enabled the French to call on the German unionists not to insist indefinitely on an ICFTU endorsement of the German cartel doctrine in ECSC.

The interplay of negotiations based on national union strength and of the appeal to labour's internationally shared values and fears is especially strikingly illustrated by the Committee's progress in agreeing to the harmonisation of fringe benefits through ECSC–wide collective bargaining. The German unions, because of their numerical strength, tight organisation and financial resources, in effect wield a veto power in the Committee. Commitment to a joint programme without their consent is impossible. Further, it was they who entertained the greatest degree of reservation toward the Renard programme because of the fear of diluting their national strength by acting as the protector of the French and Italian unions. Yet they did eventually agree to the harmonisation effort and it was Freitag's blustering which was instrumental in persuading the High Authority to interest itself actively in the programme. Apart from the change in internal German conditions, the appeals used by Renard proved to be irresistible in terms of labour's code.

In the first place, the Belgian leader's commitment is to a federally organised welfare-oriented Europe, based on supranational trade union federations. While he never hides this conviction, he also urged upon his colleagues the opportunity to extract specific pro-labour benefits from European unity:

> How did we succeed in obtaining the agreement of our union congresses to the ECSC Treaty? By telling them that ... if we create a common market, we shall obtain almost automatically other living standards, better working conditions and better wages.[30]

[30] *Report, op. cit.,* p. 87.

Further, he appealed equally to the primeval urge of European labour to protect itself against any kind of structural change implying unemployment. With respect to trade union participation in the High Authority's investment programme, he urged:

> We believe that as representatives of the working class . . . we have the right to participate in the distribution of [financial] means which will assure our jobs and those of our children.[31]

The recalcitrance of the German unionists to agree to supranational collective bargaining he met with references to working class solidarity and taunts of " nationalism." Continual emphasis over a three-year period on the economic benefits of a common market mingled with the necessity of protecting labour's share of the profits by setting minimum supranational standards and assuring readaptation benefits *without* compelling a change in trade or residence resulted in the consensus patent by 1956. The formula includes, in addition to the internationally shared values preceding the establishment of ECSC, a commitment not to block supranational action indefinitely, to negotiate " in the working class spirit " until agreement is reached and not to hold out for purely national positions, even though the effort is constantly made to introduce them into the deliberations. Because of this formula, the reluctance of the German unions did not prove an insuperable obstacle to the evolution of a general consensus. But without the presence and the efforts of a Renard, it is unlikely that the consultation formula alone was a sufficient cause for successful integration. If it had not been for the separate but converging national aims of certain unions in using supranational activity for local advantages the appeals of Renard might have continued to fall on deaf ears.

In any event, the decision-making methods of the Committee of Twenty-One, even after five years of activity, remain centred on diplomatic negotiation among sovereign equals united by common values and led by a strongly motivated personality. It is otherwise in the Christian Federation. The Christians deliberately excluded the Trade Secretariats from their work because they considered these organisations as antiquated and worthless. Contrary to the Socialists, they admitted white-collar workers' unions on a footing of equality with metalworkers and miners. Finally, since the strength of the participating German unions is not out of

[31] *Ibid.*, p. 151.

proportion to the total membership, there is no problem of over-whelming influence of any one nationally organised *bloc.*

Nor is the majority voting rule in the Christian Federation merely a paper provision. While attempts are made here as in the Committee of Twenty-One to obtain unanimity, the effort is not always successful. Yet the dissident minority is bound to implement the disputed decision and consistently complies. Thus the CFTC unions opposed a proposal to extend automatic membership rights in locals to migrant workers from other ECSC countries. Con-fronted with a majority, however, the French gave way. The residual possibility of appeal to the ICCTU by a dissatisfied member organisation has never been used.

In large part this truly " federal " code of conduct is explained by the enormous powers ceded by the national unions to their supranational secretary-general. This official, subject to instructions issued at the infrequent meetings of the Federation's Executive Committee, has the right to bind the organisation and to act on its behalf. He enjoys patronage powers of some scope which he uses to persuade hesitant national organisations. Primarily these powers hinge around his right to make nominations for appointments to the myriad High Authority expert commissions as well as the Consultative Committee, a line of access much desired by national trade unionists. A threat to withhold such an appointment from a national miners' or metalworkers' federation has been a potent stimulant to joint action. Further, the secretary-general enjoys the facility of side-stepping national trade union federation bureau-cracies by establishing direct relations with the professional economic advisers of the unions, co-ordinating their recommendations and studies, and thereby facilitating the emergence of a unified doctrine at the leadership level. An informal brain trust is thus brought into being with which the secretary-general can successfully mani-pulate the Federation. Finally, the secretary-general acts as a single lobbyist on behalf of the whole Federation, with regular access both to the High Authority and to the secretariat of the Christian-Democratic group in the Common Assembly.

Labour and Ideological Supranationalism

It is too much to claim that all pre-existing national differences among unions have been blunted and that a supranational ideology has emerged purely in response to the challenge and the stimulus of the Community. Yet, patently, a far greater degree of ideological cohesion has been achieved by labour than is true of the trade associations now functioning as supranational entities for certain purposes. Their pattern of co-operation has been characterised as " tactical," committed only to a limited field of common action in which separate national perceptions of interest happen to converge, perhaps only temporarily. No sharing of fundamental values is implied in tactical co-operation; French, German and Dutch managerial ideologies, for instance, remain far apart. The only tentative departure from this limited pattern of unity is manifest in the ranks of businessmen dubious of their own future and determined to make use of supranationalism for purposes of collectively defending a position no longer considered tenable at the national level. The insecure and frightened are the first to grope for a programme and a body of symbols implying supranational group integration, provided their previous value commitment was not solely to the national state.

In the case of labour, the same tendency has led to a far more striking espousal of supranationalism, facilitated by the possession previously of a frame of reference going beyond the national state. But it must be stressed that despite Marxist emphasis on working class unity as a tactical principle derived from the " nature " of capitalism, fear is a far more convincing explanation of this phenomenon. And it was the same fear, immeasurably magnified by the direct potential of the common market in affecting employment stability, which gave rise to the bedrock of the ECSC labour consensus, the harmonisation of living and working conditions.

However, the beginnings of a fundamental agreement on economic questions supports the conclusion that labour has developed beyond the rationale of fear in its commitment to supranational economic integration. Unlike business groups—though not without reservations and hesitations—non-Communist labour had fought for ECSC from the beginning because of the commitment in principle to democratic economic planning over the widest possible geographic space. While this sentiment included a host of conflicting national aspirations in 1951 and did not prove capable of specific and programmatic definition until 1956, it nevertheless existed as a basic shared value, as did the commitment to gain access to policy-making organs closed to unionists at the national level.

Given the dominance of a welfare ideology looking to planning rather than to a free market, the unions have no alternative but to unite in seeking to influence supranational authorities, especially if these are tempted to follow a free market doctrine. The record of ECSC processes, in their impact on trade unions, supports the conclusion that economic identification with national trade associations is neither permanent nor irrevocable if alternative courses of action are opened up which correspond to basic shared values. Hence the evolution of a European regional labour ideology is a response to a mixture of internal and external stimuli, including internationally shared values of welfare planning, disappointment with the possibilities of purely national reform, and the conviction that only united action can result in bending the policy inclinations of supranational agencies in a pro-labour direction. But a pre-existing ambivalence toward the value to labour of the national state is clearly a necessary cause for the rapid supranational re-alignment which has taken place in Europe.

Labour's " ideological " supranationalism is likely to have consequences extending far beyond the harmonisation of overtime pay in the process of regional interest group formation. The battle over the Renard programme and the desire of many unions to achieve permanent ECSC-wide collective bargaining must work itself out in the direction of more organisational and ideological cohesion, tending to establish an ever closer *rapport* between Socialist and Christian unions, united in their fight against the Communist organisations. Indeed, successful supranational collective bargaining and the progressive harmonisation of wages and working conditions is regarded by many anti-Communist labour leaders as a trump for outbidding the past appeal of the CGT in France and the CGIL in Italy.

If the principles of group behaviour prevalent in national states characterised by democracy and pluralism are projected to an integrating region earmarked by the same features—and it is the thesis of this study that the processes implied in integration are merely a special expression of the logic of pluralism—it can be predicted that labour solidarity will compel an increasing measure of supranational unity among employers. The collieries cannot refuse to bargain indefinitely if the miners' unions launch co-ordinated strikes in France, Belgium and Germany; and once they consent to bargain, they are compelled by the situation to agree on common terms among themselves and thus perhaps evolve in the direction of fundamental common thinking. The steelmakers, having agreed to the principle of bargaining already, must sooner or later take a common regional position once the possibilities of better terms at the national level are exhausted for labour. In conformity with the logic of pluralism, which tends to lead toward the formation of countervailing aggregates of economic interests, freedom of organisation and bargaining in western Europe cannot but imply a " spill-over " of labour's solidarity into the ranks of the employers.

CHAPTER 11

SUPRANATIONAL POLITICAL PARTIES

BUSINESSMEN and organised workers adjusted to the growth of a limited federation in Europe by slowly restructuring their own ideas, demands and groups toward the Luxembourg focus; and in so doing they contributed decisively to the process of political integration itself, making possible in large part the private support for the inauguration of EEC and Euratom. But the institutional facilities and pressures provided by the ECSC Treaty, the High Authority, the Council of Ministers and the Court of Justice furnished an external compulsion to organised industry and labour to which these bodies merely reacted. Parliamentarians, however, are part of the institutions which shape the emerging European political community: they do not merely react to their stimulus. Parliamentarians in the Common Assembly are crucial actors on the stage of integration for two reasons. First, they deliberately and self-consciously seek to create a federal Europe by prescribing appropriate policy for the High Authority, by stressing their own latent " legislative " powers and by stimulating the conclusion of new treaties looking toward integration. In short, they are advocates and proponents of federation in their parliamentary activity.[1] Second, the parliamentarians in their conduct have the facility of furthering the growth of practices and codes of behaviour typical of federations quite apart from the specific advocacy of substantive federal measures. Alternatively, their conduct may be such as to negate the growth of the principles they advocate. It may be suggested at the outset of our discussion that the modes of conduct evolved by the Common Assembly are probably of greater significance in tracing processes of political integration than the specific measures proposed in it.

How can we assess this dual role? Our method employs an ideal type of federal parliamentary jurisdiction, organisation and

---

[1] The most important resolutions adopted by the Common Assembly were discussed in Chap. 3. Uniformly, they represent a greater commitment to further integration along federal lines and to a maximisation of the High Authority's directing role than has been found acceptable by the other institutions of ECSC. The present chapter will be concerned with decision-making and consensus in the Assembly rather than with formal quasi-legislative measures, and hence the resolutions will not be treated in detail.

party conduct against which the Common Assembly will be measured. This should permit the making of judgments of the degree of the federal constitutional nature of the ECSC organ and of the evolution over time of modes of conduct consistent with federalism and therefore contributing to integration. While the ideal type is abstract in the sense of not being inspired by a single actual system, it nevertheless reflects United States practices more closely than, for instance, West German or Australian. This choice was made deliberately because the validity of the comparison would suffer if the rigid national European parties were pitted against the diffuse—yet clearly federal—party system characteristic of the United States. Further, since legislative conduct in federations is demonstrably influenced by the presence or absence of a separation-of-powers rule in the constitution, ECSC more closely resembles the United States than the continental European or Australian pattern.

Federal Parliaments: An Ideal Type

Inherent in the supranational activities of European parliamentarians are a number of ambiguities which make the need for a fairly rigorous scheme even greater: many of them speak as if they were federal legislators without necessarily conducting themselves in the appropriate manner. Legally, the Council of Europe, the Common Assembly and the Assembly of WEU are not legislatures; their members, however, have been determined to make these organs into true parliaments quite irrespective of federalist or nationalist convictions. The mere fact that parliamentarians are called upon to exercise an equivocal " control " over some " executive " has impelled the overwhelming majority to speak in terms of federal legislative powers. A further ambiguity arises from the intense supranational activity in Europe of national political parties, suggesting the existence of formations acting as the precursors of federal parties, similar to the Federalists in the United States or the Labour Party in Australia, engaging in active value sharing before the formal act of federation. Such a picture is, however, extremely deceiving. It will be shown that the movements in question, far from functioning as parties, approximate the same kind of international diplomatic relations which we noted in the case of trade union Internationals. On the other hand, it is equally clear that they do function as centres of communication,

facilitating contacts and value sharing to a far greater extent than
is true of other modes of inter-parliamentary relations.

The Liberal Movement for a United Europe is clearly the most
diffuse of these groupings and undoubtedly the least effective in the
role of a precursor. It is made up of Liberal parties of all Council
of Europe members and thus not limited to ECSC. Its resolutions
have been confined to praising integration in general and in
supporting whatever official scheme seemed closest to implementation. In 1953 they supported EDC, in 1954 and 1955 WEU
found favour with them, and in 1956 they turned their attention
to the New Start, stressing especially those features of the Brussels
treaties which protected free trade, free enterprise and limited
potentially dirigistic powers of supranational agencies. While
unity is far from striking on matters of detail, consensus has clearly
developed in favour of a free-enterprise Europe equipped with
a minimum of central institutions.[2] Christian-Democrats have
displayed the greatest diversity on questions of detailed economic,
military and political steps: while easily agreeing on the need to
base the new Europe on " Christian social and economic principles," their concrete decisions have been confined to supporting
first EDC, then WEU and finally the common market and Euratom.[3] There can be no question of a specific Christian-Democratic
programme for a European federation. The parties, as in the case
of the Liberals, merely express their national convictions at the
international gatherings and finally agree on a compromise resolution covering all the various particularistic conceptions.

While the Socialists also express their national positions, the
greater identity of underlying ideological commitment in their
case has made possible a far greater supranational consensus, as
expressed in the work of their Movement for the United States of
Europe. In 1953, the Movement espoused EDC and EPC, only
on the condition that democratic parliamentary control over the
agencies would be complete, and even that failed to persuade the
SPD to align with other Socialist parties. Never showing much

---

[2] For activities in 1954, see *Nouvelles de l'Europe*, December 1954, p. 26. The
resolution on the New Start is reprinted in *Informations Mensuelles*, April 1956,
pp. 63–64. Considerable detail in Heribert Krämer, *Die Stellung der politischen
Parteien in der Völkerkammer eines Künftigen Europaparlaments* (Dissertation,
Mainz, 1956), pp. 104-112.

[3] For the relevant resolutions and meetings of the Nouvelles Equipes Internationales,
see *Informations Bimensuelles*, Oct. 1, 1954, p. 26; October 1, 1955, pp. 41 *et seq*.
Krämer, *op. cit.*, pp. 112-122.

enthusiasm for WEU, the Movement in 1955 concentrated on expanding the powers of ECSC, stressing the need for economic integration through planning, business cycle control, full employment and working-class unity as a pro-European impulse. When the New Start got under way, the Socialist Movement endorsed only those proposals which would link the common market, atomic development and economic growth to planned measures of protecting the labouring population against drastic and rapid displacement. And for this purpose, the Socialists far more consistently than other groups stressed the need for federal executive and legislative institutions with planning powers independent of the national governments.[4] Their European programme is more than a vague compromise among national parties: it is a concrete scheme based on converging political needs and actively shared values, catapulting the Movement into the position of a " precursor opposition " to Liberal and Christian-Democratic pro-European sentiment.[5]

Since 1954 all European members of parliament interested in integration have been united in the Parliamentary Council of the European Movement. Certainly this organisation facilitates communication and contact among individuals and parties on a continuing basis, thus conceivably easing the birthpangs of a true European parliament. Yet on questions of programme and doctrine, the Council shows the same diversity as the constituent party movements. It has functioned as a medium of information and a forum for negotiation between national parties. It has not exercised the role of independent parliamentary agency catalysing further integration.[6] In fact, its advent followed rather than

[4] See 1954 Milan Congress of the Movement, *Agence Europe*, July 9, 1954. Decisions of June 18 and 19, 1955, in *Gauche Européenne*, July/August 1955. Decisions of October 1956 in *Informations Mensuelles*, January 1957, p. 12. Also Krämer, *op. cit.*, pp. 73-111.

[5] Among other European parties, opposition to integration is the dominant *motif*. The Communist position is well known; prior to 1955 it made use of the Cominform for co-ordinated anti-European policies in national parliaments. Parties of the extreme Right (Neo-Fascists, Poujadists, and " middle class " associations in other countries) have held sporadic international meetings, but their opposition to integration has given rise to no central institutions or programme.

[6] European parliamentary conferences were held in 1954 and 1956. The 1956 meeting was attended by 150 legislators, coming from fourteen Council of Europe member states. *Informations Mensuelles*, September/October 1956, pp. 50–53. The Conference was marked by the most insistent statements of national party positions by most major speakers, indicating continuing disagreement on the merits of the " Europe of the Six " as against that of the " Fifteen," economic *v.* political integration.

preceded the creation of the rudimentary European legislative institutions. In no case can the institutions, the party formations or the inter-parliamentary councils be considered as federal prototypes.

With the rejection of these actual institutions and formations as " international " rather than " federal," the way is cleared for stating the jurisdictional properties of our model federal parliament. Under a separation-of-powers rule, a federal parliament shares power with the executive over all spheres of activity placed under its control by the federal constitution. Over time, all federal parliaments have shown the tendency to extend their jurisdiction at the expense of the powers initially left with the federating states. Finally, in Continental Europe as in the United States, legislatures tend to assert themselves against a strong executive if that person or collegium displays evidence of preferring independent action.

An additional set of model criteria must be stated with respect to the form of organisation typical of a federal legislature. In principle, the method of state and/or popular representation in the legislature is fixed by federal law. While the representation of states on a basis of equality is common in the upper house, relative population strength guides the size of state delegations to the lower chamber. In the lower house, at least, the organisational principle is identification with the federation, not the mere representation of state interests. Further, the electoral machinery must be such as to result in the approximately fair representation of all local groups of adequate strength, *i.e.*, avoid the systematic exclusion of certain segments.[7] The legislature must be free to organise itself as it sees fit, appoint commissions, undertake investigations, request and obtain information from the executive as well as from citizens of the federation. Legislative decisions are made by simple majority vote. While absolute party solidarity certainly cannot be stipulated, it is urged that unless the voting pattern shows more solidarity on the basis of party than on the basis of regional or state identification, the " federal " nature of the legislature may well be in doubt. The same is true of votes

---

[7] Even in the United States, federal constitutional and statute law determines the composition of the Congress in principle, no matter how consistently it is ignored or violated in the states. Clearly, the southern practice of systematic discrimination against Negro voters is incompatible with our model.

in committee. Finally, the assembly is legally free to oppose the executive and to depose him (or them) by a majority vote.

The behaviour of the political parties active in the legislature provides the last and vital set of model criteria. These will be grouped as criteria relating to membership and cohesion, voting solidarity, control of the party and relations with the federal executive.[8]

Membership and Cohesion

A federation-wide political party, typically, is made up of strongly autonomous—if not independent—state and local units. The local rather than the central organisation tends to predominate. The federal party enjoys no direct contact with the citizen. It follows that locally defined conceptions of interest and value prevail within the party. This may be due to the easier sharing of values among individuals native to the same region—as in the American South, Bavaria, or Western Australia—as compared to the entire party; but it may equally well be due, as David B. Truman has shown, to the natural ease of communication among individuals coming from the same organisational context. The second explanation would seem particularly persuasive in the case of a state delegation which does not seem to differ in values from members of the same party originating elsewhere, but still displaying greater voting solidarity. Typically, some quasi-federal party formation has existed prior to the formal act of federation, again combining sharing of values with establishing channels of communication. In terms of internal cohesion, the federal party exhibits its greatest solidarity in the purely functional activity of nominating and electing federal officials. The same party may show considerable cleavages—reflecting local aims—with respect to solidarity in the election of local officials. In terms of ideological

---

[8] My treatment here owes much to the work of David B. Truman. See his " Federalism and the Party System," in Macmahon, *op. cit.*, pp. 115 *et seq.* Also his study of state party delegations in the U.S. Congress, which admits that while voting solidarity may well be attributable to ideological factors and issues, the organisational and communications advantage of the state unit makes itself felt consistently. Unfortunately, the study does not attempt an assessment of state bipartisan solidarity as against federal party solidarity. " The State Party Delegations and the Structure of Party Voting in the United States House of Representatives, " *American Political Science Review*, Vol. L, no. 4 (December 1956).

cohesion, most federal parties suffer from consistent internal strains and frequently are unable to arrive at any meaningful federal consensus.

Voting Solidarity

While members of the same party will certainly caucus consistently in the attempt to achieve voting solidarity, the principle of a binding party voting rule is not accepted. Consequently, party members are free in their possible desire to protect purely local constituency interests external to the party programme. Further, the prevalence of searing regional conflicts in the federation imposes the operational rule of avoiding voting showdowns in the federal party and to attempt the definition of a limited consensus by unceasing inter-regional negotiation and compromise within the party. This practice may approach the dimensions of diplomacy and may completely negate any specific federal programme.

Control of the Party

The programme of the party must nevertheless be a federal one, cutting across constituencies, state boundaries and regional lines. To merit the label of " federal," the party must be supported by and identified with groups enjoying federation-wide membership and interests. As far as the nomination of candidates is concerned, at least, some degree of subservience to the central organisation must exist. While the bulk of financial contributions may be locally subscribed for the benefit of the local organisation, a measure of federation-wide support not earmarked for local consumption ought to prevail. The central organisation itself may be as shadowy in its power as is true of American parties, but it must assert itself at least to that extent.

Relations with the Federal Executive

Normally, the majority party or coalition expects to select the federal executive and to be identified with it programmatically. The executive, furthermore, possesses some patronage with which to reward its supporters. The minority party, or parties, of course expect to form the opposition, carrying into the realm of legislative activity the disagreement over the selection of the executive. The usual fluidity between majority and minority status typical of the continental European multi-party system is thus assumed as part of normal parliamentary behaviour in our model federation.

JURISDICTION OF THE COMMON ASSEMBLY

The first principle of a federal legislature is clearly violated by the limited jurisdiction of the Common Assembly: the parliamentarians do *not* have the legal capacity to bind by majority vote the states from which they originate. Their only role in " legislating " for their home states resides in the possibility of participating in a revision of the Treaty.[9] Efforts to change this situation have included the anti-federal proposal of M. Maroger (France, Liberal) to charging the Assembly merely with a liaison role between the six national parliaments, as well as the clearly federal suggestion of Alain Poher (France, Chr.-Dem.) to make the Assembly the authorised representative of national parliaments, equipped with the right to receive petitions from national groups of all kinds, and able to deal directly with the spokesmen of the member states, the Council of Ministers.[10]

In any event, the routine activities of the Assembly focus around the " parliamentary control " of the High Authority. Here the absence of a true legislative power has led the members to interpret the " control " power as meaning " control in the sense of criticism . . . and direction, orientation. . . . It is a question of influence, supervision, conversations, questions, of an atmosphere to be created, etc. . . ."[11] In this sense, the total trend of Assembly assertion of jurisdiction has been extremely positive.

The struggle to achieve " parliamentary control " in the absence of true legislative powers has hinged around the triple issue of the budget of ECSC, the desire to compel the High Authority to consult the Assembly *before* undertaking new measures, and the effort to limit the role of the Council of Ministers. Naturally, these objectives were made difficult of achievement by the fact that the Treaty is more than silent on these matters. Budgetary control, under Article 78, is vested in a Commission of the Four

[9] Art. 95. This requires a three-quarters majority, representing two-thirds of the Assembly's total membership, an amending process more stringent than the rules governing constitutional amendment votes in the U.S. Congress.

[10] Jean Maroger, " L'evolution de l'Idée de supranationalité," *Politique Etrangère*, Vol. 21, no. 3, June 1956, pp. 299 *et seq*. Common Assembly, Exercise 1955–56, Doc. No. 2. " Rapport sur l'organisation à donner à L'Assemblée Commune . . .," par Alain Poher (Nov. 1955).

[11] Poher, *op. cit.*, p. 11.

Presidents and an independent Auditor; to compel the High Authority to a specific course of action requires the mobilisation of a two-thirds majority of *all* members for a censure motion; legally, the Council of Ministers is free from any organic relation with the parliamentarians.

The battle of the budget was joined early. In March of 1953, the Assembly made its first request of the High Authority to present all budget estimates for discussion before the final allocation. In more strident terms the demand was repeated in 1954, this time claiming the right to discuss the budgets of all ECSC institutions. In 1955, complaints were voiced that the High Authority had neglected to consult the Assembly for supplementary appropriations. Yet by 1956, Pierre Wigny (Belgium, Chr.-Dem.) could conclude with satisfaction that " the actions of [the Assembly's] Auditing and Administrative Commission, particularly in relation to the Commission of the Four Presidents, has proved the jurisdiction and the powers of the Assembly and has permitted it thus to exercise a much more real power, if not in law than in fact. The other institutions have accepted this gracefully." [12]

Parliamentarians of all nationalities and of all parties were one in insisting on the High Authority's submitting its plans to the confidential discussion of Assembly commissions before launching them. Unanimously the members have demanded full information from the High Authority and many objected to the invocation of the Treaty-sanctioned principle of " guarding trade secrets " when the executive was anxious to withhold information. They have made full use of their right to interpellation by posing written and oral questions, insisting on the presence of High Authority members in plenary and commission meetings, and in sending out Assembly investigating committees to look into unemployment in Italy and ore mining in Germany. Budgetary cuts or increases were advocated in accordance with individual and party preferences, thus in no way differing from standard practices in national parliaments. Irrespective of strict Treaty

[12] Vermeylen Report, Exercise 1952-53, Doc. No. 1 (March 1953); Kreyssig Report, Exercise 1954–55, Doc. No. 1 (November 1954). ECSC, Common Assembly, *Un témoignage sur la Communauté des Six*, by Pierre Wigny (Luxembourg, 1957), p. 43.

interpretation, the High Authority is treated as if it were a national cabinet responsible to parliament: the Assembly insists on introducing standard political issues and political principles of democratic accountability into the vagaries of supranational institutions. In Wigny's words:

> [The Assembly] will use all the rights which it is expressly given and, in addition, in case of doubt, it will seek solutions in the common parliamentary law and not in an unjustified comparison with non-sovereign international assemblies.[13]

Unlike the High Authority, the members of the Council of Ministers are individually responsible only to their national parliaments and collectively responsible to nobody. Sensing early that the Council may well be the real executive of ECSC, or at any rate a second executive body, federalists among the ECSC parliamentarians expressed apprehension about the Council's work and asserted the need to control it. But in view of the fact that no meaningful sanctions can be taken against the six ministers, such efforts required the voluntary co-operation of the Council. Since 1955, certain ministers have regularly attended Assembly meetings, contributed to the debate, answered questions, consented to appear at sessions of the commissions and received delegations of deputies. They have not, however, in a single instance deferred to the wishes of the Assembly or pretended regularly to consult the parliamentarians about future decisions. Only Belgium's Jean Rey, in a most significant development, has seen fit to appeal personally to the supranational parliament in his attempt to persuade his ministerial colleagues to the ECSC-wide harmonisation of working time rules. While the full Council for the first time attended an Assembly session in June of 1956, nothing was done about formally institutionalising these trends, even though such has been the demand of Assembly members. Contacts continue in an *ad hoc* fashion; the Council refuses to submit an annual report to the Assembly and its members have declined to consent to a definite schedule or plan of consultation.[14] The formal assertion of parliamentary jurisdiction has failed despite the growth of a custom of co-operation.

Far less unanimity has been apparent in a different area of the Assembly's struggle to increase its jurisdiction: the effort to extend

---

[13] *Ibid.*, p. 38.
[14] Poher Report, *op. cit.*, pp. 28–30.

the scope of European integration and thereby add to the Assembly's legislative role. One aspect of this struggle involved an assertion of direct legislative power over the High Authority. Stressed specially by the Socialists, and to a lesser extent by Christian-Democrats, the Assembly repeatedly urged the High Authority to make use of *all* the powers conferred upon it by the Treaty.[15] But the legal limitations on the Assembly's role were admitted, under constant complaints, by all members and the emphasis was therefore placed on the extension of integration. For the High Authority, many Assembly members demanded jurisdiction over all sources of classical energy, and many added atomic energy as well. Socialists and left-wing Christian-Democrats clamoured for the inclusion of welfare measures and for steps to control the business cycle. Others spoke in favour of putting all transport media under ECSC control, while the politically minded federalists sought to extend the impact of ECSC by providing for the direct election of Common Assembly members. These sentiments came to head in the resolution of December 1954, calling on the High Authority to extend its own task and creating a " Working Group " of Assembly members to make specific proposals for the intensification of European integration efforts.

The labours of this group fall into the general category of creating a federal Europe and go far beyond the scope of coal and steel. As such, they were merely the second step in a process which began in September of 1952 with the decision of the Council of Ministers to charge the Assembly with drafting a political constitution to include ECSC, EDC and political federation. In its efforts to draw up a constitution for the European Political Community, the Assembly—enlarged by nine members and rechristened " ad hoc Assembly "—in effect fulfilled the role of a constitutional Convention. The result of its labours was the still-born draft treaty for EPC, under which a federal government for coal, steel, defence, military production and procurement and the gradual

---

[15] The crystallisation of this drive is found in Common Assembly, Groupe de Travail, Sous-Commission des Compétences et Pouvoirs, Exercise 1955–56, Doc. No. 1, " Rapport sur (1) les mesures susceptibles d'assurer la pleine application des dispositions du Traité, sans modification de celui-ci; (2) l'extension des attributions de la Communauté, en matière de charbon et d'acier, nécessaires pour la pleine réalisation des objectifs assignés par le Traité," by Gerhard Kreyssig, October 1955. This report is a catalogue of unused or insufficiently used treaty provisions with guidelines for interpretations appropriate to permit an extension of jurisdiction.

economic unification of the " Six " was proposed. The draft, whose completion required the incredibly short period of six months (September, 1952–March, 1953), called for direct elections to the federal lower chamber, the creation of a federal executive strictly responsible to the legislature, and gave only truncated powers to a Council of National Ministers whose consent was to be required for any steps which might " spill over " into the unintegrated sectors.[16] The composition of the *ad hoc* Assembly and of the Constitutional Committee which prepared the actual draft is shown below:

TABLE 1

MEMBERSHIP OF THE AD HOC ASSEMBLY AND ITS CONSTITUTIONAL COMMITTEE[17]

	Germany		France		Saar		Italy		Belgium		Netherlands		Luxembourg		Total	
Christ.-Democ.	8	*4*	4	*1*	2	–	14	*4*	5	*2*	6	*2*	2	*1*	41	*14*
Socialists	8	–	4	*1*	1	*1*	6	*1*	4	*1*	3	*1*	1	–	27	*5*
Liberals	4	*2*	7	*2*	–	–	1	*1*	1	–	–	–	1	*1*	14	*6*
Unaffiliated	1	–	3	*1*	–	–	–	–	–	–	1	–	–	–	5	*1*
Totals	21	*6*	18	*5*	3	*1*	21	*6*	10	*3*	10	*3*	4	*2*	87	*26*

Clearly, the Christian-Democrats dominated the Committee out of all proportion to their real strength, a condition resulting from the boycott of the Assembly by the eight German Social Democrats who objected to the institutionalisation of EDC in EPC. The consequence was a final draft heavily weighted in a federalist direction, giving rise to considerable objections on the part of Socialists and Liberals. Already on the occasion of the Common Assembly's decision to create the ad hoc Assembly, the

[16] Ad Hoc Assembly, Secretariat of the Constitutional Committee, *Draft Treaty Embodying the Statute of the European Political Community* (Paris, 1953). For details of the fate of EPC, see Chap. 13 and, especially, Common Assembly, *Le développement de l'intégration économique de l'Europe*, Section I, " Analyse des Documents," Chap. 2, by Van der Goes Van Naters (Luxembourg, July 1955). This report relates in considerable detail how and why the draft treaty was subsequently sabotaged by the intergovernmental conference called to examine it. The Benelux delegations wished to give it a predominantly economic character by stressing the necessity of rapidly introducing a general common market through its institutions, whereupon the French Government dissociated itself from the whole effort and insisted on " reserving its entire freedom of action." Declarations of the Conference in 1954 refer only to the opinions of " the five delegations."
[17] *Ibid.*, pp. 167–175. The italicised figures refer to the Constitutional Committee.

French and Dutch Socialists had argued for an arrangement which would facilitate a federation of the " Fifteen," and not merely of the " Six." For the Gaullists, Michel Debré had unsuccessfully held out for a loose confederation instead of the tight federal union of the ECSC countries desired by the Christian-Democratic majority, a position supported by M. Struye (Belgium, Chr.-Dem.) and M. Maroger (France, Lib.). In general, therefore, it is vital to note that the Christian-Democrats acted as a united supranational majority, acting over the reservations of individual Liberals and of nationally defined Socialist clusters, notably the SFIO and the SPD.

During the drafting of the treaty these lines changed little. All Dutch delegates were united in opposing direct elections, and the Dutch and Belgians constituted national *blocs* in arguing for a maximum of economic integration immediately and the equality of small with large states in the representation formula adopted for the upper house. But these were the only instances in which nationality rather than supranational or particular national party positions determined the line-up. With one major exception, the Christian-Democratic inspired draft was accepted by the plenary Assembly; but by a vote of twenty-two to twenty-one it decided to cut down appreciably the powers initially worked out for the Council of National Ministers and strengthened the federal executive proportionately.

The Assembly accepted the amended draft by the seemingly overwhelming vote of fifty to nil, with five abstentions. One must add, however, the fact that thirty-one members were absent when the vote took place, at least fifteen of whom were known opponents of federation. Fatally and significantly, the combined abstainers and absenteeists included all German and French Socialists, two French Independent-Republicans, three French Gaullists, one Luxembourg Liberal, one Luxembourg Christian-Democrat, one Belgian Liberal and one Dutch Protestant, as well as M. Struye.[18]

---

[18] For details, see Forschungsstelle für Völkerrecht und ausländisches öffentliches Recht der Universität Hamburg, *Dokumente*, Heft X, " Die Europäische Politische Gemeinschaft " (Frankfurt, 1953), pp. 4–6. The absenteeists also included fourteen Italians who left early because of impending elections at home and the president of Belgian Christian-Social Party, M. Lefèvre. All these gentlemen were known supporters of the draft. The debates of the ad hoc Assembly are published separately. For the initial discussions of the Common Assembly, see *Débats*, compte rendu in extenso, opening session, 6th and 7th meetings, September 12, 1952, pp. 74–89, 93–104.

The record proves that by 1953 the federal logic of the Common Assembly had not succeeded in weaning two major Socialist parties away from their national programmes, while continuing to harbour within it strong pockets of national as opposed to party solidarity.

The Working Group appointed in December of 1954 took on the unenviable task of preparing the ground for further integration in the midst of the despair of " Europeans " and the anti-federal enthusiasm brought about by the defeat of EDC and EPC. But the Group acted, of course, without the slighest encouragement from either the governments or the High Authority. It issued no formal reports at first and confined itself to the advocacy of an expanded ECSC, drawing on its own tradition of urging the High Authority to make more courageous decisions in using coal and steel to bring about general economic unity.[19] The atmosphere changed dramatically, however, once the six governments committed themselves at Messina to the " New Start." From then on the Working Group, on behalf of the majority of the Assembly, regarded itself as the European parliamentary watchdog appointed to keep the government negotiators on the straight and narrow path of federal integration and to keep them from straying into the quagmire of intergovernmentalism. As a member of the Group put it, " the Working Group has essentially the task of closely following the efforts of the governments and of the High Authority on all questions of integration, and not to stop until that aim is achieved." [20]

By 1957, the results were far from impressive. Amidst considerable inter-party and international dissent in the Assembly, the general consensus which emerged was embodied in a series of quite unspectacular reports of the Group. Apart from the intensified federalism within ECSC proper advocated by MM. Poher and Kreyssig, proposals referring to the General Common Market and to Euratom failed to leave a striking impact on the deliberations of the governments. On behalf of the Group, Pierre Wigny advanced an Euratom scheme which took sharp issue with the intergovernmental OEEC Plan and closely followed the proposals of the Monnet Committee. However, he left in doubt the exact jurisdiction of the new Authority and spoke of the need to guard

[19] Common Assembly, Session Ordinaire, 1953, Doc. No. 8, Report of the Common Market Commission, by V.-E. Preusker.
[20] Common Assembly, Exercise 1955–56, Doc. No. 7, Groupe de Travail, *Rapport préliminaire*, Part II, by Van der Goes Van Naters (March 1956), p. 10.

against dirigisme and technocracy.[21] In a later report close liaison
with OEEC and Britain, co-operation with private industry, the
inclusion of overseas territories and the possibility of controls
over the military atom were also proposed.[22] With respect to the
common market, the Group contented itself with refuting economic
arguments suggesting reservations about integration, insisting on
a concerted welfare policy tied to the enlarged market, stressing
the need for generous readaptation allowances and a European
investment fund.[23]

Even in the institutional realm—the favourite stomping ground
of parliamentarians—the Group's proposals were hardly radical.
It did advocate the creation of independent Commissions to
administer both schemes but failed to object as bitterly to the
dominance of an intergovernmental Council of Ministers as it
had done in the ECSC case. Emphasis was placed instead on a
single enlarged and strengthened Common Assembly to administer
ECSC, EEC and Euratom, to be equipped with a true budgetary
power and with the right to dismiss the Commissions. Close
liaison with the Council of Ministers, along the lines of customary
development in ECSC, was stressed but no direct parliamentary
control demanded.[24] The Group warned only of the danger of a
multiplicity of supranational institutions and the need to minimise
this by giving the ECSC Assembly and Court the necessary additional powers to act as the guardian of the whole integration effort.
The danger of technocratic dominance would be averted at the
same time and by the same means.

Would this be a Europe of the Six or of the Fifteen? In a
valiant attempt to have the best of two possible worlds, the Working
Group steadfastly held to the principle that only those who were
willing to accept the supranational implications of integration
should join: *i.e.*, the Europe of the Six. But they also stressed the
need to facilitate the " association " of other countries with the

[21] Common Assembly, Exercise 1955–56, Doc. No. 6, Groupe de Travail, *Rapport
préliminaire sur le problème européen de l'énergie*, by Pierre Wigny (March 1956).
[22] Common Assembly, Exercise 1955–1956, Doc. No. 14, Groupe de Travail, *Rapport
sur le Marché commun et l'Euratom*, by Van der Goes Van Naters and Pierre Wigny.
[23] *Ibid.*, as well as the Van Naters report cited in note 20.
[24] *Ibid.*, as well as Common Assembly, Exercise 1956–1957, Doc. No. 14, *Memorandum sur la Relance Européenne*, Groupe de Travail, January 7, 1957. See especially
Common Assembly, Exercise 1955–1956, Doc. No. 28, Groupe de Travail, *Rapport
préliminaire sur certains aspects institutionnels du developpement de l'intégration
européenne*, by Gilles Gozard, (June 1956). This was *not* a unanimous report.

new Europe by following the formula worked out for ECSC–British relations, to be cemented at the inter-parliamentary level by the creation of a Common Assembly–House of Commons commission. In the economic realm, the Working Group was entirely sympathetic to any special rules which would permit Britain and others to achieve partial inclusion in the Europe of the Six,[25] such as the Macmillan Government's Free Trade Area proposal.

The evolutionary picture is thus plain: beginning with an extremely circumscribed jurisdiction far from approaching the ideal type of a federal parliament, the members of the Assembly have consistently sought to expand their role by a wide interpretation of the Treaty, by maximising the normal parliamentary techniques of control not, strictly speaking, forbidden and thus asserted themselves at the expense of High Authority and Council of Ministers independence. To some extent, this effort has been successful and has thereby contributed to the transformation of the Assembly in fact—though not in law—into a federal organ. At the same time, the members sought to influence directly the process of European integration by proposing schemes of their own and criticising the plans of intergovernmental conferences. In this attempt, their success has been far from real if influence on the official treaties is the test applied. While approaching the criteria of our ideal type as far as control over coal and steel is concerned, the will and co-operation of the six governments was the crucial element in making a reality of the " New Start," and not the reports of the Assembly's Working Group. But to the extent that political party opinion, like the aspirations of pressure groups, gave courage to the governmental delegates, the federalism of the Assembly must certainly be included as one of the many facets explaining the *Relance*.

Organisation of the Common Assembly

In a federal parliament, federal law determines the means whereby the legislators are selected. ECSC falls far short of this criterion. The Treaty merely fixes the maximum number of parliamentarians to be sent by each member state; it permits each state to use its

---

[25] Common Assembly, Session ordinaire, 1956, Doc. No. 6, Report of the Foreign Affairs and Political Commission, by Margarethe Klompé; adopted over the abstention of two Commission members. See also the report of the same Commission, Exercise 1955–1956, Doc. No. 27, by Paul Struye.

TABLE 2

DISTRIBUTION BY PARTY AND NATIONALITY OF ALL MEMBERS OF COMMON ASSEMBLY, 1952–1956

National Party Affiliation	National Total	ECSC Party Affiliation			
		Christian-Democrats	Socialists	Liberals & Aff.	Unaffiliated
Germany:	25				
CDU		12	—	—	—
SPD..........		—	8	—	—
FDP		—	—	2	—
Zentrum		—	—	—	1
DP		—	—	1	—
BHE		—	—	1	—
France:	31				
SFIO		—	7	—	—
RPF-RS-ARS		—	—	1	6
Radical-Socialists		—	—	5	—
Indep. Republicans		—	—	5	—
Peasants		—	—	2	—
UDSR........		—	—	2	—
MRP		3	—	—	—
Italy:	36				
Christian Democrats		22	—	—	—
Social-Democrats		—	6	—	—
Liberals		—	—	4	—
Republicans ..		—	2	—	—
Monarchists ..		—	—	2	—
Belgium:	14				
PSC		5	—	—	—
Socialists......		—	8	—	—
Liberals		—	—	1	—
Netherlands:	11				
Labour Party		—	3	—	—
Catholic Party		3	—	—	—
Anti-Revolutionary P.		3	—	—	—
CHU		1	—	—	—
Liberal Party		—	—	—	1

National Party Affiliation	National Total	ECSC Party Affiliation			
		Christian-Democrats	Socialists	Liberals & Aff.	Unaffiliated
Luxembourg:	5				
Christian-Democrats		2	—	—	—
Socialists......		—	2	—	—
Liberals		—	—	1	—
Saar:	5				
Christian-Democrats		4	—	—	—
Socialists......		—	1	—	—
Totals		54	37	27	8
		42·9%	29·4%	21·4%	6·3%

own procedure for selection, giving merely a choice between direct election and annual designation by national parliaments. In fact, the procedures have varied considerably. Italy, Belgium and Holland divide their delegations evenly between both houses of their parliaments; Germany ignores its Bundesrat, while the French Council of the Republic receives a lesser quota than the National Assembly. Holland, Luxembourg, Germany and Belgium have sent the same individuals to the Assembly year after year; the Italian and French delegations show great changes. Further, the predominance of local initiative in the selection process is plainly illustrated by the fact that since 1955 the Italian delegation has included only Senators because the Chamber of Deputies could not agree on its delegation, thus cutting in half the Italian membership in Strasbourg.[26]

Other variations persist, too. The Dutch Parliament debates ECSC annually, but no other legislature does so regularly. Some, but by no means all, national delegations have their own home secretariat and make annual reports to their legislatures. A good many federal activists pin their hopes for a truly federal mode of organisation to the direct election of Assembly members; but a

---

[26] Neo-Fascists combined with Communists and Nenni Socialists to defeat the Centre parties' effort to exclude the extremist groups from the delegations, resulting in deadlock. After the Saar plebiscite of December 1955, the discredited pro-French Saar delegates to the Assembly failed to make an appearance at Strasbourg, thus leaving the Saar unrepresented until 1957, when the German delegation made provision for its inclusion.

poll of German supranational parliamentarians has shown that nothing approaching general enthusiasm for the idea existed among them.[27] Carlo Schmid (SPD) argued that direct elections would yield the same results as parliamentary appointments, since the principles of proportional representation and party designation of candidates are used in either case, uniformly in all six parliaments. Other respondents urged that some real legislative powers beyond coal and steel would have to be created before any general voter interest and enthusiasm for such elections could be expected. The supranational mandate is clearly dependent upon the national mandate possessed by each member and is independent of the Assembly's rules of procedure.[28]   Clearly, this organisational criterion of federalism is most imperfectly met.

Does the Assembly represent the totality of the Community or are the parliamentarians merely the accredited spokesmen of their national states? The predominance of local influence in the selection of members might suggest that the principle of national representation governs the proceedings. Such, however, is not the case. To be sure, the Strasbourg Assembly is neither the perfect mirror of public opinion at home nor is its work closely meshed with that of its parent legislatures. Because of the tacit agreement to exclude Communists from the delegations, all the other parties are in effect considerably over-represented.[29] While Communist deputies, if represented in the Assembly, would certainly use that forum as they use national parliaments, their

[27] *Rheinischer Merkur*, December 16, 1955. Of the thirty Bundestag members who answered the poll, six favoured direct elections unconditionally, six opposed them unconditionally (including all the key SPD members of the Common Assembly), and eighteen expressed various doubts, conditions and reservations. The election and liaison issue was debated at length in the Belgian Senate on June 30, 1955. Belgium, Sénat, *Annales Parlementaires* (1955), No. 82, pp. 1485–1500.

[28] Common Assembly, Exercise 1953–1954, Doc. No. 12, Report of the Commission on Rules, Petitions and Immunities, by Gerhard Kreyssig. A suggestion to give the mandate of Assembly members some independence from the national mandate was not acted upon.

[29] If the Communists were represented on the same proportional basis which governs the delegations of other national parties, the picture in 1957 would be as follows:

Communists on national delegations

German	0
French	4
Italian	6
Belgian	0
Dutch	1
Luxembourg	0

This would make for a total of eleven Communists in the seventy-eight-member Assembly. The Italian Christian-Democratic delegation has consistently been the largest beneficiary of Communist exclusion.

presence would nevertheless eliminate one feature of artificiality from the supranational body. More thoroughgoing reforms would be required to remedy another failing of the Assembly, the poor liaison of its work with that of the national legislatures. Assembly sessions are postponed to suit the convenience of national debates. Members preoccupied with their national duties or fears fail to make an appearance at plenary or commission meetings. In case of ambivalence between national or supranational assignments, national pressure carries the day, since it is here that re-election is obtained, and not on the basis of anything said, done or voted in Luxembourg or Strasbourg.[30] The suggestions of the Poher Report, seeking to schedule co-ordinated annual debates on ECSC in all six national parliaments and to have the work at Strasbourg carried over into the national scene through parallel procedures in all six countries, have gone unimplemented.

The national principle clashed head-on with the idea that the Assembly was to represent the totality of ECSC in the 1953 debate over the establishment of permanent commissions. While the Socialists were more in favour of powerful permanent commissions than other parties, all agreed to the step readily enough. The consistent federalists, moreover, wanted to exclude any reference in the rules to a fixed representation for each state, notably the French, German and Italian Christian-Democrats. The bitter complaints of MM. Margue (Luxembourg, Chr.-Dem.), Struye, Korthals (Netherlands, Unaff.) and other Benelux spokesmen, however, resulted in the rules being so drawn as to allow for fixed national quotas *and* the recognition that all parties ought to be equitably represented.[31]

In subsequent years, the permanent commissions have remained faithful to the rules in assuring national representation according to the formula devised. When the Working Group was appointed, however, the large states were each given an additional delegate. What is far more important, however, the principle of state representation was completely abandoned in the Working Group's sub-commissions, in which the actual discussions take place. In

[30] See the complaints of Nicolas Margue (Lux., Chr.-Dem.) in *Informations Bimen-suelles*, March 15, 1955, p. 11.
[31] Common Assembly, *Débats*, compte rendu in extenso, 2ᵉ année, no. 1, February 28, 1953, pp. 50–71, 145–153. Two kinds of commissions were established, major commissions with twenty-three members and small ones with nine members. In the former the national representation formula is 5:5:5:3:3:2 and in the small ones it is 2:2:2:1:1:1.

these bodies, the parity principle among the large states has given way while some smaller countries are not regularly " represented " at all. Further, the principle of state representation is in effect inoperative to the extent that members unable to attend commission meetings may appoint substitutes. Practice has grown in such a way that a German Liberal may sit for a French party colleague, or a Dutch Socialist for a Belgian. Regardless of the nationality, the principle of party membership has become the operative rule of membership on commissions.

A final test of the role of the national state as contrasted with the collectivity is the distribution of commission report authorships and the tenor of the reports. Considerable political importance and prestige attaches to the position of " rapporteur " for a specific commission report and elections for such posts are often bitterly contested. If the principle of nationality were taken literally, one might expect the same formula which was originally applied to membership on commissions to be carried over into the assignment of rapporteurships. These figures demonstrate that such was far from being the case:

TABLE 3

NATIONAL   REPRESENTATION   IN   NUMBER   OF   REPORT AUTHORSHIPS

	Strength	Should have authored on basis of strength	Did author
Germans	18	23·0%	35·8%
French	15	19·2%	21·1%
Saar	3*	3·8%	1·2%
Italians	18*	23·0%	3·6%
Belgians	10	12·9%	13·6%
Dutch	10	12·9%	21·1%
Luxembourg	4	5·1%	3·6%

* Not corrected for incompleteness of delegations in 1955–57.
   The total number of reports issued as of January 1957 was 81.

Nor was national balance in evidence when the number and distribution of commission presidencies is analysed. Finally, it should be stressed that of the eighty-one reports issued by the beginning of 1957, all but five were adopted unanimously by the respective commissions. While this says little for the willingness of the parties to hold out for their particular viewpoints—and thus adds another artificiality as compared to our federal scheme— it does support the contention that the work of the Assembly reflects the needs of the totality and does not cater merely to the aims of particular countries. The same conclusion applies with respect to the tenor of the resolutions adopted by the plenary body. Special pleading is reserved for floor speeches but does not find an echo in collective decisions.

A federal legislature must be free to adopt its own form of organisation and plan of work. In this respect, the Common Assembly is true to the archetype. Its decision to establish permanent commissions and to undertake investigations are clear illustrations of this. An even more striking example was the decision to sanction the establishment of " political groups," or parties, and to finance their secretariats and travel expenses out of ECSC funds! This decision was made as the rules of procedure were drawn up. It was opposed by the Gaullists, Struye, Maroger, Margue and Korthals. For some time afterward these gentlemen sought to cut down the funds appropriated for this purpose during the annual budget debate, but without success.[32] It is only when the organisational demands of the Assembly depend on the co-operation of other organs or governments that the limits of freedom are reached.

Within the confines of the Treaty, the Assembly is certainly free to oppose both the High Authority and the Council of Ministers. What is more, the record shows that the parliamentarians have not been slow to take positions different from those of the two executive bodies. The tenor of resolutions passed clearly indicates an inter-party desire to persuade both executives to follow a more ener-getic federal policy. The High Authority had been exposed to this kind of criticism on the occasion of every annual debate on its general report, though the tone of opposition has been steadily intensified from year to year. In the case of the Council of Ministers, the willingness to oppose reached its high-water mark in the report of Wilmar Sabass (Ger., Chr.-Dem.), counselling the High Authority to go over the head of the Council and lobby directly with the

---

[32] For the debate on the financing of poliitcal groups, see *Débats*, compte rendu in extenso, Session Extraordinaire, March 11, 1953, pp. 4–16. As on many other occasions, the organisational issue was eased by a compromise agreement among the presidents of the three political groups.

six governments to obtain more support for integration.[33]   The
spirit of opposition to the executives, combined with the commitment to the New Start, gives the Assembly at times the role of a
supranational parliamentary lobby putting pressure for more
integration on the six governments.

Yet, despite the willingness to oppose, the voting pattern of the
Common Assembly presents a final artificiality which differentiates
this body in essence from the federal ideal type.   One difficulty,
of course, is the Treaty-imposed two-thirds majority rule required
to unseat the High Authority.   But a more serious departure from
federal practice—as opposed to law—has been the tendency of the
parties to avoid open combat.   As indicated by the seventy-six
unanimous commission reports presented, the pressure in the commissions is overwhelming to compromise clashing positions and
to reach consensus on a minimum inter-party common denominator.
Floor votes on resolutions are frequently unanimous; the number
of dissenters or abstainers hardly ever exceeds five or six.   In five
years of quasi-legislative activity, only one roll-call vote took place.
This was over the issue of the reduction by the High Authority
of the production tax, which was decided without consulting the
Assembly and in direct opposition to the investment and welfare
policy aims of the Socialists.   In the vote which ensued the alternatives were between a sharp Socialist motion criticising the High
Authority and a milder Liberal draft merely objecting to the lack
of consultation.   The Socialist and Liberal Groups were each solidly
united, whereas the Christian-Democrats split.[34]

But the general pattern is one of compromise, if not diplomatic
negotiation, not within the federal party as in the United States
but among parties.   But this pattern leads to the kind of compromising in which the maximal demands of the Socialists, in order
to be successfully compromised, entail a giving of ground by
Conservative Christian-Democrats and Liberals who otherwise
tend to fight " dirigisme " every step of the way.   Instead of opposing
ambitious programmes going beyond the will of the High Authority,
the resolutions and reports of the Assembly more and more

[33] Common Assembly, Exercise 1955–1956, Doc. No. 20, Report of the Common
Market Commission, by Wilmar Sabass, June 1956.

[34] *Débats*, compte rendu in extenso, Session Ordinaire, May 1955, pp. 466–467.   It
is interesting to note that the members of the Christian-Democratic Group did
not split along national lines.   With the exception of the Luxembourg Christians
and the Dutch Anti-Revolutionaries (two members each), each national Christian
party was divided.

consistently reflect these Socialist aims because the Conservative members do not always feel up to voting down such overtures. Examples of this trend are provided by the demands to achieve direct and continuing co-ordination of investments, to provide for planned social progress and attention to human relations in the implementation of the General Objectives, to realise the Renard programme for collective bargaining and to provide more liberal, centrally supervised re-adaptation allowances. All these measures correspond to Socialist and left-wing Christian-Democratic aims; but they are anathema to many Liberals and Conservative Christians, who voted for them just the same.[35]

In jurisdictional and organisational terms, the outstanding parliamentary artificiality of the Assembly remains its inability to bind the parent legislatures, to administer its own composition, to control its two executives meaningfully, or to co-ordinate the debates and votes of the national parliaments in such a way as to complement the supranational effort. In the absence of these powers the Assembly's routine work takes place in a vacuum: the national legislatures remain free to act as they did before; there is no evidence that they defer in any way to the resolutions of their delegates in Strasbourg. Hence the only long-range role played by the Assembly in relation to integration is the fact that continuing supranational communications channels are established physically and ideologically, probably " spilling over " eventually into the ranks of national parliamentarians not regularly deputised to go to Strasbourg.[36] It is in this connection that the role of European supranational political parties becomes crucial.

[35] See Common Assembly, Investment Commission, Report by F. de Menthon, June 1956; Social Affairs Commission, Reports by A. Bertrand, May 6, 1953, Willi Birkelbach, Doc. no. 18, Exercise 1953–1954, A. Bertrand, June 1956, G. M. Nederhorst, November 1956, Willi Birkelbach, November 1956, André Mutter, February 1957.

[36] From the viewpoint of efficient debate and the development of an expert body of coal and steel specialists among the parliamentarians, it is undoubtedly good that the same persons are consistently sent to the Assembly. Party cohesion also is probably advanced by the continuity of the personal contacts. However, it may also be argued that the scope of the communications " spill over " is limited by the fact that the total corps of legislators habitually attending Common Assembly, WEU Assembly, and Council of Europe sessions does not number more than about 150.

In 1957 evidence appeared indicating that the six national Socialist parties began to be concerned over the freedom enjoyed by their respective delegations to the Common Assembly. Anxious to reassert national control over their deputies, the parties found it essential to draw the entire national parliamentary membership into closer contact with the work of the Common Assembly. Under the presidency of SFIO Secretary-General Commin, an organisation of ECSC

MEMBERSHIP AND COHESION OF PARTIES

Our ideal type postulates that a federal political party is a multi-level and multi-unit federation itself, merely uniting autonomous formations identified with states and localities, and devoid of direct organisational contact with the individual citizen of the federation. This criterion is certainly met by the picture which obtains in ECSC. The parliamentary parties which came into immediate existence during the very first session of the Assembly are merely groupings of like-minded members of national parliaments. Each delegate is free to select the supranational group to which he wishes to belong, a pattern which results in a Dutch Liberal's (Korthals) refusing to join the Liberal Group, in the affiliation of several Italian Republicans with the Socialist Group, and in the membership of the Italian Monarchists in the Liberal Group. The Christian-Democrats, for their part, include Protestant as well as Catholic parties. Membership in the parties fluctuates annually with the individual convictions of the members possessing a mandate for the year.

As in the case of most other federations, all the Assembly groups possessed rudimentary international associations before the Treaty went into force. ECSC parliamentarians acknowledge that the ease and rapidity which characterised their formation of parties was facilitated considerably by the communications channels opened up by these early contacts as well as by the habit of inter-party consultation which had been inaugurated in the Council of Europe. The Socialists were the most determined to achieve supranational solidarity and their example stimulated their political opponents to follow suit, in the process compelling the Christian-Democrats—so far merely united in the N.E.I.—to formulate a much more detailed " European " programme than they had attempted up to that time.

Typically, the cohesion of federal parties is most strongly developed in the nomination and election of federation-wide officials. In ECSC, this pattern cannot be closely approximated because the Treaty denies the Assembly and its parties any specific

Socialist Parties was set up to exercise this kind of control. But so dependent is this organisation on the expertise of supranational officials that it made the Secretary of the ECSC Socialist Group its chief administrative official. While the initial purpose of the step was to increase national party control, its implications may well be the overcoming of the schism between the Common Assembly and the national parliaments.

role in the electoral process. It is true that members, in their capacity as national legislators, are able to lobby for the selection of pro-European national ministers. But there is no evidence, that the *federal parties* have been used to influence systematically the selection of national officials whose tasks relate to ECSC.

For the choice of the officials of the Common Assembly, the parties do function as nominating and electing media. Candidates for President and Vice-President of the Assembly are chosen first by party caucus, and later on the basis of agreement among the parties so as to avoid public controversy over the nationality of the official, giving rise to an informal rotation system. Again, inter-party compromise governs the procedure, thus approaching international diplomacy rather than spirited party conflict. For purposes of electing rapporteurs of commissions, however, the parties function very much as they do in any national legislature. Their relative success is shown in these figures:

TABLE 4

PARTY REPRESENTATION IN NUMBER OF REPORT AUTHORSHIPS

	Should have authored on basis of strength	Did author
Christian Democrats	42·9%	48·2%
Socialists...............	29·4%	37·0%
Liberals	21·4%	12·3%
Unaffiliated	6·3%	2·5%

This rough index shows the Socialists as the most successful in terms of electoral organisation, with the Christian-Democrats next, whereas the Liberals fare very poorly indeed in relation to their numerical strength.[37]

The Assembly made one supreme attempt to function as a nominating agency: it sought to be consulted in the selection of

---

[37] The scarcity of roll-call votes precludes the use of voting statistics as an index of party cohesion. The degree of absenteeism and the silence of many members during debate makes the use of content analysis hazardous as a quantitative technique of gauging cohesion. Report authorships as compared with numerical strength, given the importance attached to rapporteurships and the contests surrounding the election of rapporteurs, is therefore the only cogent quantitative index available.

Monnet's successor as President of the High Authority. Formally, it was ignored by the Council and the six governments even though it instructed its President, Signor Pella, to tour the capitals and drive home the determination of the Assembly to secure the election of a " good European." After the Messina meeting, Pella reported that in his talks with government leaders he had not suggested the candidacy of a specific individual, but had concentrated on demonstrating the need for the selection of a person with a clear pro-European record. In the choice of René Mayer, reported Pella, the Assembly's desires were amply rewarded.[38] The obvious fact remains, however, that the claim to be a nominating body went unrecognised by the governments, thus severely limiting any possible positive role for the parties.

Functional cohesion is one aspect of party solidarity. But what about ideological agreement? Commenting on the creation of the Monnet Committee in 1955, the Brussels *Pourquoi Pas*, under the heading " Good Luck, M. Monnet! " sceptically noted:

> Everybody was delighted to note that all the heads of all the parties and all the heads of all trade unions of all ECSC countries ... were among those fervently in favour of the United States of Europe. Therefore, since it is the parties who make politics and the trade unions who make economics and social relations, the integration of Europe, or of Little Europe at least, can be considered as accomplished.

> Well, we shall see . . . [39]

Five years of intensive party activity should leave some evidence of the evolution of consensus on ideological issues.[40] But the concerted work of the Liberals in the Assembly shows very little evidence of any striking degree of unity. When overproduction loomed, they favoured active High Authority co-ordination of investments; with the onset of shortages, they praised the executive for its restraint in the implementation of co-ordination rules. The

[38] *Débats*, Session ordinaire, May–June 1955. Statements of Pella (Italy, Chr.-Dem.), on pp. 198 and 505, May 6 and June 21, 1955. He also claims that his contacts with national governmental and opposition leaders led to the preparation of the documents which served as the point of departure for the discussions at Messina and the New Start.

[39] *Pourquoi Pas*, October 21, 1955, p. 16.

[40] The discussion of ideological cohesion is based on an analysis of the Assembly's debates from 1952 through January 1957. Except in the case of verbatim quotation, the footnoting of each statement has been omitted.

group unanimously favoured the reduction of the production tax. Almost all the Liberals are identified with business interests at home and thus might be expected to oppose openly the anti-cartel spirit of ECSC. But only Senator Maroger came out squarely in defence of cartels [41]; his German FDP colleagues contented themselves with praising the High Authority for its restraint and its willingness to introduce competition with " safeguards." No sweeping demands were made on the range of issues connected with coal prices and production policy. The Liberals *en bloc* had no difficulty in demanding an active ECSC housing policy but when called upon to pronounce themselves on energetic measures to promote better labour-management relations, they urged that the role of the High Authority should be that of a catalyst, merely bringing together the private parties. While not voting against the Renard programme, the Liberals were by no means stout defenders of it. The total picture shows a great deal of special pleading for local and national interests, in excess of a consistently expressed ECSC-wide consensus on the fundamental issues raised by the other parties. The fact that half of the group's members are French and that the remainder is quite heterogeneous in outlook is likely to preclude the emergence of any thoroughgoing agreement on ideology. " Liberalism " certainly has not emerged as a significant binding force. The protection of established business interests figures much more highly among the items of consensus, but since these interests tend also to be identified with purely national institutions and policies, not much supranational solace can be gained from this finding. Finally, the group not only includes several members who favour the Europe of the " Fifteen " over ECSC, but outright opponents of integration as well.

For the monistically inclined political observer the life of federal political parties is full of surprises, if not ambiguities. While ECSC Liberals show very little functional or ideological

[41] Maroger's case is an excellent example of the use of " European " symbols for anti-integration purposes, a practice by no means confined to France. Thus in *Politique Etrangère, op. cit.*, the late Independent-Republican Senator argued that integration takes place only when there is unanimous agreement among governments, deducing that the desirable United Europe of the future should be ruled by new technical High Authorities firmly subject to ministerial unanimity. He blames the smooth operation of ECSC for having resulted in its failure to achieve any of the demands of French industry, and he accuses his French colleagues in the Assembly of not seeking to arrive at common *national* policy positions before going to Strasbourg, and the Government for not trying to brief them on French needs.

cohesion, the Christian-Democrats present the interesting picture of great functional solidarity marked by considerable ideological heterogeneity, thus resembling the archetype of American parties more and more. Unlike practice in the Socialist Group, individual speakers are not very often authorised to make declarations in the name of the whole party. The Christian-Democrats succeeded in electing three out of the four Assembly presidents to date; but they have gingerly sidestepped the issue of cartels because of the divergent nationally inspired trends which dominate: the Dutch oppose them and wish for a maximum of High Authority control whereas the Germans—notably represented by Wolfgang Pohle, considered a spokesman for industry—preferred to minimise ECSC interference. In the politically charged sphere of supranational investment policy, the minimum common denominator prevailing is a tepid approval of the High Authority's modest steps, with the Dutch members expressing gratification over the executive's unwillingness to establish a preferential protected system for coal and steel and the Italians holding out for special aid to their Sardinian mines. Nor did the complex coal production and price issue lead to the evolution of a consensus. Price controls have been attacked or defended in accordance with the national economic assessments of the members, not in response to a " party line." In fall of 1956, most Christian-Democratic speakers praised the High Authority for its unwillingness to inaugurate rationing and compensation payments for coal imports; but the Italians held out for a more stringent central policy because of their coal needs. When confronted with the German Government's subsidisation of miners' wages, the Dutch defended the High Authority's arguments, while MM. Sabass and Pohle came to the aid of Bonn.

ECSC labour and welfare policy issues did not yield a Christian-Democratic consensus; but the differences within the party also ceased to coincide entirely with national assessments. True, for the CDU, MM. Kopf and Pohle acted as a brake on any ECSC harmonisation measures. But the Italians were split on this issue, uniting only to argue for the full and immediate implementation of the right to free migration. In the ranks of the PSC, M. Bertrand defended the essence of the Renard programme; but his national party colleagues showed far less enthusiasm for it. General consensus within the party on social issues is essentially confined to measures safeguarding the " dignity of workers," housing, industrial safety, and human relations.

The greatest bond of unity among the Christian-Democrats is undoubtedly their almost unanimous commitment to a United Europe. They arrive at this conclusion on the basis of anti-communism, Church doctrine, resentment of American " materialism," and of Monnet's economic arguments extolling the virtues of a large market.[42] Further, their strength on the Continent and their religious bias makes them favour the federation of the " Six." Regardless of nationality, members of the group have been consistently in favour of more integration in Little Europe, accompanied by the loose kind of association with outsiders typified by the agreement with Britain. Belgium's Paul Struye constitutes the only known exception to this rule. Hence it is not surprising that Pohle for Germany and Poher for France went out of their way to assure the Assembly in 1956 that the return of the Saar to Germany constitutes, not an undermining of ECSC, but a guarantee for continued Franco-German harmony within Little Europe.

Unquestionably the Socialist Group possesses the greatest amount both of functional and ideological cohesion of the Assembly groups. What is more, its record is one of rapid evolution toward internal consensus from initially divergent national positions, in contrast to the Liberals and Christian-Democrats who are not much more united today than they were in 1952. In principle, however, the Socialists are not yet reconciled to Little Europe. Under the pressure of the SPD and the SFIO, longings for the larger grouping of the Fifteen, and especially for the inclusion of Britain, subsist. Economic considerations as well as the expectation of gaining strength through the co-operation of the powerful British and Scandinavian Socialist parties are responsible for this attitude. Hence the Group has criticised the " foreign policy " of the High Authority for not seeking sufficient British participation. At the same time, the meandering attitudes of both the SPD and the SFIO toward the inter-connected issues of German re-unification, European integration, NATO and collective security arrangements

---

[42] An excellent example of the mixed feelings toward the United States is presented by the discussion of the loan agreement with the Export-Import Bank. All parties felt it necessary to state their disapproval of any possible secret commitment made by the High Authority to Washington, such as the rumoured concession—denied by Luxembourg—that no restrictions would be placed on the importation of American coal. For details, see Mason, *op. cit.*, pp. 95–96.

with the Soviet Union have made possible a vague rapprochement between the French and German Socialists: they both favour German unity and negotiations with the Soviet Union and accept in principle the Soviet offer of a general European collective security pact with its disarmament implications. In the process of gaining strength for such a development, however, they seek refuge in the Europe of the Fifteen rather than in ECSC.[43] The implications for integration may be crucial if the rejection of the political federation of Little Europe persists.

In view of the labour constituency of most of the ECSC Socialist parties it should come as no surprise that the demand for a systematic supranational welfare policy has constituted one of the bedrocks of Socialist consensus. However, while the Group has unanimously defended the Renard Programme in the Assembly, most of its members were not very interested in it. They placed priority on a unified economic rather than welfare policy and were satisfied with harmonisation measures achievable through treaties rather than bipartite commissions and collective bargaining. Even though the commissions were defended and their lack of success castigated by 1956, it was the trade unions and not the Socialist Group which initiated the pressure. Energetic re-adaptation and housing measures, protection of labour against the threat of automation, a guaranteed annual wage and the ECSC-wide reduction of working time were called for time and again. Further, G. M. Nederhorst, in the name of the Group, demanded in strident terms that the true test of success of ECSC was in the raising of living standards, that the High Authority become the " social conscience " of the Treaty, and that it rely on the Common Assembly for support in this struggle.

An energetic High Authority policy of steering investments and using them as an ECSC-wide anti-depression measure is regarded as the bedrock of a sane economic policy likely to yield higher wages and lower costs. Hence it was the Socialists who were most upset by the High Authority's decision to reduce the production

---

[43] For a further discussion of the SPD attitudes see Chap. 4 and Birkelbach's article, reported in *Informations Mensuelles*, February 1957, p. 10. Guy Mollet's ambivalent attitudes on these issues are well expressed in *Europe Today and Tomorrow*, June 1954, p. 12. The statement was made on the occasion of the European Parliamentary Conference of April, 1954. The SPD delegation, after its initial opposition to ECSC and to participation in it, went out of its way in 1956 to reassure the French Assembly members that the reunification of the Saar with Germany implied no blow to ECSC.

tax rate.[44]   And it is the Socialist Group which continued through 1956 to be highly critical of the inactivity of the High Authority with respect to forbidding some investments, and channelling others. But in the thinking of the Group investments tend to be an adjunct of pro-labour measures and long-range coal policy.   Unlike the other groups, the Socialists prefer to think of the entire ECSC nexus as one body of inter-related economic problems, hinging around the future of coal.

Dissatisfaction with the High Authority's famous Coal Memorandum provided the point of departure for the Socialist programme.   French members, worried about coke needs, marginal mines and the preponderance of the Ruhr, compromised their fears effectively with Belgians who were similarly motivated; Dutch Labour Party representatives worried more about cartels and high prices; the SPD delegation began to look for a supranational solution because of worry over American coal imports, rising mining costs, the competition of new fuels and the determination to increase wages while lowering prices.   The only common answer possible was to protect European mining against cheaper imports, steer investments into mines whose future seems assured, control competing fuels, maintain price ceilings, and subsidise wages by the introduction of an ECSC-wide compensation system and miners' bonuses similar to Bonn's.[45]   By mid-1956 the Socialist coal programme—supranational precisely because it relied on the harmonisation of national programmes and the pooling of national fears—was used to accuse the High Authority of doing nothing in the face of shortages and resigning its proper role to the six governments, who were doing little about concerting their anti-depression measures.

Differing initial national positions had led the Group into a firm consensus because separate national policies promised little. In the process, the free market doctrine of the High Authority was

[44] In caucus and on the floor, the entire group condemned the policy of the High Authority. The only exception was Joachim Schoene, whose affiliation with the Ruhr steel industry led him to argue that the investment needs of the firms justified a reduction of the tax. He was not supported by other SPD members.

[45] See Common Assembly, Socialist Group, Working Group for Economic and Social Questions, " Betrachtungen der Sozialistischen Arbeitsgruppe zum Memorandum der Hohen Behörde über die Kohlepolitik " (Luxembourg, mimeographed, n.d.); and *ibid.*, " Abschrift eines Briefes des Herrn René Mayer, Vorsitzender der Hohen Behörde der E. G. K. S. vom 21. November [1955], an den Genossen Guy Mollet, Vorsitzender der Sozialistischen Fraktion," (Luxembourg, mimeographed, November 21, 1955).

mercilessly mauled. An even more striking example of the formation of supranational party consensus is provided by the cartel issue, also intimately tied to the coal policy problem. In 1953 and 1954 the Dutch Socialists had joined their compatriots in attacking all cartels as illegal, while the SFIO sought to protect ATIC and the SPD wished to preserve GEORG. By 1956, the picture had changed. In the name of the whole Group and to underscore its unity, G. M. Nederhorst—the erstwhile opponent of all cartels—announced that free competition for coal was impossible. While the old cartels must be destroyed, they ought to be replaced by ECSC-wide public bodies to regulate production, equalise prices, stabilise employment and thus reduce costs and permit wage increases. Such " cartels " would be permanently controlled by the High Authority and be so organised as to keep single firms from acquiring positions of monopoly. They would also serve to keep coal imports to a minimum, and for that purpose the SPD specifically recommended the use of an ECSC-wide organ similar to ATIC.[46] As the fuel crisis of the winter 1956–57 progressed, MM. Kreyssig and Nederhorst in separate statements, but in the name of the Group, expressed their conviction that Europe's coal problem could only be solved by the " nationalisation" under ECSC of all mines.[47] The wheel had turned a full circle.

No generalisations can be made about the unaffiliated members of the Assembly. The Gaullists among them have used their membership to attack the principle of supranationalism and to embarrass the High Authority, while continuing to urge their " European " programme of a loose confederation of the Fifteen, and seeking to exploit the Saar issue to open up a Franco-German rift in Strasbourg. But M. Korthals cannot in any sense be considered an opponent of integration even though he has refused to join the Liberal Group, to which he is closest ideologically. Collectively, the unaffiliated members have played no role at all.

VOTING SOLIDARITY

Even though all three groups caucus consistently before voting or debating, no binding rule enjoining party discipline exists here

---

[46] Nederhorst's declaration was made on June 19, 1956. Common Assembly, *Débats*, compte rendu in extenso, Session ordinaire 1956, pp. 606–619. Deist's remarks on ATIC in *ibid.*, Session extraordinaire November 1956, pp. 35–40.

[47] Kreyssig in his comments on the Report of the Working Group in January 1957; Nederhorst in an article in *Socialisme en Democratie. Informations Mensuelles*, February 1957, p. 9.

any more than in American political parties. Paul-Henri Spaak was elected the first President of the Assembly with the support of some Christian votes though Brentano was the official Christian-Democratic candidate. Yet the fact that very few issues are permitted to reach the stage where a party-line vote would take place reduces the value of voting as a means to solidify the parties. The effort, instead, focuses on obtaining unanimous internal party positions in caucus and in commission sessions, which then serve as points of departure for compromises among the parties.

The success of the Socialists in achieving such internal compromises has been set forth. The Christian-Democrats have had less internal solidarity, though their caucuses have succeeded, for instance, in bringing about some rapprochement in cartel questions between Germans and Dutch. Both groups appoint individual spokesmen on specific issues only if there is unanimous agreement; but no formal votes are ever taken even in caucus! As for the Liberals, there is little evidence of any organised policy-making in their ranks. All groups, however, can make the claim that sufficient solidarity exists to prevent their members from contravening ECSC decisions or departing from ECSC positions in their activities as national parliamentarians. No such cases are known to have occurred. Nor do group members of the same nationality consistently function as a national *bloc* in the party deliberations.

One of the crucial tests of party solidarity is provided by the espousal of local constituency interests as compared to federal identification. As the American example teaches, a defence of local interests is clearly not always incompatible with the existence and functioning of a federal party. The test lies in the *extent* of such local preoccupation. Thus among the Socialists there is the barest minimum of special pleading for local interests, especially since the French, German and Dutch parties compromised their initial differences over cartel policy. True, Deist for the SPD defended the German Government's bonus to miners. But he sought to generalise the practice throughout ECSC. De Vita demanded more investment aid for Italy and Carcassonne (SFIO) argued for the equalisation of social security contributions. But these examples exhaust the special pleading among the Socialists, whose federal focus and solidarity is thus manifest once more.

Things are otherwise among the Christian-Democrats. Wigny, Bertrand and De Smet (PSC) argued heatedly for the Belgian collieries when the High Authority reorganised the Belgian compensation system. Pohle always defends the interests of the Ruhr, in Strasbourg as in Bonn. De Menthon (MRP) has been heard to argue the case of the Charbonnages de France, while almost all Italian Christian-Democrats go out of their way to claim special investment aid, protection for the Sulcis mines, more readaptation allowances and free migration rights for Italian workers. Yet these instances are perfectly compatible with the conduct to be expected of a federal party since they do not conflict with the party's basic commitment to integration.[48]

The special pleading of the Liberals is less easily reconciled with federal behaviour. Maroger spent the bulk of his time in Strasbourg demanding the canalisation of the Moselle, the equalisation of national taxes, the reduction of the ECSC levy, and ECSC participation in French overseas investments, thus never departing from a defence of purely French business aims. André Mutter, less consistently, has done the same, in addition to demanding the retention of French coal mining privileges in the Saar after the cession to Germany. Belgium's Motz has sought to assure the Belgian collieries a maximum of ECSC financial aid. By themselves, these efforts are the normal pleading of politicians for favours to their constituents. In the context of ECSC, however, the arguments come perilously close to challenging the logic of the integration process because they seek, in effect, to guard the special national position of certain industries, thus sacrificing much federal identity.

Another test of party solidarity is provided by certain crucial parliamentary situations in which national preferences could easily have been pitted against federal solidarity. One such case was the vote on the reduction of the production tax, in which federal party lines held extraordinarily well. When the Assembly was called upon to influence the Messina Conference of the foreign ministers, fears of obstructing the progress of integration were sufficiently lively to mute differences of opinion within and among the parties, thus giving rise to strongly worded resolutions in

[48] In fact, the claims of the Italians enjoyed considerable general support in the Assembly. See Common Assembly, Report of the Investment Commission, Doc. no. 21, April 1955, by Heinrich Deist; and Report of the Common Market Commission, Doc. no. 15, June 1956, by Martin Blank.

May and June of 1955 demanding that ECSC institutions be permitted to participate in the work of the intergovernmental conference to be appointed.

As the New Start made headway, the differences came to the fore again and thus provide a good test of internal party solidarity. They were symbolised by the rival positions taken by the parties at the special Assembly session called to Brussels in March of 1956 to discuss the progress of the intergovernmental conference. The Socialists in categorical fashion advanced the principles which, in their view, were to guide the drafting of the Euratom treaty. They included (1) the demand for general and controlled disarmament, implying the need for the *exclusive* dedication of Euratom to peaceful purposes; (2) " the European Community must be given exclusive title to all fissionable materials throughout the entire cycle of transformation, under effective parliamentary control. . . . The party must disapprove that an area in which the collective interest must prevail be left to private interests." [49] With respect to the common market, the Socialists insisted on the harmonisation of fiscal and economic policies, on planned welfare measures and on political institutions with true federal powers, instead of a mere relaxation of barriers to trade and capital.[50]

A less categorical resolution was advanced jointly by the Christian-Democratic and Liberal Groups. Agreeing with the Socialists that Europe's backwardness in atomic development must be made up by immediate and co-ordinated means, it nevertheless pinned its hopes (1) to a common market as such, (2) to private ECSC-wide firms—" common enterprises " in ECSC jargon—developing nuclear power, (3) supranational controls to assure industrial safety and non-diversion to military uses, (4) sufficient supranational powers to administer the system effectively and democratically, (5) membership open to all interested countries, and (6) "reserving atomic energy for peaceful purposes, with the manufacture of atomic bombs forbidden *during the first*

[49] Common Assembly, Socialist Group *Declaration concerning Euratom* (Luxembourg, mimeographed, March 20, 1956).

For the SFIO this position contains an element of hypocrisy. Domestic parliamentary pressure compelled Guy Mollet, in his capacity as Prime Minister, to water down the exclusively peaceful purpose of Euratom while his ECSC party colleagues insisted on the rigorous position formally adopted.

[50] *Ibid., Communiqué concerning the General Common Market.*

stage, and to be undertaken only under Community controls by the signatory states, as a result of a unanimous decision."[51]

In typical Assembly fashion, no vote was taken on the rival resolutions at that time. When the issue came up once more in May of 1956, a compromise had been found by the Working Group, which was adopted almost unanimously. The new resolution endorsed the work already done by the intergovernmental committee; it insisted that the common market must tend toward political unity and not merely abolish trade obstacles and that the new supranational institutions must have enough power to provide effective and democratic control; on the central issue of ownership over fissionable materials the resolution was silent whereas the issue of the military atom was merely sidestepped by declaring that the Assembly was incompetent to deal with it.[52]

The fact that adroit inter-party diplomacy had avoided a showdown does not deprive us of the opportunity to judge cohesion on this crucial issue. Thus the Christian-Democratic resolution was clearly no more than a shallow compromise even for that group. Many members, especially the Dutch, distrusted the genuineness of French interest in the *Relance*, suspecting French preoccupation with Algeria, and so were unwilling to tie their United Europe to support of French colonial policy. Also they resented the continued French demands for a special status in the common market.[53] The Italian delegation was concerned largely with the political implications of the schemes and with direct elections; only Giuseppe Pella took a marked interest in economic integration, but justified the need for intergovernmental institutions to make it work.[54] The Conservative German members (Kopf,

[51] *Informations Mensuelles*, April 1956, pp. 19–20. Italics provided.

[52] *Ibid.*, June–July 1956, p. 11.

[53] A number of Dutch suggestions were heard that perhaps a common market of the ECSC countries minus France ought to be studied, thus relying on German leadership. See Vixseboxse's statement of March 15, 1956, Common Assembly, *Débats*, compte rendu in extenso, session extraordinaire, March 1956, p. 279. Also the article by Blaisse in *Nouvelles de l'Europe*, November 1954, pp. 3–4. Credence was given to these fears by the repeated French insistence on the prior harmonisation of wage and social security costs—anathema to the Dutch—and by a closing of ranks on the Algerian issue. See, for instance, the MRP statement by Alfred Coste-Floret, " Relance Européenne et détente Internationale," *Monde Nouveau Paru* (November 1955).

[54] Giuseppe Pella, " Les fonctions de la CECA dans l'Europe nouvelle," *Bulletin de la Société Belge d'Etudes et d'Expansion*, May–June–July 1955, pp. 608 *et seq.*; also " Itineraries of European Economic Integration," *Banco di Roma, Review of the Economic Conditions in Italy*, September 1955, pp. 424 *et seq.* Pella's whole emphasis is purely economic, with interest centred on a maximum of freedom for trade and capital movements.

Pünder, Pohle) were delighted with the anti-dirigistic slant of the resolution; but the MRP delegation (Teitgen, de Menthon, Poher) favoured the opposite position. As for the Liberals associated with the resolution, their aims ranged far and wide. Mutter and Crouzier raised the issue of the equalisation of wages and social security rules before the opening of the common market; they as well as the FDP's Martin Blank welcomed the weak supranational component of the official plan. Yet René Pléven favoured strong supranational parliamentary controls and welcomed the absence of any insistence on the prior harmonisation of production costs. Most Christian-Democrats and Liberals had nothing to say about a supranational welfare policy in the General Common Market, but Alfred Bertrand made a personal point of it. Of doctrinal unity there was no trace; but once more the party demonstrated its cohesion in bringing all its members into line under one vague compromise programme, despite very strong centrifugal forces—thus clearly remaining faithful to the conduct to be anticipated of a federal party and thereby actively contributing to the integration of political movements along supranational lines.

As for the Socialists, they openly sought to make use of the debate to advance their programme of a " European welfare policy " which had taken on a firm shape in 1955. After the SPD's conversion to " Europe," a veritable supranational election fever seemed to have gripped the party. As Pierre Wigny (Belgium) taunted the Socialist spokesman Fernand Dehousse (Belgium):

> Are you very sure, M. Dehousse, that there is a chance of creating a Socialist Europe? No more, I think, than a Vatican Europe. It remains to be proved that for the developmental needs of nuclear industry fissionable materials must be public property.[55]

At the basis of this drive, of fundamental significance for the analysis of movements tending toward the integration of distinct nations, was an informal meeting of the minds of the SPD and SFIO. In 1952–53, the SPD still opposed European integration and boycotted certain ECSC activities. The SFIO opposed the " clerical " and " capitalist " Europe of the Six, with Guy Mollet declining to participate in the labours of the Ad Hoc Assembly's

[55] March 16, 1956; Common Assembly, *Débats*, compte rendu in extenso, session extraordinaire, March 1956, p. 343.

Constitutional Committee.[56]   Yet by 1955, German Socialists wrote feelingly about the need for regionally planned counter-cyclical and social security policies, directed investments and socially inspired productivity drives.[57]   While not publicly espousing European integration with the ardour of Adenauer and Brentano, they took the initiative in actually formulating policies within ECSC which would—if implemented—catapult Western Europe into a political federation within a few years.   As for the SFIO, Guy Mollet declared, in writing about the New Start, that " the risk of a new German nationalism is not a myth: if we do not have an energetic *Relance Européenne* we shall soon find this out, and not only at the European political level." [58]   While still favouring the inclusion of Britain—the issue which had plagued the SFIO in the EDC agony—Mollet was now willing to proceed within the context of the Six.   As for economics, he maintained:

> Are we always willing to pay the price of economic integration?
> For the French Socialists there is no doubt as to the answer and
> we would even wish to bypass the state of an organised economy
> in favour of a planned European economy.[59]

Both parties, for reasons initially rooted in their national political programmes, were driven to supranational fusion.   And once they began to co-operate continuously in Strasbourg and Luxembourg, the process became a two-way street whereby they persisted in synthesising differences at a higher supranational level.

The evidence for this conclusion is to be found in the unanimously defended Socialist programme for the New Start.   After Messina, the Group never wavered from its demands for a General Common Market which would include co-ordinated investment, fiscal and welfare measures and not be confined to merely recreating

---

[56] Guy Mollet, " A Warning," *Europe Today and Tomorrow*, December 1952.

[57] Details are given in Chap. 4.   On the new attitude see also the articles by Willi Birkelbach in *Soziale Sicherheit*, August 1954, and Joachim Schoene in *Jugend Europas*, November 24, 1955.

[58] Guy Mollet, " L'unification de l'Europe," *Monde Nouveau Paru*, November 1955, p. 2.

[59] *Ibid.*, pp. 3–4.   Among more doctrinaire Belgian and French Socialists, the *Relance* set off a wave of articles in which a new kind of European programme was demanded.   The struggle for or against Europe was equated with the class struggle, with the Left being the defender of Europe against the reactionary possessing classes, whose only vision of Europe could be that of larger cartels.   Hence a maximum of political integration with direct elections for the Common Assembly was urged as a device for mobilising the working classes for Europe.   See, for instance, the issue of *Gauche Européenne* for July–August 1955, particularly the articles of André Philip and Raymond Rifflet.

free trade conditions. The only discordant note was M. Vanrullen's (SFIO) suggestion that if the General Common Market did not provide for the prior harmonisation of wages and social security payments, at least these should be equalised as the market went into effect.[60] And despite the compromise resolution voted by the Assembly on Euratom, the Group continued to defend public ownership of fissionable materials and the absolute prohibition on the military use of the atom. In short, not only does the Socialist Group conduct itself thoroughly in accordance with federal principles, but its policy acts as a potent stimulus for the other groups to do the same. Its role in the political integration of Europe can hardly be overestimated even if its specific proposals remain unimplemented.

Paradoxically, a major reason for this realignment of the Socialists lies in the fundamental crisis which plagues modern Socialist doctrine. Historical determinism, a unique Socialist ethic and egalitarian culture, the substitution of new forms of social co-operation for the state—all these are being superseded by more modest, but " bourgeois," notions. The radical faith in state planning has yielded to the seductions of Keynes. " Socialist parties become parties ' like all the others,' forced into continuous political compromises, attempting to gain new members and voters from various strata unacquainted with Socialist values and traditions. This has brought with it an erosion of the former insistence on Socialist *Haltung*, of the view that Socialism implies cultural as well as economic changes, and that there should be specifically ' Socialist forms of living.' " [61]

Nor is this the full measure of the doctrinal quandary. Economic convictions firmly held in the past are also eroding. The parties are no longer sure whether—and which—prices ought to be administered or free, whether a mixed economy is a temporary phase or a permanent condition to which Socialism must adjust, whether wages ought to be administered or negotiated.[62]

The immediate results of the doctrinal crisis are found in an increased political opportunism, a distrust of visionaries and

---

[60] Common Assembly, *Débats*, Session extraordinaire, March 1956, p. 234 for Nederhorst's statement in the name of the whole party, and p. 314 for Vanrullen's statement in the name of the SFIO.

[61] Kurt L. Shell, " The Crisis of Modern Socialism," *World Politics*, Vol. IX, no. 2 (January 1957), p. 303.

[62] See R. H. S. Crossman's doubts on this score, as quoted by Shell. *Ibid.*, p. 304.

reformers and a desire to solidify the obvious social gains extracted in a mixed economy and a bourgeois order, events which themselves confute the Marxist heritage further. In the ECSC context the absence of doctrinal purity has meant that Socialists feel free to oppose their national governments and the parties composing them, indeed to capitalise on the existence of the supranational forum for this purpose. But this has carried the further consequence that when the party is in opposition nationally it is firmly supranational in action; when, however, it participates in the Government, its federal convictions may suddenly lag and its defence of Paris or Brussels blossom forth.[63] The striking cohesion of ECSC Socialists has been partly a function of the SPD's oppositional tactics and confused doctrine.

Finally, the crisis of Socialist doctrine facilitates the embracing of a practical supranationalism because the techniques implied are thought to advance the very unspectacular and modest measures of economic expansion and social welfare on which the *militants* are agreed. No drastic upheavals are involved, no expropriations, class reversals or administrative purges contemplated. ECSC planning would merely transpose to the regional level the now classic prescriptions of Keynes, rules which, Socialists think, can no longer be made meaningful in the confinement of national states. If doctrinal uncertainty breeds opportunism, ECSC is merely another device for maximising the occasions for unspectacular social advancement. After all, a United Europe may be a revolutionary step in itself and in the general historical context; but it is hardly a cataclysm in the framework of the classic Marxist millennium.

CONTROL OF THE PARTY

A federal party should be identified with groups in society overlapping state boundaries and local constituencies. Is this the case in ECSC? Certainly, the Socialist Group claims to speak for a constituency coextensive with the Community, a claim given a good deal of substance by the regular consultations between it and the

---

[63] This feature is, of course, not confined to Socialists. It has been argued that René Mayer's supranationalism is largely a function of his—probably temporary—lack of influence in Paris.

two supranational trade union organisations.[64] Further, with the advent of the commitment to a planned European welfare state, less and less emphasis is placed on local constituency pressure, as reflected in the consensus on cartel, investment and coal policy.

The question is more difficult to answer in the case of the Christian-Democrats. In essence, they remain creatures of their national party organisations in doctrine as in mandate. While faithful to their general belief in a United Europe, on concrete issues their record of merely defending the views of their national or local constituencies leads to the conclusion that control of the party remains local. As is typical in federations, this may imply extensive bargaining. Teitgen for the MRP has claimed that a United Europe must aid France in realising Eurafrica, *i.e.*, help preserve French colonial holdings. Not unreasonably, Kurt Kiesinger (CDU) agreed, provided a United Europe helps German reunification.[65] While no such " deals " seem actually to have been consummated, an intensification of supranational parliamentary activity based on strongly autonomous party wings not subject to overlapping group interests may bring them close to reality. In fact, of course, each of the national Christian parties is split into wings identified with labour, the peasantry or business. Only a small beginning has been made in carrying group identifications into the supranational realm. As for the Liberals, enough has been said about their tendency to be spokesmen for established national industrial interests as not to raise the question of supranational group identification.

Other indices of supranational control also yield little positive evidence. The supranational leadership exercises no control over the selection of national delegations. The only suggestion of financial independence is the availability of ECSC funds for meeting secretariat and travel expenses, but not for fighting election campaigns. In all groups, even in the case of the Socialists, the only supranational " control " lies in the spirit of give and take which prevails in the caucuses where, let it be said again, voting is avoided and unanimity the rule.

[64] Since G. M. Nederhorst is president of the Commission on Social Policy, he has often sought the advice and opinion of the Committee of Twenty-One and the Christian Trade Union Federation. See, for instance, the consultations on the reduction of the work week and the creation of bipartite commissions, Common Assembly Doc. AC 2155.

[65] *Informations Mensuelles*, November 1956, pp. 67–71, and February 1957, p. 11. Kiesinger's statement was not made in any ECSC organ.

However, each group has a permanent Secretary, staff, library, files, and caucus room—the only approximation to a central organisation. In the case of the Liberals this organisation is rudimentary, since the Secretary—M. Drèze (Belgium)—combines this position with activity in the Liberal International and in Belgian national politics. Meetings and consultations are extremely rare. The Christian-Democrats, by contrast, have a permanent Secretary-General, M. Opitz (Germany). This official works in close co-operation with the group's president, E. M. J. A. Sassen.[65a] He is given the power to make basic policy recommendations for adoption by the group. He undertakes studies, lobbies with High Authority members, and provides continuing liaison among the members. His policy recommendations, in effect, sometimes serve as mediating devices in the internal differences which plague the Christian-Democrats. To the extent that these services grow indispensable to extremely busy national parliamentarians who function in ECSC only on a part-time basis, a permanent party bureaucracy may eventually develop.

Things are otherwise in the Socialist Group. The Secretary and his staff in Luxembourg are little more than a communications hub for the Group, collecting and disseminating documents and memoranda. They initiate no policy. However, the Socialists early decided to enable their parliamentarians to specialise in ECSC questions and therefore released them from many national parliamentary burdens. Organised into specialised committees, the members communicate with one another continuously through the medium of permanent expert staffs in each national capital. The result is that they are better prepared in the economic niceties of coal, steel and all other issues related to further integration and possess a communications network which facilitates the evolution of consensus, a factor explaining in part why so many Socialist-inspired items find their way into unanimous Assembly resolutions. Socialist policy is carefully studied and prepared by personnel at the national capitals, enabling the delegation members to arrive on the scene with their programme largely ready, subject only to finalisation at the frequent caucus meetings. Yet the nationality issue plagued the Group at its debut, with the SPD and SFIO each insisting on the presidency. A compromise awarded the presidency to Mollet, the vice-presidency to Ollenhauer, while

[65a] Sassen was appointed to the Euratom Commission in January of 1958.

the secretariat was entrusted to a " neutral " Luxemburger. The Christian-Democrats had diplomatically avoided this issue by initially finding themselves a Dutch president, a policy imitated by the Socialists when they chose Belgium's Henri Fayat as Mollet's successor.[65b] Party central organisation, in short, remains rudimentary and based on principles closer to the international diplomatic tradition than to federal politics. Yet a start toward the creation of a central bureaucracy, especially in the case of the Socialists, has unquestionably been made.

SUPRANATIONAL POLITICAL PARTIES AND THE FEDERAL EXECUTIVE

Our final set of criteria for judging the federal nature of the Assembly's parties hinges around the desire to select the executive and be identified with its programme, and alternatively to the development of an opposition. The issue of control over the executive which relates to this aspiration has been examined before. Clearly, the institutional system of ECSC makes it impossible for the parties to function as the selectors of the High Authority members if the six governments refuse to co-operate. Stressing the structural aspect, however, comes close to glossing over the behavioural implications of this statement: the unwillingness of the governments to permit Assembly participation in the choice of the High Authority members means, in effect, that national ministers pay little or no attention to members of their own party active as supranational parliamentarians. The only success scored in this realm was the appearance of René Mayer before the Assembly immediately upon his selection, to " present his programme " in conformance with a resolution voted in December of 1954.

The local inefficacy of the Assembly's parties is manifest finally in their inability to influence decisively the selection of national ministers and civil servants who function in and about the Council of Ministers. If the work of the national legislatures could be made to dovetail more closely with activities in Strasbourg there is no reason for thinking that the federal cohesion of the parties would not suffice to marshal the necessary influence, at least in Germany and the Benelux countries. But as long as Assembly debate rages in a vacuum this is unlikely to come about. As matters stand, the parties do have some slight successes to their credit in

---

[65b] Fayat, upon becoming a member of the Belgian Cabinet in 1957, was succeeded by P.- O. Lapie (SFIO).

having cajoled the Ministers to attend their meetings and in having provoked them by bitter attacks—mostly from the Socialists—to justify themselves in public. Further, the request voted by the Assembly in 1955 calling on the Messina conferees to select a leading European political figure to head the inter-governmental conference and to solicit the participation of ECSC institutions in the *Relance* was accepted in full. But this is the extent of party " control " over the two executives of the Community. If it falls far short of the federal ideal type it nevertheless constitutes a considerable change over the wording of the Treaty and practice in 1953.

As for the executive's ability to influence the parties through the dispensing of patronage, physical and moral, the ECSC system provides little opportunity for this, and the two executive organs have deliberately avoided close identification with the parliamentarians. There is no federal patronage to distribute in the sense of a multitude of administrative positions requiring appointments. It may be suggested that appointment to various ECSC-wide and local commissions and study groups *could* be so used and that the distribution of housing and readaptation allowances *might* be considered susceptible to political manipulation. At least they would be in most democratic federal systems. In ECSC, however, both the High Authority and the Council of Ministers have scrupulously avoided close contact, relations of gratitude or mutual influence with the Assembly and consequently ignored this standard device of political integration.

A much more crucial test of behaviour consistent with and contributory to political integration is the evolution of " government " and " opposition " parties, seeking to shape policy quite irrespective of participation in the selection of the executive or the receipt of patronage from him. Here the conduct of the parties in the Common Assembly demonstrates the consequences of the supranational sharing of values in a functionally specific institutional setting: even with truncated and rudimentary legislative jurisdiction the parties have, in effect, drifted into normal federal legislative positions.

The division into pro- and anti-High Authority factions was not clearly illustrated until the session of summer 1956, when the Socialists, in connection with the discussion of the Fourth General Report, issued a general manifesto of dissatisfaction with the executive. The bill of particulars, read by Gerhard Kreyssig (SPD) on behalf of the whole Group, included these points: the High Authority ignores the will of the Assembly and undermines the federal nature of the Community by (1) doing too little in the realm of welfare policy, (2) not making use of all the powers given it by the Treaty, (3) being unwilling to follow a consistent coal policy and therefore unjustifiably removing price ceilings, (4) declining to supervise closely the implementation of the readaptation system, and (5) refusing to discuss with the Assembly problems of general economic stability, expansion and business-cycle control. The Group " consequently expresses, in the most formal way, the concern to which the policy of the High Authority has given rise." [66]

The fall session of 1956 re-enforced the separate position of the Socialists. It was here that they put forward their radical—but carefully planned and integrated—proposals for the simultaneous control of the coal market, the regulation of coal prices, investment and production, and the use of public cartels. Taking their cue from the reversion to national administrative controls over coal in the fall of 1956, the Socialists accused the High Authority of undermining its own powers by not making full use of the Treaty for a federal solution to the coal crisis.[67] In June of 1957 the attack on the High Authority was intensified in the debate over the Fifth General Report. Thus the party declared itself formally a supranational opposition to the European executive.

The logic of supranational institutions and shared ideologies may have given rise to an opposition, but did it also yield the

[66] Common Assembly, Socialist Group, " Déclaration du Groupe Socialiste," June 22, 1956 (Luxembourg, mimeographed, Doc. AC/GS/177). Also the declarations of Kreyssig and Nederhorst in *Débats*, compte rendu in extenso, Session ordinaire June 1956, pp. 768–769, 691–692. Again the declarations of Nederhorst, Vanrullen and Lapie in *ibid*, June 1957.

[67] The national measures in question were as follows. On November 29, 1956, the SPD introduced in the Bundestag a motion seeking to reimpose price control and regulation over the coal market removed earlier as a result of High Authority decisions. The Government met the opposition to the extent of increasing its subsidy to miners' housing construction and in ordering a reduction of the working week. During the same month, the Belgian Chamber of Representatives debated coal and mine safety policy and extracted a promise from the Government to undertake a national mine safety programme, implying dissatisfaction with ECSC measures. In December, the Luxembourg Government assured the Chamber of Deputies that special measures to assure coal supplies for small consumers would be taken. On November 21 and 22 the Second Chamber of the Dutch Parliament debated coal policy, with the Government expressing a preference for more stringent controls over ECSC coal sales organisations and underlining the need for purely national measures to equalise the price of imported and ECSC coal. *Informations Mensuelles*, December 1956, pp. 39–50.

evolution of a " government " party? It must be concluded that the Christian-Democrats, without having apparently wished to do so, have been forced into the position of a government party. Despite their internal divisions and despite the sympathy of several members for parts of the Socialist programme, the Party collectively opposed the Socialist attacks and came to the defence of the High Authority.[68] But rather than meet the Socialist criticism point by point, President Sassen preferred to attack the opposition for its unwillingness to make a formal censure motion of its " declaration," giving rise to a more spirited and typical parliamentary exchange of invective than had previously been witnessed in the sedate Assembly. Again on the coal issue, the Christian-Democratic Group collectively upheld the High Authority's preferences, even though many of its members individually endorsed portions of the Socialist criticism. The desire to support the only functioning European executive combines with the ideological heterogeneity of the Group—preventing a clear-cut position from being defended —to catapult the Christian-Democrats into the *de facto* position of a government party.

Are the Liberals a government or a disguised opposition party? Of the three Assembly groups the Liberal Party qualifies least for the role of a federal party. Its cohesion is almost non-existent as measured by any index; and the activities of its members support the conclusion that the " party " merely functions as a label for nationally identified pressure group spokesmen. When the position of the Christian-Democrats meets the essence of the free enterprise and autonomy wishes of the Liberals, they act as a member of a Government coalition. But when the Christian-Democrats are of two minds on High Authority policy—as they often are—the aspirations of the bulk of the Liberals come closer to meeting the role of a tacit opposition group, blackmailing the Government into inactivity by the threat of joining the opposition formally. Thus the parliamentary logic of French and Italian party life is accurately carried over into the Assembly. While this feature hardly contributes to Governmental stability, it nevertheless is so typical of continental parliamentary life as to make the Assembly

---

[68] For evidence of considerable support for the Socialist line, see the following commission reports: Investment Commission, January 1954, by F. de Menthon; *ibid.*, June 1956; Common Market Commission, two reports of November 1956 on the coal crisis and coal supplies, by Alain Poher.

a faithful mirror of regional group conflict, and therefore a vehicle of political integration.

INTEGRATION AND PARTY FORMATION

Because of their appeal to an overlapping and diffuse group constituency political parties are far more crucial carriers of political integration or disintegration than even supranationally organised interest groups. Further, the conduct of the Assembly's parties is, in the long run, a more cogent source of materials for the analysis of community formation processes than the immediate decisions of the High Authority, the Council of Ministers or the national governments. Our conclusion must be that on the basis of party behaviour trends in ECSC are not fundamentally different from conduct in "typical" federal parties. Even granting the variations between the three groups, with the sole exception of the avoidance of open party battle until 1956, the major indices of behaviour make ECSC parties quite similar to the American or Canadian prototypes. But the fact that showdown votes and insistence on party-inspired resolutions were avoided until the most recent period of the Assembly's history demonstrates also that the "precursor consciousness" which clearly motivates many of the parliamentarians has imposed checks on the freedom of normal party behaviour. Fear of offending national suscep-tibilities and of rocking the frail boat of European consciousness has been a restraining force, which is only now beginning to give way to normal partisan impulses, and thus approaches more nearly the federal pattern and the recognition of openly acting in a federal governmental organ. In general, then, it is not party conduct which has been artificial and unfederal; rather the basic clues to the strange intermediate status of the Assembly are to be found in the jurisdictional and organisational features which depart—much against the Assembly's will—from the norms accepted in federal institutions.

What, then, has been the contribution of the Assembly to western Europe's political integration and what principles of community formation can be deduced from it? Very few, if any, individual members were persuaded to the federalist creed as a result of their work in Strasbourg. With the exception of perhaps fifteen members, the bulk was more or less in favour of integration before they ever took up their supranational mandate. Nor are the specific proposals made to the governments or the Council of Ministers particularly significant contributions. The truly vital development is the growth of a code of conduct considered appropriate to supranational legislators: the right to be continually consulted by executive agencies, to put forward programmes not clearly and previously declared to be national policy, to organise, investigate and criticise on the basis of opinions and convictions developed as a result of contacts with ideologically kindred but nationally different colleagues. To make such a development possible there has to be an institutional medium in which the appropriate convictions and codes could develop. If the Common Assembly possessed more jurisdictional and organisational features making it truly federal it is certain that the codes in question would have developed even sooner.

One aspect of the code is the habit of intra-party compromising which has been developed by both Socialists and Christian-Democrats into a fine art. In the case of the Socialists this proceeds on the basis of an underlying common ideology, buttressed by converging national political needs. These have sufficed to overcome in large measure the very real national differences which existed in 1952 and 1953, and to enable the Party now to put forward its "opposition" European economic programme. However, without the energetic leadership of the SPD, after its change of heart, this would hardly have been possible. As for the Christian-Democrats, their commitment to Europe as such has provided the necessary ideological cement required to maintain consistent consensus. In both instances the acceptance of the code of intra-party compromise proceeded from an initial period of quasi-diplomatic relations to the evolution of a more truly party atmosphere, in which individual members argue with each other, seek to persuade one another, and eventually agree on a common formula without voting on it. The culminating step would be the evolution of a binding rule of party solidarity, based on a vote in caucus.

But even in the absence of such a step, the pressures generated by ECSC institutions and the prior commitments of the parliamentarians have combined to make the bulk of the members outgrow the boundaries of the national state as the referents of legislative action. All the Socialists and many of the Christian-Democrats do seek support from Europe in general, and not only from their home districts or parties. Parenthetically, it may be argued that if direct elections prevailed in ECSC it is most unlikely that this development would have taken place. Voter ignorance and indifference with respect to the purely economic issues of integration would have magnified the voices of the local pressure groups hostile to integration.

Paul Reuter, one of the foremost students of ECSC, concluded that the true federal impulse of the supranational system lay in the Assembly, and not in the two executive bodies.[69] He is right not only because of the impulses for non-national party conduct which are released by the legislative discussions, but also because of the true parliamentary aura which is given to current discussions of integration, discussions which take place in a regularly consti-tuted organ and not merely in voluntary assemblies of " good Europeans." In Wigny's words:

> We must not confuse ceremony with the political act. The members of a political assembly, whether national or international, play a double role. Very often they attend as participants in a debate in which protagonists and their roles, scenes and move-ments, the whole issue, are known in advance. It is an illusion to believe that discussion will change opinions and votes in each case. Often the decisions have already been made. The Assembly is merely the loudspeaker which, through public debate, projects previous discussions, permits them to reach the ears of the great public and thus engages the responsibility of the political parties.[70]

Federal in conduct and international in jurisdiction, the single most important contribution of the Assembly is to have served as a precursor parliament whose codes will determine the activities of the slightly more powerful legislative body foreseen for Euratom and EEC. No doubt, the bulk of the ECSC parliamentarians will be members of the enlarged Assembly. No doubt, the addi-tional national legislators to be included in the enlarged Assembly will follow the lead provided by the codes developed under their predecessors. The significance to political integration, then, is the mere fact that the hundred-odd members of the Common Assembly developed into *the* European parliamentary elite, whose very existence and functioning in the nexus of High Authority, Council of Ministers and European integration issues has given it a unique

[69] Paul Reuter, in *Droit Social* (August 1954), p. 523.
[70] *Un témoignage sur la Communaute des Six, op. cit.*, p. 45.

outlook and original channels of communication for carrying out the expanded task of "parliamentary control" which the new institutions hold in store for it.

EUROPEAN PARLIAMENTARISM AND GREAT BRITAIN

That sector integration which takes place in a broad pattern of institutional and group participation can spill over into other sectors has been demonstrated in the realm of trade associations, trade unions, governments, civil services and political parties in member states. But can a spill-over be established for political parties "associated" with ECSC, interested in its progress, concerned by the rapid momentum of the continental integration movement, but not a part of it? The relationship of Britain to the European parliamentary assemblies may provide an answer.

Given the established British rejection to any direct participation in federal or quasi-federal institutions, one may well wonder why British Governments and parliamentarians have wished and continue to desire a role in the Council of Europe, the WEU Assembly, and in the parliamentary body of the continental economic communities? The mystery deepens when one considers the appreciable federalist impetus inherent in the work of these bodies. One answer—a very cynical one with respect to British motives—maintains that Britain wishes to control the federal impetus, to keep it "manageable" and to prevent it from getting "out of hand." Participation might thus become a bloc to fruition of the movement. A less Machiavellian answer might suggest a mere desire to be present, to be represented and to be heard if and when the federalist impulse—always regarded with some scepticism in Britain—came close to establishing a European union.

This less cynical answer derives some support from Winston Churchill's remarks, blaming the Labour Government for not interesting itself actively enough in the ECSC Treaty negotiations. Again in the case of EDC Churchill argued that a warmer British reception of the Pléven proposal and an active part in the negotiations might have succeeded in watering down the federal features of the Plan while attaining German rearmament.[71]

Both interpretations of the obvious British desire to be " in " but not " a part of " the parliamentary assemblies receive support

[71] House of Commons. *Weekly Hansard*, no. 297 (July 9–15, 1954).

from the Eden Plan of 1952. While Labour's attitude toward any British role in Continental federation had been completely negative, the Conservative Government's reaction to the debut of ECSC, the signature of the EDC Treaty and the decision to draft the EPC Constitution seemed to embody a different approach. All of these events took place in the spring, summer and early Autumn of 1952: the British reaction to them might well be considered an illustration of that famous pragmatism which so readily adapts British policy to new facts, and of which the Conservatives in particular pride themselves. In March of that year, Sir Anthony Eden had proposed to the Foreign Ministers that " all European restricted Communities, such as the Coal and Steel Community, which require ministerial or parliamentary institutions, should draw upon the facilities existing here in the Council of Europe." [72] What did this mean? According to Mr. Julian Amery (Conservative) it was *not* " some Machiavellian device to secure the harlot's privilege of power without responsibility." [73] But to many delegates in the May 1952 session of the Consultative Assembly it seemed to be just that, and the proposal was greeted coolly. Eden, in the September session of the Assembly, took pains to dispel this impression. While clearly stating Britain's endorsement of supranationality among the Six, he added that his Plan was " to suggest the means, and promote the action, by which two trends to European unity, the supranational and the intergovernmental, could be linked together." [74] He denied any intention then of wishing to use the Council of Europe as a device to control ECSC, EDC and EPC, even though this was precisely the impression he had created in May.

Did the negative reception accorded by the Council to the original Eden Plan cause a change in policy? The answer is still not entirely clear.[75] What is evident is that the Council adopted a position partly meeting the Eden Plan in its recommendation that joint meetings of the Consultative Assembly and the Common

[72] Council of Europe, Consultative Assembly (4th Ordinary Session), *Official Report of Debates*, Vol. III, September 15, 1952, p. 281.

[73] *Ibid.*, Vol. II, May 29, 1952, p. 148. This whole episode is treated excellently by Allan Hovey, Jr., " Britain and the Unification of Europe," *International Organisation*, Vol. IX, no. 3 (August 1955), pp. 323–337.

[74] As cited in Hovey, *op. cit.*, p. 326.

[75] Mr. Julian Amery denied and Mr. Denis Healey persuasively claimed that a definite softening of policy had taken place in mid-1952 toward union among the Six. Hovey, *op. cit.*, p. 327.

Assembly take place once a year. Such meetings would discuss a report by the High Authority to the Council of Europe, with High Authority members in attendance to answer questions, as well as a report by the Common Assembly. This step followed an earlier recommendation calling on OEEC to submit an annual report to the Consultative Assembly and to submit to a debate by that body.[76]

Joint meetings of the two Assemblies have been held every year since 1953. In keeping with the spirit of the Eden Plan, as revised in September of 1952, no suggestion of Council of Europe control over ECSC or of a special responsibility of the Six toward the Fifteen is attached to the sessions. The High Authority and the Common Assembly render factual reports and answer—with varying degrees of frankness—questions addressed to them by parliamentarians from non-member countries. The resolutions which are adopted by the Consultative Assembly as a result of these meetings not only carry no binding force of any kind but are generally no more than endorsements of ECSC policy embroidered with appropriate references to the need for keeping the Community of the Six open to the accession of other European nations. There has been no control over ECSC through this medium; the joint meetings have the aura of ceremonial sessions rather than of parliamentary debates.

But if the joint meetings are of no particular institutional significance they may nevertheless serve as a valuable clue to the attitudes of the British parliamentarians who participate and who take an interest in ECSC. Thus for the Liberal Party, Lord Layton has been the " European " spokesman; but he seemed to take a strong interest in ECSC only in the 1953 session of the joint meeting. At that time he had many kind words for supranationalism, hoped that it would lead to the establishment of a General Common Market, proposed more active co-ordination of

---

[76] In connection with the EPC Draft Constitution, Lord Layton told the Council of Europe in January 1953 that he and Monnet had worked out an unspecified scheme of " association " between the Consultative Assembly and Political Community whereby the Fifteen could be consulted before the Six took action, including the scheme of joint meetings. On behalf of the Foreign Office, Mr. Anthony Nutting endorsed this statement and praised it for being consistent with the Eden Plan. *Chronique de Politique Etrangère*, Vol. VI, no. 3 (May 1953), p. 300.

trade and production policies between ECSC and Britain and asserted the need for a scheme of association between the two.[77] No strong sign of interest has been expressed since by Liberal Party members.

Nor has the interest shown by the Conservative Party been more striking. Mr. Ronald Bell spoke in favour of continuing friendly relations between the two entities and professed that his initial fears of federation among the Six had been dispelled by the liberal commercial policy of the High Authority. Yet he underlined his opposition to any kind of restrictive or discriminatory policy ECSC might decide to adopt eventually and hinted broadly that in the event of overproduction of steel, British and ECSC producers should logically conclude a new cartel agreement.[78] These sentiments were expressed in 1953. Subsequent sessions witnessed merely routine comments and assurances, welcoming any kind of formal and informal association which did not entail direct British membership in ECSC.

The picture is otherwise with the delegates of the Labour Party. In 1953 Mr. George Chetwynd not only praised association with ECSC but claimed that Labour deserves the credit for having insisted that the British steel denationalisation bill contain a clause making mandatory exchanges of information with ECSC. He argued further that association be the medium for assuring that no new steel cartel be formed, that investment and production plans be co-ordinated to prevent overproduction and that a joint policy be followed with respect to scrap procurement. Chetwynd summarised his detailed and well-planned programme by saying:

> In one of our debates in the House of Commons, Sir Winston Churchill, then the Prime Minister, declared that the young lady must be looked over before she is married. In my opinion, we cannot marry the young lady because we have older and stronger loves. Neither can we live in sin, enjoying all the privileges of marriage without assuming any of its responsibilities. The question for us is to know whether we can maintain understanding, tolerance, absence of passion, thanks to which a lasting platonic friendship

[77] Réunion jointe des Membres de l'Assemblée Consultative du Conseil de l'Europe et des Membres de l'Assemblée Commune de la Communauté Européenne du Charbon et de l'Acier, *Compte Rendu in Extenso des Débats* (Strasbourg: June 22, 1953), pp. 114–117.

[78] *Ibid.*, pp. 56–58.

could reign among us. Certainly there will be difficulties; but I think that it could be done.[79]

In the same session, Mr. Alfred Robens, the leader of the Labour delegation to the Council of Europe, expressed very much the same interest with respect to the welfare implications of High Authority policy that his continental Socialist colleagues were to feature in later years. But with respect to the possibility of the ECSC area developing into a restrictive and discriminatory tariff system, he expressed precisely the same fears as his Conservative and Liberal colleagues, as well as the Consultative Assembly spokesmen from Sweden, Denmark and Austria.[80] Yet his arguments in favour of the tight co-ordination of research and the sharing of its results foreshadowed not only the content of the Agreement on Association but also the tenor of the Euratom treaty.

Labour speakers continued to stress the desirability of an extended association, covering every conceivable economic and commercial topic of mutual interest, in later meetings of the two assemblies. While they never gave the impression of being eager to join ECSC, they developed the necessity of constant consultation much more deliberately and with greater attention to detail than was true of their Conservative colleagues. After the Agreement on Association went into effect, it was once more the Labour delegation which welcomed it and examined the ways in which it might be made meaningful, while continuing to stress the need to avoid any kind of direct relations between steel producers which might resemble a cartel.[81]

The pattern of British party attitudes expressed in the joint meetings is a striking one: prior to the entry into force of the ECSC Treaty, Labour was in power and showed no desire whatever to participate in continental parliamentary activity beyond the routine meetings of the Council of Europe; the opposition Conservatives, however, argued for closer co-operation with continental parties and governments. As soon as the political

---

[79] *Ibid.*, p. 29. This passage is retranslated from the French and may therefore be slightly inaccurate.

[80] *Ibid.*, pp. 62–68.

[81] Deuxième Réunion Jointe des Membres de l'Assemblée Consultative du Conseil de l'Europe et des Membres de l'Assemblée Commune de la Communauté Européenne du Charbon et de l'Acier, *Compte Rendu in Extenso des Débats* (Strasbourg: May 20, 1954), pp. 33–34, 37, 40. *Ibid.*, October 27, 1955, p. 58.

fortunes of British electoral life reversed the position of the parties, their European attitudes underwent a complete change: the Conservatives, despite the Eden Plan, showed only the most superficial and polite interest in continental parliamentary supranationalism relating to ECSC; but now it was the opposition Labour Party which carried its role in Westminster to Strasbourg by arguing in detail for an imaginative programme of association. This pattern is similar to that exhibited by a number of continental parties; interest in supranationalism seems always to increase when the party is in opposition. Powerless to influence policy meaningfully at home, it is given an extramural base from which legitimate and respectable attacks against the home government can be launched.

This feature is observable also in one of the favourite proposals of the ECSC parliamentarians, the suggestion formulated by the Common Assembly to equip the Council of Association with a parliamentary control commission. Anxious to accelerate the integration process *vis-à-vis* Britain and desirous of controlling the High Authority and the Council of Ministers in their dealings with the United Kingdom, the Common Assembly proposed in 1955 that a commission composed of nine members of the House of Commons and nine Assembly members be created to take up matters connected with association. The proposal was received coolly by the High Authority and the Council; it was politely declined by Her Majesty's Government—and therefore by the Conservative leadership. But Labour's voices spoke differently. Mr. Edwards asserted " the general principle that we must try to establish at parliamentary levels the arrangements appropriate to the new Agreement of Association."[82] In 1956 he referred to the Eden Plan itself as encouraging and justifying this arrangement, while his colleague Mr. Jenkins noted the growth of the General Common Market as making most desirable a closer inter-parliamentary liaison.[83] Being in opposition, the Labour delegation felt free to endorse the ideas of the Common Assembly, while the Conservatives accompanied their rejection of it in London with silence in Strasbourg.

Clearly, the joint meetings have led neither to any real control over ECSC by the Council of Europe nor to any considerable

[82] Third Joint Meeting . . . (Strasbourg: October 27, 1955), p. 60.
[83] Fourth Joint Meeting . . . (Strasbourg: October 20, 1956), pp. 66–67, 75.

deepening of relations between British and ECSC parliamentarians. The rejection of the Assembly's suggestion regarding the Council of Association seems to mean that the British Government in 1957 is no more anxious to establish such relations than it was in 1952. However, the obviously increasing momentum of the integration movement among the Six has left its mark on the Council of Europe and its British members. Whenever in previous years the Consultative Assembly had been presented with the spectacle of the Six wishing to conclude some form of closer union, a certain anxiety about being excluded had invariably been expressed. While the Council of Europe always endorsed whatever proposal was before it, it did so by stressing the necessity for keeping the closer union open to states who might wish to join later, as well as subject it to the kind of collective review of which the joint meetings are an example. When confronted in 1957 with the finished EEC and Euratom Treaties, the Assembly endorsed them once more while urging the necessity of maintaining democratic and parliamentary control over them. Further, it recommended to its Committee of Ministers to study all possible means whereby the common market might be made to include agricultural products and third countries, specifically Britain. Finally, it strongly urged that no new assemblies be set up, that existing assemblies of the Six be merged, and that at least half of their membership be made to be identical with the membership of the Consultative Assembly, and that Swiss and Portuguese parliamentarians be invited to join them in order to examine the work of the OEEC.[84] Those of the Fifteen who did not belong to the Six wished to assert continuing ties and re-enforce liaison with the evolving closer Community. With British support, in fact under the stimulus of a new Eden Plan—the " Grand Design " —a full-scale " rationalisation " of European institutions was demanded.

Ostensibly, the original " Grand Design " of Henri IV and Sully was to achieve the unity of western Christendom against the infidel Turk. Some equally plausible reasons have been advanced by British spokesmen for the " Grand Design " of 1957, put forward

[84] Resolution 120 (1957), Recommendation 130 (1957) and Recommendation concerning the Rationalisation of European Parliamentary Activities, adopted on January 9 and 11, 1957, Consultative Assembly, Council of Europe. Texts in *Informations Mensuelles* (January 1957), pp. 9–10, 51–54.

to rationalise the welter of European international and parliamentary bodies. Overlapping and duplication among the assemblies is to be eliminated; the pressure on members of parliaments belonging to several such organs is to be reduced and the efficiency of the assemblies increased. Furthermore, the division of Europe into two blocks, one closely united in EEC, ECSC and Euratom and the other merely held together by OEEC, NATO and the Council of Europe, is to be avoided by making one assembly the guardian of the totality.[85]

But the unexpressed purpose behind the original " Grand Design " was the assurance of French hegemony over Habsburg power. Thus many commentators in 1957 have charged that the tacit purpose behind the British scheme is once more to strengthen the machinery enabling the United Kingdom to maintain a modicum of control over the Continental federal entities which it declines to join. What is the content of the " Grand Design " and what facets of British policy toward the integrating continent does it serve?

" The Grand Design," said Mr. Ormsby-Gore at Strasbourg, " does not aim solely at creating one Assembly. It is a plan which embraces all aspects of western co-operation, political, military, economic and cultural as well as parliamentary."[86] Its purpose is to combine the rationalisation of institutions with new aims: attracting popular attention to the work of European and Atlantic agencies, putting this work before the Assembly for public criticism and stimulating the NATO governments to greater defensive efforts. Institutionally, the present assemblies of WEU, the Council of Europe and the proposed regular NATO Parliamentary Conference are to be merged into one deliberative body. This organ would examine and debate the activities of OEEC, the European Conferences of Transport and Agriculture Ministers and of NATO —all of which at present have no statutory international parliamentary control bodies—as well as of the Council of Europe's

---

[85] Thus the *Economist* (March 23, 1957) suggested that parliamentary rationalisation be accompanied (1) by the creation of a European Prime Ministers' Conference to co-ordinate all defence, commercial, economic and foreign policy problems and (2) by the appointment of a European Secretary-General to be given the task of supervising the execution of policies jointly decided. See also the speeches made during the April 1957 session of the Consultative Assembly, *Informations Mensuelles* (May, 1957), pp. 79–97.

[86] Council of Europe, Consultative Assembly, session of April 29–May 4, 1957. *Informations Mensuelles* (May, 1957), p. 91.

Committee of Ministers. There is no indication in the British plan that the debates of the single European Assembly would be any more authoritative legally than is true of the deliberations of the agencies whose place it would take.

The " Grand Design " explicitly is to assure liaison with the single parliamentary Assembly planned for ECSC, EEC and Euratom, though the British spokesmen made it clear that their assembly would have no direct jurisdiction over the activities of the Six. Joint meetings, on the model of Council of Europe–ECSC experience, are to be the means to achieve this aim, as already approved by a series of resolutions of the Consultative Assembly. Once a year, members of the enlarged single Assembly of the Seventeen would meet with representatives of the Assembly of the Six in what may presumably develop into something more than the ceremonial sessions held so far.[87] EEC and Euratom are to submit annual reports to this Assembly, which would then be discussed at the same time at which the reports of OEEC and ECSC are taken up.

While these aspects of the British proposal were accepted without much difficulty, the core of the plan ran into heavy opposition from speakers who saw no way to bring NATO and WEU discussions into the same parliamentary framework with economic matters, in view of the fact that not all governments were members of all international organisations concerned. Others objected to institutionalising the powerlessness of three parliamentary bodies into the equally powerless framework of a single one. And while the Conservative Party delegation took up the cudgels in defence of the plan and sought to demonstrate its lack of desire to " control " the aims of the Six, several Continental speakers nevertheless implied that the " Grand Design " would again give third countries the possibilities of criticism without participation.[88]

---

[87] Resolutions 123 (1957), 124 (1957), 125 (1957) and Recommendation 134 (1957) of the Consultative Assembly. *Ibid.*, pp. 90–91.

[88] The Italian Government presented a plan of its own to the May 1957 session of the Consultative Assembly. Instead of the "Grand Design " and its implied absence of any real legislative branch, the Italian Plan stressed the need for retaining what legislative powers exist already, and even to extend them. Hence it suggested the creation of a single European parliamentary Assembly, whose function would be essentially the same as that now exercised by the Council of Europe; but as " chambers " within this Assembly there would function the existing bodies, each carrying out the mandate entrusted to it by the treaty which had created it. It is hoped that the ties which would be thus formed among the separate chambers

British stress on the contributions which could be made by OEEC, emphasis on the future role of NATO, and the announcement of Mr. Ormsby-Gore that the United Kingdom was concluding *bilateral* nuclear assistance conventions with the member states of Euratom seemed to indicate that the proposal was again motivated by a desire to check the trend toward supranational integration. The only concrete purpose served by the merger of assemblies would be the elimination of duplicate mandates, thus saving the time of the members. The degree of *ad hoc* " control " already exercised by the Consultative Assembly over OEEC and by the Parliamentary Conference over NATO does not encourage the idea that the scope of effective parliamentary supervision in the unified organ would be any greater. Hence it is hard to escape the conclusion that the purpose of the scheme is to reassert the British role in continental integration. No other practicable implication seems apparent.

But it need not be assumed that the most cynical of the European interpretations of British motives is altogether accurate. It is submitted that while the Eden Plan as well as the Grand Design certainly aim at reasserting British influence over the Continental integration movement—without implying any desire to join that movement through means other than intergovernmental co-operation—reassertion should not be equated with the desire to control. It appears from such evidence as the positions taken by British trade associations and trade unions, from government statements and arguments of the Labour party, that British opinion now generally realises that the movement toward closer supranational integration is irreversible. If this is so, it becomes essential from Britain's viewpoint to make arrangements facilitating the expression of British aims and preferences, to represent British policy at all times. If this can be done in such a way as to bolster the illusion current in some European circles that Britain might soon accept the supranational aspect of the integration movement for itself, and thus extract concessions for Britain's benefit, gestures toward reconciliation with supranationalism become an even more useful tactical device. But, as close examination of the British proposals has shown, no meaningful acceptance of any aspect of federalism has ever been apparent. The aim thus remains the desire to

would lead to the organic growth of a genuine European parliament. The chambers would include all existing assemblies, EEC/ECSC/Euratom, WEU, NATO and Consultative Assembly, *Ibid.*, pp. 95–96.

participate, to speak up, to exert influence, without making any commitments other than those standard in dealings among governments, as distinguished from relations among private groups and parties.

Such a pattern cannot lead to the formation of supranational political parties even if the Grand Design were to be accepted. Certainly it can establish new channels of communication among national parties and broaden the sphere of contacts among them. As such, it may even influence the making of decisions at the interministerial level, where Britain is certain to participate far more actively than in the past. But it cannot, as the nature of our federal archetype shows, lead to the formation of trans-national political parties.

CHAPTER 12

THE HIGH AUTHORITY:

INDEPENDENT FEDERAL EXECUTIVE?

THE purpose of this analysis of the High Authority is an assessment of its contribution to the political integration of the six member states. Has High Authority policy been an active agent for the redirection of loyalties and expectations toward a federal focus? Or have the pro-integration changes of attitude described previously come about irrespective of deliberate policy in Luxembourg?

Such an inquiry makes it unnecessary to evaluate in detail the success or failure of supranational policy from a strictly economic viewpoint. Certainly in terms of the development of prices, production and investment in the coal and steel sectors the policies followed have been a success. The absence of the economic chaos predicted in 1952 supports the same conclusion. No doubt there exists a general satisfaction with supranational policy among industrialists, who have, on the whole, shown loyalty to High Authority decisions even when they opposed them. And clearly, governments have generally carried out their obligations and expressed their approval of the first experiment in functional integration. All these factors are evidence of success, and it is not the purpose of this chapter to argue otherwise. Our question refers exclusively to the deliberate contribution of supranational policy to political integration, to the code of conduct displayed by the nine members of the High Authority, their ideology, and their drive in support of growing political unity.

THE IDEOLOGY OF THE HIGH AUTHORITY

As at the close of 1957, the High Authority had enjoyed a stable membership of ten members. Only the president changed during this period, with the replacement of Jean Monnet by René Mayer in June of 1955. The essential socio-political attributes of the members can be summarised thus:

Member	Nationality	Profession	Party Affiliation
Monnet, Jean	French	businessman, diplomat, economic planner	not known, sympathies left of centre
Mayer, René	French	businessman, lawyer, administrator, politician	Radical-Socialist
Etzel, Franz [1]	German	politician, lawyer	Christian-Democrat
Coppé, Albert	Belgian	economist, politician	Christian-Democrat
Daum, Léon	French	industrialist (steel)	not known
Finet, Paul [2]	Belgian	trade union leader	Socialist
Giacchero, Enzo	Italian	engineer, politician	Christian-Democrat
Potthoff, Heinz	German	trade union leader	Socialist
Spierenburg, Dirk	Dutch	civil servant	not known
Wehrer, Albert	Luxembourg	civil servant	not known

As a decision-making organ, the High Authority is in theory and in fact a collegiate body, whose rulings usually reflect the consensus of all the members. Voting is avoided as a general practice; only if a negotiated consensus seems unobtainable does the simple majority voting rule become operative. No information of possible differences of opinion among the members is permitted to reach the public. All public statements of the members consciously are made to reflect their minimum consensus. Decisions are prepared by " working groups," committees of members joined by senior permanent officials, thus permitting a certain specialisation of the members with respect to given areas of action, while the final decision remains a collective one. Since there is a minimum of delegation of power to individual members, it seems entirely appropriate to speak of a " High Authority ideology," the total body of values and interests continually expressed, in statements and decisions, by the entire membership. Only the

[1] Resigned in autumn of 1957 to become West German Minister of Finance. Succeeded on January 1, 1958 by Franz Blücher.
[2] Succeeded René Mayer as President on January 1, 1958. Roger Reynaud took Mayer's place as member of the High Authority. Thus:

Blücher, Franz	German	Industrialist, politician	FDP until 1956; DP since then
Reynaud, Roger	French	trade union leader (CFTC)	MRP (?)

beliefs of Jean Monnet seem sufficiently different from the pattern to warrant separate statement and treatment.[2a]

Monnet's germinal importance in the origins and the negotiation of ECSC has been established above and the specific ideas he proposed to the treaty drafting conference analysed.[2b] What remains to be done is to state Monnet's personal ideology, as explaining the concrete measures he proposed in 1950 and sought to implement when chosen as president of the High Authority in 1952. His disappointment with the ECSC record—partly because of the divergence between his and the other members' outlook—and his crucial role in the *Relance Européenne* become

[2a] The rules of procedure of the High Authority are published in *Journal Officiel*, November 24, 1954. Information made available to me in Luxembourg does not suffice for an accurate decision-making analysis in terms of the roles exercised by the individual members and their reciprocal influence in the formulation of consensus. Beyond the generalisations advanced above, it can only be added that the Working Group is usually the body in which conflicting positions are compromised, after study and recommendation by the relevant division or divisions. Only when compromise cannot be achieved at this level is there likely to be a formal vote in the meeting of the full High Authority; unfortunately, details concerning such situations can be obtained only on the basis of hearsay. Henry J. Merry, after a study on the spot, suggests that dissent tends to dominate when the issue is one of restrictive as against liberal interpretation of the Treaty, when a 5 to 4 vote for narrow interpretation is likely to prevail. The dissenters included, according to this surmise, MM. Monnet, Finet, Potthoff and Giacchero: *i.e.*, the two Belgian, French and German members, respectively, voted against one another. "The European Coal and Steel Community—Operations of the High Authority," *Western Political Quarterly*, Vol. 7, no. 2 (June 1955), p. 183.

Another line of surmise is opened up by the composition of the working groups. According to the membership list published by Merry, it appears that MM. Giacchero, Wehrer and Potthoff held no chairmanships, whereas all others did. This fact corroborates the general impression obtained that these three gentlemen are least influential in shaping decisions. On the other hand, no behavioural data of this kind refutes the institutional rule laid down in the Treaty and the Rules of Procedure that the High Authority must act as a collegiate and supranational entity, independent of any national, functional or ideological constituency, at least in terms of formal instructions.

Of the 550-odd persons employed by the High Authority only about 150 are considered " personnel de responsabilité," the others being clerical, janitorial, driving, translating and interpreting staff. The professional grade can be broken down as follows by nationalities represented (based on a collation of my own survey with Wolf-Rodé, *op. cit.*, pp. 1–48–9, and applicable as of December 1955):

	Ger.	Fr.	Ital.	Belg.	Dutch	Lux.	Saar	Others or Doubtful
Directors	7	3	3	2	1	1	—	—
Assistant-Directors	4	1	—	2	1	—	—	—
Officers	31	31	14	16	12	10	2	7
Total	42	35	17	20	14	11	2	7

See especially Chap. 7.

obvious when viewed against the background of his federal doctrine.[3]

Politics and economics are inextricably intertwined in Monnet's thought pattern, with the point of departure being a definite " third force " doctrine. To Monnet, the cold war is largely the result of a disunited Europe's inviting Russian invasion and begetting permanent American counter-moves. In his words—

> In order to preserve the precariously peaceful relations which exist in the world today and develop them into a lasting peace, we must change the European situation by uniting the Europeans. In this way we shall eliminate the menace which the division and weakness of Europe constitute for herself and for others. If we remain divided as we are, the Europeans will be left exposed to

[3] Unless otherwise specified, my statement of the ideology of the High Authority is based on the following sources. (1) Speeches and explanations on policy of all High Authority members: Assemblée Commune, *Débats* (compte rendu in extenso des séances), Exercise 1954–1955, May and June 1955, no. 9; session extraordinaire, November 1955, no. 11; Exercise 1955–1956, May and June 1956, no. 13; session extraordinaire, November 1956, no. 14. (2) Monnet: " Appeals for a ' United States of Europe '," *New York Times*, June 16, 1956, p. 4; *The United States of Europe Has Begun* (speeches and addresses, 1952–1954, published as High Authority Doc. 252/553); speeches of August 10, 1952 and September 11, 1952; Address to the National Planning Association, Washington, D.C., December 13, 1954; " La création des Etats-Unis d'Europe peut seule stabiliser les rapports Est-Ouest," *Le Monde*, Paris, June 16, 1955; " L'Europe se fait," speech to the Société d'Economie Politique de Belgique, June 30, 1953; and also Gerbet, *op. cit.*, pp. 538–543. (3) Mayer: " Pour une politique Européenne," *Nouvelles de l'Europe*, June 1956; " Britain and the European Coal and Steel Community," November 16, 1955, High Authority Doc. 8102/55e; " The United States and the Community," February 5, 1956, High Authority Doc. 996/56e; *ECSC Bulletin*, June–July 1955. (4) Etzel: " Die Europäische Gemeinschaft für Kohle und Stahl," in *Die Grossen Zwichenstaatlichen Wirtschaftsorganisationen* (St. Gallen, 1955); " The European Coal and Steel Community," *European Yearbook* Vol. I (Strasbourg: Council of Europe, 1955); " Von Messina nach Brüssel," *Bulletin des Presse- und Informationsamtes der Bundesregierung*, August 4, 1955; " Montanunion und europäische Einigung," *CDU Bulletin*, December 1, 1955; " Fünf Jahre Montan-Union," *Bulletin, op. cit.*, May 12, 1955; speech to Mont Pelerin Society, Seelisberg, September 11, 1953. (5) Coppé: Speech at the National Press Club, Washington, D.C., April 20, 1955; " The Schuman Plan: Its Scope and Implications," speech at the Uebersee-Club, Hamburg, June 18, 1954. (6) Potthoff: speech at the Austrian Workers' Congress, October 2, 1953; speech at third regular Congress of I. G. Metall, September 13, 1954, *Protokoll, op. cit.*; occasional speeches and articles reported in *Stahl und Eisen, Der Gewerkschaftler, Gewerkschaftliche Monatshefte, Die Quelle, Glückauf.* (7) Spierenburg: Speech to Bundeskammer der Gewerblichen Wirtschaft, Vienna, April 23, 1954; speech to the Swedish Iron and Steel Federation, October 6, 1955. (8) Giacchero: speech to the 6th Congress of the European Union of Federalists, Luxembourg, March 2, 1956. (9) Wehrer: " Expérience d'Intégration Européenne," speech in Luxembourg, April 1, 1955; speech at Longwy, November 12, 1955; speech to the Académie Diplomatique Internationale, Paris, March 24, 1955. (10) Finet, Potthoff and others, " Quelques Aspects économiques et sociaux de la Communauté Européenne du Charbon et de l'Acier," speeches to trade union leaders, Luxembourg, December 7, 1954.

nationalist ambitions and will be forced, as happened in the past, to look for outside guarantees in order to protect themselves against each other—each one fearing the progress of the other as in the past.[4]

Only a United Europe can assure independence against both Moscow and Washington and incidentally diminish cold war tensions by reducing world bipolarity of power.

Federation, not a union of states, is the method for achieving unity because of Monnet's conviction that governments and politicians act only when prodded by a superior power. Hence, intergovernmental co-operation is condemned as futile. But federation, without an aroused public opinion demanding it, is impossible. Hence, Monnet considered it tactically useful to merge federally the economic sector which is most difficult to separate from the total economy and which most appeals to the public mind as symbolic of industrial power: coal and steel. If properly managed by a non-national, detached, technocratic body of " Europeans," such a merger would inevitably lead to full federation by confronting governments with inescapable economic *faits accomplis.*

If economics is part of political tactics, it nevertheless also occupies an independent ideological role in Monnet's doctrine. He holds that the technological revolution of our era makes possible for the first time the fulfilment of all welfare demands of all classes of society, as achieved by the United States and about to be achieved in the Soviet Union. Europe has fallen behind because of entrepreneurial stagnation, induced and protected by sealed-off and protected national economies. The competitive common market is the remedy for this condition, destined to give Europe the same industrial initiative and productivity which obtains in the United States, by multiplying the number of consumers. The common market will lead to Europe's economic revival, political stability and ultimately—through federation—to a new world position of influence rivalling that of the super-powers.

It follows that Monnet's emphasis throughout his tenure in Luxembourg was on the federal nature of ECSC institutions, as being superior in actual power to those of the member governments. He barely acknowledged the existence of the Council of Ministers, never tired of stressing the need for the immediate

[4] High Authority Doc. 252/55e, *op. cit.,* p. 61.

creation of additional federal institutions, fought publicly for EDC and EPC, and held that Britain's joining the federal movement was only a question of time, until the success of ECSC had been clearly demonstrated.

And this insistence was carried over into the functional interpretation of the Treaty, whose central aim he considers planning. " Planning today must seek to create the widest possible community of action. . . . Planning in this sense requires institutions which are developed on a scale sufficient to encourage the greatest expansion of human welfare that is possible in the twentieth century." [5] On the model of his Commissariat du Plan for the rejuvenation of French industry, such an interpretation of the Treaty was held quite consistent with free enterprise—provided that the technicians were able to force the common organisation of effort and channel the direction of development.

Hence, the role Monnet assigned to the organisation of consensus in ECSC is crucial. ECSC represents an effort for the achievement of the collective European welfare through the pooling of the resources of all. In a sense, Monnet considered the High Authority as the repository of the European General Will, with the evil governments merely the spokesmen for the selfish particular wills. The Treaty, as administered by the High Authority *is* the basic European consensus for progress, peace and federation. Monnet added that continuous consultations with interested industrial and trade union organisations would give practical effect to this consensus because groups would thus act for the common good. It may well be that here past experiences at the Commissariat du Plan shaped his doctrine. In that office, working parties for the allocation of investment funds by industrial sectors did enjoy the co-operation of trade associations; but Monnet possessed both carrot and stick to obtain consensus in the form of public funds to be distributed for investment.

Neither Mayer nor the other eight members of the High Authority shared Monnet's convictions with respect to the role of planning, the function of technicians in forcing the hands of

---

[5] Speech to the National Planning Association, *op. cit.*, p. 15. It is, of course, highly significant that Monnet's closest collaborators in the planning stage of Schuman's proposal were his aides in the Commissariat du Plan, MM. Uri and Hirsch. Their proposals were committed to formal draft form by Professor Paul Reuter, equally sympathetic to Monnet's principles even though he appeared as counsel for the French Government when the Court of Justice heard the Monnet Rebate case.

governments, or the almost mystical immanent federalism of ECSC. Their interpretation of the Treaty is far more modest and their doctrine of consensus a great deal more mechanical. Nor is the need for economic integration tied directly to the belief in the desirability of a political " third force." Only on one crucial point does Monnet's doctrine coincide with the general ideology: the creation of a competitive common market is the panacea for the revitalisation of the European industrial economy, alone capable of making it the equal of the American and Soviet patterns. For this, ECSC is considered the vital first step.

What, then, is the High Authority doctrine with respect to the virtues of supranationalism, the achievement of political federation, and the *Relance Européenne?* " The Community," said René Mayer when assuring the world that he had not been appointed president to " kill supranationalism," " is Europe's motor, its energy-giver. It is both an example for other fields of action and a lever for European action."[6] The purpose of ECSC is to demonstrate the technical and practical feasibility of economic integration and thereby act as precursor to its extension. But supranationalism is emphatically not equated with political federation: it is merely one technique, a vital one, among diplomatic and inter-governmental ways of achieving closer unity. Its vitality rests in the fact that it can promote inter-governmental efforts by studies, demonstrations and suggestions, and threaten to act unilaterally if the governments are slow to merge or coordinate their efforts. It follows, of course, that constant and intimate co-operation with the Council of Ministers is the first necessity of supranational policy-making, in sharp contrast to Monnet's preferences.

Euratom and the General Common Market are the necessary next steps, and if they should lead to political federation, the members of the High Authority would welcome and applaud such a development. But it is not the function of ECSC to further *directly* the unification of Europe. " We hear a great deal today of the necessity for further economic integration," wrote Franz Etzel. " In this, we are not claimants for but witnesses of the

[6] Speech to the Common Assembly, June 21, 1955; *ECSC Bulletin* (June–July 1955), p. 10. See also the statements of Mayer reported in *Usine Nouvelle*, August 4, 1955, and in *VWV-Vereinigte Wirtschaftsdienste-" Montan*," August 8, 1955. Also E. Vindry d'Hinvery, " Comment la C. E. C. A. forge l'Europe," *Hommes et Commerce*, January–February 1955, p. 17.

practicality of supranationalism, which alone seems to us to be able to assure the permanence of European co-operation."[7] And this line of thought dominated the participation of the High Authority in the work of the Brussels Committee of Experts which drafted the Euratom and Common Market Treaties. The purely economic need for broader union was stated and the positive experience of ECSC offered in evidence of its practicality. Some supranational organs, not necessarily as powerful as the High Authority, are essential to prevent governments from going back on their promises to integrate and to administer, free from national interference, the transitional rules for the gradual introduction of free trade: investment support, labour readaptation, transport harmonisation, removal of wage distortions, and the controlled elimination of subsidies.[8] Successful integration does *not* demand the prior harmonisation of wage, labour and tax policies. But new treaties should be more flexible than the ECSC instrument, giving the supranational authority the power to find the limits of needed competence. Mayer noted that if the High Authority had enjoyed this possibility more would have been achieved in the labour sector and in the co-ordination of overall fuel policy. Even with Euratom, he requested that the competence of ECSC over fuels be expanded and that policy in the atomic sector be closely co-ordinated with classical energy sources.

But this cautious endorsement of the *Relance* hardly amounts to an ideology of federal dynamism. One reason for this reluctance lies in a much more restrained interpretation of the planning function of supranational institutions than that held by Monnet. The Treaty, it is true, stresses the virtues of a free competitive economy and holds that increases in living standards are to be achieved as a result of more effective competition and not through direct planning. On the other hand, the Treaty also contains authorisation to use the standard techniques for " steering " an economy under conditions of " crisis," " shortages " or " surpluses " which are nowhere defined.

---

[7] " Fünf Jahre Montan-Union," *op. cit.*, p. 739.

[8] For a succinct official summary of the High Authority position toward the General Common Market, as argued in the Intergovernmental Committee in Brussels, see Pierre Uri, " Memorandum on General Economic Integration in Europe," High Authority Doc. no. 5579/55e, and Mayer's speech to the Common Assembly during the March 1956 session; *Débats, op. cit.*, no. 12, pp. 339–343. It is of the highest importance that Uri in fact *drafted the final report of the Intergovernmental committee.* The governments thus showed a high degree of confidence in the supranational example.

In the ideology of the High Authority, the free enterprise and anti-dirigist viewpoint has definitely carried the day, with repeated assurances by most members that firms must make their own decisions, that a controlled market—national or supranational—is undesirable and that the crisis powers of the High Authority should not be used without specific need, exhaustive study and general agreement.[9] Regulation of competition must be tolerated only to introduce free trade without serious hardship to workers and marginal firms, to protect employment and to control cartels and discrimination. The Treaty requires a " humane liberalism," said René Mayer.

This restricted conception of the High Authority role implies, of course, that no active steps in accelerating the " spill-over " effect be taken. That sector integration for coal and steel raises common problems as regards wages, currency, trade with third countries, general transport policy, taxes and economic stability is fully expected. The High Authority hopes that the spill-over will result in further integration, but it deliberately refuses to exploit the process in order to speed progress toward unity. It defines its purpose as exploring the issues in a test sector—coal and steel —and uses it as evidence for the successful continuation of integration policies, as initiated and implemented by others. But in view of the acceptance by the six governments of the bulk of this doctrine in the EEC Treaty, it cannot be argued that passivity has been futile or politically maladroit.

The justification for this passive attitude is " the Treaty." Albert Coppé was speaking for the entire membership when he asserted:

> It would not be wise for us to be dogmatic or base ourselves on an ideology. It is best to admit the Treaty such as it is. It was adopted by our respective parliaments, with its economic and legal techniques. Let us admit it, above the preference that we may have for one or the other ideology, for one or the other policy, or economic philosophy. Let us be faithful to a Treaty which has been signed by our six countries.[10]

Socialists and Christian-Democrats, trade unionists and industrialists on the High Authority have argued that not ideology, but

---

[9] An exception to this generalisation would be Heinz Potthoff, who on occasion defends Socialist planning principles instead. See his address to the I. G. Metall Congress, *op. cit.*
[10] *Débats, op. cit.*, no. 13, p. 554.

" the Treaty," is the bedrock of thinking, planning and action. Only what the Treaty specifically authorises can be undertaken. " The art of governing exists also for the High Authority. Its modest but permanent application is our way of assuming the responsibilities often urged upon us," warned René Mayer.[11] A wide interpretation of the Treaty is rejected therefore. The elevation of the Treaty " above " ideologies means, in fact, the institutionalisation of a restrictive interpretation as the essence of the High Authority's ideology. A membership not inclined to assume dirigistic powers, even though they could certainly be deduced from appropriate Treaty provisions, can thus find refuge in a doctrine which makes illegal the elaboration of more than a minimal regulatory programme.

The operative principle of the High Authority as an executive agency is equally passive: it seeks to organise a general consensus among its subjects before embarking on any policy. Continuous consultation with all interested parties—trade unions, industrialists and governments—is its watchword. No major decision is made before opinions have been sounded out. On some issues, such as investment policy or the co-ordination of the cyclical policies, the High Authority admits that its policy *is* whatever agreement has been worked out in the countless meetings of experts held in Luxembourg. While contacts among interest groups and national civil servants are undoubtedly multiplied enormously by this practice and while the evolution of a consensus on specific issues can certainly be demonstrated, the fact remains that the " policy " of the executive thus becomes merely the minimum common denominator in the aspirations of its constituents—the opposite of Monnet's conception. It may imply passiveness, but it is certainly *prudent* and guards against excessive charges of *dirigisme*. Said Mayer:

> My colleagues and I, the men of the High Authority, have large powers. But we do not have to use them all the time, every day, on all occasions; but we have to know when to use them, and to explain them to the interested parties. It is better to arrive at an understanding than to issue orders. It is better to find an arrangement than to hand out fines to certain firms. It is better to co-operate, to create jointly, to make your mind work in the spirit of the Treaty,

[11] *Ibid.*, p. 373.

in the spirit of the European Community than to hide behind bushes, trees, obstacles and commas.[12]

If the reluctance of the High Authority to fine tax delinquent firms or impose rigid controls on cartels and mergers rests on an interpretation of the Treaty seeking to avoid legal formalism, its reluctance to exploit the spill-over process and to work toward political unity by regarding itself as a federal executive are nevertheless justified as obedience to that instrument. The twin ideology of economic liberalism and continuous consultation, in effect, facilitates a " hands-off " approach with respect to controversial political issues and minimised the direct role of the High Authority as a vigorous coal-steel executive, or as a precursor of a larger federal pattern. However, it is equally significant that with the success of the *Relance* by 1957, stronger recommendations began to be heard in Luxembourg.

HIGH AUTHORITY POLICIES AND POLITICAL INTEGRATION

An active policy of utilising the integrated coal-steel sector for the political unification of Europe would have to go considerably beyond the belief that the purpose of ECSC is merely the establishment and maintenance of a free market. It would have to seek a maximisation of institutional growth and cater vigorously to segments of opinion seeking their advantage through supranational action. In short, High Authority policy would take its inspiration from the groups who entertain short-run and long-run positive expectations with respect to the common market, not from those who are anxious to have merely an unregulated free market. Hence, High Authority policy in fields which lend themselves to this kind of appeal and development must be critically analysed, notably measures with respect to cartels, mergers, investment labour and welfare, coal prices and distribution. Other fields of activity, while certainly important to the purely economic development of a common market, are not directly related to the political consequences which provide our focus.

Thus, cartel policy was from the first dominated by the concern to avoid federal self-assertion, though perfectly legal under the Treaty, and arrive at modifications of the coal sales organisations in Germany, Belgium and France by means of compromises acceptable to all. The High Authority was not only sympathetic

[12] " Pour une politique européenne," *op. cit.*, p. 14.

to the arguments for employment, production and distribution stability put forward by all German and French groups in justification of the cartels, but was obviously fearful of a showdown with powerful segments of industrial opinion. Hence, negotiations dragged on for over two years, only to result in a " compromise " which left the essence of the centralised sales structure intact. Formally, the High Authority justified its decisions by stressing that " the Treaty " was its sole guide, an empirical one, and that all dogmatism was thus avoided; while asserting its inability to recommend or order specific solutions to GEORG and COBECHAR, it argued that it merely has the right to allow or prohibit specific proposals made to it.[13]

But the High Authority conceded to its critics on the left and right that perfect competition among collieries was neither desirable economically nor required by the Treaty. Yet it rejected the corollary advanced by ECSC Socialists that the institution of a compulsory, publicly controlled cartel of all ECSC mines was the answer to the employment and access problems while also controlling private economic power. Such a solution would not be permitted by the Treaty, in addition to being dirigistic. Instead MM. Etzel, Mayer and Spierenburg merely gave strong assurances that the authorised sales agencies would be subject to the strictest supervision from Luxembourg.[14]

Mergers, as long as they do not lead to a monopolistic position, are actually encouraged by Luxembourg and no request for a merger has ever been disallowed, including massive German reconcentrations and the fusion of the two largest Belgian steelmakers, though some restrictions accompanied this last authorisation. But it must be admitted that on this score High Authority intentions ran into strong opposition from the Council of Ministers in 1954. Proposals for a rigid system of supervision, based on a low figure for mergers to be exempt from the authorisation requirement, were rejected by five of the six governments. German counter-proposals having the opposite aim were considered

---

[13] Albert Wehrer, " Le Plan Schuman et les Cartels," speech to the International Law Association, Luxembourg, September 24, 1954. Heinz Potthoff, " Kartelle und Zusammenschlüsse in der Montanunion," *Bergbau und Wirtschaft*, November 7, 1955, p. 525. See Etzel's campaign and compromise with German industrial opinion, especially BDI President Fritz Berg, in *Agence Europe*, April 14, 1954. For a formal statement on cartel doctrine, see High Authority answer to Michel Debré, *Journal Officiel*, May 11, 1955.

[14] Detailed statements in *Débats, op. cit.*, no. 11 (November 1955), pp. 63–75, 126–127.

unacceptable by the High Authority, with the result that an intermediate compromise was finally adopted,[15] after eight different drafts had to be considered. But the compromising went on until the unanimous agreement of the Council had been obtained even though a simple majority decision was all that was required legally, thus implying another concession by the High Authority.

The results of this policy are that German industrialists feel free to initiate merger proceedings even before formal approval from Luxembourg has been obtained. The unwillingness of the High Authority to administer the rules vigorously has led to denunciations of the whole approval system among all trade associations. And in the meantime, national clusters of industrial power, organised in only slightly revised cartels, continue to dominate industrial decision-making. If a more dirigistic interpretation of the Treaty had been adopted, Luxembourg could have been instrumental in forcing a supranational realignment of industrial groupings by systematically splitting the national trade associations by eliminating their cartels, provided supranational ententes were simultaneously controlled.

Great reluctance to guide and steer the free market so successfully established by the High Authority dominates the investment policy of ECSC. Obliged by the Treaty to publish periodically " general objectives " of production and consumption, the High Authority proceeded to publish its own forecasts in July of 1955, only to be greeted with shouts of criticism from workers for failure to include wage policy and from industrialists for its choice of statistics. Late in 1956 a more complete forecast was made public. No criticism could be made in this case since the figures were compiled on the basis of interest group and governmental participation: the results were less the High Authority's than a compromise among interested and detached experts. Even so, the general objectives hardly approach an economic plan. They merely project, on the basis of the ECSC gross national product,

---

[15] Details of the regulations in Chap. 3. The spirit of their interpretation is set forth by Léon Daum, " Devant le problème des concentrations," *Hommes et Commerce, op. cit.*, pp. 41 *et seq.* The High Authority now approaches the problem of controlling concentrations by seeking to give unofficial advice to potential investors as to whether the shares they contemplate acquiring would constitute monopolistic control *and* whether the deal would be profitable. In doing so it seeks to sidestep the anonymity of the capital market and overcome the refusal of investment banks to divulge the identity of investors they represent. The details of decision-making in the Council of Ministers are given in *Agence Europe*, April 9, 16, 26, 29, 1954.

probable consumption and production needs by 1975, predict bottlenecks, suggest areas for new investment and make some recommendations for dealing with the manpower shortage in the mines. Nothing specific is said about general economic expansion, governmental credit policy, the source of investments and the co-ordination of wage increases with price stability and growth in productivity.[16]

Under the High Authority's ideology, the fact remains that these general objectives are merely suggestions and cannot be enforced through federal policy. " Firms remain free to make their own investments. . . . The role of the High Authority is simply to announce periodic general objectives for production and modernisation. . . . It gives direction to the choice of firms. . . ." [17] One direct way of imposing the general objectives on the industries of the Community, however, is opened by the loan policy of the High Authority. Only projects justified by the general objectives are entitled, in principle, to ECSC credits or credit guarantees. Yet when the time came to distribute the $100,000,000 United States loan principle had to be adjusted to political interest. Luxembourg was confronted by mutually exclusive credit demands of French and German steelmakers and by threats of M. Louvel, French Minister of Industry, that even though the Council of Ministers had no jurisdiction over loan policy, he would watch over the interests of French steel. Wisely, the High Authority decided to finance only the relatively non-controversial coke, coal and ore sector, to permit participation by regional committees of industrialists in distributing the funds, after having split up the loan among the various countries on the basis of their contribution to the production tax. Instead of compelling industrialists to orient their financial needs to a federal focus, the High Authority considered it wiser not to antagonise national banking interests who oppose any ECSC credit policy tooth and nail. A much more consistent approach characterised the distribution of the $11,500,000 Swiss loan, though its very modesty precludes much directing effectiveness. It must be granted, however, that the loan policy did compel some reductions in commercial interest rates and eased

[16] See the useful summary of the 1956 General Objectives in *ECSC Bulletin*, January 1957, pp. 1–4.
[17] Léon Daum, " La C. E. C. A. et les investissements," *Perspectives*, November 19, 1955. Also see H. Skribanowitz, " Die Kreditpolitik zwichen zwei Etappen," *Europa*, November 1955, pp. 24 *et seq.*

a marked capital shortage. Its permanence is nevertheless far from established, especially since the Treaty forbids the use of the production tax for direct loan purposes. It was this factor which persuaded Luxembourg to reduce the rate of the levy after an adequate guarantee fund had been set up, in addition to being under continual pressure for reduction from industrialists and governments.[18]

A second way to enforce the general objectives is offered by the duty of enterprises to communicate their investment plans to Luxembourg and the right of the High Authority to pass on these and prohibit outlays based on loans and subsidies. It is through this mechanism that the French demand for the " co-ordination " of investments could be achieved.[19] Such, however, has not been the interpretation of the High Authority. Its members have argued that the co-ordination powers are only indirect and rest entirely on the wisdom of the opinions and forecasts of ECSC experts. Firms would thus make their investments on the basis only of the soundness of the advice rendered by Luxembourg, but not under any central direction. Any actual exercise of the High Authority's veto power over investments—which has not yet occurred—would fail because of the six ECSC countries only France and Holland have long-term industrial expansion programmes under public auspices. The other four would have to be persuaded by Luxembourg to initiate such plans which would then have to be harmonised with the older French and Dutch plans before any central co-ordination can be attempted. As far as is known, the High Authority has made no independent efforts to speed this process.[20] Equipped as it is with a free market doctrine it is difficult to conceive how it could do so. But by 1957 it was felt in Luxembourg that for steel at least, the investment advice function had resulted in striking voluntary co-ordination and rationalisation of outlays.

It is in the field of labour and welfare policy that Luxembourg has most consistently failed to avail itself of its potential influence and thus grievously disappointed one of its most enthusiastic group of supporters, the trade unions. This, in terms of political

[18] *Agence Europe*, May 8 and July 28, 1954.
[19] *Etudes et Documents* (May 1953) estimates that between 1948 and 1952, self-financing accounted for 40 per cent. of steel investments in all ECSC countries, thus theoretically giving the High Authority a veto power over 60 per cent. of capital sources.
[20] See the statements on this by MM. Mayer, Coppé and Daum, in *Débats, op. cit.*, no. 9, pp. 560, 640; no. 13, pp. 381, 596–597, 433.

integration, is all the more serious because the High Authority has made sporadic efforts to find a permanent supranational ally in the unions, as expressed in the housing programme, the liberal utilisation of the readaptation system and a general wooing of Labour leaders by giving them representation on expert commissions and study groups on a basis of equality with industrialists and government spokesmen.   But, in fairness, it must also be admitted that unionists have not always availed themselves of the facilities offered them by Luxembourg and that the co-operation of certain governments has been lacking.

Housing provides a crucial example.   In refuting charges that it interprets the Treaty too restrictively on welfare questions, the High Authority replies that the housing programme is not specifically authorised but was undertaken anyway.   However in reply to governmental protests over a *de facto* " spill-over " into welfare policy, Luxembourg cautiously decided not to push any housing scheme against national reservations, however muted they may be.

Readaptation payments, says the High Authority, have been granted even when it could not be clearly proved that the introduction of the common market was responsible for the difficulties. Yet, in the face of Socialist and Labour objections, the production tax was reduced in 1955 even though a larger readaptation fund could have made possible a more active policy in this area.   High Authority members have often argued that the system should be made more flexible in terms of allowable coverage and that governments should be dispensed from the requirement that ECSC allocations be matched with national payments *in excess* of normally payable unemployment compensation.   In both the Belgian and Italian readaptation cases such relaxations were eventually authorised but a French request was turned down because Paris wanted to contribute only unemployment insurance.[21]   Luxembourg blames the national governments for lack of interest and silent sabotage; yet the fact remains that whenever the Council of Ministers was approached for authorising relaxations of the rules, a unanimous willingness to do so was expressed, including the spending of readaptation funds on the retraining of workers in fields other than coal and steel.   Once more it appears that a less legalistic

[21] For details on the system of administration used see Daniel Vignes, *La Communauté Européenne du Charbon et de l'Acier* (Liége: Georges Thone, 1956), pp. 167–185. Also High Authority, " The Community's Labour Policy," Information Doc. no. 1898/55/e.

and cautious policy could reap far greater consequences in terms of a long-range positive supranational policy. Yet even Monnet insisted in 1955 that ECSC social policy was as active as the Treaty permitted. While urging that ECSC funds be used to create new industries in regions where redundant manpower has become available, Paul Finet also conceded that " the problem is outside the Community's competence." [22]

A refusal to act unless unanimous agreement on a wide interpretation of the Treaty prevails also characterises the issue of wage harmonisation. " In this important field, the High Authority can only use methods of study and advice," wrote Albert Wehrer.[23] The purpose of the common market is to achieve competition, not to equalise natural *Standortbedingungen* by artificially harmonising wages. Until it was confronted by a growing trade union clamour for action and by the specific insistence of the Belgian Government for equalising the working week, the High Authority had confined itself to the " study " aspect of its role, the collection and publication of comparable money wage and fringe benefits statistics, as well as its pioneering comparative real wage study. As for " advice," it merely wished the ILO or the Council of Ministers to conclude an international convention harmonising wages. Only the pressure of the trade unions compelled the calling of supranational labour-management commissions in 1956 to explore the possibilities of ECSC-wide collective bargaining on the secondary issues of paid vacations, overtime and holiday pay.[24]

Labour policy inactivity disappoints only the trade unions. The refusal to engage in a dirigistic course with respect to coal production, pricing and investment, however, sidesteps the positive expectations of producer groups worried by the future of coal as well as ignoring Labour and Socialist opinion. As defined

[22] *Débats, op. cit.*, no. 13, p. 715. Finet consistently calls on trade unionists to force their national governments to avail themselves of the readaptation system and blames the unions for indifference and lack of co-operation with a willing High Authority. But M. Glisenti, former director of the High Authority's Labour Problems Division, blames the High Authority for being overly sensitive to the attitudes of certain governments and not making use of its potentialities. See " Quelques Aspects économiques et sociaux de la Communauté Européenne du Charbon et de l'Acier," *op. cit.*

[23] " Le Plan Schuman," speech in Luxembourg, April 18, 1955, p. 8. See also Etzel, speech delivered at Handelshochschule St. Gallen, *op. cit.*, pp. 115–116.

[24] *Débats, op. cit.*, no. 13, p. 440, and no. 14, (November 1956) for the very explicit statement of Finet on these issues.

by the Socialist group in the Common Assembly, and endorsed by many outside it, a truly supranational coal policy would call for all of the following.   Price stability would have to be assured through permanent controls, linked with a determined effort to raise wages and welfare standards, as a means for attracting young miners as well as on doctrinal grounds.   A long-range co-ordinated policy of resource development would gear the future of coal to the rise of atomic energy and oil, necessitating investment planning, production quotas and subsidies for marginal mines. Imports of coal should be centrally controlled through an ECSC–wide compensation system and the problem of collusion among producers would be dealt with by a public, ECSC–wide, compulsory cartel.   With respect to the coal shortage which has been gripping Europe since 1955, many propose the declaration of a condition of " serious shortage " (Art. 59 of the Treaty) and the inauguration of rationing as well as price equalisation for imported coal.

A mixture of legalistic and expediential reasons have kept the High Authority from accepting this programme.   The long-range coal policy desired, based on flexible prices, was outlined above.[26] The High Authority argues that any policy of special protection for coal is impossible without an ECSC–wide energy policy.   While Luxembourg is willing to undertake the necessary statistical studies and recommend fuel policy co-ordination, the initiative is said to lie squarely with the six governments and the ultimate hope in the General Common Market, not in piecemeal ECSC efforts. As for the subsidisation of coal to attract manpower and keep prices stable, this suggestion is rejected as legally incompatible with the common market principle.

Further, as long as American coal can be imported, there is no " serious " coal shortage and the application of Article 59 cannot be considered legally.   ECSC rationing would merely reauthorise national governments to control the market since the High Authority cannot by itself administer a rationing system, thus actually triggering an anti-federal development.   When the Socialists countered that in the winter of 1956–1957, certain governments already rationed domestic coal and reimposed national price ceilings because of the absence of an ECSC programme, Franz

[26] See details in Chap. 3.

Etzel merely answered that this was indeed undesirable and should lead to the adoption of common principles.[27]

Coal price policy further demonstrates the reluctance to act. The need for price ceilings was always regretted by the High Authority and their partial continuation until 1956 was undertaken largely as a concession to national governments worried over price stability. Concern over the Treaty's provisions assuring producers of a fair return on invested capital prompted a High Authority endorsement of the Ruhr's demand for price increases in 1955, over the objections of several governments and the hesitancy of Bonn. Yet when it was decided to remove ceilings altogether in 1956, the High Authority technical staff thought that the Ruhr needed no increase whatever in order to earn a fair return. In both years the basic problem was one of wage increases being negotiated concurrently with the collieries' demanding changes in the pricing rules. If they could only be assured of a limit on wage increases or be given guarantees on tax refunds and other public aids, the Ruhr coal interests were willing to forgo some of their price demands. Luxembourg, however, steadfastly held that it could not legally intervene—even unofficially—in any wage negotiations and that the issue of direct or disguised public subsidies to hold down coal prices could be reviewed only after a specific decision was made by Bonn. Thus limiting its own role, the High Authority had no option but to approve price increases and to inveigh against the special productivity bonus decreed by the German Government in 1956 even though it probably could have influenced both situations if it had quietly intervened earlier.[28]

" There are many ways of defending powers," noted René Mayer. " Some consist of exercising them with vigour; others consist of not compromising them." [29] Clearly, the High Authority has opted for the second alternative and, in doing so, left to trade associations and governments a good many functions which in

---

[27] Statements of Mayer and Etzel in *Débats*, no. 14 (November 1956), pp. 25–31 of the *compte rendu analytique*. Details on national coal policies in winter 1956–57 in Chap. 11 and *Informations Mensuelles*, December 1956, pp. 39–50. Note, however, the change in the High Authority's coal policy with respect to buffer stocks and imports which developed in 1957. Details in Chap. 3. Some federal reassertion is in evidence here as in the investment and cartel fields.

[28] These conclusions are based on access to the relevant unpublished High Authority documents and studies.

[29] *Débats*, no. 13, p. 676.

principle were to be assumed by anonymous free market forces. Whenever the cry of crisis and the need for spectacular supranational action was raised in the coal policy field, the High Authority answered, in the words of Albert Coppé—

> This Treaty is a treaty of freedom, but with limits. Every time a crisis or shortages arise you see the rights given to the High Authority exercised, after consultation ... with the Council of Ministers. Each time you see a certain number of techniques which the High Authority can use, but which just the same must take account of a certain number of principles, notably the principle that these techniques cannot be used, no matter how, in a permanent manner because our Community is open and not autarkic.[30]

Spectacular supranational action, because it implies permanent planning, is thus in effect ruled out.

It is perhaps prudent on the part of the nine men who direct ECSC not to exploit deliberately the political implications of the spill-over process in such fields as investment, wages and the future of coal: by emphasising the absence of explicit Treaty provisions supporting an active policy they succeed in avoiding political opprobrium from such centres as the German and Dutch industrialists, financial interests in all six countries and most of the governments. Yet the influence of a federal executive grows ever more shadowy if it declines to make use of powers which it possesses beyond legal doubt. The reluctance to fine tax delinquent firms is a case in point, as is the practice of relying on national trade associations to verify the production statistics submitted by ECSC firms, figures which form the basis on which each firm's tax burden is computed.

More serious still has been the High Authority's inactivity in connection with the Saar problem. Certainly, not even committed federalists can blame Luxembourg for not intervening in the issue of whether the Saar should be German or " autonomous." But the Franco–German quarrel also included the question of access to the Warndt coal seam, which is of direct concern to the common market. Despite repeated appeals from French industrial groups, Luxembourg refused to take a hand in the negotiations on the Saar, the Warndt or on the canalisation of the Moselle, that closely connected problem bearing directly on French aspirations and on coke shipments. The amicable Franco–German settlement, under

[30] *Ibid.*, p. 556.

which Germany agreed to finance part of the Moselle Canal and give the Lorraine collieries preferential access to Warndt coal for a specific period, was reached entirely on a bilateral basis. Only after the accord was published did Luxembourg question the two governments as to whether the Warndt agreement did not violate the non-discrimination provisions of the common market. Assured by Paris and Bonn that no violation was implied, Luxembourg gave notice of closely supervising the effects of the accord, even though it is inconceivable that the High Authority would seek retroactively to upset a Franco–German deal.

But the political consequence of Luxembourg's strict neutrality was implicit in the non-federal procedure adopted for amending the ECSC Treaty with respect to the Saar. The provision calling for the inclusion of the Saar delegation to the Common Assembly in the French group had to be changed, as well as the rule giving added voting strength in the Council of Ministers to countries producing more than twenty per cent. of the Community's coal and steel. The three Saarlanders are to be absorbed into the German parliamentary delegation—without net increase in that group—while one-sixth of ECSC production will henceforth suffice to give added voting power. With the loss of Saar production, France would also have lost her privileged voting position if the 20 per cent. rule had remained unchanged. Certainly the amendments imply a remarkable German willingness to compromise, but they will come into force in the same way as did the Treaty: after ministerial signature and six parliamentary ratifications.[31]

Finally, there is the range of policy issues immediately relevant to political integration but clearly beyond the High Authority's power of initiative, under any interpretation of the Treaty. Crucial in this realm is policy assuring freedom of labour migration,

---

[31] Details concerning this episode in *Agence Europe*, November 23, 1956. In the Dutch Parliament, van der Goes van Naters questioned the Foreign Minister, M. Luns, on this very question. He elicited the information that the French Government had neglected to circulate the text of the amendments in time for speedy ratification and that the legal situation was considered so complicated that the conventional amendment procedure for international agreements was considered the simplest solution. Naters was worried also about the fact that the non-ratification by all six countries of the amendments would prevent the correct reconstitution of the Common Assembly during its session in February 1957. Luns replied that the ECSC Council of Ministers had ruled that the national delegations should be composed in conformity with the amendments even if they had not been fully ratified : *Handelingen van de Tweede Kamer der Staaten-Generaal*, January 31, 1957, Part I, pp. 484–486.

harmonised freight rates, relations with third countries and the co-ordination of general economic policy, including taxes. In the first three instances, the lack of interest of the Council of Ministers is to be blamed for whatever shortcomings supranational policy may contain. But the reluctance of the High Authority to resolve governmental disagreements by advancing independent formulas is patent. Wrote a leading ECSC transport official—

> In this field, the High Authority cannot overcome the dilemma, either in the direction of freedom or of control, without exceeding its powers. It is for the governments, in concert, to choose a solution. . . . The High Authority must merely remind them of the obligations they have incurred to find a solution which will avoid all discrimination among coal and steel consumers.[32]

In the field of general economic and tax policy, however, it is the High Authority which has refused to follow up on openings provided by the Council of Ministers. The details of this vital area of integration will be discussed in the next chapter. Suffice it to note here that when pressed on the nature of the High Authority's general economic policy, Albert Coppé contented himself by expounding the need to overcome bottlenecks and maintain a slowly rising price pattern during periods of inflationary pressure and thus even out the effects of business cycles.[33] In brief, the High Authority is unwilling to risk opposition and unpopularity by giving an energetic federal interpretation to the powers which it does possess, and thus disappoints numerous groups and some governments who expect a positive federal policy. Yet it recognises the reality of the problems posed by the co-ordination of investments and the claims of labour, by the need for more readaptation and the harmonisation of credit policies. Its answer —and this is the solution publicly adopted—is not to press for an extension of its own competence or the full use of its powers, but for the realisation of the General Common Market.

Who Influences High Authority Decision-Making?

Among the purely institutional pressures impinging on the High Authority, the role of the Court has been crucial in establishing a

---

[32] Roger Hutter, " L'Harmonisation européenne des transports," *Hommes et Commerce, op. cit.*, p. 54.
[33] Albert Coppé, " Le Plan Schuman et l'intégration économique européenne," *Revue des Sciences Economiques* (September 1953), p. 143. Also in *Débats, op. cit.*, no. 13, pp. 434 and 436.

pattern of narrow Treaty interpretation. Of the cases decided by that tribunal by the end of 1956, three stand out as important indices of constitutional interpretation because they implied varying assessments of the competence of the High Authority in applying sections of the Treaty and altering them to suit specific economic situations. In the suit of the Dutch Government challenging the legality of ceiling prices to control coal sales cartels, the Court ruled that the High Authority was free to use this kind of regulation pending the frontal assault on restrictive practices. High Authority freedom of Treaty interpretation was supported once more in the suit of the Belgian collieries, protesting against a redistribution of the ECSC compensation payments according to need and performance, alleging that the Treaty gave the High Authority no such latitude. The Court upheld the High Authority once more.[34]

However, in terms of an evolving political code of broad as against cautious interpretation, the Dutch and Belgian decisions came already too late. The Court's first rulings were on the four suits challenging the legality of the Monnet Rebate, and here the principle of strict and narrow interpretation won a smashing victory. While dismissing allegations of abuse of power and substantial procedural violations against the High Authority, the seven judges found that a violation of the Treaty had taken place in that the High Authority had wrongfully subordinated the strict language of Article 60 to the wider injunctions contained in the sections describing the Community's basic objectives, Articles 2 and 3. To this purely legalistic finding the Court added its economic conviction—to which in legal theory it was hardly entitled—that the High Authority could not claim a relaxation of price schedule publicity as a means for controlling collusion

[34] My concern is purely with the political consequences of the Court's decisions, not with their legal merits and content. The legal and institutional aspects of the Court have received far more attention in terms of monographic studies than any other part of the Community's work. The most useful such work, minimising the purely formal and textual approach which predominates among the Continental commentators, is Valentine, *op. cit.* He notes, incidentally, that Monnet in 1952 considered the Court one of the cornerstones of the federal structure which, according to Monnet, ECSC had inaugurated, while the president of the Court, M. Pilotti, confined himself to defining his role as protecting the legal rights of producers, consumers and governments against arbitrary High Authority rulings. *Ibid.*, p. 4.

among steel producers because other means for dealing with cartels had not yet been exhausted.[35]

The decision was hailed by Monnet as " a new proof of the effective functioning of the institutions of the Community " as federal organs, even though it upset one of his crucial steps.[36] It was unmercifully castigated by economists as formalistic, denounced by producers as hindering competition, and profoundly deplored by most members of the High Authority technical staff as rendering impossible in the future any functionally effective and politically expansive interpretation of the Treaty.   There is no doubt that the caution and reluctance of Luxembourg to assert itself since 1955 is very heavily influenced by the fear that any group opposing a radically federal policy can find some legal support for its position.   While subsequent Court decisions should have gone some way in dispelling this fear, the plain fact is that a majority of the seven judges does not consider itself the successor of John Marshall in the European setting; the Court has already had far-reaching restraining effects on supranationalism, not because of the continuity of its decisions, but because of the intimidating effect of its initial ruling.

Yet the Court's activity has brought with it some pro-integration consequences as well, apart from its negative role toward the High Authority.   The bulk of litigation initiated by private parties since 1955 testifies to the fact that producer and consumer organisations gladly avail themselves of supranational jurisprudence, not only against the High Authority but sometimes against their own governments.   In fact, litigation is often introduced merely as a threat against national and supranational authorities, designed to lead to a compromise on a vital decision, a thoroughly normal means of political pressure in a pluralistic community whose advent in ECSC must be regarded as evidence of progressive integration.   Further, one of the positive integrative consequences

[35] Among the many commentaries on this decision, the best published in English is Eric Stein, " The European Coal and Steel Community: the Beginning of its Judicial Process," *Columbia Law Review*, Vol. 55, no. 7 (November 1955), pp. 985 *et seq.*

[36] Quoted by Pierre Meutey, " Comment fonctionnent les institutions de la C. E. C. A.? " *Hommes et Commerce, op. cit.*, p. 40.   For an equally laudatory comment in terms of the restraint of the parties in arguing their case and the proof of Europeanism displayed by them despite the destructive effect of the decision itself, see the article by an official of the Court, Hans-Wolfram Daig, " Die vier ersten Urteile des Gerichtshofes der Europäischen Gemeinschaft für Kohle und Stahl," *Juristenzeitung*, Vol. 10, no. 12 (June 20, 1955), p. 371.

of the Monnet Rebate decision was to underscore the right of private parties to bring suits even in circumstances not clearly permitting such steps according to the Treaty. While the rigidity of the decision undoubtedly made Treaty expansion by interpretation more difficult and therefore highlights the formal and cumbersome amendment process, it is equally true and relevant to integration that the principle of judicial review—so often denied in Europe—seemed to be firmly established by the Court.

Institutionally speaking, the Consultative Committee should not be considered as an organ seeking to shape and influence High Authority decisions. According to its rules of procedure as well as the initial ideological commitments of Schuman and Monnet, the Committee is merely the loyal help-meet of the High Authority, giving technical expertise and wisdom to its decisions through the quality of the advice tendered by the members, considered as independent experts. The reality, of course, is quite the opposite. As Gilbert Mathieu described it:

> Never have the steel men or the leaders of the coal firms who sit in the Committee felt themselves to be the aides or technical councillors of the High Authority. On the contrary, they have considered themselves as representatives of their professional organisations, and have thus defended corporative viewpoints.[37]

The same may be said, incidentally, of the labour and consumer representatives on the Committee. Collectively, the interest group spokesmen have tended to regard their role as that of an economic parliament; individually, they have consistently used their relationship with the High Authority for direct lobbying purposes, in no way different from practices normal in national political settings. The pattern of access enjoyed by interest groups to individual members of the High Authority is as follows:

Dutch producers and consumers: Spierenburg.
Belgian producers and consumers: Coppé.
Belgian labour: Finet.
German producers and consumers: Etzel.
German labour: Potthoff.
French, Dutch, and Luxembourg labour: Finet and Potthoff.
Luxembourg industry: Wehrer.
French producers and consumers: Mayer.
All Italian groups: Giacchero.

[37] *Le Monde*, May 20, 1954. The rules of procedure are printed in *Journal Officiel*, January 31, 1955.

It is clear that the nationality of the members as well as their previous political and interest group connections define the pattern of access at the supranational level.

When interest group demands and expectations are paired off against the decisions made by the High Authority, it appears that the German steelmakers are by far the most successful group. The bill of particulars presented by Karl Barich in 1954—including a liberal cartel policy, unrestrained mergers, reduction of the levy and investment aid to German steel—was met consistently.[38] The Charbonnages de France have fared only slightly less well. All of their demands for price freedom, the continuation of internal compensations and subsidies and special sales access protection were granted; only the demands for the harmonisation of social security and tax burdens have so far been futile. No other producer organisation has been consistently successful in having its preferences endorsed by Luxembourg, though some demands of all groups have found satisfaction. As for the consuming industries, their major lobbying effort was aimed at the price schedule reforms embodied in the Monnet Rebate. With the outlawry of this step, specific consuming industry demands have found no consistent support in High Authority policy, other than the rigid enforcement of the fair trade code which is a distinct help to consumers under the inflationary conditions which have prevailed since 1955.

Trade unions, of course, feel that their lobbying efforts have largely gone unrewarded and that the High Authority is more receptive to producer demands than to any others. Certainly the policy picture shows only the most general endorsement of labour demands—such as the verbal assurances that rising living standards and wages, stepped up readaptation allowances and more worker housing are central to ECSC policy. In fact, the only concrete measures in response to labour activity have been the readaptation and housing projects, neither of which has satisfied the labour constituency.

Is it to be concluded from these findings that the German steelmakers and the Charbonnages de France " have the ear " of the High Authority and that Luxembourg deliberately defers to their demands? The evidence hardly warrants so sweeping a

---

[38] See Barich's speech to the general assembly of the Wirtschaftsvereinigung Eisen- und Stahlindustrie, May 5, 1954; *Stahl und Eisen*, June 3, 1954, pp. 803–806.

conclusion. The ideology and demands of a renascent Ruhr happen to coincide very largely with the convictions prevalent among the nine men in Luxembourg, as they do with the policy aims of the German Government. But it is equally true that, given the politically and economically ascendant position of German industry in contemporary Europe, the High Authority is far less willing to affront this segment of its constituency than any other single organisation. As for the French collieries, it is very likely that Luxembourg shares the general European inclination to make exceptions from free market rules for France in order not to alienate French opinion from the common market principle. The favour shown the Charbonnages may thus be fairly regarded as part of the overall gentle blackmail exercised by Paris in the movement for economic integration.

In view of the much more consistently supranational orientation of the Common Assembly, as compared to the outlook of the High Authority, it might well be surmised that the ECSC parliamentarians occupy a subordinate role in the shaping of High Authority decisions. A statistical survey of the degree of High Authority implementation of requests, voted in most cases by unanimous or near-unanimous Common Assembly resolutions, lends credence to this conclusion. The resolutions used include all specific requests for action, consultation, study or negotiation made of the High Authority between August of 1952 and November of 1956[39]:

Requests voted	Requests implemented	Requests implemented in part	Requests not implemented
110	45	32	33

The implemented resolutions include fields of action or study in which the High Authority was prepared to undertake measures or open negotiations even without Assembly prodding. Exceptions are the discussions of investment plans with the Investment Commission of the Assembly, which might not have been undertaken

[39] It should be said again that Assembly resolutions have no binding force and that the High Authority violates no Treaty rule in ignoring them. The number of " requests " computed is not equal to the number of resolutions passed. Resolutions addressed to other organs or to the Assembly itself were omitted. But separate requests included in one blanket resolution were counted separately. Source for the texts of the resolutions: August 1952 until November 1955, Assemblee Commune, *Annuaire-Manuel* (Luxembourg: 1956), pp. 369–415; November 1955 until November 1956, *Journal Officiel*, December 12, 1956, and July 19, 1956.

without continuous pressure. It is probable that the publication of production forecasts and general objectives was hastened by Assembly requests and that the cartel issue was attacked sooner than planned because of the simultaneous pressure of the Dutch Government and the Dutch members of the Common Assembly. Resolutions implemented in part include such areas as research, housing, efforts to maintain stable prices and reduce production costs, which the High Authority tried to administer without over-stepping the self-defined bounds of the Treaty. Unimplemented measures account for the bulk of demands for an active policy of investment co-ordination, vigorous readaptation not always sub-ordinated to governmental initiative, an active welfare policy and measures to deal centrally and radically with the fuel shortage. All the requests were " important " in the sense that they referred to an expanding view of the Treaty and were partisan of a wide interpretation. The unimplemented column, characteristically, includes all the areas in which the High Authority invokes the language of the Treaty as forbidding drastic or energetic action.

If the High Authority is evidently little influenced by the pro-integration bias of the Common Assembly, what is the prevalent conception of the role of the parliamentarians? Franz Etzel must have had relations of liaison and discussion in mind rather than legislation and control when he remarked—

> The High Authority has offered the Common Assembly every facility for co-operation possible under the Treaty and has so treated it, for political reasons, as if it were a fully sovereign parliament. If ECSC is to be a test for the eventual functioning of supranational institutions, political co-operation must already now be exercised in such a manner as to develop a lively and close relationship.[40]

High Authority refusal to present the ECSC budget regularly to the Common Assembly, early enough in the fiscal year to permit discussion and changes of proposed expenditures, hardly smacks of " political co-operation " with a " fully sovereign parliament." [41] Nor does the High Authority make consistent use of the Assembly in stressing the application of supranational solutions in discussions with the six governments. No effort is made, for instance, to align the European political parties functioning in the Assembly with the High Authority in jointly demanding of the Council of

[40] Speech at Handelshochschule St. Gallen, *op. cit.*, p. 105.
[41] Mayer in *Débats, op. cit.*, no. 13, p. 635.

Ministers supranational adjustments of the transport or social security issues. More important perhaps, individual members of the High Authority, in disagreement with the majority of their colleagues on narrow Treaty interpretation, do not seek support from their political friends in the Assembly.[42] In short, there is no pattern of political co-operation and mutual support between the two organs even though the logic of Etzel's formulation should dictate a maximisation of the legislative role, regardless of the Treaty's silence on this topic.

In positive terms, the High Authority grants the Assembly a role merely in praising its members for supporting European economic integration in the framework of their national legislatures. Coppé expressed his conviction that such efforts helped the High Authority immeasurably in persuading the governments to adopt a radical railway harmonisation formula and in making possible the Messina resolutions, thus launching the *Relance*. The role of the Assembly lies in persuading the national governments individually to trust to supranationalism in the future to resolve the issues over which the High Authority lacks direct and primary jurisdiction:

> Your Assembly has always distinguished ... between the important problems situated on the border between partial integration and a general integration, where action should consequently be concentrated. We are grateful to you for your efforts in the past. We count on you in the future. We can draw up an inventory of these border questions on which you could be particularly helpful in the months and years to come.[43]

Instead of using the Assembly as pro-integration forum at the *supranational* level, this formulation relegates the parliamentarians to the role of separate local pressures to be exercised at the *national* level. This looks suspiciously like the function of " harmonising " national with supranational policy which in principle should be achieved by the Council of Ministers.

The burden of this discussion would seem to indicate that the ultimate influence, direct or indirect, on High Authority decisions is the national governments acting singly or in concert through the Council of Ministers. An examination of the Council as an organ

---

[42] These points are made in a remarkably open manner by Max Kohnstamm, formerly secretary of the High Authority and since 1956 assistant to Monnet, as reported in *Informations Bimensuelles*, October 15, 1954, pp. 9–10.

[43] *Débats, op. cit.*, no. 13, p. 435.

facilitating or blocking political integration is reserved for the final chapter. Suffice it to say here that the High Authority *considers* the national governments as the crucial limits on supranational policy and therefore defers more consistently to their real or alleged intentions than to any other source of influence in the Community, except the Court. It must be stated immediately, however, that there as elsewhere the High Authority adopts a more cautious attitude than is made necessary by the actual constellation of political forces and attitudes, if a deliberate acceleration of the spill-over process into the realm of politics is the desired end.

It is the considered policy of the High Authority to consult the Council of Ministers on every major decision, whether such a step is required by the Treaty or not. The implementation of any policy is held impossible unless such consultations take place; the very nature of supranational institutions is equated with this practice. The actual pattern of consultation can be broken down into three distinct categories: (1) measures not requiring the consent of the Council; (2) measures requiring the initiative of the High Authority and the consent of the Council; (3) measures primarily reserved for the initiative of the Council, but necessitating the co-operation of the High Authority. In the first two instances, the High Authority generally defers to the Council's views, though it makes known its preferences. In the third case it subordinates its measures almost entirely to Council initiative.

Consultations with the Council are considered eminently successful by the High Authority: the Council members are praised for their detachment from national and interest group demands. " More than one Minister has admitted changing his mind in course of our discussions," either because of High Authority arguments or because of remonstrances by his colleagues from other ECSC countries.[44] However, it must be noted that it was in the course of such confrontations of opinion that the German Council member insisted on a reduction of the production tax, even though he had no jurisdiction over the question. The High Authority, for its part, has very rarely acted contrary to the views of the Council in these situations. Exceptions are the Monnet Rebate which was decreed despite Council hesitations, and Ruhr coal price ceilings which were imposed and removed over the opposition of three of the six governments.

[44] *Ibid.*, pp. 568–569.

In areas where High Authority action is contingent upon the approval of the Council, the caution observed is much greater. Here the tendency is to wait for the evolution of unanimous consensus on the Council even when the Treaty merely calls for a simple or qualified majority to back up High Authority proposals. Certainly the High Authority does not here wait for Council initiative to advance its suggestions if it considers the matter clearly under jurisdiction. Measures for controlling the scrap market, for administering the merger approval system, or relaxing the readaptation rules are cases in point.

Finally, an interpretation of the Treaty going beyond a calculated minimalism usually is given only when suggestions for this are made by the Council, or at least by certain of its members. Thus, the High Authority held that the negotiation of an agreement for the free migration of qualified coal and steel labour was a matter for the six governments. Even though it made proposals to the Council in this field, these were largely sidestepped in the modest agreement negotiated by the governments. Thereafter, the High Authority was willing to make suggestions for speeding the conclusion of a social security convention to protect migrant workers only after governmental experts failed to agree among themselves and a specific demand for active supranational proposals was advanced by the Council. Even though it had obtained Council approval for its housing programme, the informally expressed opposition of the Belgian minister concerned —" All this will be fine; we won't have anything left to do; the High Authority will do everything "—resulted in Luxembourg's subordinating its programme completely to national preferences.[45] To sum up: decisions beyond the immediate confines of coal and steel, and especially those concerning the spill-over process, are made to wait on specific indications of interest by the Council. This is true even in the field of such purely statistical studies as the varying ECSC steel industry practices on working time and

[45] These revelations were made in an extremely frank presentation of Paul Finet. *Ibid.*, pp. 709–712. In fairness, it must be admitted that the Council does not always encourage the High Authority to submit proposals seeking to maximise supranational institutional power beyond the scope of the Treaty. After the Marcinelle mine disaster, the High Authority did propose the creation of a mine safety organisation under its rule. The proposal was opposed by France and Germany, greeted with reserve by the Benelux countries, and favoured only by Italy. *Agence Europe*, August 31 and September 5, 1956. The ECSC-wide safety organ created in 1957 possesses fewer supranational powers than proposed by Luxembourg.

overtime pay, which required the insistent demand of Belgium's Jean Rey before being undertaken by a reluctant High Authority.

Yet the frequent fragmentation of government opinion, to be demonstrated in the next chapter, could be exploited by a resourceful High Authority. The unanimity rule is operative in only very few instances on the Council; even where it does prevail legally, the pattern of compromise has been so consistent as to make it quite reconcilable with the extension of supranational tasks. Short and long-term positive expectations prevail among some ministers as they do among interest groups, and no single government consistently opposes task expansion on all issues. A High Authority anxious to accelerate the spill-over process could manoeuvre in such a manner as to enlist on its side the governments favouring supranational action on one issue, even though some of the same governments might be found on the opposite side in other situations. The fluidity of positions is far from demanding a rigid High Authority attitude of waiting for the unanimous consent of the Council on each proposal. In view of the actual attitude taken by the " federal executive," however, it is clear that the six governments and the Council are, rightly or wrongly, considered to be the major influence on supranational policy.

Even recommendations for the co-ordination of general national economic policies were made dependent on continual Council encouragement, though it was Monnet who in 1953 first argued for the necessity of centralised action. The expansion of the readaptation system to non–ECSC industries has been treated in the same way. " Perhaps we could eventually envisage a revision of the Treaty which would permit direct action. But, at the moment, the governments and the High Authority insist that it be respected," shrugged Finet.[46] As for inspecting on the spot the implementation of readaptation formulas decided in Luxembourg : " We are not policemen who should watch that obligations are respected."[47] Suggestions that the Common Assembly members press governments to implement the right to free labour migration : " We do not think that this would be wise. It would be enough for one government to change its attitude and you would risk blocking everything for many more months."[48]

Timidity of this type dominated the High Authority's decision-making code during the first four years of its life. Announcements,

[46] *Débats, op. cit.*, no. 13, p. 714.   [47] *Ibid.*, p. 732.   [48] *Ibid.*, p. 442.

decisions and recommendations voiced since the autumn of 1956 suggest, however, that a more vigorous attitude toward the six governments may be in the making. With the successful completion and ratification of the EEC and Euratom Treaties it becomes politically less hazardous for the cautious executive to assert its opinions; when inflationary spirals and fuel shortages combined to threaten the logic of the common market after Suez policy in Luxembourg began to anticipate and shape national governmental decisions rather than continue to defer to the initiating nod of the Council of Ministers.

Thus the High Authority tenaciously held to its interpretation of the Treaty in its negotiations with Bonn over the legality of the miners' bonus and in its troubles with Paris over the future of ATIC. Luxembourg openly blamed the national governments for re-introducing indirect price controls in the coal and steel sectors and warned them to desist. And failing the evolution of a spontaneously co-ordinated policy to deal with the fuel shortage, imports of American coal, high ocean freight rates and the increasing unwillingness of certain French and German collieries to supply coal consumers in other ECSC countries, the High Authority suggested energetic measures to the Council and received its assurance that the six national governments will co-operate with their implementation. Specifically, this involves the drawing up of delivery schedules for the collieries, to be supervised and enforced by High Authority regulation, constant mediation by Luxembourg between coal producers and consumers, the protection of domestic coal consumers against wholesalers anxious to sell primarily to industrial consumers—to be achieved through ECSC-wide co-operation with the European Union of Retail Fuel Dealers—and co-ordinated measures to eliminate overlapping ocean transport arrangements and force freight rates down.

The last measure was approved by the Council upon failure to achieve agreement in the OEEC framework. It demonstrates once more the possibilities of exploiting the problems created by sector integration and channelling them into the direction of more integration—provided the supranational executive is willing to take the lead. The spill-over *can* be accelerated in the face of divisions of opinion among the governments and in the absence of an articulate consensus toward unity as an end in itself. All that is needed is the effective demonstration by a resourceful supranational executive that the ends already agreed upon cannot be attained without further united steps. Much the same lesson can be drawn from the problems engendered by unco-ordinated national energy resource and overall economic policies, to be explored in the final chapter.

IS THE HIGH AUTHORITY AN INDEPENDENT FEDERAL EXECUTIVE? Not all the aspects of the decision-making code of the High Authority, as it developed during the first five years of supranational activity, are inconsistent with standard practices in federal states. And at the same time it must be stressed that the bulk of High Authority practices marks a radical departure from decisions making techniques in conventional international organisation-even when it falls far short of federal practice. Thus, it is clear that the relations between the High Authority on the one hand and the Assembly and Council on the other violate the federal logic on which Monnet had insisted so strongly in 1950. The indifferent record of heeding Common Assembly requests, even though legally correct, is hardly a contribution to the emergence of an independent federal government. While strict " cabinet responsibility " to the parliamentary body would not be required in order to remain true to the federal archetype—as illustrated by the Swiss federal system—a habit of deference and respect would be necessary in any case. This, the High Authority has failed to display except in instances when it wished the Assembly to carry out the limited role which it is allotted in the executive's ideology.

At the opposite pole, deference to the intergovernmental Council of Ministers is equally inconsistent with an emerging federal practice. If carried to its logical extreme—which, thanks to the care of the Council itself, it is not—the deference pattern would result in the relegation of the High Authority to the role of technical commission facilitating the implementation of a specialised treaty under the government of an inter-ministerial conference. As things stand, the truly novel nature of the supranational principle is revealed in the practice of High Authority study, advice and recommendation frequently shaping the final decision adopted by the Council. The intensification of this process in 1957, together with its extension in EEC and Euratom, bids fair to demonstrate the inventive and pro-integration role of supranationalism.

Subservience to the Court of Justice, on the other hand, is fully compatible with federal practice even when the decisions of the Court are restrictive in nature. In fact, the growth of a vigorous ECSC–wide jurisprudence punctuated by appeals and arguments of private parties rather than governments is one of the strongest pieces of evidence in favour of progressive integration. Further, while subservience to certain powerful interest groups may not be a wise policy, it is fully consistent with federal practice. Such deference occurs in any pluralistic system, unitary or federal. It is proof of the successful access of private organisations to a governmental body and to the importance attached by these groups to the new centre of administration. Its emergence in the ECSC framework provides more evidence that political integration is taking place despite a passive High Authority outlook.

Unwillingness to accelerate the spill-over process and thereby hasten political integration, in short, is certainly timid and may reflect economic and social conservatism, but it is not by itself anti-federal. Raymond Aron argues that the achievement of European unity was hamstrung by the concentration initially on coal, a declining industry whose artificial regulation by a supra-national body is bound to engender tension and opposition rather than enthusiasm for a European policy. In rebuttal, it may be pointed out that the very challenges of the ECSC coal crisis provide a field of positive action for an energetic High Authority, anxious to cater to strands of opinion and interests clamouring for a long-range policy of regulation and gradual adjustment to nuclear energy. If this group opinion were consistently exploited, instead of being sidestepped by a restrictive interpretation of the Treaty catering to short-range and negative expectations, the very fears and difficulties engendered by the inevitable decline of coal could become the centre for a positive European policy.

CHAPTER 13

NEW FORMS OF INTERGOVERNMENTAL
CO-OPERATION

ON the bluffs overlooking the Alzette River in the city of Luxembourg, but well removed from the centre of town where the technicians of the High Authority work and constantly meet with lobbyists and politicians, on the site of an old fort, stands the section called Verlorenkost. It is host to a small and secluded modern office building which houses the Council of Ministers. The very privacy of the site is symbolic of the impression engendered by the Council. Like Plato's nocturnal council, it is credited with exercising the true government of ECSC.

Federalists complain bitterly over the powers wielded by the Council as defining the limits of High Authority action and setting the pace of integration. Anti-federalists point gratefully to the Council because it is thought to act as a conventional diplomatic brake on the integration process. Like *Perspectives*, many Europeans maintain that " we must go in the direction of a confederation, and not of a federation. We must go in the direction of a grand alliance." [1] So much the better, then, if—as is urged by many—the High Authority acts only if the omens at Verlorenkost are considered favourable.

Certainly in constitutional terms the superimposition of an intergovernmental organ like the Council over a federal executive is an anomaly violating federal legal logic and institutional neatness. This is true all the more if the federal executive tends to defer to the intergovernmental organ even in situations when this is not required by the legal texts. Yet the federalists are quite wrong in inveighing against the Council merely because it violates Monnet's programme on doctrinal grounds. It is conceivable, after all, that despite treaty provisions, the ministers are more conscious of the positive implications of the spill-over process than is true of the High Authority. Therefore the supporters of Council powers may be equally seriously

---

[1] " Un pouvoir grandissant de la CECA: le Conseil des Ministres," *Perspectives*, Vol. 10, no. 28 (July 24, 1954), p. 2. The article in question welcomes the control exercised over the High Authority and for this purpose inaccurately exaggerates the actual degree of pressure exerted by the Council. According to this view, the High Authority merely " registers agreements made at the intergovernmental level " and otherwise acts as the central bureau of a conventional cartel.

mistaken in thinking that an intergovernmental structure automatically guarantees the prevalence of diplomatic decision-making techniques and thereby controls integration.

It is impossible to assess the role of the Council in European integration merely by weighing federal against diplomatic arguments, by coming to conclusions on the basis of treaty texts. If the operational code habitually employed by the people who compose the Council can be demonstrated to result in further integration, then plainly the general level of argumentation described is beside the point. The corollary would be that institutions of a federal type do not necessarily guarantee integration, while organs of a diplomatic character may actually aid it, depending on the techniques of decision-making used. Clearly, some detailed case studies of Council decision-making are the only device to obtain answers to these leading questions:[2]

1. Do the categories of legal competence contained in the Treaty determine the pattern of decision-making? " Consultations " do not bind the High Authority; but does the Council nevertheless consider such deliberation on par with more formal decisions demanding its " agreement? " Further, does the legal possibility of decisions by simple majority, qualified majority, or unanimous vote affect the manner of compromise? Finally, does the Council act like a conventional diplomatic conference in situations where it solely is competent to initiate action?

2. What is the role of the High Authority in influencing Council deliberations in each of the categories of competence? Under what conditions is the High Authority permitted to shape or even define the scope of compromise? Under what conditions is it ignored?

3. Do certain governments habitually seek to hinder or advance integration? If so, what is the pattern of compromise? Do institutional forces and/or specific personalities exert a habitual influence?

4. Is there any evidence of changing decision-making habits over time? Toward more or less integration?

THE COUNCIL: PERSONNEL AND PROCEDURES

Even though the Council is certainly a permanent institution of

[2] The Council issues no publications and makes only the most formal and barest summary statements of the decisions it reaches. My information on decision-making, unless otherwise specified, was drawn from unpublished documents made available to me, and from interviews whose confidential nature will preclude explicit references.

ECSC, with tasks well defined in the Treaty, its membership is far more changeable than the High Authority's since it depends on the vicissitudes of national politics in six countries. Normally, the Council is composed of the ministers of economics or their substitutes. The unevenness of continuity, however, is evident from this membership list:

> Germany: Ludwig Erhard (often represented by State Secretary Westrick); (1952-   );
> France: MM. Morice, Louvel, Bourgès-Maunoury, Ulver, Ramadier;
> Italy: constantly changing representation, since mid-1955 most often Signor Cortese;
> Belgium: M. Duvieusart (1952–1954), M. Jean Rey (1954–1958); [2a]
> Netherlands: Jelle Zijlstra (1952-   );
> Luxembourg: Michel Rasquin (1952-1958). [2a]

When the subject under discussion demands it, moreover, the ministers of labour or social welfare are also present at meetings, though this does not occur very frequently. Fundamental issues, such as the inauguration of drastic new steps toward unity, are taken up by the foreign ministers.

Since members of the Council very rarely make public statements about their work, with the notable exception of M. Rey, it is impossible to construct something approaching an " ideology." Nor do internal documents indicate the existence of such a substantive doctrine. Discussion proceeds in a matter of fact way from point to point, only rarely giving way to lengthy speeches. The most that can be said is that there has evolved a common consciousness of the role of the Council in the ECSC system, a procedural code of which the compromise pattern which prevails forms an important part.[3]

In principle, the members of the Council do not deny the economic logic of the benefit of a common market or the indefinite necessity of common measures for increasing welfare. Further, the members grant that the use of supranational agencies able to

[2a] Appointed to EEC's European Commission on January 1, 1958.

[3] The following material has been drawn from published statements of three Council members, MM. Rey, Rasquin and Cortese. It is being used, even though the gentlemen in question asserted that they were speaking purely in their capacity as individuals, because the decisions and internal documents of the Council bear these sentiments out as being held generally. See Belgium, *Annales parlementaires*, Sénat, no. 83, séance de 5 juillet 1955, pp. 1510–1514, for one of Rey's declarations. Common Assembly, *Débats*, no. 9 (May–June 1955), pp. 288–292, for Rey once more. *Ibid.*, pp. 625–627 for Rasquin. *Ibid.*, no. 13, (May–June 1956), pp. 401–404 for Rey, pp. 576–580 for Cortese.

act independently is essential in all areas in which national governments are compelled to admit that they can no longer act meaningfully in isolation because of the large number of variables which escape their control. " But when we say European Community," cautioned Rey, " we do not say European state. It does not seem necessary nor proved to us that we will evolve toward the suppression of our nationalities and our uniqueness." [4] All these are too precious to be given up merely for the sake of the European federal ideal, though they do not in the least preclude the growing economic and political unification of Europe through processes analogous to ECSC. If terms such as " community " and " integration " are strong symbols to the federalists in the Common Assembly, they are acceptable equally to such anti-federalists on the Council as Erhard, Ulver and Rasquin because the institutional context in which they are to operate differs from the federal archetype. As Rasquin summarised the role of the Council in relation to Europe:

> The Council of Ministers understands that its role, which is extremely delicate and difficult, consists in facilitating the work between itself and the High Authority, as well as between itself and the Common Assembly. Even if it is not responsible to the Assembly, believe me, it still considers itself responsible to Europe.[5]

The primary task of the Council, in its own view, is to safeguard the interests of the member states. But this does not mean that it must oppose High Authority dynamism with *immobilisme*, counter the general European interest with the particularistic ones of the six governments. The Council's role is not to act as a brake on supranational action, but to safeguard national interests by:

> a harmonisation of decisions so as to avoid overly rapid or overly radical measures, which would otherwise result at any given moment in negative developments, so that the entire mechanism will be out of gear.[6]

A distinction is often drawn between the Council as an organ of the Community, in which capacity it is bound by the Treaty as is any other organ, and the six governments acting in concert but not bound by prior obligations. The whole range of issues connected with an expanded supranational task is subsumed under

---

[4] Rey in *Annales parlementaires, op. cit.*, p. 1514.
[5] Rasquin in *Débats*, no. 9, *op. cit.*, p. 626.
[6] Rasquin in *ibid.*, p. 627.

the second category.[7]   At the same time, the Council members affirm the right of the High Authority to act independently, reject allegations that they have set limits to its field of action, acknowledge that High Authority pressure was responsible for their own action in several fields, such as transport.   But they insist equally strongly that the High Authority was entirely right in consulting with the ministers on all major issues, irrespective of the Treaty text. The smooth functioning of the common market during the transitional period could not have been achieved in any other manner.

As for relations with the Common Assembly, the ministers by 1955 gladly noted the passing of the initial period of friction. At first, resentment of the anti-federal Council had prompted the Assembly to exclude ministers from plenary and commission sessions. While firmly rejecting any imputation that the Council is in any way responsible to the Assembly, or should be made responsible to it through new procedures, the ministers now not only attend Assembly meetings and testify in commission meetings, but they provide documentary information and encourage even closer informal liaison. But the ministers are firm in insisting that the principles of supranational and intergovernmental co-operation cannot be mixed organically. Thus the nocturnal council seeks to assure its autonomy in gearing supranational to national measures.

But the essence of the Council's conception of its own role is not only the harmonisation of national with High Authority policy, but the attainment and maintenance of consensus among its own members. Consequently it does *not* regard itself as a continuing diplomatic conference, whose members are free to dissent and to block joint action.   While the ministers frequently arrive with firm instructions, it is the essence of the Council's code that these may eventually be changed or even disregarded under the pressure of other views. National interests are always compromised; they are never maintained in the face of the " atmosphere of co-operation " which prevails. Two techniques for achieving this

[7] Jean Rey strongly supported, in his capacity as Belgian member of the Council, a number of proposals designed to strengthen the supranational scope of the High Authority, including a stronger investment policy, the harmonisation of wages and labour conditions, centralised deflationary measures, and permanent direct relations between the High Authority and the trade unions. He also admitted that the defence purely and simply of national interests on the Council is impossible for Belgium. In view of Belgium's dependence on Dutch and German aid for the modernisation of its collieries, Belgium cannot strongly oppose demands of those countries in such fields as transport policy, even though it possesses the legal capacity to do so. See especially his statement in *Débats*, no. 13.

atmosphere are singled out by M. Rey: the tendency of the Benelux delegations to conciliate clashing French and German aspirations and the determination not to adjourn until unanimous consent has been obtained, even when it is not required. These techniques tend all the more to be successful, since members of the High Authority attend and participate in almost all sessions of the Council.

The subordinate institutions of the Council further demonstrate the principle of a novel community-type organ as against the traditional principle of a diplomatic conference. All decisions of the Council are, in effect, prepared by a Co-ordinating Commission —" Cocor " in ECSC jargon—of six national representatives.[8] Cocor enjoys continuity and stability of membership far in excess of the Council itself. The members have grown to know one another well; negotiations tend to become less and less formal; increasingly a process is initiated of seeking the best compromise in terms of a common technical solution to a given economic problem. The Commission never votes; its purpose is to achieve consensus, which can then be easily ratified by the full Council. Yet the members are usually instructed and reluctant to take the initiative in requesting new directives when compromise seems impossible. Under such conditions, the final formula is still left to the Council whose members are frequently able to act in the absence, or even in defiance, of instructions.

Decision-making is facilitated at a still lower level of consultation by the use of permanent or long-term expert commissions. These are composed of instructed civil servants but usually work in close rapport with representatives of the High Authority, on whose co-ordinating and guiding function they rely heavily in some situations. Yet it is the experience of ECSC that civil servants at this level of consultation are even more reluctant to depart from instructions than is true of the Co-ordinating Commission. Hence the work of these expert Commissions tends to take years for successful completion through unanimously acceptable compromise. Such " *ad hoc* technical commissions " function in the realm of rail, water

---

[8] Persons who have habitually been members of the Co-ordinating Commission: Germany, von der Groeben; France, MM. Alby and Morin; Italy, MM. Bollasco and Gambelli; Belgium, M. van der Meulen; Netherlands, MM. Hyzen and Mass; Luxembourg, MM. Elvinger and Suttor. These gentlemen are all high civil servants, functioning as chiefs of divisions of international or European economic affairs, in the Ministries of Economics. M. Alby is Assistant Secretary-General of the French cabinet's inter-ministerial Co-ordinating Committee for Questions of European Economic Co-operation.

and road transport, scrap and coal policy, as well as for commercial policy matters.   The so-called " Comité mixte " is the most ambitious permanent body of this kind, charged with the harmonisation of national energy, investment, tax and social security policies. Thus the Council takes seriously the implications of the spill-over process.   It reflects its concern by the creation of appropriate machinery largely detached from national administration.   But while it grants continuous High Authority participation in these deliberations, it was careful to put the machinery under inter-governmental rather than federal direction.

Yet a new slant is given even to these measures through the function of the Council's own permanent secretariat, thus detracting further from the conventional diplomatic technique.   Decisions of the Cocor and of *ad hoc* commissions are prepared by Council technicians who no longer have any tie with national governments but are ECSC civil servants.   Their position papers and contacts with the High Authority thus find their way into intergovernmental consultations.   Since the staff members make recommendations of their own, a centralised—if technocratic—element is directly introduced into the negotiating process even at the Council level. This function, naturally, is effective in guiding Council decisions only when consensus has not yet been achieved by the six ministers. When, for opposing, converging or identical motives, they have already made up their minds on a given course of action, no amount of study and recommendation at the various lower levels of contact is relevant to the decision.   Such open-and-shut cases, however, occur very rarely.

DECISION-MAKING PATTERNS: CONSULTATIONS

The great bulk of consultations between the High Authority and the Council refers to policy questions of very minor relevance to issues of political integration.   Exceptions to this rule, however, include some of the most crucial situations with respect to supra-national decision-making: the relaxation of the fair trade code, reduction of the ECSC production tax, and the use of ceiling prices for the Ruhr.

To Monnet's request that rebates be allowed beyond the price lists submitted by steel manufacturers, the Council gave a most equivocal reply.   When the High Authority enacted its proposal regardless of the response, the French and Italian Governments felt free to proceed against the decision in their appeals to the Court. Unless the production tax is to be levied at a rate in excess of 1 per cent. of value produced, the Council lacks jurisdiction over the issue. When the High Authority consulted the Council on May 2, 1955, State Secretary Westrick, demanded that the rate be cut in half immediately, a request motivated by the assertion that the reserve fund was adequate, that coal production costs in the Ruhr must be reduced and that the collieries must be compensated for increased wages gained by I. G. Bergbau. Italy and Luxembourg supported the German claim; France was doubtful; but Belgium and Holland opposed it, citing the need for more re-adaptation and the danger of reducing taxes during an inflationary period. Yet the High Authority enacted the reduction it had planned.

The voting pattern on the central " dirigistic " question of whether ECSC price ceilings should be maintained for the Ruhr is as follows:

	voted "yes" in:	voted " no " in:	abstained or unclear in:
Germany	1954 1955	1956	
France	1954 1955 1956		
Italy	1955 1956	1954 (if prices decline)	
Belgium		1954 (if prices decline) 1955	1956
Netherlands	1955* 1956	1954	
Luxembourg	1954	1956	1955 (no increases)

* If price increases are kept low.

The pattern shows (1) that the German position was met in all cases, (2) that no unanimity was ever obtained, but that the High Authority acted anyway, and (3) that no one country was ever isolated. It should be added, however, that in the 1956 price ceiling discussion in the Cocor, the French, Italian and Dutch delegates darkly hinted at their right to re-impose national ceilings if the High Authority decided to abolish its controls.

DECISION-MAKING PATTERNS: COUNCIL AGREEMENT

A large range of issues has arisen under the Treaty calling for the agreement of the Council to a proposal of the High Authority. Many of these have been discussed in other contexts and need only be recapitulated briefly. Scrap policy is one of the chief headaches to the governments and the High Authority, with the executive having consistently sought to deal with the shortage through central price control, allocation and planning measures requiring Council approval. Yet the votes show that unanimous agreement was rarely attained during the four-year period when the issue came up repeatedly, with the High Authority proceeding to enact the measures it considered necessary: more dirigistic than the Italian Government demanded, but less than the French desired. At the same time, however, the Council considered the long-term solution of the crisis to be a " harmonisation " function under Article 26, and hence its prerogative. Therefore, it created its own expert commission to work out a final solution instead of relying exclusively on the initiative of the High Authority.[9]

Council agreement was also required for the relaxation of the rules governing national governmental participation in re-adaptation operations and in the inauguration of the ECSC housing projects. No difficulty was encountered in either of these situations at the level of the full Council, though certain members of the Cocor had expressed reserve about tax funds originating from one country being spent on non-coal and steel re-adaptation projects in other member states. While the relaxations were hedged about with conditions to keep them from becoming a precedent, the tenor of the discussions plainly showed that on none of these issues was there a determination of any single government to prevent the evolution, on principle, of federal activities even though not all members would profit equally from them.

Coal policy, and especially the coal shortage which developed from 1955 on, gave rise to some impatience among the governments. They challenged the desire of the High Authority to institute coal price flexibility as a long-range policy goal, reserved their right to examine the basic questions of investment in the coal sector in relation to other energy sources, and insisted on taking a hand in the consideration of alleviating shortages through compensation arrangements. Hence, coal policy has increasingly been confined

[9] Some details are in *Agence Europe*, July 16, 23, 26, 28, 1954.

to study and discussion in the Council's own technical commission for coal. While the High Authority is asked to co-operate with this group, it is clearly not under immediate federal jurisdiction and thus reflects a desire of the ministers to influence this vital area. But this step by no means precludes joint action in response to a more vigorous High Authority initiative, as was made clear in our discussion of Luxembourg's coal plans in 1957.

Council agreement by unanimous vote is required to empower and instruct the High Authority in dealings with third countries. Enough has already been said about the negotiation of the Agreement of Association with Britain and the Consultation Accord with Switzerland to make plain that the Council jealously guards its prerogative in this field, even though it is perfectly willing to entertain policy recommendations coming from the High Authority. However, the decision-making pattern here also reveals that the national policy most restrictive of federal initiative—France's in this instance—did not carry the day and was successfully compromised on the Council.

While paragraph 14 of the Convention on Transitional Provisions allows the High Authority to negotiate with third countries on behalf of ECSC, subject to Council instructions, the general tenor of the Treaty makes it quite clear that commercial relations with non-member countries remain the prerogative of the six governments. These have merely incurred the obligation not to violate ECSC rules in their external dealings and to harmonise their tariff structures by 1958 so as to create a true customs union. The aim of harmonisation involves not only the drastic reduction of the extremely high Italian duties, but the slight raising of the very low Benelux tariff, and especially the evening out of the intermediate level of duties typical of France and Germany.[10] In order to come to grips with this task, the Council created the Commission on Commercial Policy, whose function includes not only the long-term task of harmonisation, but the immediate one of guiding the High Authority on commercial dealings with third countries during the transitional period.

The Council's Commission has been working on harmonisation. But the very nature of the supranational system had compelled

---

[10] The legal structure and the actual tariff rates requiring harmonisation are explored in detail in Institut des Relations Internationales, *op. cit.*, pp. 248–251, and Vignes, *op. cit.*, pp. 58–62.

even before 1958 a much closer relationship with the High Authority than required by the Treaty. The rules allow the High Authority to pass on all commercial agreements negotiated by the six governments and to call to the attention of national ministers commercial policies inconsistent with ECSC directives, while also issuing recommendations for revision. Given this responsibility to Luxembourg and given the duty to arrive at a uniform tariff by 1958, the actual freedom of negotiation with third countries tends to ring hollow. The administrative problems created by it are such that the Council in 1954 invited the High Authority to occupy a much larger initial role than foreseen. As a result, it was the High Authority which, on behalf of the six governments, negotiated with Austria for a special steels accord, and within the GATT framework during the 1955–1956 session.

In these cases, the steps in the ECSC decision-making process were as follows. The Council took the initiative in expressing a desire for accords with given third countries and instructed the High Authority to prepare a draft agreement. This the High Authority did, submitting a document to the ministers requiring them to find a suitable compromise tariff level to serve as a basis for negotiation with Austria and others. Italy was by definition excepted from this, the Benelux governments declined to raise their tariffs to the level foreseen, but Germany and France then began to negotiate to align their varying levels. As this became difficult, it was the High Authority which interceded and suggested the 11 per cent. level finally adopted by both. When negotiations with Austria were opened by M. Spierenburg, Council members attended the sessions as silent observers, periodically reinstructing the High Authority as they saw fit. In actual practice, these functions of the Council were carried out by the Committee on Commercial Policy, whose final decision would guide full Council approval of any successfully negotiated agreements. Ratification by national parliaments might then still be necessary, depending on national law.

Formally, the governments retain all essential powers. In terms of regional decision-making, however, they share it not only with the High Authority, but delegate it to one of their own expert corporate bodies. The spill-over is introduced into this practice when—as at the GATT sessions—tariff bargaining on steel alone becomes impossible as concessions with respect to duties on other items are demanded. Here again the Council has accepted the challenge of the new procedures by appropriately extending the scope of its Committee on Commercial Policy. When the High Authority is challenged by other GATT members on alleged dumping or cartel practices by ECSC firms, the six governments have been unanimous in defending their agent even though it was they who denied the High Authority the right to curb such measures in 1953. In fact, therefore, the Treaty rules governing " agreement " of the Council have become the guides for action, with High Authority-sponsored discussion continuing until a compromise is found.

The classic case, not of compromise but of the complete capitulation of a tenaciously defended national position, is provided by the controversy surrounding the opening of the common market for special steels in summer of 1954. Council participation in the decision became necessary because the French Government challenged the ruling of the High Authority to abolish obstacles to trade in special steels, claiming the need for a special safeguarding clause to protect the allegedly high-cost French producers. The Consultative Committee had overwhelmingly favoured the opening, at the loud demand of German producers and dealers and over the protest of French industry spokesmen. Yet Paris made no move to repeal the special 15 per cent. tax applicable exclusively to imports of special steels.

In the Council meeting of June 24, the matter came to a head with a High Authority proposal, backed by five ministers, that the common market be definitely opened on August 1, calling on France to rescind the tax before that date. Bourgès-Maunoury agreed, *provided* a special safeguarding clause for French steels were approved at the same time. This the Council refused to grant, but agreed to instruct the High Authority to investigate the French special steels industry's needs along those lines. While French industry was in an uproar and the cabinet in Paris accused Bourgès-Maunoury of selling out French interests, the High Authority experts reported that no need for safeguarding measures could be established. The *dénouement* came during the eighteenth session of the Council, on July 27. Backed by his government, Bourgès-Maunoury first held out for the application of safeguarding measures in exchange for the repeal of the 15 per cent. tax. He was turned down by his colleagues.

He then asked for the authorisation of various administrative devices through which the imports of special steels might be temporarily controlled, only to be repulsed by the Benelux ministers. Finally he asked for a special 5 per cent. tax refund to be granted to French producers to enable them to lower their costs. Even this was branded a violation of the Treaty by the High Authority members present and by certain of the governments; but it was agreed, for " courtesy's sake," to permit such a refund during a three-months trial period, after which it would have to be removed. Thus given a slight face-saving formula, Bourgès-Maunoury capitulated and the common market was opened without special tax or safeguarding clause on August 1, 1954.[11]

DECISION-MAKING PATTERNS: COUNCIL PREPONDERANCE

In areas in which the Council possesses and claims predominant powers of initiating and approving steps relevant to political integration, however, things tend to proceed less smoothly. Crucial decisions in the fields of labour migration, transport, welfare policy, and general economic policy will be singled out for study here.

Labour Migration

Taking literally the text of the Treaty which calls on the High Authority to " orient and facilitate " the initiative of the governments in creating a free labour market, the High Authority in 1953 worked out a series of proposals. They asserted the right of qualified workers to *seek* employment free from immigration and passport restrictions, other than those concerned with health and public order, recommended the issuing of an ECSC labour card to all qualified personnel which would entitle them to migrate, noted the importance of a liberal definition of "qualified labour," and called for co-ordination among national employment services to match supply with demand, as well as a multilateral social security convention to eliminate discrimination.[12]

An inter-governmental conference was now convened to

[11] Details are reported in *Agence Europe*, June 15, 21, 24, 26, 30, July 2, 14, 19, 20, 21, 27, 28, 31, 1954. In a study of *Nouvelles de l'Europe*, January 1955, pp. 6–19, this episode is used quite unjustifiably as typical of Council willingness to heed the prodding of the High Authority.

[12] High Authority, Labour Division, Working Group for the Application of Article 69, " Bericht an die Hohe Behörde," Doc. 7523 d/1 (Luxembourg: October 1953). Information Division, " La libre circulation des travailleurs de qualification confirmée " (Luxembourg: October 27, 1954).

consider these suggestions. It revealed a division of opinion—already implicit in the positions defended by organised labour—which could not be meaningfully compromised. France and Luxembourg overtly opposed any easing of migration rules, Germany proved almost equally unenthusiastic, with only Belgium, Holland and Italy defending the High Authority ideas. All the conference managed to agree on was a far more restrictive definition of what constitutes " qualified " coal and steel labour than that advanced by the High Authority and by the Italian Government, though even this definition was more liberal than the rigid standards of vocational training demanded by the Germans. A labour card was to be issued to such personnel, but they would be entitled to migrate only to *accept* employment offered them through the medium of direct demand or national employment services. No agreement could be reached on the details of implementation.

This task was confided to the Council of Ministers and the Cocor, where a less rigidly diplomatic procedure prevailed. The ILO was charged with working out the necessary social security convention, and national employment services were to be co-ordinated through a central secretariat in Luxembourg, without powers of initiative. New techniques of intergovernmental negotiation, however, were implicit in the difficult questions of ratification and official languages. France demanded the exclusive use of French for the migration agreement, a claim hotly disputed by the Germans. A Belgian compromise formula carried the day, under which the agreement was to be considered a " resolution of the Council," and hence sidestep the question of language prestige, since such decisions need not in principle come up for parliamentary review. Other delegations, however, insisted that their national law requires formal ratification. Instead of simply accepting this assertion, the Cocor made its own review of national procedures and extracted agreement among its members either to avoid ratification or to expedite the process. Only Luxembourg refused to agree even to this concession.[13]

The resulting " agreement " was unanimously approved by the Council in October of 1954, only to remain unimplemented until

[13] *Agence Europe*, May 17, 28, July 5, 27, September 6, 23, October 11, 25, 26, 28, 1954. It should be noted that the minimalist nature of the intergovernmental negotiations resulted in a sharp attack on the Council by the Common Assembly, whose efforts to influence the treaty drafting process were repulsed by the governments.

1957. Efforts to work out the necessary multipartite social security convention failed time and again at the ILO and at the level of intergovernmental expert discussion. In December of 1956, the Council took the matter up directly, after having encouraged the High Authority to work out and circulate a compromise formula. It was confronted by the same issue which had plagued the meetings in 1954: Italy demanded that the bulk of social security contributions be borne by the country of employment, whereas all others sought to split the burden of financing more evenly between employing and home states. However, the differences were effectively compromised on the basis of High Authority intercession, leading to the conclusion of a new set of rules for all kinds of migrant workers.[14]

Transport Harmonisation

The decision-making pattern in the area of transport harmonisation is very similar to the labour migration case. ECSC activity was initiated with High Authority proposals, modified by governmental opposition, relegated to discussions of governmental experts assisted by the High Authority, confirmed in a final Council decision, with subsequent measures confided to strict Council supervision, accompanied by a minimum of federal action.

The first steps taken by ECSC involved the elimination of obvious cases of railway rate discrimination based on the nationality of shipper and consignee. A commission of governmental experts examined thirty-two separate allegations of discriminatory rates. It unanimously agreed on ordering the modification of twenty-four. The remaining cases gave rise to disputes among the delegates as to whether discrimination was involved, each national group defending its practices as legal in principle. Even here almost unanimous agreement on the details was reached, even if the principle was left in doubt. Most significantly, the experts recommended that certain practices could be brought into conformity with Treaty rules only by the introduction of uniform international through-rates, implying the abolition of fictitious frontier charges.

At this stage, the High Authority prepared a detailed scheme for harmonisation and put it before the Council for implementation. Specifically, it was requested that in cases where the Treaty clearly requires the equality of position of all coal and steel consumers,

[14] *Agence Europe*, June 5, July 24, December 11, 1956. See Chap. 3 for the details.

regardless of nationality, uniformly tapered rates must be applied irrespective of frontiers. Yet the High Authority was careful not to push this principle so far as to include the equalisation of railway tariffs at the lowest common level, to make no proposals on the actual level of the new rates, and to leave intact special rate protection accorded to certain interests unless it could be proved that these were discriminatory to coal and steel consumers. Procedurally speaking, it is interesting to note that High Authority recommendations were prepared by French and German railway experts seconded to Luxembourg, who only a few months previously had been instrumental in inventing new discriminations. For its part, the Council declined to permit the High Authority to pursue the harmonisation task independently and called for the creation of a new committee of governmental experts—representing the ministries of transport—to work out the actual arrangements. The governments were already in disagreement over the desired scope.

The labours of this committee were far from harmonious. The French, Belgian, and Luxembourg delegates, in general, endorsed the proposals of the High Authority and recommended the inauguration of a tapered through-rate system. These aims became the report of the committee even though unanimous agreement could not be secured. The Italian delegation opposed the through-rates as not required by the Treaty and harmful to the Italian steel and coke industries, as well as implying losses for the state railways. The Dutch experts thought that the report ignored the effects on carriers other than railways and failed to specify the precise rate structure. And the Germans argued heatedly that tapered through-rates were altogether unnecessary, and were bound to hurt regions and economic interests still justifiably protected by a manipulated rate structure.

Since these reservations corresponded to the opinions of the respective national ministries, a compromise had to be found if there was going to be any agreement at all. At this point, the High Authority again took the initiative by side-stepping the expert committee and approaching the national governments directly, while strongly defending the need for a supranational solution along the lines of its original proposals. It attacked the positions of the German and Italian ministers head-on. A reconvened expert commission, apparently equipped with new instructions, did agree finally to uniform tapered through-rates, meeting the German and Italian reservations by initially limiting the distances to be subject to the rules and thus permitting temporarily the protection of certain regions from competition.[15] Bonn and Rome swallowed the federal principle implied in the solution, even if the pill was sugared by certain exemptions.

When the Council was convened to approve the agreement, the earlier reluctance had by no means evaporated. The Dutch, Italian and German transport ministers seemed determined to kill the agreement even after High Authority intervention, with Bonn's Seebohm taking a particularly uncompromising stand. At the crucial point in the meeting, an adjournment was called after which the ministers of economics—the regular members of the Council—took aside their compatriots and explained to them that under the decision-making code of ECSC, the supranational principle itself is not subject to attack, though negotiations over the details are proper! Thus " converted," the recalcitrant ministers dropped their opposition and the agreement was approved by the full Council.[16]

Clearly, the final solution proved possible only because in each national capital the ministries of transport and of economics were in disagreement with one another—the former worried about losses of revenue and the latter concerned with the benefits of the common market. At the same time, national interest groups were equally divided, depending on whether they tended to rely on foreign sources of supply and markets or feared external competition. There were no strong national positions to be unanimously defended. The principle of fragmentation is again useful in explaining why a supranationally weighted compromise was realised.

Yet the sequel to this episode demonstrates that not all national governments were pleased by the crucial independent role played by the High Authority in the railway agreement. Harmonisation of rules and elimination of discrimination concerning road and

---

[15] *Agence Europe*, September 21, 22, 29, October 1, 1954. High Authority, Press Release, July 28, 1954, January 20, 1955. The details of the final agreement are given in Chap. 3.

[16] It is reported that Erhard persuaded Seebohm to change his attitude and that Spierenburg was instrumental in obtaining the acquiescence of the Dutch minister of transport. It is also reported that in the discussion between the ministers of economics and their transport colleagues, the point was strongly made that the ECSC Council of Ministers is *not* the Council of the OEEC, in which prior commitment to joint action is never taken for granted.

waterway traffic were kept out of the direct scope of High Authority initiative by national governments finding ample legal arguments for preserving inter-governmental techniques for attacking these issues.[17]   Repeated High Authority suggestions to the Council for action in these two areas were met with dilatory replies.   At first, the Council deferred to the concurrent efforts of the European Conference of Transport Ministers to work out a solution strictly along conventional diplomatic lines, while on the Rhine the pressing issue of differences between national and international freight rates was resolved by the organisation of a cartel.[18]   High Authority protests that this arrangement was contrary to the Treaty, since it included coal and involved firms under ECSC jurisdiction, had no immediate effect on the intergovernmental deliberations.[19] When early in 1956 the High Authority again called for action, the Council members agreed that the techniques of negotiation of their transport colleagues had led to no concrete results.   They charged their own expert commission on inland waterways, in co-operation with the High Authority, to submit plans for a definite solution.   While Italy and Luxembourg took no direct interest in the issue, the German and French experts favoured ECSC-imposed rate limits and publicly controlled compensation arrangements, to some degree reminiscent of the cartel approach. The Belgian and Dutch experts, however, held out for a strictly free market unobstructed by limitations of this kind.   When early in 1957 the experts and the High Authority found no common ground, the High Authority announced to the Council that it had charged one of its members to explore possible solutions directly with the six governments, thus in effect sidestepping once

[17] Details are well summarised in Bok, *op. cit.*, pp. 20 *et seq.*

[18] Under the agreement, announced in September 1955, quotas of traffic were allotted to national trade associations of shippers, as follows: Germany, 44 per cent.; Holland, 37 per cent.; France, 9 per cent.; Belgium, 8 per cent.; Switzerland, 2 per cent. *Agence Europe*, September 29, 1955.

[19] The European Conference of Transport Ministers includes most of the OEEC members.   It meets annually for exchanges of views on common problems but possesses no decision-making power.   It has no permanent staff and undertakes no independent studies, relying for such efforts on the International Railway Union, the Central Rhine Commission and such trade associations as the International Union for Inland Navigation.   Hence it is preferred both by state railway administrations and private shippers to the supranational system of the ECSC Council of Ministers, which they cannot influence directly.   On the other hand, the results obtained by the Conference are meagre because they depend exclusively on multipartite negotiations and co-operation from interested parties, whether public or private.   For details see Conseil National du Patronat Français, *Bulletin*, November 1954, p. 61 *et seq*; *Informations Bimensuelles*, March 1, 1955, pp. 31–32.

more the intergovernmental expert commission. While the agreement announced in the summer of 1957 affects only navigation on the Rhine it nevertheless represents significant concessions by both pairs of experts and underscores the mediating role of the High Authority in a setting in which governments are unable to agree but nevertheless are committed to a general solution.[19a]

Labour Policy

Quite apart from the central issue of the harmonisation of wages and working conditions throughout the ECSC area, the Council was thrown into a difficult position by the task of selecting the labour members of the Consultative Committee. According to an agreement made in 1952 between the International Confederation of Free Trade Unions and the International Confederation of Christian Trade Unions, at the suggestion of Jean Monnet, the labour groups recommended greater representation for German than for French unions in the list of candidates they presented to the Council. This was immediately disputed by the French Council member who demanded parity with Germany, and also by the Italian minister, who wanted an increased Italian workers' quota. Tedious negotiations were required to arrive at a compromise, which included a rotating system of representation under which certain unions participate as observers in alternate years.[20]

While this early difficulty clearly reflected a struggle for national prestige, distinct economic interests were involved in the later Council effort to extend the ECSC task to the harmonisation of wages and working conditions. Early in 1954 André Morice proposed that the Council study the harmonisation of social security contributions. This suggestion was backed by Luxembourg's Michel Rasquin, but opposed by everybody else. Matters became more serious when the Belgian steel industry was compelled to introduce the five-day week without loss of pay in mid-1955. Jean Rey, at the twenty-seventh session of the Council, formally

[19a] For details see Chap. 3; High Authority, *Fifth General Report* (April 1957), pp. 142–145; *Bulletin mensuel d'Information* (July 1957), p. 14.

[20] *Chronique de Politique Etrangère*, Vol. 6, no. 1 (January 1953), p. 64.

	System suggested by the ICFTU–ICCTU accord:	System adopted
Germany	5	5
France	4	5
Italy	1	2
Belgium	4	2.5
Netherlands	2	1.5
Luxembourg	1	1

put a request on the agenda that ECSC study the implications of the general introduction of the five-day week, thus hoping to pass on the Belgian cost increase to the other steel-producing members. Luxembourg once more backed the proposal energetically, as did Italy. France opposed the generalised five-day week, but was willing to go along with the study if it were linked to the harmonisation of social security contributions. The German and Dutch members, however, saw no reason why the favourable cost conditions of their steel industries should be thus hamstrung and therefore indicated that the issue was not urgent and might prejudice the competitive power of ECSC steel on external markets. Yet not even Westrick and Zijlstra could overtly oppose a measure presented as progressive social legislation though it implied the extension of ECSC activity into a new field. Hence, they reluctantly consented to the Belgian initiative by endorsing a unanimous Council resolution instructing a mixed High Authority-governmental commission to investigate the feasibility of introducing the five-day week throughout the ECSC area. But, warned Westrick, " the decision to undertake this investigation can have no prejudicial effects on a fundamental decision." [21] Irrespective of the German and Dutch reluctance to countenance the emergence of a supranational labour policy, the growing shortage of miners persuaded even these governments to endorse High Authority-sponsored recruitment measures and, in 1957, to support the drafting of an ECSC-wide bill of rights for miners.

General Economic Policy

Under Article 26 of the Treaty, it is the duty of the Council to " harmonise " the policy of the High Authority with the general economic policies of the six member states and to consult with the High Authority to this end. Article 95 gives the Council the power to call on the High Authority to undertake whatever studies may be necessary to advance the goal of integration. Action under these headings was defined initially by the Council in its famous resolution of October 13, 1953, and later undertaken by the Mixed Committee. The content of the resolution and an outline of the Mixed

---

[21] Report on the 27th Council session, September 26, 1955, *Continental Iron and Steel Trade Reports* (October 6, 1955). *Agence Europe*, September 13, 16, 26, 27, 1955. It should be noted, incidentally, that the German Ministry of Labour was far more favourably disposed toward the Belgian proposal than the German Ministry of Economics.

Committee's work were given above.[22]   What remains to be undertaken is an evaluation of this work in terms of its contribution to political integration and an assessment of the Council and its members as advancing or retarding this work.

In 1956 a commission of the Common Assembly found " that the Council has not yet made use of the possibilities offered by Article 26. . . . The choice of questions discussed by the Council and the High Authority has most often been inspired by opportunism; it has not been dictated by the desire to realise expansion, the aim assigned by the Treaty."[23]   Hence, the commission called on the High Authority to go over the head of the Council and approach the governments directly in an effort to mobilise these sections of the Treaty for the rapid integration of Europe.

A sober examination of the decision-making process in the realm of general economic policy will reveal that the fault for slowness is not solely the Council's. Thus, all the governments endorsed the proposal of the High Authority on October 12, 1953, to leave the confines of coal and steel and relate cyclical conditions in the integrated sector to overall economic policy still left in national hands. Nobody disputed Monnet's statement that the threatened slump " called for a policy of general expansion and conditions of normal competition." All the governments agreed that their coal and steel industries should be freed from administrative and fiscal handicaps which prevented optimum competition on the common market, that monetary and price policy beyond coal and steel should be designed to favour general expansion, and that investments should be encouraged.[24]   The text of the resolution endorsing the High Authority appeal for joint study and co-ordinated policies was drafted by Rasquin and enthusiastically defended by him. Again, no minister attacked the draft, while Zijlstra added to its scope by requesting that the joint study of cyclical developments become a regular part of ECSC activity.

[22] See Chap. 3. The Mixed Committee is made up of senior national civil servants plus three members of the High Authority's Economics Division. The Committee's sub-commissions are staffed by instructed national experts and High Authority specialists. It is reported that instructions have been general in nature and have stressed the need for a meaningful implementation of the Council's original resolution.

[23] Assemblée Commune, Exercise 1955–1956, Doc. no. 20, " Rapport ... sur la co-opération de la Haute Autorité et les Gouvernements des Etats membres ... ," par Wilmar Sabass, pp. 14, 19.

[24] This summary was compiled on the basis of access to High Authority Doc. 7231/2 f, and Council of Ministers Doc. CM 231/53, pp. 57–64.

A unanimous vote in favour of task extension, however, did not imply an identity of aims. France, then as later, saw in the resolution a means for equalising social security and tax burdens, controlling prices and limiting German investments. Luxembourg and Belgium agreed as to the equalisation of taxes but also favoured in principle ECSC-wide measures to control cyclical fluctuations. Holland, then as later, was preoccupied with price stability. Italy was not directly interested. The crucial role played, however, was that of Ludwig Erhard. The Minister of Economics at Bonn is known for his unflinching advocacy of the principles of the " social market economy," a doctrine opposing equally bitterly public planning and private collusion, castigating the influence of private groups on policy and extolling the state as the Hegelian guarantor of the general interest.[25] Erhard's opposition to supranationalism is based not only on his dislike of regional economic compartmentation, but to his fear of regional politicial institutions:

> The political independence of central banks and a close international co-operation among their governors is the best protection against the danger of abuses of power by pressure groups. The strict necessity of subordinating supranational authorities to supranational parliamentary control will merely result in a transposition of the pressure group problem to the supranational level.[26]

The harmonisation of general economic policies, therefore, could be defended so long as the Council alone remained in charge. But as soon as Common Assembly pressure or High Authority efforts at " dirigisme " are implied, Erhard is compelled to oppose harmonisation measures. While he spoke and voted for the resolution of October 13, 1953, his subsequent attitude has not always been consistent with his vote.

The work of the Mixed Committee under the resolution has been concerned with the study of these fields: (*a*) analysis of all economic and demographic factors conditioning general economic expansion in ECSC countries and forecasts of needs by 1960 and 1965; agreement was reached on the suppositions, definitions and hypotheses necessary for such a study and statistical material was collected;

[25] The doctrine of the " social market economy," as presented by its founders, Röpke, Eucken and Rüstow, is well summarised by Carl J. Friedrich, " The Political Thought of Neo-Liberalism," *American Political Science Review*, Vol. XLIX, no. 2 (June 1955), pp. 509 *et seq.*
[26] Erhard as quoted by Karl Albrecht, " Integration of vielen Wegen," *Wirtschaftsdienst*, September 1955, p. 504.

(*b*) estimates of long-range energy needs; data has been collected on the basis of an agreed common questionnaire; (*c*) studies of the influence of fiscal and tariff systems on the price of energy, as well as general studies on price formation for all sources of energy; again the experts agreed on the nature of the questionnaire to be used and the data to be considered relevant; (*d*) estimates of the need for and the availability of investment capital to cover future energy requirements, including a study of the general rate of investment in member countries; after considerable delays, agreement was reached on the questionnaire and the data obtained; (*e*) distortion studies, *i.e.*, analyses designed to ascertain whether six national fiscal, social security and wage systems seriously " distort " price formation and the pattern of competition; while agreement was reached on the questionnaire used, little actual data was obtained with the exception of the wage question.[26a]

By the end of 1957 no harmonisation of energy or general economic policies had been effected. In what sense, then, can the work of the Mixed Committee be considered a contribution to integration? The answer lies in the methods employed for these studies. Under the prodding of High Authority experts, the economic specialists of six governments agreed for the first time to collect and submit statistical information not previously made available to non-national organs, data which could easily find its way into supranational economic planning at some future time. They agreed to submit comparable statistics based on common definitions, unlike similar endeavours in other international organisations. The process implied, on the part of the High Authority, a deliberate reliance on key national officials in order to induce and accustom these civil servants to co-operative supranational work. Data collected on this basis engages the full responsibility of these officials and may permit no drawing back by governments in the future, once the High Authority decided to take up with the full Council the results of the studies. This is all the more germane to integration because of the reluctance of the German Government, in particular, to submit information which could be

---

[26a] The results of the energy studies, together with recommendations for investment policy, were published as Comité Mixte, *Etudes et Documents*, " Etude sur la structure et les Tendances de l'Economie énergetique dans les pays de la Communauté " (Luxembourg, 1957). In this connection, see also the parallel report by Louis Armand, Franz Etzel and Francesco Giordani, *A Target for Euratom*, May 1957.

used for planning purposes. In view of this attitude and the fear of the French officials that the Committee might be used to side-step the Council's pre-eminent role in " harmonisation," it is all the more significant that the Cocor agreed to a wide interpretation of the Committee's task and endorsed the High Authority's proposals for detailed and exhaustive questionnaires.

Apparently the decision to use these studies as a means to expand the supranational task was not made until the success of Euratom and EEC was assured. At that point, however, High Authority passivity changed to active policy: on the occasion of the Rome meeting of the foreign ministers, March 25, 1957, René Mayer urged Paul-Henri Spaak, in the latter's capacity as head of the intergovernmental committee drafting the new treaties, to bring about a clear mandate for the High Authority to make studies and propose policies in the entire energy field in order to arrive at a co-ordinated European fuel policy. The foreign ministers, through the pen of M. Hallstein, encouraged the High Authority to submit appropriate proposals to the Council of Ministers.

Such proposals were indeed submitted, based on the previous studies of the Mixed Committee, and led to the acceptance by the Council on October 8, 1957, of a protocol defining the new mission of the High Authority in the energy sector. While eschewing any desire to extend the powers of ECSC to energy sources other than coal, the Council nevertheless agreed in sweeping terms to the need for integrated and co-ordinated fuel forecasts and demand analyses in order to achieve an optimum distribution of invest-ments, tied at all levels to overall economic and foreign exchange policy. Specifically, the High Authority was charged with pre-paring studies and making recommendations for co-ordination, in co-operation with the Mixed Committee, Euratom and EEC. These studies may draw on information obtained directly from private firms and groups *not* subject to the ECSC Treaty; if these fail to co-operate, the governments are pledged to intercede on the High Authority's behalf. The High Authority's conclusions will be communicated to and discussed with the Council. Their publication may be authorised.[26b]

This clear extension of the scope of supranationality was not achieved without some hesitation by certain governments. Hence

[26b] Text of the protocol between the High Authority and the Council of Ministers in *Journal Officiel*, December 7, 1957, pp. 574–578.

the decision-making pattern is once more instructive of the nature of the spill-over process at the level of intergovernmental dealings. The points which aroused most discussion in the meeting of the Council hinged around the High Authority's right to access to non-ECSC firms, the independent role of the High Authority in the preparation of the studies (as opposed to dependence on nationally instructed experts and governments), and the possibility of publication for the reports. For Bonn, Westrick strongly urged a restricted supranational role on all three counts and he received the support of Zijlstra. However, on behalf of the High Authority René Mayer resisted these arguments, a position in which he enjoyed the strong support of the Belgian and Italian representatives. The pattern is thus clear: with a strong division of opinion among the ministers, a High Authority determined to carry its proposals won the day even in an area which clearly is not subject to its original jurisdiction. And in the interest of harmony, M. Westrick agreed finally to proposals which he had opposed at the beginning of the session.[26c]

Joint studies of cyclical conditions provide the one remaining area of Council action foreseen by the resolution of October 13, 1953. Council discussion here reveals that far more supranational action could have been achieved if the High Authority had responded affirmatively to suggestions made. Each successive report by the High Authority on business trends was criticised for being too modest in scope. Requests for specific recommendations on common credit and investment policies, inflationary or deflationary steps were made regularly by Council members, but only supplied in very sketchy form by the High Authority. Thus during the Council session of September 27, 1955, not only Morice, Rey, and Rasquin, but Zijlstra and Westrick as well called on the High Authority to make more profound and far-reaching economic analyses. But Albert Coppé replied that the Treaty does not permit such an invasion of the general economic domain and that a free-enterprise oriented ECSC should not directly deal with the policy fields implied![27]

[26c] Council of Ministers Doc. 715 f/57, October 21, 1957.

[27] The High Authority justifies its cautious attitude by pointing out that the discussions on cyclical conditions which take place in the ECSC framework are based on honest statistics and frank opinions, rather than on figures compiled for bargaining purposes. It contrasts the openness of Council discussions with the negotiating atmosphere said to prevail in similar OEEC meetings, where resolutions are merely the lowest common denominator among uncompromised

The fault for ECSC rectitude, thus, does not lie with the Council. It is apparent from the controversy over the inflationary pressures which developed after 1955 that the members would have been delighted with some kind of supranational directing mechanism to which they could have publicly shifted the blame for later adopting national policies of control and retrenchment. Accordingly the Mixed Committee was instructed in summer of 1957 to intensify its studies in such a way as to enable the Council to discuss coal and steel trends in the framework of general cyclical movements. The same willingness to defer to federal techniques in matters extending beyond the strict scope of High Authority jurisdiction is apparent in the reaction of several governments to the coal memorandum.[28] All the governments rejected the principle of coal price flexibility and thereby indicated commitment to ECSC controls. Most of them indicated more interest in centrally rationing certain kinds of coal in the winter of 1955–1956 than did the High Authority. The reluctance to adjust ECSC policy on coal price ceilings to special measures of subsidisation planned by the Bonn Government in the spring of 1956 brought forth sharp comments from the Dutch and French members of the Cocor, urging the High Authority to interest itself in this development *before* ruling on price ceilings, instead of invoking the Treaty in justification of not " officially " knowing what was afoot. Germany, France, and Belgium favoured the use of fuel oil as regulating mechanism on coal prices and argued for a closer co-ordination of energy policy. Belgium, France, and Luxembourg supported ECSC-wide measures to limit imports of coal from third countries. While only Belgium favoured the use of ECSC funds to finance coal buffer stocks during periods of glut, all the governments were agreed that coal sales organisations will continue to be necessary, though they must function under centrally administered rules. Clearly, the picture of opinion and decisions in the Council does not reveal a unanimous opposition to ECSC initative, study, and even planning.

national positions. Hence the High Authority insists on the secrecy of the proceedings, non-publication of its reports, participation of unofficial and uninstructed national experts .(usually chosen from the central banks) in the discussions, and the avoidance of any conclusion smacking of " policy." Conversely, it forgoes any intention of seeking the actual implementation by governments of the agreement in views reached on the Council. Implementation remains purely voluntary and no changes of interest rates or public spending are known to have occurred because of Council discussion.

[28] See Chap. 3. High Authority, *Bulletin Mensuel d'Information* (July, 1957), p. 2.

What principles of integration can now be extracted from the decision-making pattern legally involving High Authority participation and Council preponderance? The migration and transport decisions indicate that while the Council continues to make use of the federal mechanism for study and negotiating purposes, the operational centre of gravity has been re-asserted as lying with the ministers themselves. National governments here seem clearly to have regretted the initial exercise of authority by the federal agency. However, in both cases they eventually turned to the High Authority to mediate their disagreements and accepted the essence of Luxembourg's position. The evolution of policy in the labour and harmonisation fields, however, indicates a different trend. Here, more responsibility than desired by the High Authority was progressively delegated to it as the ministers realised that they could not singly deal with the issues involved. That the Council in all cases retained ultimate control over the activities in question does not detract from the importance of the delegation. The difference between the two opposing trends is explained by the direct involvement of vocal interest groups protesting an active federal policy in the cases of labour migration and transport harmonisation. Hence an ambitious ECSC-wide solution was politically and administratively opposed in almost all the member countries. In the labour field, some domestic groups are in favour of the federal " invasion " and the opposing groups are numerically less vital. And the issue of general economic policy harmonisation is remote from parliamentary and constituency political pressure and hence more susceptible of a federal solution, if the few civil servants directly involved are so disposed. Hence, it cannot be accurately argued on the basis of ECSC experience that in a supranational system, intergovernmental techniques will invariably cut down the federal authority and reclaim all basic powers. Not only have the ministers encouraged the federal agency in several situations, but even the intergovernmental techniques of decision-making used and re-asserted carry the imprint of new procedures and attitudes which have " spilled over " from the federal framework.

GOVERNMENTAL INITIATIVE AND EUROPEAN UNITY

This conclusion must stand even in the fundamental political decisions taken by the six governments aiming at the continuation of integration. This is true though technically such meetings do

not occur in the ECSC framework and are not subject to Council
voting rules, even when the personnel engaged in negotiation is
identical with the Council's normal membership. Yet the distinction
is unimportant in practice. Meetings of the Council have initiated
such basic new departures as the European Political Community.
Responding to a Franco-Italian suggestion, the Council at its very
first meeting in August of 1952 called on the Common Assembly
to transform itself into the " *ad hoc* Assembly "—and thus technically remain within the letter of the ECSC Treaty—to draft a
political constitution.[29]   But it was at subsequent conferences of
the six foreign ministers, or their deputies, that the French Government brought up obstacle after obstacle to block the approval of
the EPC Draft Constitution, such as the suggestion to give the
EPC Council of National Ministers a veto power over all legislation
and to limit the competence of the EPC Parliament strictly to ECSC
and EDC matters.   Similarly, the meeting at Messina was technically outside the scope of ECSC.   Yet it was here that René
Mayer was elected successor to Jean Monnet—apparently without
the consultation of the High Authority demanded by the Treaty—
and that the " New Start " was decided upon.[30]   The distinction
between Council meetings and conferences of the six governments
dealing with integration is even more blurred by the practice of
using the Council's Luxembourg secretariat in both situations.
Preparations for such meetings, unless they are handled exclusively
by foreign office personnel as was the case with EPC, may thus be
largely removed from national administrative centres.   As shown
by the Messina resolutions, the compromise obtained in this setting

---

[29] Details concerning EPC in *Chronique de Politique Etrangère*, Vol. 6, no. 1 (January
1953) and no. 3 (May 1953).   It should be noted that long before the fate of EPC
became doubtful because of the delays regarding the ratification of the EDC Treaty,
national governments expressed reservations.   Thus M. Beyen had insisted at the
Rome Conference of the six governments (February 24, 1953) that the EPC must
include a General European Common Market, much on the model of the agreement
concluded in 1957, and that a mere political federation was inadequate.   M. Van
Zeeland had warned of the dangers of EPC and the mistakes of the federal approach.
M. René Mayer, in his maiden speech as Premier in 1953, had spoken of the need
to link the unification of Europe with the internal perfection of the French Union
and thus detracted from the primacy of European unity by stressing the French
colonial problem.   M. Bidault, even though he had praised the EPC draft in warm
terms at Strasbourg, expressed himself with much more reserve—" il ne faut
pas défaire la France "—in parliament.

[30] According to the High Authority's press release of June 2, 1955, Mayer was chosen
in Messina on June 1, whereupon Bech communicated the news to Luxembourg.
The remaining eight members of the High Authority then proceeded to " elect "
Mayer on June 2.

was in no essential respect different from the pattern which has characterised the Council in general.[31]

A crucial index for gauging the evolution of new processes of intergovernmental negotiations and their contribution to political integration is provided by the work of the " New Start." It involved initial far-reaching ministerial decisions, the work of national experts advised by supranational officials, intermittent consultations among the ministers, and the presence of a " leading European political personality " as a prod to the proceedings. Events at each stage of the deliberations must now be thrown into focus.

The outstanding fact about the Messina agreement of the foreign ministers is the firm " engagement " to which it bound subsequent negotiations. While evading the institutional desires of the Benelux Memorandum, the resolutions actually went beyond Beyen's suggestions by stating, in Spaak's words, that

> The six governments recognise that a common European market free from all customs dues and quantitative restrictions is the objective of this economic policy.[32]

There was no equivocation about the engagement: a General Common Market—deliberately conceived by MM. Spaak, Beyen, and Bech as a step to political integration—was to be created, by means to be studied later. Even France, despite her hesitations, felt unable to oppose this desire of the other five ministers for fear of remaining politically and economically isolated if the others insisted on going ahead without Paris. A fundamental *political* consensus was therefore the basis of work at Brussels.

The national experts shortly appointed thereafter to confer at Brussels had as their task *the study of techniques best suited to introduce the common market, not the question of whether such a scheme should be adopted.* While they all arrived with instructions, their orders reflected this underlying political consensus. Further, their deliberations were influenced at all levels by the fact that MM. Spierenburg and Uri participated on behalf of the High Authority by putting before the experts their supranational experiences and preferences. While OEEC and British delegates were also present at Brussels as observers, their role was far less

---

[31] See Chap. 7 for the details concerning the Messina meeting.
[32] Spaak's speech to the Consultative Assembly, Council of Europe, October 21, 1955. Council doc. A.24.469, p. 5. The speech also contains a description of the function exercised by Spaak at Brussels.

pronounced in influencing the report of the experts. In addition, the supranational secretariat of the Council of Ministers furnished advice to the experts, thus departing further from the conventional pattern of diplomatic negotiation.

But it was undoubtedly the unprecedented negotiating function assigned to Spaak by his five colleagues which made the difference between success and failure during the frequently painful twenty-two months which elasped between Messina and the signature of the finished treaties. When the experts disagreed, Spaak ordered them to postpone considering the differences of opinion and to concentrate first on questions permitting agreement. He advanced the formula whereby institutional questions were reserved for discussion *after* the functional needs of the new schemes had been fixed. When obviously divergent instructions seemed to permit of no consensus, Spaak called adjournments, convened interim meetings of the foreign ministers, and persuaded them to issue more flexible instructions to their experts. When he failed to extract consensus from the ministers—as at their Nordwijk meeting in September 1955—uncertainty continued to prevail; but the matters on which disagreement continued were then merely provided with alternative conceivable solutions in the final report of the experts. Unwilling to follow a rigid federalist and institutional line in his work, Spaak merely sought in all crisis situations to advance formulas which would permit the drafting of treaties capable of growth later, even though the immediate results would be far less supranational than ECSC.

Throughout the twenty-two months of deliberations, the basic governmental positions were fairly clear. France sought maximum supranational powers and institutions for Euratom and the possibility of giving it jurisdiction over atomic arms. She sought a minimum of supranationalism for the common market, generous safeguarding clauses, a long period of adjustment with flexible stages, exemption of agriculture and the right unilaterally to re-impose trade restrictions, as well as the prior harmonisation of social legislation. The Benelux countries opposed most of these French aims as regards the common market but agreed on a maximalist position for Euratom. Germany argued for an extensive system of free trade, a minimalistically conceived Euratom close to the scheme suggested by OEEC, and opposed especially the creation of new supranational institutions. But in deference to the SPD, the German negotiators were unwilling to equip Euratom with jurisdiction over atomic arms.   Continuous compromising by all parties was thus strikingly necessary to achieve final consensus.

The experts finished their work early in 1956.   Their agreement was extensive and provides the essence of the economic aspects of the two treaties.   But they did not reach agreement on the institutional question, except to advance the possibility that the common market could well be administered by an intergovernmental system assisted by a permanent expert commission possessing the powers of study, advice and the capacity to ease intergovernmental compromising by advancing appropriate formulas.   In short, the role exercised by the High Authority in relation to the Council in matters not clearly under ECSC jurisdiction was simply transposed to the common market.   On the delicate question of the prior harmonisation of social legislation, France lost most of her point in the experts' solution of not requiring complete equalisation before the opening of the common market and to rely on normal competitive forces to achieve it in the long run, even though "drastic distortions" could be studied for special action.   Complete agreement on the length of the transitional period and the rigidity of stages could not be obtained, but the principle of a common external tariff caused relatively little difficulty.   While the need for safeguarding clauses was admitted by all, their text remained controversial as did the central issue of the permissibility of reintroducing exchange controls if balance of payments difficulties developed.

Yet most of these difficulties were ironed out at the next level—deliberations of the heads of delegations.   This group reported to the home governments in April of 1956.   Its report was drafted very largely by Pierre Uri, whose official role in Brussels had been merely that of the ECSC High Authority representative.   It represented not only the actual political compromising performed at the expert level, but the translation of the High Authority's integration doctrine into concrete policy.

Thus the dispute over balance of payments crises was resolved by the heads of the delegations by permitting the invocation of difficulties as reason for demanding relaxation of the common market rules; but the administration of the exemption was made rigorously dependent upon approval by EEC organs. Disagreement over the treatment of agriculture was resolved by proposing two formulas:

agricultural commodities could be treated competitively as if they were identical with other goods in the common market; but in the event of resistance and difficulties, a " common organisation " of agriculture could be instituted instead. It was, of course, the second solution which was adopted by the ministers who approved EEC in 1957. Furthermore, the very delicate issue of the staging of the transitional period for the introduction of the common market, and the allied problem of how to compute tariff reductions, was resolved by Uri for the heads of delegations essentially in the form which found expression in the completed Treaty. As for Euratom, the heads of delegations opted in favour of a complete purchase priority for the European Commission in the acquisition of fissile materials, gave it extensive powers over the direction of private investments—which were later watered down by the ministers—and insisted on stringent supranational controls to assure security. However, the heads of delegations, like the experts before them, sidestepped the institutional problem. In the case of EEC their suggestions were the sketchiest, with ample powers left by inference to the intergovernmental organs. Even in the case of Euratom, most of the stringent central powers were explicitly claimed for the " Community " rather than for the European Commission particularly. And the heads of the delegations, like their subordinates, preferred to remain silent on the issue of whether Euratom should take part in the development of nuclear weapons.[33]

At this level of negotiation, France made most of the central concessions, with the essence of the free trade position of the Benelux and German Governments left intact. Italy, however, got her investment and re-adaptation funds. As regards Euratom, the German delegation conceded most by minimising its free enterprise advocacy. The institutional picture was clouded further by the preference of most delegations that certain ECSC organs be converted to serve Euratom and the common market. The French Government, having promised its rightist supporters to avoid close identification with ECSC, disputed this approach. In March of 1956 Spaak appealed to the Common Assembly that even though

[33] On the Brussels Conference and the reports written by it, see the bibliography cited in Chap. 8 as well as American Committee on United Europe, " Euratom and the Common Market " (New York, December 1956). I have used the unofficial translations of the reports prepared by the Information Division of the High Authority, *viz. The Brussels Report on the General Common Market* (Washington, D. C., June 1956) and *The Brussels Report on Euratom* (Washington, D.C., May 1956).

the solutions were neither drastic nor federal, they were the best obtainable in the political environment then prevailing.

The final scene, however, was played once more on the stage of ministerial meetings and it was here that France re-introduced most of her earlier demands. At the Venice meeting of the foreign ministers, May 30, 1956, the report of the heads of delegations, with all its lacunae, was accepted as the basis for the drafting of the treaties, followed by the convening of another conference to undertake this task, once more headed by the skilful M. Spaak. While Spaak's supranational mediating role was the same as at the preceding expert conference, the subsequent activities were punctuated by more frequent basic quarrels and the need to reconvene the ministers every few months.

In February of 1956, Christian Pineau had launched the French counter-offensive by hinting that consultations with trade associations were essential before the common market provisions could be drafted—a hint which carried overtones of sabotage by publicity. He also re-affirmed the French desire to keep open the question of the military atom, the institutional issue, and the insistence to give Euratom a monopoly over the procurement and ownership of fissile materials. While the others did not agree to all the French claims, enough consensus emerged in February to permit Spaak, in the name of the six governments, to defend the Euratom scheme in the meeting of the OEEC Council of Ministers. At Venice, the counter-offensive was carried forward by Pineau's demand that overseas territories be included in the two treaties (an issue which had contributed to the death of EDC). And in later meetings, the French argued for the right to exclude agriculture from the common market, continue to levy a surtax on " freed " commodities imported from other ECSC countries, the need to bring German fringe benefits and labour legislation into line with French practice, and to extract financial contributions from the other five countries to spur investment in Africa—or tying " Eurafrica " to the common market.[34] It looked almost as if all previously arranged compromises would be questioned again.

[34] On the Brussels Conference, February 12, 1956, see *La Documentation Française*, no. 0.319, February 14, 1956, and *Agence Europe*, February 6, 8, 12, 1956. On the Venice Conference, see *La Documentation Française*, no. 0.363, May 31, 1956. Later ministerial meetings and their compromises are discussed in ECSC, *Bulletin*, December 1956, February-March, 1957. Special French demands are found in *Agence Europe*, July 18, September 10, October 4, October 5, October 20, 1956, February, 7, 1957. It is reported that the onslaught of new French demands

But with almost angelic patience, point after point was re-discussed, restudied, and eventually recompromised. France was granted the right to levy a special surtax and to exclude her agriculture from the common market subject to periodic review by the European Commission. Agreement was worked out, especially with Bonn, on the specific contributions to be made to French African investments, subject to the proviso that if after a five-year trial period no benefits were apparent, the project would be discontinued. The problem of the military atom was solved by authorising Euratom to transfer fissile materials to the Western European Union, thus involving the same governments but in a different structural and legal context. On fringe benefits, Germany agreed to copy immediately the French practice of equal pay for women and agreed further to introduce the forty-hour week by the end of the first four-year lap during the transitional period. And Euratom's monopoly problem over fissile materials was solved by permitting private firms to procure such materials independently if the world price is more favourable than Euratom's, or if a shortage exists. At the same time, the ministers endorsed the Monnet Committee's call of urgency with respect to nuclear energy by appointing the " Three Wise Men " to make recommendations for an immediate atomic programme.

The compromise pattern, once more, closely resembles that of the ECSC Council of Ministers. In no essential instance was the principle of collective action and collective review over national policy sacrificed to specific national demands. On the other hand, the governments were uniformly sympathetic to each other's fears and requests, and therefore arrived at compromise formulas implying concessions by *all*. The rule of simple intergovernmental bargaining from fixed positions was abandoned in favour of delegation of power to experts and mediation by a " respected European political figure," strikingly similar to the role of the High Authority in some ECSC negotiations. France was granted

during 1956 was prompted by a desire to scuttle the General Common Market or to make French participation in it unattractive to the other members. It is therefore extremely significant for the study of the decision-making pattern in ECSC-type ministerial meetings that France did not care to question outright the principle of the common market and the impetus to political integration which it would furnish, and that the other governments preferred to grant France a number of very unpopular and economically questionable concessions rather than proceed alone. If this interpretation of French motives in 1956 is correct, the results demonstrate not only the inability of M. Pineau to shake the European commitment of his opposite numbers but the depth of his and their " engagement."

most of her requests through this formula, but not in the form of the clear unilateral rights claimed initially by Paris.[35]   On the question of separate organs for Euratom and the common market, for example, the French Government was persuaded completely to abandon its earlier position.   The negotiations, in short, were far more " supranational " in technique and attitude than those leading to the ECSC and EDC Treaties, carrying over into fundamental ministerial dealings the code of conduct developed in the ECSC Council.

Intergovernmentalism and Supranationality

All this evidence, quite obviously, is inadequate to dispute the basic institutional fact that the Council of Ministers is an intergovernmental organ.   In what way, then, can it be contrasted with similar organs and the pattern of its decisions assessed in competition with other intergovernmental bodies in which parallel problems are at issue?   The OEEC seems an appropriate agency for this comparison.   Its Council includes the same persons who are active in Luxembourg, it is subject to the unanimity rule, possesses a self-conscious and active secretariat, and is, in principle at least, concerned with European economic integration.

Apart from its initial activity in " slicing up the pie " of Marshall Plan funds among the sixteen recipient countries, the basic fact concerning OEEC activity is its failure to contribute to long-term integration.   Investment co-ordination, siphoning funds to European underdeveloped regions, plant modernisation, co-ordinated monetary policies, free movement of capital and manpower, general and sector common market schemes were all suggested and discussed, but never fully implemented, by the OEEC Council in its ten years of activity.   Successful policy decisions were confined to the twin short-range aims of abolishing quantitative restrictions and introducing convertibility.   Yet even here no

[35] Hence, it is highly significant to note the difference in emphasis given by official German commentators on the agreements.   Adenauer and Brentano agreed in stressing the long-range fundamental political implications, and in so doing endorsed completely the unity ideology of Monnet.   Erhard ignored the General Common Market and Euratom schemes—both of which he opposed as protectionistic and dirigistic—and praised only the probability of creating a larger area of globally unprotected trade through the Free Trade Area formula of association with Britain and the Sterling bloc.   West German Information Agency, *Bulletin*, February 21 and 28, 1957.   The negotiations and parliamentary debates over ratification of both treaties are discussed by Miriam Camps, *The European Common Market and Free Trade Area* (Princeton: Center of International Studies, 1957).

finally binding measures were ever evolved. Trade liberalisation
is subject to national vetoes, escape clauses and annual authorisa-
tions. Convertibility is confined to the special rules of the
European Payments Union and annually subject to conflicting
national claims for reduction and expansion, with uneasy compromises of continuing the status quo emerging as the interim
solution. In such crucial areas as transport and agricultural
harmonisation, activities are confined to inter-ministerial exchanges
of opinion.

" OEEC experience should be carefully considered," concludes
a former official of that organisation. " It demonstrates that a
simple international organisation, paralysed by the right to use
the veto, is unable to create a common market in Europe: national
particularism and private interests are too powerful. An organic
tie is necessary to limit the sovereignty of nation-states. It also
demonstrates that Britain is not disposed to accept an organic union
with the Continent." [36] British efforts and threats to use her veto
have certainly been significant in limiting the role of OEEC and
are partly responsible for the weaknesses of the trade liberalisation
and convertibility programmes. But French efforts have run a close
second to British recalcitrance. A study of a series of OEEC Council
decisions with respect to demands for special safeguarding measures
in favour of British and French policy, as compared to similar
demands by Bonn, indicates that the reluctance expressed by these
Governments in the face of Council opposition went a long way
in excluding energetic collective measures. [37] Why, then, should

---

[36] Guy de Carmoy, *op. cit.*, pp. 179–180.

[37] Jens Trock (in a seminar paper prepared at the University of California, Berkeley,
January 1955). A different interpretation is advanced by Lincoln Gordon, in " The
Organisation for European Economic Co-operation," *International Organisation*,
Vol. 10, no. 1 (February 1956), pp. 1–11. Gordon argues that the decisions in
question reflected genuine corporate thinking and prevented even more extreme
French and British disregard for OEEC rules. Further, he believes that the concept of " engagement " has a reality in OEEC circles and explains some of the
genuinely " European " solutions worked out in the framework of that organisation.
Former OEEC Secretary-General Robert Marjolin agrees by arguing that the
unanimity of rule has compelled not only compromises but has implied the
rigorous adherence of member governments to those compromises because they
felt " engaged " by them and unwilling to violate the code of conduct implied
by the process of negotiation which led to them. See his *Europe and the United
States in the World Economy* (Duke University Press, 1954). Yet Marjolin
resigned his position in 1955 because he felt dissatisfied with OEEC's contribution
to integration. His successor, René Sergent, confessed that progress toward
economic integration demanded a federal rather than an intergovernmental
structure. See his " Schritt für Schritt zum Gemeinsamen Markt," *Europa*,
October 1955, pp. 24 *et seq.*

the same French ministers on the ECSC Council display a different attitude? Why should an organ possessing similar institutional qualities nevertheless consistently produce decisions which endorse progressive economic integration? National interests and pressure groups certainly express themselves more directly and forcefully in the ECSC setting than in OEEC; but their demands are compromised without being reduced to the minimum common denominator, as in OEEC. How is one to account for the difference?

One plausible explanation is the fact that France, in ECSC, is face to face with four governments committed to common market thinking, while Italy is equally sympathetic in principle though sometimes desirous of arguing the case of her defensively minded heavy industries. In OEEC, by contrast, the German and Benelux position enjoys no clear and consistent majority. But this fact alone does not suffice to explain the French refusal to use the veto power, and the good record of eventually complying with ECSC orders. It is suggested that the concept of " engagement," already introduced in connection with the Messina Conference, provides a convincing explanation, combining institutional and ideological causes.[38]

The concept of " engagement " postulates that if parties to a conference enjoy a specific and well-articulated sense of participation, if they identify themselves completely with the procedures and codes within which their decisions are made, they consider themselves completely " engaged " by the results even if they do not fully concur in them. This is especially applicable to international conferences of governments united by certain fundamental common assessments and beliefs—as in OEEC, NATO, the Scandinavian setting, Benelux and ECSC—but subject to the unanimity rule. Identification with the purposes of the organisations, dedication to an informal code of conduct among the members impose a reluctance to exercise the right to veto. Since, however, disagreements do prevail and unanimity is required for a decision, continuous negotiation until consensus is attained is the only alternative. Once a resolution is adopted, its implementation is accepted as well, even though formal means of organisational

---

[38] The concept of " engagement " is developed as an adaptation from a similar principle in small group psychology by G. Chaumont, " The Evolutionary Aspect of International Organisation and International Co-operation," *International Social Science Bulletin*, Vol. 5, no. 2 (1953), pp. 257–277.

enforcement may not exist. If a simple consensus were all the concept requires, the pattern of agreement in OEEC would be covered by it. But if consensus is to mean more than a resolution based on the least co-operative attitude expressed—though this may be more than complete refusal to take any measures whatever—the concept describes the ECSC Council of Ministers much more accurately.

There can be no question that in ECSC all six governments are firmly " engaged " to maintaining the common market for coal and steel and to extending it—though changes in attitude are, of course, not precluded. Hence, they cannot indefinitely oppose meeting to some extent the maximalist demands put forward by one of their treaty partners, thus begetting a compromise pattern going beyond the minimalist position perhaps desired. The code of the Council clearly demands, though the Treaty does not, that all decisions other than consultations requested by the High Authority be made by unanimity. Governments, knowing that binding opinions could be made in some situations despite their negative vote and that some agreement is called for in any case, are extremely unwilling to be forced into the position of being the single hold-out, thus to be isolated and exposed as " anti-European." Governments placed in a majority position, moreover, realising that they may at some future time be put in the place of the dissenter, prefer not to isolate their colleagues. Hence the search for unanimously acceptable decisions meeting the logic of accelerated integration goes on until a formula is found. All the participants know that the dispenser of concessions today may be tomorrow the claimant for the consideration of the others. Fifty years is a long period to be " engaged."

The decision-making code which emerges from the series of case studies presented shows that the categories of legal competence of the Treaty do not determine all votes. True, no effort is made to achieve unanimity on simple consultations and no pretence is made to bind the High Authority to their content. But all other decisions are in fact made on the basis of unanimity and certainly the Council members do not expect the High Authority to act contrary to their deliberations even if the Treaty did permit this latitude. This, however, leaves open the question of what the Council might do if the High Authority acted in accordance with a majority viewpoint, especially if it tended to meet certain ardently

defended national views in so doing. It cannot be argued, therefore, that different kinds of compromises are reached merely because
the Treaty may require simple agreement in one situation or unanimity in another. At the same time, it is equally true and vitally
significant that, even in situations calling for unanimity, the Council
pattern of compromise is far more federal in nature than would
be indicated by the customary practices of intergovernmental conferences. In fact, such conferences in Europe have taken on the
pattern of Council deliberations in content and technique.

The participation of the federal " executive," the High
Authority, is vital in explaining these developments. It has been
extremely difficult for recalcitrant governments to resist the facts
and recommendations put before the Council by the High Authority,
partly because government experts had been bound to the accuracy
and relevance of the necessary statistics while they were being
compiled. Negotiations are thus freed of the preliminary issue of
the reliability of the facts alleged by the parties. Continual prior
contact among the personnel engaged in the talks reduces the
possibility of bluffing, idle speechmaking and bargaining in defiance
of the technical demands of the issue at stake. When the governments are determined to agree but find themselves unable to formulate the necessary compromise, the High Authority is asked to
step in and mediate. While it is true that earlier High Authority
efforts to prod the governments on some issues were resented, the
fact remains that such pressure was eventually effective. When
the governments, for identical or converging reasons, are determined *not* to find a federal solution to their problems, however,
High Authority initiative will be neither solicited nor respected.

But the pattern also shows that no single government habitually
seeks to hinder or to advance integration. The specific issue at
stake determines the position argued, which may be minimalist
in one context and maximalist in the next. Thus France habitually
seeks to slow down measures to do away with national protectionism; but she supports energetic measures of supranational
dirigisme. Germany habitually objects to High Authority regulation
of industry, but supports ECSC-wide scrap control schemes when
there is a scrap shortage. While Italy will defend the fears of her

steelmakers in Luxembourg, and France the desires of her collieries, the fact that there are no permanent voting *blocs* in the Council means that such special pleading is doomed to failure unless the resistance to integration happens to be shared by other governments.

Does the power of a national government determine the pattern of compromise or do the institutional peculiarities of the Council system mitigate the normal consequences of national strength? France was forced to capitulate time and again. Italian demands have been frequently ignored or cut down. Germany compromised her claims repeatedly at Luxembourg, as at Messina and at Brussels. Tiny Luxembourg held up the implementation of the labour agreement and Holland sometimes blocked agreement to strong ECSC-wide scrap controls. The formula of continuous negotiation, High Authority participation, insistence on unanimity coupled with the principle of engagement seems to assure a mutual concession pattern in which no one government consistently " wins " or " loses." Personalities are far less important in this context than institutional forces.

Yet the evolution of Council activity and attitudes suggest that the scope of independent High Authority action has been somewhat reduced since 1955. But this implies no slowdown of the process of integration: it merely means that the Council itself has taken a greater direct interest in channelling the spill-over process instead of permitting the High Authority—which is reluctant in any case—to proceed on its own. It also means that the ministers have realised their inability to act in the context of their " engagement " unless there is a federal arena for action. Hence, they have called for more High Authority initiative in the realm of general economic policy and analysis.

Five years of supranational activity show that the " federal " executive has grown less federal in nature and the " intergovernmental " control body more so. Governments, in their mutual relations in ECSC, tend to act more and more like sensitive politicians in a federal state plagued by severe regional, cultural and economic differentials. Generally, a showdown through the medium of strict majoritarian decisions is avoided in such settings. Interminable " negotiations " and *ad hoc* compromises worked out in caucus rooms, cabinet meetings and personal understandings take their place. While this inevitably limits federal initiative, it does not invariably preclude all change. In ECSC, the emergence of the Council's decision-making code has meant *gradual* change in economic and political relations in the direction of unity. The satisfaction of the six governments with this formula is reflected by its insertion into the machinery for Euratom and the General Common Market. True, it restricts the initiative of the federal executive as compared to ECSC. But it maximises the role already fulfilled by the ECSC Council and institutionalises the mediating function of the High Authority in the powers conferred upon the European Commission. Since the intergovernmental machinery, under the institutional logic of the common market and the ideological impulsion of political and economic expectations released by earlier integration measures, has moved strikingly in the direction of certain federal decision-making methods, there is no reason for thinking that the new European institutions will not carry this process further.

Hence, in the focus of processes tending toward political community, it is unimportant that the High Authority has not always exploited the spill-over. Governments, partly because they are administratively and doctrinally committed to integration and partly because the institutional logic of the common market permits them no meaningful alternative, are alive to the expanding drive inherent in sector integration and seek to channel it through new techniques of supranational action. Thus the symbiosis of inter-ministerial and federal procedures has given rise to a highly specific, and certainly corporate, series of techniques whose tendency to advance integration is patent even though it is neither clearly federal nor traditionally intergovernmental.

Yet this symbiosis and the codes connected therewith are the essence of supranationality. It is *sui generis* not only in the legal and institutional sense but also in terms of the relationships it sets up among civil servants and ministers, trade unionists and cartel executives, coal consumers and administrative lawyers. Even though supranationality in practice has developed into a hybrid in which neither the federal nor the intergovernmental tendency has clearly triumphed, these relationships have sufficed to create expectations and shape attitudes which will undoubtedly work themselves out in the direction of more integration. As compared with conventional international organisations, the supranational variety clearly facilitates the restructuring of expectations and attitudes far more readily. Though not federal in nature, its consequences are plainly federating in quality merely because it activates socio-economic processes in the pluralistic-industrial-democratic milieu in which it functions, but to which conventional international organisations have no access. And to this extent the vision of Jean Monnet has been clearly justified by events.

BIBLIOGRAPHY

1. BIBLIOGRAPHIES AND HANDBOOKS

Armbruster, H. and Engel, F.-W., ed., *Handbuch der Montanunion,* Frankfurt am Main: Agenor Druck- und Verlags-GmbH, 1953– . (serial).

Bibliographie zum Schumanplan, 1950–52, Bibliographien, Index der amtlichen Unterlagen, Buecher, Broschueren und Beitraege, Frankfurt: Institut fuer Europaeisch Politik und Wirtschaft, 1953.

Bulletin mensuel de bibliographie, service de documentation de l'Assemblée Commune (quarterly since 1956), Luxembourg.

European Coal and Steel Community, Common Assembly, *Bibliographie Analytique du Plan Schuman et de la Communauté Européenne du Charbon et de l'Acier,* Luxembourg: 1955.

European Coal and Steel Community, Common Assembly, *Catalogue Analytique du Fonds, Plan Schuman—C.E.C.A.,* Luxembourg, 1955.

Speckaert, G. P., ed., *International Institutions and International Organisation,* a select bibliography, published with assistance from UNESCO, Brussels: Union of International Associations, 1956.

Wolf-Rodé, Karl, ed., *Handbuch fuer den gemeinsamen Markt,* Frankfurt: Montan und Wirtschaftsverlag, 1955.

2. DOCUMENTS OF THE EUROPEAN COAL AND STEEL COMMUNITY

British Iron and Steel Federation, *Treaty Establishing the European Coal and Steel Community,* London: no date.

European Coal and Steel Community, *Agreement Concerning the Relations Between the European Coal and Steel Community and the United Kingdom of Great Britain and Northern Ireland,* and related documents, Luxembourg: December, 1954.

European Coal and Steel Community, Common Assembly, *Annuaire-Manuel de l'Assemblée Commune,* Luxembourg, 1956 and 1957.

European Coal and Steel Community, Common Assembly, *Informations mensuelles* (before January, 1956: *Informations bimensuelles*), Luxembourg, monthly.

European Coal and Steel Community, Common Assembly, *Le développement de l'intégration économique de l'Europe,* by M. van der Goes van Naters, Luxembourg, July, 1955.

European Coal and Steel Community, Common Assembly, *Rapport préliminaire sur le développement de l'intégration économique de l'Europe,* by M. van der Goes van Naters, Luxembourg, March, 1956.

European Coal and Steel Community, Common Assembly, *Rapport sur le marché commun et l'Euratom,* by P. Wigny and van der Goes van Naters, doc. no. 14 (1955–56).

European Coal and Steel Community, Common Assembly, *Un Témoignage sur la Communauté des Six,* by Pierre Wigny, Luxembourg, 1957.

European Coal and Steel Community, Cour de Justice, *Recueil de la Jurisprudence de la Cour,* serial.

European Coal and Steel Community, *Débats de l'Assemblée Commune,* édition de langue française, compte rendu in extenso des séances, serial.

European Coal and Steel Community, High Authority, *Bulletin from the European Coal and Steel Community,* Washington, bimonthly, (monthly before April, 1955).

European Coal and Steel Community, High Authority, *Bulletin Mensuel d'Information,* monthly, since January, 1956.

European Coal and Steel Community, High Authority, *Bulletin Statistique,* Luxembourg, bimonthly, since 1953.

European Coal and Steel Community, High Authority, *General Reports on the Activities of the Community,* with annexes, Luxembourg, 1953, 1954, 1955, 1956 and 1957.

European Coal and Steel Community, High Authority, Information Service, *Treaty Establishing the European Atomic Energy Community,* provisional translation, Washington, D.C., April 22, 1957.

European Coal and Steel Community, High Authority, Information Service, *Treaty Establishing the European Economic Community,* provisional translation, Washington, D.C., May 6, 1957.

European Coal and Steel Community, High Authority, *Real Income of Workers in the Community,* Luxembourg, January, 1957.

European Coal and Steel Community, High Authority, *Report on the Activities of the High Authority,* annual, until November, 1955.

European Coal and Steel Community, High Authority, *Report on the Situation of the Community,* Luxembourg, January, 1953, January, 1954 and November, 1954.

European Coal and Steel Community, High Authority, *Special Report : The Establishment of the Common Market for Steel,* supplement to the General Report on the Activities of the Community, Luxembourg, May, 1953.

Journal Officiel de la Communauté Européenne du Charbon et de l'Acier, édition de langue française, serial.

3. Documents of Other European International Organisations

Ad Hoc Assembly for the Establishment of a European Political Community, Constitutional Committee, *Draft Treaty Embodying the Statute of the European Community, and Documents,* October, 1952–April, 1953, Paris, 1953.

Council of Europe, Consultative Assembly, *Informations mensuelles,* monthly.

Council of Europe, Consultative Assembly, *Official Reports of Debates,* serial.

Organisation for European Economic Co-operation, *Historique et structure,* 5th edition, Paris, 1956.

Organisation for European Economic Co-operation, *La coopération économique européenne. Rapport établi pour le Conseil d'Europe,* Paris, 1956.

Organisation for European Economic Co-operation, *Possibilities of Action in the Field of Nuclear Energy,* Paris, January, 1956.

Organisation for European Economic Co-operation, *Rapports Annuels,* serial.

4. DOCUMENTS OF NATIONAL GOVERNMENTS

Belgium, Chambre des Représentants, *Annales Parlementaires,* no. 70 (June 3, 1952), 3–8, 12–14; no. 71 (June 4, 1952), 6–9, 13–18; no. 74 (June 11, 1952), 2–3, 4–6; no. 75 (June 12, 1952), 8–12; (May 9, 1957).

Belgium, Chambre des Représentants, *Documents,* no. 379—1955–56 (1); no. 361—1951–52; no. 457—1951–52; no. 410—1951–52.

Belgium, Sénat, *Annales Parlementaires,* no. 15 (January 29, 1952), 288–301; no. 16 (January 30, 1952), 304–332; no. 17 (January 31, 1952), 334–360; no. 18 (February 5, 1952), 363–377.

Belgium, Sénat, *Documents,* nos. 84, 90, 93, 107 (1951–52).

Federal Republic of Germany, *Bundesgesetzblatt,* II, 445 (April 29, 1952); no. 14 (May 13, 1955); no. 47 (December 28, 1955).

Federal Republic of Germany, Bundesrat, *Drucksachen,* no. 470/51, 631/51, 775/51.

Federal Republic of Germany, Bundesrat, *Sitzungsberichte,* no. 61 (July 27, 1951), 439–456; no. 66 (September 6, 1951), 608–610; no. 67 (September 13, 1951), 612; no. 68 (September 29, 1951), 620; no. 69 (October 5, 1951), 684.

Federal Republic of Germany, Bundestag, 1. Wahlperiode, *Drucksachen,* nos. 2401, 2484, 2950, 2971, 2972, 2973, 2974, 2951.

Federal Republic of Germany, Bundestag, 1. Wahlperiode, *Sitzungsberichte,* no. 161 (July 12, 1951), 6499–6556; no. 182 (January 9, 1952), 7582–7650; no. 183 (January 10, 1952), 7652–7686, 7787–7791; no. 184 (January 11, 1952), 7792–7817, 7833–7836.

France, Journal Officiel de la République Française, *Débats Parlementaires* Assemblée Nationale, no. 150 (December 6, 1951), 8870–8873; no. 151 (December 7, 1951), 8918–8921, 8926–8928; no. 152 (December 11, 1951), 9000–9001, 9008–9009.

France, Journal Officiel de la République Française, *Débats Parlementaires,* Conseil de la République, no. 29 (March 25, 1952), 712–740; no. 30 (March 27, 1952), 755–764, 773–775.

France, Journal Officiel de la République Française, *Documents,* Conseil Economique Français, " La Communauté Européenne du Charbon et de l'Acier "; " Rapport de la délégation française sur le traité instituant la Communauté Européenne du Charbon et de l'Acier et la Convention rélative aux dispositions transitoires." (October, 1951.)

Great Britain, Foreign Office, *Der Schuman-Plan, der britisch-franzoesische Gedankenaustausch ueber die franzoesischen Vorschlaege fuer die westeuropaeischen Kohle-, Eisen- und Stahlindustrien,* ed. by Publications Branch, British Information Services, Hamburg, May–June, 1950.

Great Britain, House of Commons, Debates, *Weekly Hansard,* no. 361, July 5, 1956.

Italy, Senato della Repubblica, Atti Parlamentari, *Resoconti delle Discussioni,* 1948–52, vol. 32, no. 780 (March 11, 1952), 31480–31528; (March 12, 1952), 31567–31609; (March 13, 1952), 31615–31671; (March 14, 1952), 31677–31713; (March 15, 1952), 31719–31746, 31750–31889.

United States, Department of State, Publication no. 4173, *Draft Treaty Constituting the European Coal and Steel Community, Draft Convention Containing the Transitional Provisions,* European and British Commonwealth Series no. 22, Washington, D.C., April, 1951.

United States, High Commission for Germany, *Sixth Quarterly Report on Germany,* January–March, 1951.

5. SECONDARY SOURCES

Books

Auboin, Roger, *The Bank for International Settlements, 1930–1955,* Essays in International Finance no. 22, Princeton, New Jersey: Princeton University, May, 1955.

Bally, G. and Thuerer G., ed., *Die Integration des europaeischen Westens,* Veroeffentlichungen der Handelshochschule St. Gallen, Zuerich, St. Gallen: Polygraphischer Verlag AG, 1954.

Beaumont, Pierre de, *L'harmonisation des fiscalités Européennes,* Paris: Librairie Générale de droit et de jurisprudence, 1955.

Bok, Derek Curtis, *The First Three Years of the Schuman Plan,* Princeton Studies in International Finance no. 5, Princeton, New Jersey: Princeton University, 1955.

Bosch, Werner, *Die Saarfrage, eine wirtschaftliche Analyse,* Veroeffentlichungen des Forschungsinstituts fuer Wirtschaftspolitik an der Universitaet Mainz, vol. 4, Heidelberg: Quelle & Meyer, 1954.

Breitling, Rupert, *Die Verbaende in der Bundesrepublik,* Reihe Parteien, Fraktionen, Regierungen no. 8, Meisenheim am Glan: Anton Hain K.G., 1955.

Buchanan, William and Cantril, Hadley, *How Nations See Each Other,* Urbana: University of Illinois Press, 1953.

Camps, Miriam, *The European Common Market and American Policy,* Princeton, New Jersey: Center of International Studies, November 1956.

Delperée, Albert, *Politique Sociale et Intégration Européenne,* Liège: Thone, 1956.

Deutsch, Karl W., *Nationalism and Social Communication,* New York: Wiley and Sons, 1953.

Deutsch, Karl W., et al., *Political Community and the North Atlantic Area,* Princeton, New Jersey: Princeton University Press, 1957.

Deutsch, Karl W., *Political Community at the International Level,* New York: Doubleday, 1954.

Erhard, Ludwig, *Deutschlands Rueckkehr zum Weltmarkt,* Duesseldorf: Econ-Verlag GmbH, 1953.

Florinsky, Michael T., *Integrated Europe?,* New York: Macmillan, 1955.

Goormaghtigh, J., "European Coal and Steel Community," *International Conciliation,* no. 503, May, 1955.

Die grossen zwischenstaatlichen Wirtschaftsorganisationen, Veroeffentlichungen des schweizerischen Instituts fuer Aussenwirtschafts und Marktforschung an der Handelshochschule St. Gallen, no. 17, Zuerich, St. Gallen: Polygraphischer Verlag, 1955.

Guetzkow, Harold, *Multiple Loyalties: Theoretical Approach to a Problem in International Organization,* Center for Research on World Political Institutions, publ. no. 4, Princeton, New Jersey: Princeton University Press, 1955.

Hahn, Horst Carl, *Der Schuman-Plan,* Munich: Pflaum Verlag, 1953.

Haines, C. Grove ed., *European Integration,* Baltimore: Johns Hopkins University Press, 1957.

Haussmann, Frederick, *Der Schumanplan im Europaeischen Zwielicht,* Munich and Berlin: C. H. Becksche Verlagsbuchhandlung, 1952.

Haviland, H. Field, Jr., ed., *The United States and the Western Community*, Haverford: Haverford College Press, 1957.

Hellwig, Fritz, *Westeuropas Montanwirtschaft*, Schriftenreihe des Deutschen Industrieninstituts, Koeln: Deutsche Industrieverlags-GmbH, 1953.

Henle, Günther, *Der Schumanplan vor seiner Verwirklichung*, Sonder-veroeffentlichung des Rheinisch-Westphaelischen Instituts fuer Wirtschaftsforschung, Essen, 1951.

Herchenroeder, K. H., Schaefer, Johann and Zapp, Manfred, *Die Nachfolger der Ruhrkonzerne*, Duesseldorf: Econ-Verlag, 1954.

Hexner, Ervin, *The International Steel Cartel*, Chapel Hill: University of North Carolina Press, 1943.

Institut des Relations Internationales, *La Communauté Européenne du Charbon et de l'Acier*, Brussels, 1953.

Isay, Rudolf, *Deutsches Kohlenwirtschaftsrecht im Rahmen des Schuman-planes*, Muenchen und Berlin: C. H. Beck, 1952.

Juergensen, Harald, *Die westeuropaeische Montanindustrie und ihr gemeinsamer Markt*, Forschungen aus dem Institut fuer Verkehrs-wissenschaft an der Universitaet Muenster, Ld. 10, Goettingen: Vandenhoeck & Ruprecht, 1955.

Kiersch, Guenter, *Internationale Eisen- und Stahlkartelle*, Schriftenreihe des Rheinisch-Westfaelischen Instituts fuer Wirtschaftsforschung Neue Folge, no. 4, Essen: Rheinisch-Westfaelisches Institut fuer Wirtschaftsforschung, 1954.

Knorr, Klaus, *Nuclear Energy in Western Europe and United States Policy*, Princeton, New Jersey: Center of International Studies, 1956.

Koever, J. F., *Le Plan Schuman, ses mérites—ses risques*, Paris: Nouvelles Editions Latines, 1952.

Krawielicki, Robert, *Das Monopolverbot im Schumanplan*, Tuebingen: J. C. B. Mohr, 1952.

Kunze, Hans Juergen, *Die Lagerungsordnung der westeuropaeischen Eisen- und Stahlindustrie, im Lichte ihrer Kostenstruktur*, Kieler Studien, Heft 30, Kiel: Institut fuer Weltwirtschaft, 1954.

Langwieler, Wilhelm, *Die Sozialpolitische Problematik der Montanunion*, Frankfurt: Lutzeyers Fortsetzungswerke GmbH, 1953.

Lerner, Daniel and Aron, Raymond, *France Defeats EDC*, New York: Praeger, 1957.

Lorwin, Val, *The French Labor Movement*, Boston, Mass.: Harvard University Press, 1954.

Macmahon, Arthur, ed., *Federalism, Mature and Emergent*, Garden City: Doubleday, 1955.

Mason, Henry L., *The European Coal and Steel Community*, The Hague: Nijhoff, 1955.

Meade, James E., *The Belgium-Luxembourg Economic Union, 1921–39*, Essays in International Finance, no. 25, Princeton, New Jersey: Princeton University, 1956.

Meade, James E., *Negotiations for Benelux: An Annotated Chronicle, 1943–1956*, Princeton Studies in International Finance, no. 6, Princeton, New Jersey: Princeton University, 1957.

Neuordnung der Eisen- und Stahlindustrie im Gebiet der Bundesrepublik Deutschland, Bericht der Stahltreuhaendervereinigung, Muenchen-Berlin: C. H. Beck, 1954.

Northrop, F. S. C., *European Union and United States Foreign Policy*, New York: Macmillan, 1954.

Perroux, François, *Europe sans Rivages,* Paris: Presses Universitaires de France, 1954.

Philip, André, *L'Europe unie et sa place dans l'économie internationale,* Paris: Presses Universitaires de France, 1953.

Pritzkoleit, Kurt, *Bosse, Banken, Boersen,* Wien, Muenchen, Basel: Kurt Desch, 1954.

Racine, Raymond, *Vers une Europe Nouvelle par le Plan Schuman,* Neuchâtel: Éditions Baconnière, 1954.

Reuter, Paul, *La Communauté Européenne du Charbon et de l'Acier,* Paris: Librairie Générale de droit et de jurisprudence, 1953.

Rieben, Henri, *Des Ententes de Maitres de Forges au Plan Schuman,* Lausanne: Epalinges, H. Rieben, 1954.

Robertson, Arthur H., *The Council of Europe,* London: Stevens & Sons, Ltd. 1956.

Sainte-Lorette, Lucien de, *L'Intégration économique de l'Europe,* Paris: Presses Universitaires de France, 1953.

Schregle, Johannes, *Europaeische Sozialpolitik,* Koeln-Deutz: Bund-Verlag, 1954.

Valentine, D. G., *The Court of Justice of the European Coal and Steel Community,* The Hague: Nijhoff, 1954.

Van Wagenen, Richard W., *Research in the International Organization Field: Some Notes on a Possible Focus,* Princeton, New Jersey: Center for Research on World Political Institutions, Publication no. 1, 1952.

Vignes, Daniel, *La Communauté Européenne du Charbon et de l'Acier,* Liège: Georges Thone, 1956.

Weir, Sir Cecil, *The First Step in European Integration,* London: The Federal Educational and Research Trust, 1957.

Wightman, David, *Economic Co-operation in Europe,* United Nations Economic Commission for Europe, London: Stevens and Sons, Ltd., 1956.

Articles

Abraham, Jean-Paul, "Les Entreprises comme sujets de droit dans la Communauté Charbon-Acier," *Cahiers de Bruges,* no. 3 (October, 1954).

Almond, Gabriel, "Attitudes of German Businessmen," *World Politics,* VIII no. 1 (January 1956).

Antione, Anik, "La Cour de Justice de la Communauté Européenne du Charbon et de l'Acier et la Cour Internationale de Justice," *Révue Générale de Droit International Public,* no. 2 (April–June, 1953).

Bayer, Wilhelm, "Das Privatrecht der Montanunion," *Zeitschrift fuer auslaendisches und Internationales Privatrecht,* XVII, no. 3 (1952).

Bebr, Gerhard, "Labor and the Schuman Plan," *Michigan Law Review,* LII (May, 1954).

Bertrand, Raymond, "The European Common Market Proposal," *International Organization,* X, no. 4 (November, 1956).

Blondcel, J. L. and Van der Eycken, Henri, "Les Emprunts de la Communauté Européenne du Charbon et de l'Acier," *La Revue de la Banque,* nos. 3 and 4, 1955.

Cois, Daniel, "La renaissance de la sidérurgie allemande," *L'Economie,* XI, nos. 518–520 (December 8, 15, 22, 1955).

Deutsch, Karl W., "The Growth of Nations," *World Politics,* V, no. 2 (January, 1953).

Ehrmann, Henry W., "The French Trade Associations and the Ratification of the Schuman Plan," *World Politics,* VI, no. 4 (July, 1954).

Gehrels, Franz and Johnston, Bruce F., "The Economic Gains of European Integration," *Journal of Political Economy* (August, 1955).

Gerbet, Pierre, "La Genèse du Plan Schuman," *Révue Française de Science Politique,* VI, no. 3 (September, 1956).

Gordon, Lincoln, "Economic Aspects of Coalition Diplomacy—the NATO Experience," *International Organization,* X, no. 4 (November, 1956).

Goriély, Georges, "L'opinion publique et le Plan Schuman," *Revue Française de Science Politique,* III, no. 3 (September, 1953).

Green, L. C., "Legal Aspects of the Schuman Plan," *Current Legal Problems,* V (1952).

Haas, Ernst B., "The United States of Europe," *Political Science Quarterly,* LXIII, no. 4 (December, 1948).

Hellwig, Fritz, "Die Unternehmerorganisation in der westeuropaeischen Eisen- und Stahlindustrie," *Stahl und Eisen,* LXXI (1951), no. 7.

Hellwig, Fritz, "Die westeuropaeische Montanwirtschaft," *Stahl und Eisen,* LXX (1950).

Hommes et Commerce (January–February, 1955), ECSC issue.

Hovey, Allan, Jr., "Britain and the Unification of Europe," *International Organization,* IX, no. 3 (August, 1955).

Juergensen, Harald, "Die Montanunion in den Funktionsgrenzen der Teilintegration," *Wirtschaftsdienst,* XXXV, no. 11 (November, 1955).

Kirchheimer, Otto, "West German Trade Unions," *World Politics,* VIII, no. 4 (July, 1956).

Koever, J. F., "The Integration of Western Europe," *Political Science Quarterly,* LXIX, no. 3 (September, 1954).

Leites, Nathan and de la Malène, Christian, "Paris from EDC to Western Union," *World Politics,* IX, no. 2 (January, 1957).

Lerner, Daniel, "Franco-German Relations: Politics, Public Opinion and the Press," *International Affairs,* X, no. 2 (1956).

Mendershausen, Horst, "First Tests of the Schuman Plan," *Review of Economics and Statistics,* XXXV, no. 4 (November, 1953).

Merry, Henry J., "The European Coal and Steel Community—Operations of the High Authority," *Western Political Quarterly,* VII, no. 2 (June, 1955).

Northrop, F. S. C., "United States Foreign Policy and European Union," *Harvard Studies in International Affairs,* IV, no. 1 (February, 1954).

Parker, W. N., "The Schuman Plan—A Preliminary Prediction," *International Organization,* VI, no. 3 (August, 1952).

Peco, Franco, "Progress of the Italian Steel Industry," *Review of the Economic Conditions in Italy,* VIII, no. 2 (March, 1954).

"Le Plan Schuman," *Etudes Economiques,* nos. 81 and 82 (November, 1951).

"Le Plan Schuman," *Nouvelle Revue de l'Economie Contemporaine,* nos. 16 and 17 (1951).

Rabier, J.-R., "Le pool Charbon-Acier: Échec ou Réussite?" *Revue de l'Action Populaire* (February, 1955).

Reuter, Paul, "La conception du pouvoir politique dans le Plan Schuman," *Revue Française de Science Politique,* I, no. 3 (July–September, 1951).

Roux, René, " Le plan Schuman et la condition ouvrière," *Revue Internationale du Travail* (March, 1952).

Schilling, Karl, " Der Europaeische Wirtschaftsrat und die E.G.K.S.," *Europa-Archiv,* No. 1 (January 5, 1953).

Schuman, Robert, " Origin et Elaboration du ' Plan Schuman,' " *Cahiers de Bruges,* no. 4 (December, 1953).

Sethur, Frederick, " The Schuman Plan and Ruhr Coal," *Political Science Quarterly,* LXVII, no. 4 (December, 1952).

" La Communauté Européenne du Charbon et de l'Acier," *Sondages,* XVII, no. 2 (1955).

Stein, Eric, " The European Coal and Steel Community: the Beginning of its Judicial Process," *Columbia Law Review,* LV, no. 7 (November, 1955).

Strange, Susan, " The Schuman Plan," *Yearbook of World Affairs,* V (1951).

Taylor, A. J. P., " France, Germany and the Saar," *International Journal* (Winter, 1952–53).

Vaglio, M., " The European Coal and Steel Pool and the Italian Economy," *Review of the Economic Conditions in Italy,* VIII, no. 2 (March, 1954).

Van der Meulen, J., " L'intégration économique Européenne: Essay de synthèse," *Annales des Sciences Economiques Appliquées,* XIII, no. 3 (August, 1955).

Vernon, Raymond, " The Schuman Plan," *American Journal of International Law,* XLVII, no. 2 (April, 1953).

Vinck, François, " Les Performances du Marché Commun," *Synthèses,* X, no. 110 (July, 1955).

Zawadski, K. K. F., " The Economics of the Schuman Plan," *Oxford Economic Papers,* V, no. 2 (June, 1953).

INDEX